D0687555

From the
Library of:

Brother Mark McVann
F.S.C.

WORD
BIBLICAL
COMMENTARY

General Editors
David A. Hubbard
Glenn W. Barker †

Old Testament Editor
John D. W. Watts

New Testament Editor
Ralph P. Martin

WORD

BIBLICAL

COMMENTARY

VOLUME 34A

Mark 1-8:26

ROBERT A. GUELICH

WORD BOOKS, PUBLISHER • DALLAS, TEXAS

Word Biblical Commentary
MARK 1:1–8:26
Copyright © 1989 by Word, Incorporated

All rights reserved. No portion of this book may be reproduced in any form without the written permission of the publisher.

Library of Congress Cataloging-in-Publication Data
Main entry under title:

Word biblical commentary.

   Includes bibliographies.
   1. Bible—Commentaries—Collected Works.
BS491.2.W67   220.7′7   81–71768ISBN 0–8499–0233–9 (vol. 34a)   AACR2

Printed in the United States of America

The author's own translation of the Scripture text appears in italic type under the heading *Translation.*

   39   AGF   98765432

To my parents
who have faithfully served
in the ministry of the Word
for over fifty years

Contents

Contents

Editorial Preface

The launching of the *Word Biblical Commentary* brings to fulfillment an enterprise of several years' planning. The publishers and the members of the editorial board met in 1977 to explore the possibility of a new commentary on the books of the Bible that would incorporate several distinctive features. Prospective readers of these volumes are entitled to know what such features were intended to be; whether the aims of the commentary have been fully achieved time alone will tell.

First, we have tried to cast a wide net to include as contributors a number of scholars from around the world who not only share our aims, but are in the main engaged in the ministry of teaching in university, college, and seminary. They represent a rich diversity of denominational allegiance. The broad stance of our contributors can rightly be called evangelical, and this term is to be understood in its positive, historic sense of a commitment to Scripture as divine revelation, and to the truth and power of the Christian gospel.

Then, the commentaries in our series are all commissioned and written for the purpose of inclusion in the *Word Biblical Commentary.* Unlike several of our distinguished counterparts in the field of commentary writing, there are no translated works, originally written in a non-English language. Also, our commentators were asked to prepare their own rendering of the original biblical text and to use those languages as the basis of their own comments and exegesis. What may be claimed as distinctive with this series is that it is based on the biblical languages, yet it seeks to make the technical and scholarly approach to a theological understanding of Scripture understandable by— and useful to—the fledgling student, the working minister, and colleagues in the guild of professional scholars and teachers as well.

Finally, a word must be said about the format of the series. The layout, in clearly defined sections, has been consciously devised to assist readers at different levels. Those wishing to learn about the textual witnesses on which the translation is offered are invited to consult the section headed *Notes.* If the readers' concern is with the state of modern scholarship on any given portion of Scripture, they should turn to the sections on *Bibliography* and *Form and Structure.* For a clear exposition of the passage's meaning and its relevance to the ongoing biblical revelation, the *Comment* and concluding *Explanation* are designed expressly to meet that need. There is therefore something for everyone who may pick up and use these volumes.

If these aims come anywhere near realization, the intention of the editors will have been met, and the labor of our team of contributors rewarded.

General Editors: *David A. Hubbard*
Glenn Barker †
Old Testament: *John D. W. Watts*
New Testament: *Ralph P. Martin*

Author's Preface

One can hardly exaggerate the significance of Mark's Gospel for the Christian Church. From a literary standpoint, the evangelist's designation of his work as the "gospel of Jesus Messiah, Son of God" (1:1) not only set in motion the process by which the first four books of the New Testament came to be known as "gospels," but he most likely was the first to pen the story of Jesus. In fact, Mark's Gospel may well have spawned the writing of the other Gospels. Though there is still some dispute today (e.g., C. S. Mann's *Mark* in the Anchor Bible Commentary), the consensus of biblical scholarship accepts as axiomatic the thesis that both the Gospels of Matthew and Luke use Mark as their foundational source.

From a theological standpoint, the evangelist wrestled with the heart of the Christian gospel in addressing the questions about who Jesus was, what was the nature and content of his ministry, and why he died. At the same time, Mark struggled with the issue of the believer's response to Jesus—the life of discipleship, in a hostile world. And he subtly did all this by composing a portrait of Jesus and the disciples drawn from the early church's preaching and teaching about Jesus' ministry.

In the history of Gospel studies, Mark stands out again today. As is often the case with initial contributions, the Gospel of Mark early in the life of the Church was eclipsed by the succeeding Gospels, with their fuller narratives. Ironically, interest in the larger Gospels as the primary source for the life and teaching of Jesus led to the rediscovery of Mark as a primary source for Matthew and Luke in the nineteenth-century quests for the historical Jesus. But not until the development of redaction criticism during the fifties of this century were Mark and the other Gospels appreciated in their own right as verbal "portraits" of Jesus and his ministry. Now the literary critical focus on Mark as narrative has helped us to see it as a whole as the "gospel of Jesus Messiah, Son of God" in story form.

This commentary on Mark, begun under the gracious invitation of Professor Ralph Martin, has evolved into a two-volume work in an attempt to do justice to the very extensive discussion and literature on almost every facet of Mark's Gospel. Even so, I make no claim to having exhaustively covered the literature that continues to appear as I write (e.g., B. Mack's *A Myth of Innocence* [Philadelphia: Fortress Press, 1988]). I only trust that the selection is representative and the treatment is fair. The reader will soon discover how indebted I am to those who have gone before in Markan studies.

I take great pleasure in expressing my gratitude for the students, colleagues, and administration at Northern Baptist Theological Seminary as well as for the people and staff of the Colonial Church of Edina, Minnesota, who have listened and sustained me during the years of work on this volume. I also am very grateful for the Markan Seminar of the Society of New Testament Studies and my co-chair Prof. Dieter Luehrmann for providing a forum and stimulating discussion on Markan themes over the past six years. I express thanks too for the Alexander von Humboldt Foundation who funded the initial year of my research on this commentary at the University of Tübingen, Germany, where Prof. Dr. Martin Hengel was my host. Last but certainly not least, I gratefully acknowledge the critical work of Olive Brown, who carefully read and corrected the proofs of this complex undertaking.

Only those whose hours have been consumed by writing books can appreciate the investment of patience, understanding, and encouragement of my family, especially my wife Joyce, who has been a constant expression of amazing grace. I dedicate this work to my parents, the Reverend and Mrs. Robert S. Guelich, who not only first taught me the Bible but instilled in me the hunger to understand God's word intellectually and experientially.

September, 1988   ROBERT W. GUELICH
Fuller Theological Seminary

Abbreviations

A. General Abbreviations

A	Codex Alexandrinus	n.d.	no date
א	Codex Sinaiticus	Nestle	Nestle (ed.) *Novum*
Aq	Aquila's Greek		*Testamentum Graece*[16]
	Translation of the OT		rev. by K. and B. Aland
Apoc.	Apocrypha	N.F.	*Neue Folge*, new series
B	Codex Vaticanus	NS	New Series
C	Codex Ephraemi Syri	NT	New Testament
ca.	*circa*, about	OT	Old Testament
cent.	century	p., pp.	page, pages
cf.	*confer*, compare	*pace*	with due respect to, but
chap(s).	chapter(s)		differing from
contra	in contrast to	// , par(s)	parallel(s)
D	Codex Bezae	par.	paragraph
DSS	Dead Sea Scrolls	passim	elsewhere
ed.	edited by, editor(s)	pl.	plural
e.g	*exempli gratia*, for example	Q	Quelle (Sayings source for
et al.	*et alii*, and others		the Gospels)
ET	English translation	q.v.	*quod vide*, which see
EV	English Versions of the	rev.	revised, reviser, revision
	Bible	*sic*	an unusual form exactly
f., ff.	following (verse or verses,		reproduced from the
	pages, etc.)		original
fem.	feminine	sing.	singular
frag.	fragments	s.v.	*sub verbo* under the word
FS	Festschrift, volume	sy	Syriac
	written in honor of	Symm.	Symmachus
hap. leg.	*hapax legomenon*, sole	Tg.	Targum
	occurrence	Theod.	Theodotion
ibid.	*ibidem*, in the same place	Tr.	translator, translated by
id.	*idem*, the same	UBSGT	The United Bible
i.e.	*id est*, that is		Societies Greek Text
lat	Latin	v, vv	verse, verses
LXX	Septuagint	viz.	*videlicet*, namely
masc.	masculine	v.l.	*varia lectio*, alternative
MS(S)	manuscript(s)		reading
MT	Masoretic text (of the Old	vol.	volume
	Testament)	x	times (2x = two times,
n.	note		etc.)

B. Abbreviations for Translations and Paraphrases

AB	Anchor Bible	JB	Jerusalem Bible
AV	Authorized Version = KJV	KJV	King James Version
GNB	Good News Bible = Today's		(1611) = AV
	English Version		

Moffatt	*A New Translation of the Bible* (NT 1913)	NJB	New Jerusalem Bible (1985)
NEB	New English Bible (NT 1961; OT and Apoc. 1970)	RSV	Revised Standard Version (NT 1946, OT 1952, Apoc. 1957))
NIV	New International Version (1978)	RV	Revised Version (1881)

C. Abbreviations of Commonly Used Periodicals, Reference Works, and Serials

AB	Anchor Bible	*BJRL*	*Bulletin of the John Rylands University Library of Manchester*
AGJU	Arbeiten zur Geschichte des antiken Judentums und des Urchristentums		
		BN	Biblische Notizen
AnBib	Analecta Biblica	*BR*	*Biblical Research*
ATAbh	Alttestamentliche Abhandlungen	*BT*	*The Bible Translator*
		BTB	*Biblical Theology Bulletin*
ATANT	Abhandlungen zur Theologie des Alten und Neuen Testaments	BWANT	Beiträge zur Wissenschaft vom Alten und Neuen Testament
ATD	Das Alte Testament Deutsch	*BZ*	*Biblische Zeitschrift*
		BZNW	Beihefte zur *ZNW*
ATR	*Anglican Theological Review*		
		CBQ	*Catholic Biblical Quarterly*
BASOR	*Bulletin of the American Schools of Oriental Research*	CBQMS	CBQ Monograph Series
		CNT	Commentaire du Nouveau Testament
BBB	Bonner biblische Beitrage		
BDB	E. Brown, S. R. Driver, and C. A. Briggs, *Hebrew and English Lexicon of the Old Testament* (Oxford: Clarendon, 1907)	CGTC	The Cambridge Greek Testament Commentary
		ConB	Coniectanea biblica
		Concil	*Concilium*
		ConNT	*Coniectanea neotestamentica*
BDF	F. Blass, A. Debrunner, and R. W. Funk, *A Greek Grammar of the New Testament* (University of Chicago/University of Cambridge, 1961)	EKK	Evangelisch-katholischer Kommentar zum Neuen Testament
		EKL	*Evangelisches Kirchenlexikon*
		EstBib	*Estudios biblicos*
BETL	Bibliotheca ephemeridum theologicarum lovaniensium	*ETL*	*Ephemerides theologicae lovanienses*
BET	Beiträge zur evangelischen Theologie (BEvT)	EvK	Evangelische Kommentar
		EvQ	*Evangelical Quarterly*
BGD	W. Bauer, *A Greek-English Lexicon of the New Testament and Other Early Christian Literature*, ET, ed. W. F. Arndt and F. W. Gingrich; 2d ed. rev. F. W. Gingrich and F. W. Danker (University of Chicago, 1979)	*EvT*	*Evangelische Theologie*
		EWNT	*Exegetisches Wörterbuch zum Neuen Testament*, ed. H. Balz and G. Schneider, 3 vols. (Stuttgart: Kohlhammer, 1980–83)
		ExpTim	*The Expository Times*
Bib	*Biblica*	FRLANT	Forschungen zur Religion und Literatur des Alten und Neuen Testaments
BibLeb	*Bibel und Leben*		

FTS	Frankfurter Theologische Studien	MM	J. H. Moulton and G. Milligan, *The Vocabulary of the Greek Testament* (London: Hodder, 1930)
GKC	*Gesenius' Hebrew Grammar*, ed. E. Kautzsch, tr. A. E. Cowley	MNTC	Moffatt NT Commentary
GNS	Good News Studies	MTS	Marburger theologische Studien
HKNT	Handkommentar zum Neuen Testament	NCB	New Century Bible (new ed.)
HNT	Handbuch zum Neuen Testament	*Neot*	*Neotestamentica*
		NGS	New Gospel Studies
HNTC	Harper's NT Commentaries	NICNT	New International Commentary on the New Testament
HTKNT	Herders theologischer Kommentar zum Neuen Testament		
		NovT	*Novum Testamentum*
HTR	*Harvard Theological Review*	NovTSup	Supplement to *NovT*
		NRT	*La nouvelle revue théologique*
ICC	International Critical Commentary	*NTA*	*New Testament Abstracts*
		NTAbh	Neutestamentliche Abhandlungen
IEJ	*Israel Exploration Journal*		
Int	*Interpretation*	*NTS*	*New Testament Studies*
JAAR	*Journal of the American Academy of Religion*	OTNT	Oekumenischer Taschenbuchkommentar zum Neuen Testament
JBL	*Journal of Biblical Literature*		
JBR	*Journal of Bible and Religion*		
JETS	*Journal of the Evangelical Theological Society*	*PEQ*	*Palestine Exploration Quarterly*
		PJ	*Palästina-Jahrbuch*
JQR	*Jewish Quarterly Review*		
JR	*Journal of Religion*	*RAC*	*Reallexikon für Antike und Christentum*
JSJ	*Journal for the Study of Judaism*		
		RB	*Revue biblique*
JSNT	*Journal for the Study of the New Testament*	RechBib	Recherches bibliques
		RevExp	*Review and Expositor*
JSNTSup	JSNT Supplement Series	*RevScRel*	*Revue des sciences religeuses*
JTS	*Journal of Theological Studies*	RGG	*Die Religion in Geschichte und Gegenwart*
KD	*Kerygma und Dogma*	RNT	Regensburger Neues Testament
LD	*Lectio divina*	*RQ*	*Revue de Qumrân*
LEC	Library of Early Christianity	*RSPT*	*Revue des sciences philosophiques et théologiques*
LSJ	H. G. Liddell and R. Scott, *A Greek-English Lexicon*, rev. H. S. Jones (Oxford: Clarendon, [9]1940; with supplement, 1968)	*RSR*	*Recherches de science religieuse*
		RTL	*Revue théologique de Louvain*
		SANT	Studien zum Alten und Neuen Testament
MeyerK	H. A. W. Meyer, Kritisch-exegetischer Kommentar über das Neue Testament	SBLDS	SBL Dissertation Series
		SBM	Stuttgarter biblische Monographien

SBS	Stuttgarter Bibelstudien	*TLZ*	*Theologische Literaturzeitung*
SBT	Studies in Biblical Theology	*TQ*	*Theologische Quartalschrift*
ScEs	*Science et esprit*	*TS*	*Theological Studies*
Scr	Scripture	*TSK*	*Theologische Studien und*
SE	*Studia Evangelica I, II, III*		*Kritiken*
	(= TU 73 [1959], 87 [1964],	TTS	Trier theologische Studien
	88 [1964], etc.)	*TTZ*	*Trierer theologische Zeitschrift*
SJT	*Scottish Journal of Theology*	TU	Texte und Untersuchungen
SNT	Studien zum Neuen	*TynB*	*Tyndale Bulletin*
	Testament	*TZ*	*Theologische Zeitschrift*
SNTSMS	Society for New Testament		
	Studies Monograph Series	*USQR*	*Union Seminary Quarterly*
SNTU	Studien zum Neuen		*Review*
	Testament und ihrer		
	Umwelt	*VuF*	*Verkündigung und Forschung*
SR	*Studies in Religion / Sciences*	*VT*	*Vetus Testamentum*
	Religieuses		
ST	*Studia theologica*	WBC	Word Biblical Commentary
Str-B	H. Strack and P. Billerbeck,	*WD*	*Wort und Dienst*
	Kommentar zum Neuen	WMANT	Wissenschaftliche
	Testament, 4 vols. (Munich:		Monographien zum Alten
	Beck'sche, 1926–28)		und Neuen Testament
StudNeot	Studia neotestamentica		
SUNT	Studien zur Umwelt des	*ZAW*	*Zeitschrift für die*
	Neuen Testaments		*alttestamentliche Wissenschaft*
		ZDPV	*Zeitschrift des deutschen*
TB	Theologische Bücherei		*Palästina-Vereins*
TDNT	G. Kittel and G. Friedrich,	*ZKT*	*Zeitschrift für katholische*
	eds., *Theological Dictionary of*		*Theologie*
	the New Testament, 10 vols.,	*ZNW*	*Zeitschrift für die*
	ET (Grand Rapids:		*neutestamentliche Wissenschaft*
	Eerdmans, 1964–76)	*ZRGG*	*Zeitschrift für Religions- und*
THKNT	Theologischer		*Geistesgeschichte*
	Handkommentar zum	*ZTK*	*Zeitschrift für Theologie und*
	Neuen Testament		*Kirche*

D. Abbreviations for Books of the Bible with Apocrypha

OLD TESTAMENT

Gen	2 Chron	Dan
Exod	Ezra	Hos
Lev	Neh	Joel
Num	Esth	Amos
Deut	Job	Obad
Josh	Ps (Pss)	Jonah
Judg	Prov	Mic
Ruth	Eccl	Nah
1 Sam	Cant	Hab
2 Sam	Isa	Zeph
1 Kgs	Jer	Hag
2 Kgs	Lam	Zech
1 Chron	Ezek	Mal

NEW TESTAMENT

Matt	1 Tim
Mark	2 Tim
Luke	Titus
John	Philem
Acts	Heb
Rom	James
1 Cor	1 Pet
2 Cor	2 Pet
Gal	1 John
Eph	2 John
Phil	3 John
Col	Jude
1 Thess	Rev
2 Thess	

APOCRYPHA

Bar	Baruch	Sir	Ecclesiasticus (Wisdom of
Jdt	Judith		Jesus the son of Sirach)
1 Macc	1 Maccabees	Tob	Tobit
2 Macc	2 Maccabees	Wisd Sol	Wisdom of Solomon

E. Abbreviations of the Names of Pseudepigraphical and Early Patristic Books

Adv. Haer.	Irenaeus, Against All Heresies	*Gos. Eb.*	Gospel of the Ebionites
		Gos. Heb.	Gospel of the Hebrews
Apoc. Abr.	Apocalypse of Abraham (1st to 2nd cent. A.D.)	*Gos. Pet.*	Gospel of Peter
		Gos. Thom.	Gospel of Thomas
2-3 Apoc. Bar.	Syriac, Greek Apocalypse of Baruch	Herm. *Sim.*	Hermas, *Similitudes*
		Jub.	Jubilees
Apoc. Mos.	Apocalypse of Moses	*Odes Sol.*	Odes of Solomon
Apoc. Pet.	Apocalypse of Peter	*Pss. Sol.*	Psalms of Solomon
As. Mos.	(See *T. Mos.*)	*Sib. Or.*	Sibylline Oracles
Did.	Didache	*T. Judah*	Testament of Judah
1-2-3 Enoch	Ethiopic, Slavonic, Hebrew Enoch	*T. Levi*	Testament of Levi, etc.
		T. Mos.	Testament of Moses
Ep. Arist.	Epistle of Aristeas	*Vita*	Life of Adam and Eve

F. Abbreviations of the Names of Dead Sea and Related Texts

CD	Cairo (Genizah text of the) Damascus (Document)	1QS	*Serek hayyahad* (*Rule of the Community, Manual of Discipline*) from Qumran Cave 1
1QH	*Hôdayôt* (*Thanksgiving Hymns*) from Qumran Cave 1	1QSa	Appendix A (*Rule of the Congregation*) to 1QS
1QIsaa,b	First or second copy of Isaiah from Qumran Cave 1	1QSb	Appendix B (*Blessings*) to 1QS
		4QFlor	*Florilegium* from Qumran Cave 4
1QpHab	*Pesher on Habakkuk* from Qumran Cave 1	4QTestim	*Testimonia* from Qumran Cave 4
1QM	*Milhāmāh* (*War Scroll*) from Qumran Cave 1		

G. Abbreviations of Rabbinic Works

Bab.	*Babylonian*	*Rab.*	*Rabbah* (following abbreviation for biblical book)
Bar.	*Baraita*		
Kalla	*Kalla*		
Mek.	*Mekilta*	*Sipra*	*Sipre*
Midr.	*Midraš,* abbreviation for biblical book	*Sipre*	*Sipre*
		Sop.	*Soperim*
Pal.	*Palestinian*	*Tg. Onq.*	*Targum Onqelos*
Pesiq. R.	*Pesiqta Rabbati*	*Tg. Isa.*	*Targum of Isaiah*
Pirqe R. El.	*Pirqe Rabbi Eliezer*		

H. Abbreviations of Orders and Tractates in Mishnaic and Related Literature

(Italicized *m, t, b,* or *y* used before name to distinguish between same-named tractates in Mishna, Tosepta, Babylonian Talmud, and Jerusalem Talmud)

ᵓAbot	*Pirqe Abot*	*Ber.*	*Berakot*
Bek.	*Bekorot*	*B. Qam.*	*Baba Qamma*

Git.	Gittin	Nid.	Niddah
Hal.	Halla	Qidd.	Qiddušin
Hor.	Horayot	Sanh.	Sanhedrin
Hul.	Hullin	Šabb.	Šabbat
Ker.	Keritot	Šeb.	Šebiʿit
Ketub.	Ketubot	Šebu.	Šebuʿot
Kil.	Kilʾayim	Sukk.	Sukka
Mak.	Makkot	Taʿan.	Taʿanit
Meg.	Megilla	Yad.	Yadayim
Ned.	Nedarim	Yoma	Yomā
Neg.	Negaʿim	Zer.	Zeraʿim
Nez.	Neziqin		

Note: The textual notes and numbers used to indicate individual manuscripts are those found in the apparatus criticus of *Novum Testamentum Graece*, ed. E. Nestle and K. Aland et al. (Stuttgart: Deutsche Bibelgesellschat, 1979[26]).

Main Bibliography

A. Works Cited by Author Only

Anderson, H. *The Gospel of Mark.* NCB. London: Oliphants, 1976. **Bultmann, R.** *The History of the Synoptic Tradition.* Tr. J. Marsh. Rev. ed. Oxford: Blackwell/New York: Harper & Row, 1963. **Cranfield, C. E. B.** *The Gospel According to Saint Mark.* CGTC. Cambridge: Cambridge UP, 1963. **Dibelius, M.** *From Tradition to Gospel.* Tr. B. L. Woolf. Cambridge: James Clark, 1971/Greenwood, SC: Attic Press, 1982. **Ernst, J.** *Das Evangelium nach Markus.* RNT. Regensburg: Pustet, 1981. **Gould, E. P.** *A Critical and Exegetical Commentary on the Gospel According to Saint Mark.* ICC. New York: Scribners, 1907. **Gnilka, J.** *Das Evangelium nach Markus.* EKK 2/1–2. Zürich: Benzinger/ Neukirchen-Vluyn: Neukirchener Verlag, 1978, 1979. **Grundmann, W.** *Das Evangelium nach Markus.* THNT 2. Berlin: Evangelische Verlagsanstalt, 1977. **Haenchen, E.** *Der Weg Jesu: Eine Erklärung des Markus-Evangeliums und der kanonischen Parallelen.* Berlin: Töpelmann, 1966. **Klostermann, E.** *Das Markusevangelium.* HNT 3. Tübingen: Mohr, 1950. **Lagrange, M.-J.** *Evangile selon saint Marc.* Paris: J. Gabalda, 1929. **Lane, W. L.** *The Gospel According to Mark.* NICNT. Grand Rapids: Eerdmans, 1974. **Lohmeyer, E.** *Das Evangelium Des Markus.* MeyK 2. Göttingen: Vandenhoeck & Ruprecht, 1963. **Lührmann, D.** *Das Markusevangelium.* HNT 3. Tübingen: Mohr, 1987. **Mann, C. S.** *Mark.* AB 27. Garden City, NY: Doubleday, 1986. **Meyer, H. A. W.** *Critical and Exegetical Handbook to the Gospels of Mark and Luke,* Vol 1. Tr. R. E. Wallis. Edinburgh: T. & T. Clark, 1930. **Nineham, D. E.** *The Gospel of St Mark.* Pelican New Testament Commentaries. Harmondsworth, England/New York: Penguin Books, 1963. **Pesch, R.** *Das Markusevangelium.* HTKNT 2/1-2. Freiburg: Herder, 1977. **Rawlinson, A. E. J.** *St Mark.* London: Metheun, 1947. **Schmid, J.** *Das Evangelium nach Markus.* RNT 2. Regensburg: Pustet, 1958. **Schmidt, K. L.** *Der Rahmen der Geschichte Jesu. Literarkritische Untersuchungen zur ältesten Jesusüberlieferung.* Berlin: Trowitsch & Sohn, 1919. **Schmithals, W.** *Das Evangelium nach Markus.* OTNT 2/1-2. Gütersloh: Mohn, 1979. **Schniewind, J.** *Das Evangelium nach Markus.* NTD 1. Göttingen: Vandenhoeck & Ruprecht, 1963. **Swete, H. B.** *The Gospel According to St Mark.* London: Macmillan, 1913/Grand Rapids: Eerdmans, 1952. **Schweizer, E.** *The Good News According to Mark.* Tr. D. H. Madvig. Richmond, VA: John Knox Press, 1970. **Taylor, V.** *The Gospel According to St Mark.* 2d ed. London: Macmillan/New York: St Martin's Press, 1966. **Wellhausen, J.** *Das Evangelium Marci.* 2d ed. Berlin: Reimer, 1909. **Williamson, L.** *Mark.* Atlanta: John Knox Press, 1983.

B. Frequently Cited Works

Best, E. *Following Jesus: Discipleship in the Gospel of Mark.* JSNTS 4. Sheffield: University of Sheffield, 1981. **Black, M.** *An Aramaic Approach to the Gospels and Acts.* 3d ed. Oxford: Clarendon Press, 1967. **Dodd, C. H.** *The Parables of the Kingdom.* Rev. ed. New York: Scribners, 1961. **Egger, W.** *Frohbotschaft und Lehre: Die Sammelberichte des Wirkens Jesu im Markusevangelium.* FTS 19. Frankfurt: Knecht, 1976. **Jeremias, J.** *New Testament Theology: The Proclamation of Jesus,* Vol 1. Tr. J. Bowden. New York: Scribners, 1971. ———. *The Parables of Jesus.* Tr. S. H. Hooke. New York: Scribners, 1963. **Kelber, W.** *The Kingdom in Mark: A New Place and a New Time.* Philadelphia: Fortress, 1974.

Kertelge, K. *Die Wunder Jesu im Markusevangelium: Eine redaktionsgeschichtliche Untersuchung.* SANT 23. München: Kösel, 1970. Koch, D.-A. *Die Bedeutung der Wundererzählungen für die Christologie des Markusevangeliums.* BWNT 42. Berlin: DeGruyter, 1975. Kümmel, W. G. *Introduction to the New Testament.* Trans. H. C. Kee. Nashville: Abingdon, 1975. Kuhn, H.-W. *Ältere Sammlungen im Markusevangelium.* SUNT 8. Göttingen: Vandenhoeck & Ruprecht, 1971. Maloney, E. C. *Semitic Interference in Marcan Syntax.* SBLDS 51. Chico, CA: Scholars Press, 1981. Marxsen, W. *Mark the Evangelist: Studies on the Redaction History of the Gospel.* Tr. J. Boyce et al. Nashville: Abingdon, 1969. Metzger, B. *A Textual Commentary on the Greek New Testament.* New York: United Bible Societies, 1971. Meye, R. P. *Jesus and the Twelve: Discipleship and Revelation in Mark's Gospel.* Grand Rapids: Eerdmans, 1968. Moule, C. F. D. *Idiom-Book of New Testament Greek.* 2d ed. Cambridge: Cambridge UP 1959. Neirynck, F. *Duality in Mark: Contributions to the Study of Markan Redaction.* Leuven: Leuven UP 1972. Pryke, E. J. *Redactional Style in the Marcan Gospel.* SNTSMS 33. Cambridge: Cambridge UP 1978. Reploh, K. G. *Markus—Lehrer der Gemeinde: Eine redaktionsgeschichtliche Studie zu den Jüngerperikopen des Markusevangeliums.* SBM 9. Stuttgart: Katholisches Bibelwerk, 1969. Roloff, J. *Das Kerygma und der irdische Jesus: Historische Motive in den Jesuserzählungen der Evangelien.* Göttingen: Vandenhoeck & Ruprecht, 1970. Schenke, L. *Die Wundererzählungen des Markusevangeliums.* SBB. Stuttgart: Katholisches Bibelwerk, 1974. Theissen, G. *The Miracle Stories of the Early Christian Tradition.* Tr. F. McDonagh. Edinburgh: T. & T. Clark/Philadelphia: Fortress, 1983. Weeden, T. J. *Mark: Traditions in Conflict.* Philadelphia: Fortress, 1971. Wrede, W. *The Messianic Secret.* Tr. J. C. G. Greig. Edinburgh: T. & T. Clark/Greenwood, SC: Attic Press, 1971.

Introduction

GENRE

Bibliography

Aune, D. E. "The Gospels as Hellenistic Biography." *Mosaic* 20 (1987) 1–10. ———. "Greco-Roman Biography." In *Greco-Roman Literature and the New Testament,* ed. D. E. Aune. SBL Sources for Biblical Study 21. Atlanta: Scholars Press, 1988. ———. *The New Testament in Its Literary Environment.* LEC 8. Philadelphia: Westminster Press, 1987. **Best, E.** *Mark: The Gospel as Story.* Philadelphia: Fortress, 1987. **Bilezikian, W.** *The Liberated Gospel: A Comparison of the Gospel of Mark and Greek Tragedy.* Grand Rapids: Zondervan-Baker, 1977. **Cameron, R.** *The Other Gospels: Non-Canonical Gospel Texts.* Philadelphia: Westminster, 1982. **Guelich, R. A.** "The Gospel Genre." In *Das Evangelium und die Evangelien,* ed. P. Stuhlmacher. WUNT 28. Tübingen: Mohr, 1983. 183–20. **Gundry, R. H.** "Recent Investigations into the Literary Gattung 'Gospel.'" In *New Dimensions in New Testament Study,* ed. R. Longenecker and M. C. Tenney. Grand Rapids: Zondervan, 1974. 97–114. **Hengel, M.** *Studies in the Gospel of Mark.* Tr. J. Bowden. Philadelphia: Fortress, 1985. **Kee, H. C.** *Community of the New Age: Studies in Mark's Gospel.* Philadelphia: Westminster, 1977. **Lang, F. G.** "Kompositionsanalyse des Markusevangeliums." *ZTK* 74 (1977) 1–24. **Perrin, N.** "The Literary Gattung 'Gospel'—Some Observations." *ExpTim* 82 (1970–71) 4–7. **Reicke, B.** *The Roots of the Synoptic Gospels.* Philadelphia: Fortress, 1986. **Robinson, J. M.,** and **H. Koester.** *Trajectories through Early Christianity.* Philadelphia: Fortress, 1971. **Standaert, B. H. M. G. M.** *L'Evangile selon Marc. Composition et genre littéraire.* Zevenkerken-Brugge, 1984. **Talbert, C. H.** *What Is a Gospel? The Genre of the Canonical Gospels.* Philadelphia: Fortress, 1977. **Via, D. O.** *Kerygma and Comedy in the New Testament.* Philadelphia: Fortress, 1975. **Vorster, W. S.** "Der Ort der Gattung Evangelium in der Literaturgeschichte." *VuF* 29 (1984) 2–25. ———. "Kerygma/History and the Gospel Genre." *NTS* 29 (1983) 87–95.

With the words "the beginning of the gospel concerning Jesus Messiah, Son of God," Mark provided the early Church with a distinctive literary genre, the gospel. Although he did not intend to call his literary work a "gospel," his work most likely served as a pattern for Matthew and Luke and contributed to the eventual use of "gospel" as a literary designation in the early Church (e.g., Irenaeus, *Adv. Haer.* 3.1.2 and the *"Gospel" of Thomas*).

Numerous early Christian writings are called "gospels" (see Cameron, *Gospels*), and many attempts have been made to identify more precisely the literary genre of the Gospels in general and Mark's Gospel in particular (see Guelich, *Evangelium,* 185–204; Gundry, *Dimensions,* 97–114). The variety of recent suggestions includes an apocalypse (e.g., Perrin, *ExpTim* 82 [1970–71] 4–7; cf. Kee, *Community,* 76), a drama (Lang, *ZTK* 74 [1977] 1–24; Bilezikian, *Gospel*; Via, *Comedy*; Standaert, *Marc*), a hellenistic aretalogy (Schmithals, 1:46), and a biography (e.g., Talbert, *Gospel*; Hengel, *Studies,* 32–34; Aune, *Environment,* 46–59; *Mosaic* 20 [1987] 1–10). Though disputed, the issue is critical, since the genre provides an interpretative framework for reading Mark.

The canonical Gospels and apparently some related, noncanonical gospels (e.g., *The Gospel of the Nazoreans, The Gospel of the Ebionites, The Gospel of the Hebrews*) focused on the person and ministry of Jesus. Mark and John begin their narratives about Jesus with the baptism of John the Baptist; Matthew and Luke begin with stories about Jesus' birth. Mark ends with the note of the resurrection; Matthew, Luke, and John end with the resurrected Lord's appearances to the disciples after Easter. Furthermore, except for the flashback about the death of the Baptist in Mark 6:17–29, one has the distinct impression of following a linear chronology running from Jesus' baptism to his death and resurrection in Mark's arrangement of the episodic materials. The same can be said of John's Gospel and all the more of Matthew's and Luke's which begin their respective stories with the birth narratives. Thus these Gospels are clearly biographical. "Biographical," however, does not necessarily imply that they belong to the literary genre of biography, since biographical accounts can come in various genres, for example, in comedic or tragic dramas.

Other writings called "gospels" also exist which are not in the least biographical. These gospels consist almost exclusively of sayings (e.g., *The Gospel of Thomas, The Gospel of the Egyptians, The Gospel of Philip, The Gospel of Truth, The Gospel of Mary*). The existence of such writings called "gospels" raises the question of how they came to be so called by the Christian movement, for whom "gospel" as literary designation was unique. The answer may well supply the necessary clue in the search for the literary genre of the Gospels.

Only Mark uses the term "gospel" in his heading or incipit (1:1; cf. Matt 1:1; Luke 1:1). Yet he uses "the gospel" to refer to the content of his narrative and not as a literary designation for his work (see *Comment* on 1:1). The literary designation "The Gospel according to Mark" (cf. "According to Mark" in B ℵ, which is a later abbreviation—so Hengel, *Studies*, 66–67; Reicke, *Roots*, 151–52; Lührmann, 4) came to be applied later as an inscription in some manuscripts and as a subscription in others (Hengel, *Studies*, 64–84).

"The Gospel according to . . ." gives us two important items of information. First, it implies the existence of more than one such literary work which necessitated the distinction according to author (cf. Luke 1:1–3). This implication is confirmed by the existence, for example, of four such works in the NT. Second, "gospel" has become a literary designation for these works. But how did the Church come to refer to these literary works as "The Gospel according to ⁙ . . . ?" One could answer that Mark's own heading in which he refers to his story as "the gospel" gave rise to the later use of "gospel" as a designation for literary works of similar content even though Matthew refers to his Gospel as a "book" (βίβλος, 1:1) and Luke to his work as a "narrative" (διήγησις, 1:1). This answer, however, fails to account for the use of "gospel" with reference to the noncanonical gospels of dissimilar content like *The Gospel of Thomas.*

Instead of Mark 1:1 giving the direct occasion for the subsequent use of "gospel" as a literary designation, this heading indicates what "the gospel" was for the writer of the Second Gospel. On the one hand, "the gospel" (1:1) was about the person and ministry of Jesus Messiah, Son of God, as seen in the content of Mark's narrative (1:4–16:8), the "beginning" of which is 1:1–15. On the other hand, the evangelist notes that "the gospel" has its roots in Isaiah's promise (cf. 1:2a, see *Comment*) as seen in the coming of the Baptist, Jesus' baptism and temptation, and the summary of Jesus' preaching (1:14–15). Jesus came proclaiming the "gospel of God" (1:14, see *Comment*) as promised in Isa 52:7 and 61:1. The "gospel concerning Jesus Messiah, Son of God" then was God's promised good news about God's eschatological deliverance, salvation, expressed in the person and ministry of Jesus.

Mark, however, was not the first to make the identification between Isaiah's promise of the eschatological gospel and Jesus' ministry. The similar content of John's Gospel with no apparent direct literary linkage to Mark or the Synoptic Gospels, the underlying outline of many of the sermons in Acts (cf. esp. 10:34–43; see Guelich, *Evangelium*, 211–13) and the presence in the early Church of various traditions concerning Jesus' earthly ministry strongly suggest that the identification had preceded Mark. Mark's achievement lies in his being the first to put the story or the "gospel" in writing and thus giving it a shape followed to a great extent by Matthew and Luke. The writer of the Fourth Gospel would later provide another such written story.

Since the *gospel* concerning Jesus Messiah, i.e., the good news about God's salvation in and through Jesus' ministry according to the Scriptures, was essentially the *message* of Mark's story, it is only logical that this and similar writings should receive the designation of "The *Gospel* according to . . ." in the early Church for whom this message had been the "gospel." Furthermore, the shift within the gnostic Christian movement away from any emphasis on Jesus' earthly life and ministry would explain the prominence in gnostic circles of the revelatory discourse as bringing the *message* of salvation. This shift (cf. the incipit of *Gos. Thom.*—"These are the secret words which the living Jesus spoke, and [which] Didymus Judas Thomas wrote"—with the "title," "The Gospel according to Thomas," at the end) corresponds to the docetic tendency and a view of salvation gained through divinely imparted knowledge characteristic of this movement. To the extent that these other writings were viewed as containing the *message* or "good news" of salvation by some circles of the early Church they too could be called "The Gospel . . ." Consequently, "gospel" as a literary designation had more to do with the content ("good news") than the form of the document (e.g., biography or revelatory discourse).

This conclusion means that the Gospels were viewed by the early Church and most likely by the evangelists as shaped by the content of the *message*, i.e., the "gospel concerning Jesus Messiah, Son of God," rather than by any desire to appropriate a literary genre such as biography. The content influenced the form, rather than the form the content (Best, *Mark,* 140–41). That the gospel of God's promised salvation was directly related to Jesus of Nazareth and could be expressed in a narrative of Jesus' ministry resulted in writings that might fall into the broad, complex category of ancient Greco-Roman biography (Talbert, *Gospel*; Aune, *Mosaic* 20 [1987] 1–10; idem, *Literature,* 107–26). But the view shared by Mark and the early Church that the narrative was the *gospel* of God about promised salvation effected through the ministry of Jesus (1:1, 14) clearly makes the canonical and their content-related noncanonical gospels a distinctive "subtype of Greco-Roman biography" (Aune, *Environment,* 46).

Formally, then, these gospels belong to the broad category of hellenistic biography (e.g., Justin, *Apol.* 106.3, "memoirs of the Apostles" [ἀπομνημονεύματα]); materially, they are *sui generis* (e.g., Irenaeus, *Adv. Haer.* 3.1.2, "gospels"). Therefore, one can legitimately refer to them as "gospels," and one must interpret them in view of the broader and narrower literary categories (on Greco-Roman biography, see Aune, *Literature*, 107–26).

MARK AS NARRATIVE

Bibliography

Best, E. *Mark: The Gospel as Story.* Philadelphia: Fortress, 1983. **Hahn, F.,** ed. *Der Erzähler des Evangeliums.* SBS 118/119. Stuttgart: Katholisches Bibelwerk, 1985. **Kingsbury, J. D.** *The Christology of Mark's Gospel.* Philadelphia: Fortress, 1983. **Malbon, E. S.** *Narrative Space and Mythic Meaning in Mark.* San Francisco: Harper & Row, 1986. **Peterson, N. R.** "'Point of View' in Mark's Narrative." *Semeia* 12 (1978) 97–121. ———. *Literary Criticism for New Testament Critics.* Guides to Biblical Scholarship. Philadelphia: Fortress, 1978. ———. "When Is the End Not the End?" *Int* 34 (1980) 151–66. **Rhoads, D.,** and **D. Michie.** *Mark as Story.* Philadelphia: Fortress, 1982. **Schmidt, K. L.** "Die Stellung der Evangelien in der allgemeine Literaturgeschichte." In *EUCHARISTERION* II, FS H. Gunkel, ed. H. Schmidt. Göttingen: Vandenhoeck & Ruprecht, 1923. 50–134. **Tannehill, R. C.** "The Gospel of Mark as Narrative Christology." *Semeia* 16 (1979) 57–98. ———. "The Disciples in Mark: The Function of a Narrative Role." *JR* 57 (1977) 386–405.

For centuries Mark was read as a narrative. With the dawn, however, of form criticism early in the twentieth century Mark came to be seen more as a collection of traditional units, each with a distinctive form and historical setting. The evangelist's role became that of a stringer of pearls (e.g., Schmidt, *EUCHARISTERION,* 127–28) and a mere collector of traditions (e.g., Dibelius, 3) as he constructed his Gospel. The result, according to Bultmann (347–48), was a combination of the "hellenistic kerygma about Christ, whose essential content consists of the Christ myth as we learn of it in Paul (esp. Phil 2:6 ff.; Gal 3:24) with the tradition of the story of Jesus." According to Dibelius (230), Mark is a "book of secret epiphanies." But instead of focusing on Mark's Gospel as a whole, Bultmann's and Dibelius' work along with that of the succeeding generation of form critics sought primarily to deconstruct the Gospel by defining the "original" form of its traditional units and locating their respective sociohistorical setting(s) in the developing faith of the Church.

The rise of redaction criticism during the 1950s refocused attention on the Gospels as such. The work of Marxsen on Mark, Bornkamm on Matthew, and Conzelmann on Luke examined the Gospel as a distinctive portrait of Jesus and his ministry. These portraits came from the evangelists' selection, arrangement, and modification of traditional units. Naturally, this understanding changed the role of the evangelist from a passive collector of tradition to the more active role of author. Consequently, much of the discussion for the next two decades concentrated on determining what was "redactional" and on distinguishing "redaction" from "tradition." Eventually, under the influence of literary criticism (see Peterson, *Criticism*) the discussion has shifted more to the Gospel as a whole viewed as the literary product of the evangelist. Mark has again come to be seen as a narrative in its own right (e.g., Peterson, *Criticism*; idem, *Semeia* 12 [1978] 97–121; idem, *Int* 34 [1980] 151–66; Rhoads and Michie, *Mark*; Best, *Mark*; Tannehill, *JR* 57 [1977] 386–405; idem, *Semeia* 16 [1979] 57–98; Kingsbury, *Christology*; Hahn, *Erzähler*). When viewed as a narrative in its own right, the Gospel reflects certain literary features. The object of literary criticism per se has been to analyze the literary work with these features in mind. A broad look at two such features, point of view and plot, reveals how the story is told and the broad strokes of the story line. Both features condition how we read the Gospel.

Point of View. A story may have several points of view. The primary point of view in Mark's Gospel, however, is that of the narrator. This story is told by an unnamed, intrusive narrator who has an "omniscient point of view" (e.g., Peterson, *Semeia* 12 [1978] 105). The narrator not only knows all the events of the story but also the thoughts, feelings, emotions, and intentions of the various characters. This knowledge allows him as an "intrusive" narrator to intrude into the world of the characters or into any scene to give additional comments and explanations to the reader (e.g., 6:52).

The narrator or teller of this story is not one of the story's characters. Furthermore, no one character in the story qualifies as an eyewitness of all that transpires. The narrator uses the same voice throughout and he always stands external to what is narrated as though he were above or beyond it. At the same time, the narrator will enter inside the mind of the characters or into the events of the story when, for example, he tells of events such as Jesus' temptation, his prayer in the Garden, or his private instruction to the disciples. In this way, the "omniscient" narrator invites the reader to trust him and his comments as reliable.

A story's point of view contains numerous aspects (see Peterson, *Semeia* 12 [1978] 106–19, following B. Uspensky, *A Poetics of Composition*, tr. V. Zavarin and S. Wittig [Berkeley and Los Angeles: University of California Press, 1973]), one of which is an "ideological" or evaluative moment that reflects a set of values about what is right or wrong, good or bad, proper or improper. In Mark's story with many characters, each with their own evaluative point of view, the narrator consistently identifies his with Jesus' point of view from which all other points of view are weighed (Peterson, *Semeia* 12 [1978] 107). Kingsbury has additionally noted that Jesus' evaluative point of view in Mark is identical with God's (Kingsbury, *Christology*, 48) as seen by the narrator's use of the OT (e.g., 1:1–2), God's own voice (1:11; 9:7), and Jesus' stated concern to align himself with God's point of view (e.g., 10:18; 10:40; 14:36). This corresponds with what appears to be two fundamentally opposing points of view in Mark's narrative that shape to a great extent the conflict of Mark's plot. Using the language of the Gospel (8:33), these opposing points of view are: (a) "thinking the things of God" or (b) "thinking the things of human-kind."

The implications of the narrator's point of view for his reliability and authority become obvious. Since the *narrator* identifies with Jesus' point of view regarding himself, the events, and the characters of the story, and since *Jesus* identifies with God's point of view about himself, the events, and other characters of the story, the narrator's story is normative for the reader who wants to "think the things of God." The "gospel concerning Jesus Messiah Son of God" (1:1) is the "gospel of God" (1:14).

One could hardly confuse the intrusive, omniscient narrator with the actual writer or author of Mark's Gospel. We have no indication of a first-person, eyewitness account. The narrative often outstrips the physical, temporal, and personal limitations of the writer of the Gospel. Yet the commentary follows the common practice of using "Mark" or "the evangelist" to refer both to the writer of the Gospel (see *Author* below) as well as to the narrator. Only context can differentiate between the two referents. The two are combined because the evangelist called Mark in the early Church employs the omniscient narrator as his literary device for telling his story as the "implied author." To that extent, then, the narrator speaks for the writer of the Gospel.

The Plot. At the risk of sounding simplistic, the plot of Mark's Gospel is given to the reader in the heading of 1:1. It revolves around the "gospel" or "good news" concerning "Jesus Messiah, Son of God," which for Mark's Gospel lies in the events of the story. The plot has to do with Jesus' effective proclamation through his words and actions of the "gospel" or "good news" from God. This "good news" declares that God's promised redemptive rule is near, *the* promised moment in time has come to fruition, and all are summoned to surrender in repentance and faith to God's redemptive rule (1:14–15). It calls one to respond in faith, to "think the thoughts of God" (8:33).

This plot or the events that compose it involves conflict that gives flow to the story line (see Rhoads and Michie, *Mark,* 73–100, for more detailed discussion). For example, we find conflict between Jesus and the demonic (e.g., 1:12–13, 21–27; cf. 3:23–27), between Jesus and the Roman authorities (e.g., 15:2–15), between Jesus and the Jewish authorities (e.g., 2:1–3:6; 12:13–44), between Jesus and his family (e.g., 3:20–21, 31–35; cf. 6:1–6), between Jesus and his disciples (e.g., 4:40; 8:14–21; 14:26–31), and even between Jesus and God (e.g., 14:35–36; cf. 15:34). On the one hand, Jesus overcomes the conflict by resisting Satan's temptation and freeing victims of demonic possession, by forgiving sinners, healing the sick and raising the dead, by feeding the hungry and subduing the forces of nature, and ultimately by defeating the grave itself. On the other hand, Jesus voluntarily succumbs to the fatal designs of his enemies and drinks "the cup" that the Father has for him, a role that was prefigured by the Baptist (1:14; 6:17–29; 9:11–13) and plotted by his opponents (e.g., 3:6; 11:18; 12:12; 14:10; 15:15) as part of the Father's will (cf. 12:1–12; 14:36).

A corollary to the conflict motif growing out of the "gospel" is the question of Jesus' identity. This question runs throughout the narrative. Made explicit for the reader in the heading of 1:1, supported by the voice of God at the baptism (1:11), confirmed by the stifled demonic cries (1:25, 34; 3:11–12; 5:7), reenforced by the heavenly voice at the Transfiguration (9:7), acknowledged before the high priest (14:61–62), and climactically declared without qualification by the Roman centurion (15:39), the text claims that Jesus is the "Messiah, Son of God" with the accent on the phrase "Son of God" (see Kingsbury, *Christology,* 47–155). Yet apart from the demons, the full significance of this identity escapes the story's characters until after the crucifixion. This phenomenon is enhanced in Mark, on the one hand, by Jesus' own command of silence to the demons, the healed, and the disciples as well as his reference to himself with the less than explicit self-designation, the Son of man. On the other hand, the question of Jesus' identity is enhanced not only by his rejection at the hands of the religious authorities, the people of his hometown and his family, but by the surprising lack of understanding on the part of even his disciples, who are his closest followers and companions.

Indeed, the disciples' response to Jesus is a major portion of the plot. As people specially called and touched by Jesus, they respond in "repentance and faith" to Jesus as the one effectively proclaiming the "gospel of God," as those "to whom the mystery of the Kingdom has been given" (4:11). They receive special instruction from Jesus, participate in his ministry, and some are even commissioned to do that ministry. Yet they repeatedly demonstrate a lack of understanding about who Jesus is as well as about the implications of Jesus' identity for the life of discipleship. They waffle between "thinking the things of God" and "thinking the things of humankind."

This story is set in an unspecified time span between Jesus' baptism and his death. The shift in locale from Galilee (1:16–7:23) to the area north and east of Galilee (7:24–9:29, cf. 9:30–52) then to the Transjordan (10:1–52) and eventually to Jerusalem (11:1–16:8) gives movement to the story without offering a precise travelogue. The tight framework and the reference to the single Passover in Jerusalem toward the end of the story leaves the impression that the events took place within a time span of one year. This conclusion, however, assumes that the writer intended to give a short chronological account that included the scope of Jesus' ministry, an assumption that need not be the case either from the pattern of Greco-Roman biography or in the light of the framework and content of the Fourth Gospel. Though seeking to provide the reader with a connected narrative, the evangelist makes no claim about either the extent of the chronology or the completeness of his story (see on *Date* and *Place* below regarding where the author stands in terms of the story's chronology and locale).

AUTHOR

Bibliography

Hengel, M. *Studies in the Gospel of Mark.* Tr. J. Bowden. Philadelphia: Fortress, 1985. **Körtner, H. J.** "Markus der Mitarbeiter des Petrus." *ZNW* 71 (1980) 160–73. **Kümmel, W. G.** *Introduction to the New Testament.* 1975. **Kürzinger, J.** "Der Aussage des Papias von Hierapolis zur literarischen Form des Markusevangeliums." *BZ* 21 (1977) 245–64. **Niederwimmer, K.** "Johannes Markus und die Frage nach dem Verfasser des zweiten Evangeliums." *ZNW* 58 (1967) 172–88. **Reicke, B.** *The Roots of the Synoptic Gospels.* Philadelphia: Fortress, 1986. **Schoedel, W. R.** *The Apostolic Fathers: A New Translation and Commentary, V,* ed. R. M. Grant. London: Nelson and Sons, 1967.

The Second Gospel, like the other three, is anonymous. It does not even allude to authorship (cf. Luke 1:1–4; John 21:24). Though perhaps without significance, since, for example, the author may simply have assumed the reader's knowledge of who he was (e.g., Luke 3:1–3), the anonymity may have derived from the nature of the literary work. Anonymity may imply that the *Gospel* (literary work) does not come from the pen of a writer or an author but is the *gospel* (message) from God promised by Isaiah (e.g., 52:7; 61:1) and expressed in the teachings of and stories about Jesus Messiah (1:1, 14).

The wording of the titles supports this explanation. Instead of the more common construction with a genitive of authorship (e.g., "The Gospel *of* Mark") we find "The Gospel *according* to Mark" (Hengel, *Studies*, 65). Even the form of the later fourfold Gospel as "The Gospel" with the abbreviated "*According* to . . ." (κατά . . .) pointing to four accounts of "The Gospel" rather than the four "Gospels" makes clear that the "gospel" was an entity in itself not derived from any one author (Hengel, *Studies*, 65–67). Consequently, anonymity belonged inherently to the genre of the Gospels. Both the authors and the Church viewed the literary work as "The Gospel *according* to Mark" and not "The Gospel *of* Mark." It was the "gospel *of* God."

For us, however, the Gospels are not anonymous. We refer to them by a title that denotes authorship, e.g., "The Gospel according to Mark." According to Hengel (*Studies*, 70; similarly, Reicke, *Roots*, 154), these titles go back to the end of the first century. If so, they contribute the earliest information about the authorship of these documents. Thus we have "The Gospel according to Mark."

But who was Mark? That Mark (*Marcus*) was one of the most common Roman names of that era only complicates matters. But the answer has generally been based on information from a lost five-volume work of Papias, the bishop of Hieropolis (Λογίων κυριακῶν ἐξηγῆσις, *Interpretation of the Lord's Sayings*, A.D. 120/30) cited by Eusebius (*H.E.* 3.39.15):

> And this is what the Elder said, "Mark, who became Peter's interpreter, accurately wrote, though not in order (τάξει), as many of the things said and done by the Lord as he had noted (ἐμνημόνευσεν). For he neither heard the Lord nor followed him, but afterwards, as I said, he followed Peter who composed his teachings in anecdotes (χρείας) and not as a complete work (σύνταξιν) of the Lord's sayings. So Mark made no mistake in writing some things just as he had noted (ἀπεμνημόνευσεν) them. For he was careful of this one thing, to leave nothing he had heard out and to say nothing falsely."

This information associating Peter and Mark is echoed later in the anti-Marcionite prologue (160/80) that also refers to Mark as being "stubby fingered" (κολοβοδάκτυλος). Irenaeus (*Adv. Haer.* 3.1.1) from roughly the same time period (180) also makes the association of Mark with Peter. Toward the end of the second century, Clement of Alexandria attributes the writing to Mark in Rome during Peter's lifetime (Eusebius, *H.E.* 6.14; cf. 2:15). Yet all these writers appear dependent on Papias's tradition. This places the weight of evidence for Mark's identity on Papias.

Papias's testimony has received many treatments, both positive and negative. Papias does not claim to be the original witness but purports to pass on tradition which he had received from the "Elder." Accordingly, Mark is identified as Peter's "interpreter" (ἑρμηνευτής) who wrote down what the Lord said and did based on his notations of Peter's preaching which Peter had adapted. "Interpreter" can mean either a "translator" (e.g., from Aramaic to Greek) or, what is more likely in this context so full of semitechnical rhetorical language, the "transmitter" ("middleman") of Peter's preaching to others. Papias's statement also indicates that Peter presented his material in anecdotes (χρείαι) rather than as a completed work (τάξις) and that Mark's notes (cf. ἐμνημόνευσεν, ἀπεμνημόνευσεν, cf. Justin, *Dial.* 106.3) of this preaching became the source for his Gospel (see Kürzinger, *BZ* 21 [1977] 251–52; Schoedel, *Fathers*, 106–7).

Papias's statement makes two explicit value judgments about Mark's account. First, Mark wrote "without order." Second, he wrote accurately, carefully, completely, and honestly. The latter comment is almost stereotypical in Greco-Roman prologues to historical works (Hengel, *Studies*, 49, n. 67) and stands as an endorsement for the reliability of Mark's work. The charge that he wrote "without order" (τάξις) is less certain. On the one hand, some scholars have taken this as a disavowal of Mark's chronological order (e.g., Pesch, 1:5; Hengel, *Studies*, 48). On the other hand, "order" (τάξις) has been taken more technically as rhetorically referring to artistic arrangement (e.g., Schoedel, *Fathers*, 106, 108; Kürzinger, *BZ* 21 [1977] 252–53, Aune, *Environment*, 67). The latter seems more appropriate in view of the other rhetorical expressions in this statement and alludes to the paratactic, anecdotal style of Mark (cf. Pesch, 1:5, n. 5).

How is one to accept Papias's testimony? On the one side, the preponderance of scholarship over the centuries has accepted this witness in total. It has its defendants among critical scholars today (e.g., Cranfield, 5; Kürzinger, *BZ* 21 [1977] 245–64; Hengel, *Studies*, 47–50). On the opposite side, many contemporary scholars have totally rejected Papias's views (e.g., Niederwimmer, *ZNW* 58 [1967] 172–88; Kümmel, *Introduction*, 97; Körtner, *ZNW* 71 [1980] 171). Somewhere in the middle are those who accept Papias's identification of the writer as Mark but question his explanation of Mark's material as reminiscences of Peter's preaching (e.g., Pesch, 1:9; Ernst, 21; Lührmann, 5).

Without doubt a close examination of Mark's material will show that the evangelist did not simply write his Gospel based on his notes or memory of Peter's teachings. The amazing similarity in language, style, and form of the Synoptic tradition between the Markan and non-Markan materials of Matthew and Luke (cf. John's Gospel) hardly suggests that Mark's materials were shaped by one man, be he either Peter or Mark. Furthermore, the *Commentary* will demonstrate the presence of multiple traditional milieus (e.g., the two Feedings), stages in the development of traditional units (e.g., 5:1–20), and the thematic combination of units into collections (e.g., 4:1–34) within the Markan materials that point to a more complex traditional background than mental or written notes of another's preaching. Therefore, while Papias may accurately identify the author as Mark, his description of Mark's source and content is oversimplified at best.

Papias's testimony that identifies Mark as the writer of a Gospel does concur with the title, "The Gospel according to Mark," an apparently early, independent reference to authorship. The credibility of a Markan authorship grows when considered with the relative insignificance of a "Mark" in the early Church. Unless a "Mark" stood behind this Gospel, it is difficult to imagine why the early Church would have assigned this foundational document pseudonymously to such a nondescript Roman name, especially when the "Mark" of the NT was so relatively obscure.

But who was Mark? Assuming that the name refers to a definite person and not simply a pseudonym (e.g., Kümmel, *Introduction*, 97) we note two possibilities. First, and more traditionally, "Mark" has been identified with the Mark of 1 Pet 5:13; Acts 12:12, 25; 13:13; 15:37–39 and the Pauline corpus (e.g., Philem 24; Col 4:10; 2 Tim 4:11). He was "John Mark" (e.g., Cranfield, 5–6; Ernst, 19–20), an associate of the two giants of the early Church, Peter and Paul, and a member of the primitive community in Jerusalem which met in the upper room of his mother's home (Acts 12:12), where Jesus may have celebrated the last supper (Mark 14:14–15; Acts 1:13–14). This connection has even led to the pure speculation that Mark was the lad carrying the water pot of Mark 14:13 and even perhaps the boy fleeing naked into the night from the garden (14:51–52). Second, and more recently, several scholars have distinguished between "Mark" and the "John Mark" of the NT. For example, Lührmann (5–6), based on the consistent references to "Mark" as an associate of Peter rather than Paul in the tradition of the second and third centuries, has sought to distinguish "Mark" the associate of Peter in 1 Pet 5:13 from "John Mark" the associate of Paul in Acts and the Pauline corpus. Pesch (1:9–11) considers the evangelist to have been an "unknown Mark," possibly a Palestinian Jewish Christian in Rome, who through the influence of Papias's use of 1 Pet 5:13 came to be associated with the "John Mark" of the NT. And Niederwimmer (*ZNW* 172–88, esp. 178–185) identifies him as an unknown, gentile Christian ignorant of Palestinian geography and basically unfamiliar with Jewish customs.

The Commentary will show, contrary to the argument of Niederwimmer and others, that the evangelist was indeed well aware of Jewish customs but writing for, at least in part, a non-Jewish audience. Furthermore, Hengel (*Studies*, 46) comments: "I do not know any other work in Greek which has as many Aramaic or Hebrew words and formulae in so narrow a space as does the second Gospel." Even the questions raised by the apparent lack of knowledge about the geography of Galilee (cf. Mark 6–8) make unjustified assumptions about both the nature of the geographical references as well as the writer that need not disqualify a former resident of Jerusalem. Apart from the fact that such questions unfairly assume that a native of Jerusalem would know the detailed geography of Galilee and always seek precision when making geographical references to it, the *Comment* on Mark 6–8 will show that even the problematic references are not as improbable as has often been maintained.

The attempt to distinguish between the evangelist Mark and the later identification of the evangelist with the John Mark of the NT requires special pleading. We really do not have any basis for this distinction in the Church tradition. That the writer Mark is always associated in references to the Gospel with Peter and never with Paul reflects the influence of Papias's comments which purportedly came from the Elder. Furthermore, 1 Pet 5:13, regardless of the date of 1 Peter, can hardly support this distinction, since the mention of both Silvanus and Mark in 1 Pet 5:12–13 makes clear that "Mark" was the John Mark of Acts and the Pauline corpus who along with Silvanus (Silas) had also been a companion of Paul. Therefore, the traditional identification of Mark as being the John Mark of the NT seems to stand.

Ultimately, however, the question of authorship is moot for our reading of the Gospel. The writer makes no pretense of giving either his own or another's eyewitness account of the Gospel events for which his identity would either assist our understanding or guarantee the accuracy of the details. Furthermore, the traditional nature of the Markan material in particular and the Synoptic materials in general renders any association with Peter as the direct source useless as a guide for interpreting the material. Consequently, the identity of the author is more a historical curiosity than an exegetical necessity.

PLACE

Bibliography

Dschulnigg, P. *Sprache, Redaktion und Intention des Markus-Evangeliums: Eigentümlichkeiten der Sprache des Markus-Evangeliums und ihre Bedeutung für die Redaktionskritik.* SBB 11. Stuttgart: Katholisches Bibelwerk, 1986. **Hengel, M.** *Studies in the Gospel of Mark.* Tr. J. Bowden. Philadelphia: Fortress, 1985. **Kümmel, W. G.** *Introduction to the New Testament.* 1975. **Marxsen, W.** *Mark the Evangelist.* 1969. **Schreiber, J.** "Die Christologie des Markusevangeliums." *ZTK* 58 (1961) 154–83. **Schulz, S.** *Die Stunde der Botschaft: Einführung in die Theologie der vier Evangelisten.* Hamburg: Furche, 1967. **Smith, M.** *Clement of Alexandria and a Secret Gospel of Mark.* Cambridge, MA: Harvard UP, 1973. **Standaert, B. H. M. G. M.** *L'Evangile selon Marc: Composition et genre littéraire.* Zevenkerken-Brugge, 1984. **Vielhauer, P.** *Geschichte der urchristlichen Literatur: Einleitung in dem Neue Testament und den Apokryphen und den apostolischen Väter.* Berlin: DeGruyter, 1975.

Though numerous places have been suggested, including, for example, Galilee (Marxsen, *Mark,* 64–66), the Decapolis (Schulz, *Stunde,* 9), Syria (Vielhauer, *Literatur,* 347; Lührmann, 6–7), Tyre, Sidon, or the Decapolis (Schreiber, *ZTK* 58 [1961] 183), or more vaguely, "a gentile Christian community in the East" (Kümmel, *Introduction,* 97–98; similarly, Lührmann, 6–7), the majority of scholars concur with the early tradition in guardedly assigning Mark's Gospel to Rome. The anti-Marcionite prologue (160/180) places it in the "regions of Italy" and Clement of Alexandria (Eusebius, *H.E.* 2.15; 6.14.6) indicates Rome by noting Peter's approval of it there for the reading in the churches. Though Papias gives no hint of locale, the association of Mark's writing with the person of Peter may well explain how Mark came to be identified with Rome. 1 Pet 5:13 not only connects Peter and Mark but also locates them in "Babylon," an obvious allusion to Rome.

Some scholars have found internal evidence for Rome in Mark's disproportionately numerous Latinisms consisting of several Latin words which Mark simply transliterates into Greek and Latin expressions (e.g., Dschulnigg, *Sprache*, 276–78; Standaert, *Marc*, 470–73; Hengel, *Studies*, 29). Most notable is the explanation of the Greek coin (λεπτόν [νόμισμα]), the "widow's mite," as being a *quadrans* (12:42). Similarly, in 15:16 "inside the courtyard" (ἔσω τῆς αὐλῆς) has the Latin explanation (ὅ ἐστιν πραιτώριον). Such redactional comments would make more sense for an audience in Rome than one in the East for whom the Greek expression would hardly have needed the Roman/Latin explanation. Hengel (*Studies*, 29; Standaert, *Marc*, 473–78) has also noted that the description of the Syrophoenician woman as a "Greek-speaking, *Syrophoenician* by birth" ('Ελληνίς, Συροφοινίκισσα τῷ γένει) would make more sense in Rome than in Syria where "Phoenician" would have been clear. In Rome, by contrast, the Carthaginians were called Λιβυφοίνικες (cf. Συροφοινίκισσα) to distinguish them from the Phoenicians (Φοίνικες).

Mark's Gospel itself offers no concrete basis for determining location other than the noted disproportionate number of Latinisms. Since these can be attributed in part to the currency of these terms in semitechnical military and trade terminology (Kümmel, *Introduction*, 98), this evidence has generally been dismissed by those who would locate it somewhere "in the East" (e.g., Lührmann, 8). Ironically, however, proponents for a location other than Rome have even less basis for judgment. It appears that the rejection of Rome stems more from the rejection of the Papias's tradition associating Mark with Peter than from any hard evidence. Papias's tradition certainly needs revising regarding the source of Mark's material, but that need not mean the tradition of Mark's association with Peter and thus with Rome has any less credibility than a place arbitrarily posited elsewhere. At this point, the evidence of Mark's Latinisms, as suspect as it might be, would seem to tip the scale in favor of the tradition.

The only variation in the early tradition comes from John Chrysostom (*Matthaeum Homilae* 1.3) who suggests that Mark wrote his Gospel in Egypt. This witness has generally been discounted as a misreading of Eusebius's comment that Mark had been the first to proclaim in Egypt the Gospel which he had written (*H.E.* 2.16.1). But a recent discovery by Morton Smith of a supposedly lost letter of Clement of Alexandria indicates that Mark wrote a second edition, the so-called Secret Gospel, in Alexandria. If this is an authentic letter, it merely affirms Rome to be the original place of Mark's Gospel (*Secret Gospel*, 1.16), since, as Smith indicates, the Gospel we have is not the "Secret Gospel" (*Clement*, 88–97)

As with authorship, the lack of clear internal evidence for location makes the question of place moot as an exegetical tool. The Gospel does not address its readership from the standpoint of any particularly identifiable geographical location the knowledge of which would help us better understand the text. The narrator tells the story without importing geographical details from outside the narrative that might influence the reader's interpretation of the events. As an "intrusive narrator" he can tell the story as though present in the wilderness, by the sea, in a private home, in Herod's palace, in the synagogue or Temple, on a mountain, in a boat, in Galilee, in the area of Tyre and Sidon, in Caesarea Philippi, in the Decapolis, in Bethany, and in Jerusalem. Though specific details have come under question, the difficulties are not impossible to understand and certainly do not allow for deducing the Gospel's place of origin.

DATE

Bibliography

Guthrie, D. *New Testament Introduction: The Gospels and Acts.* Chicago: InterVarsity Press, 1965. **Hengel, M.** *Studies in the Gospel of Mark.* Tr. J. Bowden. Philadelphia: Fortress, 1985. **Kümmel, W. G.** *Introduction to the New Testament.* 1975. **Robinson, J. A. T.** *Redating the New Testament.* Philadelphia: Westminster, 1976.

Our earliest tradition (ca. A.D. 160/180) dates Mark's Gospel after Peter's death in Rome (anti-Marcionite prologue; Irenaeus, *Adv. Haer.* 3.1.1). Since it is generally assumed that Peter along with Paul met his death during an intense persecution by Nero of the Roman Christians in A.D. 64/65, the Gospel would have had to have been written subsequent to that time. By contrast, Clement of Alexandria implies that Mark wrote in Rome during Peter's lifetime (*Hypotyposeis* 6, cited by Eusebius, *H.E.* 6.14.5–7; similarly, *Secret Gospel,* 1.18–19), a view evidently followed by Eusebius (see *H.E.* 2.14–16). Should this dating be correct, the question shifts to when Peter was in Rome. The earliest traditional date places Peter in Rome during Claudius's rule (ca. 42, Eusebius, *H.E.* 2.14.6; 17.1; *Chronicle of Jerome*).

With few exceptions (e.g., Robinson, *Redating,* 107–17; cf. Guthrie, *Introduction,* 70–71), contemporary scholarship has opted for the later dating. The larger debate has centered on whether Mark wrote before or after the fall of Jerusalem in A.D. 70. On the one side, commentators like Anderson (25–26), Cranfield (8), Lane (17–21), Nineham (42), Schweizer (25), and Taylor (32) place its writing during the earlier stages of the war (A.D. 65–68). On the other side, Ernst (22), Gnilka (1:35), Grundmann (25), Pesch (1:14), Schmithals (1:61), and Lührmann (6) (similarly, Kümmel, *Introduction,* 98) date it sometime shortly after the fall of Jerusalem (ca. A.D. 70–73). The crux for this debate is Mark 13.

Mark 13 has been used to support both a prewar and postwar dating. But a detailed analysis of Mark 13:14 set against the historical background of the war in 67–70 (cf. *Comment* on Mark 13 and Hengel, *Studies,* 14–28) shows that the events associated in much of the current scholarship with the fall of Jerusalem and the destruction of the Temple simply do not fit with this verse that contains both a reference to the "abomination of desolation" and the note about fleeing "into the hills." Yet, since Mark places the discourse of 13:3–37 in the context of the predicted fall of the Temple (13:1–2, see *Comment* on 13:3) and as the answer to the question about when "these things" (including the predicted destruction of the Temple) would take place (see *Comment* on 13:4), 13:14 fits more appropriately a setting preceding the destruction of the Temple in A.D. 67–69, when the evangelist could foresee the impending doom of Jerusalem and the Temple. Thus, a date sometime after the Romans began their military campaign under Vespasian in 67 against the Jews in Palestine but before the final siege of Jerusalem under Titus in the summer of 70 seems to fit the perspective of Mark 13 best (see *Comment* on 13:14).

As was the case with authorship and place, the debate over a precise dating of the Gospel indicates above all how little solid internal evidence we have to go on. Coupled with few and conflicting traditional witnesses, the date has little to offer as a guide for interpreting the Gospel apart from perhaps the details of Mark 13 and related warnings of suffering. This conclusion concurs with the amazing consistency with which the author maintains the integrity of the story line almost free from anachronistic interpolations.

Mark writes for readers who live subsequent to and distant from the events narrated. Not only is this seen by the explanations made for the reader, but in 13:14 the narrator specifically warns the reader to take note of what had been promised and was now imminently expected. They live in the time frame of 13:10, when the gospel is "preached to all nations." The narrative itself, by contrast, takes place in an earlier time period beginning with the appearance of the Baptist and concluding with the women's discovery of Jesus' empty tomb.

SOURCES

Bibliography

Best, E. "Mark's Preservation of the Tradition." In *Disciples and Discipleship: Studies in the Gospel according to Mark.* Edinburgh: T. & T. Clark, 1986. 31–48. **Crossan, J. D.** *Four Other Gospels: Shadows on the Contours of Canon.* Philadelphia: Fortress, 1985. **Dschulnigg, P.** *Sprache, Redaktion und Intention des Markus-Evangeliums: Eigentümlichkeiten der Sprache des Markus-Evangeliums und ihre Bedeutung für die Redaktionskritik.* SBB 11. Stuttgart: Katholisches Bibelwerk, 1986. **Devisch, M.** "La relation entre l'évangile de Marc et le document Q." In *L'Evangile selon Marc. Tradition et rédaction*, ed. M. Sabbe. BETL 34. Gembloux: Leuven UP, 1974. 59–91. **Farmer, W. R.** *The Synoptic Problem: A Critical Analysis.* New York: Macmillan, 1964. ———, ed. *New Synoptic Studies: The Cambridge Gospels Conference and Beyond.* Macon, GA: Mercer UP, 1983. **Kelber, W.** *The Oral and Written Gospel.* Philadelphia: Fortress, 1983. **Koester, H.** "History and Development of Mark's Gospel (From Mark to Secret Mark and 'Canonical Mark')." In *Colloquy on New Testament Studies: A Time for Reappraisal and Fresh Approaches*, ed. B. Corley. Macon, GA: Mercer UP, 1983. **Kuhn, H.–W.** *Ältere Sammlungen im Markusevangelium.* 1971. **Laufen, R.** *Die Doppelüberlieferungen der Logienquelle und des Markusevangeliums.* BBB 54. Bonn: Peter Hanstein, 1980. **Lüderitz, G.** "Rhetorik, Poetik, Kompositionstechnik im Markusevangelium." In *Markus-Philologie: Historische, literargeschichtliche, und stilistische Untersuchungen zum zweiten Evangelium*, ed. H. Cancik. WUNT 33. Tübingen: Mohr, 1984. 165–203. **Neirynck, F.** *The Minor Agreements of Matthew and Luke Against Mark with a Cumulative List.* BETL 37. Leuven: Leuven UP, 1974. ———. "The Redactional Text of Mark." *ETL* 57 (1981) 144–62. **Peabody, D. B.** *Mark as Composer.* NGS 1. Macon, GA: Mercer UP, 1987. **Pryke, E. J.** *Redactional Style in the Marcan Gospel.* SNTSMS 33. Cambridge: Cambridge UP, 1978. **Reiser, M.** *Syntax und Stil des Markusevangelium.* WUNT 2, 11. Tübingen: Mohr, 1984. **Schenk, W.** "Der Einfluss der Logienquelle auf das Markusevangelium." *ZNW* 70

[1979] 141– 65. **Schulz, S.** *Die Stunde der Botschaft: Einführung in die Theologie der vier Evangelisten.* Hamburg: Furche, 1967. **Zerwick, M.** *Untersuchungen zum Markus-Stil: Ein Beitrag zur stilistischen Durcharbeitung des Neuen Testaments.* Rome: Pontifical Biblical Institute, 1937.

The clearly traditional nature of Mark's materials may have considerable bearing on the questions of authorship, place, and date. A close look at the Gospel reveals that the evangelist made extensive use of traditional material as the source for his work. In fact, the *Commentary* will show that we lack convincing evidence for arguing that the writer, though actively involved in reworking material, ever creatively composed *de novo* one single pericope (cf. Schmithals, 1:44–45). Even the rare pericopes composed by the evangelist consistently reflect a use of traditional materials and motifs appearing elsewhere in the Gospel tradition (e.g., see *Comment*, 6:7–13 or 8:14–21). That the writer was so heavily indebted to familiar traditional material may help explain why he wrote anonymously without attempting to claim "authorship" of his materials.

Yet the indebtedness to tradition hardly relegates the evangelist's role to that of a collector of traditions (Dibelius, 3). The way the materials have been selected and combined has indeed produced a distinctive literary work. This work contains the added thumbprints of comments, arrangement, motifs, style, and even vocabulary that brings a particular nuance to the varied traditions. The result is a distinctive portrait of Jesus and his ministry.

At the same time, the evangelist appears to have been conscientious about preserving the integrity of the place and time found in the tradition. He seeks continually to work within the given geographical and temporal framework of the materials, even when providing his own transitional comments that connect discrete traditions. This too may explain why subsequent readers removed from the writer's own temporal and geographical context have such a difficult time determining the place of origin and date of the Gospel's composition.

But what were Mark's traditional sources? Apart from those who take a neo-Griesbach position, according to which Mark used Matthew and Luke, led especially by the work and concern of W. R. Farmer (*Problem*; *Studies*), the consensus of the past century has viewed Mark to be a source for Matthew and Luke instead of vice versa. This approach has proven the more obvious to this writer when repeatedly tested on pericopes with parallels in Matthew and/or Luke. Therefore, one cannot look to Matthew or Luke as a source for Mark. This conclusion holds true in spite of the so-called minor agreements which can be as readily explained as coincidental or attributable to the living, oral tradition (see Neirynck, *Agreements*).

At the same time, Mark reflects some parallels with material found in the special sayings collection (commonly referred to as "Q") used by Matthew and Luke. Furthermore, these parallels cover more than simply "sayings" material (e.g., 4:21–25, 30–32; 8:38; 9:42–50; 12:38–40) when one considers the account of the Baptist (1:4–8), the Temptation (1:12–13), the Beelzebul incident (3:22–30), the sending of the Twelve (6:7–13) and the request for a sign (8:11–13). Though some have attributed the differences to Mark's redaction of the Q-material (e.g., Schenk, *ZNW* 70 [1979] 141–65; Schulz, *Stunde*, 363, n. 24), Mark's material appears better explained as an independent witness to an earlier tradition of which Q is generally the older witness (Lührmann, 12; Devisch, *Marc*, 49–95; similarly, Laufen, *Doppelüberlieferungen*). The same can be said for the similarities between Mark and John, especially in the combination of the Feeding and a Crossing (6:34–52; cf. 8:1–9), the events of the Triumphal Entry (11:1–11, 15–19), and the passion narrative.

As to the extracanonical materials, Mark seems to be independent of the *Gospel of Thomas*, the *Gospel of Peter*, and Egerton Papyrus 2 (1:40–45). The recent suggestion by Crossan (*Gospels*, 89–121) that canonical Mark represents a revision of the work referred to by Clement of Alexandria as the *Secret Gospel* (cf. similarly, H. Koester, *Colloquy*, 35–57) not only lacks any basis in Clement's comments, which declares that Mark wrote his "shorter" Gospel in Rome (see M. Smith, *Secret Gospel*, 1, 18–19), but has no real support in the Markan text. This view along with Schmithals's (1:44–51) *Grundschrift* represents but the latest variation on the oft rejected *Urmarkus* theory about an earlier version of Mark (see Cranfield, 13). Therefore, one looks in vain for one specific traditional source for Mark's material.

Despite the excesses of form criticism, that discipline and subsequent studies on oral tradition have shown that Mark consists of numerous traditional units. For example, we find various miracle stories, controversy and didactic stories, brief stories about Jesus and the Baptist, various kinds of parables, and sayings. These units apparently began as oral traditions and were doubtless used in various settings of the early Church's preaching and teaching. The oral character of the tradition most likely means that Mark's audience was also familiar with his materials. One cannot assume that the evangelist was writing to an audience for whom this tradition, oral or written, was unfamiliar. Furthermore, the traditional units betray little evidence of being simply mental or written notes based on Peter's preaching from his first-hand witness, a conclusion that impugns part of Papias's testimony but does not necessarily disparage the veracity or the value of the traditional units. We have, for example, many other traditional units in Luke's Gospel whose veracity one would not question but whose source has not been attributed directly to any one disciple or eyewitness (cf. Luke 1:1–4).

Some of the related, individual units appear to have been combined into larger units, perhaps even available to the evangelist as written sources, prior to his use of them. The extent of this grouping of materials has been debated (cf. Kuhn, *Sammlungen*), but the Commentary will point out evidence for, among others, a day in Capernaum behind 1:29–39, a collection of controversies in 2:15–28, a series of "Kingdom" parables behind 4:1–34, a collection of miracle stories around the Sea of Galilee behind 3:7–12; 4:35–5:43; 6:32–56 and at least the rudiments of a passion narrative underlying 14:1–16:8. Other smaller collections or combinations of traditional units may also have taken place (e.g., 8:34–9:1; 13).

Nevertheless, the many attempts at delineating even a clear, consistent distinction between redaction and tradition have proven futile. Mark did not wear gloves when handling his material which means that he left his redactional fingerprints even on the tradition (Dschulnigg, *Sprache,* 269–73, 289). At the same time, the evangelist had no inhibitions about employing traditional motifs, vocabulary, and style in his own redaction. Consequently, for the most part, one can only speak generally and tentatively when seeking to delineate between tradition and redaction. This conclusion does not dispute Mark's use of traditional materials or the availability of multiple sources, but it does mean that one cannot precisely reconstruct or always identify the exact content of his source or sources.

Therefore, the concern of the Commentary lies more in determining what the evangelist has actually done with the traditional material in writing his Gospel than in attempting to isolate the tradition for its own sake. The ultimate purpose in identifying the form-, source-, and redaction-critical elements of each pericope is to highlight the evangelist's adaptation and use of the respective material for his narrative as a means toward our primary goal of understanding, as best one can, what the evangelist wanted to communicate to his readers. By noting, where possible, the distinction between redaction and tradition, we enhance our perspective of the evangelist's intent as seen in his use of his traditional materials as well as our perspective of how the reader, most likely also familiar with the tradition, perceived the Markan use of that material.

For some of an Evangelical Christian persuasion, this more "critical" approach to the Gospels may appear much too complex a task in view of the generally assumed perspicuity of the Scriptures. Unfortunately, the latter view is based on the false assumption that the Scriptures were written *to* us as the primary audience rather than *for* us, a much later audience in a very different place and time. At the same time, such a critical approach may appear as though the exegete stands over the text rather than that the exegete stands under the scrutiny of the text. Yet one of the cardinal teachings of the Evangelical Christian community about the Scriptures has maintained that Scripture is our ultimate authority for faith and practice. This authority is based on what the Scriptures "said" as written by writers inspired by the Holy Spirit and not what the Scriptures "mean to me." Since what was "said" is determined both by the writer, his readers and the sociohistorical context and since the contemporary reader is so removed from that context, the insistence on determining what the text said necessitates that all who seek a normative witness must use every available literary and historical means to gain a more accurate understanding of what the evangelist "said" when he wrote the Gospel of Mark.

STRUCTURE

Bibliography

Ellis, P. F. "Patterns and Structures of Mark's Gospel." In *Biblical Studies in Contemporary Thought,* ed. M. Ward. Somerville, MA: Greeno, Hadden and Co., 1975. 88–103. **Hartmann, G.** *Der Aufbau des Markusevangeliums.* Münster: Aschendorff, 1936. **Koch, D.–A.** "Inhaltliche Gliederung und geographischer Aufriss im Markusevangelium." *NTS* 29 (1983) 145–66. **Kümmel, W. G.** *Introduction to the New Testament.* 1975. **Lang, F. G.** "Kompositionsanalyse des Markusevangeliums." *ZTK* 74 (1977) 1–24. **Perrin, N.** "Toward an Interpretation of the Gospel of Mark." In *Christology and A Modern Pilgrimage,* ed. H. D. Betz. Claremont, CA, 1971. 1–78. **Schenke, L.** "Der Aufbau des Markusevangeliums—ein hermeneutischer Schlüssel?" *BN* 32 (1986) 54–82.

One might well despair of finding any structure or outline for Mark's Gospel based on a consensus. The suggestions are as diverse as the individual commentators. In fact, one finds little consensus around even a principle for determining Markan structure. While some have found a geographical basis (e.g., Kümmel, *Introduction,* 82–83; Taylor, 105–13; Cranfield, 13–14), others have looked more toward thematic or Christological themes (e.g., Gnilka, 1:31–32; Lührmann, 23–24). Some commentators have tried a combination of the two (e.g., Ernst, 17–19; Koch, *NTS* 29 [1983] 145–66). More recently, literary or rhetorical bases have surfaced (e.g., Pesch, 1:32–40; Lang, *ZTK* 74 [1974] 1–24).

The breakdown usually comes in the subdivision of 1:1–8:26 and 8:27–16:8. Most scholars (cf. Lang, *ZTK* 77 [1977] 1–24; Ernst, 17–19) concur that the pericope of Caesarea Philippi represents the turning point that divides the Gospel into at least two major sections (1:1–8:26; 8:27–16:8). From this point on, Jesus' ministry focuses more narrowly on the disciples, and the ominous threat of his impending death becomes much more explicit. The conflict motif mounts and the events leading to his arrest, trial, and execution shape the narrative. Here one can find broader agreement on Mark's structure.

Three subsections emerge fairly neatly, although one cannot make the divisions based exclusively on either geographical or thematic criteria. In 8:27–10:52, Jesus begins the journey toward Jerusalem during which he instructs his disciples. The subsection is built around three passion predictions (8:31; 9:31; 10:33–34). In 11:1–13:37 Jesus arrives in Jerusalem and conflict arises almost immediately (e.g., 11:18). This conflict eventually leads to his death. Finally, in 14:1–16:8 the story reaches its climax, the passion narrative proper which ends with the account of the empty tomb.

The first half (1:1–8:26) also consists of three subsections plus an introduction. But here one looks in vain for agreement among scholars. The structure followed in this Commentary, however, is based more on literary considerations which were more likely coincident with Mark's telling of the story than with his conscious desire to follow a design. The "beginning" of the story, its introduction (1:1–15), is set under the heading of 1:1–3 as congruent with Isaiah's promise which provides the redemptive historical setting for the emergence of the Baptist and Jesus with their respective messages.

In 1:16–8:26 Mark's narrative breaks into three subsections (1:16–3:12; 3:13–6:6; 6:7–8:26) according to a literary pattern common to all three. Each subsection begins with a pericope involving the disciples (1:16–20; 3:13–19; 6:7–13) and concludes with a note of rejection followed by a summary relating to Jesus' ministry as seen in the preceding section (3:1–6, 7–12; 6:1–6a, 6b; 8:10–21, 22–26). Only 8:22–26, the Blind Man at Bethsaida, breaks this pattern, as a miracle story rather than a summary statement. Yet it too functions as a summary of Jesus' ministry for his disciples. The story of 8:22–26 not only looks backward but forward to set the stage for the change in the story's direction found in 8:27–16:8. After having given the disciples sight, seen as partial in 1:16–8:21 (esp. 8:13–21) and in what follows in 8:27–16:8 (esp. 8:27–33), Jesus will restore their sight completely, as the reader knows, after Easter.

Though one can sense a flow in Mark's story with different directions and themes, it seems impossible to give an adequate title either to the two major sections or to the six subsections that make up these two parts without simply being arbitrary. Since the story line follows Jesus' ministry and its ensuing response that takes place from Galilee and beyond until it ends in Jerusalem, various thematic and geographical divisions have naturally arisen. None works consistently. We have simply chapters in a story, as suggested by the following outline.

OUTLINE

1A. Introduction: "The Beginning" (1:1–15)
2A. Jesus' Public Ministry (1:16–8:26)
    1B. Jesus' Authority (1:16–3:12)
    2B. Jesus' Teaching (3:13–6:6)
    3B. Jesus and Mission (6:7–8:26)
3A. Jesus' Death (8:27–16:8)
    1B. Jesus' Instruction of the Disciples (8:27–10:52)
    2B. Jesus Confronts Jerusalem (11:1–13:37)
    3B. Jesus' Death and Resurrection (14:1–16:8)

THE THEOLOGY OF MARK

Bibliography

Ambrozic, A. M. *The Hidden Kingdom: A Redaction-critical Study of the References to the Kingdom of God in Mark's Gospel.* CBQMS 2. Washington, DC: CBA, 1972. **Best, E.** *Disciples and Discipleship: Studies in the Gospel According to Mark.* Edinburgh: T. & T. Clark, 1986. ———. *Mark: The Gospel as Story.* Edinburgh: T. & T. Clark, 1983. **Kealy, S.** *Mark's Gospel: A History of Its Interpretation.* New York: Paulist, 1982. **Kee, H. C.** *Community of the New Age: Studies in Mark's Gospel.* Philadelphia: Westminster, 1977. **Kelber, W.** *The Kingdom in Mark.* 1974. **Kingsbury, J. D.** *The Christology of Mark's Gospel.* Philadelphia: Fortress, 1983. **Koch, D.–A.** *Die Bedeutung der Wundererzählungen für die Christologie des Markusevanageliums.* 1975. **Lohmeyer, E.** *Galiläa und Jerusalem.* FRLANT 34. Göttingen: Vandenhoeck & Ruprecht, 1936. **Luz, U.** "Das Geheimnismotiv und die markinische Christologie." *ZNW* 56 (1965) 9–30. **Martin, R. P.** *Mark: Evangelist and Theologian.* Grand Rapids: Zondervan, 1973. **Marxsen, W.** *Mark the Evangelist.* 1969. **Minette de Tillesse, G.** *Le Secret Messianique dans l'Evangile de Mark.* Paris: Cerf, 1968. **Perrin, N.** "Toward an Interpretation of the Gospel of Mark." In *Christology and a Modern Pilgrimage,* ed. H. D. Betz. Claremont, CA, 1971. 1–78. **Räisänen, H. *Das "Messiasgeheimnis" im Markusevangelium.* Helsinki: Lansi-Suomi, 1976. **Reploh, K. G.** *Markus—Lehrer der Gemeinde.* 1969. **Schreiber, J.** "Die Christologie des Markusevangeliums." *ZTK* 58 (1961) 154–83. **Tuckett, C.,** ed. *The Messianic Secret.* Philadelphia: Fortress, 1983. **Vielhauer, P.** "Erwägungen zur Christologie des Markusevangeliums." In *Aufsätze zum Neuen Testament.* TB 31. Munich: Kaiser, 1965. 199–214. **Weeden, T. J.** *Traditions in Conflict.* 1971. **Wrede, W.** *The Messianic Secret.* Tr. J. C. G. Greig. Greenwood, SC: Attic Press, 1971.

Since the work of W. Wrede (*Secret,* German ed., 1901), Mark has been seen as having a distinctive theological message rather than simply being an account of the historical Jesus' ministry. Wrede saw it as an early Christological apology explaining the anomaly of the primitive Church's recognition of Jesus as the Messiah after Easter and the nonmessianic character of the tradition from Jesus' earthly ministry. The evangelist supposedly accounts for the failure to recognize Jesus' messianic role until after Easter by shaping his material to conform to the so-called messianic secret. Bultmann (347–48) viewed Mark as the combination of two kerygmas current within the early Church: the "Hellenistic kerygma about Christ" and the "tradition of the story of Jesus." Dibelius (230) labeled Mark a "book of secret epiphanies." Yet the study of a Markan theology per se really began to flourish after Marxsen's *Mark the Evangelist* (German ed., 1956).

One can see the diversity of the many works since Marxsen's in the surveys by Martin (*Mark: Evangelist and Theologian*) and Kealy (*Mark's Gospel*). Generally speaking, the major thrust of the various approaches to Markan theology have fallen into one of three categories: (a) eschatology, (b) Christology, and (c) discipleship and paraenesis.

Eschatology. Marxsen (similarly, Lohmeyer, *Galiläa*) initiated the eschatological approach. He argued that the evangelist used the Jesus-tradition to write the Gospel as a "visualized" kerygmatic summons to the Jerusalem Church after the outbreak of the Jewish War to go to Galilee where their imminently returning Lord would meet them. By contrast, Kelber (*Kingdom*), following Lohmeyer and Marxsen, accepts the eschatological locus of Galilee but argues that the fall of Jerusalem and the destruction of the Temple by A.D. 70 also destroyed an imminent eschatology connected with the "false concept of time and wrong choice of place: the Kingdom did not come at its appointed time and promised place" (*Kingdom,* 139). Therefore, Mark's Gospel offers a positive response to this crisis by means of a spatio-temporal redefinition of the Kingdom that now sets in motion the fundamental program for the realization of the Kingdom in Galilee.

Kee (*Community,* 106) also interprets Mark apocalyptically but defines the constituent element of apocalyptic as being a "community which regards itself as the recipient of a revelation through a God-sent prophet concerning the destiny of the world and its own eschatological vindication, which is to occur in the near future." Accordingly, Mark's community sees itself in the "time between" Jesus' inauguration of the Kingdom and its future consummation as promised. Thus the Gospel reflects an apocalyptic community, its Christology, and ethics.

Ambrozic (*Kingdom,* 244) finds the "primary message" of the Gospel to be the Kingdom of God, "a Kingdom yet to come which is, paradoxically, already present." Concurring with Kee's emphasis on the "time between," this study contrasts with Marxsen's imminent and Kelber's realized eschatology of Mark. Ambrozic argues that Jesus inaugurates God's Kingdom by his words, deeds, and destiny. But the Kingdom's presence remains "hidden" until its future manifestation at the end of time. The pertinence of Mark's Gospel for his readers lies in that little, except for the messianic secret which ended with the events of Jesus' death and resurrection, has changed between the time of Jesus' ministry and Mark's day. As in Jesus' ministry, God continues to work through the words and deeds of the community to establish the "hidden" Kingdom. As with the Twelve, the "hidden" character of the Kingdom makes the believers in Mark's day vulnerable to weakness of faith, discouragement, and rejection. Yet the Gospel reminds the readers that a "radical obedience to Jesus' call and selfless service to others" remains the sign of the present, though hidden, Kingdom (*Kingdom*, 244).

Christology. Wrede, of course, was the first to see a Christological motif as giving shape to Mark's Gospel. His so-called messianic secret, though seldom left unmodified, has continued to figure prominently in Markan studies (cf. Minette de Tillesse, *Secret*; Räisänen, *Messiasgeheimnis*; Tuckett, *Secret*). Bultmann's (347–48) thesis that Mark wedded the hellenistic kerygma with its Christ or gnostic redeemer myth and the tradition of the story of Jesus has also found several exponents. For example, Vielhauer (*Aufsätze*, 199–214) points to the prominence of "Son of God" in 1:1 that is used positively (cf. 1:24; 3:11; 5:7) in 1:11 (baptism); 9:11 (transfiguration); and 15:39 (crucifixion) in a supposed correlation with an ancient Egyptian enthronement ceremony of adoption, presentation, and enthronement. Accordingly, Mark's story relates Jesus' mission as the divine Son who passes incognito through the realm of time and space. Similarly, Schreiber (*ZTK* 58 [1961] 154–83) has taken the motif and structure for Mark's Gospel to be the structure of the hymn behind Phil 2:6–11 in which a divine being yields to humiliation by death at which time he is exalted and vindicated.

A recent trend finds in Mark's Gospel a corrective to a false Christology. Though this view is implicit in Wrede's reconstruction, it generally has focused on the Bultmannian distinction between a "hellenistic" Christology and one more akin to the primitive Jesus-tradition. Best known is Weeden's (*Traditions in Conflict*, 1971; similarly, Luz, *ZNW* 56 [1965] 9–30; Perrin, *Christology*, 1–78; Koch, *Wundererzählungen*) thesis that Mark counters an exalted Christology reflecting the hellenistic "divine man" (θεῖος ἀνήρ) pattern as found in the stories of Jesus' mighty, miraculous works and represented by the Twelve (1:1–8:26) with a theology of the suffering Son of man (8:27–16:8).

Martin (*Mark*, 160–61) rejects Weeden's scenario but finds Mark to be addressing Paul's "dubious legacy on the later church" which was vulnerable to the overemphasizing of Christ the heavenly figure "out of touch with earthly reality" and the "historical events underlying his kerygma." Accordingly, the evangelist provides a supplement to Paul's kerygma through writing a "dramatization in the life of Jesus" by joining selective materials drawn from the Jesus-tradition and a passion narrative to focus on the humiliation and the enthronement of the Lord, the "twin elements" of Paul's preaching (161).

Using a literary-critical approach to Mark as narrative, Kingsbury (*Christology*) rejects such a "corrective" approach to Mark's Christology. He has concluded that Mark's Gospel focuses above all on the meaning of Jesus' identity as the "Messiah Son of God" (1:1) which, except to Jesus himself, remains a secret throughout the Gospel. The secret is first revealed when the centurion publicly declares the fact in view of the events of the crucifixion (15:39) and in the anticipatory comments at the tomb by the young man in white (16:7) which imply that the "disciples and Peter" will fully receive their "sight" in Galilee (cf. 8:22–26). Jesus, who thinks "the thoughts of God," recognizes the full meaning of his royal Sonship in contrast to those who think "the thoughts of man" (cf. 8:27–33). Thus Mark's Gospel invites the reader to abandon "human thinking" and adopt "divine thinking" by aligning with the will of God through conformity to the life of Jesus (*Christology*, 155): "If anyone would come after me, let him deny himself and take up his cross, and let him follow me" (3:34).

Discipleship. In addition to those who understand Mark's theology to have been primarily eschatological or Christological in character, other scholars have taken Mark to have been aiming primarily at the meaning of discipleship. This approach should not be surprising in the light of the prominence given the disciples in the structure of his Gospel.

Reploh (*Lehrer*) treats Mark's Gospel as essentially the evangelist's use of the Jesus-tradition to instruct his community that was struggling to understand the significance of the Jesus-tradition. Accordingly, the role of the disciples in Mark has been greatly reworked by the evangelist to represent primarily his own community and their need to understand and believe (1:14–15, *Lehrer*, 228–30). Above all, the community needed to recognize that following Jesus involved the way of the cross (8:27–10:52). Similarly, Best finds that the disciples "generally represent the community as a whole" (*Disciples*, 128), and he has attributed Mark's purpose to a pastoral concern to edify his readers in the faith (*Mark*, 95). In particular, Mark addresses their "failure to appreciate the sacrifice required from the members if they were to be true followers of the Lord" (*Mark*, 144).

This brief survey of varied statements of Markan theology merely indicates the diversity of focus and viewpoint in Markan theology. Mark's gospel about Jesus Messiah, Son of God, however, inherently involves eschatology, Christology, and discipleship. To single out one of these themes as primary not only distorts the gospel but distorts Mark's Gospel.

THE PURPOSE OF MARK'S GOSPEL

Mark 1:1 clearly indicates that the evangelist set out to write the "gospel concerning Jesus Messiah, Son of God." In determining the writer's purpose, one must start here. This statement, however, only gives the reader the "what" but not the "why" of this narrative. By referring to the story that follows as the "gospel concerning Jesus Messiah, Son of God," the evangelist tells the reader how he perceives his narrative. It is "the gospel." But why does he put the "gospel" comprised of numerous traditional units in writing? Unfortunately, we are left to reading between the lines for the answer.

Perhaps the more traditional answer for why Mark wrote the Gospel has to do with the concern to preserve the tradition. Assuming that the first generation eyewitnesses and guarantors of the tradition were either dying out or being killed, the evangelist would have put the "gospel" in writing lest it be lost or distorted with the passing of time. In Mark's case, this theory corresponds with the traditionally close connection between Peter and the evangelist so that the death of the former precipitated the writing by the latter.

This answer, however, makes at least two false assumptions. First, it wrongly assumes a much later view that tradition could be better preserved in written than oral form, a view disputed by Papias's own reliance on oral tradition a generation later (e.g., Eusebius, *H.E.* 3.39.4). Second, it wrongly assumes that Mark was merely recording rather than himself reworking the tradition in a way doubtless parallel to his community's own handling of the tradition. It is inconceivable that Mark could have done what he did with the tradition, if such practice had not been an accepted procedure in the earlier transmission of the tradition. Certainly, Matthew and Luke handled the tradition in the same manner, as their reworking of Mark indicates. Therefore, even the pre-Markan oral tradition had a dynamic life/lives of its own which no one Gospel could preserve.

A more recent approach to discovering Mark's purpose has focused on clues within Mark's Gospel that might betray a specific setting or occasion for its having been written. For some writers (e.g., Lührmann), the Jewish war led to a crisis in the early Church's eschatology which Mark addressed by writing his Gospel. For others (e.g., Weeden), a Christological heresy growing out of the increasing "hellenization" of the mission needed countering with a more orthodox Christology. Apart from the fact that these theories fail to answer why Mark wrote a "gospel," none has proved convincing. In fact, they have all been shown to lack sufficient basis in Mark's Gospel when read as a whole. Yet these theories have correctly noted that Mark's "gospel" does have to do with the "Kingdom of God" and with the identity of Jesus.

For Mark the "gospel" clearly depicts Jesus as inaugurating God's sovereign rule, the Kingdom, through his words and deeds. The evangelist makes this point evident at the outset in both the heading of the introduction, "the gospel concerning Jesus Messiah, Son of God" (1:1), and the programmatic summary of Jesus' preaching "the gospel of God" about the Kingdom and the fulfillment of time at the end of the introduction (1:14–15). At the same time, for Mark the "gospel concerning Jesus Messiah, Son of God," has a future component when the Kingdom of God will appear "in power" (9:1) at the coming of the Son of man to bring God's salvation to its consummation (13:26–27).

This message or "gospel concerning Jesus Messiah, Son of God" represents the fulfillment of Isaiah's promised gospel of God's rule and salvation (Isa 52:7; cf. 61:1) proclaimed by Jesus (1:14). But it also raises the dilemma of how the Kingdom could be both present and future. More particularly, in what sense could one say that it was present in Jesus' ministry? The dilemma was no less problematic for Mark's audience than for that of Jesus. The response to the gospel continued to be confused and mixed, the rejection and even persecution of those who did respond had intensified, and the "Messiah, Son of God" had been crucified rather than crowned in Jerusalem.

This confusion appears particularly in Mark's handling of the disciples. Taking motifs found in the tradition and doubtless reflecting the confusion of Jesus' own followers, Mark accents these to depict the "disciple" from the standpoint of his community as one both privileged and perplexed. On the one hand, the disciples and Mark's audience had been specially called to follow Jesus, to be with him on the way. They had been given the mystery of the Kingdom; they had experienced in their own lives God's redeeming activity. Privy to special instruction, they were even empowered to act in Jesus' name to preach the gospel, to heal, to exorcise, and to teach. Yet, on the other hand, they have misunderstood. They have become confused and afraid. When adversity set in, they reflected little faith and hardness of heart. This confusion had eaten away at their fundamental perception of who Jesus was, in short, the essence of the gospel.

Mark, consequently, writes the "gospel concerning Jesus Messiah, Son of God" to proclaim anew for his audience the "gospel of God" to address their confusion. He reminds them that Jesus had indeed come as God's promised, Spirit-anointed, royal Son to herald and inaugurate the Kingdom by defeating Satan and his forces, healing the sick, forgiving the sinner, feeding the hungry, and raising the dead—all indications of the promised day of salvation. He reminds the reader that Jesus is the Messiah, Son of God, not only by introducing him that way (1:1) but by repeatedly affirming this identity throughout the narrative (1:11; 3:11–12; 5:7; 9:7; 14:61–62; 15:39).

At the same time, the evangelist developed his narrative to show that Jesus' message risked a triumphalist misunderstanding by those who saw primarily the glory of the final Kingdom in contrast to its vulnerable beginning. In Jesus' first extended teaching focusing on the Kingdom, the Kingdom parables (4:1–34) declare that the Kingdom is here but depict the Kingdom as a vulnerable seed (4:1–20), a seed growing on its own (4:26–29), and the smallest of seeds (4:30–32), and warn the "hearer" not to mistake its presence (4:21–25). In Jesus' last extended teaching, the Olivet Discourse (13) promises salvation in the future consummation, but warns that meanwhile conditions appear to go from bad to worse. By accenting silence commands, by dropping hints of a mortal conflict, by depicting the rejection by the religious authorities and even Jesus' family, by repeating Jesus' reference to his coming death, and by the centurion's climactic statement at the crucifixion, Mark qualifies "Messiah, Son of God" in terms of suffering and the cross.

Mark also uses the "gospel concerning Jesus Messiah, Son of God" as the basis for a discipleship paraenesis. At stake for Mark's audience is not only the issue of who Jesus Messiah, Son of God, is in relation to the cross and the Kingdom present and future but also the implications of this "gospel" for the cost of discipleship. Right thinking and right faith must issue in right living. Right living meant following Jesus' way, the way of the cross (8:27–10:52).

Therefore, Mark wrote the Gospel pastorally to address a community under duress. This duress had given rise to questions about who Jesus was and the nature of the "Kingdom" he had come to inaugurate. Mark points back to the "good news concerning Jesus Messiah, Son of God," to remind them of who Jesus was and what he had come to do as well as what he would do. This Gospel offered a renewed basis for their faith, made clear the dangers and pitfalls along the way, and offered the hope of the Kingdom future, the day of harvest, the mustard tree, the resurrection, and the ultimate consummation of God's rule.

The reader may wish a more precise definition of the community, its setting, and the occasion for this Gospel. But apart from the evidence that the readers were not at home in Aramaic or many of the Jewish laws and customs, which necessitated the evangelist's explanations, and apart from the fact that the thrust of the Gospel was more for Christian believers than for either the unbelievers in their mission or their adversaries, little more can be said in spite of many attempts to say more. The evidence permits one to place the audience in various time periods and locales. This trait gives a universal character to Mark's Gospel that explains why it addresses the modern disciple in much the same manner as it did the first readers. It continues to be the "gospel concerning Jesus Messiah, Son of God."

I. The Beginning of the Gospel according to Isaiah   (1:1–15)

Bibliography

Bacon, B. W. "The Prologue of Mark: A Study of Sources and Structure." *JBL* 26 (1907) 84–105. **Dautzenberg, G.** "Die Zeit des Evangeliums. Mk 1,1–15 und die Konzeption des Markusevangeliums." *BZ* 21 (1977) 219–34. **Feneberg, W.** *Der Markusprolog: Studien zur Formbestimmung des Evangeliums.* SANT 36. Munich: Kösel, 1974. **Gibbs, J. M.** "Gospel Prologues." *SE* 6 = *TU* 112 (1974) 154–88. **Guelich, R. A.** "The Beginning of the Gospel, Mark 1:1–15." *BR* 27 (1982) 5–15. **Iersel, B. F. W. van,** and **Schoonenberg, P.** "Die Theologie über die exegetische Detailarbeit: Ein Exeget und ein Theolog über Markus 1, 1–15." *Concil* 7 (1971) 715–24. **Keck, L. E.** "The Introduction to Mark's Gospel." *NTS* 12 (1965–66) 352–70. **Langkammer, H.** "Tradition und Redaktion im Prolog zum Markusevangelium." *RTK* 20 (1973) 37–57. **Lightfoot, R. H.** *The Gospel Message of St. Mark.* Oxford: Clarendon, 1950. **Lührmann, D.** "Biographie des Gerechten als Evangelium: Vorstellungen zu einem Markus-Kommentar." *Wort und Dienst* 14 (1977) 23–50. **Pesch, R.** "Anfang des Evangeliums." In *Die Zeit Jesu,* FS H. Schlier, ed. G. Bornkamm and K. Rahner. Freiburg: Herder, 1970. 108–44. **Robinson, J. M.** *The Problem of History in Mark.* SBT 21. London: SCM, 1957. **Schnackenburg, R.** "Das Evangelium' im Verständnis des ältesten Evangelisten." In *Orientierung an Jesus,* FS J. Schmid, ed. P. Hoffmann. Freiburg: Herder, 1973. 309–24. **Schweizer, E.** "Anmerkungen zur Theologie des Markus." In *Neotestamentica et Patristica,* FS O. Cullmann. NovTSup 6. Leiden: Brill, 1960. 1–13. **Seitz, O. J.** *"Praeparatio Evangelica* in the Marcan Prologue." *JBL* 82 (1963) 201–6.

Introduction

The Gospel of Mark opens with a series of vignettes depicting the beginning of the ministry of Jesus Messiah, the Son of God. The focus on Jesus' coming begins with the OT promise (1:2–3) of a precursor that is fulfilled by John the Baptist (1:4–6) whose own role as a prophet, indicated by his food and clothing (1:6), culminates in his heralding of Jesus' coming (1:7–8). The Baptist's preaching and baptism set the stage for the divine declaration that attests Jesus to be the Son of God (1:9–11) who resists Satan in the wilderness temptations (1:12–13) and who himself emerges in Galilee to herald the fulfillment of time, the good news of God's reign (1:14–15). Thus the opening section sets forth the "beginning of the gospel of Jesus Messiah, Son of God" (1:1).

Yet this opening section has given rise to a variety of opinions regarding its proper designation, its limits and its sources. Cranfield (33) reflects the diversity in the passage's designation by entitling the section "The Beginning" and then noting that it serves as a "prologue" to the Gospel that "introduces" Jesus of Nazareth. It has become rather common to refer to these opening verses as a "prologue" (e.g., Bacon, *JBL* 26 [1907] 84; Grundmann, 34; Lane, 39; Pesch, 71–72; Seitz, *JBL* 82 [1963] 201), while others prefer the more neutral "introduction" (e.g., Dautzenberg, *BZ* 21 [1977] 3; Keck, *NTS* 12 [1965–66] 352–70; Lightfoot, *Message,* 15; Taylor, 151) or "preface" (e.g.,

Anderson, 63). The evangelist (1:1) apparently referred to this section as the "beginning" (so Cranfield, 33; Gnilka, 1:39 ["initium"]; Lohmeyer, 9; Schweizer, 28).

Behind the choice of terminology lies the basic question of the section's relationship to the rest of the Gospel. Whereas "prologue" and "preface" connote a more self-contained section, "introduction" and clearly "beginning" signal a more integral relationship between this material and the rest of the Gospel. The answer ultimately lies in the significance of the opening verse.

The limit of this opening section has been variously set as 1:1–8, 1:1–13, and 1:1–15 (Feneberg, *Markusprolog,* arbitrarily chose 1:1–11 apparently for the purposes of his survey). The division of 1:1–8 found in the Greek texts of Westcott and Hort, Nestle, and the GNT (cf. Nestle[26]) has few followers today (e.g., Haenchen, 28–51, and Schmithals, 1:73–82, without comment). Since the appearance and preaching of the Baptist (1:4–8) hardly represent the "beginning of the gospel" for Mark and since the thrust of 1:2b–3, 7–8 points to the one who would follow John, Mark's opening section must include at least 1:1–13 (e.g., Bacon, *JBL* 26 [1907] 87–88; Cranfield, 32–60; Lane, 39–62; Lightfoot, *Message,* 15–20; Lohmeyer, 9–28; Schniewind, 44–50; Schweizer, 28–43; Taylor, 151–64).

Yet the grounds for drawing the line at 1:13 rather than 1:15 are seldom stated. They are implied by the headings given the following sections. For most of the above commentators, 1:14–15 represent the outset of Jesus' public or Galilean ministry. Thus by implication 1:1–13 merely set the stage for Jesus' entry into his public ministry. Since, however, such a chronological orientation appears at best to be of secondary importance to the evangelist both in 1:1–13 as well as in the following pericopes that lead to the passion narrative, one wonders if it should be accorded such significance in the relationship of 1:1–13 to 1:14–15. The evidence suggests a third option.

The recent trend has been to include 1:14–15 within the opening section (e.g., Anderson, 63–64; Dautzenberg, *BZ* 21 [1977] 219–34; Gibbs, *TU* 112 [1974] 154–88; Gnilka, 1:39–40; Grundmann, 34; Keck, *NTS* 12 [1965–66] 352–70; Langkammer, *RTK* 20 [1973] 57; Pesch, 1:71–73; Mann, 193–94). Three arguments support this option. First, terminologically εὐαγγέλιον forms an inclusion between 1:1 and 1:14–15 and the related term κηρύσσειν links John and Jesus in 1:4, 7, 14. Second, thematically John the Baptist as the forerunner provides the foil for Jesus' appearance in 1:9–15. In addition to the contrast explicitly stated in 1:2–8, the threefold division of the traditional units regarding John and Jesus respectively parallel each other in such a manner as to accent this contrast. For example, both units open with an identifying word from God (1:2b–3, 11), contain a reference to their person and work (1:4–6, 12–13), and climax with a reference to their preaching (1:7–8, 14–15). Third, structurally the second major section of the Gospel (1:16–8:26) can be divided into three subsections, each beginning with a reference to discipleship (1:16–3:12; 3:13–6:6; 6:7–8:26; so Keck, *NTS* 12 [1965–66] 362–63) that supports the break between 1:15 and the call of the four disciples in 1:16–20.

This opening section consists of several traditional units. At issue in the discussion of sources is the extent of the evangelist's redactional contribution to and the shaping of the material. On the one side, some have argued for a preevangelist traditional unit (1:1–15) with little redactional activity by the evangelist (e.g., Langkammer, *RTK* 20 [1973] 57; Pesch, 1:71–108; Schnackenburg, *Orientierung*, 318–19). Accordingly, this material would have come to the evangelist as the product of the community's previous combination of traditional materials. On the other side, several have assigned the combination of the traditions in 1:2–8 and at least the shaping, if not the whole, of 1:14–15 to Mark (e.g., Dautzenberg, *BZ* 21 [1977] 226–27; Gnilka, 1:39–40; Grundmann, 34–35; van Iersel, *Concil* 7 [1971] 717–18).

Based on an examination of this material, Mark appears to have formed the opening of his Gospel from a mixed quotation (1:2b–3) taken either from a setting similar to 1:4 or found as an isolated *testimonium*, a traditional unit on the appearance and ministry of John the Baptist (1:4–8), a tradition of Jesus' baptism by John (1:9–11) previously combined with an account of Jesus' temptation in the wilderness (1:12–13) and a summary statement consisting of several traditional formulas to summarize Jesus' message (1:14–15). The evangelist has aligned these units under his heading of 1:1–3 to show how the "beginning of the gospel of Jesus Messiah, Son of God" corresponds to Isaiah's promise. In this way, he introduces and identifies John the Baptist and the main character of his story, Jesus Messiah, Son of God.

A. The Heading (1:1–3)

Bibliography

Arnold, G. "Mk 1,1 und Eröffnungswendungen in griechischen und lateinischen Schriften." *ZNW* 68 (1977) 121–27. **Bowman, J. W.** "The Term *Gospel* and its Cognates in the Palestinian Syriac." In *New Testament Essays*, FS T. W. Manson, ed. A. J. B. Higgins. Manchester: Manchester UP, 1959. 54–57. **Dautzenberg, G.** "Die Zeit des Evangeliums: Mk 1,1–15 und die Konzeption des Markusevangeliums." *BZ* 21 (1977) 219–34. **Feneberg, W.** *Der Markusprolog: Studien zur Formbestimmung des Evangeliums.* SANT 36. Munich: Kösel, 1974. **Fitzmyer, J. A.** "The Use of the Explicit Old Testament Quotations in Qumran and the New Testament." *NTS* 7 (1960–61) 297–33 = *Essays on the Semitic Background of the New Testament.* London: Chapman, 1971. 3–58. **Iersel, B. F. W. van,** and **P. Schoonenberg.** "Die Theologie über die exegetische Detailarbeit: Ein Exeget und ein Theologe über Markus 1,1–15." *Concil* 7 (1971) 715–24. **Kazmierski, C. R.** *Jesus, the Son of God: A Study of the Markan Tradition and Its Redaction by the Evangelist.* Forschung zur Bibel 33. Würzburg: Echter Verlag, 1979. **Kingsbury, J. D.** *The Christology of Mark's Gospel.* Philadelphia: Fortress, 1983. **Lamarche, P.** "Commencement de l'Evangile de Jésus, Christ, Fils de Dieu (Mc 1,1)." *NRT* 92 (1970) 1024–36. **Martin, R. P.** *Mark, Evangelist and Theologian.* Grand Rapids: Zondervan, 1972. **Marxsen, W.** *Mark the Evangelist.* 1969. **Pesch, R.** "Der Anfang des Evangeliums Jesu Christi: Eine Studie zum Prolog des Markusevangeliums (Mk 1:1–15)." In *Die Zeit Jesu*, FS H. Schlier, ed. G. Bornkamm and K. Rahner. Freiburg: Herder, 1970. 108–44. **Schnackenburg, R.** "'Das Evangelium' im Verständnis des ältesten Evangelisten." In *Orientierung an Jesus*, FS J. Schmid, ed. P. Hoffmann. Freiburg: Herder, 1973. 309–24. **Schweizer, E.** "Die theologische Leistung des Markus." *EvT* 19 (1964) 337–

55. **Seitz, O. J. F.** "*Praeparatio Evangelica* in the Marcan Prologue." *JBL* 82 (1963) 201–6. **Slomp, J.** "Are the Words 'Son of God' in Mark 1:1 Original?" *BT* 28 (1977) 143–50. **Snodgrass, K. R.** "Streams of Tradition Emerging from Isaiah 40:1–5 and Their Adaptation in the New Testament." *JSNT* 8 (1980) 24–45. **Strecker, G.** "Das Evangelium Jesu Christi." In *Jesus Christus im Historie und Geschichte*, FS H. Conzelmann, ed. G. Strecker. Tübingen: Mohr, 1975. **Stuhlmacher, P.** *Das paulinische Evangelium— 1: Vorgeschichte.* FRLANT 95. Göttingen: Vandenhoeck & Ruprecht, 1968. **Turner, C. H.** "Marcan Usage: Notes, Critical and Exegetical, on the Second Gospel." *JTS* 26 (1925) 145–56. **Wikgren, A.** "ΑΡΧΗ ΤΟΥ ΕΥΑΓΓΕΛΙΟΥ." *JBL* 61 (1942) 11–20.

Translation

[1] *The* [a] *beginning of the gospel concerning* [b] *Jesus Messiah, Son of God,* [c] [2] *as written by the prophet* [d] *Isaiah:* [e] *"Take note, I send my messenger before you who will prepare your way.* [f] [3] *A voice of one crying in the wilderness:* [g] *'Prepare the way of the Lord; make straight his* [h] *paths.'"* [i]

Notes

[a] Anarthrous Greek construction may signal the function as a heading (e.g., Hos 1:2; Prov 1:1; Eccl 1:1; Cant 1:1; Matt 1:1; Rev 1:1).

[b] Genitive (Ἰησοῦ Χριστοῦ) offers possibility of subjective genitive or objective genitive. Context determines the choice (see *Comment* on 1:1).

[c] "Son of God" (υἱοῦ θεοῦ) is missing in ℵ* Θ 28 sy[pal] Iren[gr,lat1/3] Or[gr,lat] but present in ℵ[1] B D L W pc latt sy co; Iren[lat2] (A reads υἱοῦ τοῦ θεοῦ). Though broadly and strongly attested, its omission in several MSS provides basis for question. The internal argument favors the reading (cf. Pesch, 1:74, n. 1; Slomp, *BT* 28 [1977] 143–50). Not only does the evangelist use the title to introduce Jesus in 1:11 but the Roman centurion's recognition of Jesus as "Son of God" in 15:39 offers the climactic counterpart of that revelation (cf. 1:11; 5:7; 9:7; 14:61). Although a homoioteleuton at the beginning of a work seems unusual (Slomp, *BT* 28 [1977] 148), the series of six genitives and the normally abbreviated ΙΥ ΧΥ ΥΥ ΘΥ (Turner, *JTS* 26 [1925] 150) make this suggestion the best explanation for its absence.

[d] Several MSS (A L W) read τοῖς προφήταις for τῷ Ἡσαΐᾳ τῷ προφήτῃ in an attempt to adapt this introduction to the mixed citation of 1:2b–3.

[e] The question of punctuation pertains to the function of 1:1 and its relationship to 1:2–4. As a heading, 1:1 could stand as independent and verbless concluded by a period (e.g., Nestle[26] and most commentaries). Since, however, καθώς alone never begins a sentence in Mark or elsewhere in the NT (cf. Taylor, 153; Anderson, 67–68; Haenchen, 39), the καθώς of 1:2 implies a syntactical relationship with 1:1 (Arnold, *ZNW* 68 [1977] 123–24; Cranfield, 35; Feneberg, *Markusprolog*, 186–87; Lagrange, 1–2; Turner, *JTS* 26 [1925] 150).

[f] Some MSS (e.g., A f1 f13 sa bo Or Eus) read additionally ἔμπροσθέν σου adapted from Matt 11:10 // Luke 7:27.

[g] Although "wilderness" designates where one "prepares the way" in the Hebrew text of Isa 40:3, it locates the "voice of one crying" in the LXX and the Targum. Thus the shift has its history in Judaism.

[h] The Western text (D it) substitutes τοῦ θεοῦ ἡμῶν for αὐτοῦ in keeping with the Hebrew and LXX text of Isa 40:3.

[i] The period ends the "heading" of 1:1–3. As will be seen below, 1:1–3 is the heading for 1:4–15 and not simply 1:4–8 as suggested by an intermediate punctuation mark (e.g., comma: so Nestle[26]; semicolon: so Taylor, 154; dash: so RSV).

Form / Structure / Setting

Mark 1:1 beginning with an anarthrous noun (ἀρχή) and containing no verb has the form of a heading, title or superscription (e.g., LXX Hos 1:2;

Prov 1:1; Eccl 1:1; Cant 1:1; Matt 1:1; Rev 1:1). Although it is frequently designated the title or superscription for the entire Gospel (Anderson, 66; Gnilka, 1:42; Haenchen, 38–39; Pesch, 1:74–75; Schnackenburg, *Orientierung,* 322–23; Taylor, 152), syntactical considerations and comparable literary models make such a designation most improbable (Arnold, *ZNW* 68 [1977] 121–27).

Syntactically, to function as a title 1:1 would need to stand grammatically independent from the following verse(s), since the content of 1:1–2 (3) could hardly form the title for the Gospel that follows. But this is not the case. First, καθώς never introduces a sentence in either Mark or the rest of the NT documents except in the unrelated καθώς/οὕτως combination (cf. Taylor, 153; Anderson, 67–68; Haenchen, 39). Second, when καθώς occurs in a formula with γέγραπται, it always refers to the preceding rather than to the succeeding material (cf. Schmidt, 18; Haenchen, 39; Marxsen, *Mark,* 32–33). Therefore, 1:2 clearly requires a close syntactical relationship with 1:1.

From a literary standpoint, 1:1 compared with similar openings in extrabiblical literature indicates that similar headings refer either to the immediate introduction of a work (e.g., Isocrates, *Phil.* 1; Philo, *de Sob.* 1; *de Spec. Leg.* 1; Tacitus, *Hist.* 1.1.1—cited by Arnold, *ZNW* 68 [1977] 124–25) or to the opening of the main part of that work in contrast to the preliminary comments (Polybius 1.5.1; Dionysius Halic. 1.8.4; Josephus, *War* 1.30) and not to the work as a whole. The frequent reference to the apparent parallel of Hos 1:2 merely offers a comparable sentence, since the analogy breaks down when one recognizes that Hos 1:1 rather than 1:2 is the title of the book. Indeed, Hos 1:2 provides the heading for the following section. Therefore, 1:1 designates the heading of the initial section as the "beginning of the gospel" rather than entitling the Gospel as a whole (Arnold, *ZNW* 68 [1977] 123–27; Cranfield, 34–35; Feneberg, *Markusprolog,* 186–87; Lane, 42; Lohmeyer, 9–11; Schweizer, 30).

But where does the heading end? Apart from the majority of commentators who would place the period at the end of 1:1, some, recognizing the syntactical impossibility of this alternative, have settled for 1:1–4 with the quotation of 1:2a–3 being parenthetical (e.g., Feneberg, *Markusprolog,* 186–87; Lagrange, 1–2; Lane, 42; Turner, *JTS* 26 [1925] 146). But this reading deemphasizes what Mark has emphasized, namely, that which was "written by the prophet Isaiah." Therefore, it seems most logical to place the final period at the end of 1:3, even though this leaves us with a clumsy heading signaled by the evangelist's use of an anarthrous ἀρχή and a verbless opening statement (1:1) materially connected to the quotation of 1:2b–3 by the introductory formula of 1:2a.

Mark 1:2b–3 is a composite citation of three OT passages. The first (1:2b) corresponds to the LXX text of Exod 23:20; the second (1:2c) to the Hebrew text of Mal 3:1; the third (1:3) to the LXX of Isa 40:3. The interplay, however, of the Hebrew text of Exod 23:20 and Mal 3:1 reflected in the LXX rendering of the respective texts (Exod 23:20 [מלאך] has τὸν ἄγγελόν μου, cf. מלאכי of Mal 3:1; Mal 3:1 [הנני] has ἰδοὺ ἐγώ, cf. הנני אנכי of Exod 23:20) and the similarity of the LXX text and the *Tg. Isa* 40:3 cautions one against concluding too readily that Mark 1:2bc simply reproduces the respective LXX and Hebrew texts (Pesch, 1:78). The presence of the same composite citation (1:2bc) in a Q context pertaining to the Baptist (Matt 11:10 // Luke 7:27) as well as the same composite citation in Rabbinic circles to refer to the "forerunner" (e.g., *Exod. Rab.* 23:20; Str-B, 1:597; Snodgrass, *JSNT* 8 [1980], 24–45) demonstrates the traditional character of the citation in 1:2bc and precludes its being the product of Markan redaction (cf. Marxsen, *Mark*, 37, n. 28).

Comment

1   "The beginning" (ἀρχή) has various nuances (BGD, s.v.; G. Delling, *TDNT* 1 [1964] 479–84). Its position in 1:1 is reminiscent of Gen 1:1 (LXX) and John 1:1. Yet the difference in content between "in the beginning" referring to a time prior to creation in John 1:1–2 and the "beginning of the gospel" quickly becomes evident. Thus the ἀρχή of 1:1; Gen 1:1 and John 1:1 have little in common apart from their location in the respective works.

"Beginning" can also mean more than the starting point implying a chronological *when* to which one can return by proceeding backwards or from which one begins (e.g., 10:6; 13:19, cf. Marxsen, *Mark*, 41). It can also denote the "first things," "elementary principles" or the "rudimentary elements" (BGD, s.v.; Wikgren, *JBL* 61 [1942] 16–19; e.g., LXX Ps 110:10; Prov 1:7; 9:10; Sir 1:14). Consequently, the ἀρχή of the gospel could lexically signify the "starting point" or "outset" of the gospel as its "beginning," or it could point to the "rudiments" of the gospel as comprising its ultimate "origin." The meaning of ἀρχή ultimately depends on the meaning of the qualifying phrase, "the gospel of Jesus Messiah, Son of God," and the relationship of 1:1 to what follows.

"Of the gospel" (τοῦ εὐαγγελίου). A comparison with the other Gospels indicates that Mark alone uses the noun εὐαγγέλιον in the absolute (1:15; 8:35; 10:29; 13:10; 14:9; cf. Acts 15:7). Matthew follows Mark four times but always with a qualifier ("the gospel of the Kingdom"—4:23; 9:35; 24:14— and "this gospel"—26:13). Both Matthew (11:5 // Luke 7:22) and Luke (10x, Acts 15x) use the verb εὐαγγελίζειν, which is missing from Mark. The data appear to support Marxsen's suggestion that Mark "has introduced the noun εὐαγγέλιον into the synoptic tradition" (*Mark,* 125). It remains to be seen in the discussion of the respective passages, however, whether or not these occurrences stem from Mark's redaction or his tradition.

"The gospel of Jesus Messiah, Son of God" (1:1) represents what Schweizer has called the "theological accomplishment" of the evangelist (*EvT* 19 [1964] 339). Does, however, this "achievement" represent a *novum*? Was Mark the first to perceive Jesus' earthly ministry as part of the "gospel"? Did Mark's achievement consist in his setting forth in literary fashion what was already commonly accepted as inherent to the "gospel," namely, the Christian message of salvation through Jesus Christ? In other words, does Mark's "achievement" lie in the literary creation of the gospel genre by being the first to write out the gospel as understood and preached by the Church (so apparently Schweizer, *EvT* 19 [1964] 339) or does his "achievement" lie in his altering the content of the Church's mission proclamation of Jesus' death, resurrection and exaltation by setting it within Jesus' earthly ministry (so apparently Marxsen, *Mark*, 117–50)? The answer to this question lies in 1:1–15.

It has become common consensus that εὐαγγέλιον in 1:1 refers to at least the content of the literary work that follows. Drawing on other common mission terminology of his day, the evangelist makes reference to the "gospel" as the proclaimed message six times and designates his work as such at the outset. But in what sense is his work "the gospel"? Although it sets the stage for the development in the second century (e.g., Justin, *Apol.* 66.3), "the gospel" of 1:1 can hardly be taken as intended merely to name a literary genre. Rather εὐαγγέλιον here also refers to the good news as proclaimed, though set forth here in written form. The clue to the evangelist's intent lies in the genitive qualifier, "concerning Jesus Messiah."

"Concerning Jesus Messiah." The "gospel of Jesus Christ" can mean "the gospel concerning Jesus Christ" with Ἰησοῦ Χριστοῦ being an objective genitive (e.g., Klostermann, 3–4; Lane, 44–45; Pesch, 1:75; Schnackenburg, *Orientierung*, 322; Schweizer, 30–31; Taylor, 6) or the "gospel proclaimed by Jesus Christ" with Ἰησοῦ Χριστοῦ being a subjective genitive (e.g., Cranfield, 35–36; Dautzenberg, *BZ* 21 [1977] 223–24; Schniewind, 44; Strecker, *Jesus Christus*, 535). Several have taken the construction to include both objective and subjective elements (e.g., Anderson, 66–67; Ernst, 33; Friedrich, *TDNT* 2 [1964] 798; Gnilka, 1:43; Grundmann, 35; Marxsen, *Mark*, 131–33).

Of these three options, the last poses a grammatical difficulty, since one or the other emphasis has to dominate. The second generally results from the misplaced emphasis on 1:14 from which 1:1 has been interpreted rather than interpreting 1:14 in terms of 1:1 with the latter providing the redactional setting for the traditional reference of the former (see *Comment* on 1:14). The objective genitive not only corresponds with the use of εὐαγγέλιον in the Church's mission but also with the other redactional uses of εὐαγγέλιον in Mark (8:35; 10:29; 13:10; 14:9). Therefore, the εὐαγγέλιον is the message of "good news concerning Jesus Messiah" whose very content includes both the word and works of Jesus for Mark.

"Jesus Messiah." Is Ἰησοῦ Χριστοῦ a proper name or a name and title? Once again the opinions vary between the former (Gnilka, 1:43; Grundmann, 35; Pesch, 1:76; Schnackenburg, *Orientierung*, 322; Taylor, 152) and the latter (Cranfield, 37; Dautzenberg, *BZ* 21 [1977] 229; Lamarche, *NRT* 92 [1970] 1033–34; Lane, 44). Certainly, the Pauline corpus demonstrates the common use of "Jesus Christ" as a proper name in the Church prior to the writing of the Gospels. And Mark 9:41 implies that "Christ" served as a name in Mark's community, while 8:29; 12:35; 13:21; 14:61 and 15:32 show it maintained its function as a title. Yet "Jesus Christ" could hardly be interchangeable with "Jesus" in the Gospels. Luke's Gospel only uses "Jesus" (c. 85x, cf. "Jesus Christ" in Acts c. 10x), while Matthew and Mark only use Ἰησοῦς Χριστός at the outset of their Gospels (cf. Matt 1:1, 18; John 1:17; 17:3) in contrast to their use of "Jesus" (Matthew c. 150x; Mark c. 80x, cf. John c. 17x).

One may at least say that Χριστός has not lost its messianic significance in the double name so that both Matthew and Mark deliberately choose to use the double name to introduce their Gospels about "Jesus Messiah" (cf. Acts 10:36; Rom 1:2–4). Furthermore, the title "Messiah" plays a pivotal role in 8:29 where Peter's confession leads to the fourth major section (1:16–3:12;

3:13–6:6; 6:7–8:26; 8:27–10:52; 11:1–16:8) of Mark's Gospel. Therefore, "Jesus Messiah" more adequately renders Ἰησοῦ Χριστοῦ. It is comparable to our use of "Lord Jesus" in which "Lord" as part of the double name connotes more than simply a proper name.

"The Son of God." The Gospel's focus lies clearly on the person "Jesus Messiah" who is further identified as the "Son of God," a designation of great importance for Mark's Gospel (see 1:11). Apart from the centurion's confession of the crucified Messiah (15:32) as the "Son of God" (15:39), Jesus' own death sentence by the Jewish leaders comes after his positive response to the high priest's question of whether he was the "Messiah, the *Son of the Blessed*" (14:61–64). This same combination of "Jesus Messiah" and "Son of God" occurs, perhaps more than coincidentally, along with the mention of the OT promise (cf. 1:2a) in Paul's reference to the gospel at the outset of Rom 1:2–4.

"As written" (καθὼς γέγραπται). This formula (Fitzmyer, *Essays*, 8–9) has a direct counterpart in the Qumran literature (כאשר כתוב, *ka'ăšer katûb*, e.g., 1QS 5.17; 8.14; CD 7.19; 4QFlor 1.12), a parallel in the LXX (2 Kgs 14:6; Dan 9:13 Theod.), numerous parallels in Paul (Rom 14x; 1 Cor 1:31; 2:9; 2 Cor 8:15; 9:9), three in Luke-Acts (2:23; Acts 7:42; 15:15) and two other references in Mark (9:13, cf. 9:12 and Matt 17:12–13; 14:21 // Matt 26:24, cf. Luke 22:22). With the exception of the variant reading in Dan 9:13, only Mark 9:13 and 14:21 // Matt 26:24 stand without a specific quotation that follows.

Since in every other instance the formula refers to the preceding context and combines a subsequent quotation with the statement that immediately preceded, we can conclude that either Mark has redactionally added the formula in 1:2a in terms of the definitely redactional 1:1, or if the formula introduced the quotations of 1:2b–3 in the pre-Markan tradition, 1:2a must on syntactical grounds have had a different setting following another statement (perhaps 1:4; cf. Matt 3:1–3).

"By Isaiah the prophet" (ἐν τῷ Ἡσαΐᾳ τῷ προφήτῃ) has caused difficulties, since the subsequent quotation consists of material from Exod 23:20; Mal 3:1 and Isa 40:3. Some have solved the difficulty by attributing the non-Isaiah material to a later gloss (e.g., Taylor, 153); others have considered it to be typical of a collection of *testimonia* consisting of thematically related texts without precision as to authorship (Fitzmyer, *Essays*, 62–63); still others have attributed the use of Isaiah to the preponderance of Isaiah's role with reference to the coming messianic age (Grundmann, 36).

The actual key may lie in Mark's redaction. By setting the subsequent citations at the outset and combining the Baptist materials (1:4–6, 7–8), the evangelist has constructed a section involving a parallel between the Baptist and Jesus: (a) 1:2b–3, God's word of introduction, cf. 1:9–11; (b) 1:4–6, a wilderness motif, cf. 1:12–13; and (c) 1:7–8, preaching, cf. 1:14–15. The "beginning of the gospel . . . written by Isaiah the prophet" would then become the complex of events of 1:2b–15 regarding both the Baptist and Jesus that fulfilled Isaiah's promise (cf. John's appearance and role—Isa 40:3; Jesus' appearance—Isa 42:1 and role—Isa 52:7; 61:1). Thus the "beginning of the gospel" (1:2b–15) transpires "as written by the prophet Isaiah."

2 "My messenger" (τὸν ἄγγελόν μου) in Exod 23:20 refers to an angel sent by God to precede Israel as her guardian and guide into the land. Mal 3:1 refers to the messenger (ἄγγελος, LXX) who will prepare the way for the Lord's coming like a "refiner's fire" and a "fuller's soap" (3:2). But Mal 4:5 (MT, 3:23) identifies this messenger with Elijah whom God will send before the "just and terrible day of the Lord" to "turn the hearts of the fathers and their children" lest they be cursed (4:6). Thus the angel of Exod 23:20 becomes Elijah, the eschatological messenger promised for the age of salvation in Mal 3:1; 4:5. The combination of these two texts also appears in rabbinic thought (*Exod. Rab.* 23.20), a combination also reflected in the LXX rendering of the two texts (see above, p. 7–8). The "messenger" in Mark 1:2b parallels the "voice of one crying in the wilderness" in 1:3 that sets the stage for the Baptist's appearance in the "wilderness" as the precursor, a motif found also in the Q tradition of Matt 11:7–10 // Luke 7:24–27.

"Who will prepare" shifts the thought from the angel's role of guiding and guarding the people in Exod 23:20 to the messenger's task in Mal 3:1 (MT) of preparing the way (κατασκευάσει, cf. ἐπιβλέψεται of Mal 3:1) of the Lord. The nature of the preparation of the heart follows in the description of Elijah's sending in Mal 4:5–6. Consequently, the composite citation in Judaism as in Mark 1:2bc points to the coming of one who will prepare God's people for the eschatological day of the Lord.

"Before you" (πρὸ προσώπου σου). In Exod 23:20 the "angel" preceded the people, but in Mal 3:1 the "messenger" precedes the Lord and in Mal 4:5–6 Elijah is sent to precede the Day of the Lord. Here "before you" clearly refers to the "Lord" of 1:3 whom 1:1–15 identifies as Jesus Messiah, Son of God. Though Jesus has not yet personally entered the scene, the evangelist assumes the reader understands Jesus to be the "Lord" of 1:3 and thus the "you" of 1:2b whose way is prepared by the following events in 1:4–8.

3 "A voice crying in the wilderness" applies Isa 40:3 to the Baptist's role as a herald "proclaiming" (κηρύσσων, 1:4, 7) a repentance-baptism and the coming of a greater one. The "wilderness" (ἐρήμῳ) locates the "voice" in Isa 40:3 (LXX) as here, whereas in Isa 40:3 (MT) it locates the preparation of the way of the Lord.

"Prepare the way of the Lord" reflects Isaiah's call to make ready for a triumphal march to be led by God himself. This motif (ἑτοιμάσατε) parallels the statement of 1:2c (κατασκευάσει) and applies both the "you" of Exod 23:20 (πρὸ προσώπου σου) and the "Lord" of Isa 40:3 (κυρίου) to Jesus. This identification with Jesus becomes clear in the substitution of "his" (αὐτοῦ) for Isaiah's "our God" (τοῦ θεοῦ ἡμῶν), an identification that Mark concurs with as is seen by 1:2b–15 in general and 1:1–2a in particular. The pre-Markan character of 1:3 and his use of the material in 1:4–15 precludes any redactional "messianic secret" motif (cf. Schmithals, 1:75).

Explanation

Mark opens his Gospel in a manner similar to other hellenistic writings with a heading (1:1–3) for the introductory section (1:1–15) of his work. This heading designates the appearance of both John (1:4–8) and Jesus

(1:9–15) as the beginning of the gospel corresponding to the promises of Isaiah. The "beginning" of the gospel, therefore, refers specifically to the events of 1:4–15 that stand at the outset of the message of good news about the presence of the long-anticipated age of salvation.

Yet Mark's usage of "gospel" in 1:1 stands in contrast with its previous NT usage. Whereas the "gospel" had come to signify the distinctive message of salvation proclaimed in the Church's mission and based in the death, resurrection and return of Jesus Christ (e.g., Rom 1:2–4; 1 Cor 15:1–7; 1 Thess 1:5, 9–10) in contrast to "gospel" as used in Judaism and Hellenism, Mark's usage includes Jesus' earthly ministry "beginning" with John's and Jesus' respective appearances.

To this extent Mark's Gospel amplifies the outline of Peter's sermon to Cornelius in Acts 10:36–38 and indicates the broader scope of the Church's preaching than simply the death, resurrection, and Parousia of Jesus Christ, supposedly characteristic of Paul's writings. Furthermore, Mark by designating his *written* account as the "gospel" (1:1) broke with the traditional use of "gospel" to refer to the *proclaimed* message of the Church's preaching. Thus the evangelist prepared the way for the Church's later practice of calling the four similar Christian documents "Gospels."

Mark qualifies the "gospel" as the "gospel concerning Jesus Messiah, Son of God." But this gospel concerning Jesus Messiah includes by virtue of its content the gospel proclaimed by Jesus both in word and deed during his earthly ministry. Indeed, the gospel concerning Jesus Messiah (1:1) consists of Jesus' preaching, teaching, and acts of mercy and healing that created conflict and led to his ultimate rejection in death.

In Mark, therefore, Jesus' proclamation of the good news by word and deed in view of the Kingdom expectation of the OT promise (cf. 1:14–15) comes together with the Church's proclamation of the good news with Jesus' death, resurrection and return as the primary focus. Jesus' coming and ministry fulfill the OT promise of the age of salvation typified especially by Isaiah but do so in the one who suffers rejection and death only to be vindicated by the resurrection to return in glory. The heart of the gospel, therefore, is Jesus Messiah, Son of God (cf. 1:11; 8:29; 14:61–64; 15:32, 39).

The composite citation of Exod 23:20; Mal 3:1; and Isa 40:3 in 1:2b–3 sets the stage for John's and Jesus' appearance against the background of redemptive history. Not only does God's promise to his people during the exodus (Exod 20:23) find its expression in the promise to God's people of a messenger to prepare the way for the age of salvation (Mal 3:1–2; 4:5–6), but both texts now combine with Isa 40:3 to identify the Baptist's coming and ministry in the wilderness as the fulfillment of that promise for the coming of the "Lord."

Isaiah's promise of the coming of the Lord clearly applies to Jesus. Thus this "heading" includes events beyond the appearance and message of the Baptist. The beginning of the gospel according to Isaiah's promise extends to the events that mark Jesus' appearance (1:9–11, 12–13) and message (1:14–15). Mark 1:1–15, therefore, sketches the "beginning of the gospel about Jesus Messiah, Son of God, as written by Isaiah the prophet."

Excursus: ΕΥΑΓΓΕΛΙΟΝ

Εὐαγγέλιον has a complex background. In the Hebrew scripture, the noun בשׂרה, *bĕśorâh*, occurs only with a nontheological, secular meaning of "reward for good news" (2 Sam 4:10; 18:22) or the "good news" of deliverance from the enemy (e.g., 2 Sam 18:20, 25, 27; 2 Kgs 7:9). By contrast, the verb בשׂר, *bāśar*, has both the neutral sense of "to announce," usually in conjunction with a military victory, (e.g., 1 Kgs 1:42; 1 Sam 4:17) and the theologically pregnant sense of "proclaiming the good news of God's reign" (cf. Isa 52:7; 61:1; Nah 2:1). In particular, the participial form מבשׂר, *mĕbāśśer*, designated the "messenger" in both a secular sense (e.g., 2 Sam 18:26) and more importantly in the religious sense of the one who will declare "the good news of God's reign" (e.g., Isa 52:7; Ps 96:2–10; cf. Isa 61:1). In Hebrew-Aramaic speaking Judaism, the same phenomenon obtains with an increasing stress on the "messenger" as the expected one who would announce the day of salvation (G. Friedrich, *TDNT* 2 [1964] 715–17). The noun itself does not occur in a theological sense in Qumran. Its use primarily in Targumic materials takes on a more theological tone by referring to angelic messages, messages of God's blessing, comfort, and mercy (Stuhlmacher, *Evangelium*, 129–35). None of these examples, however, comes close to the NT absolute usage of εὐαγγέλιον.

In the Greek-speaking world, the verb εὐαγγελίζεσθαι and the nouns εὐαγγέλιον, εὐάγγελος ("messenger") occur in a variety of settings including the announcement of victory over the enemy, the birth of a son, a wedding, an oracular pronouncement as well as the announcement of the court appearance of Apollonius of Tyana (G. Friedrich, *TDNT* 2 [1964] 710–14; 721–27). This terminology carries into the LXX with slight modifications. First, the verb translates בשׂר, *bāśar*, only when it has a positive sense. Second, the noun (εὐαγγέλια, neuter plural) occurs only once with the meaning of "reward for good news" (2 Sam 4:10; cf. 18:22), and εὐαγγελία (feminine singular) has the meaning of "good news" in 2 Sam 18:20, 25, 27, and 2 Kgs 7:9. Third, εὐάγγελος has been replaced by the more literally translated participle εὐαγγελιζόμενος for מבשׂר, *mĕbāśśer*. Philo and Josephus follow the secular usage of these terms, but each does use the εὐαγγελ- root apparently within the context of the imperial cult. Philo refers to the enthronement of Gaius as εὐαγγελιζομένη (*Leg.* 231) and Josephus refers to the accession of Vespasian as εὐαγγέλιον (*War* 2.618).

The references by Philo and Josephus in the context of the imperial cult suggest for many the immediate religious background of the NT usage of the noun εὐαγγέλιον (e.g., A. Harnack, *Reden und Aufsätze* I, 2d ed. [Giessen: Töpelmann, 1906]; Strecker, *Jesus Christus*, 510–12; G. Friedrich, *TDNT* 2 [1964] 724–25; for lit., see Stuhlmacher, *Evangelium*, 11–19). The publication in 1899 of the oft-cited Priene inscription from 9 B.C. regarding the birth of Augustus set the stage ("The birthday of the god was for the world the beginning of joyful messages [εὐαγγελίων] which have gone forth because of him," so G. Friedrich, *TDNT* 2 [1964] 724). The emperor with his divine nature (cf. "birthday of a god"), miraculous powers, and the deliverance or peace he brings to the state incorporates many of the traits of the hellenistic heroes and divine men. The subsequent use of εὐαγγελ-terms for the Caesar's birth, coming of age (see G. Friedrich, *TDNT* 2 [1964] 724, n. 37) and accession to the throne (see G. Friedrich, *TDNT* 2 [1964] 725) supposedly offers the immediate background for the NT usage of εὐαγγέλιον, particularly within the milieu of the gentile mission where such a background would influence one's understanding of the concept (so most recently, Strecker, *Jesus Christus*, 511–12).

Stuhlmacher, however, in a thorough reexamination of the hellenistic use of these terms in reference to divine men, heroes and the imperial cult (*Evangelium*, 191–206) has concluded that such a background for εὐαγγέλιον concedes too much in view of the evidence. Apart from the late provenance of the writings pertaining to divine men and the popular philosophers (third century C.E.), he (*pace* G. Friedrich, *TDNT* 2 [1964] 711–12) has shown that the use of this word group does not indicate any particular religious significance drawn from the character or role of the divine man (e.g., Philostratus, *Vit. Apoll.* 1.28; 8.26–27) or the popular philosophers (Heliodoros, *Ethiop.* 10.1–3). Rather the use of the εὐαγγελ- terms corresponds rhetorically and stylistically with the secular usage of the hellenistic world (*Evangelium*, 191–96).

In three inscriptions of the fourth century B.C. εὐαγγέλια (always plural) does denote messages involving earthly "salvation" (σωτηρία) resulting from the contribution of a certain Greek hero, but the interchange between εὐαγγελ-/ἀγγελ- terms in these inscriptions (J. Schniewind, *TDNT* 1 [1964] 57, 61, 66, 69) suggests that even here one does not find a fixed terminology. As to the imperial cult, the same rhetorical and stylistic rather than clearly religious concerns apply to the use of these terms regarding the emperor's coming of age and accession to the throne. These concerns most likely explain the usage noted above by Philo and Josephus (Stuhlmacher, *Evangelium*, 196–203).

The one clear exception is the Priene inscription referring to the birth of Augustus who brings relief from wars, establishes peace, and thus fulfills all the hopes expressed in previous promises (εὐαγγέλια). Here one finds εὐαγγέλιον connoting a message of salvation to be effected by the emperor. But the lack of similar parallels elsewhere in the Greco-Roman world and the use of the plural εὐαγγελίων that splits this message into separate messages according to the emperor's accomplishment of the expected deliverance and establishment of the life of peace indicate how remote this use of εὐαγγέλιον stands from the ultimate message of the NT (Stuhlmacher, *Evangelium*, 201). Thus one might legitimately question not only the direct influence of the imperial cult on the NT use of εὐαγγέλιον but also to what extent the term εὐαγγέλιον in the ears of those hearing the Christian message in its Gentile setting would necessarily remind the hearer of any "technical" usage from the political and rhetorical setting of the imperial cult. Stuhlmacher concludes, therefore, that the roots of the NT usage lie in the distinctive mission and message of the primitive Church in terms of Jesus Christ and the OT promise (*Evangelium*, 207–44).

The pre-Pauline materials of 1 Thess 1:9–10; Rom 1:2–4; 1 Cor 15:3–5 clearly show that Jesus' death, resurrection and exaltation comprised the substance of the εὐαγγέλιον of the early mission. Paul's own use (nearly 50x without counting the six of Ephesians and Colossians or the four of the Pastorals) accepts this meaning as a given, and expands on it. But we also have indications (e.g., Rev 14:6–7; Matt 11:4–6; Mark 1:14) of a gospel within the Palestinian church prior to the Gentile mission (Hahn, *Mission*, 40–41; Stuhlmacher, *Evangelium*, 210–44; *pace* Strecker, *Jesus Christus*, 513–24) that speaks primarily of the coming of the Kingdom of God.

This raises the question of whether Jesus himself proclaimed the "gospel of the Kingdom" and, if so, how the one proclaiming the gospel of the coming Kingdom himself became the content of the gospel in terms of his death, resurrection, and exaltation. To attribute this change in focus in the "gospel" to the shift in the Church's mission from a Palestinian mission among the Jews to the hellenistic mission among the Gentiles represents a much too facile approach, particularly at the expense of Mark's own contribution to the resolution of this dilemma, which we shall pursue in our discussion of the respective passages.

B. The Promised Precursor (1:4–8)

Bibliography

Bammel, E. "The Baptist in Early Christian Tradition." *NTS* 18 (1971–72) 95–128.
Becker, J. *Johannes der Täufer und Jesus von Nazareth.* Biblische Studien 63. Neukirchen:
Neukirchener, 1972. ———. *Untersuchungen zur Entstehungsgeschichte der Zwölf Patriarchen.* AGJU 8. Leiden: Brill, 1970. **Best, E.** "Spirit-Baptism." *NovT* 34 (1959–60) 236–
43. **Betz, O.** "Die Proselytentaufe der Qumransekte und die Taufe im Neuen Testament." *RevQ* 2 (1958) 213–34. **Böcher, O.** "Ass Johannes der Täufer kein Brot (Luk.
vii. 33)?" *NTS* 18 (1971–72). ———. "Wölfe in Schafspelzen: Zum religionsgeschicht-
lichen Hintergrund vom Matth. 7, 15." *TZ* 24 (1968) 405–26. **Brownlee, W. H.** "John
the Baptist in the New Light of Ancient Scrolls." In *The Scrolls and the New Testament,*
ed. K. Stendahl. London: SCM, 1958. 33–53. **Bruce, F. F.** "Qumran and Early Christianity." *NTS* 2 (1955–56) 176–90. **Cullmann, O.** "ὁ ὀπίσω μου ἐρχόμενος." In *Vorträge und
Aufsätze, 1925–62.* Tübingen: Mohr, 1966. 169–75. **Dahl, N.** "The Origin of Baptism."
In *Interpretationes ad Vetus Testamentum Pertinentes Sigmundo Mowinckel.* Oslo: Land og
Kirke, 1955. 36–52. **Dibelius, M.** *Die urchristliche Überlieferung von Johannes dem Täufer.*
FRLANT 15. Göttingen: Vandenhoeck & Ruprecht, 1911. **Dunn, J. D. G.** *Christology
in the Making.* Philadelphia: Westminster, 1980. ———. "Spirit-and-Fire Baptism."
NovT 14 (1970) 81–92. **Dupont-Sommer, A.** *The Essene Writings from Qumran.* Cleveland:
World, 1962. **Eisler, R.** *The Messiah Jesus and John the Baptist.* London: Methuen,
1931. **Elliott, J. K.** "*Ho baptizon* and Mark 1.4." *TZ* 31 (1975) 14–15. **Feneberg, W.**
Der Markusprolog. Studien zur Formbestimmung des Evangeliums. SANT 36. Munich: Kösel,
1974. **Gnilka, J.** "Die essenischen Tauchbäder und die Johannestaufe." *RevQ* 3 (1961)
185–207. **Grobel, K.** "He That Cometh after Me." *JBL* 60 (1941) 397–401. **Guelich,
R. A.** "'The Beginning of the Gospel,' Mark 1:1–15." *BR* 27 (1982) 5–15. **Hengel,
M.** *The Charismatic Leader and His Followers.* New York: Crossroad, 1981. **Hess, J. J.**
"Beduinisches zum Alten und Neuen Testament." *ZAW* 35 (1915) 120–31. **Hill, D.**
Greek Words and Hebrew Meanings: Studies in the Semantics of Soteriological Terms. SNTSMS
5. Cambridge: Cambridge UP, 1967. **Jeremias, J.** "Proselytentaufe und Neues Testa-
ment." *TZ* 5 (1949) 418–28. **Jonge, M. de.** "Christian Influence in the Testaments of
the Twelve Patriarchs." *NovT* 4 (1960) 182–235. **Joüon, P.** "Le Costume d'Élie et
celui de Jean Baptiste. Etude Lexicographique." *Bib* 16 (1935) 74–81. **Kraeling,
C. H.** *John the Baptist.* New York: Scribners, 1951. **Lang, F.** "Erwägungen zur eschatolo-
gischen Verkundigung Johannes der Täufers." In *Jesus Christus in Historie und Geschichte,*
FS H. Conzelmann, ed. G. Strecker. Tübingen: Mohr, 1975. 459–73. **Leivestad, R.**
"Exit the Apocalyptic Son of Man." *NTS* 18 (1971–72) 243–67. **Lindars, B.** "Re-Enter
the Apocalyptic Son of Man." *NTS* 22 (1975–76) 52–72. ———. *Jesus Son of Man: A
Fresh Examination of the Son of Man Sayings in the Gospels.* Grand Rapids: Eerdmans,
1983. **Lohmeyer, E.** "Zur evangelischen Überlieferung von Johannes dem Täufer."
JBL 51 (1932) 300–319. **Manson, T. W.** "Baptism in the Church." *SJT* 2 (1949) 391–
403. **Marxsen, W.** *Mark the Evangelist.* 1969. **Mauser, U. W.** *Christ in the Wilderness.*
SBT 39. London: SCM, 1963. **Michaelis, W.** "Zum jüdischen Hintergrund der Johan-
nestaufe." *Jud* 7 (1951) 81–120. **Robinson, J. A. T.** *Twelve New Testament Studies.*
SBT 34. London: SCM, 1962. 11–52. **Rowley, H. H.** "The Baptism of John and the
Qumran Sect." In *New Testament Essays,* FS T. W. Manson, ed. A. J. B. Higgins.
Manchester: Manchester UP, 1959. **Schütz, R.** *Johannes der Täufer.* ATANT 50. Zürich:
Zwingli, 1967. **Scobie, C. H. H.** *John the Baptist.* London: SCM, 1964. **Thyen, H.**
"ΒΑΠΤΙΣΜΑ ΜΕΤΑΝΟΙΑΣ ΕΙΣ ΑΦΕΣΙΝ." In *Zeit und Geschichte,* FS R. Bultmann, ed.
E. Dinkler. Tübingen: Mohr, 1964. 97–125. **Turner, C. H.** "Marcan Usage: Notes,

Critical and Exegetical, on the Second Gospel." *JTS* 26 (1925) 145–56. **Vielhauer, P.** "Tracht und Speise Johannes der Täufers." In *Aufsätze zum Neuen Testament.* TB 31. Munich: Kaiser Verlag, 1965. 47–54. **Windisch, H.** "Die Notiz über Tracht und Speise des Täufers Johannes und ihre Entsprechungen in der Jesus-Überlieferung." *ZNW* 32 (1933) 65–87. **Wink, W.** *John the Baptist in the Gospel Tradition.* SNTSMS 7. Cambridge: Cambridge UP, 1968. **Wolf, H. W.** "Das Thema 'Umkehr' in der alttestamentlichen Theologie." *ZTK* 48 (1951) 129–48. **Yates, J. E.** "The Form of Mark i. 8b." *NTS* 4 (1958) 334–38.

Translation

⁴ *John the Baptizer* ᵃ *appeared* ᵇ *in the wilderness proclaiming a repentance* ᶜ*-baptism for* ᵈ *the forgiveness of sins.* ⁵ *The whole area of Judea and all the people of Jerusalem went out to him. Confessing their sins, they were baptized by him in the Jordan River.*

⁶ *John wore* ᵉ *a garment of camel hair* ᶠ *and a leather belt around his waist, and he ate locusts and wild honey.*

⁷ *He proclaimed: "The one greater than I comes after me. So much greater is he that I am not worthy of bowing and untying the straps of his sandals.* ⁸ *I baptize you with water, but he will baptize you with the Holy Spirit."*

Notes

ᵃὁ βαπτίζων occurs in two of four textual variants: (a) ὁ βαπτίζων ἐν τῇ ἐρήμῳ κηρύσσων, B 33 282 WH Nestle¹⁷; (b) ὁ βαπτίζων ἐν τῇ ἐρήμῳ καὶ κηρύσσων, ℵ L Δ *pc* bo Nestle²⁶; (c) cf. βαπτίζων ἐν τῇ ἐρήμῳ καὶ κηρύσσων, A K P W UBSGNT, Nestle¹⁷; (d) ἐν τῇ ἐρήμῳ βαπτίζων καὶ κηρύσσων, Δ Θ 29 *pc* lat syᴾ. It functions as a Markan synonym (cf. 6:14, 24) for βαπτιστής (e.g., 6:25; 8:28; and elsewhere in the NT and Josephus). Of the four variants, ὁ βαπτίζων . . . καὶ κηρύσσων represents the more difficult reading, but it represents a description of John as "the one baptizing . . . *and* proclaiming." The anarthrous construction (βαπτίζων . . . κηρύσσων) reflects an alteration of the unusual Markan participial (ὁ βαπτίζων, e.g., 6:14, 24) rather than nominal (ὁ βαπτιστής, so 6:25 and 8:28) apposition. Thus ὁ βαπτίζων . . . κηρύσσων not only corresponds to Mark's redactional style in 6:14, 24, but also serves as the basis for the change to the alternative readings (e.g., Turner, *JTS* 26 [1925] 150; Lohmeyer, 13, n. 1; Marxsen, *Mark*, 31–34; Elliot, *TZ* 31 [1975] 14–15; cf. Metzger, *Textual Commentary*, 73).

ᵇἐγένετο stands as the main verb in a Semitic construction, "John appeared" (cf. John 1:6; 1 John 2:18). The distance from κηρύσσων makes periphrastic usage unlikely (Lohmeyer, 13, n. 1; Cranfield, 40).

ᶜμετανοίας, genitive of description: "repentance-baptism."

ᵈεἰς ἄφεσιν to express purpose. John's repentance-baptism was for the purpose of the forgiveness of sins.

ᵉἦν . . . ἐνδεδυμένος . . . ἐσθίων reflects Mark's use of the periphrastic to express habitual action: "John was customarily dressed in . . . and habitually ate. . . . "

ᶠτρίχας for δέρριν (D a), a later alignment with Zech 13:4 (cf. Turner, *JTS* 26 [1925] 151) at the expense of καὶ ζώνην . . . αὐτοῦ (D it) from 2 Kgs 1:8.

Form / Structure / Setting

The Baptist and his ministry are rather abruptly set forth in five rather unconnected statements: 1:4–5, 6, 7–8. Identifying him only as the "Baptizer" (1:4) with the sole biographical note pertaining to his clothing and food (1:6), the evangelist assumes the reader's knowledge of John. The material divides roughly into two sections: one dealing with the Baptist's appearance and proclamation of his baptism (1:4–6), the other with his proclamation of the "Greater One" (1:7–8). The latter consists of a double saying comparing John with the Greater One (1:7) and then explicating the comparison by contrasting their respective baptisms (1:8). This double saying appears in chiastic form in the Q-tradition (Matt 3:11 // Luke 3:16).

Rather than a block or blocks of tradition, Mark 1:4–8 most likely consisted of traditional elements from the Baptist tradition selected and shaped by the evangelist under the influence of Isa 40:3 (cf. 1:3; 1:2a). In 1:4 John appears as "the voice in the wilderness" proclaiming a repentance-baptism whose aim was the forgiveness of sins. Each item rooted in the tradition of John's ministry now connotes his role as the one sent to prepare the way by baptizing the penitent with water in preparation for the one who would bring forgiveness of sins. John's identity as the "voice in the wilderness" finds further support in the reference to his dress and diet typical of the wilderness. Finally, this unit concludes with his prophetic message of preparation which explicitly proclaims the coming of the Greater One whose baptism by the Holy Spirit effects the goal of John's repentance-baptism (1:8; cf. 1:4).

The exclusive emphasis on salvation in the Baptist's message without any trace of the judgment motifs of Q (Matt 3:7–12 // Luke 3:7–9, 15–18) most likely stems from the evangelist's deliberate portrait of John. As the "voice in the wilderness," John prepared for the good news of God's eschatological salvation. This promised proclamation comes to pass in Jesus' appearance and ministry as depicted in 1:9–15 according to Isaiah's promise (see *Comment* on 1:2).

Comment

4 "John the Baptizer" (Ἰωάννης ὁ βαπτίζων). Mark alone uses the participial form to identify John. As a substantival participle, "the Baptizer" conveys a more dynamic tone than the synonymous "the Baptist" (βαπτιστής, so 6:25; 8:28; Matt 3:1; 11:11, 12; 14:2, 8; 16:14; 17:13; Luke 7:20, 28, 33; 9:19; Josephus, *Ant.* 18.117).

John's surname connotes his trademark. Yet baptism was hardly distinctive of him. Apart from the OT ritual cleansings practiced and expanded by the Pharisees (Dahl, *Interpretationes*, 36–52) and the first-century practice of prose-lyte-baptism (Jeremias, *TZ* 5 [1949] 418–28; Rowley, *Essays*, 313–14; Cranfield, 43), the discovery of Qumran has provided another example of the rite as practiced in John's day (Cullmann, *Aufsätze*, 18–32; Betz, *RevQ* 2 [1958] 213–34; Gnilka, *RevQ* 3 [1961] 185–207).

The Baptist's distinctiveness lay in the form and significance of his baptism. In form, John *himself* (ὑπ' αὐτοῦ) immersed (1:5) those coming to him in an *unrepeatable* baptismal act. Whereas proselyte baptism, whose origins and dates are most obscure (Michaelis, *Jud* 7 [1951] 100–120; Vielhauer, *RGG* 3 [1959] 806), and the Qumran rite of initiation (Brownlee, *Scrolls*, 38–39; Betz, *RevQ* 2 [1958] 216–20; Scobie, *Baptist*, 104–6, assuming such a rite; cf. Rowley, *Essays*, 218–19; Gnilka, *RevQ* 3 [1961] 189–91) were also once for all, each was self-administered like the OT and Pharisaic lustrations. And in contrast to the respective initiatory character of proselyte and Qumran's baptism by which a Gentile became a part of a Jewish community or a novitiate entered into full standing within the Essene community, John's baptism had no initiatory significance. His was a "repentance-baptism" for the "forgiveness of sins" in view of the imminent eschatological day of the Lord. Thus John was called "the Baptist" because the specific form and meaning of his baptism was his own "original creation" (Vielhauer, *RGG* 3 [1959] 806; cf. Taylor, 154–55; Bruce, *NTS* 2 [1955–56] 176–90).

"Appeared" (ἐγένετο) in conjunction with 1:1–3 connotes the "happening" of what had been promised and sets the Baptizer's appearance within redemptive history as an event that comes to pass (Lohmeyer, 12–13, n. 4). What follows in 1:4–8 "happens" in keeping with Isa 40:3 (so 1:2a). This theological premise doubtless conditioned the evangelist's selection of the materials, and it unifies the disparate elements of 1:4–8.

"In the wilderness" (ἐν τῇ ἐρήμῳ) for some reflects a later Christian interpretation (e.g., Schmidt, 21; Bultmann, 246; Marxsen, *Mark*, 36–37; Schmithals, 1:77). But the reference to the Baptizer's wilderness appearance in the Markan (1:4 and parallels) and Q (Matt 11:7 // Luke 7:24) traditions, the eschatological role of the "wilderness" for the prophets, for messianic figures (e.g., Acts 21:38 cf. Matt 24:26; Josephus, *War* 2.259, 261; 6.351; 7.438), for Qumran and for John's typically wilderness garb and diet (see 1:6, cf. Matt 11:8 // Luke 7:25; Matt 11:18 // Luke 7:33), all suggest the likelihood and authenticity of this tradition (Vielhauer, *RGG* 3 [1959] 805; Becker, *Täufer*, 20–21).

The "wilderness" motif expresses the eschatological hope of the Exodus typology found in Hos 2:14; 12:9 (cf. Micah 7:14–15) and especially in Isaiah (e.g., 40:3–4; 41:18–19; 43:19–20; 48:20–21; 51:9–11). The "wilderness" represented the place where God would once again act to deliver the people. Thus Mark, who did not create the theme here, did make deliberate use of it in 1:4 in the light of the promise of Isa 40:3 cited in 1:3 in order to indicate that John was the promised "voice in the wilderness" come as the precursor for "the way of the Lord" (see 1:9–14). The evangelist's failure to locate the Baptist's ministry more specifically in either the "wilderness of Judea" (Matt 3:1) or "around the Jordan" (Luke 3:3; cf. John 1:28) suggests that the "wilderness" had more theological than geographical importance for him.

"Proclaiming" (κηρύσσων) has as its subject in Mark the Baptizer (1:4, 7), Jesus (1:14, 38–39), the Twelve (3:14; 6:12) and other messengers (1:45; 5:20; 13:10; 14:9). Although "to proclaim a baptism" (κηρύσσων βάπτισμα) parallels the proclamation of a fast in 2 Chron 20:3 and Jonah 3:5, this verb in the NT refers almost exclusively to the redemptive act of God, the "gospel of the Kingdom" (G. Friedrich, *TDNT* 3 [1965] 710–12). Consequently, "proclaiming" in 1:4 picks up "the voice crying" of Isa 40:3 (cf. 1:3) within the framework of the Baptizer's preparatory activity that heralded the dawn of God's new day.

"Repentance-baptism" (βάπτισμα μετανοίας, see *Note* c). μετάνοια denotes in Greek a change of mind. Used, however, in this context, the verb (μετανοεῖν) translates the Hebrew שוב, *šûb*, which means to "turn back" or "return." In the OT, this verb, especially in the prophets (e.g., Jer 18:11; Isa 55:7; Zech

1:4), connoted a whole-hearted "return to Yahweh" and taking Yahweh seriously as "Israel's God" (E. Würthwein, *TDNT* 4 [1967] 984–86; Wolf, *ZTK* 48 [1951] 129–48). Such an abandoning of one's wrong ways and a return to God's ways in obedient surrender belonged to the prophetic hope for the age of salvation (e.g., Mal 4:5–6 [MT 3:23–24]; Ezek 11:19; 36:25–26; Dan 9:13; Sir 48:10). Repentance was also fundamental to the Qumran sect (e.g., 1QS 5.1, 14, 22; 1QH 2.1; 6.6; 16.17). It involved a voluntary renunciation of one's previous ways and a decision to join the community in radical obedience to the Law as interpreted there.

"Repentance-baptism" suggests that the call to repentance and the act of baptism were integrally related in John's ministry. The moral and ethical content of his preaching in Q (Matt 3:7–10 // Luke 3:7–9; cf. Luke 3:10–14) indicates that "repentance" included appropriate conduct (so Josephus, *Ant.* 18.117) without which the baptismal act would doubtless have been futile. Thus one can hardly speak of John's baptism in a strictly "sacramental" sense (cf. Lohmeyer, 19; Thyen, *Geschichte*, 98; Grundmann, 37; Schütz, *Johannes*, 46–48). By submitting to John's baptism one demonstrated a readiness to repent.

At the same time, the baptismal act itself conveyed the certainty that one's repentance was valid and acceptable to God—providing that it was expressed in genuine fruits of repentance (Gnilka, *RevQ* 3 [1961] 203–4; Matt 3:8 // Luke 3:8; Josephus, *Ant.* 18.117). Therefore, John's "repentance-baptism" demanded and gave expression to one's repentance—"the transformation of the total direction of one's life" (Schweizer, 32). The goal of John's proclaiming "repentance-baptism" was the forgiveness of sins, i.e., salvation.

"For the forgiveness of sins" (εἰς ἄφεσιν ἁμαρτιῶν) expresses the "highest hopes" of the prophets (Schniewind, 45; e.g., Jer 31:34; Isa 33:24; 53:5–6; Ezek 18:31; 36:25–27; Zech 13:1; Mic 7:18). Apart from its early Christian usage (Matt 26:28; Luke 24:47; Acts 2:38; 5:31; 10:43; 13:38; 26:18; Col 1:14; Heb 10:18), the phrase occurs with reference to the Baptist here (par Luke 3:3) and in Luke 1:77 (cf. Josephus, *Ant.* 18.117). Several have ascribed the usage here to a Christian interpretation of John's message and baptism (e.g., Lohmeyer, 15; Grundmann, 37; cf. Taylor, 155). But the reference to "forgiveness of sins" in Luke 1:77, Mark 1:4, and in the oblique reference of Josephus (*Ant.* 18.117) combined with the tendency to subordinate John's ministry to Jesus' in the Christian tradition (cf. Matt 3:11) speaks for the authenticity of this concept in John's ministry (Thyen, *Geschichte*, 102; Becker, *Täufer*, 22, 38; Gnilka, *RevQ* 3 [1961] 203).

But how does John's baptism relate to "forgiveness of sins"? The question of whether "forgiveness of sins" was the goal of repentance (μετανοίας) or of baptism (βάπτισμα, see Gnilka, 1:45–46; cf. Schweizer, 32) is moot, since John's was a "repentance-baptism." For John baptism without repentance was futile; repentance without baptism inconceivable. Did, however, the "forgiveness of sins" accompany the act of baptism (e.g., Thyen, *Geschichte*, 93–101; Becker, *Täufer*, 22, 38–39) or was the "forgiveness of sins" the goal of but separate from the act of baptism (so Josephus, *Ant.* 18.117; Schniewind, 45)? A comparison with Qumran proves instructive.

"Repentance," "baptism," "forgiveness of sins," and the "Spirit" all appear in the Essene writings. The "forgiveness of sins," however, corresponds to one's "repentance"—the renouncing of one's wicked ways and the obedient submission to life according to the Community—and is granted by the "Spirit of the true counsel of God," the Holy Spirit (1QS 3.6–8; cf. 11.14; CD 3.18; 4.6, 9.10; 1QH 4.37; 7.30; 11.10, 30–31; 16.12). The waters of baptism do not effect forgiveness (1QS 8.4–5). "Forgiveness" is granted by the Spirit on the basis of "repentance" and not the waters of baptism (so Gnilka, RevQ 3 [1961] 194–95). Indeed, the "forgiveness of sins" displayed by a life of obedience was a necessary prerequisite for entering the waters for the "purification of the many" (1QS 6.16–23) and expressed a present experience of the future, final "forgiveness of sins" through the lustration of God's Spirit at the eschaton (1QS 4.20–23).

John's baptism had repentance—though expressed differently from Qumran—as its focus. Like Qumran's lustrations, John's baptism signified one's readiness to repent and offered the certainty of God's acceptance of a candidate's repentance. Unlike Qumran where the Community screened one's repentance and the accompanying forgiveness of sins as measured by one's life lived under the scrutiny of the Community, John called for repentance and its corresponding conduct and offered a confirming baptism as the necessary prerequisite for the "forgiveness of sins" that was yet to come. This "forgiveness" was to accompany the Greater One. Thus John's baptism marked one's turning back to God in total surrender as preparation for the Greater One who would bring salvation, i.e., the "forgiveness of sins." John's proclaiming a "repentance-baptism for the forgiveness of sins" in 1:4 gains further exposition by the comparison in 1:8 of his water-baptism and the Greater One's Spirit-baptism (see *Comment* on 1:8).

5 "The whole area of Judea and all the people of Jerusalem" (πᾶσα ἡ Ἰουδαία χώρα καὶ οἱ Ἰεροσολυμῖται πάντες). Clearly hyperbolic, this statement corresponds with Josephus' note on John's impact (*Ant.* 18.117). The reference to Judea (cf. 3:7) and Jerusalem implies what the Q tradition (Matt 3:7–10 // Luke 3:7–9) states. The Baptist was calling *all* Israel to repentance.

"Confessing their sins" (ἐξομολογούμενοι τὰς ἁμαρτίας) denotes the acknowledgment of sin and a renouncing of sinful ways (cf. 1QS 1.24–26). Such an act belongs implicitly, if not explicitly, to the meaning of repentance.

"Jordan River." The ford of Chadschle located south of Jericho near the Wadi-el-Kelt has been the traditional location of John's baptism. Since the lower Jordan Valley belongs to the wilderness area (cf. Josephus, *War* 3.515), John's preaching "in the wilderness" and his baptizing "in the Jordan" do not necessarily stand in conflict. Elijah's association with the Jordan (2 Kgs 2:6–14; cf. Elisha's in 5:8–14) is most likely coincidental. Early rabbinic tradition specifically excludes the Jordan River as a place of purification (*m. Para* 8.10).

6 "A garment of camel hair and a leather belt" (ἐνδεδυμένος τρίχας καμήλου καὶ ζώνην δερματίνην) adds a brief biographical note whose roots most probably extend to the Baptist's ministry since both his food and clothing correspond to his ministering "in the wilderness." A "garment of camel hair" suggests a cloak of roughly woven camel's hair rather than the quality material of that description today. A "leather belt" refers to a wide strip of leather drawn around one's waist and abdomen. Several have seen an intentional parallel between the Baptist's and Elijah's clothing (e.g., Joüon, *Bib* 16 [1935] 74–81; Taylor, 156; Hengel, *Leader*, 36, n. 71; Wink, *Baptist*, 3; Pesch, 1:81; Grundmann, 28). The reference to a "leather belt around his waist" does correspond to the description of Elijah's belt in 2 Kgs 1:8 LXX (cf. MT), and the reference to a hair garment has a distant parallel with Zech 13:4 LXX (ἐνδύσονται δέρριν ἢ μιχίνην).

By combining 2 Kgs 1:8 and Zech 13:4 several have interpreted 2 Kgs 1:8 to read, "He wore a garment of haircloth with a girdle of leather around his loins" (rsv, so Joüon, *Bib* 16 [1935] 74–81; Hengel, *Leader*, 36, n. 71), a reading quite similar to Mark 1:6. Unfortunately, such a reading of 2 Kgs 1:8 corresponds neither to the Hebrew (איש בעל שער, ʾîš baʿal śēʿār—"hairy man" or "man with thick hair," cf. Gen 27:11, 23) nor the LXX (ἀνὴρ δασύς, "hairy man"). Furthermore, Zech 13:4 refers to the clothing of prophets without any trace of an analogy with Elijah (see Vielhauer, *Aufsätze*, 47–54). Even should one argue by analogy that "hairy man" in 2 Kgs 1:8 referred to a garment of hair (so Hengel, *Leader*, 36, n. 71), why the specific reference in Mark 1:6 to "camel's hair," when sheepskin provided the usual raw material (μηλωτή—1 Kgs 19:13, 19; 2 Kgs 2:8, 13, 14; Heb 11:37)? Even the reference to a "leather belt" need not be a direct reference to 2 Kgs 1:8, since such belts belonged to the dress of the wilderness nomad (Hess, *ZAW* 35 [1915] 120–31; Gnilka, 1:47).

John's garb, therefore, corresponds to the nomadic attire of the wilderness in general and to the prophetic dress in particular (so Zech 13:4; Heb 11:37, Böcher, *TZ* 24 [1968] 408–11). To be dressed in simply a cloak and a belt befits John's prophetic role as one living and ministering "in the wilderness" (cf. 1:3, 4; Matt 11:7–8 // Luke 7:24–25) and leaves little basis for any direct allusion to Elijah. At most one might find a similar ascetic note in his attire, a note supported by his diet.

"Locust and wild honey" (ἀκρίδας καὶ μέλι ἄγριον) also bespeaks the wilderness (Taylor, 156; Schweizer, 33; Pesch, 1:81). But Böcher (*NTS* 18 [1971–72] 91) has noted that "locust," like fish, served as suitable substitute for meat in the ancient world (see Lev 11:22–23; *m. Ḥul.* 8.1; *m. Taʿan.* 4.7). Similarly, "honeywater" served as a suitable substitute for wine (Böcher, *NTS* 18 [1971–72] 91; cf. Plato, *Symp.* 2036; Luke 24:42 *v.l.* cf. 1QS 6.4–5; 1QSa 2.17–21). Thus Mark 1:6 would correspond to Luke 7:33 // Matt 11:18 (cf. לחם, *leḥem*, "bread" behind ἄρτος, so Böcher, *NTS* 18 [1971–72] 92) which declares that John neither ate meat nor drank wine, a practice found among late Jewish prophets (*Vitae Prophetorum* 16.8–10; cf. Dan 1:8; *Mart. Isa.* 7.11).

7 "He proclaimed" (ἐκήρυσσεν) resumes John's function as the "voice in the wilderness" (1:3, 4) and announces his prophetic message. It consists of a double saying (1:7, 8) and has close parallels in John 1:26–27 and Q (Matt 3:11 // Luke 3:16). The difference from the chiastic form of Q may well derive from Mark's own redactional interest in depicting John as the voice in the wilderness who prepares the way for another (1:4–5; cf. 1:2a, 3; Isa 40:3). Accordingly, John's prophetic proclamation begins with a direct reference to the coming of the Greater One rather than to his own repentance-baptism (cf. Matt 3:11 // Luke 3:16). The evangelist would then be responsible for changing the participle (ὁ ἐρχόμενος, Matt 3:11) to the indicative construction (ἔρχεται—1:7 // Luke 3:16). Furthermore, John's proclamation in 1:7–8 focuses exclusively on the eschatological salvation with no trace of the judgment theme present in Q (Matt 3:7–12 // Luke 3:7–9, 16–17).

"One greater than I" (ὁ ἰσχυρότερός μου). Various forms of the root underlying "greater" (ἰσχυρότερος) appear in the LXX and NT with reference to God (e.g., 2 Sam 22:31; 23:5; Ps 7:12; cf. 1 Cor 10:22; Rev 18:8), angels (Rev 10:1; 18:21), the oppressors (Isa 49:25; cf. 53:12; Rev 6:15; 19:18) and Satan (Mark 3:27). A similar expression occurs in the Hebrew text of Isa 9:6 (cf. μεγάλης—LXX) in reference to the messiah. But this variety of referents prevents one from taking the "Greater One" as a technical messianic designation. An emerging motif in the biblical usage, however, does suggest that "greatness" belongs to God even when ascribed to the oppressors and Satan, since those who are "great" or "strong" are being or will be overcome by God or God's agents demonstrating that God is the "Stronger" or "Greater One" (cf. Isa 49:25; Rev 6:15–17; 18:21; 19:17–18; Mark 3:27).

To apply the comparative motif literally to John himself in 1:7 would imply incongruously that John saw himself among those to be overcome. Yet the comparison within the context of John's ministry (1:4–8) does suggest a radical break between himself, the precursor of the way, and the one who comes as God's eschatological agent of salvation. The latter's "strength" or "greatness," if not referring to God himself, comes from God as seen in his work. Consequently, the designation the "Greater One" corresponds in part to the biblical attribution of greatness or strength ultimately to God.

But whom was John expecting as the "Greater One"? At least five possibilities have surfaced in the discussion: (a) God (e.g., Thyen, *Geschichte*, 100; Grundmann, 38; cf. Lane, 52), (b) the messiah (e.g., Cranfield, 48; Dunn, *NovT* 14 [1970] 91–92; cf. Taylor, 156; Schweizer, 34), (c) the Son of man (e.g., Becker, *Täufer*, 34–37; Pesch, 1:84; Lang, *Jesus Christus*, 469–71), (d) the eschatological prophet (e.g., Robinson, *Studies*, 30–31), and (e) an unknown eschatological figure (Vielhauer, *RGG* 3 [1959] 895). The choice of an unknown figure offers a solution of last resort, and the eschatological prophet fails to correspond to the rest of the Baptist tradition which calls for repentance in view of the coming judgment. Most have decided for one of the first three options, which in turn conditions, or is conditioned by, the further description of the Greater One in 1:8 (cf. Matt 3:11 and Luke 3:16). One of the keys lies with whether John considered the Greater One to be baptizing with (a) fire, (b) the Spirit, (c) wind and fire, or (d) the Holy Spirit and fire (see *Comment* on 1:8).

Option (a) appears as the most likely on the basis of Exod 23:20, Mal 3:1 and Isa 40:3, the verses that comprise the citation of 1:2b–3. This option also fits with the promise of 1:8, since the coming of the Day of the Lord bespoke judgment (cf. "with fire"). The giving of the Holy Spirit belongs exclusively to God's domain in the OT (cf. "with the Holy Spirit"). Nevertheless, assuming that the Baptist was expecting God to come in person, the use of the comparative "One Greater than I" and the rather mundane reference to untying his shoes stand out as most inappropriate (Haenchen, 43). Consequently, one either dismisses the comparisons as later Christian interpretations (e.g., Gnilka, 1:47) or one looks for someone else more compatible with the context of John's ministry.

For some, the Son of man fits this figure (e.g., Becker, *Täufer*, 34–37). In the *Similitudes of Enoch, 4 Ezra,* and Dan 7 the Son of man comes as a transcendent, heavenly figure to initiate the final, eschatological judgment of the world. He appears to fit the profile of John's "Greater One" (heavenly figure) (cf. Matt 3:7–12 // Luke 3:7–9, 15–18). The weakness of this suggestion lies in its sources. The assumption of the existence of a fixed, transcendent figure known as the Son of man who would come to judge the world cannot be firmly documented as pre-Christian (e.g., Leivestad, *NTS* 18 [1971–72] 243–67; Dunn, *Christology*, 67–82; Lindars, *Son of Man*, 1–16). While one could argue that the Baptist himself first applied the vision of Dan 7 to a specific eschatological figure, the Son of man, one still stumbles over the motifs of fire-judgment and Spirit-salvation which characterize the work of this figure. Neither of these motifs stands out in Dan 7 where the one "like a son of man" was given "dominion over all" by the Ancient of Days (7:13–14).

Others have considered a messiah figure to stand behind the "Greater One." They point to the Baptist's proclamation of a hope of salvation (cf. "forgiveness of sins"—1:4 and "the Holy Spirit"—1:8 // Matt 3:11, Luke 3:16) as well as an imminent judgment (see 1:8). Two hurdles have consistently been encountered with this option. First, could the messiah baptize "with the Holy Spirit"? and second, why the oblique reference here when clear messianic designations were at hand?

The answer to the first question depends on one's reading of 1QS 4.20–21; *T. Levi* 18.6–8 and *T. Judah* 24.2–3. The highly debatable pre-Christian provenance of *T. Levi* 18.6–8 and *T. Judah* 24.2–3 (cf. de Jonge, *NovT* 4 [1960] 200–208; Dupont-Sommer, *Writings*, 301–5; Becker, *Patriarchen*, 291–93; 319–21) makes the use of these texts very tenuous. The cleansing function of the Spirit in 1QS 4.20–21, however, does correspond to the role of the Spirit in the messianic hymn of *T. Levi* 18.6–8. Further, 1Q^{Isa} suggests that Qumran even had a concept of an "anointed one" who would "sprinkle" others (so Brownlee, *Scrolls*, 43–44; Dunn, *NovT* 14 [1970] 90). Therefore, whether or not the expectation of a final cleansing by the Spirit was directly associated with the messiah's own experience of the Spirit in Qumran, their juxtaposition in Qumran was such that a prophet like John might readily have taken the next step and combined them in his proclamation of a "Spirit-baptism," a step hardly more novel than one taken in the proclamation of his unique water-baptism (so Dunn, *NovT* 14 [1970] 91–92).

If the Baptist had a messiah figure in mind, we can only speculate about why he did not use a more direct messianic designation. Some observations, however, can be made. First, if John did indeed expect another—regardless of his identity—to come after him, this simple reference in 1:7 (cf. Matt 3:1 // Luke 3:16) could hardly have exhausted his vocabulary or means of referring to the "coming one." Second, should the comparative references to the Greater One have been the product of the Christian community, would not the absence of a more direct reference to Jesus, for example, the messiah, Son of man, or Son of David, have been even more enigmatic—especially if the saying were forged in polemics? Third, if this saying was preserved by the early Church in the debate with the Baptist's circles, how better could the Church have identified John than by showing his secondary relationship to Jesus through the use of the Baptist's own words? Therefore, such a saying might well have had its historical roots in the Baptist tradition. While "the Greater One" lacks technical messianic precision, one could hardly doubt that the Baptist was referring to an eschatological figure through whom God would effect his promised activity for the eschaton. The explanatory comparison in 1:8 makes that clear.

"After me" (ὀπίσω μου). Though this phrase makes a temporal statement in 1:7; Matt 3:11 cf. Luke 3:16, it does serve at times as a more technical expression for discipleship (see *Comment* on 1:17, 20; Grobel, *JBL* 60 [1941] 397–401). Some (e.g., Lohmeyer, 18; Lane, 52; cf. Pesch, 1:83) have assigned that usage to the underlying Baptist tradition which implies that the Baptist saw "the Greater One" as coming from among his disciples (see John 1:26). The rabbinic use of the servant-master analogy for the pupil-teacher relationship in the reference to untying one's shoes (*b. Ketub.* 96a) could add support to this interpretation. Irony would then play a significant role in the statement. The pupil or disciple surpasses the teacher to such an extent that the teacher is unworthy of being a pupil of the former disciple. This subtle comparison, however, has been lost in the temporal force of the Markan usage. Furthermore, the emphasis on the chronological sequence and not the disciple-master relationship in the early Christian polemics with the Baptist circle strongly supports the chronological reference within the Baptist tradition as well (e.g., Cullmann, *Vorträge*, 169–75).

"The straps of whose sandals." This graphic description of the contrast between the Baptist and "the Greater One" has its background in the slave-master relationships. Despite the fact that such activity belonged to the role of a slave (Str-B, 1:121; 2:1), *Mek. Exod.* 21.2 and the analogous reference to the pupil-master in *b. Ketub.* 96a expressly state that untying the master's sandals was the one demeaning task never required of a Hebrew servant. To be unworthy of such a task would be to lower oneself below the status of a slave.

8 "I baptize . . . but he will baptize" (ἐγὼ ἐβάπτισα . . . αὐτὸς δὲ βαπτίσει). This half of the double saying explains the contrast made in the first half (1:7). It sets the baptism of "the Greater One" in antithetical parallelism to that of the Baptist. The use of the personal pronouns, "I" (ἐγώ) and "he" (αὐτός), resumes and accentuates the comparison. "I baptize" (ἐβάπτισα) in the aorist tense reflects a Semitism, the Hebrew perfect with present force (Taylor, 157), rather than a temporal statement implying the end of the Baptist's activity (Lagrange, 7; Pesch, 1:83; Gnilka, 1:48). The Baptist's proclamation in 1:7–8 parallels rather than supersedes the message of 1:4. The baptism by "the Greater One" still belongs to a future time, as the future tense (βαπτίσει) indicates.

"Baptize with the Holy Spirit" (βαπτίσει ἐν πνεύματι ἁγίῳ). See *Excursus: Baptism with the Spirit and/or Fire* for background. The phrase "Spirit-baptism" that has become prominent in certain circles today owes its derivation to this element inherent in the Baptist's message (Matt 3:11 // Luke 3:16; John

1:33; cf. Acts 1:5; 19:1–7). John, focusing on his baptism as the trademark of his ministry, used baptism metaphorically to contrast his ministry with that of "the Greater One." The bestowal of the Spirit expressed metaphorically as a baptism signified God's eschatological act of salvation promised long ago by the prophets (e.g., Isa 32:15; 44:3; Ezek 11:19; 36:26–27; 37:14; Joel 3:1–2 [2:28–29]); *T. Jud.* 24.3; *T. Levi* 18.11). Therefore, the Baptist was declaring the dawn of a new day of salvation, not simply a new baptism.

Rather than interpret "the baptism with the Holy Spirit" in terms of the Spirit's coming in Acts as a gift (2:38; 5:32; 8:19; 10:45; 11:15–17) of power (1:8; 4:31; 6:10; 8:15–19) signifying the age of salvation (2:16–21), perhaps one should interpret 1:8 (cf. Matt 3:11 // Luke 3:16) in view of the Baptist's expectation of the ultimate forgiveness of sins. Taken this way, the Spirit would be a cleansing agent parallel to water-baptism (so Yates, *NTS* 4 [1958] 334–38; Dunn, *NovT* 14 [1970] 87–92; Hill, *Words,* 238–41; Gnilka, *RevQ* 3 [1961] 194–97).

This usage would then be analogous to that of Qumran (e.g., 1QS 3.7–9; 4.20–21; 1QH 16.11–12; cf. *T. Levi* 18.6–7), a similarity that should be neither surprising nor disturbing. Whereas the Baptist may not have been raised and trained in Qumran, it is hardly fantasy to suppose some sort of familiarity and contact with a community that lay so close to his place of ministry (see H. Braun, *Qumran und das Neue Testament* [Tübingen: Mohr, 1966] 2:2–3). One can certainly find a degree of similarity with Qumran in his eschatological orientation, his wilderness setting, his ascetic lifestyle, his use of water-baptism, his priestly background, his stress on repentance for all Israel, and his warning of the coming judgment. Thus a similar expectation of the Holy Spirit as the agent of ultimate cleansing would hardly be novel.

To view the Spirit as the agent of cleansing, the one bringing the eschatological forgiveness of sins, corresponds with the Baptist's preaching of a repentance-baptism to be lived out in one's daily life with view to the ultimate forgiveness of sins (1:4). Those submitting to John's baptism (cleansing clearly implied) prepare themselves for the Greater One's baptism by the Holy Spirit (cleansing also implied) who ultimately forgives their sins as an eschatological act of salvation (1:8). This role of the Spirit accompanying God's promise of salvation for his own has its roots in Ezek 36:25–27: "I will sprinkle clean water on you . . . you shall be clean from all your uncleanness. . . . I will put my Spirit within you and cause you to walk in my statutes." Therefore, the Baptist's proclamation in 1:4 of a repentance-baptism for the forgiveness of sins corresponds directly to his proclamation in 1:8 of his water-baptism and the Greater One's Spirit-baptism.

This conclusion would imply that the evangelist did not intend for "the baptism with the Holy Spirit" to be read through the Lukan eyes of Acts. Jesus himself receives the Holy Spirit in 1:10 through whom he has the power and authority to heal the sick, forgive sins (e.g., 2:1–12), defeat Satan (1:12–13; 3:22–30), and ultimately to give his life "for the many" (14:24; cf. 10:38–40, 45). Through Jesus' life (ministry) and death, one receives the "baptism with the Holy Spirit," i.e., the salvation promised for the new age (1:14–15; 1:16–18). We have no hint of his bestowing the Spirit as a gift of power on his followers.

This conclusion would also imply that the evangelist truncated the tradition as seen in Q (Matt 3:11 // Luke 3:16) by eliminating "and with fire." Similarly, he has chosen not to include any reference to the Baptist's warning of judgment (cf. Matt 3:7–12 // Luke 3:7–9, 15–18). The controlling principle behind his redaction might again be found in 1:2a, his perception of the opening events of the Gospel as the fulfillment of Isaiah's promise. John fulfilled his task as the forerunner, "the voice in the wilderness," by baptizing with a repentance-baptism that prepared for the Greater One to consummate this ministry with a Spirit-baptism that brings the eschatological salvation, the forgiveness of sins, promised by the Baptist. Consequently, Mark's focus falls on the persons and their roles in announcing and effecting the gospel, the good news of salvation (1:14–15), rather than on the coming judgment.

Explanation

The counterpart of the prophetic promise in 1:2b–3 follows in 1:4–8. As the heading in 1:1–3 suggests, Mark, drawing on traditional elements about the Baptist and his ministry, describes the man and his ministry in four brief, disjointed statements that relate him to Isaiah's prophecy, especially Isa 40:3 (1:3). Assuming the reader's familiarity with the Baptist, the evangelist seeks primarily to underscore the Baptist's identity as the actual voice in the wilderness who has come to prepare the way of the Lord as seen in 1:9–15.

John appears "in the wilderness" without biographical introduction or specific geographical location (1:4). Ample evidence supports a wilderness setting for his ministry. Yet Mark focuses on the wilderness primarily in view of Isa 40:3 as the place of the one preparing the way of the Lord. The disconnected reference to the Baptist's dress of camel's hair with a wide, leather belt and to his diet of locusts and wild honey characteristic of a wilderness habitat (1:6) reinforces John's identity as the "voice crying in the wilderness" of Isa 40:3.

As the "voice crying in the wilderness," the Baptist's proclamation dominates this brief vignette in keeping with his role as herald (1:4, 7–8). In 1:4, he appears proclaiming a repentance-baptism with view to the forgiveness of one's sins. In 1:7–8, he proclaims the coming of a Greater One for whom he has come to prepare the way. On the one hand, the Baptist proclaims his own baptism for the present that fulfills Isaiah's promise of the preparation of the way. On the other hand, he proclaims the Greater One who will supersede him and his baptism with the ultimate eschatological salvation. As the voice of one crying in the wilderness, he stands as the point between the past promise and the future fulfillment of redemptive history with his own role representing both accomplishment and anticipation of that history.

He was known as "the Baptizer" because of his special baptism. Through this particular act, he carried out his task of preparing the way. Like the prophets of old, the Baptist called all God's people, regardless of their standing in Israel (cf. 1:5) to repentance. Repentance connoted much more than sorrow or remorse. It included the reorientation of one's total life (cf. Matt 3:7–10 // Luke 3:7–9, 10–14). As a sign and seal of this personal commitment, the Baptist offered a baptism, an act of immersion by him in the Jordan (1:5). This baptism was both an acknowledgment of one's sins and one's desire to repent and an acknowledgment of God's acceptance of that repentance. The ultimate goal of repentance-baptism was the forgiveness of sins and acceptance by God in the coming day of salvation.

By calling all Israel to repentance, John, the voice in the wilderness, prepared the way for the Greater One (1:7) whose coming would supersede his ministry by bringing, through his own "baptism" with the Holy Spirit, the promised salvation for those who had repented. This "baptism with the Holy Spirit" by the Greater One graphically expresses the actual forgiveness of sins and eschatological cleansing anticipated by John's preparatory ministry and the promise of Isaiah. Thus by proclaiming a repentance-baptism and pointing to the coming Spirit-baptism, John fulfills the promise of Isa 40:3 and accomplishes the task of the "voice of one crying in the wilderness to prepare the way of the Lord."

Excursus: Baptism with the Spirit and/or Fire

The Q material (Matt 3:11 // Luke 3:16) refers to a baptism "with the Holy Spirit and fire" rather than simply "the Holy Spirit" (1:8 cf. John 1:33). This difference has led to considerable debate about the original wording of the Baptist's message. Three options have emerged: (a) a baptism "with fire," meaning judgment; (b) a baptism "with wind ($\pi\nu\epsilon\dot{\upsilon}\mu\alpha\tau\iota$) and fire," meaning judgment; (c) a baptism "with the Holy Spirit and fire," meaning salvation and judgment.

Since "fire" was a familiar symbol of judgment in the OT (e.g., Amos 7:4; Isa 31:9; Mal 3:2; see F. Lang, *TDNT* 6 [1968] 936–37) and since John's preaching contained a strong judgment motif in Q (Matt 3:7–12 // Luke 3:7–9, 15–18), few doubt that the earlier tradition contained a reference to it, although absent in Mark. Further, many have found Mark's saying (cf. John 1:33) too similar to the Church's interpretation of the Pentecost experience and have consequently attributed it to a later Christian adaptation of the Baptist's message. That earlier message appears now in Matthew's and Luke's conflated reading of Mark and Q (e.g., Dibelius, *Täufer*, 43–55; Taylor, 157, Manson, *SJT* 2 [1949] 391–403; Pesch, 1:83; Thyen, *Geschichte*, 93–101; Becker, *Täufer*, 23–25). When one considers the lack of OT evidence for the bestowal of the Spirit by any except God personally, a fairly strong case emerges for "he will baptize you with fire" as having been the earlier reading.

This conclusion, however, leaves us with a hypothetically reconstructed reading referring only to fire for which there is little more than circumstantial evidence. Acts 19:1–7 contributes little to the discussion, since "we have never even heard that there is a Holy Spirit" (19:2) could hardly be taken literally as an indication that the Baptist never mentioned the Spirit in view of both the OT and current Jewish hope for the Spirit. One could equally argue that Acts 19:2 meant that John's disciples, baptized with his repentance-baptism (19:4), did not know that the Spirit had actually come through Jesus. They then were baptized in Jesus' name (19:5–6). More importantly, the hypothetical reading "with fire" stresses too narrowly John's role as a prophet of doom rather than one proclaiming a repentance-baptism which had to have included an element of hope.

The second option that takes $\pi\nu\epsilon\dot{\upsilon}\mu\alpha\tau\iota$ as "wind" (Eisler, *Jesus*, 275–80; E. Schweizer, *TDNT* 6 [1968] 399; Best, *NovT* 34 [1959–60] 240–42) has all the advantages of the first, since "wind" and "fire" are both symbols of judgment (e.g., Isa 29:6; 30:27–28; 40:24; Jer 23:19; 30:23; Ezek 13:11–13; cf. *4 Ezra* 13.1–22). In addition it offers a transitional basis for the Christian reading of πνεύματι = "Spirit" and avoids the problem of a hypothetically reconstructed text (cf. Dunn, *NovT* 14 [1970] 84–85). Further this parallelism has its supposed counterpart in the winnowing analogy employing "wind" and "fire" that follows in the Q material (Matt 3:12 // Luke 3:17). However, one should note that the text reads πνεύματι ἁγίῳ or "Holy Spirit," an anarthrous construction untypical of Mark (cf. 1:10, 12; 3:29; 12:36; 13:11).

Though "wind" belongs inherently to the analogy of winnowing that follows, the judgment in Matt 3:12 // Luke 3:17 takes place in the "fire" and not in the winnowing process itself. One could argue that the "wind" provides the purifying agent that separates the wheat and chaff leading to the double result of gathering grain into the granary and the destruction of the chaff. The double result of gathering wheat and burning the chaff also warns against focusing too narrowly on the judgment motif in the Baptist's message.

In the third option, "with the Holy Spirit and fire," two difficulties stand out. First, the one direct object, "you" (ὑμᾶς), is the apparent recipient of both baptisms— "He will baptize you with the Holy Spirit and fire." Second, we lack any previous parallel to any but God as being the giver of the Holy Spirit. This problem carries significant weight. But as an argument from silence, it cannot be controlling. We find a similar absence of parallel to the Baptist's nonrepeated water-baptism of repentance. Further, we have noted in 1:7 that the juxtaposition of all the constituent elements—the messiah anointed with the Spirit (cf. Isa 11:2; *Pss. Sol.* 17.37; 18.7; *T. Levi* 18.6–8; *T. Judah* 24.2; *1 Enoch* 49.3; 62.2), the prophetic expectation of the Spirit as a sign of the eschaton, and the expectation of the Spirit as an agent of cleansing from sins (1QS 4.20–21; 1QH 16.11–12; cf. Ezek 36:25–26)—lay at hand in the Baptist's setting.

Therefore, just as the Baptist drew upon his times by prophetically combining the mode of baptism, the call to repentance, and the promise of forgiveness of sins in view of the coming day of the Lord to shape his ministry of baptism, so he could have shaped his expectation of the Greater One's baptism. The roots of his own ministry lie deep in the OT prophets' call to repentance. The roots of the "Spirit-baptism" lie close to the promise of Ezek 36:25–27.

Some have avoided the problem of the one direct object by considering it to have been a later insertion (e.g., Lohmeyer, 17; Gnilka, 1:48), a solution lacking any textual basis. One might well argue for much the same result by taking the "you" to refer to the Baptist's audience in general rather than to specific, baptized individuals. Whereas the Baptist proclaimed a baptism by water to his audience ("you," ὑμᾶς), he also proclaimed to his audience ("you") that the Greater One would baptize them with the Holy Spirit and fire.

This solution, however, appears to break down since the Baptist offered only one baptism and the Greater One offers two. But such a division in ranks was also implicit to the Baptist's ministry. Those submitting to his repentance-baptism and living accordingly stood in contrast to those who did not, a distinction to be clarified by the coming judgment. The Greater One will show himself to be greater because his "baptism" with the "Holy Spirit" offers the ultimate salvation, the forgiveness of sins, anticipated and proclaimed by the Baptist (1:4), and his "baptism" with "fire" effects the final judgment also anticipated by the Baptist for the unrepentant or unprepared (cf. Matt 3:7–10 // Luke 3:7–9). Consequently, we might legitimately read the saying without the "you": "I baptize with water, he will baptize with the Holy Spirit and fire."

C. The Baptism of Jesus (1:9–11)

Bibliography

Beasley-Murray, G. R. *Baptism in the New Testament.* Grand Rapids: Eerdmans, 1962. **Bousset, W.** *Kyrios Christos: A History of the Belief in Christ from the Beginnings of Christianity to Irenaeus.* Tr. J. E. Steely. Nashville: Abingdon, 1970. **Bretscher, P.** "Exodus 4:22–23 and the Voice from Heaven." *JBL* 87 (1968) 301–11. **Buse, I.** "The Markan Account of the Baptism of Jesus and Isaiah lxiii." *JTS* 7 (1956) 74–75. **Chilton, B. D.** *A Galilean Rabbi and His Bible: Jesus' Use of the Interpreted Scripture of His Time.* GNS 8. Wilmington, DE: Michael Glazier, 1984. **Cranfield, C. E. B.** "The Baptism of Our Lord: A Study of St. Mark 1:9–12." *SJT* 7 (1955) 53–63. **Cullmann, O.** *The Christology of the New Testament.* Rev. ed. Philadelphia: Westminster, 1963. **Dalman, G.** *The Words of Jesus Considered in the Light of Post-biblical Jewish Writings and the Aramaic Language.* Edinburgh: T. & T. Clark, 1902. **Feuillet, A.** "Le baptême de Jésus." *RB* 71 (1964) 321–51. ———. "Le symbolisme de la columbe dans les récits évangéliques du baptême de Mc 1,11 (et parallèles)." *RSR* 46 (1958) 524–44. **Fuller, R.** *The Mission and Achievement of Jesus.* SBT 12. London: SCM, 1963. **Gaboury, A.** "Deux Fils uniques: Isaai et Jésus; Connexions vétéro-testamentaires de Mc i, 11." *SE* 4 (1968) 198–204. **Garnet, P.** "The Baptism of Jesus and the Son of Man Idea." *JSNT* 9 (1980) 49–65. **Gero, S.** "The Spirit as a Dove at the Baptism of Jesus." *NovT* 18 (1976) 17–35. **Jeremias, J.** *Abba: Studien zur neutestamentlichen Theologie und Zeitgeschichte.* Göttingen: Vandenhoeck & Ruprecht, 1966. ———. *New Testament Theology.* 1971. **Kazmierski, C. R.** *Jesus the Son of God: A Study of the Markan Tradition and Its Redaction by the Evangelist.* Forschung zur Bible 33. Würzburg: Echter, 1979. **Keck, L. E.** "The Spirit and the Dove." *NTS* 17 (1970–71) 41–67. **Kingsbury, J. D.** *The Christology of Mark's Gospel.* Philadelphia: Fortress, 1983. **Lentzen-Deis, F.** *Die Taufe Jesu nach den Synoptiken: Literarkritische und gattungsgeschichtliche Untersuchungen.* FTS 4. Frankfurt: Knecht, 1970. **Maloney, E. C.** *Semitic Interference in Marcan Syntax.* 1981. **Marshall, I. H.** "Son of God or Servant of Yahweh? A Reconsideration of Mk 1, 11." *NTS* 15 (1968–69) 326–36. **Mauser, U. W.** *Christ in the Wilderness.* SBT 39. London: SCM, 1963. **Richter, G.** "Zu den Tauferzählungen Mk 1:9–11 und Joh 1:32–34." *ZNW* 65 (1974) 43–54. **Schürmann, H.** *Das Lukasevangelium.* HTKNT 3/1. Freiburg: Herder, 1969. **Theissen, G.** *Miracle Stories of the Early Christian Tradition.* 1983. **Turner, C. H.** "ὁ υἱός μου ἀγαπητός." *JTS* 27 (1925–26) 113–29. **Vielhauer, P.** "Erwägungen zur Christologie des Markusevangeliums." In *Aufsätze zum Neuen Testament.* TB 31. Munich: Kaiser, 1965. 199–215. **Vögtle, A.** "Die sogenannte Taufperikope Mk 1, 9–11. Zur Problematik der Herkunft und des ursprünglichen Sinns." *EKK* 4 (1972) 15–29.

Translation

⁹*In those days, Jesus came*[a] *from Nazareth in Galilee and was baptized in*[b] *the Jordan by John.* ¹⁰*At the moment*[c] *he came up out of the water, Jesus*[d] *saw the heavens split and the Spirit like a dove coming down to him.* ¹¹*Then a voice came*[e] *from heaven: "You are my son, the beloved one. I am very pleased with you."*

Notes

[a] καὶ ἐγένετο . . . ἦλθεν to express a past event is a Semitic idiom consisting of καὶ ἐγένετο, temporal expression, and second verb without καί, drawn either from first-century Aramaic or

the LXX (e.g., Gen 4:3) that "never occurs in nonbiblical Greek" (Maloney, *Interference*, 85). It reappears in 4:4 (cf. 2:15 and 23).

[b] εἰς occasionally takes over the function of ἐν in Hellenistic Greek (BDF, § 205).

[c] εὐθύς occurs adverbially 87 times in NT (51 as εὐθύς; 36 as εὐθέως) and almost exclusively in narrative units (W. Pöhlmann, *EWNT* 2:194–95; Theissen, *Miracle Stories*, 199). Mark has 47 occurrences (26 as εὐθύς); 11 in this chapter. Despite the frequency in Mark, one must use caution before assigning the term to Markan redaction (Theissen, *Miracle Stories*, 199; Pesch, 1:18–19, 89–90). It serves at times a temporal ("immediately" or "suddenly") and at times a stylistic function merely to focus one's attention.

[d] Romanized words added from context.

[e] ἐγένετο (cf. 9:7) read by Nestle[26] and UBSGNT following ℵ A L (W) *f*[1] *f*[13.] Majority text lat sy co. Omitted by Taylor (161; Lohmeyer, 20, n.3; Cranfield, 54) following ℵ* D as an assimilation to Luke 3:22 (cf. Matt 3:17) of an "overliteral translation of an Aramaic original."

Form / Structure / Setting

This pericope consists of the baptismal event (1:9) and an ensuing revelatory scene (1:10–11) formally described as a "calling-vision" (*Berufvision*) based on the OT calling of a prophet (e.g., Jeremias, *Theology*, 55), an epiphany "myth" (Dibelius, 271–72), a biographical "legend" (Bultmann, 249) or an interpretative vision (*Deutevision*) based on similar scenes from the Targums (e.g., Lentzen-Deis, *Taufe*, 195–248).

Related to the formal question is the historical question: Did this scene have its roots in Jesus' experience? If so, was it to interpret (*Deutevision*) his baptism with sinners as the atoning servant (e.g., Cullmann, *Christology*, 66–67)? Was it the moment of his calling (*Berufvision*), the birth of his messianic consciousness (e.g., Fuller, *Mission*, 36–89) or the clarification and confirmation of his person and ministry (e.g., Taylor, 162)? Or was it a scene to reveal him to Israel and/or to John (e.g., Lagrange, 11–13) or to give him a sign or impulse to begin his ministry (e.g., Feuillet, *RB* 71 [1964] 321–52)?

If not anchored in Jesus' ministry, did the community create the tradition for Christological reasons to set Jesus' sonship and messianic role at the outset of his ministry (e.g., Conzelmann, *RGG* 3:627; Dibelius, 271–72; cf. Schmithals, 1:84–89)? Was it intended paradigmatically as the prototype for Christian baptism (Haenchen, 62)? Or did the community create the revelation scene as an apologetical counter to the question of why the Greater One, the Messiah, submitted to John's baptism (e.g., Vögtle, 134–39)? Answers to these questions require a closer exegetical analysis of the pericope and its setting in Mark.

Apart from the redactional use of "in those days" (ἐν ἐκείναις ταῖς ἡμέραις) and possibly "at the moment" (καὶ εὐθύς), the material stems from pre-Markan tradition. The question of whether other traditional baptism accounts also existed (e.g., Q, see Schürmann, *Lukasevangelium* 1:197, 218–19; other accounts, cf. Jeremias, *Theology*, 49–50) must remain open at this point. The anarthrous use of "Jesus" and "John," the absolute use of "the Spirit," and the reference to the Jordan stand in contrast to similar uses in 1:4–8 and suggest that this traditional unit existed separately from that behind 1:4–8 (Pesch, 1:88). The evidence indicates that the evangelist brought this unit into conjunction with 1:2b–8 to form his prologue under the heading of 1:1–3.

The setting of 1:9–11 in the context of 1:2b–8 places Jesus in comparison with the Baptist. The promised precursor (1:7–8) of the OT (1:2b–3) offers the setting (1:9) for the coming of the Greater One (1:7, 11) who will baptize with the Spirit as the one bringing the age of salvation (1:10–11, 14–15), according to Isaiah's promise (1:1–2a). Therefore, for Mark the account of Jesus' baptism not only has significance of its own, but it culminates in and validates the Baptist's ministry as Isaiah's "voice in the wilderness."

Comment

9 "Jesus" (Ἰησοῦς). The evangelist obviously assumed the reader's greater familiarity with Jesus' identity (cf. 1:1). He begins without further biographical information. The absence of a birth narrative (cf. Matt 1–2; Luke 1–2) more than likely arises from his intention to introduce Jesus in the framework of redemptive history (1:2b–15) as the fulfillment of Isaiah's promise for the day of salvation (1:1–2a), the proclaimer of the "good news" (1:14–15), rather than from any lack of knowledge about such a narrative.

"From Nazareth of Galilee" (ἀπὸ Ναζαρὲτ τῆς Γαλιλαίας) could qualify "Jesus" (e.g., Lohmeyer, 20; Schweizer, 39) as "Jesus of Nazareth" (so John 1:45, 46; Acts 10:38; cf. Mark 1:24; 14:67; 16:6) or "came" (ἦλθεν) as "came from Nazareth" (e.g., Klostermann, 8; Taylor, 159). The further qualification "of Galilee" suggests the latter. Were "Jesus of Nazareth" meant to be a name, "Galilee" would have been redundant. As a place of origin, little known Nazareth might well have needed the further geographical qualifier. Furthermore, Jesus' coming stands in contrast to the coming of those from Judea and Jerusalem in 1:5.

"Was baptized by John." The passive verb (ἐβαπτίσθη) and the genitive of direct agency (ὑπὸ Ἰωάννου) implies that Jesus was immersed by John in the Jordan as the agent of and not merely as the witness to the baptism (cf. Jeremias, *Theology*, 51). The Baptist's hesitance in Matt 3:14–15, the location of the notice of John's imprisonment in Luke 3:19–20, the absence of his name in Luke 3:21–22, and the absence of the baptism account entirely in John suggest the increasing concern felt by the Church with this event as such and support its historical roots in Jesus' experience (cf. Haenchen, 60–63).

10 "At the moment" (καὶ εὐθύς), whether added by the evangelist or part of his tradition, underscores the relationship of the vision (εἶδεν) in 1:10–11 with the event of the baptism (1:9). It expresses the continuity between John's and Jesus' ministry, while setting the stage for the discontinuity. In other words, the baptismal act completes the Baptist's preparatory ministry by providing the setting for the vision that sets Jesus apart as the Greater One.

"He came up" (ἀναβαίνων) corresponds to the Spirit's "coming down" (καταβαῖνον). At the same time, the sequence of events indicates that the baptismal act itself was completed (cf. 1:9, ἐβαπτίσθη, aorist tense). Thus, John's baptism was the occasion rather than the means of the Spirit's coming to Jesus and the voice speaking from heaven. The Baptist's "water baptism" remains distinct from and discontinuous with the eschatological moment that sets off the Greater One (cf. 1:7–8). Furthermore, the distinction between the awkward event of 1:9 and the events of 1:10–11 precludes the creation and use of

Jesus' baptism by the primitive Church as a prototype of Christian baptism (cf. Haenchen, 62–63).

"He saw" (εἶδεν) can only refer to Jesus, the subject of 1:9 and the one addressed in 1:11 (so Matt 3:16; cf. John 1:32, 33). "Seeing" in the context of heaven opening often connotes a visionary experience (e.g., Acts 7:56; 10:11; Rev 19:11; *T. Levi* 2.6; *T. Jud.* 24.2; *2 Apoc. Bar.* 22.1). Luke 3:22 drops the verb and Matt 3:16 changes the formula and has Jesus simply seeing the descending Spirit.

"The heavens split" (σχιζομένους τοὺς οὐρανούς). Matt 3:16 and Luke 3:21 have a "minor agreement" (ἀνοίγειν, cf. σχίζειν). While a Q parallel would account for the difference, the rarity of σχίζειν in this construction together with the more common use of ἀνοίγειν in similar settings might well account for a coincidental change in Matthew and Luke (e.g., Gen 7:11; Ps 77:23 LXX; Isa 24:18; Ezek 1:1; John 1:51; Acts 7:56; 10:11; Rev 4:1; 11:19; 19:11; *T. Levi* 2.6; 5.1; 18.6; *T. Jud.* 24.2; cf. esp. קרע, *qāraʿ* = σχίζειν but rendered stylistically with ἀνοίγειν in Isa 63:19 LXX). Mark 1:10 may in fact be a play on the prayer of Isa 63:19 MT for Yahweh "to *rend* the heavens and come down" (Buse, *JTS* 7 [1956] 74–75; C. Maurer, *TDNT* 7 [1971] 962; Feuillet, *CBQ* 21 [1959] 458–90; Grundmann, 41; Gnilka, 1:52; Lentzen-Deis, *Taufe,* 101–3, cf. Pesch, 1:91). If so, Matthew and Luke either missed this motif or aligned the reference more closely with the LXX of Isa 63:19. If Isa 63:19 MT does indeed lie behind Mark's text, it would then reflect a setting familiar with the Hebrew text.

"The Spirit coming down." The splitting of the heavens does not provide further visionary material as such (cf. Ezek 1:1; Acts 7:56; Rev 4:1; 11:19; *2 Apoc. Bar.* 22:1). It enabled the Spirit to descend (cf. Gen 7:11; Ps 77:23 LXX; Acts 10:11; Rev 19:11). This may explain the order ἠνεῴχθησαν . . . εἶδεν in Matt 3:16 and simply ἀνεῳχθῆναι in Luke 3:21 and further support Isa 63:19 as the background text. The suggestion that the absolute use of "the Spirit" (τὸ πνεῦμα) betrays a Hellenistic influence and setting (e.g., Bultmann, 247; Vielhauer, *Aufsätze,* 205–6; Schmithals, 1:83–84) has been sufficiently disproved by similar usage in Qumran, e.g., 1QS 4.6; 1QH 12.11–12; 13.18–19; 16.11; E. Schweizer, *TDNT* 6 [1968] 400). Rather, the background of the Spirit's coming appears to be more the OT promises for the new age such as Isa 11:2; 61:1 (cf. Mark 1:14–15 and 1:2a) and especially Isa 42:1 (cf. also 63:11).

"Like a dove" (ὡς περιστεράν) has been taken as secondary by some (e.g., Gero, *NovT* 18 [1976] 18–19). However, the evidence (absence from the *Gos. Heb.*) hardly implies an early, separate tradition. Read in conjunction solely with the noun (πνεῦμα) and participle (καταβαῖνον), the phrase can be either adjectival, i.e., "the Spirit (appearing) *like* a dove," or adverbial, i.e., "coming down *as* a dove (does)." The latter adverbial use has some supporters (e.g., Jeremias, *Theology,* 52; Gnilka, 1:52; esp. Keck, *NTS* 17 [1970–71] 41–67). The phrase must be read in the larger context. Jesus "sees" (εἶδεν) the heavens *and* the Spirit, a construction implying a visual form of the Spirit. Jesus could hardly have "seen" an invisible Spirit descending "as a dove" (Haenchen, 53–54). Furthermore, all parallels (Matt 3:16; Luke 3:22; John 1:32–34; and

Gos. Eb.) follow explicitly the adjectival understanding of the Spirit appearing "like a dove." Consequently, most commentators (e.g., Taylor, 160–61; Grundmann, 42; Lohmeyer, 23; Pesch, 1:19; see esp. Richter, *ZNW* 65 [1974] 43–45) have taken the phrase adjectivally. At the same time, the absence of clear precedent for identifying the dove symbolically with the Spirit, despite the extensive literary use of the dove in ancient literature (see Str-B, 1:123–25; H. Greeven, *TDNT* 6 [1968] 64–67; Lentzen-Deis, *Taufe*, 170–83), makes any symbolic explanation of the dove's role in this pericope (cf. Feuillet, *RSR* 46 [1958] 524–44; Lentzen-Deis, *Taufe*, 269–73) tenuous at best (so Schweizer, 37).

11 "A voice from heaven" (φωνή . . . ἐκ τῶν οὐρανῶν). Some have identified this "voice" with the Bath Qol (e.g., Taylor, 161; Chilton, *Rabbi*, 126–27) of rabbinic writings (Str-B, 1:125–32). Yet the relative inferiority of this sound, compared at times to an echo, in contrast to God's word as spoken through the prophets, makes this connection unlikely. The parallel and contrast between the voice referring to Jesus in 1:11 and the prophetic word referring to the Baptist in 1:2b–3, the direct discourse of 1:11 compared to the narrative style of 1:2b–3, and the private audition of Jesus within the context of the vision (1:10–11 // Luke 3:22; cf. Matt 3:17) suggest that God was personally speaking (so O. Betz, *TDNT* 9 [1974] 298).

Many have looked to the OT for a key to understanding the meaning of the statement from the heaven. Some see it in Ps 2:7 (e.g., Justin, *Dial.* 88.8; Vielhauer, *Aufsätze*, 205–6); others in Isa 42:1 (e.g., J. Jeremias, *TDNT* 5 [1967] 701–2), Gen 22:2, 12, 16 (e.g., Turner, *JTS* 27 [1925–26] 113–29; Gaboury, *SE* 4 [1968] 198–204), or Exod 4:22–23 (e.g., Bretscher, *JBL* 87 [1968] 301–11). Yet no single text adequately accounts for the statement as a whole.

"You are my son" (σὺ εἶ ὁ υἱός μου) has most commonly been viewed as a rendering of Ps 2:7 LXX (υἱός μου εἶ σύ). However, the unique word order (cf. Ps 2:7 LXX; Acts 13:33; Heb 1:5; Luke 3:22 *v.l.*) and the absence of further parallels despite the continuation of both Ps 2:7 and Mark 1:11 have led to other explanations.

Several have turned to Isa 42:1 (e.g., Dalman, *Words*, 276–80; Bousset, *Kyrios Christos*, 97–98; Jeremias, *Abba*, 191–98; *TDNT* 5 [1967] 701–2; Cullmann, *Christology*, 66; Gnilka, 1:50). This alternative accounts for the similarity in context (the coming of the Spirit) and content between 1:11 and Isa 42:1 as well as the dissimilarity between Ps 2:7 LXX and Mark 1:11. Accordingly, "my son" (υἱός μου) represents a later interpretation of an earlier, ambiguous "my servant"/"child" (παῖς μου) as found in Isa 42:1 LXX. Granting the possibility of such a shift from ambiguous παῖς to υἱός, this view suffers from the absence of evidence for an earlier παῖς Christology in the baptismal setting and has the additional difficulty of explaining the exchange of παῖς to υἱός in a ("hellenistic") Church where παῖς consistently connoted "servant" when used as a title (e.g., Matt 12:18; Luke 1:54, 69; Acts 4:25, 27, 30; cf. 3:13, 26; *Did.* 9.2–3). Furthermore, we lack any hard, textual evidence that υἱός replaced παῖς in this account (Marshall, *NTS* 15 [1968–69] 327–32).

The change in word order and the discontinuation of Ps 2:7 as a parallel may well point to the significance of the heavenly voice. Instead of accenting the enthronement (Bultmann, 248) or adoption (Dibelius, 272) motifs of Ps 2:7, the opening "you are" (σὺ εἶ) points directly to the addressee and his identity. This emphasis carries through the third person construction of Matt 3:17 and the Transfiguration accounts (9:7; Matt 17:5; Luke 9:35; cf. 2 Pet 1:17) where the identification of the son supersedes any emphasis on the Father's role. But does "my son" connote a messianic title (e.g., Taylor, 162; Gnilka, 1:53) or a filial relationship (e.g., Pesch, 1:93; Grundmann, 43)? The subsequent modifier, "the beloved one" (ὁ ἀγαπητός), supplies our clue.

The adjective ἀγαπητός gains in significance because it is missing in Ps 2:7 LXX (though present in the late Targum of the Psalms [חביב, ḥabbêb]). It never renders בחיר, bāḥîr ("chosen" or ἐκλεκτός), of Isa 42:1 anywhere in the LXX. (The presence of ἀγαπητός in Matthew's rendering of Isa 42:1 [12:18] might as easily reflect the influence of the baptismal narrative as a non-LXX translation of Isa 42:1.) This adjective indicates affection, such as "beloved one," in classical and LXX Greek. When used, however, with "son" or "daughter," it can connote uniqueness or "only" (Turner, JTS 27 [1925–26] 113–29; Kazmierski, Son, 54–55). For example, Gen 22:2, 12, 16 LXX supply a parallel (hardly more, cf. Gaboury, SE 4 [1968] 198–204; Pesch, 1:93) when this term designates Isaac as Abraham's "only" son (ἀγαπητός = יחיד, yāḥîd). Therefore, the heavenly voice identifies Jesus as one having a special relationship with the Father—his "only son," a motif developed in John's Gospel (cf. μονογενής). The final phrase helps us delineate the character of that special relationship.

"I am very pleased with you." (ἐν σοὶ εὐδόκησα). This phrase most likely renders רצתה, rāṣtâh, of Isa 42:1 (MT has "my soul is well pleased"; LXX has προσεδέξατο αὐτὸν ἡ ψυχή μου; cf. εὐδοκεῖν in Α Θ Σ and Matt 12:18; Tg. Isa. has "my word is well pleased"). It stands in conjunction with "my chosen" (ὁ ἐκλεκτός μου, cf. Luke 9:35; John 1:34 v.l.). Isa 42:1 LXX and similar uses of this verb connote an election motif (G. Schrenk, TDNT 2 [1964] 739–40). Chilton (Rabbi, 129–30) has noted that "I am well pleased" occurs "fairly frequently" in Tg. Isa. with "to choose" (בחר, bĕḥar = ἐκλέγεσθαι, e.g., Isa 41:8–9; 43:10 with reference to the "servant"). "Well pleased" corresponds with the Markan "only/beloved (ἀγαπητός) son" which also underscores the primary motif of affection, delight and pleasure inherent in εὐδοκεῖν. The voice consistently addresses Jesus both in terms of his role (Ps 2:7, "son" = the anointed king; Isa 42:1, "my chosen" = the servant) and his relationship to the Father ("my son, the only/beloved one," cf. Gen 22:2; "very pleased," εὐδόκησα instead of the more explicit ἐκλεκτός of Isa 42:1).

The juxtaposition of role and relationship in the words of the heavenly voice leaves open the enigmatic nature of that role and relationship. The role combines that of messianic king (Ps 2:7) and that of God's chosen servant (Isa 42:1). The special "filial" relationship ("beloved son," cf. Gen 22:2; and "very pleased," Isa 42:1) remains unspecified. Yet it is precisely this enigma in Jesus' role and relationship with the Father that marks his earthly ministry as depicted in the Gospels. The focus from here on in Mark's narrative, as in the other Gospels, turns ultimately to Jesus' ministry (1:12–13, 14–15) to address this enigma.

Explanation

Without further biographical information about Jesus or any apparent concern about why Jesus went to John for baptism, Mark combines the tradition of the baptism (1:9–11) directly to the Baptist materials of 1:2b–8. In so doing, the evangelist qualifies Jesus theologically in terms of the Baptist who came in the wilderness as the precursor to prepare the way for the Greater One who would bring in the age of salvation (1:2b–8). Jesus is the Greater One of John's proclamation (1:7–8).

Yet in Mark's account, Jesus' actual identity comes neither from John nor his baptism as such but from the event, couched in the language of visionary experiences, that immediately followed the baptism (1:10–11). As Jesus came out of the water, he saw the heavens splitting and the Spirit like a dove descending and heard a heavenly voice that set the Spirit's coming in perspective. Consequently, John's baptism of Jesus provides for Mark the redemptive historical setting for the event (1:10–11) that expresses the eschatological discontinuity between John and Jesus anticipated by the Baptist's comparative statements about the Greater One in 1:7–8.

Although the dove has subsequently become a popular symbol for the Holy Spirit, the occurrence of the imagery in 1:10 appears to stand without previous parallel, a fact that should discourage any attempt at finding a symbolic meaning behind this reference. The importance of the event lies in the Spirit's coming. It corresponds to the OT hope integral to the age of salvation (e.g., esp. Isa 11:2; 42:1; 61:1; cf. 63:10–64:1), a motif fundamental to John's comparison between his baptism and that of the Greater One (1:8). The Spirit comes, therefore, as God's enabling presence to equip Jesus for his ministry.

The reader permitted to share in this private audience with Jesus expectantly listens to the voice from heaven. But the voice from heaven apparently gives a mixed signal. It begins with a royal messianic designation of sonship drawn from Ps 2:7 and concludes with the servant motif of Isa 42:1. Mark's heading of 1:1–3, which aligns the events of 1:4–15 with Isaiah, may weight the balance in favor of Isa 42:1 where the Spirit is given to the servant. But the tension continues throughout Mark's narrative. Both the royal messianic sonship and the servant figure persist. One might also maintain that what is true of Mark's narrative holds true for his tradition. The combination of Jesus' "sonship" including his messianic role and his servanthood permeate the tradition behind the Gospels. Therefore, we should not be surprised that this tension should appear explicitly at the scene of Jesus' introduction in Mark.

One can no longer determine with certainty the original context of the baptism narrative. The present third-person narration betrays its use in the Church's tradition. Yet the correspondence between the Christological tension in this scene to that found in the Jesus tradition in general suggests two things. First, it suggests that the roots of this narrative extend to the beginning of Jesus' ministry. Second, it suggests that Mark's use of the material in his Gospel differs little from that of the Church who sought to declare the good news about who Jesus was and why he died. In Mark's alignment of 1:9–11 with 1:2b–8, the voice of the prophets introduces John (1:2b–8) and the voice from heaven introduces Jesus (1:9–11)—both by using Isaiah's promise. John was the promised precursor; Jesus the Spirit-equipped Bringer of the age of salvation.

D. *The Temptation of Jesus* (*1:12–13*)

Bibliography

Best, E. *The Temptation and the Passion: The Markan Soteriology.* SNTSMS 2. Cambridge: Cambridge UP, 1965. **Dupont, J.** "L'arrièrefond biblique du récit des tentations de Jésus." *NTS* 3 (1956–57) 287–304. ———. "L'origine de récit des tentations de Jésus an desert." *RB* 73 (1966) 30–76. ———. *Die Versuchung Jesu in der Wüste.* SBS 37. Stuttgart: Katholisches Bibelwerk, 1969. **Fascher, E.** "Jesus und die Tiere." *TLZ* 90 (1965) 561–70. **Feuillet, A.** "L'épisode de la tentation d'après l'Evangile selon saint Marc (1,12–13)." *EstBib* 19 (1960) 49–73. **Funk, R.** "The Wilderness." *JBL* 78 (1959) 205–14. **Grässer, E.** "ΚΑΙ ΕΝ ΜΕΤΑ ΤΩΝ ΘΗΡΙΩΝ (Mk 1,13b): Ansätze einer theologischen Tierschutzethik." In *Studien zum Text und zur Ethik des Neuen Testaments,* FS H. Greeven, ed. W. Schrage. Berlin: DeGruyter, 1986. 144-57. **Jeremias, J.** "Nachwort zum Artikel von H. G. Leder." *ZNW* 54 (1963) 278–79. **Kelley, H. A.** "The Devil and the Desert." *CBQ* 26 (1964) 190–220. **Leder, H. G.** "Sündenfallerzählung und Versuchungsgeschichte." *ZNW* 54 (1963) 188–216. **Mahnke, H.** *Die Versuchungsgeschichten im Rahmen der synoptischen Evangelien.* BBET 9. Frankfurt: P. Lang, 1978. **Marxsen, W.** *Mark the Evangelist.* 1969. **Neugebauer, F.** *Jesu Versuchung: Wegentscheidung am Anfang.* Tübingen: Mohr, 1986. **Pokorný, P.** "The Temptation Stories and Their Intention." *NTS* 20 (1973–74) 115–27. **Riesenfeld, H.** "The Messianic Character of the Temptation in the Wilderness." In *The Gospel Tradition.* Philadelphia: Fortress, 1970. 75–93. **Robinson, J. M.** *The Problem of History in Mark.* SBT 21. London: SCM, 1957. 26–28. **Schnackenburg, R.** "Der Sinn der Versuchung Jesu bei den Synoptikern." *TQ* 132 (1952) 296–326. **Schulze, W. A.** "Der Heilige und die wilden Tiere: Zur Exegese von Mc 1,13b." *ZNW* 46 (1955) 280–83. **Stegner, W. R.** "Wilderness and Testing in the Scrolls and in Matthew 4:1–11." *BR* 12 (1967) 18–27.

Translation

[12] *Then the Spirit drove Jesus[a] immediately into the wilderness.* [13] *He was[b] in the wilderness for forty days, tempted by Satan. He was with the wild animals and the angels waited on him.*

Notes

[a] Romanized words added from context.

[b] The use of καὶ ἦν in 1:13b and καὶ οἱ ἄγγελοι διηκόνουν in 1:13c and the *v.l.* ἐκεῖ ("there") in 1:13a suggest that ἦν serves as the finite verb of 1:13a (Taylor, 163; Dupont, *Versuchung*, 75, n. 10) and not as a periphrastic with πειραζόμενος (Schnackenburg, *TQ* 132 [1952] 305, n. 1; Pesch, 1:94).

Form / Structure / Setting

Mark's brief account of Jesus' temptation (cf. Matt 4:1–11 // Luke 4:1–13) has given rise to several explanations: (a) Mark's tradition underlies the expanded form behind Matthew and Luke (e.g., Bultmann, 253–54); (b) Mark is an abbreviation of the tradition behind Matthew and Luke (Feuillet, *EstBib* 19 [1960] 49–73; Dupont, *Versuchung,* 79–92); or most commonly (c) Mark used a tradition more or less independent of Matthew and Luke (Taylor, 162–63; Pokorný, *NTS* 20 [1973–74] 115–17). The reference to the wild animals and the distinctive role of the angels (1:13, cf. Matt 4:11) provide strong support for this explanation, particularly since they seem to introduce a Paradise motif in contrast to the Exodus motif of Matthew and Luke.

This account consists of four separate statements, each introduced by καί ("and") and related by the explicit or implicit theme of the wilderness. In 1:12 the Spirit drives Jesus "into the wilderness"; in 1:13a Jesus is "in the wilderness" forty days; in 1:13b he is with the wild animals whose habitat is the wilderness; and in 1:13c angels wait on him in the otherwise inhospitable setting of the wilderness. In contrast to the prominence of the temptation motif in Matthew and Luke, the reference to Satan's tempting Jesus comes as a corollary to Jesus' presence in the wilderness (1:13). Thus the focal point lies in Jesus' being in the wilderness rather than in his being tempted by Satan.

In terms of the larger context (1:1–15) set under the promise of Isaiah (1:1–3), one might view this wilderness motif as picking up the thread of Isa 40:3 found in 1:3–4 referring to the "voice in the wilderness" preparing the way for the coming one whose path lay in the wilderness. Or one might point to the Paradise motif underlying this scene that also corresponds to Isaiah's promise of similar conditions for the age of salvation (e.g., Isa 11:6–9; 32:14–20; 65:25). In either case, the events of 1:12–13 as in 1:9–11 correspond to Isaiah's promise (1:1–3) and help introduce Jesus as the Greater One of 1:7.

Does not this correspondence with Isaiah indicate Markan redaction behind 1:12–13? No more than does the Isaianic correspondence of the events of the baptism. If Mark's account and the parallel account in Matthew and Luke are independent, as the content and structure suggest, the combination of the temptation narrative and baptism narrative in Matthew and Luke would also support the pre-Markan existence and combination of these traditions behind Mark (Taylor, 162–63; Gnilka, 1:56).

Furthermore, the Adam-Christ (Paradise) theme of 1:12–13 and the Israel-Christ (Exodus) theme of Matthew and Luke represent the interpretations by the early Church of a temptation account whose roots most likely extend to Jesus' ministry (Dupont, *Versuchung,* 104–26) rather than the apologetical or catechetical needs of the Church (e.g., Dibelius, 274; Bultmann, 253–54, cf. Dupont, *Versuchung,* 92–104). Mark's contribution lies in his preserving the tradition intact with the baptism of 1:9–11 and his aligning this scene along with the others in 1:4–15 under the heading of Isaiah's promise in 1:1–3.

Comment

12 "Then the Spirit drove Jesus" (εὐθὺς τὸ πνεῦμα αὐτὸν ἐκβάλλει). Perhaps a transitional verse composed from the absolute use of "the Spirit" in 1:10 (Gnilka, 1:56), but the presence and different use of the "Spirit" and "wilderness" motifs in Matt 4:1 and Luke 4:1 suggest that both temptation narratives opened in this fashion. The rendering "drove" (ἐκβάλλει) strikes some as unnecessarily strong (e.g., Pesch, 1:94, n. 35; Gnilka, 1:56–57) causing them to prefer the less forceful "led" (cf. ἄγειν in Matt 4:1; Luke 4:1). In either case, the context conveys the impression of the Spirit's coming (1:10) and taking control of Jesus (cf. Luke 4:1) illustrated by his impelling Jesus to go into the wilderness.

"Into the wilderness" (εἰς τὴν ἔρημον). The Spirit takes Jesus into the "wilderness," not directly into temptation (cf. Matt 4:1). Given the setting of 1:4–11, the reference here within Mark's narrative pertains most likely to the same Judean wilderness of John's appearance (Pesch, 1:94; Grundmann, 46; Funk, *JBL* 78 [1959] 207–14). Yet "wilderness" with its variety of meanings in the OT and Judaism may also play a figurative role in this narrative. For example, the "wilderness" represents the place of God's coming deliverance (cf. Qumran; Isa 40; Matt 24:26; G. Kittel, *TDNT* 2 [1964] 658; Stegner, *BR* 12 [1967] 18–21), a place of eschatological testing (Stegner, *BR* 12 [1967] 21–27), the abode of Satan and evil (Taylor, 163; Lohmeyer, 27; Pesch, 1:94; Marxsen, 26–28), and the inhospitable habitat of wild animals (Gnilka, 1:57). What follows helps specify the significance of Jesus' wilderness experience here.

13 "In the wilderness forty days." The reiteration of the "wilderness" underscores its significance in the Markan narrative (cf. Matthew and Luke). "Forty" has a rich OT background in the flood story (Gen 7:4, 12), Israel's years in the wilderness (Exod 34:28) and Elijah's flight without food (1 Kgs 19:4–8). The majority of these references (including *Adam and Eve* 6.1–2) include the theme of sustenance and/or fasting. Mark has no hint of fasting (cf. Matt 4:2; Luke 4:2), but he does mention the sustenance by angels (1:13c). Thus, Jesus is in the wilderness for a period of time under the control of the Spirit and sustained by God's providence.

"Tempted by Satan" (πειραζόμενος ὑπὸ τοῦ Σατανᾶ). Using the more Semitic name "Satan" (3:23, 26; 4:15; 8:33; cf. διάβολος in Matt 4:1; Luke 4:2), Mark's account introduces the motif of temptation as part of Jesus' experience in the wilderness. Nothing further is said regarding the nature or the means of this temptation. The outcome remains implicit to the account. Consequently, one must be cautious about assigning too much significance to Jesus' "defeat" of Satan in the Markan narrative (cf. Robinson, *History,* 26–28; Best, *Temptation,* 3–60).

In the Scriptures, "temptation" consists either of testing (e.g., Israel's time in the wilderness—Deut 8:2; cf. Gen 22:1–14) or of tempting one by evil (e.g., Gen 3:1–7, although the terminology is missing, so Best, *Temptation,* 44–60). The accounts of Matthew and Luke appear set against the Exodus background of Israel's testing as God's son, but the "wild beasts" and "angels" of Mark suggest a setting in Paradise that may underlie the Markan tradition.

"With the wild animals" (μετὰ τῶν θηρίων). This phrase, distinctive to Mark's account, holds the key to his temptation narrative. "Wild animals" intensify the foreboding character of the wilderness (W. Foerster, *TDNT* 3 [1965] 134). They frequently appear in league with the forces of evil (e.g., Ps 91; Ezek 34:5, 8, 25; *T. Naph.* 8.4; Lohmeyer, 27; Marxsen, *Mark,* 47). Hostility marks their relationship with humanity after the fall (*Apoc. Mos.* 10.1–11:4; *Vita*

37–38). μετά with the genitive (BDF, § 227.2; W. Grundmann, *TDNT* 7 [1971] 797), however, indicates that Jesus was living peaceably with the animals, a relationship found only at creation (Gen 1:28; 2:19–20) and expected for the age of salvation, the new creation (Isa 11:6–9; 65:17–25; Hos 2:18; *2 Apoc. Bar.* 73.6). Thus Jesus' peaceful coexistence "with the wild animals" boldly declares the presence of the age of salvation when God's deliverance would come in the wilderness and harmony would be established within creation according to the promise, especially of Isaiah (11:6–9 and 65:17–25).

Jesus' presence with the wild animals may also point to an Adam-Christ typology (cf. Exodus typology behind Matthew's and Luke's account) underlying the Markan temptation narrative (so J. Jeremias, *TDNT* 1 [1964] 141; Gnilka, 1:58; cf. Leder, *ZNW* 54 [1963] 203–6). Both Adam and Christ were tempted while living at peace with the animals (Gen 1:28; 2:19–20; Mark 1:13b; cf. *Apoc. Mos.* 11.2–4). But Satan's victory over the former led to the enmity and fear within creation (e.g., Ps 91:11–13; *Apoc. Mos.* 10.1–11.4; *Adam and Eve* 37–38, cf. *T. Naph.* 8) that was reconciled and removed by the coming of the latter whose victory over Satan signaled his being the new obedient Adam (Pesch, 1:96). This typology finds further support in the role of the angels which follows.

"The angels were waiting on him" (οἱ ἄγγελοι διηκόνουν αὐτῷ). The verb (διηκόνουν) and its context suggest that the angels were feeding Jesus during this period (Best, *Temptation,* 9–10; cf. Matt 4:2 // Luke 4:2; Matt 4:11). One finds a similar reference in Elijah's life (1 Kgs 19:1–8), but the closer analogy comes from the Jewish references to the angel's sustenance of Adam and Eve in the Garden (*Adam and Eve* 4, cf. 2; *b. Sanh.* 59b; J. Jeremias, *TDNT* 1 [1964] 141). Taken together, Jesus' temptation by Satan, his peaceable existence with the wild animals, and his sustenance by the angels form an impressive counterpoint to Adam and bear witness to the coming of the second Adam and the new creation.

Explanation

Mark most likely found this tradition of Jesus' temptations already combined with the baptismal narrative. The underlying tradition may well have reflected an Adam-Christ typology used by the early Church to interpret Jesus' temptation (cf. the Exodus typology behind the Q tradition). Traditional Jewish references to Adam in the Garden help explain the references to Jesus' being tempted by Satan, his presence with the wild animals, and his being waited on by the angels. The contrasting disobedience of Adam and the obedience of Christ occurs in the familiar passage of Rom 5:12–21 (cf. Luke 3:38; 1 Cor 15:22, 45–49). Whereas Adam succumbed to his tempter resulting in hostility within creation and hardship in his own life, Jesus overcame the tempter, restored harmony within the creation, and lived by God's sustenance as a sign of the new creation. Jesus is the second Adam, the obedient one.

This typology, if present, appears to have held little attraction for Mark. His interest stated in the heading of 1:1–3 focused more on Jesus' presence in the wilderness where he not only confronted Satan but lived in harmony with the wild animals. Isaiah's promise of the coming deliverer's appearance in the wilderness (e.g., Isa 40, cf. Mark 1:12, 13a) and the ensuing conditions of Paradise (e.g., Isa 11:6–9; 65:17–25) find their fulfillment and indicate that Jesus is indeed the promised one as proclaimed by John (1:7–8) and identified at the baptism (1:9–11).

This Christological theme of Jesus as the fulfillment of Isaiah's promise rather than any stress on the defeat of Satan, which goes unmentioned, characterizes the setting and significance of Jesus' temptation for Mark. For him, Jesus is the promised deliverer whose ministry begins under the control of the Spirit (1:12) in the wilderness (1:12–13a) where he resists Satan (1:13a) and lives in harmony with creation (1:13b, c) befitting the presence of the new age of salvation.

E. The Fulfillment of Time (1:14–15)

Bibliography

Ambrozic, A. M. *The Hidden Kingdom: A Redaction Critical Study of the References to the Kingdom in Mark's Gospel.* CBQMS 2. Washington: CBA, 1972. **Beasley-Murray, G. R.** *Jesus and the Kingdom of God.* Grand Rapids: Eerdmans, 1986. **Berkey, R. F.** "ΕΓΓΙΖΕΙΝ, ΦΘΑΝΕΙΝ, and Realized Eschatology." *JBL* 82 (1963) 177–87. **Black, M.** "The Kingdom of God Has Come." *ExpTim* 63 (1951) 289–90. **Campbell, J. Y.** "'The Kingdom of God Has Come.'" *ExpTim* 48 (1936–37) 91–94. **Clark, K. W.** "Realized Eschatology." *JBL* 59 (1940) 367–83. **Dautzenberg, G.** "Die Zeit des Evangeliums: Mk 1,1–15 und die Konzeption des Markusevangeliums." *BZ* 21 (1977) 219–34. **Dodd, C. H.** *The Parables of the Kingdom.* 1935. **Egger, W.** *Frohbotschaft und Lehre.* 1976. **Fuller, R. H.** *The Mission and Achievement of Jesus.* SBT 12. London: SCM, 1963. **Jeremias, J.** *New Testament Theology.* 1971. **Keck, L. E.** "The Introduction to Mark's Gospel." *NTS* 12 (1965–66) 352–70. **Kelber, W.** *The Kingdom in Mark: A New Place and a New Time.* 1974. **Kümmel, W. G.** *Promise and Fulfillment.* SBT 23. London: SCM, 1961. **Ladd, G. E.** *Jesus and the Kingdom.* New York: Harper & Row, 1964. **Marxsen, W.** *Mark the Evangelist.* 1969. **Mussner, F.** "Gottesherrschaft und Sendung Jesu nach Markus 1,14f." In *Praesentia Salutis: Gesammelte Studien zu Fragen und Themen des Neuen Testaments.* Dusseldorf: Patmos, 1967. 81–98. **Popkes, W.** *Christus Traditus: Eine Untersuchung zum Begriff der Dahingabe im Neuen Testament.* ATANT 49. Zurich: Zwingli, 1967. **Reploh, K. G.** *Markus—Lehrer der Gemeinde.* 1969. **Schnackenburg, R.** "'Das Evangelium' im Verständnis des ältesten Evangelisten." In *Orientierung an Jesus: Zur Theologie der Synoptiker,* FS J. Schmid, ed. P. Hoffmann. Freiburg: Herder, 1973. 309–24. ———. *God's Rule and Kingdom.* Montreal: Palm, 1963. **Stuhlmacher, P.** *Das paulinische Evangelium.* 1. *Vorgeschichte.* FRLANT 95. Göttingen: Vandenhoeck & Ruprecht, 1968. **Turner, C. H.** "Marcan Usage: Notes, Critical and Exegetical on the Second Gospel." *JTS* 26 (1925) 12–20. ———. "Text of Mark 1." *JTS* 28 (1927) 150–58.

Translation

[14]*After[a] John had been handed over, Jesus came into Galilee and preached the gospel[b] from God,* [15]*saying[c]: "The[d] appointed time has come to pass. The Kingdom of God has come in history. Repent! Believe[e] the gospel!"*

Notes

ᵃ MSS vary between καὶ μετά (B D it sy^s bo^{Pt}) and μετὰ δέ (א A W Θ λ φ *pl* lat sy^P sa Tisch WH Nestle^{26}). Controlling argument for μετὰ δέ is Turner's observation (*JTS* 28 [1927] 152) that Mark apparently used δέ at turning points in his Gospel (7:24; 10:32; 14:1, so Taylor, 165; Mussner, "Gottesherrschaft," 82). But 7:24 and 10:32 are not critical junctures and 1:14–15 forms the concluding element of the prologue (1:1–15). The δέ might well reflect a later misconstruing of the function of 1:14–15 or more likely a desire to set Jesus' coming and preaching in sharper relief from that of the Baptist (Egger, *Frohbotschaft*, 44, n. 21).

ᵇ Some MSS (A D W *pm* lat sy^P) read an interpolated τῆς βασιλείας after εὐαγγέλιον under the influence of 1:15 (cf. Matt 4:23; 9:35).

ᶜ καὶ λέγων is omitted as redundant in א* C sy^s. καί with λέγων is rare in Mark (cf. 1:7) and is omitted by A D F G *pm* it sa bo, but the καί functions epexegetically (Mussner, "Gottesherrschaft," 83) indicating that the statement sets forth the content of the "gospel" of God."

ᵈ ὅτι-recitative introduces direct quotation almost fifty times in Mark.

ᵉ πιστεύειν ἐν occurs only here in the NT. It is a Semitism (Taylor, 167: Lagrange, 16; Cranfield, 68; Pesch, 1:103).

Form / Structure / Setting

This unit has the form of a summary report. Some (e.g., Mussner, "Gottes-herrschaft," 90–91; Pesch, 1:100) have gone further based on texts such as Isa 56:1; Ezek 7:3, 12; 9:1; Lam 4:18 to set this summary more specifically within the genre of a prophetic summons as an opening statement ("*Eröffnungslogion*," Mussner, "Gottesherrschaft," 90–91) or "preamble" (Reploh, *Lehrer*, 23–24). Egger (*Frohbotschaft*, 44–45) has countered by arguing that the supposed OT parallels are unfounded and misleading. Whereas Isaiah, Ezekiel, and Lamentations have a summons beginning with an imperative followed by a future event, Mark 1:15 begins with a perfect indicative and moves to an imperative. Furthermore, 1:14–15 functions primarily as a summary statement and not an opening statement. At stake in the debate over form lies the function or setting of 1:14–15 for Mark's Gospel as a whole and Mark's understanding of the "gospel" (cf. 1:1) in particular.

As to the source of 1:14–15, a few have assigned the whole summary to a pre-Markan tradition (e.g., Lohmeyer, 29–30; Pesch, 1:103), some to Mark's redaction (e.g., Marxsen, *Mark*, 132–35; Reploh, *Lehrer*, 14–15; Ambrozic, *Kingdom*, 4–5; Schmithals, 1:95) and some have assigned 1:14 to Mark's redaction and 1:15 to his tradition (e.g., Mussner, "Gottesherrschaft," 84–85; Kelber, *Kingdom*, 3–4; Gnilka, 1:64–65). Egger's (*Frohbotschaft*, 46–64; similarly, Beasley-Murray, *Kingdom*, 71–72) detailed examination, however, has pointed out the complexity of the problem by arguing that the summary is redactional but only in the sense that the evangelist has made use of traditional materials stemming from Jesus' earthly ministry and the Church's mission.

Structurally, 1:14 serves as an introduction for the message in 1:15. The introduction moves Jesus into Galilee after John's arrest and singles out his preaching activity in preparation for 1:15. The message itself consists of two pairs of statements, each constructed in synthetic parallelism (Mussner, "Gottesherrschaft," 81–82). The first pair make declarative statements and are set in the perfect indicative; the second pair are admonitions set in the present imperative and grow out of the declarations.

The account of Jesus' ministry that follows in 1:16–16:8 is synonymous with Jesus' preaching as expressed in 1:14–15 (Mussner, "Gottesherrschaft," 90–98; Keck, *NTS* 12 [1965–66] 362–68; Reploh, *Lehrer*, 23–26; Ambrozic, *Kingdom*, 3–31). His work and words in 1:16–16:8 declare the coming of the appointed time and proclaim the Kingdom of God. To this extent, 1:14–15 does represent a summary of Mark's Gospel, but not as a "programmatic summary" or an "opening statement." In the context of 1:1–3, 1:14–15 represents the concluding element in Mark's "beginning" of the gospel concerning Jesus Messiah, Son of God, according to Isaiah's promise (1:1–3).

In 1:4–8 John comes as the voice in the wilderness preparing the way. In 1:9–11 Jesus comes designated by God as the promised deliverer and equipped by the Spirit under whose control in 1:12–13 he enters the wilderness where he resists Satan and establishes harmony within creation in keeping with the promised age of salvation. Against this background Jesus comes from the wilderness into Galilee in 1:14–15 to proclaim this good news from God about the coming of the Kingdom (cf. 1:7–8). The final component (1:14–15) of Mark's introduction (1:1–15), as did the others, has its basis for Mark in Isaiah's promise. Therefore, this summary of Jesus' preaching in 1:14–15 functions primarily as the conclusion of Mark's "beginning" (1:4–15) for which 1:1–3 serves as the heading. All of 1:4–15, Mark's "beginning," sets the stage for 1:16–16:8 and not simply 1:14–15.

Comment

14 "After John had been handed over" (μετὰ δὲ τὸ παραδοθῆναι τὸν Ἰωάννην). The summary opens with a vague setting of time and place that corresponds with Acts 10:37 (cf. Mussner, "Gottesherrschaft," 81; Egger, *Frohbotschaft*, 54) and appears to conflict with the data of John 3:22–24; 4:1. Although some have sought to reconcile these differences (e.g., Cranfield, 61), Mark's primary concern here appears to be more theological than chronological (Schmidt, 34). He returns later (6:17–29) to John's arrest and death. For now the evangelist appropriately concludes the Baptist's ministry with a final precursory note whose formulation may well anticipate Jesus' own end.

The absolute use of παραδοθῆναι ("to be handed over") with its various meanings most likely corresponds to a similar use with reference to the Son of man in 9:31; 10:33; 14:21, 41. Behind the human scenario at the end of John's and Jesus' ministries stands God's purpose and activity expressed by the divine passive (e.g., Lohmeyer, 29; Cranfield, 62; Marxsen, *Mark*, 38–40; Popkes, *Christus*, 143–45; Pesch, 1:101). Thus, in terms of the "beginning" of 1:1, John's role as the promised precursor ends with the coming (ἦλθεν) of the "Greater One" who would "baptize with the Spirit" (1:9–13).

"Jesus came into Galilee." Jesus had "come" (ἦλθεν) from Galilee to John (1:9). He now "comes" (ἦλθεν) into Galilee preaching the good news. To describe this event in 1:14 as "epiphanic" (e.g., J. Schneider, *TDNT* 2 [1965] 668; Mussner, "Gottesherrschaft," 82) may well be too strong, but the verb does take up John's promise in 1:7 of the "coming" of the "Greater One." The geographical location of the outset of Jesus' ministry has its roots in the tradition of Jesus' earthly ministry rather than in the redactional interests of Mark (Egger, *Frohbotschaft*, 54–55, cf. Marxsen, *Mark*, 58–60). Galilee was Jesus' home, the home of his disciples, the location of much of his ministry and thus the "land of the gospel" (Lohmeyer, 29; Pesch, 1:104; Gnilka, 1:69–71).

"And preached the gospel from God" (κηρύσσων τὸ εὐαγγέλιον τοῦ Θεοῦ). The evangelist appears to have used terminology drawn from the Church's mission situation to describe Jesus' activity in Galilee (cf. Rom 1:1; 15:16; 2 Cor 11:7; 1 Thess 2:2, 8; 1 Pet 4:17, so Stuhlmacher, *Evangelium*, 1:237–38). Yet 1:14 depicts Jesus' coming in terms of Isaiah as the one who heralds the good news from God (e.g., 52:7; 61:1). Thus, once again Isaiah's promise offers the background for Mark's "beginning" (1:1–3). At the same time, Jesus' "preaching" sets him in stark contrast with the Baptist who also came "preaching" (1:7). Whereas John proclaimed a repentance-baptism and the coming of the "Greater One," Jesus demonstrates himself to be the "Greater One" by proclaiming as the promised one of Isaiah the "good news from God." The content of this "gospel" is set forth in the message of 1:15 that is epexegetic to 1:14.

15 "The appointed time has come to pass" (πεπλήρωται ὁ καιρός). The epexegetic use of καὶ λέγων and the ὅτι-recitative leads to the specific message setting forth the "gospel from God." The message opens with two synthetically parallel declarations. The first speaks of the fulfillment of time; the second speaks of the coming of the Kingdom. Some have assigned these declarations to the evangelist (e.g., Bultmann, 118; Schmidt, 33; Marxsen, *Mark*, 132–34; Ambrozic, *Kingdom*, 4–6) but most today assign this material either to the tradition of Jesus' earthly ministry (e.g., Egger, *Frohbotschaft*, 56–61; Pesch, 1:101–2) or at least to the tradition of the earliest Church which correctly depicted Jesus' earthly message (Schnackenburg, "'Das Evangelium,'" 318–21; Mussner, "Gottesherrschaft," 82–83; Stuhlmacher, *Evangelium*, 1:236–38; Grundmann, 48–49; Gnilka, 1:64–65).

The first declaration is set against a prophetic-apocalyptic background that corresponds to the expectation of Dan 7:22; Ezek 7:12; 9:1; 1 Pet 1:11; Rev 1:3. The term "appointed time" (καιρός) generally connotes a decisive moment in time, an appointed time, a fixed season (cf. 11:13; 12:2) rather than an expanse or period of time. The verb πεπλήρωται thus has its redemptive historical connotation of "fulfillment" or "coming to pass" rather than "completion." Instead of announcing a period of time reaching its conclusion, Jesus announces the coming to pass of a decisive moment in time. The voice and tense of πεπλήρωται support this meaning. The perfect tense indicates that the event has come to pass now with lasting significance, and the passive voice indicates that God is at work in bringing it to pass (Grundmann, 50; Egger, *Frohbotschaft*, 56). It is God's "appointed time" that has come—the eschaton (Schweizer, 45; Gnilka, 1:66; Schmithals, 1:100).

"The Kingdom has come into history" (ἤγγικεν ἡ βασιλεία τοῦ Θεοῦ). This declaration confirms and explicates (by synthetic parallelism) the other. Jesus comes as the herald of Isa 52:7 and 61:1 who announces the good news of God's rule. Mark uses "Kingdom" (c. 15x) considerably less than Matthew (c. 50x) or Luke (c. 40x), and the occurrences most likely stem from the pre-Markan tradition. But set here as the content of Jesus' message and synonymous with the "gospel" (1:14, 15), one can see the "Kingdom's" great importance for Mark's understanding of Jesus' ministry.

But what does Jesus proclaim about the "Kingdom of God"? The key to this perplexing statement lies in the verb ἤγγικεν and the structural relationship of this statement with the preceding parallel statement. Lexical studies of ἐγγίζειν have produced mixed results alternating between the meaning of "nearness" and of "arrival." Dodd, claiming a common Semitic term (נגע, nāgaʿ—Hebrew; מטא, mĕṭaʾ—Aramaic) behind ἐγγίζειν and φθάνειν (Matt 12:28 // Luke 11:20) in the LXX, posited the meaning, "has come," from the Semitic terms (Parables, 28–30). Kümmel, by contrast, concluded, after examining the NT use of ἐγγύς and ἐγγίζειν, that the terms consistently denoted "nearness" rather than "arrival" (Promise, 19–25; so Campbell, ExpTim 48 [1936–37] 91–94, and Clark, JBL 59 [1940] 367–83). Fuller (Mission, 20–35) concurred with Kümmel's analysis but suggested with Black (ExpTim 63 [1951–52] 289–90; cf. Clark, JBL 59 [1940] 370) and Ambrozic (Kingdom, 16) that another Semitic term (קרב, qārab) might underlie ἐγγίζειν, a term that has both the meaning of "nearness" (qal stem) and "arrival" (hiphil stem). After examining the numerous options, Berkey (JBL 82 [1963] 177–87) reached the obvious conclusion that a philological approach merely demonstrates the "ambiguity" of the Greek and the underlying Semitic terms.

Since ἐγγίζειν has a specific context in 1:15 and that context has a very straightforward statement about something having happened, several have recently followed Dodd's conclusion—even if for different reasons (e.g., Black, ExpTim 63 [1951–52] 289–90; Reploh, Lehrer, 20; Ambrozic, Kingdom, 21–23; Kelber, Kingdom, 7–11; Beasley-Murray, Kingdom, 72–73). Thus one is left with a context denoting "arrival" and a Greek verb which generally denotes "nearness"—an apparent syntactical contradiction.

Schnackenburg has taken the tension as intentional and inherent in Jesus' proclamation of a Kingdom with present and future dimension (Rule, 141–42; so Berkey, JBL 82 [1963] 177–87, Ambrozic, Kingdom, 23; Beasley-Murray, Kingdom, 73). Rather than referring exclusively to the present aspect of the Kingdom (e.g., Dodd, Parables, 28–35; Kelber, Kingdom, 9–11) or the future (e.g., Kümmel, Promise, 19–24; Marxsen, Mark, 132–34), the ἤγγικεν of 1:15 maintains both the present but "hidden" fulfillment of the Kingdom in Jesus' ministry (cf. the "good news" of 1:1 and 1:14) and the future consummation of the Kingdom in power (cf. parables in Mark 4 and 13). Thus the Kingdom of God has "come into history," the appointed time "has been fulfilled," even though the full appearance is yet to come.

Both elements are important to Mark (4:11; 9:1; 13). But the thrust of 1:1–15, the context of 1:14–15, and the synthetic parallelism of 1:15 underscore the presence of the Kingdom as the theme of Jesus' message. Whether one assigns this statement with its deliberate ambiguity to Jesus' ministry (cf. Matt 19:7 // Luke 10:9; Jeremias, Theology, 32–34) or to the tradition of the Church's mission, the content certainly corresponds to Jesus' own ministry (Kümmel, Promise, 141–55; Schnackenburg, Rule, 114–59; Ladd, Presence, 145–238).

"Repent! Believe the gospel!" (μετανοεῖτε καὶ πιστεύετε ἐν τῷ εὐαγγελίῳ). Two imperatives follow the previous declarations. The combination elsewhere of "repent" (μετανοεῖν) and "believe" (πιστεύειν, e.g., Acts 11:17, 18; 20:21; Heb 6:1) and the construction πιστεύειν ἐν in the light of a Markan tendency to use εἰς for ἐν (Turner, JTS 25 [1925] 14–20) point to a pre-Markan tradition (Schnackenburg, "'Das Evangelium,'" 320–21; Egger, Frohbotschaft, 50–53;

Pesch, 1:103; cf. Mussner, "Gottesherrschaft," 85; Marxsen, 133–36; Reploh, *Lehrer,* 22). This would mean then that at least this use of "gospel" in Mark would have been traditional (see on 1:1) and would reflect a "gospel" whose content was the announcement of the Kingdom of God (Schnackenburg, "'Das Evangelium,'" 320–21; Stuhlmacher, *Evangelium,* 1:236).

The setting of the call to repentance within a proclamation context (cf. κηρύσσειν—1:4, 14–15; 6:12) suggests that "repent" (μετανοεῖν) most likely carries the OT prophetic import of שוב, *šûb,* meaning "to go back again," "return" and connotes the prophetic call to "turn to Yahweh with all one's being" (E. Würthwein, *TDNT* 4 [1967] 985). Much more is at stake than the more literal "changing of one's mind," "regret," or "sorrow" of μετανοεῖν. Thus Jesus called one to turn from one's wayward ways in total surrender to God.

The call to "believe the gospel" stands in synthetic parallelism with the preceding summons. This relationship helps determine the meaning of the somewhat unusual construction of "believe in" (πιστεύειν ἐν). Although some have given ἐν its full weight in the sense of "on the basis of" (Lohmeyer, 30; Marxsen, *Mark,* 135; Ambrozic, *Kingdom,* 26), the broader context of 1:14–15 and the immediate setting of the call to repentance in 1:15 indicates that Jesus, who fulfills the promise of Isa 52:7; 61:1 by proclaiming the good news of the fulfillment of time and the coming of God's rule into history, summons one to "believe the good news" (1:15), which is the "good news from God" (1:14). Thus one "repents," turns in total surrender to God, as one "believes the gospel" about God's rule.

Explanation

Using the form of a summary statement, the evangelist draws together traditional formulas in 1:14–15 to conclude his "beginning of the gospel" from the perspective of Isaiah's promise (1:1–3). This redemptive historical perspective pervades the introduction of Jesus' public ministry in Galilee.

First, Jesus' ministry begins "after" John has been "handed over" (1:14a). Rather than precise chronological data for the outset of Jesus' ministry, the evangelist uses John's role of precursor (1:2b–3), according to Isaiah's promise, to set the ultimate stage for Jesus' ministry. Not only does the ministry come logically "after" John's preparation but John's anticipatory role may well extend to Jesus' own being "handed over" (cf. 9:31; 10:33; 14:21, 41).

Second, Jesus, who came to John "from Galilee" (1:9), comes from the wilderness "to Galilee" (1:14). The lack of geographical precision corresponds to the summary character of the statement and points to Galilee as the focus of Jesus' ministry, the "land of the gospel."

Third, Jesus' ministry in Galilee clearly reflects the setting of Isa 52:7; 61:1. Jesus is introduced as "proclaiming" or "heralding the good news from God." To this extent, Mark portrays Jesus as the eschatological messenger who announces the coming of God's rule into history. This message is then explicated by the statements in 1:15 that summarize Jesus' message.

The message in 1:15 consists of two declarative and two imperative statements, each pair set in synthetic parallelism. The good news from God proclaimed by Jesus concerns the coming to pass of God's appointed time, the coming of God's rule into history. The initial statement clearly declares that

God is at work bringing to pass the appointed time, the time of salvation anticipated by the prophets including the Baptist. The coming of God's appointed time meant no less than that God's rule had entered into history. Yet the language chosen to express the latter, the "coming" of the Kingdom, connoted a complex event of arrival and nearness.

Thus, one finds both a present and future dimension implied in the statement, a dual aspect characteristic of Jesus' teaching elsewhere regarding the Kingdom. Given this dual aspect within the statement taken by itself, the immediate context suggests that the accent here falls on the present coming of the Kingdom into history. This was the element of Jesus' ministry that was the most difficult to grasp and called for one to turn in total surrender to God, to believe the good news.

Taken in isolation this summary would suggest that Mark viewed Jesus as the eschatological messenger promised in Isa 52:7 and 61:1 who would announce the arrival of God's rule and deliverance, the "good news from God." But such an understanding of 1:14–15 overlooks the larger context of 1:1–15 and the portrait of Jesus that emerges in 1:16–16:8. Jesus not only proclaimed that God's appointed time had occurred; it had occurred with his own coming. Jesus not only proclaimed that the Kingdom had come into history; his work was effecting God's rule in history.

John had prepared the way (1:2b–3, 5–8) by proclaiming a repentance-baptism promising the forgiveness of sins and the coming of a Greater One who would effect that salvation (1:7–8). The coming of the Spirit and the voice from heaven (1:9–11) clearly indicated that Jesus was the one of whom John had preached. Furthermore, the Spirit's leading Jesus into the wilderness, the place of the promised one, where he resisted Satan's temptations and lived in harmony with the wild animals and was nourished by the angels (1:12–13) points to the new age of God's deliverance. God's appointed time had come. Therefore, as the climactic expression of Isaiah's promise, 1:14–15 concludes the "beginning" referred to in 1:1.

For Mark, Jesus was both the one who proclaimed the good news from God in terms of the coming of God's promised redemptive rule and the one through whom this good news was effected in history. Jesus, the one preaching the gospel of God, thus himself becomes part of that which is preached as the gospel. Consequently, Mark could open his Gospel with the heading: "The beginning of the gospel concerning Jesus Messiah, Son of God, as written by the prophet Isaiah . . ." (1:1–3).

II. New Wine in Old Wineskins (1:16–3:12)

Introduction

Mark's Gospel falls rather neatly into two halves (1:1–8:26 and 8:27–16:8). Since the "beginning" of 1:1–15 serves the whole Gospel, the first half actually consists of 1:16–8:26. No consensus, however, has arisen regarding how to subdivide the first half into subsections. Neither a thematic nor a geographical approach provides a clear criterion.

We have chosen to divide the material into three sections based on a formal structure. Mark appears to have structured these three sections in a similar fashion. Each opens with an account pertaining to the Twelve (1:16–20; 3:13–19; 6:7–13); each closes with a summary report about or an event in Jesus' ministry that provides a summary and transition to the next section (3:7–12; 6:6b; 8:22–26). Mark 8:22–26 is a healing story rather than a summary in form, but it functions as a summary of the disciples' response to Jesus' ministry in the third section and leads quite naturally into the events of the second half of the Gospel.

The first section (1:16–3:12) opens with Jesus calling four disciples. This story placed at the outset of Jesus' public ministry and preceding as it does a "day in Capernaum" demonstrates the importance of the disciples for Mark's narrative. Not only are they there "from the beginning," but they along with Jesus are the main characters of this story. Like Jesus, they are almost always in the story. Their function is varied. But two aspects of their role stand out. Along with the supporting cast they act as a foil in Mark's depiction of who Jesus is. They enhance the definition of the other main characters. At the same time, they act as a foil for Mark's own readers who doubtless can identify with the disciples and their relationship with Jesus. These and other features will emerge throughout the narrative.

Numerous features of Jesus' ministry stand out in this initial section. The events clearly express the meaning of the "gospel of God" as summarized in 1:15. But the note of "authority" rings louder than the others. The "authoritative" calling of the four disciples depicted by the manner of their call and response (1:16–20), the crowds' astonishment at Jesus' authority (1:21–28), the submission of the demonic (1:23–27, 34), Jesus' forgiving sins explicitly and implicitly (2:1–12, 13–17), his healing the sick and ritually defiled (1:29–45), and his claim regarding the sabbath law (2:23–3:6), all lead inevitably to a confrontation with the religious and political "authorities." It is new wine in old wineskins. That new wine is the embodiment of the message of 1:15 in Jesus' ministry. From the outset we begin to discern who Jesus is and why he died. Mark returns in the second half of his Gospel to develop the passion motif. In sections two (3:13–6:6) and three (6:7–8:26) of the first half, he concentrates primarily on who Jesus is and the response to him and his message.

Mark brings several traditions and traditional units together to form this first section. Behind 1:21–45 lies a traditional unit which has been called "a day in Capernaum." This includes 1:29–39. The evangelist extends the "day" by beginning it with an exorcism (2:23–28). He then makes the transition to a series of conflict stories (2:1–3:6) by using a healing story with hints of conflict in 1:40–45. The conflict stories of 2:1–3:6 have as their core a traditional group of three similar in form, content, and personnel (2:15–28). Again Mark has extended this core by adding a complex healing/conflict story at the outset (2:1–12) and conclusion (3:1–6). Not only are these stories more similar structurally, but both contain an ominous note that corresponds with a similar theme at the heart of the traditional core (2:18–22). Finally, Mark concludes this section with a summary report (3:7–12), drawn most likely from a collection of miracle stories behind 4:35–5:43; 6:32–56, which depicts Jesus ministering to the crowds by healing the sick and exorcising the possessed. The same motifs dominate the opening "day in Capernaum" (1:21–29).

A. The Calling of the First Disciples   (1:16–20)

Bibliography

Best, E. "The Role of the Disciples in Mark." *NTS* 23 (1976–77) 377–401 = *Disciples and Discipleship: Studies in the Gospel according to Mark.* Edinburgh: T. & T. Clark, 1986. 98–130. **Cullmann, O.** *Peter: Disciple, Apostle, Martyr.* New York: World, 1958. **Hengel, M.** *The Charismatic Leader and His Followers.* New York: Crossroad, 1981. **Keck, L. E.** "The Introduction of Mark's Gospel." *NTS* 12 (1965–66) 352–70. **Klein, G.** "Die Berufung des Petrus." *ZNW* 58 (1967) 1–44. **Mánek, J.** "Fishers of Men." *NovT* 2 (1957) 138–41. **Meye, R. P.** *Jesus and the Twelve.* 1968. **Pesch, R.** "Berufung und Sendung, Nachfolge und Mission. Eine Studie zu Mk 1,16–20." *ZKT* 91 (1969) 1–31. **Reploh, K. G.** *Markus—Lehrer der Gemeinde.* 1969. **Schmahl, G.** *Die Zwölf im Markusevangelium.* TTS 30. Trier: Paulinus, 1974. **Schulz, A.** *Nachfolgen und Nachahmen: Studien über das Verhältnis der neutestamentlichen Jungerschaft zur urchristlichen Vorbildethik.* SANT 6. Munich: Kösel, 1962. **Smith, C. W. F.** "Fishers of Men: Footnotes on a Gospel Figure." *HTR* 52 (1959) 187–203. **Wuellner, W.** *The Meaning of "Fishers of Men."* Philadelphia: Westminster, 1967.

Translation

[16] *While passing[a] by the Sea of Galilee, he saw Simon and Andrew, Simon's brother, casting[b] their nets into[c] the sea. For they were fishermen.* [17] *Jesus said to them, "Come, follow me[d] and I shall make you fishers of men."* [18] *Immediately leaving their nets they followed him.*

[19] *Proceeding a little further[e] he saw James, the son of Zebedee, and John, his brother,[f] putting their nets in order.* [20] *He then called them. And they, leaving their father, Zebedee, in the boat with the hired hands, followed him.*

Notes

[a]Some MSS (K A W Θ λ *pm*) read περιπατῶν with Matt 4:18 to avoid the redundant παράγων παρά (B ℵ D φ *al* lat bo).

ᵇ ἀμφιβάλλειν used absolutely is a technical expression for using a casting net, but text tradition indicates attempts to add the missing object for verb (cf. βάλλοντας ἀμφίβληστρον, Matt 4:18).

ᶜ ἐν for εἰς reflecting tendency in Hellenistic Greek to interchange these prepositions.

ᵈ ὀπίσω μου, "after" or "behind me" used here and in 1:20 to express the action of "following Jesus."

ᵉ ὀλίγον, adverbial expression of extent.

ᶠ καὶ αὐτούς omitted as grammatically redundant in English.

Form / Structure / Setting

In form and structure, this pericope corresponds more to a calling narrative (e.g., Pesch, 1:109; Schmal, *Zwölf,* 63–64; Hengel, *Leader,* 5) comparable to Elisha's call (1 Kgs 19:19–21) than a biographical apothegm (Bultmann, 56–61) or an epiphany story (Lohmeyer, 33). This form, which also appears in 2:14 (cf. Matt 8:18–22) consists of a setting (1 Kgs 19:19a; Mark 1:16, 19), call (1 Kgs 19:19b; Mark 1:17, 20a) and a response (1 Kgs 19:20–21; Mark 1:18, 20b). The pericope itself consists of two scenes (1:16–18, 19–20) with the first containing a specific call and promise (1:17a,b; cf. 1:19). In the second scene the call lies implicitly in καλεῖν (1:20) and the response (1:20). The men's common lot as fishermen makes the promise of the first scene appropriate for the second.

Mark appears to have found this material more or less intact in his tradition. The suggestion that he molded 1:19–20 after the scene of 1:16–18 (e.g., Schulz, *Nachfolgen,* 98; Schmithals, 1:98) fails to recognize the lack of parallel construction (no actual call or promise), the difference in details and even the difference in expressions, hardly befitting an imitative composition (so Gnilka, 1:72; Reploh, *Lehrer,* 28–30). Thus Mark's own redactional contribution lies in his locating the material at this particular point in his narrative. Furthermore, the colorful and pertinent details, the unusual use of the phrase "fishers of men" in 1:17 and the association of Peter, James, and John with the sea (cf. John 21:1–3) give indication of the historical roots of these scenes (Taylor, 168; Grundmann, 54–55; Pesch, 1:18–25; cf. Bultmann, 28, 56–57; Schmithals, 1:105; and Klein, *ZNW* 58 [1967] 1–44).

Mark's setting for this pericope (cf. Matt 4:18–22; Luke 5:1–11) has significance for two reasons. First, by placing the call of the disciples at the outset of Jesus' ministry, the evangelist attests that the disciples were present at the beginning and thus legitimate bearers of the tradition, a motif which has traditional support (cf. Luke 1:1–2; Acts 1:21–22; 10:37–39). Second, by opening each of the sections of Jesus' ministry (1:16–3:12; 3:13–6:6; 6:7–8:26) leading to the climax of Caesarea Philippi with discipleship pericopes (1:16–20; 3:13–19; 6:7–13) the evangelist also indicates the integral relationship for him of Christology and discipleship. This interplay of Christology and discipleship offers one of the central themes in Mark's Gospel.

Comment

16 "By the Sea of Galilee." The rather redundant and unusual παράγων παρά plus accusative may stem from Mark's redactional alignment of 1:16–20 with 1:14–15 (Taylor, 168; Lohmeyer, 31). Whereas the tradition would simply have referred to Jesus' "passing by" (παράγων), the addition of παρὰ τὴν θάλασσαν τῆς Γαλιλαίας locates the first disciples along with Jesus (1:14–15) in the area of Galilee (cf. John 1:35–42).

"Sea of Galilee" (τὴν θάλασσαν τῆς Γαλιλαίας), one of two occurrences in Mark (cf. 7:31). This body of water has several names around the time of Jesus: Sea of Tiberias (John 21:1; cf. 6:1; t. Sukk. 3.3); Sea of Gennesar (Josephus, War 3.10.7); Lake of Gennesaret (Luke 5:1; cf. 8:22, 33; Pliny, Nat. Hist. 5.15.71) and Sea of Galilee in the Gospels. Both the underlying Hebrew/Aramaic ם‍‍‍‍י, yām, and θάλασσα in Koine can be rendered either "sea" or "lake." Since, however, θάλασσα more commonly means "sea" (cf. Num 34:11 LXX) and since only Luke 5:1 uses the more precise "lake" (λίμνη) for this body of water in the Gospels, we will continue the more common English translation of "sea," i.e., "Sea of Galilee" recognizing that this "sea" is an inland, fresh-water lake.

"Simon and Andrew, Simon's brother." Andrew ('Ανδρέας) is strictly a Greek name without a Hebrew/Aramaic equivalent. Simon, a Greek name, does have a similar-sounding Hebrew counterpart in "Simeon" (Gen 29:33, שמעון, Šimʿōn = Συμέων in Acts 15:14; 2 Pet 1:1). According to John 1:44, Philip, the other disciple with a strictly Greek name, came from the same town of Bethsaida as Andrew and Peter. The Greek names may well suggest the extent of "hellenization" in Palestine at that time (Cullmann, Peter, 22; Wuellner, "Fishers of Men," 30–31; Hengel, Judaism, 61–65). The double reference to Simon most likely indicates his relative stature in Mark's Gospel, which refers to Simon (7x) and Peter (10x) proportionately more than does either Matthew or Luke (Taylor, 169).

"Casting their nets." The verb ἀμφιβάλλοντας connotes the casting of a net, most likely a round casting net thrown by one person at a school of fish (BGD, s.v.; Wuellner, "Fishers of Men," 39). Some have concluded that Simon and Andrew were wading (Grundmann, 56; Haenchen, 81). But a casting net was also used from boats (Wuellner, "Fishers of Men," 39), and the lack of reference to a boat in 1:16–18 need not imply the absence of one (cf. 4:1, 35).

"For they were fishermen." This explanatory parenthesis informs us of the disciples' occupation and sets the stage for Jesus' call to become "fishers of men" (1:17). Wuellner's study has demonstrated the fallacy of the prevalent caricature of "fishermen" in Jesus' day as being simple, illiterate, lower class laborers. Providing one of the staples of the Palestinian diet, fishing was a very profitable business in the Greco-Roman world—including Palestine (Wuellner, "Fishers of Men," 36–63). While the common image of the biblical fisherman had its validity for the "hired hands" in the fishing business (cf. 1:19–20), these four disciples most likely belonged to another class who owned and operated the boats and fishing equipment. They were more the "managers" than the "laborers" in the fishing business (Wuellner, "Fishers of Men," 47–61).

17 "Come, follow me" or literally "Come after me" (δεῦτε ὀπίσω μου) offers one of several expressions for following Jesus (cf. ἀκολουθεῖν—1:18; 2:14–15; 8:34; ἔρχεσθαι ὀπίσω—8:34 v.l.; ἀπέρχεσθαι ὀπίσω—1:20). The imagery graphically depicts the pupil's role and relationship to the master illustrated

by the disciples' following the teacher who leads the way. In appearance, therefore, Jesus and his disciples looked like the rabbinical schools of his day (Str-B, 1:187–88; Schulz, *Nachfolgen*, 7–32). But Hengel warns about deriving "discipleship" and "following after" from a model of the rabbinical scribes. He notes that "following after" never was used to describe becoming a student of the Law (*Leader*, 51). Used in rabbinic sources in the concrete sense of "walking behind the teacher" when traveling, the phrase "almost never takes the general meaning 'when I was a pupil with Rabbi N.N'" (Hengel, *Leader*, 52). Therefore, "follower," the familiar synonym for "disciple," has its roots in the Christian rather than Jewish usage.

Hengel goes on to note that this call in 1:17 underscores the radical difference between Jesus and the Rabbis (*Leader*, 51). Rather than being chosen by his disciples as a Rabbi (cf. Matt 8:19) in order to study the Law, Jesus authoritatively summons his own disciples to join him in sharing his life and ministry (1:17; 3:14; 6:7). Theirs was not to learn and transmit his teaching of the Law (cf. Matt 23:8) but to become "fishers of men."

"I shall make you fishers of men." The future tense (ποιήσω) indicates what will transpire in the disciples' lives and anticipates their future ministry (cf. 6:7). "Fishers of men" (ἁλιεῖς ἀνθρώπων) as such does not occur in the OT. Jer 16:16 refers to "fishers" and "hunters," and several other passages mention the use of a "hook" (e.g., Ezek 29:4–5; Amos 4:2; Hab 1:14–17; cf. 1QH 3.26; 5.7–8; Wuellner, *"Fishers of Men,"* 88–133). Each of these references carries a negative tone of judgment, a meaning hardly appropriate here (cf. Smith, *HTR* 52 [1959] 187–203). A more approximate usage can be found in hellenistic literature (e.g., Diogenes Laert. 2.67; *Ep. Arist.* 2.23b; see Wuellner, *"Fishers of Men,"* 67–75), but it cannot justify locating the saying's origin in the hellenistic mission (e.g., Schmithals, 1:105).

The common use by Jesus of metaphors drawn from everyday life such as servants, sheep, wolves, and farmers suffices to explain the "novel" usage here, especially set in the context of the disciples' vocation as "fishermen" (Grundmann, 54; Pesch, 1:110; Hengel, *Leader*, 76–78). Jesus' call, therefore, changes the disciples' vocation implying a radical break with their former way of living. Instead of living by the fishing business, they will live to reach others.

18 "Immediately leaving their nets" (εὐθὺς ἀφέντες τὰ δίκτυα). Their response is immediate (εὐθύς) and positive (cf. 1 Kgs 19:20–21). Without necessarily implying that Jesus had had no previous contact with these fishermen or that they were meeting Jesus for the first time, the stark narrative focuses attention on Jesus' call and their obedient response. Jesus had taken the initiative and they had responded accordingly. They left their nets, indicating the change in their life's calling, as they obeyed his summons and followed (ἠκολούθησαν) him.

19 "Proceeding a little further" (προβὰς ὀλίγον) indicates proximity between the two sets of brothers and corresponds to their relationship as "partners" (κοινωνοί) according to Luke 5:10.

"James, the son of Zebedee, and John, his brother." James, the son of Zebedee, who is only mentioned in connection with his sons, differs from James, the brother of Jesus (6:3), James, the son of Alphaeus (3:18), and

James, the Less (15:40). According to Acts 12:1–2, Herod put this James to death in an attack upon the Church. John emerges as one of the leaders of the primitive Church alongside Peter in Acts 3–4 and Gal 2:9. These brothers appear in Mark mostly in company with Simon to form an inner circle of disciples at key points in Jesus' ministry (5:37; 9:2; 13:3 with Andrew; 14:33). In 10:33, 41 they come together to request the privilege of sitting on Jesus' right and left.

"In the boat putting their nets in order." The scene differs in detail from that in 1:16–18. Whereas Peter and Andrew were using casting nets that could be handled by one person standing on or near shore or from a boat, James and John appear to be using much larger nets that involved several persons and the use of a boat. Often rendered "mending," a task done after the fishing had been completed and thus supposedly incompatible temporally with the previous scene (e.g., Lohmeyer, 33), καταρτίζοντας may simply refer to the brothers "preparing" or "folding" their nets (δίκτυα) for use (Wuellner, "Fishers of Men," 37).

20 "He called them" (ἐκάλεσεν αὐτούς). Their response indicates that this statement in context connotes the same call and promise of discipleship of 1:17.

"Left their father . . . with the hired hands" (ἀφέντες τὸν πατέρα . . . μετὰ τῶν μισθωτῶν). Whereas Peter and Andrew left their occupation (their "nets," 1:18), James and John left their father and their occupation. "Hired hands" (μισθωτῶν) suggests the size and stature of Zebedee's business.

"They followed him" (ἀπῆλθον ὀπίσω αὐτοῦ). This is another way of expressing discipleship (cf. 1:17, 18).

Explanation

Drawing on tradition set in the form of a calling narrative (cf. 1 Kgs 19:19–21), Mark introduces Jesus' ministry in 1:16–3:12 with the calling of four disciples. Simon, Andrew, James, and John are not only among the better known of the Twelve but often form an inner circle of companions for Jesus (1:29; 5:37; 9:2; 13:3; 14:33).

This traditional pericope reveals three significant aspects about discipleship in Jesus' ministry. First, rather than the disciple taking the initiative in choosing the master, as was characteristic among the Jews, Jesus emerges as the central figure who dominates the scene and calls his own disciples by means of an authoritative summons. The absence in Mark's narrative of any previous context that might make such an event intelligible, such as a previous awareness of or contact with the persons involved (cf. John 1:35–42), serves only to heighten the centrality of Jesus' call and the disciples' obedient response.

Second, the disciples respond negatively and positively. Negatively, they leave their occupations, and James and John also leave their father (1:18, 20). Discipleship means leaving behind their way of life and former ties. This motif of the cost of discipleship will intensify throughout the Gospel. Positively, they "followed him." The disciples join themselves to Jesus, to accompany him and to participate in his life (see 3:14).

Third, the promise of 1:17 anticipates their new vocation—to become "fishers of men" rather than students of the Law. The disciples will not only accompany Jesus but he will enable them to share his ministry and eventually continue it. Perhaps even the sets of two brothers reflect the mission setting of witness by two-by-two (cf. 6:7).

Mark's redactional contribution apart from setting the scene by the Sea of Galilee (1:16) lies in his placing this pericope at this juncture in his Gospel. Although 1:1–15 culminates with the summary of Jesus' preaching in Galilee (1:14–15), 1:16–20 lies in its shadow. To a great extent, the disciples' response of leaving their way of life and following Jesus into a new way of life illustrates the demand to "repent and believe the gospel" of 1:15. But one should not make the mistake of viewing 1:16–20 as the response to Jesus' preaching in 1:14–15, since the disciples respond specifically to Jesus' call to discipleship.

By placing 1:16–20 at the outset of the material in 1:16–3:12, the evangelist sets the stage for the disciples to accompany Jesus in his ministry but he also places them with Jesus "from the beginning" as witnesses to and participants in his ministry. Furthermore, this combination of the Christological thrust in 1:1–15 carried over in the authoritative nature of the call in 1:16–20 and the prominence given to this pericope on discipleship sets the thematic tones of Christology and discipleship for Mark's Gospel.

B. Jesus' Teaching with Authority   (1:21–28)

Bibliography

Argyle, A. W. "The Meaning of *Exousia* in Mark 1:22, 27." *ExpTim* 80 (1969) 343. **Bächli, O.** "Was habe ich mit Dir zu schaffen?" *TZ* 33 (1977) 69–80. **Bauernfeind, O.** *Die Worte der Dämonen im Markusevangelium.* BWANT 44. Stuttgart: Kohlhammer, 1927. **Best, E.** *The Temptation and the Passion: The Markan Soteriology.* NTSMS 2. Cambridge: Cambridge UP, 1965. **Burkill, T. A.** *Mysterious Revelation: An Examination of the Philosophy of St. Mark's Gospel.* Ithaca: Cornell University Press, 1963. **Daube, D.** "Ἐξουσία in Mark 1:22 and 27." *JTS* 39 (1938) 45–59 = *The New Testament and Rabbinic Judaism.* London: Athlone Press, 1956. 205–33. **Dideberg, D.,** and **P. Mourlon Beernaert.** "'Jésus vint en Galilée': Essai sur la structure de Marc 1, 21–45." *NouRevThéol* 98 (1976) 306–23. **Egger, W.** *Frohbotschaft und Lehre.* 1976. **Guillemette, P.** "Mc 1,24 est-il une formule de défense magique?" *ScEs* 30 (1978) 81–96. **Hengel, M.** *The Charismatic Leader and His Followers.* New York: Crossroad, 1981. 42–50. **Kee, H. C.** "The Terminology of Mark's Exorcism Stories." *NTS* 14 (1967–68) 232–46. **Kertelge, K.** *Die Wunder Jesu im Markusevangelium.* 1970. **Koch, D. A.** *Die Bedeutung der Wundererzählungen für die Christologie des Markusevangeliums.* 1975. **Loos, H. van der.** *The Miracles of Jesus.* NTS 8. Leiden: Brill, 1965. **Luz, U.** "Das Geheimnismotiv und die markinische Christologie." *ZNW* 56 (1965) 9–30. **Marxsen, W.** *Mark the Evangelist.* 1969. **Meye, R. P.** *Jesus and the Twelve.* 1968. **Mussner, F.** "Ein Wortspiel in Mk 1,24?" *BZ* 4 (1960) 285–86. **Neirynck, F.** *Duality in Mark.* 1972. **Osten-Sacken, P. von der.** "Streitgespräch und Parabel als Formen markinischer Christologie." In *Jesus Christus in Historie und Geschichte,* FS H. Conzelmann, ed. G. Strecker. Tübingen: Mohr, 1975. 375–93. **Pesch, R.** "Ein Tag vollmächtige Wirkens Jesu in Kapharnaum (Mk 1:21–34, 35–39)." *BibLeb* 9 (1968) 61–77, 114–28, 177–95. **Robbins, V. K.** *Jesus the Teacher: A Socio-Rhetorical Interpretation of Mark.* Philadelphia: Fortress, 1984. **Robinson, J. M.**

The Problem of History in Mark. SBT 21. London: SCM, 1957. **Schweizer, E.** "Er wird Nazoräer heissen (zu Mc 1,24; Mt 2,23)." In *Judentum, Urchristentum, Kirche,* FS J. Jeremias, ed. W. Eltester. BZNW 26. Berlin: Töpelmann, 1964. 90–93. **Starr, J.** "The Meaning of 'Authority' in Mark 1,22." *HTR* 23 (1930) 302–5. **Stein, R. H.** "The 'Redaktionsgeschichtliche' Investigation of a Markan Seam (Mc 1:21 f.)." *ZNW* 61 (1970) 70–94. **Theissen, G.** *The Miracle Stories of the Early Christian Tradition.* 1983.

Translation

21 *They proceeded into Capernaum. Then* [a] *on the sabbath,* [b] *after entering the synagogue,* Jesus [c] *began teaching.* 22 *And the people* [d] *were overwhelmed at his teaching. For he was teaching them as one having authority and not as the scribes.* 23 *Suddenly* [e] *there was a man with* [f] *an unclean spirit in their synagogue. He yelled,* 24 *"What do we have in common,* [g] *Jesus the Nazarene?* [h] *Have you come to destroy us? I know* [i] *who you are,* [j] *the Holy One of God."* 25 *Jesus subdued him, saying, "Be silent and come out of him!"* 26 *And the unclean spirit after convulsing him and crying out with a loud voice came out of him.* 27 *All were so astounded that they argued* [k] *saying, "What* [l] *is this? A new teaching with authority. He orders the unclean spirits and they obey him."* 28 *And his fame immediately spread in all directions into the whole region surrounding Galilee.* [m]

Notes

[a] εὐθύς functions as a transitional connective here without its more literal meaning of immediacy (cf. 1:23, 28).

[b] τοῖς σάββασιν can be rendered as singular or plural, but context suggests the singular force here.

[c] Romanized words supplied from context.

[d] ἐξεπλήσσοντο is impersonal third person plural, "the people."

[e] εὐθύς has descriptive force, "suddenly," since attention is shifted abruptly from Jesus' teaching to another person.

[f] ἐν . . . πνεύματι, a Semitism rendering the Hebrew preposition ב (Taylor, 173).

[g] ἡμῖν . . . σοί, literally "What is it to us and to you?" may render a Hebrew expression (מה לי ולך; cf. John 2:4; Matt 8:29; 2 Sam 16:10; 19:23; 1 Kgs 17:18).

[h] Ναζαρηνέ—Mark's designation for Jesus (e.g., 10:47; 14:67; 16:6), cf. Ναζωραῖος in Matt 2:23; 26:71; Luke 18:37; John 18:5, 7; 19:9. Despite various accountings for these terms (Taylor, 177–78; H. H. Schaeder, *TDNT* 4 [1967] 874–79), Schaeder has demonstrated how both Ναζωραῖος and Ναζαρηνός could come from the same Aramaic root (נצרא/נאזרא) derived from the town's name (נאצרת) rendered Ναζαρέτ in Greek and how the radicals shift on occasion from the usual (צ)=σ to (צ)=ζ in Greek (*TDNT* 4 [1967] 875–79).

[i] οἴδαμεν (א pc bo) for οἶδα adapts plural subject with ἡμῖν of the previous statement.

[j] οἶδά σε uses proleptic accusative σε, the predicate nominative of τίς εἶ.

[k] πρὸς ἑαυτούς added for smoothness in C A D W Θ pm, see 8:11; 9:10; 12:28.

[l] τί . . . ἐξουσίαν (א B L) differs from Luke 4:36 (τίς ὁ λόγος οὗτος· ὅτι ἐν ἐξουσίᾳ . . .) whose reading may have influenced the MS tradition (cf. [A] C lat sy[pi,h] and D [W it sy[s]]). Lohmeyer's suggestion (34) of an original τίς διδαχὴ ἐκείνη offers an explanation of Mark's διδαχὴ καινή and a common denominator between Mark and Luke. But the awkward character of the more accepted reading in 1:27 may, along with some redactional interests (see below), support its originality.

[m] τῆς Γαλιλαίας may be an epexegetic or appositional use of the genitive to specify "the surrounding region, namely, Galilee" (Lohmeyer, 38, cf. 1:39). The distinction between groups from Galilee and from areas beyond Galilee in 3:7–8 (see *Comment* on 3:7–8) makes Mark's reading this as a genitive of description, "the area surrounding Galilee" (cf. Matt 4:24; cf. Mark 3:7–8), more probable.

Form / Structure / Setting

Mark 1:21–22 opens with a summary report of Jesus' teaching (Egger, *Frohbotschaft*, 146–47) that sets the stage and locale for the exorcism of 1:23–28. The exorcism itself reflects the classic exorcism form of encounter (1:23), defense (1:23b–24), command to depart (1:25), exorcism (1:23) and reaction of bystanders (1:27). Yet the crowd's response to Jesus' "new teaching with authority" in 1:27 forms an inclusion with their response to his teaching "with authority" in 1:22 and makes 1:21–22, 23–28 into a single literary complex (Taylor, 171; Theissen, *Miracle Stories*, 163–64).

Numerous signs point to Mark's redactional activity in this complex. He may well have drawn the Capernaum setting (1:21a) from an earlier context in 1:29–31 (e.g., Pesch, 1:171–72, cf. Taylor, 171). Furthermore the thematic (Jesus' teaching, crowd's astonishment, role of scribes), lexical (εἰσπορεύεσθαι, εὐθύς, διδαχή), and stylistic (dual use of related verbs, impersonal plural, historical present, periphrastic, γάρ-explanatory) characteristics of Mark (e.g., Egger, *Frohbotschaft*, 147–48; Stein, *ZNW* 61 [1970] 83–91) betray his role in shaping the setting of 1:21–22. Thus one might conjecture that 1:21a originally introduced 1:29–31 and 1:21b (cf. 3:1) introduced 1:23–28 before being combined and expanded by 1:21c (καὶ ἐδίδασκεν) and 1:22. Mark would then have located the exorcism story, whose traditional form and Semitisms suggest a pre-Markan tradition (Lohmeyer, 36), in Capernaum (1:21a) and modified it in terms of Jesus' authoritative teaching (1:22). He then rounded off the complex by reworking the observers' startled question and response in 1:27 in terms of Jesus' "new teaching with authority."

The setting of 1:21–28 has often been linked with the larger section of 1:21–34 (35–39) under the heading of a Day in Capernaum (Taylor, 170–71; Grundmann, 57; Pesch, 1:116–17; *idem, BibLeb* 9 [1968] 114–28). The traditional complex of 1:29–39 has been expanded by Mark to include and open with 1:21–28. After calling four disciples by the sea (1:16–20), Jesus enters Capernaum on a sabbath (1:21a). An account of his teaching (1:21–22, cf. 1:27), an exorcism (1:23–28), a healing (1:29–31), a summary account of more healings and exorcisms (1:32–34) all follow with Jesus leaving Capernaum on the next day (1:35–39). At the same time, by focusing on Jesus' authoritative teaching (1:22, 27) and by identifying it with his exorcism ministry (1:21–28) in the opening pericope, the evangelist uses 1:21–28 as a programmatic introduction for Jesus' authoritative ministry of healing and exorcisms with its counterpart in the summary report in 1:35 of Jesus' ministry in all Galilee (cf. 1:35–38).

Comment

22 "His teaching" (διδαχὴ αὐτοῦ). The prominence of Jesus as teacher in Mark (Meye, *Jesus*, 30–60) becomes clear not only in the three references to teaching in this brief setting but in the frequency with which the evangelist refers to Jesus' "teaching" (διδαχή, 5x), to Jesus as "teacher" (12x, and only in reference to Jesus), and to his use of "to teach" (17x, 15x pertaining to Jesus). Thus the redactional expansion of 1:21c–22 and the location of 1:21–

28 at the outset of Jesus' public ministry after calling his first disciples correspond to Mark's interest in Jesus as teacher.

"As having authority" (ὡς ἐξουσίαν ἔχων). Daube has suggested that "authority" (ἐξουσία) has the more technical meaning here of "license" (רשות, rēšût)
to teach the Law as an ordained rabbi on a higher level than the more elementary level of a scribe who simply passed on tradition (JTS 39 [1938] 45–59;
idem, Rabbinic Judaism, 205–33). But Argyle has correctly argued that, apart
from the valid question of whether such levels of authority existed within
Judaism in Jesus' day, not one of the fifty occurrences of ἐξουσία in the LXX
renders רשות, the suggested Hebrew term behind ἐξουσία in 1:22 (ExpTim
80 [1969] 343). Furthermore, the accompanying exorcism (1:23–28) and the
obedience of the unclean spirits of 1:27 in particular demonstrates the nature
of Jesus' startling "authority" and shows that the contrast in 1:22 lies between
Jesus' teaching and that of the scribes rather than between an ordained rabbi
and the scribes of lesser training.

Since the "deed explains the word" (Gnilka, 1:80; Hengel, Leader, 67),
more than style differentiated Jesus' teaching from that of the scribes. His
failure to allude to the authorities or make use of scribal tradition may have
set him off (Taylor, 173; cf. Lohmeyer, 35, who argues that the scholastic
chain of tradition postdates Jesus' day; Hengel, Leader, 45–50, 67–71). But
his distinguishing "authority" is bound up with his being the "Holy One
from God" who "teaches" (1:21–28), "heals" (1:29–34), "exorcizes" (1:23–
28, 32–34, 39) and "preaches" (1:39, cf. 1:14–15).

"The scribes" (οἱ γραμματεῖς) were a special group who concerned themselves
professionally with the Law. Although various religious groups, such as the
Pharisees, Sadducees, and Essenes, each had their own scribes, the vast majority
of scribes seem to have belonged to the Pharisees in Jesus' day (cf. 2:16).
The scribes, also called "Rabbi" at times (Hengel, Leader, 42–44), had at least
three tasks regarding the Law (Gnilka, 1:79): (a) to develop and interpret
the Law pertinent to the times, (b) to teach students the Law, and (c) to act
in judicial situations. In Mark the "scribes" always appear at counterpoint to
Jesus (von der Osten-Sacken, "Streitgespräch," 376–81)—alone (1:22; 2:6;
3:22; 9:11, 14; 12:28, 38), with the Pharisees (2:16; 7:15), with the chief priests
(10:33; 11:18; 14:1; 15:31) and with the elders and chief priests (8:31; 11:27;
14:43, 53; 15:1).

23 "The unclean spirits" (τὰ πνεύματα τὰ ἀκάθαρτα) represents a common
Jewish designation for demons (cf. δαιμόνια). The two expressions appear
synonymously in Mark (3:30 cf. 3:22; 7:25 cf. 7:26, 29, 30) with the latter
always used in the context of "to cast out" (ἐκβάλλειν, see 1:34). Mark uses
"unclean spirit" eleven times (cf. Matt 10:1; 12:43; Luke 4:33, 36; 8:29; 9:42;
11:24), six of which occur in two stories (1:23, 26, 27; 5:2, 8, 9, cf. 7:25; 9:25),
which may have influenced his composition of 3:11–12.

24 "What do we have in common?" This rhetorical question is the first
of a series of comments uttered by the "unclean spirit" speaking at times in
the plural and generically for the unclean spirits and at times in the singular
for himself (cf. ἡμῖν, ἡμᾶς and οἶδα). A formulaic question (cf. 5:7 // Matt 8:29;
Luke 8:28 and John 2:4) with an OT background (e.g., 2 Sam 16:10; 19:23;
1 Kgs 17:18; 2 Kgs 3:13; Judg 11:12; 2 Chron 35:21; Bächli, TZ 33 [1977]

69–80), it is almost always posed by an inferior or by one in an inferior position to a superior. Thus, the question has the defensive function of placing the one questioned in the position of responsibility for what follows and thereby creates an irreconcilable distance between the two parties (Bächli, *TZ* 33 [1977] 79–80). The question betrays the unclean spirit's recognition of his own status, particularly in the light of Jesus' authority. This reading gains confirmation from the following statements.

"The Holy One of God" (ὁ ἅγιος τοῦ Θεοῦ). The demon addresses Jesus as "Jesus, the Nazarene." After asking about the purpose of Jesus' coming, the spirit then demonstrates his knowledge of Jesus' true identity, "The Holy One of God." The naming of a name frequently has been viewed to be a defense, an apotropaic device, typical of exorcism stories by which the demon seeks to gain power over the exorcist (e.g., Bauernfeind, *Worte*, 3–10; Burkill, *Revelation*, 72–80; cf. Guillemette, *ScEs* 30 [1978] 81–96). But Koch (*Wunderer-zählungen*, 57–61), in a survey of supposed parallels, has noted that the use of a name by the demon in an exorcism is extremely rare. And instead of being an apotropaic device to gain control over the exorcist, the few parallels where a name is given indicate the recognition and acknowledgment of the exorcist's deity and the subordination of the demon. For example, "You come in peace, you great god who expels demons . . . I am your servant" (see K. Thraede, "Exorcism," *RAC* 8 [1967] 48). The demon recognizes the deity and, as in Mark 1:24 and 5:7, acknowledges the exorcist to be superior. Therefore, this announcement shows the demon's awareness of who Jesus is and that Jesus is his superior (Best, *Temptation*, 17). In so doing he identifies Jesus for Mark's audience or reader.

"The Holy One from God" occurs in the OT and variously refers to Aaron (Ps 106:16), Elisha (2 Kgs 4:9) and Samson (Judg 16:17 *v.l.*) and in John 6:69 to Jesus. Despite the attempts of some to view this as a Christological reference to a messianic high priest whose task would be to bind Beliar (e.g., *T. Levi* 18.12; so Grundmann, 60), the occurrence here may rather stem from a play on words in the two designations for Jesus (e.g., Mussner, *BZ* 4 [1960] 285–86; Pesch, 1:122, n. 20; Schweizer, 91–93). The radicals behind Nazareth (נצר, *nṣr*) and "holy one" (נזיר, *nzyr*) lend themselves to such a wordplay. But even the LXX translates נזיר, *nāzîr*, in two ways (ναζιραῖον Θεοῦ, Judg 13:7 A, cf. ἅγιον Θεοῦ, 13:7 B; cf. ναζιραῖος Θεοῦ/ἅγιος Θεοῦ) with reference to Samson, a text that might be the key to this passage (Pesch, 1:122, n. 20). Therefore, the designation indicating Jesus' background ("Jesus of Nazareth [Ναζαρηνέ]") leads to his true identity (the "Holy One [ὁ ἅγιος] of God"). Furthermore, the "Holy One of God," the one set apart, consecrated by God, may even take on more significance ironically from his encounter with an "unclean" spirit (1:23). In any event, this use of "Holy One of God" does indicate a special relationship, though unspecified here, between Jesus and God.

25 "Jesus subdued him" (ἐπετίμησεν αὐτῷ). Kee has shown that this verb (ἐπιτιμᾶν) has a technical meaning coming from the underlying Hebrew word גער, *gāʿar*, meaning a commanding word "uttered by God or by his spokesman, by which evil powers are brought into submission" (Kee, *NTS* 14 [1967–68] 235). The uttering of this word corresponds to the demon's question about "their" ultimate destruction (ἀπολέσαι ἡμᾶς) and indicates that Jesus was seen as the one in whom God was overcoming Satan and his rule.

"Saying, 'Be silent.'" Literally φιμοῦν means to "tie shut" or "to muzzle." The command for silence was standard procedure for an exorcism (Pesch, 1:123; Luz, ZNW 56 [1965] 19; Burkill, Revelation, 73; van der Loos, Miracles, 380). Whether or not this pericope supplies partial support for Mark's "messianic secret" must remain somewhat open (Burkill, Mysterious Revelation, 79–85; Luz, ZNW 56 [1965] 9–30; cf. Wrede, 24–34, and Kertelge, Wunder, 56). Since, however, the demons openly identify Jesus in Mark, especially in 3:11 and 5:7 where they use the title, "Son of God," used by the voice from heaven in 1:11 and 9:7, perhaps the evangelist took the traditional "Holy One of God" to have the same meaning. Thus, the demons' statements would have an additional function, namely, to give Jesus' true identity, as well as or instead of an apotropaic function for Mark. That Mark takes the command to silence as more than simply Jesus' counter to an apotropaic maneuver becomes clear at least in 1:34b and 3:12 (see Comment there).

"Come out of him!" (ἔξελθε ἐξ αὐτοῦ). Again, following the ritual of the exorcism, Jesus commands the demon to depart, which sets the stage for the crowd's amazement at his "authority" in 1:27.

26 "The unclean spirit . . . came out of him." Following the command verbatim, the spirit departs after convulsing the man, a final abuse of the victim. Yet his crying "with a loud voice" (φωνῆσαν φωνῇ μεγάλῃ), a death wail, signals the fact of the spirit having been vanquished.

27 "All were so astounded that they argued" (ἐθαμβήθησαν ἅπαντες ὥστε συζητεῖν). The response typical of the healing/exorcism miracle follows but this time in the form of a question (cf. 4:41), which might indicate the traditional setting of the pericope within the Church's mission context (e.g., Kertelge, Wunder, 55; Pesch, 1:124–25). But the motif of argument or intense discussion (συζητεῖν) seems rather characteristic of Mark (cf. Luke 4:36; Mark 6x without parallel; Luke 2x).

"What is this?" (τί ἐστιν τοῦτο;). Cf. Luke 4:36—"What is this matter?" (τίς ὁ λόγος οὗτος ὅτι . . . ;). Mark 4:35–41 has a similarly constructed narrative concluding with the appropriate question (τίς ἄρα οὗτός ἐστιν, ὅτι . . . ;). The similarity of narrative construction and the focus in both contexts on Jesus, the exorcist (cf. personal pronouns in 1:27–28), strongly suggests an underlying traditional question here—"Who is this?" (τίς . . . οὗτός ἐστιν;)—which Mark has adapted to his own context (Kertelge, Wunder, 51; Pesch, 1:124–25). The present form of the question (τί ἐστιν τοῦτο;) clearly sets the stage for the answer.

"A new teaching with authority" (διδαχὴ καινὴ κατ᾽ ἐξουσίαν). Although some have disputed Mark's redactional role behind this phrase because of its use of the mission terminology of Acts 17:19 and the lack of evidence for Mark's use of "new" (καινή, cf. 2:21) elsewhere (e.g., Theissen, Miracle Stories, 164–65; Gnilka, 1:77, 82), its presence here correlates with Mark's redactional setting of 1:21–22 for 1:23–28 that stressed Jesus' startling teaching with authority (cf. 1:22). Furthermore, the "new" underscores the amazing character of Jesus' "teaching with authority" in terms of its eschatological basis.

Jesus' coming not only threatens the unclean spirit, it forebodes for Mark the ultimate, eschatological destruction ("Have you come to destroy [ἀπολέσαι] us?" 1:24) of the Satanic forces in the new age (Kertelge, *Wunder*, 59; J. M. Robinson, *History*, 35–38). It signifies the coming of the Kingdom (1:14– 15). Thus "new" does not qualify simply the "teaching" of the Church (so Theissen, *Miracle Stories*, 165) but Jesus' "teaching with authority" (διδαχὴ κατ᾽ ἐξουσίαν) as epexegetically clarified (καί) by the unclean spirit's obedience of Jesus' command (1:26, 27b). The eschatological character of Jesus' authoritative teaching is demonstrated by the exorcism, indicating that "teaching in Mark consists of Jesus' claim found in his words *and* works" (Kertelge, *Wunder*, 56).

28 "His fame spread" (ἐξῆλθεν ἡ ἀκοὴ αὐτοῦ). This reference may also support the missionary setting of the tradition (Pesch, 1:125). The wide circumference of Jesus' fame (πανταχοῦ εἰς ὅλην τὴν περίχωρον) may have been limited or specified by Mark's addition (Marxsen, *Mark*, 60; Lohmeyer, 38) of τῆς Γαλιλαίας (cf. 1:14 and 3:7–12) in keeping with his locating the exorcism in Capernaum (1:21, cf. Luke 4:31, 37). Mark has numerous double expressions of locality (Neirynck, *Duality*, 50–51, lists: 1:38; 4:5; 5:1, 11; 6:3, 45; 11:4; 13:3; 14:54, 66, 68) in which a second member makes specific a general expression. But one could equally argue that Mark found "Galilee" in the tradition enabling him to align the material with Capernaum (cf. Schmidt, 51), particularly since he does not develop the Galilee motif or mention it again until the summary report of 1:39 (cf. 1:32–34 with reference to Capernaum, esp. 1:33).

Explanation

After calling the four disciples (1:16–20), Jesus opens his public ministry with them in Capernaum (1:21) where his astounding, authoritative teaching (1:21–22, 27) expresses itself in an exorcism (1:23–26).

The exorcism narrative, shaped most likely within the context of the Church's mission preaching, had as its focal point Jesus' encounter with an unclean spirit. The possessed man played no role apart from the opening scene. Without any embellishment Jesus exorcised the unclean spirit (1:26) by silencing him (1:24–25) and ordering him out. The unclean spirit's use of the generic plural ("us," 1:24), the reference to Jesus' coming to destroy them (1:24) and the rather technical connotation suggesting God's activity behind Jesus' "subduing" the unclean spirit (1:25a) indicate the eschatological character of Jesus' action in defeating the Satanic forces. Furthermore, the story in its mission setting would have reached its climax with the Christological question, "Who is this that commands and the unclean spirits obey?" The answer, in part, lay in the spirit's address of Jesus, "I know who you are, the Holy One of God . . . come to destroy us" (1:24). Therefore, the thrust of this story corresponds to Mark 3:22–27 and Matt 12:22–28 // Luke 11:14– 20, which refer to the eschatological character of Jesus' exorcisms, namely, the presence of the Kingdom in his ministry (Matt 12:28 // Luke 11:20), the "plundering of the house of the strong man" (Mark 3:27).

Mark does not change this Christological and eschatological thrust of the tradition. By introducing the exorcism into a setting of Jesus' teaching in a synagogue which had left the hearers astounded at the contrast between his teaching and that of the scribes (1:21–27) and by having the observers in the synagogue react to the exorcism by referring to his "new" teaching (1:27), the evangelist redirects the thrust of the tradition to underscore Jesus as teacher whose teaching reveals who he is. Jesus offers a "new teaching with authority," meaning the eschatologically "new" in his words and work. Both Jesus' words and his works—the "new teaching"—declare for Mark who Jesus is.

But why this stress on Jesus as teacher and his teaching? Mark's emphasis appears even more deliberate when compared with Matthew who does not carry the pericope and with Luke 4:31–37 who has separated the setting (4:31–32 // Mark 1:21–22) and exorcism story (4:33–37 // Mark 1:23–28). Perhaps the context of the previous pericope involving the call of disciples supplies a clue. To learn from a teacher represents one of the primary roles of a disciple and, as we shall see, Jesus relates to the disciples throughout Mark as a teacher with varying degrees of success.

By opening Jesus' ministry with the call of disciples (1:16–20) and a portrait of him as teacher (1:21–22), Mark sets the tone for Jesus' relationship with his disciples both in terms of his earthly ministry and also as a paradigm for Jesus' relationship with the "disciples" in Mark's congregation who are to learn from Jesus, their teacher. But even more importantly, as a prelude to Jesus' ministry throughout the Gospel, Mark sets Jesus off at the outset of his Gospel not only as a teacher but as one different from the usual rabbi or scribe (1:22) by virtue of his "new teaching" (1:22, 27), the eschatological claim inherent in his words and works in 1:21–28. This pericope, therefore, serves, above all, a Christological purpose to highlight Jesus as "teacher" and his relationship with his "disciples." At the same time, it serves a programmatic function of introducing Jesus' authoritative ministry of healing and exorcisms of 1:29–34.

C. The Healing of Peter's Mother-in-law (1:29–31)

Bibliography

Best, E. *Following Jesus.* 1981. **Kertelge, K.** *Die Wunder Jesu in Markusevangelium.* 1970. **Koch, D. A.** *Die Bedeutung der Wundererzählungen für die Christologie des Markusevangeliums.* 1975. **Roloff, J.** *Das Kerygma und der irdische Jesus.* 1970. **Theissen, G.** *The Miracle Stories of the Early Christian Tradition.* 1983. **Trocmé, E.** *The Formation of the Gospel according to Mark.* Philadelphia: Westminster, 1975. **Wuellner, W.** *The Meaning of "Fishers of Men."* Philadelphia: Westminster, 1967.

Translation

[29] *And departing immediately from the synagogue, they*[a] *went to the house of Simon and Andrew with James and John.* [30] *Simon's mother-in-law lay ill with a*

fever, and they spoke[b] *to him concerning her.* [31]*Approaching and seizing her hand, he raised her. The fever left her, and she began to serve them.*

Notes

[a] B λ φ al bo read singular verb and participle (ἐξελθὼν ἦλθεν) consistent with Jesus as subject of 1:21–28 and making a smoother sentence (Wellhausen, 11–12; Taylor, 178–79). The larger context (1:16–31, cf. 1:21) and redactional character of 1:29, however, support the plural reading (ἐξελθόντες ἦλθον) of א A C L vg sy[h] bo[pt], despite the awkward sentence with "they" as subject followed by "Simon and Andrew's house with James and John." The four disciples and Jesus are the contextual (1:16–20, 21) antecedents of "they." The suggestion of a later third person modification ("they") of an underlying first person Petrine "reminiscence" (e.g., "we . . . came into my/our house with James and John") accounts for the present awkwardness (Taylor, 178) but lacks MS support. It also assumes that "with James and John" (cf. "of Andrew") was present in the tradition rather than being a redactional addition binding 1:29–31 to the larger context of 1:16–20, 21.

[b] λέγουσιν only historical present in the pericope.

Form/Structure/Setting

The form, despite the pericope's brevity, contains all of the constituent elements of a healing narrative: (a) setting (1:29–30) with description of illness and request (implied) for healing, (b) healing (1:31a, b) and (c) demonstration (1:31c). The pericope's function is less obvious, especially in Mark 1:29–31, cf. Luke 4:38–39, since Mark's account does not betray any explicit kerygmatic tendencies. Consequently, the vast majority of commentators have concluded that its association with Peter attests to its source and explains its presence in the Church's tradition (e.g., Schmidt, 55–56; Klostermann, 18; Lohmeyer, 40; Taylor, 178; Haenchen, 80; Pesch, 1:129; Grundmann, 62; cf. Gnilka, 1:83; Roloff, *Kerygma*, 115–17).

Mark most likely found this pericope in a traditional complex with the two that follow. They were set in Capernaum in and around Simon's house according to a temporal sequence: (a) during the day (1:29–31), (b) after sunset (1:32–34) and (c) early the next morning (1:35–38). As the opening pericope, 1:29–31 provided the setting for the two that followed and a specific example of the multiple healings and exorcisms of 1:32–34.

Mark's redactional activity appears to have been limited to the opening verse. If, as suggested in 1:21–28, the original location for this pericope in Capernaum was preempted by Mark for the setting in 1:21a, much of 1:29 would then be redactional as well. The reference to the "synagogue" and "their departure" (ἐξελθόντες ἦλθον) would be drawn from 1:21–28 and the naming of the four disciples from 1:16–20. In fact, a redactional modification of 1:29 most likely accounts for the awkwardness of the sentence. Assuming that the healing narrative contained a reference to Jesus' going to Simon's house (1:29b), the redactional context (1:16–20, 21, 36) of the disciples accompanying Jesus (ἐξελθόντες, plural) from the synagogue may have led to the evangelist's also adding "and Andrew's" to "into Simon's house." The larger context implied that Jesus departed "with" Simon and Andrew as well as "with James and John."

As to the broader setting of this pericope, some have seen it as simply part of a traditional complex beginning with 1:21 that focuses on a day in Capernaum (e.g., Taylor, 170–71). Others attributing more redactional responsibility to Mark for the arrangement have pointed to the stark contrast between the public and private settings, the synagogue and the house, the clamor and the quietness in this and the previous narrative (e.g., Grundmann, 62). Still others view the pericope combined with the exorcism of 1:21–28 as offering the setting for the summary of Jesus healing the sick and casting out demons in 1:32–34 (e.g., Koch, *Wundererzählungen*, 135).

Comment

29 "Simon's house." According to John 1:44, Peter and Andrew along with Philip came from Bethsaida. Many have resolved this geographical difference by conjecturing that Peter had moved to Capernaum, perhaps at the time of his marriage (e.g., Lohmeyer, 40; Pesch, 1:131). As commercial fishermen, they might also have had more than one place of residence (cf. Wuellner, *"Fishers of Men,"* 30).

Jesus continues to meet in Mark with his disciples apart from the crowds "in a house" (e.g., 7:17; 9:28, 33; 10:10, cf. 2:1), and some have identified this "house" with Simon's in Capernaum (e.g., Taylor, 179; Pesch, 1:132). In contrast to this traditional reference specifically to "Simon's house," the other passages appear to be a redactional device to convey a note of privacy and separateness from the crowds where the disciples question Jesus (7:17; 9:28; 10:10) or are questioned by Jesus (9:33). But one can hardly conclude from this setting that Mark distinguishes deliberately between the synagogue and the house church (Gnilka, 1:83–84; Trocmé, *Mark,* 162–63; cf. Best, *Jesus,* 226). Furthermore, the "synagogue" in 1:21–28 and "Simon's house" in 1:29–31 belong in the traditional framework of 1:23–28 (synagogue setting) and 1:29–31 (house setting).

30 "Simon's mother-in-law" (ἡ πενθερὰ Σίμωνος). This note corresponds to Peter's marital status as given by Paul in 1 Cor 9:5.

"Lay sick with a fever" (κατέκειτο πυρέσσουσα) might also be translated, "laid low by a fever." The healing here corresponds to the perception in antiquity of fever as an illness itself rather than a symptom of an illness. Luke's account reflects the common association of a fever and the demonic when the healing is described in the language of an exorcism (e.g., 4:39— ἐπετίμησεν τῷ πυρετῷ, cf. Mark 1:25). Only the immediate context of 1:21–28 (cf. 1:32, 34) hints at such a connection for Mark.

31 "Seizing her hand" (κρατήσας τῆς χειρός). The healing transpired along formulaic lines. Str-B (1:2–3) documents a similar combination of taking persons by the hand and raising them in rabbinic narratives. The "seizing her hand" (cf. 5:41; 9:27) represents one of several kinds of physical contact between the healer and the sick (e.g., laying on hands—5:23; 7:32; touching— 3:10; 8:22; the touching of a garment—5:28; 6:56, cf. Theissen, *Miracle Stories,* 71–72; see *Comment* on 3:10). It was assumed that strength was conveyed in this manner from the healer to the weakness of the sick (cf. ἀσθενής = "weak"). "Raised her" (ἤγειρεν) also belongs to the formulas of healing narratives, although often in the imperative (e.g., 2:9, 11; 5:41; 9:27; cf. 3:3; 10:49).

"She began serving them" (διηκόνει αὐτοῖς). The basic meaning of serving (διακονεῖν) implies to serve them a meal. Despite the rabbinic evidence from the fourth century against a woman serving men at the table (Str-B, 1:480), one has no indication that this action was out of the ordinary. Her serving them also fulfills the formal function of demonstrating her having been healed.

Explanation

As the briefest healing narrative in the Gospels, this pericope may well be one of our oldest traditional units with its roots in Peter's experience. As a part of a pre-Markan traditional complex (1:29–38), it provided the setting (cf. 1:29, 33, 35) and persons (1:29, 36) for Jesus' healing in Capernaum. As a part of Mark's redactional complex (1:16–39), its setting in Capernaum provided the context for the outset of Jesus' public ministry (1:21) and an illustration of Jesus' healing ministry (1:29–31). The association with Simon's house (1:29–38) may even have spawned the use and expansion of the traditional complex of 1:29–38 to include the calling of the four disciples (1:16–20). Consequently, the thread of the disciples runs throughout this block (1:16–20, 21, 29, 36, 39a).

D. Healings at Evening Time (1:32–34)

Bibliography

Egger, W. *Frohbotschaft und Lehre.* 1976. Kertelge, K. *Die Wunder Jesu im Markusevangelium.* 1970. Koch, D.-A. *Die Bedeutung des Wundererzählungen für die Christologie des Markusevangeliums.* 1975. Neirynck, F. *Duality in Mark.* 1972. Snoy, T. "Les miracles dans l'Evangile de Marc: Examen de quelques études recentes." *RTL* 4 (1973) 58–101.

Translation

[32] *When evening had come and the sun set,[a] they continually brought to him all the ill and the demon possessed.* [33] *The whole city was gathered at the door.* [34] *And he healed those ill with various diseases and cast out the demons. And he did not allow the demons to speak because they knew him.*

Notes

[a] Majority of MSS (א A C L W Θ 0133) have the second aorist ἔδυ (Nestle[26]) of classical Greek, whereas B D 28 1424 support the hellenistic ἔδυσεν.

Form / Structure / Setting

This pericope has the form of a summary report but in the sense of expanding Jesus' ministry to include the sick of the city rather than simply generalizing the themes of exorcism and healing from 1:21–31 (Egger, *Frohbotschaft*, 65–66). The source has become more disputed with many assigning its core to the pre-Markan tradition (e.g., Schmidt, 57; Lohmeyer, 41; Taylor, 180; Schweizer, 54; Kertelge, *Wunder*, 31–32; Egger, *Frohbotschaft*, 66–71) and others assigning it totally to Mark's redaction (Koch, *Wundererzählungen*, 161–66; Snoy, *RTL* 4 [1973] 70–71; Gnilka, 1:86). This discussion holds part of the key to the larger question concerning the extent of the pre-Markan tradition behind the complex of 1:16–39 and the particular question regarding the meaning and function of this pericope for Mark.

Word statistics offers little help here distinguishing between tradition and redaction, since no clear pattern emerges in 1:32–34. The strongest evidence lies in the contextual relationship between 1:32–34 and 1:21–28, 29–31 and in the contrast between this summary and other Markan summaries (Egger, *Frohbotschaft*, 68–69). Contextually, the temporal (1:32a) and local (1:33) relationship between 1:32–34 and 1:29–31 provides strong positive support for the common traditional status of 1:29–31 and 1:32–34. Such specific temporal and local concerns do not at all reflect Mark's typical redactional activity (Schmidt, 57–58). Further, the absence of any verbal correspondence between 1:21–28 (cf. τὸ πνεῦμα τὸ ἀκάθαρτον, ἐπιτιμᾶν/φιμοῦν) and 1:32–34 (cf. δαιμόνιον, ἐκβάλλειν) and between 1:29–31 (κατέκειτο πυρέσσουσα, ἐγείρειν) and 1:32–34 (κακῶς ἔχοντας, νόσοις, θεραπεύειν) hardly corresponds to a redactional summary generalizing the previous pericopes. The only contact with 1:21–31 appears in the clearly redactional interpretation of the silence command (cf. 1:25) in 1:34b.

By comparison with other Markan summaries, this one also has the gathered crowds and heightened language ("all of the city," "all the sick") but lacks the indefinite setting in time and place and any reference to Jesus preaching and/or teaching. As to content, only the summaries of 1:32–34; 3:7–12 and 6:53–56 focus exclusively on Jesus' healing and exorcism ministry (cf. Egger, *Frohbotschaft*, 69, see 3:7–12 and 6:53–56). This evidence suggests a pre-Markan traditional section (1:32–34a) combined with 1:29–31.

Structurally, the pericope consists of an introduction (1:32a) and two parallel statements about the ill and possessed (1:32b, 34a) set around the description of the size and location of the gathered crowds (1:33) to form an inclusion (aba'). Some (e.g., Grundmann, 63–64; Schmithals, 1:130) have also found a chiastic structure in the larger context of 1:21–34 with exorcism and healing (1:21–28, 29–31) followed by healings and exorcism (1:34a).

If indeed this pericope belonged to 1:29–31 in the tradition, the setting shifts the focus from Jesus' healing in the private confines of Simon's house to a much more public scene "at the door" (of Simon's house) with the "city" (Capernaum) turning out with all their sick and the demon possessed. In the tradition no basis or occasion was given for the city's actions, which would also correspond to the "reminiscent" character of the materials in 1:29–34. Yet Mark's redactional location of the exorcism narrative (1:21–28) in the synagogue of Capernaum (1:21) would now account for the city's thronging to Jesus. At the same time, this pericope with its healings and exorcisms in the evening set the stage for Jesus' early morning withdrawal and the seeking throngs in the following pericope (1:35–38).

Comment

32 "When evening had come." This phrase, a genitive absolute (ὀψίας δὲ γενομένης), occurs five times in Mark (Matthew 7x, four parallel with Mark; Luke has none) with three in seams as one part of a two-step temporal progression (1:32; 4:35; 15:42) and two within a narrative (6:47; 14:17). Conveying the general meaning of "evening" (4:35; 6:47; 14:17 and 15:42), the second temporal comment here specifies "after sunset." Neirynck (*Duality*, 46) assigns this "two step progression" to Markan redaction (see *Comment* on 4:35). Others, however, have attributed it to the pre-Markan tradition (e.g., Kertelge, *Wunder*, 32; Egger, *Frohbotschaft*, 68; Pesch, 1:133, n. 2). Perhaps Mark's redactional hand can be seen in constructing the "two step progression," but that need not mean he created both temporal elements. The rather unusual occurrence of δέ rather than the more typical Markan καί would support this conclusion.

"After the sun had set" (ὅτε ἔδυ ὁ ἥλιος). This phrase denoted the end of the Jewish day and here it specifies the end of the sabbath (cf. 1:21). Numerous commentators have considered this expression to allow the setting for what follows, since the sabbath restrictions would have ended with "sunset." If so, this temporal element may have been the original temporal clause reflecting an earlier stage in the tradition when such fine points regarding the Law were more pertinent than for Mark or his audience.

"They continually brought." The deliberate use of the imperfect ἔφερον might well underscore the repeated act of bringing the ill, a formula common to the settings of healing narratives (2:3; 7:32; 8:22; 9:17–20).

"All the ill." "All" (πάντας) has a hyperbolic meaning here as frequently in Mark. This scene is set with hyperbole—"all the ill" and "the whole city" (1:32–33). "The ill" expressed as τοὺς κακῶς ἔχοντας occurs here, in 2:17 and in 6:55.

"The demon possessed" (δαιμονιζομένους). This expression occurs only here and at the end of the Gerasene demoniac narrative in 5:15, 16, 18 (see *Comment* on 5:14–16). There is little evidence to support Mark's having introduced it (e.g., Pesch, 1:134; Kertelge, *Wunder*, 32), since he could easily have stayed with the terminology of 1:23–28 (τὸ πνεῦμα ἀκάθαρτον, cf. 1:23) and the tradition in 1:32 (τοὺς κακῶς ἔχοντας) by adding "those having unclean spirits" (τοὺς τὰ πνεύματα τὰ ἀκάθαρτα ἔχοντας, cf. 3:30; 7:25; 9:25, cf. 9:17).

33 "The whole city was gathered at the door." This verse probably holds the key to the source question not only for 1:32–34 but for the relationship of 1:32–34 to 1:29–31 and 1:35–38. Apart from the unusual function of the dual chronological expression in 1:32, the specificity in 1:33 that picks up the previous references to the "city" of Capernaum (1:21) and the "door" of Simon's house (1:29) hardly reflects Mark's redactional tendencies (so Schmidt, 57–58) and definitely not those of his summaries (Egger, *Frohbotschaft*, 69). Furthermore, these indications of locale belong structurally at the heart of the material (1:32b, 34a and 33, see above) rather than in the margin or in a seam.

Mark 2:2 does come close in content by referring to the gathering of so many that access was blocked to the "door," but there the evangelist has the more common verb συνάγειν rather than the heightened form used here (ἐπισυνἄγειν, cf. 13:27). One could argue that Mark's setting in 2:2 redactionally betrays the suggestive force of the traditional material in 1:33 (Egger, *Frohbotschaft*, 69). Thus, the evidence appears quite strong that Mark found a complex, traditional unit consisting of 1:29–31; 1:32–34 and 1:35–38 to which he simply made some redactional modifications (cf. 1:29, 34b, 38b).

34 "Many . . . many . . ." (πολλούς . . . πολλά). Some have found a tension here between the "all" (πάντας) of 1:32 and the "many" (πολλούς/ά) of 1:34a (e.g., Pesch, 1:134–35; Schmithals, 1:131–32; Gnilka, 1:87). Most have followed Lohmeyer's explanation of πολλούς/ά as a Semitism meaning "all" (41; Lagrange, 26; Taylor, 181; Lane, 79; see J. Jeremias, *TDNT* 6 [1968] 541). If such a limitation were intended by Mark's account, neither Matthew nor Luke reflect it (Matt 8:16; Luke 4:40), and it remains undeveloped in Mark.

The hyperbolic character of the material in 1:32, 33 should not force one to conclude either that by rendering "many" = "all" Jesus would have indiscriminately forced his healing on those without faith (Schmithals, 1:131–32) or that the crowd would have had no cause to seek him on the next day (cf. 1:37, Pesch, 1:134–35). The tone of this account struck by the use of "all" and "the whole city" seems rather to be carried through in the healings of 1:34a by the reference to Jesus' curing not only the sick but "the sick with various illnesses" (ποικίλαις νόσοις).

"He cast out many demons" (δαιμόνια πολλά ἐξέβαλεν). The shift from "unclean spirits" (πνεύματα ἀκάθαρτα) of 1:23–28 to the terminology here may reflect the consistent use of "demon" (δαιμόνιον) in conjunction with "to cast out" (ἐκβάλλειν). All ten occurrences of "demon" (δαιμόνιον) in Mark come either directly with "to cast out" (ἐκβάλλειν, 1:34, 39; 3:15, 22; 6:13; 7:26; 9:38) or in the immediate context (1:34b; 7:29, 30).

"He did not allow the demons to speak" (οὐκ ἤφιεν λαλεῖν). At this point we move to Mark's redaction and into a motif that will recur in Mark involving Jesus' identity, Wrede's so-called "messianic secret." Whereas the command to silence in 1:25 belonged to the traditional formula as part of the exorcism ritual, Mark has Jesus silencing the demons "because they knew him" (cf. 1:24, οἶδά σε, "Holy One of God," and "Son of God" in 3:11; 5:7). Thus Mark has apparently taken a motif from the tradition (cf. οἶδά σε and φιμώθητι) and given it his own special significance of veiling Jesus' identity (see *Comment* on 3:12).

Explanation

In contrast to the private, personal setting of the healing of Simon's mother-in-law (1:29–31), this summary report set in hyperbole accents Jesus' multiple healings of "various illnesses" (1:32, 34a) in a very public fashion as the "whole city" (cf. 1:21) gathers "at the door" (1:33). The underlying tradition behind 1:29–38 gives no occasion for this public response. The scene simply shifts from inside Simon's house (1:29–31) to the door of the house after sunset (1:32–34). The crowd's knowledge of Jesus and his ability to heal is implied by their bringing the sick and possessed to him (1:32).

Apart from a possible "reminiscent" and thus biographical value of this complex (1:29–38), the Church doubtless preserved this material in terms of its two motifs: (a) Jesus' healing and exorcism ministry (1:34 cf. 1:31) as well as (b) the corresponding attraction of the needy (1:32, "all the sick and possessed") and curious (1:33, "the whole city gathered"). Yet the simple, straightforward, unembellished statement of Jesus' actions here (1:34a) and in 1:31a prevent one from extrapolating what, if any, Christological implication might lie behind this complex.

The occasion for the city's response in 1:32–34 might now come as an unintentional by-product of the evangelist's expanding the traditional complex of 1:29–38 to include the synagogue exorcism with its startling, public effect in 1:21–28. Mark leaves this summary report intact and merely adds a note regarding Jesus' silencing the demons in 1:34b. By adding this note, he interprets the silence command of 1:25 in terms of Jesus' avoiding public recognition as the explanatory clause ("because they knew him," cf. 1:24) indicates.

This statement comes as the first hint of a recurring tendency in Mark in which not only the demons (e.g., 3:12) but also those healed (e.g., 1:45) and even the disciples (e.g., 8:30) are bound to silence. Furthermore, this command to silence stands in tension with a context that assumes a broad public "knowledge" of Jesus, at least, as one who heals and exorcizes (1:32–33). This raises the question regarding a possible difference between Jesus' popular image as a miracle worker and his true identity as known by the demons. But why would Jesus appear to prefer the former at this stage? See *Comment* on a similar passage in 3:7–12.

E. Preaching in Surrounding Areas (1:35–39)

Bibliography

Egger, W. *Frohbotschaft und Lehre.* 1976. **Neirynck, F.** *Duality in Mark.* 1972. **Turner, C. H.** "Marcan Usage: Notes, Critical and Exegetical, on the Second Gospel," *JTS* 26 (1925) 145–56.

Translation

[35] *Arising very early while it was still dark, he went out* [a] *to an uninhabited place, and there he prayed.* [36] *Simon and his companions* [b] *pursued him,* [37] *found him and said* [c] *to him, "Everyone is looking for you."* [38] *He said* [c] *to them, "Let us go in another direction to the neighboring towns in order that I might preach there also. For I came out* [d] *to do that."* [39] *And he went into all Galilee preaching in their synagogues and casting out demons.*

Notes

[a] "Went out" renders a typical Markan redundancy of doubling the verbs (ἐξῆλθεν καὶ ἀπῆλθεν, Turner, *JTS* 26 [1925] 155; Neirynck, *Duality,* 33, 77–81). Pesch's association of ἐξῆλθεν with

reference to the house and ἀπῆλθεν with reference to the city appears too exacting for the Markan usage.

    b "His companions," literally, "those with him" (οἱ μετ᾽ αὐτοῦ).

    c Both verbs (λέγουσιν and λέγει) are in historical present in contrast to the rest of the account.

    d "Came out" ἐξῆλθον (א B C L Θ 33 pc) cf. ἐξῆλθεν in 1:35. Some MSS read ἐξελήλυθα (A D K Γ 0104. 0133 f¹ 700 1010 1241 pm; others read ἐλήλυθα (W Δ 090 f¹³ 28 565 892 pm).

Form / Structure / Setting

This pericope defies formal classification, a fact that might indicate its integral relationship in the pre-Markan tradition with the two preceding pericopes (1:29–31, 32–34). Without an independent existence in the tradition, the material would have had no occasion to take on a particular form of its own. Some have accounted for this lack of traditional form by relegating the material entirely to the evangelist's redactional activity (e.g., Bultmann, 155; Gnilka, 1:88). But lexical (Σίμων, καταδιώκειν, ἀλλαχοῦ, τὰς ἐχομένας κωμοπόλεις) and thematic (προσηύχετο) grounds support its pre-Markan existence in the tradition.

The evangelist appears to have taken over this pericope—like the previous one (1:32–34)—intact and to have made his redactional modifications at the end. As it now stands, one detects a tension between Jesus' "departure" (ἐξῆλθεν) in 1:35 to pray in a deserted place and his "departure" (ἐξῆλθον) in 1:38 to preach to the surrounding towns in all Galilee and thus to avoid the searching crowds in Capernaum (1:37). The one "departure" (1:35) contains a repose motif, the other (1:38) a redirection of ministry motif (1:38b, 39). One can resolve this tension by attributing the reference to Jesus' preaching and the explanatory clause (1:38b, c) to Mark's redaction as a prelude for the redactional summary of 1:39 (Egger, Frohbotschaft, 74–75). Thus Mark would have explained the traditional reference to Jesus' avoiding the searching crowd (1:37, 38a) in terms of his preaching mission to all Galilee (1:38b, c, 39).

Structurally, 1:35–39 opens with a statement about Jesus' withdrawal to pray. Then Simon pursues him and announces the crowd's search for him (1:36–37) to which Jesus responds by leaving the city for the neighboring villages (cf. 6:45–46). The present account concludes with a new reason for the withdrawal (1:38b, c).

In context, this pericope concludes a series of three traditional pericopes that were joined by temporal sequence, location and personnel. Simon's house in Capernaum (1:29, cf. 1:21) offers the location for a single healing in 1:29–31, multiple healings and exorcisms at "the door" in 1:32–34, and finally a place of departure for solitude in 1:35–38. Simon and his companions (1:29, 36) and the "crowds" (1:32, 33, 37) provide continuous threads running throughout the temporal shift in scenes from daytime (1:29–31) to after sunset (1:32–34) to early in the morning (1:35).

Mark, who expanded these three pericopes by adding the setting and exorcism of 1:21–28, now uses this pericope to set the stage for Jesus' broader ministry in Galilee (1:38b, c, cf. 1:14), which he summarizes in 1:39. Jesus began this section (1:21–39) by teaching and exorcizing in the synagogue of Capernaum (1:21–22, 27) and he concludes it by preaching and exorcizing in the synagogues of all Galilee (1:39).

Comment

35 "Very early . . . still dark." Just as in 1:32 the second temporal reference (ἔννυχα) further specifies the first (πρωΐ . . . λίαν).

"Uninhabited place" (ἔρημον τόπον) is one of Mark's five references (1:35, 45; 6:31, 32, 35) to a place of solitude. Each of the three contexts (1:35; 1:45; 6.31–95) carry the connotation of an out of the way place where one might avoid the crowds. Of these five occurrences, 1:45 may well be a redactional adaptation of 1:35 for the conclusion of 1:40–45 and 6:31–32 appears to be a redactionally constructed transitional scene that appropriates the traditional "uninhabited place" from the setting of the Feeding narrative (6:35). Consequently, rather than a typically Markan expression, "uninhabited place" has its roots when added by Mark (1:45; 6:31–32) in the tradition behind 1:35; 6:35.

36 "Prayed" (προσηύχετο). Luke's parallel in 4:42 surprisingly does not follow Mark in view of the former's emphasis on prayer (cf. Luke 5:16 with Mark 1:45, where the motif may reappear). The same motif of Jesus departing for prayer in an out of the way place after his ministry to the crowds does occur again in 6:46. The imperfect tense (προσηύχετο) as in 1:32 (ἔφερον) may connote durative action (Taylor, 183).

"Pursued" (καταδιώκειν). The only NT occurrence of this rather strong verb conveys the sense of urgency in Simon's actions. The following verse explains why "Simon and his companions" (Andrew, James and John from the redactional context of 1:29) felt such urgency.

37 "Everyone is looking" (πάντες ζητοῦσιν). "Everyone" belongs with the hyperboles of 1:32–34, and the context of 1:32–34 gives ample basis for this eagerness to find Jesus. They came to him because of his healings and exorcisms. Yet Jesus rejects the opportunity to return to the city. One might ask why Jesus would have healed the sick and cast out demons before the "whole city" the night before and then reject their interest in finding him the next day. A similar issue arises in the following pericope (1:40–45). The answer lies not in Jesus' aversion to healing the sick or exorcising the demons (cf. 1:39; 1:40–45), which he had done the night before (1:32–34), but apparently in the crowd's response (cf. 1:45).

38 "Let us go . . . towns" (ἄγωμεν . . . κωμοπόλεις). Jesus invites his disciples to accompany him to the "neighboring towns." If, as suggested above, the traditional unit concluded with this comment, the implication would be twofold: (a) Jesus continued his ministry (cf. plural—τὰς ἐχομένας κωμοπόλεις) and (b) he rejected the city's response without explanation (cf. 1:45). Thus this pericope gives two traditional reasons for Jesus' "withdrawing." The first was to be alone to pray (1:35); the second to avoid the public clamor (1:38a).

"In order . . . preach there also." This purpose clause gives a very specific reason for Jesus' going to the towns. The Markan interest in the verb "to preach" (κηρύσσειν, 12x, cf. Matthew and Luke, 9x each), its setting the stage for 1:39 and its correlation with Jesus' coming to minister in Galilee summarized in 1:14 all point to Markan redaction (e.g., Pesch, 1:137–38; Egger, *Frohbotschaft*, 74–75). Jesus came to proclaim the "good news from God" (1:14) apparent in his "teaching" (1:21–28), healing and exorcism (1:29–34).

"For I came to do this." Mark in his typical use of a γάρ-explanatory now makes the reason (εἰς τοῦτο) for Jesus' departure (ἐξῆλθον, cf. 1:35) explicit. According to Mark, Jesus withdrew from Capernaum (1:35) to go to the neighboring towns throughout Galilee and preach. The context makes the rendering of "came out" (ἐξῆλθον) to mean "coming out from God" and thus a developed theological statement about Jesus' coming (e.g., Lohmeyer, 43; Gnilka, 1:89; cf. Luke 4:43—ἀπεστάλην) most unlikely, especially in the context of Mark's redactional intention of moving Jesus from Capernaum (1:1–38) to all of Galilee (1:39, 40–45, cf. 1:14 and 2:1).

39 "Into all Galilee . . . preaching . . . and casting out demons." This summary report stems most likely from the evangelist who drew on previous motifs to conclude the material beginning with 1:21 (see Egger, *Frohbotschaft*, 76). There Jesus entered the synagogue of Capernaum where he taught and exorcised an unclean spirit (1:21–28); here he goes throughout the synagogues of Galilee where he preached and exorcised the demons (1:39). Both Jesus' teaching and his preaching declare the fulfillment of time, the presence of the Kingdom, as seen in his ministry of healing (1:29–31, 32–34) but particularly of exorcism (1:21–28, 39a, b). Again we see that, for Mark, word and deed communicate Jesus' message summarized in 1:14–15.

Explanation

This pericope most likely concluded the traditional complex of 1:29–38 combined by a temporal and local sequence of shifts from the event at Simon's house during the day (1:29–31), the healings and exorcisms at the door after sunset (1:32–34) and finally the departure early in the morning (1:35–38). Furthermore, Jesus stands as the central figure but the reference to Simon in 1:29 and again in 1:36 helps unify the complex.

After the clamor and activity of the healings and exorcisms in the evening (1:32–34), Jesus withdrew to a private place for prayer (1:35, cf. 6:45–46). The contrast speaks graphically for itself (cf. Pss 5:3; 88:13). Then Simon and his companions pursued Jesus, found him and reported that "everyone" was looking for him (1:36–37). Jesus responds surprisingly by going with his disciples to the neighboring towns (1:38a).

Within the traditional pericope, therefore, Jesus withdrew to be alone and pray (1:35) and then withdrew from the searching crowd to move elsewhere (1:37–38a). But why such an unexpected reaction to the crowd's response, one that obviously caught even the disciples by surprise? That Jesus continued his ministry becomes evident in his decision to go to the neighboring towns. But why not back to Capernaum? Here lies the point of the pericope.

Jesus had publicly healed and exorcized and this activity had led to "everyone's" looking for him. But he deliberately rejected their quest by taking his ministry elsewhere. One can only conclude from the pericope's understatement that Jesus' decision to move on stemmed from the city's response rather than its needy whom he had helped the previous night. Thus one may well have in this pericope a pre-Markan "seed" of a "messianic secret" embedded in the tradition itself (cf. 1:45). Jesus avoids the crowds whose quest arises from his mighty works but without any explanation (cf. John 6:26).

Mark again preserves the tradition intact but modifies its conclusion to underscore Jesus' continuing ministry implied in 1:38a by making it explicit in 1:38b, c, 39. For Mark, however, the ultimate purpose of Jesus' withdrawal (cf. 1:35, 38c) centers in his intention to preach in other areas of Galilee (1:38b, c, 39). Consequently, the evangelist interprets the tradition not in terms of Jesus' rejecting the searching throngs of Capernaum, a "messianic secret," but in terms of Jesus' preaching in Galilee beyond the confines of Capernaum (cf. 1:14–15, 39). Mark will return later to develop the traditional motif of Jesus' avoidance of the throngs (cf. 1:45).

The pericope concludes with a summary report of Jesus' preaching and exorcism activity throughout the synagogues of all Galilee, a summary that stands as the counterpart for the opening scene of this present complex in the synagogue of Capernaum where Jesus teaches and exorcizes (1:27–28). Jesus' preaching like his teaching remains unspecified, except by the accompanying exorcisms in both cases that indicate the eschatological content (cf. 1:14–15). Jesus clearly ministers as the one in whom God is at work, the bringer of the new age of salvation (cf. 3:22–27). Yet one finds no hint that anyone (1:22, 27, 37) apart from the demons (1:25, 34b) actually recognized him for who he was.

F. Healing of the Leper   (1:40–45)

Bibliography

Bonner, C. "Traces of Thaumaturgic Technique in the Miracles." *HTR* 20 (1927) 171–81. **Burkill, T. A.** *Mysterious Revelation: An Examination of the Philosophy of St. Mark's Gospel.* Ithaca: Cornell, 1963. **Cave, H. C.** "The Leper: Mark 1.40–45." *NTS* 25 (1978–79) 245–50. **Elliott, J. K.** "The Conclusion of the Pericope of the Healing of the Leper and Mark 1,45." *JTS* 22 (1971) 153–57. ———. "The Healing of the Leper in the Synoptic Parallels." *TZ* 34 (1978) 175–76. ———. "Is ὁ ἐξελθών a Title for Jesus in Mark 1:45?" *JTS* 27 (1976) 402–5. **Kee, H. C.** "Aretalogy and Gospel." *JBL* 92 (1973) 402–22. **Kertelge, K.** *Die Wunder Jesu im Markusevangelium.* 1970. **Kilpatrick, G. D.** "Mark i 45 and the Meaning of λόγος." *JTS* 40 (1939) 389–90. **Koch, D.-A.** *Die Bedeutung der Wundererzählungen für die Christologie des Markusevangeliums.* 1975. **Lachs, S. T.** "Hebrew Elements in the Gospels and Acts." *JQR* 71 (1980) 31–39. **Lake, K.** "Ἐμβριμησάμενος and Ὀργισθείς (Mark 1:40–43)." *HTR* 16 (1923) 197–98. **Loos, H. van der.** *The Miracles of Jesus.* NTS 8. Leiden: Brill, 1965. **Luz, U.** "Das Geheimnismotiv und die markinische Christologie." *ZNW* 56 (1965) 9–30. **Pryke, E. J.** *Redactional Style in the Marcan Gospel.* 1978. **Schenke, L.** *Die Wundererzählungen des Markusevangeliums.* 1974. **Theissen, G.** *The Miracle Stories of the Early Christian Tradition.* 1983.

Translation

⁴⁰*And a leper came*ᵃ *appealing to* Jesusᵇ *and kneeling said, "If you want, you can make me clean."* ⁴¹*Being angered,*ᶜ *Jesus stretched out his hand and touched*

him and said, "I do. Be clean." [42]*And immediately the leprosy left him and he was cleansed.* [43]*Silencing him,*[d] *Jesus sent him away*[e] *immediately* [44]*and said to him, "See that you say nothing to anyone. But go, show yourself to the priest and make the offerings commanded by Moses for your cleansing as evidence against them."* [45]*But after departing,*[f] *he began to proclaim many things*[g] *and spread the word, so that Jesus was no longer able to enter a city publicly. Rather he remained outside in the uninhabited places. And people*[h] *continued to come to him from everywhere.*

Notes

[a] ἔρχεται, historical present as λέγει in 1:41, 44.

[b] Romanized words added from context.

[c] ὀργισθείς/σπλαγχνισθείς offers a genuine textual dilemma. Both expressions are attested in Jesus' ministry ("anger," cf. John 11:33, 38; Mark 7:34; 9:19, 23; "compassion," cf. Mark 6:34; 9:22). Only D a ff² r¹ support ὀργισθείς, but it represents the more difficult reading (Taylor, 187; cf. Lachs, *JQR* 71 [1980] 33–35). The disturbing presence of ὀργισθείς might account for the absence of either participle in Matt 8:3; Luke 5:13, who do use σπλαγχνίζεσθαι elsewhere (e.g., Matt 9:36; Luke 7:13). Perhaps the strongest argument for ὀργισθείς lies in its apparent correspondence to ἐμβριμᾶσθαι in 1:43, cf. John 11:33, 38 and στενάζειν in Mark 7:34 (G. Stählin, *TDNT* 5 [1967] 427, n. 326).

[d] ἐμβριμησάμενος, uncommon verb whose meaning remains obscure. In classical Greek it meant "to snort" or "puff" like a disturbed horse or an expression of anger and agitation. "Anger" comes across in the LXX (Lam 2:6; Dan 11:30) and underlies NT references (Mark 14:5; John 11:33, 38). Matt 9:30 and Mark 1:43, however, use the verb in a miracle context, leading some to interpret it as "pneumatic excitement" or "prophetic frenzy" in a miracle worker (e.g., Bonner, *HTR* 20 [1927] 171–78; Theissen, *Miracle Stories,* 57–58). Kee (*JBL* 92 [1973] 418, n. 123) traces this verb to its Indo-European root, *bhrem* = "growl, grumble, mutter," which also translated the Semitic root גער, *gā˓ar*, as did ἐπιτιμᾶν (see *Comment* on 1:25).

[e] "To send away" renders ἐξέβαλεν with milder force in this context (cf. 1:12; 5:40) than the harsher "to cast out."

[f] ὁ ἐξελθών syntactically ambiguous, referring to either the leper or Jesus. Context suggests the healed man as subject whose "preaching" prevented Jesus from publicly entering the city. Mark 7:36 offers a parallel of one healed "preaching," despite Jesus' command to silence.

[g] Though some have taken this as adverbial (cf. 3:12; 5:10, 23, 38, 43; 6:20; 9:26), the direct object of κηρύσσειν is in line with 4:2 and 6:34 (διδάσκειν).

[h] "People" renders impersonal third person plural ἤρχοντο.

Form/Structure/Setting

The form follows essentially that of a healing narrative: (a) setting with encounter and specific request for healing (1:40), (b) healing with healer's reaction and healing gesture and word (1:41–42), and (c) demonstration implicit in the command to go to priest for confirmation (1:43–44). The response in 1:45, however, plays its own role rather than the usual, formal one.

The absence of any local, temporal, or personal connections with the previous pericopes in 1:29–38 strongly indicates that Mark found this unit as a separate pericope and was responsible for introducing it into the present context. He connected it thematically to what preceded by his redactional conclusion in 1:45 that picks up the traditional motif of Jesus avoiding reentering the city, a motif left undeveloped in the preceding pericope (1:35–38).

Structurally, the narrative becomes a bit awkward in the transition from the healing (1:41–42) to the demonstration (1:43–44). The demonstration opens with a statement of rebuke (ἐμβριμησάμενος, "silencing him") and a strong verb of dismissal (ἐξέβαλεν, "sent him away") before the dual commands to observe secrecy and to go to the priest. Both terms could function quite naturally in an exorcism setting (see *Comment* on 1:43), but do not fit structurally into the present healing component of 1:41–42. This raises the question about the integrity of the pericope or whether it might incorporate more than one healing component.

In its larger narrative context, 1:40–45 now functions in a dual capacity. First, it forms the climax for 1:21–45. Jesus' ministry had reached its peak in Capernaum in the evening healings and exorcisms (1:21–34) that caused him to withdraw from the crowds to preach in neighboring towns (1:35–39). But now his fame had spread to such an extent that he had to avoid all cities for the less populous places (1:45). Thus what had become true in Capernaum (1:33–38) had now become true for "all of Galilee." His fame had reached a high point. Second, this pericope serves as a transition and introduction for the pericopes that follow in 2:1–3:12. Apart from the rather ominous comment about Jesus' inability to enter any city publicly (1:45) with its suggestion of conflict, the pericope's specific content involving Jesus' ministry and the Mosaic Law (1:44) helps set the thematic stage for the following conflict narratives in 2:1–3:6 involving issues of the Law. This thematic connection with what follows may explain the evangelist's selection and use of this particular pericope here.

Comment

40 "A leper" (λεπρός). The designation "leper" or "leprosy" in the OT and NT most likely included a variety of other skin diseases along with the disease of leprosy (van der Loos, *Miracles*, 465–68). The "leper" (cf. λέπειν = "to scale or peel off") was considered ceremonially unclean (cf. Lev 13–14), often prevented from entering the Holy City of Jerusalem, and socially ostracized from everyday life for prophylactic reasons (cf. *m. Nega'im*). Frequently regarded as divine punishment for serious sin, this disease belonged among the worst evils to afflict one, a living death whose healing was equivalent to being raised from the dead (2 Kgs 5:7; Str-B, 4:745).

"If you will" (ἐὰν θέλῃς). This request for healing follows a rather awkwardly constructed sentence describing the leper's "coming," "appealing," "kneeling" and "saying." By addressing Jesus at the level of his will rather than his ability, the supplicant believingly acknowledges that Jesus' ability or power (δύνασαι) correlates with his will (θέλῃς). Thus, his request arises out of his confidence rather than doubt in Jesus' ability to heal him. Lachs notes that leprosy was considered the punishment for slander, "one of the most reprehensible sins" in rabbinic circles. Consequently, the leper questioned Jesus' willingness to heal him, a slanderer (*JQR* 71 [1980] 36).

"You can make me clean" (δύνασαί με καθαρίσαι). The verb (καθαρίζειν) can mean to declare one to be clean or to make one to be clean. The pericope itself suggests the latter meaning (cf. Cave, *NTS* 25 [1978–79] 246). Consequently, the man was requesting healing from his illness and not simply official recognition of his cleanliness, which was to come from the priest (1:44).

41 "Being angered" (ὀργισθείς). Choosing the more difficult reading (see *Note* c) over the better-attested one (σπλαγχνισθείς) leaves the problem of the meaning and cause of Jesus' anger. His actual "touching" the leper (1:41) disputes his being angered by the man's inconsiderate, defiling, disregard for the legal regulations by approaching him (cf. Rawlinson, 21–22; Schmid, 50; Burkill, *Revelation*, 38–39).

Some have sought to attribute this expression to the ritual agitation felt by the miracle worker (e.g., 1:41; 3:5; 7:34; 8:2; cf. 6:34 and 9:19; John 11:33, 38) as the miracle-working power stirs within one when confronted by the physical need (Bonner, *HTR* 20 [1927] 171–81; Schenke, *Wundererzählungen*, 136–37; Pesch, 1:144; Theissen, *Miracle Stories*, 57–58; Gnilka, 1:93). But the lack of uniformity of expressions makes this view unlikely and, despite the claim, none of these NT examples leave the impression of Jesus being taken over by or under the control of a spiritual power that vents itself in various ways.

If the anger was not directed at the man or his actions and if it does not play a formal role in the narrative, it must stem from the setting of the illness and what it represented as a distortion of God's creature by the forces of evil (Taylor, 188; Grundmann, 68; Schweizer, 58; Kertelge, *Wunder*, 67; cf. Cave, *NTS* 25 [1978–79] 246–47). A similar mood occurs in the healing scene of Mark 7:34 and in the face of death in John 11:33, 38. Therefore, Jesus' anger is a "righteous anger" that recognizes the work of the Evil One in the sick as well as the possessed (Kertelge, *Wunder*, 67).

"Touched him" (αὐτοῦ ἥψατο). Although touching frequently belonged to the healing ritual (see 1:31), one cannot escape the additional implications of touching a leper. Jesus' healing power overrode the defiling condition of the leper. He then confirmed this healing gesture with a healing word by repeating the man's request in the affirmative. "I do. Be clean!"

Jesus' healing goes beyond a simple priestly declaration of the man's ritual cleanliness (cf. Cave, *NTS* 25 [1978–79] 246–49). Consequently, the miracle points to more than a messianic high-priestly Christology (Grundmann, 69), it approximates to the work of God himself. According to Judaism, God alone can heal the leper or raise the dead (Str-B, 4:751). Furthermore, healing the leper and raising the dead were characteristic of the presence of the age of salvation (Matt 11:5 // Luke 7:22). Thus, the healing of the leper along with the exorcisms and healings of 1:21–39 sets forth Jesus' preaching and teaching as the good news about God's sovereign rule (1:14–15).

43 "Silenced him" (ἐμβριμᾶσθαι). This verb conveys a strong emotional response of displeasure or anger in the LXX and other NT usages (cf. *Note* d). Yet taken in this manner here, 1:43 would stand in tension with what has just transpired by introducing an unexplainable note of harshness on Jesus' part. Consequently, some have posited an underlying combination of more than one version of the story (Lohmeyer, 47), a doublet in 1:43 cf. 1:41 (Kertelge, *Wunder*, 68) or a redactional insertion in 1:43 in anticipation of the behavior in 1:45 (Koch, *Wundererzählungen*, 76–78). Furthermore, neither Matthew nor Luke carry this observation, although Matthew, who uses this pericope to *open* his collection of miracles in 8:1–9:38, does have a similar comment appended to his *last* Markan miracle (9:27–31 // Mark 10:46–52) in his collection (9:30–31; cf. Mark 1:43, 45).

In contrast to the other occurrences of ἐμβριμᾶσθαι, 1:43 and Matt 9:30 (under the influence of Mark 1:43?) offer no occasion for anger, personal agitation or even "prophetic frenzy" on Jesus' part. The anger mentioned in 1:41 at the illness or situation (cf. John 11:33, 38) would hardly carry over, since the healing has been completed. And, despite the subsequent failure of those healed to comply with Jesus' order for silence, one can hardly attribute his "feelings" in advance (1:43) to a premonition of their unruly behavior (1:45).

Jeremias, in harmony with the context, follows a suggestion by E. E. Bishop (*Jesus of Palestine* [London: Lutterworth, 1955] 89), and interprets ἐμβριμᾶσθαι as "oriental sign-language" for silence. This sign consisted of the placing of one's hand on the lips and blowing air in puffs through the teeth (*Theology*, 92, n. 1). Thus the verb would function somewhat like ἐπιτιμᾶν in 3:12; 8:30; 10:48 (e.g., Pesch, 1:145). The command in 1:44 (cf. Matt 9:30) would make the sign explicit.

Kee, however, has taken this verb in a more technical sense to be the equivalent of ἐπιτιμᾶν as an alternate rendering of the Hebrew גער, gāʿar (see *Note* d). Both ἐπιτιμᾶν and ἐμβριμᾶσθαι would then have the technical function in an exorcism setting of "subduing" the demon. The rather surprisingly harsh ἐξέβαλεν = "to cast out" would follow more naturally. If so, then 1:43 could represent a remnant of a variant tradition of the healing described in 1:41. We would then have traces of two "healings," one by touch and word (1:41) and one by exorcism (1:43).

44 "Say nothing . . ." (μηδενὶ μηδὲν εἴπῃς). The double negative emphatically prohibits the healed man from talking about what had happened. This secrecy command may have its closest formal parallel in the magical papyri in which a stereotyped silence command forbad the passing on of the effective formulas or actions used in a healing (e.g., Theissen, *Miracle Stories*, 68–69, 140–45, for extensive examples; cf. 5:43; 7:36). Thus it differed in purpose from the silencing of a demon inherent to the exorcism rite (see 1:25), and it may have belonged formally to the healing narrative (cf. Bultmann, 212; Koch, *Wundererzählungen*, 75; Schenke, *Wundererzählungen*, 132, who take this as redactional). In other words, we may find that the formal roots of Mark's "secrecy" motif, which now has its own theological function (e.g., 1:34; 3:12), extend to the traditional use of the silence commands form-critically in exorcisms and healings. In the one case, the silence command countered the demon's apotropaic use of the exorcist's name, and in the other the secrecy command prohibited the one healed from relating the healing process to others. At issue then is whether Mark found the command in the tradition or added it for his own purposes.

The strongest argument for the redactional character of this injunction stems from similar injunctions in 5:43 and 7:36 as well as the similarity between 1:44a and 16:8b. Yet the redactional character of the secrecy command in 7:36 is frequently posited but not beyond question (see *Comment* on 7:36). Furthermore, we have no lexical or stylistic basis for positing Markan redaction in 5:43 (see *Comment* on 5:43). And despite the similarity between "say nothing to anyone" (μηδενὶ μηδὲν εἴπῃς) and "they said nothing to anyone" (οὐδενὶ οὐδὲν εἶπαν) of 16:8b, it does not necessarily follow that Mark was responsible for both. Either or both could have been redactional. The imperative use of "see that!" (ὅρα) and the separation of the injunction (1:44a) from the contrary behavior (1:45a) by the demonstration for the priests (1:44b) suggests that the secrecy command may well have been in the tradition. It pertained to the miracle of the healing/cleansing.

Mark's own use of the secrecy motif, however, is much more complex and has often been related to a "messianic secret" motif. He uses the command twice with reference to the demons (e.g., 1:34; 3:12), three times in healing contexts (1:44; 5:43; 7:36 cf. 8:26) and twice with reference to the disciples (8:30; 9:9). The demons and the disciples are and remain silenced because they "know who he is," while two healing stories report a flagrant violation of the silence command (1:45; 7:36). This difference has led Luz to posit a "messianic secret" that remains a secret in the first case with demons and disciples and a "miracle secret" that cannot remain "hidden" in the second (Luz, ZNW 56 [1965] 9–30).

Apart from the question of Mark's "messianic secret," Luz's interpretation of the secrecy command in healing contexts has numerous weaknesses. First, Mark only has the silence command in three healing stories (1:44; 5:43; 7:36 cf. 8:26) despite numerous other healing accounts. Second, it is not clear that 1:44; 5:43 and 7:36 are the redactional products of Mark, especially the commands of 1:44 and 5:43. Finally, the presence of the silence command in 5:43 without the corresponding conduct of the parents and daughter to the contrary (cf. 8:26) as well as Jesus' instruction to the Gerasene demoniac to proclaim what had happened to him should warn against attributing such a pattern as found in 1:44–45 and 7:36–37 to Mark's understanding of a "miracle secret."

The contrary behavior given in 1:45a and 7:36b to the silence injunction may well show that Mark found the command as formally belonging to the healing narratives but understood it as an expression of Jesus' desire to avoid publicity. In the larger context of 1:40–44, Jesus left the crowds in 1:35–38 and in 1:45 they again stream to him as a result of the man's "preaching." The same is true in 7:36–37. Jesus leaves the Galilee area for the territory of Tyre in 7:24 wanting no one to know where he was. After healing the Syrophoenician, he travels to Sidon and then through the middle of the Decapolis where he heals the deaf-mute. Perhaps because of the Gentile setting, he seeks to avoid further publicity. The result, however, of their "preaching" is the four thousand of 8:1–9. Therefore, the "secrecy command" and its violation serves an ironic purpose for Mark to show the drawing power of the "preaching" of those healed.

"Show yourself to the priest" (σεαυτὸν δεῖξον τῷ ἱερεῖ). Without doubt Jesus had already "cleansed" the man (1:41–42). But he orders the leper to remain silent about the healing and to submit to the priest who alone, according to the Mosaic provision, could declare him "clean" (Lev 13–14). Formally, this action constitutes the demonstration of the healing. It appears to attest to Jesus' concern to comply with the Law.

"As evidence against them" (εἰς μαρτύριον αὐτοῖς). This concluding phrase must be read with the previous imperatives: "Show yourself . . . make the offerings commanded by Moses." But what is the nature of the evidence and to whom (αὐτοῖς) is it to be given? Some have rendered this phrase by

the dative of advantage as evidence of the man's healing for the priests or
the people with whom he is to resume living (e.g., Klostermann, 24; Lagrange,
30–31; Taylor, 190; Pesch, 1:146; Gnilka, 1:91). To this extent the phrase
explicated the formal function of the demonstration of the healing. But the
phrase has also been rendered as the dative of disadvantage as incriminating
evidence of Jesus' eschatological healing directed at the "unbelieving" (H.
Strathmann, *TDNT* 4 [1967] 503), the "priests" (van der Loos, *Miracles,* 489)
or as evidence of Jesus' concern for the Law against the "representatives of
the Law" (Kertelge, *Wunder,* 69).

The normal function of μαρτύριον with the dative to connote incriminating
evidence against a defendant (so H. Strathmann, *TDNT* 4 [1967] 502–3)
strongly supports that rendering here. That the phrase taken in this manner
introduces a polemical note to an otherwise straightforward healing apothegm
(Gnilka, 1:91) may only indicate a pre-Markan modification of the tradition
for this purpose. To find the antecedent of αὐτοῖς in the "unbelievers" reflects
too narrowly the influence of 6:11 on the interpretation of 1:44 (H. Strathmann, *TDNT* 4 [1967] 503) and to focus on the "priests" (van der Loos,
Miracles, 489; Schweizer, 58) limits unduly the plural (αὐτοῖς) in a singular
context (cf. τῷ ἱερεῖ, "the priest"). This phrase appears to underscore Jesus'
compliance with the Mosaic regulations in 1:44 despite his having healed
and "cleansed" the man by his touch and his word of healing.

Consequently, "as evidence against them" may well reflect a pre-Markan
context for a pericope whose roots may extend to Jesus' ministry and whose
preservation in the tradition not only bore witness to Jesus' eschatological
healing of lepers but also to Jesus' attitude toward the Law. Thus like the
Temple Tax (Matt 17:24–27) and the advice of Matt 5:23–24, this pericope
may have played a role in the early Church's struggle within Judaism. This
account, with Jesus' specific instruction to comply with the Law, offered "evidence against them" who accused Jesus of having disregarded the Law. Mark,
though the issue of Jesus and the Law was not his primary concern, took
this pericope from what may have been a collection of controversy narratives
and used it for his own purposes in 1:21–45. Thus its thematic relationship
with the controversies in 2:1–3:6 is more coincidental than redactional.

45 "But he departed" (ὁ δὲ ἐξελθών). This verse represents the formal
response of the healing narrative, but it may well have come totally from
Mark's redaction (Luz, *ZNW* 56 [1965] 15; Gnilka, 1:91; Koch, *Wundererzählung-
en,* 74–75). Mark does appear to use the missionary language of "proclaiming
many things" (κηρύσσειν πολλά, cf. 1:14, 38, 39; 3:14; 5:19–20; 7:36; 13:10;
14:9) and he likes ἤρξατο with the infinitive and the ὥστε-result clause (Pryke,
Style, 79–87, 115–18) that resumes the motif of 1:37–38 (Pesch, 1:146;
Schenke, *Wundererzählungen,* 144) with Jesus in the "uninhabited places" (ἐπ᾽
ἐρήμοις τόποις, see *Comment* on 1:35).

"To proclaim many things" (κηρύσσειν πολλά) along with "to spread the
word" (διαφημίζειν τὸν λόγον) that follows sets the healed man within the language and context of the early Christian mission as well as in line with Jesus'
own preaching (1:14–15, 38, 39; 3:14; 6:12; 7:36, etc.).

"The word" (τὸν λόγον). Mark uses λόγος to mean "the sum of the Christian
proclamation" (e.g., 2:2; 4:14–20, 33; cf. 8:32), and he may have taken it in

this sense here (Kilpatrick, *JTS* 40 [1939] 389–90; Luz, *ZNW* 56 [1965] 16; cf. Pesch, 1:146, n. 39).

"So that . . ." The result of the leper's behavior meant that Jesus could no longer publicly enter a city, but people sought him out in "the uninhabited places." Mark picks up the motif of Jesus' avoiding the crowds in 1:35–39 applicable to Capernaum and applies it now to all of Galilee. But he adds that the leper's preaching means Jesus cannot enter a city publicly. Jesus' authoritative ministry that opened in Capernaum (1:21–34) has now reached its zenith. Yet Mark's portrait of Jesus' ministry contains a subtle enigma. Whereas Jesus continues his ministry, moving from Capernaum to the other towns in Galilee (1:35–39) and eventually to the uninhabited places (1:45) where the people "continue coming to him from all around," his ministry and its "proclamation" receives such a response that he can no longer enter the cities publicly.

What is there about the cities, their leaders and/or their throngs of clamoring people (cf. 1:37) that Jesus shuns? Is it misunderstanding? conflict? or both? That Jesus' ministry entails conflict becomes explicit in the accounts of 2:1– 3:6. The stage is now set for the controversy narratives.

Explanation

This pericope, a classic healing story, most likely existed independently of the previous narratives. It lacks any temporal, local or personal ties with the preceding. It also contains a novel motif of conflict or judgment (cf. 1:44, "as evidence against them") arising from Jesus' ministry that may suggest a traditional setting among controversy narratives like those in 2:1–3:6.

Two elements stand out in the traditional story: (a) Jesus' healing of a leper and (b) his compliance with the Mosaic Law. First, as a healing narrative the account focuses on Jesus' healing a leper who in Judaism can only be healed by God, a feat comparable to the raising of the dead. Both the healing of the leper and the raising of the dead were to be characteristic of the age of salvation (cf. Matt 11:5 // Luke 7:22). Thus, the account portrayed Jesus' eschatological role in his healing.

Second, Jesus complies with the Mosaic Law by ordering the man to follow the legal procedures for reentering society. The phrase, "as evidence against them" (1:44) may suggest that the primary function of this pericope at one time in the tradition was to dispel the charge that Jesus had disregarded or set aside the Law. In other words, Jesus' compliance with the Law more than his healing of the leper (1:41–42) may have become the focal point of the narrative within the pre-Markan tradition.

Yet this account of Jesus' support for the Law appears to be in tension with the following controversy narratives in which Jesus' conduct conflicts with the Law (2:15–17, 18–20, 23–28; 3:1–6), conduct that could well have led to the charge of his accusers. The question of Jesus and the Law can best be handled in the respective pericopes as they occur. From this account, however, similar in thrust to the Temple Tax in Matt 17:24–27, one can deduce that Jesus did not disparage the Law or arbitrarily set it aside. He recognized the Law at least in its social function. Although the man had been healed and "cleansed" (1:41–42), the way back into Jewish society for the leper was by following the prescribed ritual. In this case, one might say that the Law recognized and facilitated God's work in Jesus. On the one hand, one can see that the Law had not become passé for Jesus; on the other hand, one cannot read this account as giving a blanket endorsement of the Law.

The evangelist has little interest in the question per se of Jesus and the Law in spite of its relevance for the pericopes that follow. For him the significance of this pericope lay in Jesus' healing of the leper and the response which he adapts for his own purposes. We have seen that the materials of 1:21–45 have at their core an earlier collection of units around a "day in Capernaum" involving teachings beginning with Peter's mother-in-law (1:29–31) followed by other healings in the evening and Jesus' departure from Capernaum (1:32–39). Mark expanded this material and set the tone of Jesus' authoritative ministry with a call for disciples in 1:16–20 and an exorcism (1:21–28) that displayed Jesus' unique, eschatological authority over the demons (1:27–28). He now concludes this material with Jesus' healing of a leper, a further indication of the eschatological character of Jesus' ministry as summarized in his preaching of 1:14–15 and recapitulated in 1:39. The eschatological significance of opening Jesus' work with an exorcism (1:21–28) and climaxing it with the cleansing of a leper (1:40–45) can hardly be coincidental. The evangelist has selected and located this pericope because of what it said about Jesus and his ministry.

This conclusion gains more support from the way he then modifies the response of 1:45. Not only does Jesus' work of exorcism and healing correspond to his word of teaching and preaching (cf. 1:21–22, 27, 32–34, 38–39) of the Kingdom (1:14–15) but in 1:45 the one healed himself becomes a proclaimer of the message. But the man's conduct in 1:45 stands in stark contrast with Jesus' specific order to "tell no one anything" (1:43–44).

The structure of the narrative prevents one from speculating about any failure to carry out Jesus' orders to go to the priest in keeping with the Law. The disobedience lies solely between Jesus' emphatic command to secrecy (1:44a) and the leper's spreading the matter (1:45a). Consequently, one might assume that he carried out the other orders sooner or later.

But why the apparently laudable disobedience? Perhaps the clue lies in the formal character of the secrecy command in healing narratives where these commands pertain to the means of the healing, which are not to be repeated or passed on. The man's conduct in 1:45 would then represent not so much an act of disobedience as the impossibility of Jesus' healings remaining hidden. Jesus' healing rather than the man's conduct becomes the thrust of the response in 1:45. This conclusion gains support from the concluding comment about the continued stream of people to Jesus.

Thus Jesus' ministry culminates in attracting many to him (1:32–34, 37, 45), but it also contains an ominous note. He left the crowds behind in Capernaum (1:38) and he now can no longer enter a city publicly (1:45). What was true of Capernaum becomes true for "all Galilee," the location of Jesus' public ministry. The very nature of Jesus' ministry reaches out to the needy. Yet it remains guarded (1:34) and contains the ultimate seeds of conflict which become evident in the accounts that follow (2:1–3:6).

G. The Healing of the Paralytic   (2:1–12)

Bibliography

Albertz, M. *Die synoptische Streitgespräche.* Berlin: Trowitzsch und Sohn, 1919. **Böcher, O.** *Christus Exorcista: Dämonismus und Taufe im Neuen Testament.* BWANT 16. Stuttgart: Kohlhammer, 1972. **Boobyer, G. H.** "Mark II.10a and the Interpretation of the Healing of the Paralytic." *HTR* 47 (1954) 115–20. **Branscomb, H.** "Mark 2:5, 'Son Thy Sins Are Forgiven.'" *JBL* 53 (1934) 53–60. **Ceroke, C. P.** "Is Mark 2:10 a Saying of Jesus?" *CBQ* 22 (1960) 369–90. **Dewey, J.** "The Literary Structure of the Controversy Narratives in Mark." *JBL* 92 (1973) 394–401. ———. *Markan Public Debate: Literary Technique, Concentric Structure, and Theology in Mark 2:1–3:6.* SBLDS 48. Chico: Scholars Press, 1980. **Donahue, J. R.** *Are You the Christ? The Trial Narrative in the Gospel of Mark.* SBLDS 10. Missoula: Scholars Press, 1973. **Dunn, J. D. G.** *Christology in the Making.* Philadelphia: Westminster, 1980. **Duplacy, J.** "Mc 2,10: Note de syntaxe." In *Mélanges bibliques redigés en l'honneur de Andre Robert.* Paris: Bloud et Gay, 1957. 420–27. **Feuillet, A.** "L'*exousia* du Fils de l'Homme d'après Mc. ii,10–28 et parr." *RSR* 42 (1954) 161–92. **Fuller, R. H.** *Interpreting the Miracles.* Philadelphia: Westminster, 1963. **Gnilka, J.** "Das Elend von dem Menschensohn (Mk 2,1–12)." In *Jesus und der Menschensohn,* FS A. Vögtle, ed. R. Pesch and R. Schnackenburg. Freiburg: Herder, 1975. 196–209. **Hay, L. S.** "The Son of Man in Mark 2:10, and 2:28." *JBL* 89 (1970) 69–75. **Hooker, M. D.** *The Son of Man in Mark.* Montreal: McGill University Press, 1967. **Hultgren, A.** *Jesus and His Adversaries: The Form and Function of the Conflict Stories in the Synoptic Tradition.* Minneapolis: Augsburg, 1979. **Janow, H.** "Das Abdecken des Daches (Mc 2,4/Lc 5,19)." *ZNW* 24 (1925) 155–58. **Jeremias, J.** "Die älteste Schicht der Menschensohn-Logien." *ZNW* 58 (1967) 159–72. ———. *New Testament Theology.* 1971. **Kelber, W.** *The Kingdom in Mark: A New Place and a New Time.* 1974. **Kertelge, K.** "Die Vollmacht des Menschensohnes zur Sündenvergebung (Mk 2, 18)." In *Orientierung an Jesus: Zur Theologie des Synoptiks,* FS J. Schmid, ed. P. Hoffmann, N. Brox, and W. Pesch. Freiburg: Herder, 1973. 205–13. ———. *Die Wunder Jesu im Markusevangelium.* 1970. **Kiilunen, J.** *Die Vollmacht im Widerstreit: Untersuchungen zum Werdegang von Mk 2,1–3,6.* Helsinki: Suomalainen Tiedeakatemia, 1985. **Klauck, H.-J.** "Die Frage der Sündenvergebung in der Perikope von der Heilung des Gelähmten." *BZ* 15 (1981) 223–48. **Koch, D.-A.** *Die Bedeutung der Wundererzählungen für die Christologie des Markusevangeliums.* 1975. **Koch, K.** "Messias und Sündenvergebung in Jesaja 53-Targum." *JSJ* 3 (1972) 117–48. **Kuhn, H.-W.** *Ältere Sammlungen im Markusevangelium.* 1971. **Lindars, B.** *Jesus Son of Man: A Fresh Examination of the Son of Man Sayings in the Gospels.* Grand Rapids: Eerdmans, 1983. **Loos, H. van der.** *The Miracles of Jesus.* NTS 8. Leiden: Brill, 1965. **Lührmann, D.** "Die Pharisäer und die Schriftgelehrten im Markusevangelium." *ZNW* 78 (1987) 169–85. **Maisch, I.** *Die Heilung des Gelähmten.* SBS 52. Stuttgart: Katholisches Bibelwerk, 1971. **Mead, R. T.** "The Healing of the Paralytic a Unit?" *JBL* 80 (1961) 348–54. **Osten-Sacken, P. von der.** "Streitgespräch und Parabel als Formen markinischer Christologie." In *Jesus Christus in Historie und Geschichte,* FS H. Conzelmann, ed. G. Strecker. Tübingen: Mohr, 1975. 375–93. **Perrin, N.** "The Creative Use of the Son of Man Tradition by Mark." *USQR* 23 (1968) 237–65. = *A Modern Pilgrimage in New Testament Christology.* Philadelphia: Fortress, 1974, 84–93. **Schenke, L.** *Die Wundererzählungen des Markusevangeliums.* 1974. **Schweizer, E.** *Lordship and Discipleship.* SBT 28. London: SCM, 1960. **Thissen, W.** *Erzählungen der Befreiung: Eine exegetische Untersuchung zu Mk 2,1–3,6.* Forschung zur Bibel. Freiburg: Echter, 1976. **Tödt, H. E.** *The Son of Man in the Synoptic Tradition.* Philadelphia: Westminster, 1965. **Tuckett, C.** "The Present Son of Man." *JSNT* 14 (1982) 58–81. **Vermes, G.** "The Use of *bar nash/bar nasha* in Jewish Aramaic." In M. Black, *An Aramaic Approach to* the Gospels and Acts. 3d ed. Oxford: University Press, 1967. 210–38. ————. *Jesus the Jew.* New York: Macmillan, 1973. **Weeden, T. J.** *Traditions in Conflict.* 1971. **Wrede, W.** "Zur Heilung des Gelähmten (Mc 2,1 ff.)." *ZNW* 5 (1904) 354–58.

Translation

¹ *When, after some days,*[a] *Jesus*[b] *had again entered*[c] *Capernaum, it was learned that he was in the house.*[d] ² *Many gathered so that there was no longer any room, not even near the door.*[e] *He began speaking the word to them.*

³ *And they came bringing to him a paralytic carried by four people.* ⁴ *Not being able to bring him to Jesus because of the crowd, they unroofed the roof where he was. After digging through, they let down the mat*[f] *on which the paralytic lay.* ⁵ *Jesus, seeing their faith, said to the paralytic, "Son, your sins are forgiven."*

⁶ *But some of the scribes were sitting there and reasoned in their hearts,* ⁷ *"Why does he speak in this manner? He blasphemes. Who is able to forgive sins except the One God?"* ⁸ *Jesus, knowing immediately in his spirit that they reasoned among themselves in this manner, said to them, "Why do you reason these things in your hearts?* ⁹ *Which is easier, to say to the paralytic, 'Your sins are forgiven,' or to say, 'Arise, pick up your mat and walk?'* ¹⁰ *But in order that you might know that the Son of man has authority to forgive sins on earth"—he says to the paralytic,* ¹¹ *"I say to you, 'Arise, pick up your mat and go to your house.'"*

¹² *He arose, immediately picked up his mat, and went out before them all, so that all were amazed and glorified God saying, "We have never seen such a thing."*

Notes

[a] δι' ἡμερῶν, a classical expression of time, meaning "through" a period of time. Best rendered "after some days" (BDF 223.1).

[b] Romanized words added from context.

[c] εἰσελθών introduces an adverbial clause with no direct syntactical relation to main verb (cf. ἠκούσθη), an anacoluthon or "broken construction" not uncommon in Mark (e.g., Taylor, 192).

[d] ἐν οἴκῳ has stronger support (P⁸⁸ B D L W Θ) than εἰς οἶκον (A C 090). Anarthrous construction may have implied "at home" or "in a house" known from the traditional setting of the pericope. In present context (cf. "again"), the phrase most likely refers to "Simon's house" in 1:29 (Taylor, 193; Pesch, 1:153, n. 5).

[e] χωρεῖν . . . θύραν literally: "so that not even the area near the door had room any longer." τὰ πρὸς τὴν θύραν is an accusative of reference with the infinitive.

[f] κράβαττος often a "poor man's bed" (BGD, s.v.) in contrast to the more common "bed" or "stretcher" (κλίνη).

Form / Structure / Setting

As to form, this pericope defies any neat classification along the lines of healing or controversy narratives. The pericope contains the basic elements of a healing narrative: (a) setting, including healer, the ill and the request for healing acted out, so to speak, by the extra effort needed to reach Jesus (2:4); (b) healing (2:5b, 11); (c) demonstration (2:12a); and (d) response (2:12b). Yet at the heart of the narrative lies a controversy between Jesus and the scribes over the issue of forgiveness of sins (2:6–10). But this controversy material, whose setting (2:5b) and resolution (2:10–11) are integral to the narrative and whose controversy lies in the unexpressed "reasoning" of the scribes, could hardly have existed as an independent narrative (cf. Hooker, *Son of Man*, 87). Thus most have considered the pericope to be an expanded healing miracle (e.g., Wrede, *ZNW* 5 [1904] 354–58; Bultmann, 14–16; Taylor, 191; Schweizer, 60; Pesch, 1:151–52; Gnilka, 1:95–96). By contrast, Dibelius (66–67) represents one of the few who see here a "pure" form, more precisely, a "pure type" of paradigm.

The multiple arguments against the pericope's integrity (see Maisch, *Heilung*, 29–39; Mead, *JBL* 80 [1961] 348–49; Klauck, *BZ* 15 [1981] 225–31) consist primarily of literary issues. Formally, the narrative fails to represent either a healing or pronouncement story. Stylistically, the vividness of 2:1–5, 11–12 contrasts with the abstraction of the debate in 2:6–10. Structurally, one can remove the content and characters of 2:6–10 without affecting the basic story, and the choral response in 2:12 appeals to the healing in 2:1–5, 11, with no response to the act of forgiveness. Syntactically, the change in persons in 2:10, 11 is awkward and unexpected. And in terms of content, two separate issues emerge: healing in 2:1–5, 11–12 and forgiveness of sins in 2:6–10.

The arguments for the pericope's integrity often begin with the thematic issue (e.g., Cranfield, 96; Lane, 97–98; Mead, *JBL* 80 [1961] 348–54). Theissen has even argued form-critically by noting that the statement of forgiveness (2:5b) corresponds formally to the assurance (*Zuspruch*) often found in healing narratives (*Miracle Stories*, 58, 164–65). This assurance anticipated but seldom directly introduced the healing. By virtue of its distinctive content here, it would have led to the intervening discussion (2:6–10). Thus the discussion and its resolution are germane to the healing story.

The question of form and integrity may well be unanswerable, but it pertains only to the history of the tradition. From the standpoint of Jesus' ministry as perceived by the early Church and by Mark, the question is moot. Clearly the Church perceived Jesus as one who healed the sick (e.g., 1:21–45) and offered his friendship to sinners (e.g., 2:15–17). Furthermore, the common association of sin and sickness (e.g., John 5:14; 9:2; cf. Ps 103:3; Str-B, 1:495; Kertelge, *Wunder*, 79) as well as the prophetic hope of healing and forgiveness indicating the age of salvation, all make the combination of healing and forgiveness within a single pericope quite understandable. In fact, the explicit combination of healing and forgiveness in this pericope is surprising only to the extent that the combination rarely occurs elsewhere in the tradition (e.g., John 5:14).

Consequently, this pericope makes a fundamental statement about the nature of Jesus' healing ministry. Healing the sick and forgiving the sinner represent a single issue after all. They both point to the eschatological character of Jesus' ministry that placed him in conflict with the religious authorities. In other words, this complex pericope offers a cameo of Jesus' ministry.

In terms of source, the major question concerns whether Mark found this pericope as part of a traditional collection or whether he selected this traditional unit and placed it here in his arrangement of the materials. Despite the frequent association of 2:1–12 with a traditional block of controversy narratives in 2:1–3:6 (e.g., Albertz, *Streitgespräche*, 5–16; Schmidt, 104; Taylor,

91–92, 191; Thissen, *Erzählungen*, 40; Hultgren, *Adversaries*, 151–54) or more recently in 2:1–28 (e.g., Kuhn, *Sammlungen*, 53–98, Dewey, *JBL* 92 [1973] 400–401, and *Debate*, 193), the redactional presence of 2:13 (14?), the rather formulaic use of καὶ γίνεται (2:15) to open a complex, the consistent use of controversy without any hint of miracle (cf. 2:1–12; 3:1–6), the same cast (Jesus, opponents and disciples), and the common motif of Jewish praxis pertaining especially to eating (ceremonial cleanliness, fasting, and Sabbath observances) suggest a more homogeneous combination of 2:15–28 in form and content (e.g., Maisch, *Heilung*, 112–20; Pesch, 1:149–51; Grundmann, 71–72; Gnilka, 1:131–32; Koch, *Wundererzählungen*, 52–55).

Furthermore, Mark's selection and location of this pericope focusing on Jesus' authority corresponds to his redactional activity in setting the opening pericope of 1:21–28 which also focuses on Jesus' authority at the outset of a "day in Capernaum" (1:29–39). This "authority" which raises questions about the capital crime of "blasphemy" (14:64) among the "authorities" anticipates the caucusing of the "authorities" in 3:6 to plot Jesus' death. Consequently, 2:1–12 continues the ministry depicted in 1:21–45 and introduces the resulting implications for conflict as they arise in 2:1–3:6 with hint of their ultimate results in 3:1–6.

Most have limited the evangelist's redactional activity to the setting in 2:1–4, which offers numerous possibly redactional elements. This activity merely supplied the setting for the pericope 2:1a and developed themes drawn from previous narratives (e.g., "Capernaum"—1:21, 33 cf. 2:1; recluse period—1:45 cf. 2:1; [Simon's] "house"—1:29 cf. 2:1; crowds "at the door"—1:33 cf. 2:2, 4, and speaking the "word"—1:45 cf. 2:2). Several exegetes (e.g., Kelber, *Kingdom*, 19, following Perrin, *Christology*, 88–89; Koch, *Wundererzählungen*, 49–50; Donahue, *Trial*, 81–82; Lührmann, 58) have recently attributed the insertion of 2:6–10 to Mark (cf. Boobyer, *HTR* 47 [1954] 115–20, and Lane, 97–98, who take 2:10 as an editorial comment for the reader). If Mark also inserted the controversy element in 2:6–10, the evangelist would then have been responsible for substantially altering the tradition. But the stylistic evidence to support this position is ambiguous at best (see *Comment* on 2:6–10 below). The weak link in the argument ultimately involves the function of the Son of man saying in 2:10 and the use of the "title" in Mark (see *Comment* on 2:10). Thus, Mark's redactional effort appears limited to the "seam" of 2:1–2.

Structurally, Dewey's rhetorical critical analysis of 2:1–3:6 led her to posit a tight concentric pattern in the five conflict stories (*Debate*, 67–74, 80–85, 89–94, 95–100, 101–4). The first (2:1–12) and fifth (3:1–6), second (2:13–17) and fourth (2:23–28) pericopes consisting of three structural elements and containing numerous other structural parallels between each pair contrast with the third and central pericope with two structural elements (2:18–22). The heart and focus of the concentric pattern in 2:18–22 is thematically related to the second and fourth pericopes through the motif of eating/fasting and to the first and fifth through the motifs of death/resurrection (*Debate*, 109–16). She attributes this construct to Mark's redaction based on similar constructions elsewhere (e.g., 1:1–8; 4:1–34; 12:1–40, *Debate*, 143–71).

Kiilunen, who critiques Dewey's suggested parallelisms between the respective pairs, accepts the concentric pattern but also poses the difficult questions of such a proposal (*Vollmacht*, 71–80). Was the writer as conscious, and thus as deliberate, of the detailed parallels as a modern exegete who meticulously examines the material? Was the reader so sophisticated as to discern these parallelisms? Most importantly, how deliberate or coincidental are the parallels in terms of the very nature and content of the stories themselves? In other words, could not this collection of material have come about without such a structural design? The answer determines the amount of weight one gives then to the structure in determining the meaning of 2:1–3:6 in Mark's narrative.

Kiilunen also finds a linear structure (a, a¹, b, c, c¹) in 2:1–3:6 (*Vollmacht*, 68–70). The first (2:1–12) is thematically paired with the second (2:13–17) through "sin/sinners"; the fourth (2:23–28) with the fifth (3:1–6) through the sabbath question. The third (2:18–22) comes into play because of the related theme of eating in the surrounding stories of 2:1–17 and 2:23–28. The thread running through all five is the increasingly aggressive role of the opponents (2:6 [inward], 2:16 [indirect], 2:18, 23 [direct]; 3:2 [calculated]).

As to setting, this pericope introduces a series of conflict scenes (2:1–3:6) that give expression to an adversarial motif latent to 1:35–38, 45. At the same time, the focus on Jesus' authority hardly appears to be coincidental to the Markan accent on Jesus' authority implicit in 1:16–20 and explicit in 1:21–28 which introduced 1:21–45. Thus Mark selected this introductory narrative to maintain the theme of 1:16–45 but to set it in a different key, one stated eventually at the conclusion of a comparable pericope in 3:1–6.

Comment

1 "Again into Capernaum" (πάλιν εἰς Καφαρναούμ). Mark frequently uses πάλιν at the outset of a pericope to refer to a previous place or event (e.g., 2:13; 3:1, 20; 4:1; 5:21; 7:31; 8:1; 10:1, 10, 32; 11:27). "Capernaum" (cf. 1:21) renames the setting for the events of 1:21–38 and "after some days" (δι' ἡμερῶν) bridges the time span of 1:33–45.

2 "Began speaking the word to them" (ἐλάλει αὐτοῖς τὸν λόγον). "The word" (ὁ λόγος) occurs throughout the NT as a technical expression for the primitive Christian missionary preaching (see BGD, *s.v.*), sometimes as "the word" (e.g., Mark 4:14–20; Acts 6:4; Gal 6:6; Col 4:3), "the word of the Lord" (e.g., Acts 8:25; 1 Thess 1:8; 1 Tim 6:3), "the word of God" (e.g., Luke 5:1; Acts 4:29, 31; Phil 1:14; Heb 13:7), or with an object ("the word of the Kingdom," Matt 13:19; ". . . of the cross," 1 Cor 1:18; ". . . of life," Phil 2:16).

With the exception of 1:45, "the word" in Mark always refers to Jesus' message (e.g., 2:2; 4:14–20; cf. 4:33; 8:32). In 4:14–20, 33 "the word" consists of Jesus' message regarding the Kingdom expressed "in parables" (Kelber, *Kingdom*, 33; cf. 1:14–15), but in 8:32 "the word in boldness" pertains to the coming passion (see 8:33). Given the contextual difference between 4:14–20, 33–34 and 8:32, one might well take "the word" here and in 4:14–20, 33 as synonymous with the summary in 1:14–15, namely, Jesus' message concerning the Kingdom (cf. Kiilunen, *Vollmacht*, 87). Thus Jesus' "word" in 2:2 correlates with his works in 1:21–45, expressive of the "gospel of the Kingdom," and sets the stage for 2:5–12. There is little evidence of a "secret gospel" preached by Mark's opponents (cf. Weeden, *Traditions*, 151).

4 "Unroofed the roof where he was" (ἀπεστέγασαν τὴν στέγην ὅπου ἦν). This clause stands as somewhat redundant to the following one. Schenke (*Wundererzählungen*, 152, so Gnilka, 1:97; Kiilunen, *Vollmacht*, 88) attributes this to Mark's redaction, since it supposedly refers to a western tile rather than an oriental thatched roof. Such a reading draws too heavily on Luke 5:19 (which refers to "tiles" but does not use this phrase!). Each phrase contributes vital information. The first indicates their presence on the roof (στέγην). The second notes not only how they "unroofed the roof," namely, by "digging through" (ἐξορύξαντες) but also that they "lowered" (χαλῶσι) the man into Jesus' presence (cf. Matt 9:2). "Digging through" specifies the mode of entry as well as the mud and thatch construction of a Palestinian roof (cf. Luke 5:19).

Although some have described the approach through the roof as a desire to conceal the building's main entry from the demon responsible for the illness (Janow, *ZNW* 24 [1925] 156; Böcher, *Exorcista*, 72; Schenke, *Wundererzählungen*, 152; Gnilka, 1:97–98), this pericope reflects no other signs of exorcistic influences (Kertelge, *Wunder*, 77).

5 "Seeing their faith" (ἰδὼν . . . τὴν πίστιν αὐτῶν). Formally the effort to reach Jesus functions as a nonverbal request for healing (Pesch, 1:158). Materially, however, these actions are designated as "faith" that becomes the basis for the subsequent assurance and healing.

Some would limit "faith" to the confident trust in Jesus' healing power (e.g., Taylor, 194; Pesch, 1:158), a trust or attitude—even when unexpressed (e.g., 1:29–31, 40–45)—that existed by definition in each healing miracle when one made an intentional effort to gain Jesus' help. Others define "faith" in such contexts more broadly and Christologically as being paradigmatic for true faith in the proclamation about Jesus. The passages would then give basis for and clarify faith in Jesus to those who hear them (Maisch, *Heilung*, 74–75; Gnilka, 1:99).

Both the broader and narrower definition fail to do justice to the use of "faith" in Mark's miracle stories. The noun or verb appears in four healing narratives (2:1–12; 5:25–34; 5:21–24, 35–43; 10:46–52; cf. 6:5–6a). It always involves actions that transcend human obstacles or limitations and cross social boundaries (crowds—2:4 and 10:48; futility and shame—5:26–27, 33; death—5:35). And in each case faith is seen in the actions taken to receive Jesus' help rather than on any specific Christological content. The woman's actions in 5:25–34 prove to be an expression of her "faith" and a paradigm for similar efforts by others in 3:10 and 6:56 to "touch" Jesus (see *Comment* on 5:34). Yet Mark's careful location of the story of Jesus' rejection in Nazareth after a series of healing stories shows that more than conduct was involved in healing faith (see *Comment* on 6:5–6a). Faith denoted an attitude expressed in conduct (cf. *Comment* on 6:6). Theissen (*Miracle Stories*, 132) has noted that faith (πίστις/πιστεύειν) preceding the miracle sets the NT miracle stories off from their counterparts where faith always follows the miracle.

"Your sins are forgiven" (ἀφίενταί σου αἱ ἁμαρτίαι). If one takes this construction as a divine passive (e.g., Jeremias, *Theology*, 114; Schweizer, 61; Pesch,

1:156; Grundmann, 76), Jesus declares that God forgives the paralytic his sins (similarly, 3:28; 4:12; Luke 7:47–48; John 20:23). Or if Jesus authoritatively declares that the man's sins are forgiven, he himself usurps God's prerogative to forgive sins. The latter reading corresponds to the ensuing controversy that peaks in the statement of the Son of man's authority in 2:10. Consequently, many have read this clause as part of the inserted section of 2:5b–10 (e.g., Bultmann, 14–15; Taylor, 191; Maisch, *Heilung*, 39–48; Koch, *Wundererzählungen*, 47; Gnilka, 1:96; Lührmann, 57).

As a divine passive, however, the statement would function formally as a statement of assurance (*Zuspruch*) integral to healing narratives (Theissen, *Miracle Stories*, 58–59; van der Loos, *Miracles*, 124, 443, n. 3; Fuller, *Miracles*, 50–51; Schweizer, 61; Kertelge, *Wunder*, 76–77). In such a case, this statement belonged to the healing narrative as a statement of encouragement. God forgives him his sin. Consequently, Jesus can and will heal him (Pesch, 1:156).

Problems arise with either reading. On the one hand, taken as a formula of assurance within a healing narrative, one must admit that a statement of forgiveness would be a unique expression of the assurance formula, the most common, though not exclusive, expression being "take heart" (θάρσει, so Matt 9:2). On the other hand, taken as an expression of Jesus' authoritative action and part of the complex of 2:5b–10, one is pressed to explain why the conflict section was added at this point in this pericope. To say that the close association of sin and sickness in Judaism sufficed (e.g., Gnilka, 1:99; Lührmann, 57) begs the question, since no other healing story gives rise to similar expressions. Thus, the very presence of 2:6–10 would seem to support the prior existence of 2:5b in the healing narrative (Pesch, 1:156).

Even if one were to take the word of forgiveness as a divine passive and integral to the original healing story (2:1–5b, 11–12), its meaning set in the context of Jesus' ministry would imply more than simply a formulaic word of encouragement like "take heart!" Although Jesus explicitly pronounces forgiveness on only one other occasion in the Synoptics and this with reference to a "sinner" (Luke 7:36–50, 48), his teaching often included figurative expressions of forgiveness (e.g., Matt 18:27, Luke 7:42; 15:5, 9, 11–32; 18:14) and his fellowship with "sinners" offers a material parallel to the forgiveness statement (Jeremias, *Theology*, 113–15). Furthermore, the stage is now set by this pericope for the following story in which Jesus' table fellowship with "sinners" (2:15–17) is explained in terms of his coming for both the "sick" and the "sinners" (2:17).

Healing the sick and forgiving the sinner correspond to the prophetic hope for the age of salvation. Thus, the pronouncement of forgiveness in this healing context makes explicit the fundamental character of Jesus' healing ministry (see Maisch, *Heilung*, 86–90; Klauck, *BZ* 15 [1981] 241–42). His healing, not limited to the symptomatic treatment of the illness, represents the wholeness of the new age (Matt 11:3–5 // Luke 7:18–23; see *Comment* on 7:37). Jesus' healing of the sick (2:1–12) like his exorcism of the demons (1:21–28) proclaims the "gospel of the Kingdom." This issue lies at the heart of the conflict between Jesus and the religious authorities.

6 "Some of the scribes" (τινες τῶν γραμματέων). The "scribes" (γραμματέων) appeared in 1:22 in the negative comparison drawn between Jesus' and their teaching. Without warning, they suddenly emerge in this scene to raise the question about his statement of forgiveness. They do so by "reasoning in their hearts" (διαλογιζόμενοι ἐν ταῖς καρδίαις αὐτῶν). Just as the formal request for healing characteristic of the healing narrative remained unspoken (2:4), so the formal question characteristic of the controversy narrative remains unspoken (cf. *Comment* on 2:16, 18, 23; 3:2).

"He blasphemes [βλασφημεῖ]. Who is able . . . except the One God?" The controversy opens with the scribes' charge of blasphemy based on Jesus' pronouncement of forgiveness (2:5b). Should the pronouncement have belonged to the earlier healing narrative as a word of assurance expressed as a divine passive, the question of 2:6–10 takes it as a declaration by one who had usurped for himself God's prerogative to forgive sins (e.g., Exod 34:6–7; Isa 43:25; 44:22). Accordingly, the "One God" (εἷς ὁ Θεός) probably reflects the wording of Deut 6:4 LXX with its emphasis on the singularity of Israel's God, an appropriate emphasis for this context. In other words, Jesus was not being accused of claiming to be God but of blaspheming against God by claiming to do what God alone could do.

The question accurately reflects the contemporary Jewish perception that the forgiveness of sins was exclusively God's prerogative. This was the consistent pattern of the OT and the intertestamental literature. Furthermore, no evidence has emerged to indicate that the Jews expected even the Messiah, regardless of how one defined this expectation, or any other eschatological figure, to have the right to forgive sins. Koch's finding Messianic forgiveness in the *Tg. Isa.* 53 (*Wundererzählungen*, 117–48) goes beyond the actual text of Isa 53. The Servant does make intercession for the sins of the guilty, but God alone forgives (*Tg. Isa.* 53:5–12, so Klauck, *BZ* 15 [1981] 238–39). The same obtains for the eschatological High Priest (e.g., *T. Levi* 18.9) whose pronouncement of forgiveness was bound up with the cult and sacrifices, as in the OT priesthood.

Of all the charges leveled against Jesus in 2:1–3:6, this one is the most serious, because the Law pertaining to blasphemy called for the death penalty (Lev 24:15–16) and it was invoked at Jesus' trial (cf. Mark 14:64). Yet the call for Jesus' death does not surface until 3:6 in the last of this series of conflict narratives. Thus the opening (2:1–12) and closing (3:1–6) narratives of this controversy section underscore the magnitude of the conflict.

One of the strongest arguments against the integrity of 2:1–12 lies in the difference between the pronouncement of forgiveness in 2:5b, expressed in the divine passive mode, and the implicit charge in 2:7, which becomes explicit in 2:10, that Jesus claimed for himself the right to forgive sins. Whereas the scribes might have questioned Jesus' right in 2:5b to pronounce forgiveness in God's name apart from the cult and without demanding repentance, or even to pronounce God's forgiveness of sins now rather than in the eschaton, their implicit charge does not arise from the divine passive of 2:5b. Rather it focuses on the issue expressed in 2:10, Jesus' usurping God's authority to forgive sins. The answer to the scribes' question, "Who except God . . . ?" is clearly, "the Son of man" (2:10). Therefore, the issue of 2:6–10 is thematically related to 2:5b (i.e., the forgiveness of sins) and perhaps occasioned by it but differs at its core.

7–8 Jesus knows, however, their reasoning "in his spirit" (τῷ πνεύματι). More than likely "his spirit" means "in himself" rather than a reference to the Holy Spirit, for which the context offers no support (Taylor, 196). Pesch (1:159) has suggested that by knowing their thoughts "in their hearts" (2:6) Jesus acts as a prophet in God's stead, since in the OT God is described as the "knower of hearts" (καρδιογνώστης: e.g., 1 Sam 16:7; 1 Kgs 8:39; Ps 7:9 [LXX 10]; Jer 11:20; Sir 42:18–20; cf. Acts 1:24; 15:8; Luke 16:15). Such a parallel becomes all the more interesting in view of the scribes' question in 2:6. He confronts them by directly asking, "Why do you reason these things in your heart?"

Donahue (*Trial*, 78–82, 141–43) has found a Markan redactional technique behind 2:6–8 and 2:9–10 which he has labeled "Marcan insertions." Accordingly, Mark has inserted important material into a passage on more than twenty occasions by repeating almost verbatim a phrase at the beginning and the end (2:6b, cf. 2:8b; 2:9b, cf. 2:11a). The second repeated phrase can easily be omitted, and Matthew and Luke alter the tautology. This would mean that Mark redactionally added at least 2:6–10.

While the repetition of phrases may indeed be a sign of the "insertion" of additional material into an existing unit, the example of 2:6–10 should warn against prematurely assigning this phenomenon to Markan redaction. First, the reference to the scribes' deliberations (2:6–8) based on Jesus' statement in 2:5 could hardly have existed as a free-floating traditional unit. Second, while the Son of man saying in 2:10 could have been a free-floating tradition, it hardly corresponds to Mark's more typical use of Son of man in a passion setting (see *Comment* on 2:10). Third, the repetition in 2:11a in the form of a command for the man to take up his bed is hardly formally or materially redundant. Fourth, a block (2:6–10) consisting of two "insertions" would seem to be awkward at best.

In this case, the repetition in 2:8b sets the stage for Jesus' counter in 2:9 (cf. 2:16, the next story!), and the repetition in 2:11a performs the healing and carries out the alternative posed in that counter (2:9b). We have little evidence that the repetitions betray a redactional hand at all. In fact, as Donahue has noted, repetition in language is a very common phenomenon in Mark (*Trial*, 143).

9 "Which is easier . . . (τί ἐστιν εὐκοπώτερον;)?" Jesus counters with his own rhetorical question, half of which picks up the word of assurance in 2:5b (forgiveness) and the other half picks up the word of healing in 2:11 (healing). This construction drawn from 2:5, 11 gives strong indication that 2:6–10 never existed as an independent traditional unit.

The context suggests that verifiability determines degree of easier/harder. One can verify the word of healing through observation, whereas the word of forgiveness cannot be empirically verified. Therefore, the word of healing (harder) being verified by observation would imply the validity of the word of forgiveness (easier) by reasoning from the greater (harder) to the lesser (easier). This is the argument implicit to the Son of man statement that follows.

10 "In order that you might know" (ἵνα . . . εἰδῆτε). This statement consists exclusively of a ἵνα-clause. Some have resolved this awkward syntactical construction by translating ἵνα . . . εἰδῆτε as an imperative: "Know that the Son of man . . . !" (Duplacy, *Mélanges,* 420–27; Lane, 97–98; Moule, *Idiom-Book,* 144–45). Hooker (*Son of Man,* 85) takes the clause as an ellipsis with a verb like γέγονεν supplied: "These things have happened that you may know. . . ." Yet neither alternative is necessary in view of the context. This statement offers a partial, verbal response to the rhetorical question of 2:9. The heart of the answer comes in Jesus' healing of the paralytic (2:11–12). Thus Jesus' command to walk (2:11; cf. 2:9b) gives the evidence for his statement of forgiveness (2:5b; cf. 2:9a), a demonstration to his audience of the Son of man's authority (2:10). Rather than an ellipsis, the action of turning from the scribes (2:6–10) to address the paralytic (2:10b–11) implies a nonverbal command to watch or listen to what follows. This is the significance of the narrator's almost parenthetic, "He said to the paralytic" (λέγει τῷ παραλυτικῷ, 2:10b).

"The Son of man" (ὁ υἱὸς τοῦ ἀνθρώπου). We meet here the first of fourteen occurrences of this designation in Mark. Twelve of the fourteen, however, occur after the episode at Caesarea Philippi (8:27–30), and both 2:10 and 2:28 in contrast to the other sayings express the Son of man's authority "on earth" in matters of God's prerogative (forgiveness of sins and the sabbath law).

Following Bultmann, the Son of man sayings have often been grouped into three categories: (a) present Son of man sayings, focusing on the earthly ministry; (b) passion Son of man sayings, focusing on rejection, suffering and death; and (c) Parousia or future Son of man sayings, focusing on the future coming in power and glory. Mark 2:10 and 28 belong to the first category, but the emphasis on "authority," a feature of the third category, in a context of controversy and hint of death ("blasphemy," 2:7; cf. 14:64; 2:20; 3:6) characteristic of the second category cautions us from drawing the lines between the categories too sharply (so Hooker, *Son of Man,* 180–81; Tuckett, *JSNT* 14 [1982] 70).

"Son of man" in 2:10 has received at least three major interpretations: (a) an Aramaic expression for humanity in general (Wellhausen, 15–16; C. Colpe, *TDNT* 8 [1972] 402–4); (b) an Aramaic circumlocution for "I" or the speaker (Bultmann, 15–16; Vermes, "Jewish Aramaic," 310–28, *idem, Jesus,* 160–91; cf. C. Colpe, *TDNT* 8 [1972] 430; Jeremias, *Theology,* 262); and most commonly (c) a Christological title, the "Son of man."

The first option supposedly based on the "usual" Aramaic meaning of the expression would mean that authority to forgive sins on earth had been given to humankind. Support for this interpretation comes from the crowds' response in Matt 9:8, ". . . they glorified God, who had given such authority to men," and from a similar usage in 2:28 taken in a parallelism with 2:27 (Wellhausen, 16). This view has found few followers because the context clearly focuses on Jesus and his claim of special authority (Bultmann, 15; Tödt, *Son of Man,* 126–27). Furthermore, 2:28 offers contrary evidence (see below, 2:28) and Matt 9:8 can hardly interpret 2:10 (cf. 2:12).

The second choice also stems from a supposed idiomatic Aramaic usage as a circumlocution for "I." "I have the right to forgive sins" (Bultmann, 15; Vermes, "Jewish Aramaic," 310–28; *idem,* 180). Although Colpe (*TDNT*

8 [1972] 403) and Jeremias (*ZNW* 58 [1967] 159–72; *Theology*, 261, n. 1) have questioned Vermes' philological basis for rendering the Aramaic expression as "I," their alternative for 2:10 has the same effect. While each wants to protect the more inclusive third person force of "a man," or "one" over the more exclusive first person "I" (similarly, Lindars, *Son of Man*, 44–47), their translation of 2:10 makes it clear that "Son of man" is a circumlocution referring to the speaker (Jeremias, *Theology*, 262: "But that you may know that (not only God in heaven but in my case also) a man on earth has the right to forgive sins." Cf. Colpe, *TDNT* 8 [1972] 430: "Not only God may forgive, but man too in me, Jesus"). In either case, Jesus would have made the claim for himself had he used the Aramaic [א]שנא רב, *bar 'ĕnāšā* (similarly, Lindars, *Son of Man*, 17–28).

The first two options operate with an underlying Aramaic expression stemming from the accepted fact that the Greek ὁ υἱὸς τοῦ ἀνθρώπου is an Aramaism. Part of the confusion over the designation arises from the possible Aramaic phrases and meanings. Yet the major confusion arises over the meaning of "Son of man" in the Greek-speaking communities. For example, ὁ υἱὸς τοῦ ἀνθρώπου in 2:10 within the context of 2:1–12 does not render an idiomatic Aramaic "humankind" (cf. ἀνθρώποις, Matt 9:8) or even a "man" (cf. ἄνθρωπος). Therefore, neither the first nor second option obtains for Mark 2:10 as it stands now in the Greek text. Here "Son of man" (ὁ υἱὸς τοῦ ἀνθρώπου) clearly refers as a self-designation to Jesus the speaker.

The third possibility takes "Son of man" to be a Christological title. The suggested content of this title, however, runs the gamut from a supposed apocalyptic, preexistent, heavenly being about whom Jesus spoke and with whom he later became identified to simply a phrase without any "messianic" connotations characteristically used by Jesus to refer to himself and preserved by the Church as Jesus' self-designation.

Assuming it to be pre-Markan, we can only conjecture about the earlier import of "Son of man" in 2:10. But the use of the phrase here and in 2:28 prior to Caesarea Philippi (8:31), the repeated use of "Son of man" in the passion setting (8:31–14:21) and the recurrent theme in Mark of Jesus' silencing those who might confess who he is (e.g., 1:25, 34, 44) indicate that the phrase or "title" had little of the apocalyptic import for Mark that "Son of man" supposedly had in the early Church. In other words, "Son of man" appears to be little more than a way for Jesus to refer to himself which the evangelist found in the tradition. To that extent, "Son of man" functions here quite similarly to the underlying Aramaic expression as suggested by Colpe, Jeremias and Lindars above, a circumlocution for "I" or the speaker (cf. Vermes, *Jesus*, 164–68).

"Authority" (ἐξουσίαν). Both 2:10 and 28 refer specifically to the Son of man's "authority" in areas of God's prerogative. Tödt has grouped these with four Q-sayings (Matt 11:19 // Luke 7:34; Matt 12:32 // Luke 12:10; Matt 8:20 // Luke 9:58; and Luke 6:22) which make implicit claim to authority by the Son of man on earth (*Son of Man*, 113–25). This verse, however, is the only specific reference to ἐξουσία in the group.

"To forgive sins" (ἀφιέναι ἁμαρτίας). The active verb (ἀφιέναι) agrees with the implied question in 2:7 but contrasts with the passive (ἀφίενται) of 2:5 and 2:9. Whereas the passive voice attributes the action of forgiveness to

God, the active voice in 2:7 and 10 makes clear that one besides God was forgiving sin. Therefore, 2:10 directly answers the question, "Who besides the One God?" (2:7), with "the Son of man." This verse provides the only direct statement that Jesus or the Son of man personally could or did forgive sinners (for Luke 7:47 as a divine passive, and 7:48–49 as a secondary expansion akin to 2:6–10, see H. Schürmann, *Das Lukasevangelium*, I. HKNT 3. [Freiburg: Herder, 1969] 440).

"On earth" (ἐπὶ τῆς γῆς) sharpens the contrast between God in heaven and the "Son of man" on earth. Jesus is not claiming to be God. He does not respond to the scribes' question by agreeing with their premise, "Who besides the One God." Rather he answers directly. "The Son of man" has authority to forgive sins on earth. He leaves his inquisitors to resolve how this might be or whether indeed it is blasphemy.

The emphasis on the Son of man's authority on earth in contrast to Mark's later emphasis on the Son of man's suffering and the two, isolated occurrences of this designation prior to Caesarea Philippi has led most to trace these Son of man sayings to pre-Markan tradition. But a growing number of interpreters are now assigning 2:10 to Mark's redaction.

First, several scholars have taken 2:10 to be an editorial comment directed at the Christian reader rather than as part of the traditional unit (e.g., Boobyer, *HTR* 47 [1954] 115–20; Cranfield, 100; Duplacy, *Mélanges*, 420–27; Ceroke, *CBQ* 22 [1960] 369–90; Lane, 97–98; Hay, *JBL* 89 [1970] 69–75). Apart from the absence of any indication in the text of such a change in audience from 2:9 and 2:10b, this verse would be the only example in the Gospels where "Son of man" would not be used by Jesus himself. Whereas such an exception may be possible, the absence of any indication of this being an editorial comment rather than the words of Jesus makes it most improbable. Furthermore, Son of man is also used in Jesus' response to the Pharisees in 2:28 and to the High Priest in 14:62.

Second, others have found a distinctive Markan motif behind the use of "Son of man" here. According to Schmithals (1:152–53), Mark was the first to apply the apocalyptic Son of man designation to Jesus and did so in the interest of his "messianic secret." By using an ambivalent designation meaning both "a man" and a Christological title "the Son of man," Mark indicated to the reader, who already knew, that Jesus was referring to himself when speaking of the Son of man. By contrast, Jesus' contemporaries simply thought he was speaking of a yet unidentified person, "a man." This view labors under numerous assumptions about the Son of man tradition and the Markan messianic secret. But its greatest weakness lies in its inability to account for the distribution and use of Son of man in Mark, especially the redactor's limited use of this designation in 2:10 and 2:28 prior to Caesarea Philippi when he was responsible for every other occurrence except 8:38; 13:26; and 14:62–63 (Schmithals, 1:153).

According to Perrin, the stress on "authority" corresponds to Mark's accenting of Jesus' authority in 1:16–3:6 (Perrin, *Christology*, 88–89; Kelber, *Kingdom*, 18–19; Koch, *Wundererzählungen*, 49–50). But one must again ask why "Son of man" was limited to just 2:10, 28 within this larger section, if the Son of man's authority is the key? More specifically, why is "Son of man" missing in 1:21–28 and 11:27–33 where the question of "authority" (ἐξουσία) is explicit

(Tuckett, *JSNT* 14 [1982] 66), not to mention the other pericopes where Jesus' authority is implicitly involved? Thus, the evidence for "authority" and the "Son of man" being distinctively Markan is meager at best.

According to Tuckett, the Son of man sayings in 2:10, 28 take their primary coloring from the controversy context of 2:1–3:6 (*JSNT* 14 [1982] 65–66; cf. Kiilunen, *Vollmacht*, 117–19, who combines motifs of authority and passion). The reference to blasphemy (2:7), the removal of the bridegroom (2:20), and the council to put Jesus to death (3:6) point so deliberately to Jesus' coming death that Son of man in this context corresponds with Mark's emphasis on the suffering Son of man in 8:31–10:45. Granted that 2:1–3:6 underscores the conflict between Jesus and his opponents, the primary characteristic, however, of the "Son of man" in 2:10 and 2:28 is undeniably his "authority." We have no immediate reference either in 2:1–12 or 2:23–28 to the suffering or even the rejection of the "Son of man." Any passion overtone comes from the context rather than from the immediate pericope. Thus, Mark's redaction may be seen in his use of traditions containing the "Son of man" references (e.g., 2:10 in context with 2:28) rather than in his composition of 2:10 and/or 2:28.

If Mark most likely found this reference to the "Son of man" in the tradition, where does it have its origin? Some would place the origin of the saying alongside of the expansion (2:6–10) of the healing story (e.g., Kertelge, "Vollmacht," 211; Schenke, *Wundererzählungen*, 157–58). But most have treated it as having been an independent logion adapted syntactically, to be sure, for this context (e.g., Bultmann, 130, 149–50; Tödt, *Son of Man*, 128–29; Gnilka, "Elend," 204–5).

Of those writers assuming that 2:10 was woven of the same cloth as 2:6–10, most assign the setting for the controversy to either the Church's debate with Judaism (Grundmann, 73; cf. Pesch, 1:161) or the early Church debates between the stricter Jewish-Christians who, like the Jews, relegated forgiveness to God's future action and the Christians who claimed the right to forgive sins now (Kertelge, "Vollmacht," 208–11; Kuhn, *Sammlungen*, 90–91; Klauck, *BZ* 15 [1981] 244; Ernst, 88–89; Hultgren, *Adversaries*, 108; cf. Pesch, 1:161). Accordingly, the Son of man's authority to forgive sins becomes the paradigm for the Church's healing and forgiving of sins.

Such an ecclesiological reading of 2:6–10 may reflect more the influence of Matt 9:8 than Mark 2:1–12 and fails to recognize the strong Christological emphasis of the latter (Dibelius, 66–68; Maisch, *Heilung*, 101–4; Gnilka, 1:101). The debate is between the scribes and Jesus. The question is "Who except the One God . . . ?" (2:7); the answer is "the Son of man" (2:10). Furthermore, the Church expressed forgiveness in Jesus' name (Acts 2:38), centered on his death (1 Cor 15:3; Gal 1:4; Rom 8:3; Matt 26:28; cf. Heb 9:22), and based its right to forgive sins, not on the model of the Son of man (Matt 9:8 being Matthew's redactional application, cf. Mark 2:12 // Luke 5:26) but on Jesus' direct command (Matt 18:18; John 20:23). The thrust, therefore, of 2:10 and 2:6–10 is primarily Christological, that is, it is a statement about Jesus.

The strongest argument for the saying's existence as an independent logion is its material parallels in 2:28 and Q (Matt 11:19 // Luke 7:34; Matt 8:20 // Luke 9:58; Matt 12:32 // Luke 12:10). Each of these sayings shares a common theme of the Son of man's "authority" in his ministry "on earth" (Tödt, *Son of Man*, 114–33), and each of these sayings can stand alone, apart from a context. Furthermore, as an independent saying 2:10 could easily have generated 2:6–10, given the context of 2:1–5, 11–12, while 2:6–9 does not need 2:10 to have Jesus counter the scribes' question. Perhaps, the rather clumsy transition in 2:10 betrays its giving rise to the setting (2:6–9) rather than the setting giving rise to the pronouncement (2:10).

Where might such a Christological statement about the Son of man's authority to forgive sins have found its setting, either as an expansion of the miracle story (2:6–10) or as an independent logion (2:10) since the content is the same? Some have focused on the theme of "authority" shared with 2:28 and the Q-sayings and have traced the roots of this "authority" to Dan 7:14 where the LXX actually refers to the giving of "authority" (ἐξουσία) to the Son of man (Feuillet, *RSR* 42 [1954] 171–75; Hooker, *Son of Man*, 89–93; Pesch, 1:160).

Yet the "authority" at stake in 2:10 pertains specifically to God's exclusive right to forgive sins. Since there is no other history-of-religions parallel for such authority, the roots of this specific authority doubtless go back to Jesus' own ministry in which he preached the coming of the Kingdom and shared table fellowship with sinners. In Tödt's words (*Son of Man*, 129): "Jesus' preaching of the coming of God's reign not only summoned men to turn round in repentance in face of this coming but also included the assurance of God's forgiveness. How else could entry into God's Kingdom be possible?" Even more indicative of Jesus' ministry was his acceptance of sinners into his fellowship. "The question whether or not Jesus himself expressly promised the forgiveness of sin is far less relevant than the fact that by his actions he has brought the forgiveness of sin as an actual event" (Schweizer, *Lordship*, 14). In other words, 2:10 and Matt 11:19 // Luke 7:34 are material parallels. For the Son of man to be a "friend of tax collectors and sinners" is for the Son of man to have the "authority to forgive sins."

Therefore, either as an independent logion or as a part of an expansion of a miracle story, 2:10 and 2:6–10 give explicit expression to what was implicit in Jesus' ministry. Jesus had the authority to forgive sins. Consequently, to the extent that the content of the saying concurs with the implication of Jesus' ministry, the question of whether the saying came from Jesus or from the Church is moot. The fact that Jesus does not personally forgive sins elsewhere in the Gospel tradition and indeed does not do so even in 2:5b (divine passive) may suggest that 2:10 refers more generally to Jesus' ministry to sinners, a ministry that created question and controversy with the "scribes" on numerous occasions. And whether Jesus' deliberate ministry to the sick and sinners (see 2:17) could have been expressed by him or by the early Church in the self-conscious statement of 2:10 depends ultimately on whether and how one attributes the use of "Son of man" to Jesus or the early Church (see Dunn, *Christology*, 87–92; cf. Tödt, *Son of Man*, 138–40).

It appears that Mark selected a pericope that originally consisted of a healing (2:1–5, 11–12) with a specific declaration of God's forgiveness (2:5b). An independent logion expressing the Son of man's authority to forgive sins (2:10), a motif implicit to Jesus' ministry and an irritant to the Jewish religious authorities, gave rise to a later expansion (2:6–10) of the miracle story (2:1-5, 11-12) with its reference to the forgiveness of sins (2:5b). The story became an expression of Jesus' ministry in miniature, a ministry to restore wholeness of body for the sick and broken relationships with God for the sinner. Yet it was the latter which created major conflicts between Jesus and the religious leaders, a theme reflected in the controversy of 2:6–10 and illustrated in the following pericope (2:13–17).

The issue of authority certainly stands out in reference to the "Son of man" in 2:10 and 2:28, a theme which Mark has highlighted at the outset of Jesus' ministry (cf. 1:21–28). But Mark's primary interest here lies in the resultant conflict occasioned by Jesus' claim to authority. The placing of this pericope into a larger controversy context of 2:1–3:6 with ominous references to Jesus' death (2:7; cf. 14:64; 2:20 and 3:6) does align the Son of man sayings materially with Mark's more characteristic use of them in 8:31–14:62. This traditional background and the unique coming together of the themes of authority and conflict may well explain why the only other occurrence of this designation prior to 8:31 occurs in this controversy complex (Tuckett, *JSNT* 14 [1982] 65–66).

11 "I say to you" (σοὶ λέγω) resumes the narrative of 2:5.

12 "All were amazed and glorified God" (ἐξίστασθαι πάντας καὶ δοξάζειν τὸν θεόν). The lack of mention of the scribes and the doxological response appear to refer back to the setting of 2:1–5 and the healing of 2:11. The conflict theme of the larger context (2:1–3:6) would hardly suggest that the scribes had been convinced by Jesus' response to their charge (2:6–10). Therefore, whereas the pericope centered upon a healing story, Mark selected the story in light of the controversy in 2:6–10 and—unlike Matt 9:8 cf. Luke 5:26—left the response unaltered.

Explanation

This story combines two motifs, Jesus' healing of a paralytic (2:1–5) and a question about his authority to forgive sins (2:6–10). The latter comes to a head in a Son of man saying (2:10). This dual theme may reflect two stages in the development of the tradition. The earliest stage consisted of a healing story involving a paralytic, his friends, Jesus, and the crowds. The second stage developed the former by concentrating on the Son of man's authority to forgive sin on earth and involved the scribes and Jesus. Consequently, the pericope uniquely combines Jesus' ministry of healing and forgiving.

As a miracle story certain elements stand out. First, the story is marked by the extra effort exerted by the four friends to bring the man to Jesus. Jesus acknowledges their actions not only as an unspoken request for help but as an expression of their faith (2:5). The context does not suggest any specific content of their faith except that Jesus could heal their friend (cf. 1:30, 32, 42). But this singling out of their faith corresponds to other Markan references to faith in healing settings where individuals have transcended human obstacles or limitations (5:25–34; 21–24, 35–43; 10:46–52). Therefore, at a minimum, faith in Mark is an attitude that issues in appropriate conduct.

Jesus addressed the man with an unusual word of assurance. Instead of the more common, "Take heart" or "Cheer up," Jesus announced, "Your sins are forgiven." By declaring that God had forgiven the paralytic his sins, Jesus makes two statements. On the one hand, the declaration points to the integral relationship of sin and sickness, a theme common to the OT, Judaism and even the NT (cf. James 5:15–16). Yet one cannot go so far as to see an implicit causal relationship (cf. John 9:2–3), since the actual healing comes later (2:11). On the other hand, the declaration makes clear Jesus' concern to bring wholeness to the person, not just a healing of a physical infirmity. Thus, his healing of the sick corresponds to his fellowship with sinners, and the expression of God's forgiveness is congruent with the healing of the body. Both elements were integral to Jesus' ministry and gave evidence that God's moment of salvation or wholeness had come (1:14–15).

The story concludes with Jesus telling the lame man to arise, take up his mat and go home (2:11). The healing given by a verbal command was then followed by its demonstration in the man's obedient response. Finally, the crowds break out in a doxology at what they have seen (2:12). In so doing, they focus attention on the nature of Jesus' work. Rather than expressing astonishment at Jesus or claiming some powers of deity for him, they attribute the event to God's work. This response correctly reflects the thrust of Jesus' ministry as one in whom God is at work in history, and it reflects the import of the miracle story as used by the Church to bear witness to this understanding of who Jesus is.

The specific reference to forgiveness in the healing story may have triggered the controversy about Jesus' right to forgive sinners (2:6–10). Whereas the divine passive, "your sins are forgiven," implies that God is the subject, the controversy between the scribes and Jesus revolves around "who except the One God" (2:7). This issue has its roots in Jesus' conduct with sinners and in his preaching of the coming of the Kingdom rather than in his healing the sick. That does not mean that the sick were not perceived by Jesus or their contemporaries as being sinners. We have noted above the close association of sickness and sin in Jewish thought, so the sick and sinner would naturally correspond. But Jesus' healing of the sick did not give rise to charges of "blasphemy" or of transgressing the Law. It was his friendship with "tax collectors and sinners" and his apparent offer of the Kingdom to those least "qualified" that brought the strongest charge from his opponents. This is the issue in 2:6–10.

The key verse, of course, is the Son of man saying (2:10). As an isolated logion, it along with the statement of forgiveness in the healing story (2:5b) might have given rise to the controversy section in 2:6–9. Together, 2:1–5, 11–12 and 2:6–10 affirm that Jesus both healed the sick and forgave the sinner and did so as the Son of man. All three elements have their place in Jesus' earthly ministry. It is seldom questioned that he healed the sick and offered God's forgiveness to the sinners through his fellowship (an indirect, if not direct, act of forgiveness). And the evidence seems overwhelming that he referred to himself as the Son of man.

Whether the origin of 2:10 and thus 2:6–10 lies in the teaching of the early Church or in Jesus' own ministry, this material certainly coheres with Jesus' ministry. The most the early Church could have contributed in reworking the tradition would be the explication of the implication of Jesus' ministry. Therefore, the miracle of healing and the statement of forgiveness attest to who Jesus is and the nature of his ministry. It offers a paradigm of Jesus' ministry to the sick and the sinners.

The evangelist's redaction is limited to his adaptation of the setting (2:1–2) to what has gone before (1:21–45) and to his selection and location of the pericope to introduce another traditional complex (2:15–28). On the one hand, the use of previous motifs (Capernaum, several days later, in a house, with crowds at the door) in 2:1–2 indicates the continuation of the ministry begun in 1:21–45. On the other hand, just as Mark used the exorcism story woven around the theme of authority in 1:21–28 to introduce a traditional complex (1:29–38), so he uses this pericope that focuses on the Son of man's authority to introduce another traditional complex (2:15–28). Just as Jesus appeared in a synagogue teaching the people (1:21), he is again in Capernaum "speaking the word" (2:2). In 1:44, 45 we begin to get hints of conflict or opposition when Jesus is no longer able to enter a city publicly, and this controversy emerges in the scribes' charge of blasphemy in 2:7. Ultimately, this conflict theme results in a consultation by the authorities of how they might put him to death (3:6).

The redactional location of this pericope at the outset of several conflict scenes makes clear that the dispute between the scribes and Jesus over the forgiveness of sins (2:6–10) was Mark's primary concern. That is not to diminish the force of the healing of the paralytic, but the question of "authority" and the controversy set the tone for what follows.

This context may also make intelligible the occurrence of "Son of man" in 2:10 and 28. While each underscores Jesus' authority, this authority runs a collision course with the "authorities" who reject the claim of Jesus' ministry. Therefore, the Son of man as seen in the larger context of 2:1–3:6 has very close ties to the suffering Son of man so characteristic of Mark in 8:31–14:21.

For Mark, this pericope continues Jesus' ministry of healing the sick but introduces the accompanying resistance to Jesus and his ministry. This opposition goes to the very heart of Jesus' work, his authority as the one preaching the "gospel of God" about the presence of the Kingdom, the "fulfillment of time." When the healing of the sick is combined with the forgiveness of the sinner, one is confronted by the question of who Jesus really is. He claimed to be doing God's work "on earth" (2:10), a claim that would eventually lead to his death (cf. 2:7 and 14:64).

H. The Call of Levi and a Feast with Toll Collectors and Sinners (2:13–17)

Bibliography

Bartsch, H. W. "Zur Problematik eines Monopoltextes des Neuen Testament." *TLZ* 105 (1980) 92–96. **Baumgarten, A. I.** "The Name of the Pharisees." *JBL* 102 (1983) 411–28. **Best, E.** *Following Jesus.* 1981. ———. "Mark's Use of the Twelve." *ZNW* 69

(1978) 11–35 = *Disciples and Discipleship: Studies in the Gospel according to Mark*. Edinburgh: T. & T. Clark, 1986, 131–61. **Betz, H. D.** *Nachfolge und Nachahmung Jesu Christi im Neuen Testament*. BHT 37. Tübingen: Mohr, 1967. **Carlston, C. E.** *The Parables of the Triple Tradition*. Philadelphia: Fortress, 1975. **Dewey, J.** *Markan Public Debate: Literary Technique, Concentric Structure, and Theology in Mark 2:1–3:6*. SBLDS 48. Chico, CA: Scholars Press, 1980. **Donahue, J. R.** "Tax Collectors and Sinners: An Attempt at Identification." *CBQ* 33 (1971) 39–61. **Dunn, J. D. G.** "Mark 2:1–3:6: A Bridge between Jesus and Paul on the Question of the Law." *NTS* 30 (1984) 395–415. **Hill, D.** *Greek Words and Hebrew Meanings: Studies in the Semantics of Soteriological Terms*. SNTSMS 5. Cambridge: University Press, 1967. **Hultgren, A.** *Jesus and His Adversaries: The Form and Function of the Conflict Stories in the Synoptic Tradition*. Minneapolis: Augsburg, 1979. **Jeremias, J.** *The Eucharistic Words of Jesus*. 2d ed. New York: Scribners, 1966. ———. *Jerusalem in the Time of Jesus*. Philadelphia: Fortress, 1969. ———. *New Testament Theology*. 1971. ———. "Zöllner und Sünder." *ZNW* 30 (1931) 293–300. **Kiilunen, J.** *Die Vollmacht im Widerstreit: Untersuchungen zum Werdegang von Mk 2,1–3,6*. Helsinki: Suomalainen Tiedeakatemia, 1985. **Kruse, H.** "Die 'dialektische Negation' als semitisches Idiom." *VT* 4 (1954) 385–400. **Kuhn, H.-W.** *Ältere Sammlungen im Markusevangelium*. 1971. **Lührmann, D.** "Die Pharisäer und die Schriftgelehrten im Markusevangelium." *ZNW* 78 (1987) 169–85. **Malbon, E. S.** "Τῇ οἰκίᾳ αὐτοῦ: Mark 2:15 in Context." *NTS* 31 (1985) 282–92. **Maloney, E. C.** *Semitic Interference in Marcan Syntax*. 1981. **Meye, R. P.** *Jesus and the Twelve*. 1968. **Neusner, J.** *From Politics to Piety*. Englewood Cliffs, NJ: Prentice-Hall, 1973. **Pesch, R.** "Levi-Matthäus (Mc 2,14/Mt 9,9; 10,3): Ein Beitrag zur Lösung eines alten Problems." *ZNW* 59 (1968) 40–56. **Schmahl, G.** *Die Zwölf im Markusevangelium*. TTS 30. Trier: Paulinus, 1974.

Translation

[13] *And Jesus[a] went out again by the sea. And all the crowd continued to come to him, and he continued to teach them.* [14] *As he was passing by, he saw Levi,[b] the son of Alphaeus, sitting at his toll booth. And he said to him, "Follow me!" Arising, he followed him.*

[15] *And it happened that, while dining[c] in his[d] house, that many toll collectors and sinners were dining with Jesus and his disciples, for there were many of them.* [16] *The scribes of the Pharisees also followed him.[e] And when they saw that he was eating with sinners and toll collectors, they began to say to his disciples, "Why[f] does he eat with toll collectors and sinners?"* [17] *When Jesus heard this, he said to them,* [g] *"The healthy do not need a physician, but those who are ill do. I did not come to call the righteous but the sinners."*

Notes

[a] Romanized words added from context.

[b] D Θ *f*[13] 565 *pc* it; Tat read Ἰάκωβον to align this disciple with the listing of the Twelve in 3:18.

[c] κατακεῖσθαι αὐτόν functions as a temporal expression in the Semitic idiom καὶ γίνεται . . . καὶ . . . συνανέκειντο . . . ("It happened that . . . ," Maloney, *Interference*, 85–86).

[d] αὐτόν . . . αὐτοῦ could have Jesus, Levi, or both respectively as the antecedent. Thus either Levi or Jesus could be the host. Most commentators, however, concur with Luke 5:28 (similarly Matt 9:10) that Levi was the host and thus the antecedent for at least αὐτοῦ (cf. Malbon, *NTS* 31 [1985] 282–92).

[e] Nestle[26] reads: 2:15 καὶ ἠκολούθουν αὐτῷ. 2:16 καὶ οἱ γραμματεῖς following B W sa[pt]. The

translation follows: 2:15 αὐτῷ καὶ γραμματεῖς τῶν Φαρισαίων; 2:16 καὶ ἰδόντες of ℵ L (Δ) 33 pc b bo^mss. Metzger (*Textual Commentary*, 78) argues for the former (cf. UBSGNT[1]), ἀκολουθεῖν used with "disciples" rather than for those "hostile" to Jesus. ἀκολουθεῖν, however, occurs elsewhere in Mark in a nontechnical sense of simply to follow or accompany Jesus (3:7–8; 5:24: 10:32; 11:9; 14:13, 54). Bartsch (*TLZ* 105 [1980] 94) argues that the later perception of the word as a technical expression of discipleship led to the textual revision above (cf. text variations in 3:8 and 10:32) and that the second reading actually has the stronger MSS evidence.

f ὅτι = τί or διὰ τί (cf. Matt 9:11; Luke 5:30), see BDF, 300(2).

g ὅτι = *recitativum*, see BDF, 397(5).

Form/Structure/Setting

The pericope's complex tradition history explains its form-critical complexity. We have a biographical apothegm or more specifically a calling narrative (2:14) and a pronouncement story in the form of a controversy narrative (2:15–17). Together the two forms constitute a controversy narrative thematically related through Levi's vocation as toll collector, Jesus' dinner companions (2:14, 16) and Jesus' purpose in coming to call sinners (2:17b, 14).

Mark clearly has taken over traditional material in this pericope. The only questions pertain to the extent and shape of the tradition. Whereas Dibelius (64, n. 1) assigned the calling of Levi to the tradition (2:14, 16b–17) and the meal setting (2:15–16a) to Mark, Pesch has limited the underlying tradition to the festive meal at Levi's house (2:15–17) from which Mark constructed the calling scene (2:14) along the lines of 1:16–20 (*ZNW* 59 [1968] 43–44; similarly Grundmann, 79; Dewey, *Debate*, 86–87; Dunn, *NTS* 30 [1984] 398; Kiilunen, *Vollmacht*, 133–34). Many, however, have attributed the call of Levi (2:14) and the meal (2:15–17) to two separate traditions (e.g., Lohmeyer, 54–55; Taylor, 201–4; Schweizer, 63; Gnilka, 1:104; Ernst, 94; cf. Cranfield, 101, and Schmithals, 1:165).

If Mark, as suggested above (pp. 82–83), added 2:1–12 to a previous collection of three controversy stories (2:15–28), he either developed 2:14 from the story in 2:15–17 or added it to serve as an appropriate transition to 2:15–17 which underscores Jesus' purpose in coming (2:17b). The common themes of eating, presence of the disciples, and Jesus' opponents in the three controversy narratives of 2:15–17, 18–22, 23–28 make it most likely that the complex began with the scene in 2:15 rather than a call narrative in 2:13–14. Furthermore, Mark's redaction is most apparent in 2:13 with its distinctively Markan terms and concepts.

The addition of 2:13–14 to 2:15–17 may well account for the awkwardness in the flow of the story line. As the pericope now stands, Levi responds to Jesus' call by arising and following him (2:14) but presumably to Levi's house (2:15). Yet after his call, he plays no further role in the story (2:15–17). Furthermore, Jesus' response to the scribes' question specifically mentions "sinners" (2:17b) rather than "toll collectors" or both. These difficulties disappear when one treats the two stories as separate entities (e.g., Lohmeyer, 54–58; Taylor, 201–4; Lagrange, 41–44; Lane, 99–107).

Structurally, 2:13–17 shares a parallel with 2:23–28 (Dewey, *Debate*, 212–14). Within the complex of 2:1–3:6, both these stories specifically include the disciples and each focuses on the questionable behavior of Jesus or the disciples regarding the Law. The topos is eating. Yet by prefacing 2:15–28 with 2:1–12 and adding the call of Levi in 2:13–14, Mark clearly seeks to underscore the motif of forgiveness in Jesus' ministry. Furthermore, by the appending of a second sabbath controversy in 3:1–6 to 2:23–28 the evangelist shifts the focus in the latter from eating to the sabbath per se.

As to setting 2.19–17 now continues the theme of Jesus' forgiving sinners from 2:6–10. As noted in 2:10, the Son of man's authority to forgive sins is materially related to his friendship and fellowship with toll collectors and sinners. Furthermore, both occasion questions from the "scribes" (2:7, 15/16).

Comment

13 This verse serves as a redactional seam. It includes the distinctive Markan terms (ἐξῆλθεν; cf. εἰσελθών in 2:1a; πάλιν, see 2:1) and themes (Jesus by the sea, crowds coming to him, his teaching them; cf. 1:21; 4:1). The seam provides a general transition for what follows rather than a specific background for the calling of Levi. That calling appears to be as abrupt as the calling of the four brothers (2:14; cf. 1:16).

14 The calling and response of Levi transpires with minimal details. Verbally and structurally this verse parallels 1:16, 18 (παράγων . . . εἶδεν Λευίν [Σίμωνα καὶ Ἀνδρέαν] . . . καὶ λέγει [εἶπεν] αὐτῷ, ἀκολούθει μοι [δεῦτε ὀπίσω μου] καὶ ἀναστὰς [ἀφέντες τὰ δίκτυα] ἠκολούθησεν αὐτῷ). Consequently, Pesch (*ZNW* 59 [1968] 43–45) has ingeniously suggested that Mark took the name Levi, which he found in the following story (2:15), and constructed 2:14 along the lines of 1:16, 17. Gnilka (1:104) disputes this, since nothing in 2:15–17 would suggest that Levi was a toll collector. Therefore, either the calling of Levi and the brothers reflects a stereotyped structure of a calling scene found in the tradition or Mark has adapted from the tradition an account of the calling of Levi to conform to the scene in 1:16–18 (Best, *Following Jesus,* 176–77).

"Levi, the son of Alphaeus." The name Levi for a disciple occurs only here and in Luke's parallel (5:27). The further specification, "the son of Alphaeus," suggests and the absence of other references to a Levi in the NT supports a historical reminiscence.

Matt 9:9 refers to the man as "Matthew" and Matt 10:3 has "the toll collector" after Matthew's name in the list of the Twelve. Many interpreters have explained this difference by following Lagrange's (42, so Lane, 100, n. 29) lead of assigning two Semitic names to the same individual (Levi/Matthew), although the practice of having a Semitic and Greek/Roman name (Saul/Paul, John/Mark, Simon/Peter) was the more common pattern. Pesch, however, has shown that Matthew carefully distinguishes between his use of ὁ λεγόμενος to give names, surnames, and titles to known persons (cf. 4:18; 10:2; 26:3; 26:15) and λεγόμενος to introduce a new individual (Matt 27:16; cf. Mark 15:7). The use of "a man named (λεγόμενος) Matthew," therefore, does not imply either that the "man" was well known or that he had a surname (e.g., Λευὶν τὸν λεγόμενον Μαθθαῖον / τὸν λεγόμενον Μαθθαῖον after ἄνθρωπον). Furthermore, Matthew closely aligns his list of the Twelve with the scene of their calling and thus the appositive, "the toll collector," in 10:3 (ZNW 49 [1968] 46–49). Pesch concludes, therefore, that the evangelist changed the names because of his desire to limit the disciples to the Twelve. That he chose Matthew from the list can be attributed to the role Matthew, the Disciple, played either for the evangelist or his community that eventually led to the title The Gospel according to Matthew (ZNW 49 [1968] 56).

But how did Mark perceive the relationship of Levi to the Twelve? Did Mark like Matthew take Levi to be another name for Matthew? Not only does Mark give no support for this, but Pesch has shown that Matt 9:9; 10:3 do not support this alternative. Could Levi have been James, "the son of Alphaeus," from 3:18, either according to the dubious Western reading or assuming Mark understood them to be the same person? Again this possibility lacks any Markan support. Some scholars, noting the irreconcilable differences in the lists of the Twelve in the Synoptics and Acts 1:13, have concluded that Mark carefully preserved the tradition behind 2:14 and assumed it to be somehow compatible with his view of the Twelve. Thus Mark attests to the limited and perhaps confused information in the early Church about the Twelve (Taylor, 202–3; Cranfield, 102; Meye, Jesus, 140–42).

More recently several have questioned the identity of the "disciples" and "the Twelve" in Mark (e.g., Betz, Nachfolge, 32; Schmahl, Die Zwölf, 113–14; Best, Following Jesus, 204; idem, ZNW 69 [1978] 11–35). This position appears to gain support from a Markan comment in 2:15c. Best (Following Jesus, 176–77) has noted the care which Mark has taken in his list of the Twelve (3:13–19). Peter was known only as Simon until the listing which mentions Jesus giving him the name Peter from which point on he is known only as Peter. Identifications in the list represent either names given by Jesus (e.g., Peter, Boanerges to James and John) or qualifications to prevent confusion (Simon the zealot, not to be confused with Simon Peter; James the son of Alphaeus, not to be confused with James the son of Zebedee). Thus Best concludes that Mark did not consider "Levi" to have been one of the Twelve (Following Jesus, 177). Kiilunen (Vollmacht, 134) supports this conclusion by noting two significant differences between the calling of the Four (1:16–20) and that of Levi. First, a comparable task ("fishers of men") is missing here. Second, Levi "arises" (ἀναστάς) whereas the two sets of brothers "leave" (ἀφέντες) their business and family respectively to follow Jesus. The Four had a distinctive calling.

Yet the almost verbatim parallel between the call of Levi and that of Peter, Andrew, James and John, who were of the Twelve, as well as the technical use of ἀκολουθεῖν to mean discipleship makes very clear that Mark understood Levi to be called to be a disciple. Mark makes clear to his readers that Jesus called a "toll collector," a "sinner," in the same way he called the Four (cf. 2:17).

"Toll booth." This rendering of τελώνιον reflects more accurately Levi's position and role in the tax structures of that day. Although Levi represents a group commonly known as "tax collectors," Donahue has shown that "toll collector" may come closer to identifying this group (CBQ 33 [1971] 42). In the first century, taxation was divided between "direct taxes" such as poll or head taxes, land taxes and "indirect taxes" such as sales taxes, custom taxes, taxes on transport and various tolls. The former were under the central authorities or rulers; the latter were farmed out to individuals. The term τελώνης applied to the latter group. Thus, Levi most likely sat at a toll booth along the roadside. One can only speculate about the kind of tolls he collected.

"Arising, he followed him" (ἀναστὰς ἠκολούθησεν αὐτῷ). Levi's response is expressed as a matter of fact, just as was his calling. Despite the succinctness of the statement, "to follow" (ἀκολουθεῖν) is pregnant with connotations in such a setting. Levi, a "toll collector," is called and responds to become a "follower" of Jesus. We find the same invitation in 1:16–20.

15 καὶ γίνεται often introduces a traditional narrative. This opening lends further support for beginning the traditional controversy complex (2:15–28) here rather than in 2:14.

"Dining" (κατακεῖσθαι) indicates reclining at the meal. The Jewish custom, according to Jeremias, was for people to sit down for their ordinary meals. They reclined on pillows or rugs only on festive occasions or when special guests were present (*Words,* 48–49). The context implies that Levi arranged a banquet to celebrate his call to discipleship.

"His house": αὐτοῦ is ambiguous meaning either Jesus' or Levi's house (see *Note* d). If the evangelist combined the call of Levi with Jesus' dining with toll collectors and sinners, then he may have added αὐτοῦ to what may simply have been ἐν τῇ οἰκίᾳ (cf. Matt 9:10). The drift of the pericope seems to point to Levi as the host. Thus, we have a material parallel to the Zacchaeus story in Luke 19:1–10.

"Toll collectors" (τελῶναι) is one of several "despised trades" listed in various places in the Mishnah and Babylonian Talmud (see Jeremias, *Jerusalem,* 303–12). Although they are often considered to have been despised because of the frequent contact with Gentiles in their line of duty and even at times considered to be "quislings" because of their cooperation with the Roman authorities, Donahue has shown that their reputation came more from their dishonesty (*CBQ* 33 [1971] 49–61).

The singling out of this vocation above all others and combining it with the more encompassing "sinners" may be appropriate in the context of 2:14, but an almost formulaic "toll collectors and sinners" most likely underlay the tradition in 2:15–16 (Kiilunen, *Vollmacht,* 15–56). It recurs in Matt 11:19 // Luke 7:34 and Luke 15:1. This prominence of "toll collectors" in the Synoptic tradition may reflect the high level of disdain for that vocation, but it most likely comes from a historical setting in Jesus' ministry that included the particular reference to "toll collectors" like Levi and Zacchaeus.

"Sinners" (ἁμαρτωλοί). Just as the formulaic character of "toll collectors and sinners" speaks against viewing τελῶναι as an addition to a story regarding Jesus' ministry to "sinners" (2:17b), the same applies to ἁμαρτωλῶν (2:16) as an addition to a pericope originally pertaining to "toll collectors" (so Pesch, 1:165; Schweizer, 64).

"Sinners" could refer to one of two different groups in Jesus' day. Specifically, it designated those who in terms of the OT lived an immoral lifestyle (murderers, robbers, adulterers, a more criminal element) or had a dishonor-

able trade or vocation (usually because of the dishonesty or defilement associated with the job). Generally, it designated all who failed from the Pharisees'
perspective to live according to the ritual law, the so-called "people of the
land" (עם הארץ, ʿam hāʾāreṣ). Since Jesus and his disciples fell in the latter
category and thus would hardly have been faulted for eating with similar
people, "sinners" here refers more specifically to people of ill-repute.

"His disciples" (μαθηταῖς αὐτοῦ) provides the first mention (46x) of "disciple"
in Mark. Their sudden appearance on the scene results from Mark's use of
a traditional block where the disciples play a key role (2:15–28). It is useless
to speculate about the identity and number of these disciples in the pre-
Markan tradition. For Mark, however, we can assume they would have certainly
included the Four called in 1:16–20 who accompanied Jesus during his "day"
in Capernaum (1:21–39). But did μαθηταῖς include even a larger group for
Mark? The answer depends on one's reading of the next couple of clauses.

"For there were many" (ἦσαν γὰρ πολλοί). Many follow the textual reading
that includes the next clause "and they were following him" (see Note e).
Taken together the two clauses stand in parataxis, as a Semitism in which
the second clause acts as a relative clause to the former (Taylor, 205). It
would then read: "And there were many who were following him." If one
were to take ἠκολούθουν technically as in 2:14, this reading would imply that
either Mark, who may be making a parenthetical comment (Taylor, 205;
Gnilka, 1:104), or the tradition envisaged a large group of disciples. The
stage would then be set for Jesus to call out a special group of Twelve (3:13–
19). But if ἠκολούθουν has the nontechnical meaning of simply to follow,
then these clauses might be a further explanation of the number of toll collectors and sinners and how they came to be at the meal (cf. Meye, Jesus,
142–45).

If we follow the reading of the translation and end the verse with "for
there were many," the γάρ-clause would appear to be a Markan comment
pertaining to the disciples. The toll collectors and sinners are already qualified
by "many" (πολλοί, cf. "many toll collectors and sinners"). What would then
be the significance of this comment but to indicate that Jesus had a larger
number of disciples than the Twelve? Consequently, Levi's call to discipleship
also fits with this larger circle of disciples for Mark (Best, ZNW 69 [1978]
32).

16 "Scribes of the Pharisees" (οἱ γραμματεῖς τῶν Φαρισαίων) represents
an unusual combination appearing only here in Mark. If Mark added 2:1–
12 to this context, he might have drawn "the scribes" (see Comment on 1:22)
from the setting in 2:6 and combined it with "the Pharisees" of this tradition
(Kiilunen, Vollmacht, 141). The Pharisees were one of the leading Jewish
religious parties alongside of the Sadducees and Essenes in Jesus' day. Their
roots are difficult to trace, but they appeared as a group by the second century
B.C., perhaps emerging from the Hasidim of the post-Exilic period. The name
itself apparently means "separatist" or "specifiers" (Baumgarten, JBL 102
[1983] 411–28). The name was doubtless descriptive of their attitude and
role in Jewish life, especially regarding ritual purity and the Law (see Comment
on 7:3).

Consisting of lay people from all walks of life, their focus was clearly on doing and teaching the Law of Moses. Accordingly they developed a "hedge" around the Law with their oral interpretation of it known as the "tradition of the elders" (see 7:1–13). This interpretation itself came to have the validity of the Law of Moses. After the fall of Jerusalem they became a dominant force in Judaism by rallying the people around the Law. This concern for the Law makes them the natural opponents of Jesus in these controversies concerning ritual purity, fasting, and the Sabbath laws.

"Were following him" (ἠκολούθουν αὐτῷ). This use of ἠκολούθουν (see *Note* e) simply informs the reader of how the "scribes of the Pharisees" came into this scene. It certainly has no technical implications of discipleship. Neither can one push this detail to the point of creating an artificial scene in which the Pharisees have "accompanied" Jesus so closely as to be in danger of defiling themselves (cf. Hultgren, *Adversaries,* 109). The story maintains its credibility by having them ask Jesus' disciples why "*he* was eating" (ἐσθίει).

"Seeing that he was eating with sinners and toll collectors" may be a secondary (but pre-Markan) addition to supply the basis for the ensuing question. The present context makes it rather redundant and the terms "sinners and toll collectors" are reversed, perhaps under the influence of Jesus' answer in 2:17b rather than the situation of 2:14–15.

"Why is he eating with toll collectors and sinners?" In contrast to the question posed in the minds of the "scribes" in 2:6, the Pharisees do voice their question but indirectly through the disciples. This is the second step in an increasing aggressiveness on the part of Jesus' opponents (cf. *Comment* on 2:6, 18, 23; 3:6). From the standpoint of the Pharisees, Jesus was doing that which was ritually defiling through disregard for the laws concerning table fellowship and clean and unclean foods. Neusner (*Piety,* 83–90) has pointed out the importance of these concerns among the Pharisees before A.D. 70. Part of the concern grows out of fear that one not only will be ritually defiled but also be morally contaminated by such company. Eating with someone had special connotations. "It was an offer of peace, trust, brotherhood and forgiveness; in short, sharing a table meant sharing life" (Jeremias, *Theology,* 115). Eating together created a special bond or fellowship through the eating of the broken bread over which the host had spoken the blessing (Grundmann, 82). Therefore, guests were selected very carefully.

The Pharisees raised the question of Jesus' behavior and more importantly they challenged his basis for such conduct. Jeremias notes that the tone of the question is more of a challenge to the disciples than a mere quest for information (*Theology,* 118, n. 2). For some this story reflects the debates within the early Church between Jewish and Gentile Christians over the issue of table fellowship, not unlike the scene in Gal 2:11–18 (e.g., Kuhn, *Sammlungen,* 94–95; Gnilka, 1:106). Others assign it to the debates between the Church and Judaism who accused the Church of taking into its fellowship the עם הארץ, *'am hā'āreṣ,* "sinners," rather than those concerned about doing the Law (e.g., Hultgren, *Adversaries,* 108). Yet both explanations ignore the fact that it is Jesus and not the disciples who is "eating" (ἐσθίει). Neither "toll collectors" nor "sinners" functioned in the early Church as a synonym for "Gentiles." The story serves best to explain the phenomenon of Jesus' ministry, his acceptance of the unacceptable even into table fellowship. This story not only explained why that was so in light of Jesus' coming, but the community used it doubtless to explain their own practice of taking into their fellowship people of ill repute.

17 Jesus responds with parallel sayings. The first takes the proverbial form of a metaphor concerning the healthy and the sick. The second is an "I have come" (ἦλθον-) saying in the form of a "dialectical negation" (Pesch, 1:166) concerning the righteous and the sinners. The first appears easily transmitted as an independent logion, and *2 Clem.* 2.4; *Barn.* 5.9 and Justin, *Apol.* 1.15.8, indicate that the second was used as an independent saying. Yet the metaphorical and thus generalizing character of the first saying and the specification of the second saying in context corresponds with a similar pattern in the following pericopes (cf. 2:19, 20 and 2:27, 28) and suggests that both were constituent parts of 2:15–17 from the beginning (cf. Bultmann, 92; Pesch, 1:166).

"Those who are well . . . those who are sick." This saying has numerous Greek parallels (e.g., Plutarch, *Apo. Lac.* 230–31; Diogenes Laertius, *Antisth.* 6.1.6), but the popular motif need not imply that the saying has its origins in a hellenistic community (e.g., Schweizer, 63; Hultgren, *Adversaries,* 110). Both its literal and metaphorical meanings certainly correspond to Jesus' ministry regarding the sick and the needy. This is particularly true of the broader context of 2:1–12 and 3:1–6. Healing the sick, forgiving the sinner, and offering table fellowship to toll collectors and sinners, all have the same significance in Jesus' ministry.

The syntax of this saying distinctively places the accent on the "patients" rather than the physician as a trait that typified Jesus' mission. The object of his concern was those in need. This was integral to God's promises for the day of salvation (e.g., Isa 61) and does not mean that the healthy were disregarded. God's concern and Jesus' concern was that all should be healthy. Unfortunately, some of the "healthy" showed their inherent "illness" in their attitude toward Jesus' ministry to the "sick." But until they recognized their need, they could not utilize the help of the Physician and thus excluded themselves.

"I did not come to . . . but to . . ." is one of two sayings in Mark specifically dealing with Jesus' coming (10:45). Bultmann (152–56) assigned all ἦλθον-sayings to a later stage in the tradition because they purportedly contain later reflections on Jesus' ministry. But there is no solid basis for disputing that this saying goes back to Jesus' ministry (cf. Carlston, *Parables,* 114–15). Its content is certainly congruent with his ministry as consistently depicted throughout the Synoptic tradition. Its structure as a "dialectical negation" is Semitic in keeping with OT counterparts (Kruse, *VT* 4 [1954] 385–400) as is the contrast "righteous" and "sinners."

Although some have interpreted the saying as being ironical (Lane, 105) or forged in polemics (Gnilka, 1:109), set in the form of a dialectical negation the statement simply accents the positive member of two counter-statements. In a dialectical negation one statement, often the first, is placed in the negative in order to accentuate the other (Kruse, *VT* 4 [1954] 386). Therefore, the import of the saying is found in the second statement about Jesus' coming to call sinners. One cannot place the same weight on the first half and thus conclude that he meant to exclude the righteous.

The "righteous" (δικαίους) like the "sinners" receives its meaning from the context. Some, consequently, have taken it ironically to mean, "all who think themselves righteous" (Klostermann, 130; Lane, 105). But this rendering would no longer stand in parallelism with the first saying ("those who are well" does not mean "those who only think they are well") and such a rendering has no other parallel in the NT (Hill, *Greek Words*, 130–31). If "sinners" refers to those in society whose lifestyle and conduct betrayed a broken and rebellious relationship to God (either in terms of the Mosaic Law in general or the specification of the Law by certain groups like the Essenes or Pharisees), the "righteous" referred to those whose conduct and lifestyle reflected a right relationship with God. Naturally, the lines were drawn depending on one's starting point. Unlike the Pharisees and the Essenes, Jesus, as far as the tradition indicates, never delineates where the lines are drawn. He simply makes use of the vocabulary at hand.

Jesus came to offer God's redemptive fellowship by announcing the coming of God's sovereign rule in history and "calling" all to respond. This invitation went to all to declare a time of wholeness and the establishment by God of a new relationship with those who respond to his action in history. Thus, the Kingdom in one sense includes all who are "well" and offers healing to the sick; includes all the "righteous" but invites the "sinners" to come into this new relationship. To that extent Jesus' ministry was all-inclusive. The shepherd did not dispense with the ninety-nine sheep when he sought and found the one lost sheep (Luke 15:3–7); nor did the woman discard the nine coins in favor of the one she found (Luke 15:8–10). Rather Jesus focused his ministry on reaching out to those aware of their need of God's redemptive activity in their lives. In the process, however, some of the "healthy" and "righteous" showed themselves to be less than whole and in need of a right relationship with God (Luke 15:25–32). Consequently, to the extent that Jesus' ministry was rejected by the "healthy" and "righteous" it was exclusive. But the accent of 2:17 is on the positive ministry to those in need.

Explanation

The story of Levi's call comes without any extraneous details. Levi, a son of Alphaeus, appears nowhere else in the NT and receives no further description either here or in the listing of the Twelve (3:13–19). Since the Church's tendency would be to use familiar names if creating such accounts, we can assume that the story has solid historical substance and addressed the singling out of "toll collectors" as a particularly reprehensible vocation of Jesus' companions (cf. Luke 19:1–10; Matt 11:19 // Luke 7:34).

The call of Levi would mean that Jesus' disciples included more than the circle of the Twelve. At the same time, Jesus' call of a toll collector to be a disciple illustrates the scope of his ministry, since this group was especially alienated not only from God but from their fellow Jews. They were known as "sinners" (Luke 15:7).

Thematically Jesus' eating with toll collectors and sinners had the same significance as his calling one to be a disciple. His table fellowship with sinners conveyed by action the forgiveness that was given verbally in 2:5. Therefore, his being a "friend of toll collectors and sinners" (Matt 11:19 // Luke 7:34) had a fundamental significance extending far beyond the question of friendliness. Just as his calling of disciples went beyond the normal rabbi/disciple relationship and as his healing the sick went beyond the symptomatic relief of their illness so his eating with the social and religious misfits meant more than a gracious acceptance of their hospitality. Each depicted the gospel of God's activity in calling together a new people of the Kingdom, the promise of wholeness of the age of salvation and the forgiving reconciliation of God with his alienated people.

This ministry moved inevitably on a collision course with those who expected God to act on a very different basis. The question or challenge of the scribes of the Pharisees echoes their consternation and condemnation. According to their expectation, God would act on behalf of the righteous rather than the sick and the sinners. Therefore, Jesus' twofold response to the question sharpens the point of difference. On the one hand, it draws direct attention to his intentional ministry to the sick and the sinners. Through him God was extending his redemptive activity of healing and forgiveness to the needy. The sick were being made healthy and the sinners were brought into a right relationship with God ("righteous"). On the other hand, to the extent that the "healthy" and "righteous" rejected Jesus' ministry as being God's promised activity for his own, they showed themselves to be the needy, alienated from the Father (e.g., Luke 15:25–32).

Mark's combination of the call of Levi with the story of Jesus' dining with toll collectors and sinners has a thematic correspondence with his previous redaction. By using a pericope that concludes with a reference to the "sick" and the "sinners," the evangelist picks up the theme of healing and forgiveness in 2:1–12. An aura of authority surrounds the rather abrupt call of Levi and his immediate response to discipleship similar in character and setting to the call of Peter, Andrew, James and John in 1:16–20; cf. 1:21–27, and the authority issue has just surfaced again in 2:10. Furthermore, Jesus' authority stands once again in relationship to the scribes (1:21–22; 2:6; 2:16).

The pericope as a whole sets forth Jesus' ministry of forgiveness as noted in 2:1–12 by focusing on the call of Levi, a toll collector, to discipleship and Jesus' table fellowship with toll collectors and sinners. The "call" of Levi in 2:14 explicitly illustrates the purpose of Jesus' coming to "call" sinners (2:17). Therefore, the thrust of this pericope is primarily Christological for Mark. Jesus and his actions remain at the heart of a story which answers the incriminating charge about his conduct toward those alienated from God and from his people. Jesus' conduct was commensurate with the purpose of his coming, namely, to heal the sick and restore the sinner. In this way, the story also illustrates the width of the circle of "disciples," a circle wide enough to include "toll collectors and sinners."

I. The Question about Fasting   (2:18–22)

Bibliography

Bacon, B. W. "Pharisees and Herodians in Mark." *JBL* 39 (1920) 102–12. **Braumann, G.** "'An jenem Tag' Mk 2,20." *NovT* 6 (1963) 264–67. **Burkill, T. A.** *New Light on* *the Earliest Gospel: Several Markan Studies.* Ithaca, NY: Cornell University Press, 1975. **Carlston, C. E.** *The Parables of the Triple Tradition.* Philadelphia: Fortress, 1975. **Cremer, F. G.** *Die Fastenaussage Jesu: Mk 2,20 und Parallelen in der Sicht der patristischen und scholastischen Exegese.* BBB 23. Bonn: Peter Hanstein, 1965. ————. "Die Söhne des Brautgemachs (Mk 2,19 parr) in der griechischen und lateinischen Schrifterklärung." *BZ* 11 (1967) 246–53. **Daube, D.** "Responsibilities of Master and Disciples in the Gospels." *NTS* 19 (1972–73) 1–15. **Dewey, J.** *Markan Public Debate: Literary Technique, Concentric Structure, and Theology in Mark 2:1–3:6.* SBLDS 48. Chico: Scholars Press, 1980. **Dodd, C. H.** *The Parables of the Kingdom.* 1961. **Ebeling, H. J.** "Die Fastenfrage (Mark 2.18–22)." *TSK* 108 (1937–38) 382–96. **Flusser, D.** "Do You Prefer New Wine?" *Immanuel* 9 (1979) 26–31. **Hahn, F.** "Die Bildworte vom neuen Flicken und vom jungen Wein." *ET* 31 (1971) 357–75. **Hultgren, A.** *Jesus and His Adversaries: The Form and Function of the Conflict Stories in the Synoptic Tradition.* Minneapolis: Augsburg, 1979. **Jeremias, J.** *The Parables of Jesus.* 1963. **Kee, A.** "The Old Coat and the New Wine: A Parable of Repentance." *NovT* 11 (1969) 13–21. ————. "The Question about Fasting." *NovT* 12 (1970) 161–73. **Kiilunen, J.** *Die Vollmacht im Widerstreit: Untersuchungen zum Werdegang von Mk 2,1–3,6.* Helsinki: Suomalainen Tiedeakatemia, 1985. **Kuhn, H.-W.** *Ältere Sammlungen im Markusevangelium.* 1971. **Kümmel, W. G.** *Promise and Fulfillment.* SBT 23. London: SCM, 1961. **Roloff, J.** *Das Kerygma und der irdische Jesus.* 1970. **Rordorf, W.** *Sunday.* London: SCM, 1968. **Schäfer, K. T.** "'. . . und dann werden sie fasten, an jenem Tage' (Mk 2,20 und Parallelen)." In *Synoptische Studien,* FS A. Wikenhauser. Munich: Karl Zink, 1953. 124–47. **Ziesler, J. A.** "The Removal of the Bridegroom: A Note on Mark II,18–22 and Parallels." *NTS* 19 (1972–73) 190–94.

Translation

[18] *And John's disciples and the Pharisees were fasting. And they came and said to him, "Why do the disciples of John and the disciples of the Pharisees fast but your disciples do not fast?"* [19] *And Jesus said to them, "The groomsmen are not able to fast while the bridegroom is with them are they?" As long as they have the bridegroom with them, they are not able to fast.* [20] *But the days shall come when the bridegroom will have been taken from them, and then they will fast on that day.*

[21] *No one sews a patch of unshrunken cloth on an old garment. Otherwise, the patch would tear away from it, the new from the old, and the rip would become worse.* [22] *And no one puts new wine into old wineskins. Otherwise, the wine would burst the wineskins, and the wine be destroyed and the wineskins.* [a] *Rather they put new wine into new wineskins.*

Notes

[a] Syntactically, this clause forms a second, contrasting element in the main clause (2:22a, c), leaving the middle clause as parenthetical (2:22b). The three clauses are rendered as sentences above.

Form / Structure / Setting

Set within a series of conflict narratives, one expects the form of a controversy narrative. The usual elements of setting, action, question and response appear in 2:18–19a. But the response continues in 19b–20, drawing on themes from 2:19a, and in 21–22 with two parallel constructed parables. Dewey has argued that rhetorically 2:18–20 form a symmetrical pattern of contrasts and wordplay but that 2:21–22 with its own rhetorical structure has no direct links with 2:18–20 apart from context and logical ties (*Debate*, 89–94). This conclusion would support the ancillary role of 2:21–22 to the specific controversy of 2:18–20. Once again, as in 2:13–17, we have here an expanded controversy narrative.

This complexity in form as well as the apparent tension in the content within the unit have led to numerous attempts to reconstruct a history of this tradition. The earliest component appears to have been 2:18b–19a, either reflecting a setting in Jesus' ministry or a saying (2:19a) with roots in Jesus' ministry. At issue was the disciples' behavior regarding fasting. This unit was then expanded and modified by the addition of 2:19b–20, supposedly reflecting the early Church's practice or struggle with the practice of fasting (Burkill, *New Light*, 41–42; Kuhn, *Sammlungen*, 71; Pesch, 1:171–74; Gnilka, 1:111–12; Carlston, *Parables*, 121–24; cf. Hultgren, *Adversaries*, 81). Whether 2:21–22 belonged to the earlier unit (Lohmeyer, 59; Schweizer, 67), was added to the earlier unit (Gnilka, 1:111) or to 2:18–20 pre-Markan (Burkill, *New Light*, 41–42; Kuhn, *Sammlungen*, 71; Pesch, 1:177) or by Mark (Bultmann, 19; Taylor, 212; Grundmann, 88; Roloff, *Kerygma*, 234; Hultgren, *Adversaries*, 82) is more difficult to say and depends to an extent on how one interprets each component.

Nearly all commentators assign at least part of this material to a pre-Markan collection of controversy narratives. Most also concur that tradition lies behind the material on fasting in 2:18–20 and the parables in 2:21–22. Mark's redactional role, however, either in constructing elements (2:19b, e.g., Schweizer, 65; 2:19b–20, e.g., Schmithals, 1:179; 2:18a, 21b, e.g., Gnilka, 1:112; 2:20c, e.g., Lohmeyer, 60–61) or in combining 2:21–22 to 2:18–20 is more debatable. In either case, three traditional parabolic sayings (2:19a, 21, 22) comprise the pericope as it now stands in Mark.

As to structure, 2:18 offers the setting and question to which 2:19–22 is the response. The response begins with a proverbial saying (2:19a; cf. *Gos. Thom.* 104) that is explicated in 2:19b–20. This response centers upon the themes of fasting, groomsmen and the presence/absence of the bridegroom. Then 2:21–22 concludes the response with two parables about old and new that are thematically and structurally parallel to each other.

The pericope lies at the core of a concentric pattern of the five conflict stories (2:1–3:6). Its relationship to the two surrounding stories (2:15–17, 23–28) comes through the common theme of Jewish praxis regarding eating/fasting. All three scenes focus on the presence of Jesus with his disciples and are based on the mutual accountability of master-disciple (see Daube, *NTS* 19 [1972–73] 1–15). With the addition of 2:1–12 and 3:1–6 and their passion overtones, the theme of the bridegroom's removal connects with the motif of Jesus' death, a motif that would be clear to Mark's readers during the time of the bridegroom's absence.

Comment

18 Fasting was a common rite in Judaism with roots deep in the OT. At times it was an expression of mourning for the loss of someone or something

(1 Sam 31:13; 2 Sam 1:12). More often it was an expression of contrition and penitence, a sign of repentance marked by the symbols of mourning (Matt 6:16). Combined with prayer, fasting was a statement of self-denial and self-humiliation depicting one as self-effacing and submissive to God's will.

"John's disciples" (οἱ μαθηταὶ Ἰωάννου, 6:29; Matt 11:2 // Luke 7:18; Matt 14:12; Luke 11:1; John 1:35, 37; 3:25) may offer a bridge between this pericope and the banquet setting of 2:13–17. It does shift the focus from Jesus' conduct in 2:13–17 to that of the disciples. It may suggest the historical context for the pericope and depict the contrast between the Baptist's and Jesus' ministry (Roloff, *Kerygma,* 228). The material counterpart in Q (Matt 11:16–19 // Luke 7:31–35) describes "this generation" as petulant children who refuse to play either to John's tune of asceticism or Jesus' tune of celebration. John's fasts were doubtless associated with his ascetic lifestyle ("neither eating nor drinking," Matt 11:18 // Luke 7:33, see *Comment* on 1:6) and corresponded to his call to repentance as a sign of penitence and humility before God in view of the coming Kingdom. Jesus' ministry by contrast was marked by festive meals ("eating and drinking," Matt 11:19 // Luke 7:34) and table-fellowship even with "sinners" (e.g., 2:13–17), in which those who followed him experienced God's acceptance and forgiveness, the blessings of the Kingdom.

"The Pharisees" (οἱ Φαρισαῖοι) shared in common with John's disciples the practice of fasting. In addition to the three major fasts in Judaism (the Day of Atonement, New Year, and a national fast for previous calamities, so Str-B, 4:77–114) and personal fasts expressing penitence and contrition by individuals, at least some Pharisees fasted twice a week, on Monday and Thursday (Luke 18:12; *Did.* 8.1). Consequently, John's disciples with their ascetic lifestyle marked by fasting and the Pharisees for whom fasting was an important characteristic of their piety provided a stark contrast to Jesus' disciples.

Yet some have viewed the reference to the Pharisees as indicating a shift of emphasis in the pericope that betrays a development in the tradition. Whereas the question raised by John's disciples was *whether* to fast (2:19a, Roloff, *Kerygma,* 225–29), the question raised by the Pharisees' fasts was *when* to fast (2:19b–20, Kuhn, *Sammlungen,* 61–72). Accordingly, "the Pharisees" and "the disciples of the Pharisees" would have been added to the pericope when it was modified by the addition of 2:19b–20 (see *Comment* on 2:20).

This reconstruction obviously depends on a particular interpretation of 2:18–20 that sets the Christian practice of fasting over against that of the Pharisees. The "Pharisees" may well be secondary but they could also have been added as the literary thread drawn from the surrounding conflict stories with the Pharisees when these controversy narratives were brought together as a collection (Taylor, 210; Schweizer, 67).

"They came . . . they said" (ἔρχονται καὶ λέγουσιν) may well have begun the narrative as impersonal verbs (Pesch, 1:171; Gnilka, 1:112). The indefinite subject assuming the absence of any immediate context would then have been "the people." Placed in the larger context of 2:15–28, the logical subject becomes "the Pharisees" or their "scribes" (2:6, 16; similarly 3:2, later identified in 3:6 as the "Pharisees"). Here and in the following pericope, Jesus' opponents come to him directly and confront him with their question (cf. *Comment* on 2:6, 16).

"The disciples of the Pharisees" presents an awkward moment, since the Pharisees were a religious party and technically did not have "disciples" (cf. Matt 9:14). While one might attribute disciples to the "scribes (rabbis) of the Pharisees," the preceding reference to the "scribes of the Pharisees" is too remote to be applicable for this phrase in 2:18b. Most likely the phrase suggests a secondary construction along the lines of "the disciples of John" and may only be a loose usage of μαθητής ("disciple") comparable to Matt 22:16 rather than an indication of limited historical knowledge about the Pharisees (e.g., Carlston, *Parables*, 118). One might also add the rhetorical force created by the parallel phrase "disciples of John/the Pharisees" in contrast to "your disciples" (οἱ δὲ σοὶ μαθηταί) as a consideration in the use of this phrase (Dewey, *Debate*, 90).

19 Jesus responds to the question in rabbinical style by posing a counter-question (2:19a). The question itself uses a wedding analogy to make the point. Then it is restated in the form of a declaration (2:19b). At issue, however, is whether the declaration simply restates the question and emphasizes the answer or whether it modifies the question and changes the basic thrust of Jesus' answer.

"The sons of the bridegroom" (οἱ υἱοὶ τοῦ νυμφῶνος) is a Semitic expression (literally, "sons of the bridechamber") meaning either "wedding guests" or "groomsmen." The repeated reference to the "bridegroom" supports the latter.

"While the bridegroom is with them" (ἐν ᾧ . . . ἐστιν) can mean symbolically "during the wedding festival" (Dodd, *Parables*, 116, n. 2; J. Jeremias, *TDNT* 4 [1967] 1103; *Parables*, 52, n. 14; Klostermann, 28; Kuhn, *Sammlungen*, 62; Nineham, 103–4; Gnilka, 1:114) or more literally the time period of the bridegroom's personal presence (Kümmel, *Promise*, 57, n. 123; Cranfield, 109; Carlston, *Parables*, 123–24). In other words, taken independently and metaphorically this secular proverb describes the conditions of the day of salvation in the imagery of a wedding feast. Taken contextually in 2:19–20, it is a parabolic saying with an obvious correspondence between Jesus and his disciples and the bridegroom and the groomsmen.

If one limits Jesus' response to 2:19a and attributes 2:19b–20 to a later modification, the metaphorical reading seems in order. Although no solid parallels exist in Judaism of a bridegroom = messiah identification (Jeremias, *Parables*, 52, n. 13; Carlston, *Parables*, 122, n. 33), marriage and wedding feast symbolism with roots in the OT imagery of Israel as Yahweh's bride did come into play in Jewish hope (J. Jeremias, *TDNT* 4 [1967] 1103). Consequently, the use of an aphorism involving a wedding celebration would be an appropriate expression for the age of salvation. "During the wedding festival" would then be a metaphor for "during the age of salvation."

This reading of 2:19a becomes more attractive when set against the background of "John's disciples" whose fasting doubtless reflected the ascetic lifestyle of the Baptist and signified their repentance and contrition in view of the coming Kingdom. Jesus' conduct and that of his disciples was more in keeping with the coming of the Kingdom and the presence of the age of salvation typified in their fellowship around a meal that even included unsavory company (e.g., 2:13–17). What John's disciples were fasting with view toward,

Jesus and his disciples were celebrating, namely, God's acceptance and forgiveness characteristic of the day of salvation. Joy and celebration rather than grief and mourning marked their lifestyle (cf. Matt 6:16–18; Matt 11:18–19 // Luke 7:33–34). Therefore, the focus of 2:18–19a would be primarily on the significance of fasting rather than on rules for fasting or not fasting. The contrast between the old and the new (2:21–22) could not be sharper (Schweizer, 65; Gnilka, 1:111).

Read in this manner the temporal clause does not accent a limited time period ("only as long as") but a time period itself ("during the bridegroom's presence"). It simply accounts for the disciples' disregarding of fasting practices during Jesus' ministry and may well reflect an original core of this conflict story with a setting in Jesus' ministry. What follows, however, in 2:19b–20 appears to jeopardize or at least modify this metaphorical rendering of 2:19a.

"As long as they have the bridegroom with them" (ὅσον χρόνον ἔχουσιν) makes a declaration and specifies the "while" (ἐν ᾧ) as the period of time (ὅσον χρόνον) of the bridegroom's presence. This statement appears to remove all ambiguity by accenting the temporal aspect of the bridegroom's presence and setting the stage for the prophetic statement of 2:20 referring to a future time of the bridegroom's absence. Thus, in light of 2:20 an allegorical identification of the bridegroom as Jesus in 2:19 seems unavoidable. Rather than a response in terms of the presence of the age of salvation, 2:19b explains the disciples' questionable behavior as temporary and dependent upon Jesus' presence with them. Accordingly, 2:19b qualifies Jesus' answer in 2:19a by focusing on the time of the bridegroom's presence and anticipating a time of his absence (2:20). The repetitive references to "fasting" (6x in 2:18–20) and the bridegroom's presence/absence (2:19a, b, 20) underscore this reading of 2:18–20. Furthermore, 2:20 moves the focus from the issue of not fasting to the affirmation of fasting when the bridegroom has been removed. Consequently, many have attributed at least the final shape of this controversy narrative to the etiological concerns of the early Church either to explain why they now fasted and/or when they did (J. Jeremias, *TDNT* 4 [1967] 1096; Burkill, *New Light*, 41; Kuhn, *Sammlungen*, 71; Pesch, 1:171–74; Gnilka, 1:112; Grundmann, 85; Schweizer, 67; Carlston, *Parables*, 121–24; Hultgren, *Adversaries*, 81).

20 Few would argue that this verse belonged to the earliest form of the pericope. The shift of emphasis from the presence to the absence of the bridegroom, from not fasting to fasting, and from a veiled to a more obvious identification of the bridegroom with Jesus all suggest a shift in theme from 2:19a (Roloff, *Kerygma*, 230).

"But the days will come . . ." (ἐλεύσονται δὲ ἡμέραι) introduces a temporal contrast to what has been stressed in 2:19 (cf. ἐν ᾧ ["while"]; ὅσον χρόνον ["as long as"]). Gnilka (1:115) notes that elsewhere this phrase "announces an eschatological event" (e.g., Luke 17:22; 21:6; LXX Jer 16:14; 19:6; 23:5; 28:52; 38:27, etc.) but hardly the period of the messianic woes when the messiah will be removed from his own, as suggested by Ebeling (*TSK* 108 [1937–38] 382–96) or Braumann (*NovT* 6 [1963] 264–67). Such an expectation finds no support in Judaism or in the NT (Kümmel, *Promise*, 76). Most likely this opening phrase simply contrasts one period of time (2:19) with another period and has no technical connotations apart from giving the statement a prophetic aura.

"Will have been taken away" (ἀπαρθῇ). The use of the aorist tense between the two future clauses indicates antecedent action (Schäfer, *Synoptische Studien*, 131–32; Roloff, *Kerygma*, 231–32) and accentuates the period of time after the bridegroom is removed in contrast to the time of his presence in 2:19.

At this point the allegorical application of the bridegroom to Jesus becomes obvious through the allusion to his "removal." First, in Jewish wedding custom the guests leave rather than the bridegroom. Consequently, the idea of the bridegroom being removed from the wedding scene comes as a jarring surprise. Second, this verb (ἀπαίρεω) simply mentions the "removal" of the bridegroom. But it may imply the use of force and may be an echo of a similar use of the verb in Isa 53:8 to refer to Jesus' death (Taylor, 211; Lohmeyer, 60). The motif of Jesus' death actually fits the larger conflict context (cf. 3:6) and would, therefore, be the first passion prediction in Mark. Furthermore, death, funeral and mourning would form a sharp contrast to bridegroom, wedding and joyous celebration, the very contrast at issue in 2:19, 20.

"Then . . . on that day." "Then" (τότε) underscores the temporal contrast and points toward the concluding "on that day" (ἐν ἐκείνῃ τῇ ἡμέρᾳ) which Matt 9:15 drops as redundant and Luke 5:35 changes to "in those days" (ἐν ἐκείναις ταῖς ἡμέραις) to correspond with the plural ἡμέραι of 2:20a. Obviously, Matthew and Luke took Mark's "on that day" as being synonymous with "the days will come" that begins the verse.

Many, however, have taken "on that day" to be distinct from "the days" of 2:20a. The more technical eschatological phrase of "that day" (ἐκείνη ἡμέρα, e.g., Matt 7:22; 24:36; Luke 10:12; 17:31; 21:34 cf. Zech 12:3–4, 6, 8–9; 13:1–2, 4, etc.) is irrelevant in this context (cf. Braumann, *NovT* 6 [1963] 264–67). And Kuhn rejects BGD's translation of ἡμέρα = "time" or "period of time" as lacking specific biblical and extrabiblical support (*Sammlungen*, 64–65). Therefore, a specific "day" has been sought, in particular a day having to do directly with Jesus' death such as the Quatrodecimens' Passover fast (e.g., J. Jeremias, *TDNT* 5 [1957] 902, n. 50), Good Friday (Lohmeyer, 59), Holy Saturday (before Easter, Rordorf, *Sunday*, 126) and a weekly Friday fast (Klostermann, 28; Burkill, *New Light*, 116; Kuhn, *Sammlungen*, 65–68; Haenchen, 116; Schweizer, 68; Pesch, 1:175; Ernst, 99; Hultgren, *Adversaries*, 81).

Kuhn rejects all suggested annual fast days because of lack of evidence before the beginning of the second century (*Sammlungen*, 68; E. Lohse, *RGG*[3] 4:1735). The weekly Friday fast would seem the most likely candidate for "that day" when the bridegroom was removed and the disciples returned to fasting. So the verse states that the days were coming when the bridegroom would be removed or killed and then, "on that day," Friday, the disciples would fast. Accordingly, the Church used this to justify a Friday fast as the Christian alternative to the Pharisee's fasts on Monday and Thursday. And this supposedly accounts for the controversy behind the pericope in 2:18–20 as it now stands. This would also account for the reference to the "Pharisees" and their "disciples" in 2:18 and the difference between the old and the new in 2:21–22 (Kuhn, *Sammlungen*, 69–72; Hultgren, *Adversaries*, 81). Therefore, from an earlier controversy narrative involving whether to fast or not (2:18–19a), we have a narrative that apparently centers upon the question of when to fast.

This interpretation of 2:18–20, however, suffers from several weaknesses. First, *Did.* 8.1 indicates that by the turn of the century the Church celebrated two weekly fasts on Wednesday and Friday in contrast to the Jews. One must assume that a weekly fast was expanded to a twice a week fast which diminishes the significance of Friday, the day the Lord died or the day the "bridegroom was removed." Second, neither Matthew nor Luke read Mark as specifying a particular day. Third, the aorist tense of ἀπαρθῇ indicates action prior to the main verbs, so that "the days/that day" refers to time after the bridegroom's removal rather than the day of his removal. Fourth, John 14:20; 16:23, 26 use "that day" in the same way to refer to the period of time after Jesus' removal/death (Roloff, *Kerygma*, 232, n. 101). Therefore, the shift from the plural "the days" to the singular "that day" does not necessarily mean a specification of a single day or anything other than what was intended by "the days that will come" in 2:20a.

Consequently, 2:20 picks up the motif of the bridegroom's presence from 2:19 and speaks of a time when he no longer is present. This temporal aspect could hardly be more pronounced ("the days will come . . . when . . . then . . . in that day") and structurally it centers upon the removal of the bridegroom. Consequently, 2:19 deals with the time of Jesus' ministry on earth with his own; 2:20 deals with the time when his personal presence has been removed.

"They will fast" (νηστεύσουσιν) contrasts to their not being able to fast in 2:19a, b. Does this imply, as has often been suggested, that the Church added this saying to the tradition of 2:19 to justify their fasting? Whose criticism would this verse answer? Hardly that of the Jews (cf. "Pharisees" in 2:18) who would have nothing against Christians fasting and for whom this Christological argument would carry little weight. Presumably, then, the force of 2:20 would only reach its mark when aimed at those in the early Church who mistook Jesus' response in 2:19a as a categorical rejection of all fasting (Burkill, *New Light*, 39–47; Carlston, *Parables*, 121–24). But given that possibility, what group and what context of the early Church would be involved? The antinomians would hardly have made use of 2:19 with its basis being the bridegroom's presence as an argument for dispensing with fasting. Even so, read in this fashion the double sayings that follow in 2:21–22 would have little point of contact with 2:19–20, unless the "old" has the greater value.

The larger context of 2:18–22 suggests still another way of interpreting 2:19–20 which focuses less on the issue of conflict (2:18) and more on the nature of Jesus' response in 2:19–20. If one takes 2:20 to be more a statement of the bridegroom's coming absence than a principle for fasting, fasting can play a more metaphorical role as in 2:19a. Whereas in 2:19a, "not fasting" at a wedding celebration was indicative of the joy of the age of salvation experienced in the company of the bridegroom, "fasting" in 2:20 becomes a symbol for the sorrow and mourning accompanying the loss of the bridegroom (Roloff, *Kerygma*, 233). The same theme occurs without the fasting symbolism in John 16:16–20.

In other words, whereas 2:19 is a statement about the presence of the new age embodied in the presence and company of the bridegroom, 2:20 is essentially a passion prediction of the loss of the bridegroom. The old and the new are mutually exclusive (cf. 2:21–22). Therefore, 2:19b, 20a change the focus of 2:19a but not the meaning. Both deal with fasting but more metaphorically than principally—the one with reference to Jesus' earthly ministry, the other with reference to his death.

21 The first of two parallel constructed parabolic sayings of folk wisdom regarding old and new items occurs in a different context and in inverted order in *Gos. Thom.* 47. The original context is obviously lost to us, but Hahn traces their roots to Jesus' ministry (*ET* 31 [1971] 357–75; cf. Carlston, *Parables*, 125–29). How and when they came into this context depends to a great extent on how one interprets the thrust of 2:18–20.

"No one sews a patch of unshrunken cloth . . ." states a maxim from everyday experience. No value judgments are made apart from the contrast in the cloth of an old garment and an unshrunken patch.

"Otherwise" (εἰ δὲ μή) introduces the hypothetical result.

"The new from the old" (τὸ καινὸν τοῦ παλαιοῦ) underscores the "new," mentioned explicitly for the first time, and the "old." Redundant and interrupting the flow of the sentence, this phrase may be secondary (Gnilka, 1:112; Hahn, *ET* 31 [1971] 362–63). Perhaps it is redactional reflecting a Markan emphasis on the "new" (καινός, see 1:27).

22 The saying regarding new wine follows the same syntactical structure as 2:21. It opens with a "no one"- maxim followed by the hypothetical results introduced by "otherwise."

"The wine is destroyed and the wineskins" (ὁ οἶνος ἀπόλλυται καὶ οἱ ἀσκοί) does bring a slight surprise, since according to the parallelism in 2:21b one would only expect the destruction of the wineskins. The mention of the wine as well as the wineskins may again indicate the absence of any value judgments favoring either the new or the old, since both have their value which is lost. Yet the destruction of the "new wine" may reflect the passion implications of 2:19–20, the "removal" of the bridegroom.

"Rather they put new wine into new wineskins" comes as an added statement that disrupts the parallelism with 2:21. This too emphasizes the "new" by referring to "*new* wine" (οἶνον νέον) and "*new* wineskins" (ἀσκοὺς καινούς) as well as by dropping any reference to "old wineskins" (cf. ἱμάτιον παλαιόν). This accent on the new may again be Markan and correspond to the additional comment in 2:21 and the description of Jesus' ministry as "new teaching" (διδαχὴ καινή) in 1:27.

How then do these parables relate to 2:18–20? For those who take 2:19b–20 to be the justification of Christian fasting, this contrast is somewhat blurred. The old and new would then correspond to the difference between Jewish and Christian fasting (Kuhn, *Sammlungen*, 71–72; Carlston, *Parables*, 128). Kee finds the context so incompatible that he treats 2:18–20 and 21–22 as separate units (*NovT* 11 [1969] 13–21). Such an extreme measure arises from his misreading of 2:18–20 as rules for fasting at odds with Jesus' teaching (*NovT* 12 [1970] 161–73).

If, however, the original conflict narrative focused on the contrast between the "disciples" of John and Jesus (Lohmeyer, 59; Schweizer, 67; Gnilka, 1:111–12) or even the "Pharisees" regarding fasting, the "old" and "new" order would correspond with these parabolic sayings. As such, these sayings could logically belong to the earlier traditional unit behind 2:18–19b. The later addition of 2:19b–20, perhaps occasioned by the negative consequences of 2:21–22, would also explain why the connection between 2:21–22 and 2:18–20 is so loose.

The contrast between the old and new certainly corresponds to the contrast between the conduct of John's and Jesus' disciples. For that matter, John's disciples and the Pharisees represent in their own way the hope of Judaism for God's action on their behalf. Their conduct has its roots deep in Israel's history. To that extent they represent the old. Jesus comes announcing the good news about God's action in history. He effects this in the experience of those who come to him in need and join him in fellowship.

The new, however, and the old do not mix. They are incompatible with each other. The "new" patch and new wine will destroy the "old" garment and wineskins. Thus, the point of correspondence between the parables and the import of 2:18–19a is this incompatibility of the new and the old orders. Consequently, 2:21–22 could have been added originally to 2:18–19a to illustrate the incompatibility of the old and the new. At the same time, this incompatibility becomes highly apparent when it leads to the bridegroom's death, a still later explication in 2:19b–20. As a result, the sayings of 2:21–22 now following 2:18–20 and the reference to the "Pharisees" in 2:18 underscore the passion prediction of 2:20 as a consequence of this incompatibility of the new and the old.

Therefore, one need not attribute the combination of 2:18–20 and 2:21–22 to Mark (cf. Bultmann, 19; Taylor, 212; Grundmann, 88; Roloff, *Kerygma*, 234; Hultgren, *Adversaries*, 81). Yet the additional comments in 2:21b and 2:22c reflect his emphasis on the "new" in Jesus' ministry that "tears from the old garment" and is "put into new wineskins," elements that enhance the passion motif of 2:19b–20. This passion emphasis corresponds with the capital charge of blasphemy in 2:1–12 and in the collaboration of the opponents to destroy Jesus in 3:1–6, two accounts added most likely by Mark into the controversy complex of 2:1–3:6.

Explanation

On the surface, the pericope has two parts, one dealing specifically with the question of fasting (2:18–20), the other consisting of two parables about old and new items (2:21–22). But a closer analysis reveals that even the first part has two different thrusts built around the same theme of a wedding celebration and the presence/absence of the bridegroom (2:18–19a; 2:19b–20).

The heart of the story most likely concerned the difference between the lifestyles of John's and Jesus' disciples (2:18b–19a). We have a material parallel in Q comparing the reaction of the public to Jesus and John (Matt 11:16–19 // Luke 7:31–35). John's disciples fasted as a way of life commensurate with his preaching of repentance. Consequently, the use of the wedding celebration would offer a stark contrast to the ascetic lifestyle of John's disciples. The reference to the Pharisees (2:18), who fasted as a part of their ritual concern for piety before God, most likely came from the context of 2:13–17 and 2:23–28 at the time when these stories were combined. This addition was possible since the Pharisees fasted, as did John's disciples, and thus stood in contrast to Jesus' disciples.

Jesus' response (2:19a) to the question about his disciples' behavior makes use of a common symbol for the age of salvation in Judaism, the wedding celebration. But by comparing the disciples' conduct with that of the groomsmen in the presence of the bridegroom, the story claims the presence of the age of salvation, God's promised redemptive activity, in Jesus' person and ministry. At the same time, since the bridegroom-messiah typology does not appear to have been current in Judaism, this claim of the presence of the eschaton is somewhat veiled. The metaphorical use of the wedding scene as figurative for the age of salvation makes the claim possible but uncertain for the audience.

Yet the analogy clarifies the significant contrast between the lifestyle of John's disciples and Jesus'. John came preaching repentance and a lifestyle befitting repentance before God in view of the coming judgment. So fasting by his disciples represented the posture of anticipation expressed in symbols of mourning and penitence. Jesus came preaching the good news of God's action in history on behalf of the needy. Through his person and ministry God was at work bringing wholeness to the broken and forgiveness to the wayward. This is epitomized in his ministry to the sick and his table fellowship with the sinners. Consequently, the wedding celebration with its expression of joy represented the presence of the new day of God's redemptive activity in the person and ministry of Jesus. Thus fasting as a lifestyle for those in Jesus' company would have been as inappropriate as sewing a patch of new cloth on an old garment or pouring new wine into old wineskins (2:21–22). It is no wonder that the meal became the symbol of Christian fellowship for the Church, both in respect to the presence of our Lord and in anticipation of the ultimate wedding feast of the Lamb.

The stress on the bridegroom's presence contained within the analogy the possibility of his absence. The stage is set in 2:19b for the temporal limits of his presence, and 2:20 speaks of the coming days of his absence. When the bridegroom has been removed, then his companions will fast. But if the import of 2:19a was not primarily with fasting per se but as an expression of a lifestyle that was incompatible with the joy of the age of salvation, fasting in 2:20 may also have a metaphorical function of expressing the sorrow and mourning that will accompany the removal of the bridegroom from their presence (see John 16:16–20). Understood in this manner, 2:20 would be the first hint in Mark of the coming death of the "bridegroom" as seen in the companions' future fasting in mourning.

In making this shift from focusing on the presence of the age of salvation in Jesus' ministry in 2:19a to focusing on the coming death of the bridegroom (2:20), one need not conclude that the age of salvation would then have ended with the death of the bridegroom. That would only be a logical necessity if 2:19b–20 were of the same cloth as 2:18–19a. In 2:19a the emphasis is on the presence of the age of salvation in and through Jesus' ministry. In 2:20 we have a later development not of that particular theme but of the temporal element in 2:19a ("while") that led to a statement about "when" the bridegroom would be removed.

In other words, fasting from the standpoint of John's disciples in 2:18–19a refers to a lifestyle that contrasts with that of Jesus' disciples. Fasting in 2:19b–20 refers to the mourning that accompanies the loss of a loved one and contrasts with the celebration of wedding guests. The issue is no longer the question of the presence of the age of salvation (the question in 2:18–19a). The story now (2:18–20) contrasts the joy of being with Jesus with the mourning that accompanies his death. The pericope has become essentially a passion prediction and this may explain its place in this collection of controversy narratives.

The concluding parables (2:21–22) about new and old make no value judgments about either. The theme of each is the incompatibility and thus impossibility of combining the new with the old. This theme corresponds directly to Jesus' response to the question about fasting in 2:19a. John and his disciples represented the old order. Fasting and wedding celebrations just do not go together. Regardless of the original context for these parables, their point would have been the same and their use by Jesus in similar context most likely. And it may well be that these sayings were combined with 2:18b–19a before the addition of 2:19b–20. In either case, the destructive consequence of trying to combine unshrunk cloth and an old garment and new wine and old wineskins parallels the consequence of the incompatibility of Jesus' ministry with that of his opponents. It led to the removal of the bridegroom and mourning.

Mark's own contribution to this section is minimal. Yet he may well have added the comments "the new from the old" in 2:21 and "new wine into new wineskins" in 2:22. This emphasis on the "new" corresponds with his depiction of Jesus' teaching with authority in 1:27 that is implicit to 2:18–20.

The thrust of this pericope is clearly Christological, despite all attempts to take the story etiologically for the Church's practice of fasting. The nature of Jesus' ministry sets implicit claim to the presence of something new, the new age of salvation. This claim is not only evident in his eating with toll collectors and sinners (2:13–17), his healing the sick (2:1–12) but even in the lifestyle of his disciples. This theme continues in the following story of their behavior on the Sabbath.

J. Reaping on the Sabbath (2:23–28)

Bibliography

Abrahams, I. *Studies in Pharisaism and the Gospels.* First Series. Cambridge: University Press, 1917. 129–35. **Aichenger, H.** "Quellenkritische Untersuchung der Perikope vom Ahrenrauffen am Sabbat, Mk 2,23–28 par." In *Jesus in der Verkündigung der Kirche*, ed. A. Fuchs. SNTU 1. Linz: A. Fuchs, 1976. 116–53. **Banks, R.** *Jesus and the Law in the Synoptic Tradition*. SNTSMS 28. Cambridge: University Press, 1975. **Beare, F. W.** "The Sabbath Was Made for Man." *JBL* 79 (1960) 130–36. **Berger, K.** *Die Gesetzesauslegung Jesu: Ihr historischer Hintergrund im Judentum und im Alten Testament*. I. WMANT 40. Neukirchen: Neukirchener, 1972. **Bussmann, W.** *Synoptische Studien, I: Zur Geschichtsquelle*. Halle: J. C. Hinrichs, 1925. **Cohn-Sherbok, D. M.** "An Analysis of Jesus' Arguments Concerning the Plucking of Grain on the Sabbath." *JSNT* 2 (1979) 31–41. **Cohon, S. S.** "The Place of Jesus in the Religious Life of His Day." *JBL* 48 (1929) 82–106. **Daube, D.** *The New Testament and Rabbinic Judaism*. London: Athlone Press, 1956. ———. "Responsibilities of Master and Disciples in the Gospels." *NTS* 19 (1972–73) 1–15. **Dewey, J.** *Markan Public Debate: Literary Technique, Concentric Structure, and Theology in Mark 2:1–3:6*. SBLDS 48. Chico, CA: Scholars Press, 1980. **Doeve, J. W.** *Jewish Hermeneutics in the Synoptic Gospels and Acts*. Assen: van Gorcum, 1954. **Dunn, J. D. G.** "Mark 2.1–3.6: A Bridge between Jesus and Paul on the Question of the Law." *NTS* 30 (1984) 395–415. **Hay, L. S.** "The Son of Man in Mark 2:10 and 2:28." *JBL* 89 (1970) 69–75. **Hooker, M. D.** *The Son of Man in Mark*. Montreal: McGill University Press, 1967. **Hübner, H.** *Das Gesetz in der synoptischen Tradition*. Witten: Luther, 1973. **Hultgren, A. J.** "The Formation of the Sabbath Pericope in Mark 2:23–28." *JBL* 91 (1972) 38–43. ———. *Jesus and His Adversaries: The Form and Function of the Conflict Stories in the Synoptic Tradition*. Minneapolis: Augsburg, 1979. **Jeremias, J.** "Die älteste Schicht der Menschensohn-Logien." *ZNW* 58 (1967) 159–72. **Käsemann, E.** "The Problem of the Historical Jesus." In *Essays on New Testament Themes*. SBT 41. London: SCM, 1964. **Kiilunen, J.** *Die Vollmacht im Widerstreit: Untersuchungen zum Werdegang von Mk 2,1–3,6*. Helsinki: Suomalainen Tiedeakatemia, 1985. **Kuhn, H.-W.** *Ältere Sammlungen im Markusevangelium*. 1971. **Lindars, B.** *Jesus Son of Man: A Fresh Examination of the Son of Man Sayings in the Gospels*. Grand Rapids: Eerdmans, 1983. **Lindemann, A.** "'Der Sabbat ist um des Menschen willen geworden': Historische und theologische Erwägungen zur Traditionsgeschichte der Sabbatperikope, Mk 2:23–28 parr." *Wort und Dienst* 15 (1979) 79–105. **Lohse, E.** "Jesu Worte über den Sabbat." In *Judentum, Urchristentum und Kirche*, FS J. Jeremias, ed. W. Eltester. BZNW 26. Berlin: Töpelmann, 1960. 79–89. **Maloney, E. C.** *Semitic Interference in Marcan Syntax*. 1981. **Manson, T. W.** "Mark II.27 f." *ConNT* 11 (1947) 138–46. ———. *The Sayings of Jesus*. London: SCM, 1957. **Morgan, C. S.** "When Abiathar Was High Priest." *JBL* 98 (1979) 409–10. **Neirynck, F.** "Jesus and the Sabbath: Some Observations on Mark ii,27." In *Jésus aux origines de la christologie*, ed. J. Dupont. BETL 40. Gembloux: J. Duculot, 1974. 227–70. **Rogers, A. D.** "Mark 2.26." *JTS* 2 (1951) 44–45. **Roloff, J.** *Das Kerygma und der irdische Jesus*. 1970. **Rordorf, W.** *Sunday*. London: SCM, 1968. **Schweizer, E.** "The Son of Man." *JBL* 79 (1960) 119–29. **Suhl, A.** *Die Funktion der alttestamentlichen Zitaten und Anspielungen im Markusevangelium*. Gütersloh: Mohn, 1965. **Tödt, H. E.** *The Son of Man in the Synoptic Tradition*. Philadelphia: Westminster, 1965. **Tuckett, C.** "The Present Son of Man." *JSNT* 14 (1982) 58–81. **Wenham, J. W.** "Mark 2.26." *JTS* 1 (1950) 156.

Translation

[23] *It happened*[a] *that Jesus*[b] *was going through the grainfields on a sabbath, and his disciples began to make their way*[c] *picking the heads of wheat.* [24] *And the Pharisees said to him, "Look, why are they doing what is illegal on the sabbath?"* [25] *He said to them, "Have you never read what David did when he had need, when he and the ones with him were hungry?* [26] *How he went into the house of God during the time of Abiathar, the high priest, and ate the loaves of shewbread,*

which were illegal for any one to eat except the priests, and also gave them to those with him?" [27] *And he said to them, "The sabbath was made for man's sake, man was not made for the sake of the sabbath,* [28] *so that the Son of man is lord also of the sabbath."*

Notes

[a] Maloney (*Interference*, 85–86) points out the awkwardness in Greek and Hebrew/Aramaic of the construction of καὶ ἐγένετο followed by a temporal expression (ἐν τοῖς σάββασιν), an accusative with an infinitive clause (αὐτὸν πορεύεσθαι) and a καί and aorist indicative (καὶ ἤρξαντο) expressing past event. Such a construction is without parallel in biblical and nonbiblical Greek (see *Comment* on 1:9; cf. 2:15 and 4:4). He attributes it to a confused rendering of a Semitic idiom.

[b] Romanized words added from context.

[c] ὁδὸν ποιεῖν literally means "to make a way." Most likely it should be read like the classical ὁδὸν ποιεῖσθαι meaning simply "to make their way" or "to travel" (Lat. *iter facere*) as in Judg 17:8 LXX. Matt 12:1 and Luke 6:1 smooth out this construction.

Form/Structure/Setting

Again we have to do with the form of a controversy narrative whose constituent elements of setting, question, and response are complicated by an extended response (see 2:18–22). On the surface, Jesus seems to give three responses to the critics' question: a counter-question (2:25–26); a gnomic saying (2:27); and a Christological statement (2:28). This complex response has led to the positing of multiple stages in the development of the pericope in the tradition.

The view is almost unanimous that our present pericope represents a composite of two or more traditions (see Neirynck, *Jésus*, 227–70, for extended discussion and bibliography). The various suggestions include numerous configurations: (a) 2:23–26 + 27–28; (b) 2:23–26 + 27 + 28; (c) 2:23–24, 27 + 28 + 25–26; (d) 27 + 23–24 + 25–26, 28. These suggestions, however, fall into two broad categories.

Some have divided the narrative into an original story in 2:23–26 with 2:27–28 being added later either as a unit or in two stages (Bultmann, 16; Taylor, 214; Lane, 119–20; Neirynck, *Jésus*, 227–70; Pesch, 1:179; Gnilka, 1:119–20; Schmithals, 1:183–87; Roloff, *Kerygma*, 58–59; Kiilunen, *Vollmacht*, 197–203). The common use of καὶ ἔλεγεν αὐτοῖς ("And he said to them," 2:27a) as an introductory formula and the apparent difference in the thrust of the response from 2:25–26 are the usual reasons given.

Others have divided the narrative into an original story in 2:23–24, 27 (28) with 2:25–26 (28) being added later (Klostermann, 29; Haenchen, 119–21; Grundmann, 89–90; Kuhn, *Sammlungen*, 72, 74; Ernst, 102; Hultgren, *Adversaries*, 113; Lührmann, 64). According to Hultgren (*JBL* 91 [1972] 38–43; *idem, Adversaries*, 114–15; similarly, Lindemann, *Wort und Dienst* 15 [1979] 83–86), 2:27, a Jesus logion, gave rise to 2:23–24 with 2:25–26, 28 added later. The unusual use of scripture rather than a direct response in 2:25–26 (cf. 2:27–28) and the failure to answer the sabbath question in 2:25–26 are the reasons most commonly given.

The controlling factor in the question of form and history of the tradition has generally been the premise that the pericope provided primarily an apologetic for the early Church's sabbath practices. Our study below will show that the focus was more Christological and that the first alternative in the development of the history of the tradition is the more likely. The addition of 2:27–28 correlates with and explicates the answer in 2:25–26.

This pericope also belonged to the pre-Markan collection of three controversy stories involving the Pharisees, the disciples, and Jesus in conflict over praxis concerning eating or not eating (2:15–17, 18–22, 23–28). This story raises the serious question about behavior specifically contrary to the Law.

Structurally, the opponents pose a question based on observed behavior of the disciples (2:25a). Jesus counters with two questions. The first sets the stage with reference to David and his companions' need and hunger (2:25b). The second describes what David did to assuage his and his companions' hunger (2:26). The question and counter-question are interrelated verbally and thematically (Dewey, *Debate*, 97). Then Jesus responds with two additional statements. The first, a gnomic saying, speaks directly to the sabbath issue. The second, a Christological statement, declares the Son of man's authority over the sabbath. These statements have no direct verbal linkage to the counter-questions in 2:25–26, but they do have a logical connection in showing that Jesus has the authority to provide for his own just as David did (Dewey, *Debate*, 98–99). Therefore, the pericope does hang together as a logical unit, despite its complex history of tradition.

The setting follows two other controversy narratives between Jesus and his opponents over issues of food. Yet eating, implicit in 2:23 and explicit in 2:25–26, merely provides the occasion for the transgression of the sabbath. The conflict over the sabbath continues in 3:1–5 where it culminates in the opponents taking counsel on how they might kill Jesus (3:6), a theme implicit in Jesus' response about the bridegroom in 2:19b–20.

Comment

23 This verse provides the temporal and local setting, a grainfield ripe for harvest on the sabbath. Although the setting has often been viewed as created by the Church to set forth Jesus' teaching on the sabbath (e.g., Bultmann, 16; Beare, *JBL* 79 [1960] 133; Schweizer, 71; Hultgren, *JBL* 91 [1972] 38–43; *idem, Adversaries,* 111–15; Lindemann, *Wort und Dienst* 15 [1979] 89–91), Haenchen (122) argues for an occasion in Jesus' ministry since it was hardly the habit of the Christians to stroll through fields on the sabbath and eat the wheat (also Manson, *Sayings,* 190). That the disciples' conduct should raise a question for Jesus their leader corresponds to the mutual responsibility between a master and his disciples in Judaism (Daube, *NTS* 19 [1972–73] 1–15; see *Comment* on 2:16).

"Picking the heads of wheat" (τίλλοντες τοὺς στάχυας) corresponds to a specific regulation given in Deut 23:25: "When you go into your neighbor's standing grain, you may pluck the ears with your hand . . ." Yet it gives rise to the Pharisees' question in 2:24. Since both Jesus, who is unnamed in this pericope, and his disciples are walking through the field, it is this "picking of the grain" on the sabbath that is called illegal rather than a transgression of a sabbath's journey (a half mile). They were "reaping" (τίλλοντες) on the sabbath. At the same time, their action also implied eating the wheat (cf. Matt 12:1; Luke 6:1). This implication provides a point of contact for Jesus' response about David and his companions' eating the shewbread in 2:25–26. The implicit issue of food also represents the common thread running through the three conflict stories of 2:15–28.

24 "The Pharisees" (οἱ Φαρισαῖοι) again pose the question (so 2:15, 18; cf. 3:6). It is moot to ask how they came into the scene, when the story has most likely been stylized (cf. Haenchen, 119, who suggests they might have been farmers).

"What is illegal on the sabbath" (ὃ οὐκ ἔξεστιν) focuses on the sabbath law, which had vital importance for Judaism. Anchored in the Decalogue (Exod 20:8–11; Deut 5:12–15), this law was kept with varying degrees of rigor in contemporary Judaism. The book of *Jubilees* took the sabbath law as its theological foundation and viewed the sabbath as a special sign given only to Israel (*Jub.* 2.19). The *Damascus Document* of the Essenes, offering the most rigorous interpretation of this law (CD 10.14–11.18), even forbids giving help to a birthing animal or one fallen into a pit or cistern (CD 11.13–14 cf. Matt 12:11; Luke 13:15; 14:5) and likewise for a human being (CD 11.16–17). The Pharisee and rabbinic tradition was less rigorous but vitally concerned with delineating what could and could not be done as seen in the listing of thirty-nine proscribed major works in *m. Šabb.* 7:2 that were later broken down into six sub-categories each and a further list in *m. Beṣa* 5:2 (E. Lohse, *TDNT* 7 [1971] 12–14; Str-B, 1:615–18). This specification of proscribed activities reflects their concern to avoid all possibilities of transgressing the sabbath law. Only life-threatening situations or dire personal needs could supersede the sabbath law (*Mek. Exod.* 31:12).

25 "Have you never read what David did?" Jesus replies by referring to the scriptures. This change to an indirect response has led some to assign 2:25–26 to the Church's use of scripture as a basis for their conduct (Klostermann, 29; Haenchen, 119–21; Grundmann, 89; Berger, *Gesetzesauslegung*, 579; Ernst, 102; Hultgren, *JBL* 91 [1972] 38–43; Hübner, *Gesetz*, 120–21; cf. Kuhn, *Sammlungen*, 74, who assigns it to Mark). If, however, Jesus could make use of proverbial or parabolic sayings (2:17, 19a, 21–22), it is arbitrary to deny his having used scripture.

This use of scripture has also been viewed as an example of scribal or rabbinic casuistry (Cohon, *JBL* 48 [1929] 97; Nineham, 105; Rordorf, *Sunday*, 72; Doeve, *Hermeneutics*, 106–7). But Daube (*Rabbinic Judaism*, 71) and Cohn-Sherbok (*JSNT* 2 [1979] 31–41) have shown that Jesus' response would have been invalid because of the choice and use of 1 Sam 21. Were this intended to be a "rabbinical" use of *gezerah shawah*, argument based on two related texts, (so Cohon, *JBL* 48 [1929] 97; Doeve, *Hermeneutics*, 106–7), the analogy would have to have been based on identical wording in two different scriptural passages (Cohn-Sherbok, *JSNT* 2 [1979] 34). Not only does Jesus fail to use two different biblical texts, the narrative in 2:25–26 does not correspond verbally at any point with 1 Sam 21. Furthermore, his argument would not be persuasive as scribal casuistry because he uses a story from a historical book, a haggadah, to make his case rather than an actual legal precept found in the Scripture, a halakah. A haggadah could illustrate or corroborate a halakah but not serve as its basis (Daube, *Rabbinic Judaism,* 71). Therefore, had Jesus' reply been intended as a rabbinical argument, his opponents could have dismissed it as invalid.

"When he had need, when he hungered and those with him" describes David's circumstances. This passage received considerable attention in rabbinic studies which attempted in several ways to justify David's behavior (Str-B, 1:618–19). Since the shewbread was exchanged each sabbath, this event was often seen by the rabbis as a sabbath occurrence. But this plays no role in Jesus' response. The mention of David's "need" and "hunger" would appear to reflect the general tendency by the rabbis to justify David's actions as being from one ravenously hungry whose life was in danger. "Those with him" (οἱ μετ᾽ αὐτοῦ) stands out because David acted alone in 1 Sam 21:1. The same point is made in 2:26c.

26 "Entered the house of God" (εἰσῆλθεν εἰς τὸν οἶκον τοῦ θεοῦ) is missing in 1 Sam 21. Rather the priest goes to meet David when he arrives in Nob (1 Sam 21:1).

"During the time of Abiathar, the high priest" (ἐπὶ Ἀβιαθὰρ ἀρχιερέως) obviously conflicts with the text of 1 Sam 21:1, 2, 8 which has "Ahimelech," Abiathar's father. Matt 12:4 and Luke 6:4 drop this reference, as do several of the Western MSS (D W it sy⁵). Wenham's suggestion that ἐπί has the meaning "entitled" as in 12:26 to indicate the section in 1 Samuel pertaining to Abiathar (*JTS* 1 [1950] 156; similarly Lane, 119) was rejected long ago by Meyer (45) and Lagrange (53). Though the better known of the two, Abiathar does not appear until 1 Sam 22:20 and then not as "high priest." Furthermore, to function as a heading ἐπί would need to follow ἀνέγνωτε more closely rather than several clauses later (Meyer, 45; Rogers, *JTS* 2 [1951] 44). Therefore, with no strong MSS evidence of this being a later gloss, we must assume that the name "Abiathar," a high priest during David's reign, was exchanged here with his father's name, "Ahimelech."

"He ate . . . and gave to those with him" makes explicit what was implied in the story. David does mention some companions whom he was to meet and vouches for their purity when asked by the priest. The issue of ritual purity is the only "legal" question asked in 1 Sam 21. But nothing explicit is stated about either David's or his men's eating of the shewbread. Consequently, 2:26 underscores that David ate what was unlawful and gave it to those with him.

In what sense does this response answer the Pharisees' question? One approach takes 2:25–26 as an attempt to justify the disciples' conduct by use of a precedent from the life of David. Read in this fashion, 2:25–26 offers for some an answer by use of rabbinic casuistry (e.g., a *gezerah shawah*). Others find the choice of David's conduct with his special status in Judaism to be a reminder to the Pharisees that the Law can on occasion be broken with impunity and a corrective to their rigidity regarding the ritualistic law (e.g., Klostermann, 30; Lohmeyer, 65; Cranfield, 115; Lane, 117). Still others see the analogy far more sweeping, "necessity knows no law" (Beare, *JBL* 79 [1960] 134; Schweizer, 72).

This approach, however, falters on two counts. First, Daube and Cohn-Sherbok, as noted above, have demonstrated the inadequacy of this reply from the standpoint of rabbinic argument in principle (haggadah cannot provide basis for halakah) and in hermeneutics (*gezerah shawah* necessitates verbal analogies between passages). Second, the analogy between the David story and the disciples' conduct breaks down completely. Whereas the conduct of David and his men comes in question, Jesus' conduct does not. Whereas David is said to have been hungry and in need, nothing comparable is said of the disciples (cf. Matt 12:1). Whereas David's conduct involved illegally eating the shewbread, the disciples' conduct involved illegal work on the sabbath. Consequently, the only apparent common ground lies in the doing of something forbidden by law. Such a basis establishes anarchy rather than precedent.

Another approach takes 2:25–26 to offer a typology between David and Jesus rather than an OT precedent for the disciples' conduct (Roloff, *Kerygma*, 56–58; Banks, *Jesus*, 116–23; Pesch, 1:182; Gnilka, 1:122). In addition to the lack of verbal correspondence between 2:25–26 and 1 Sam 21:1–6, the difference in detail, noted above, highlights David's rather than the priest's actions, the presence and actions of David's companions, and David's responsibility in doing what was forbidden by the Law. Roloff has taken this rather arbitrary rendering of the David story to be the clue to the correspondence between David and his companions on the one hand and Jesus and his disciples on the other (*Kerygma*, 22). Just as David had the authority and freedom to eat illegally and to give those with him to eat the shewbread illegally, so Jesus had the authority and freedom to permit his disciples who had left all to follow him (Matt 19:27) to eat food gathered illegally on the sabbath.

Jesus could hardly have been laying claim for humanity to David's prerogative, since the correlation is not between David's conduct and Jesus' disciples but between David with his companions and Jesus with his disciples as the Pharisees' question indicates. He was responsible for his disciples' conduct (Daube, *NTS* 19 [1972–73] 1–15). Therefore, the argument runs *a fortiori* from David to Jesus with the precise nature of his relationship to David left unstated and veiled, a trait presumably more characteristic of Jesus than the early Church for whom Jesus was the Davidic Messiah. Instead of an apology for the disciples' (Church's) sabbath conduct, this response like those of 2:10, 17, 19a makes a Christological statement about Jesus and his ministry.

27 This verse has been variously interpreted across the spectrum from a scribal gloss (Bussmann, *Studien*, 92, 142–44) to the saying that occasioned the original controversy narrative (e.g., Schweizer, 71; Hultgren, *JBL* 91 [1972] 38–43; *idem*, *Adversaries*, 114–15; Lindemann, *Wort und Dienst* 15 [1979] 83–86). Several have taken it to be the original response to the Pharisees' question in 2:24 (Klostermann, 29; Rordorf, *Sunday*, 61; Haenchen, 119–21; Kuhn, *Sammlungen*, 72; Grundmann, 89; Hübner, *Gesetz*, 120; cf. Beare, *JBL* 79 [1960] 130–36, with 2:28). Others have viewed it as a later addition to 2:23–26 (Bultmann, 16; Taylor, 218; Lane, 119–20; Nineham, 106; Neirynck, *Jésus*, 264; Pesch, 1:179; Gnilka, 1:119–20). Furthermore, neither Matthew nor Luke carries the verse in their parallels. Although some have attributed this absence to different sources or editions of Mark (e.g., Hübner, *Gesetz*, 116–22; Aichenger, *Verkündigung*, 110–53), most have attributed this difference to the redactional interests of Matthew and Luke.

"And he said to them" (καὶ ἔλεγεν αὐτοῖς) has been seen as a common

Markan connecting formula (4:11, 13, 21, 24; 6:10; 7:9, 14; 8:21; 9:1, 31; see *Comment* on 4:11). This has led many to take the following statements as a later expansion of 2:23–26. Since, however, 2:25a (cf. 2:24a) also begins with the same phrase (καὶ λέγει αὐτοῖς), this expression in itself does not necessarily indicate primary and secondary material or even Markan redaction (cf. Neirynck, *Jésus,* 264).

"Man" (ἄνθρωπον) stands as a generic term for the human creature. But it could hardly have the universalizing force of "humanity" here which would imply the extension of the sabbath law from Israel who saw herself as one specially gifted by God with the sabbath (e.g., *Jub.* 2) to all of humanity. Neither is there any evidence that ἄνθρωπος represents a mistranslation of an Aramaic נשא בר, *bar nāšā᾿,* parallel with 2:28 and meaning collectively Israel (e.g., Dan 7) or new Israel composed of Jesus and his disciples (Manson, *ConNT* 11 [1947] 138–46). "Man" in this context stems from the creation setting of Gen 1 (cf. "was made" [ἐγένετο]).

"The sabbath was made for man" (τὸ σάββατον διὰ τὸν ἄνθρωπον ἐγένετο) has been interpreted at times as the equivalent of "man is the measure of all things." The sabbath law would now be subject to human caprice as illustrated by the disciples' behavior in 2:23. By emphasizing a fundamental human freedom over against the sabbath, the saying represents a radical break with the "sabbath theology of post-exilic Judaism" (Rordorf, *Sunday,* 62). Yet apart from the question of so radical a critique of the sabbath law in Jesus' ministry, such a reading of 2:27 takes the saying out of context. It has little in common either with the response of 2:25–26 or 2:28 to the Pharisees' question. Therefore, 2:25–26 must be eliminated either as irrelevant or a later addition and 2:28 viewed as a subsequent qualification. We are left with the unlikely result of a controversy narrative consisting of three nonhomogeneous responses (2:25–26, 27, 28).

Others have found 2:27 to be much more compatible with Judaism in principle (Abrahams, *Studies,* 129; Roloff, *Kerygma,* 60–61; Nineham, 105–6; Lane, 119). They cite an apparent parallel saying of R. Simeon b. Menasya (ca A.D. 180) in *Mek. Exod.* 31:13–14 (cf. *b. Yoma* 85b): "The sabbath was delivered to you, not you to the sabbath." Thus Jesus would be reminding the Pharisees of their own teaching. Hultgren (*Adversaries,* 140, n. 62), however, has pointed out the difference in context. The rabbinic saying speaks of Israel's privilege in having received the sabbath, a distinctive which assumes she will keep it. Str-B (2:5) and others have noted that rabbinic casuistry used the principle in life-threatening situations rather than as a general maxim. Perhaps a similar understanding underlay the Maccabean provision for fighting on the sabbath (1 Macc 2:41, so Abrahams, *Studies,* 130). Accordingly, 2:27 would only have carried weight if the disciples had been in danger of starving. Yet the setting in 2:23 does not even mention their hunger.

Perhaps the key lies in the saying's starting point in creation. We find a similar response based on the order of creation in the divorce question of 10:2–9. Rather than accent "man" or humanity in general, the saying places both the "sabbath" and "man" in the context of creation in Gen 1 (Lohmeyer, 65; Haenchen, 121; Pesch, 1:184; Gnilka, 1:123). Consequently, the sabbath as a part of creation must be taken seriously and not lightly dismissed.

The issue is one of priorities as seen in the antithetical parallelism. The sabbath was created for the benefit of the human creature and as God's created gift stands at the service of humanity, not humanity at the service of the sabbath. This view hardly represents a radical departure from Judaism even with its starting point in creation. It certainly is akin to the theology of *Jub.* 2 that perceived the sabbath as a special gift from God to his people for their enjoyment (Hooker, *Son of Man,* 96). But this begs the question of the disciples' conduct, if indeed one is to take the sabbath seriously.

In other words, either we have a saying that affirms the human freedom to set aside the sabbath law without any qualifications, or we have a saying that affirms the value of the sabbath as God's provision at creation but as a benefit for "man," the human creature, with no prescribed or proscribed guidelines for sabbath conduct. Given the alternatives, only the former answers the Pharisees' question. But, as we have noted, that answer stands in tension with 2:25–26 and 2:28. The decisive clue lies in the next saying.

28 This saying has often been viewed as an isolated logion that was added to either 2:27 in the pre-Markan tradition (Rawlinson, 33; Taylor, 218; Haenchen, 121; Kuhn, *Sammlungen,* 74; Grundmann, 90; Ernst, 102) or to 2:23–27 (Lane, 120; Lohse, "Jesu Worte," 83; Gnilka, 1:124; Lindemann, *Wort und Dienst* 15 [1979] 92–93). Lindars (*Son of Man,* 103–6; Lührmann, 64) assigns it to Mark's composition in line with 2:10. These suggestions, however, founder on the conjunction ὥστε.

"So that" (ὥστε) introduces a result clause that connects 2:28 syntactically with 2:27. Therefore, to take 2:28 as a summary of 2:23–27 (Lane, 120; Gnilka, 1:124; Lindemann, *Wort und Dienst* 15 [1979] 92–93) or even the larger context of 2:1–26 (Kuhn, *Sammlungen,* 77, 83) is to ignore the logic and syntax of "so that" in 2:28 which results from the content of 2:27. But how does 2:28 follow from the content of 2:27? The answer depends on how one understands "Son of man."

From time to time "Son of man" (ὁ υἱὸς τοῦ ἀνθρώπου) has been taken as synonymous with "man" (ἄνθρωπος) in 2:27 by positing the same Aramaic expression (בר נשא, *bar nāšā*ʾ), behind the differing Greek translations. According to one view, 2:27 (ἄνθρωπος) correctly renders the Aramaic idiom for "humankind" that has been mistranslated as "Son of man" in 2:28 (e.g., Bultmann, 16; C. C. Torrey, *The Four Gospels,* [New York: Harper, 1933] 73; Jeremias, *ZNW* 58 [1967] 165; cf. Hay, *JBL* 89 [1970] 73–75). Consequently, 2:28 would follow logically from 2:27. If the sabbath was created for "man" (2:27), it follows that "man" then is "lord of the sabbath" (2:28).

However, this reading expresses a position "wholly inconceivable in any Jewish teacher, including Jesus" (Beare, *JBL* 79 [1960] 130–36). Thus, Beare has argued along with T. W. Manson, though with different conclusions, that "Son of man" is the correct rendering of both sayings (2:27–28) and represents a "surrogate for the personal pronoun 'I' " (*JBL* 79 [1960] 131–32) rather than a collective or corporate term for Israel (Manson, *ConNT* 11 [1947] 138–46). In this case Jesus (or the early Church) declared that the sabbath was made for "the Son of man" or "me" and thus "the Son of man" or "I" is/am "lord of the sabbath." This reasoning may account for the logic of 2:27–28 assuming an Aramaic text, but it does not explain the difference in the Greek translation "man/Son of man" of the supposedly same Aramaic phrase and in sayings with the same supposed import. We are still left with the apparent *non sequitur* of the Greek text.

The logical problem only becomes worse when, with the majority of commentators, we take "Son of man" as a titular, messianic designation. Käsemann (*Essays*, 39, so Rordorf, *Sunday*, 65; Haenchen, 121; Kuhn, *Sammlungen*, 74; cf. Suhl, *Funktion*, 84; Lohse, "Jesu Worte," 83; Neirynck, *Jésus*, 244, who posit the opposite) has argued that the Son of man saying serves to limit what Schweizer (71) has called the "frightening" statement of 2:27. In other words, whereas 2:27 offers a general maxim of human freedom regarding the Sabbath, 2:28 limits the scope of this freedom to the authoritative discretion of the Son of man. Thus, the Son of man represents the figure of authority (Tödt, *Son of Man*, 131) who ultimately sanctions the disciples' (community's) conduct (Lohse, "Jesu Worte," 82–83). But this rendering ignores the logical hurdle of ὥστε that introduces 2:28. It makes little sense, if "Son of man" connotes a messianic title of authority, to argue that the "Son of man" has authority over the sabbath (2:28) because the sabbath was made for "man" (2:27).

If, however, "Son of man" (ὁ υἱὸς τοῦ ἀνθρώπου) literally renders the Aramaic (בר נשא, *bar nāšāʾ*) behind 2:28 and "man" (ἄνθρωπος) literally renders an Aramaic expression behind 2:27, we would have the possibility of a wordplay in Aramaic not unlike Ps 8:4 (i.e., "man"/"son of man," so Roloff, *Kerygma*, 61–62) that escapes us now in Greek and English. Read one way, the sayings declare in synonymous parallelism that the sabbath was made for "man, so that the son of man"(= "man" or "humankind," cf. Ps 8:4) has authority over the sabbath. Read another way, the sayings declare that the sabbath was made for "man" so that "the Son of man"(= "I," self-designation) has authority over the sabbath. The one gives to humanity the authority over the sabbath; the other gives authority to Jesus. Yet the ambiguous "Son of man" (בר נשא, *bar nāšāʾ*) leaves the claim for authority veiled in 2:28 (Roloff, *Kerygma*, 61–62; Grundmann, 93–94), much as it did in 2:10 (cf. Matt 9:8).

The play on words is lost in Greek, which may help explain why Matt 12 and Luke 6 have dropped 2:27. Mark, however, may well have taken "Son of man" as a nontitular self-designation by Jesus (see *Comment* on 2:10). This would also explain why Mark despite the "messianic secret" could openly use this designation here (2:10, 28). Jesus in 2:10 and 2:28 was expressing his claim of authority "as" the Son of man not "by virtue" of being the Son of man.

Such a reading of 2:28 also explains the force of 2:27. Rather than a self-contained response to the Pharisees that asserts human freedom with the potential of doing as one pleases on the sabbath, 2:27 affirms the sabbath as God's created provision for "man," the human creature, but offers neither guidelines for human conduct nor a concrete answer to the Pharisees' question. This saying simply provides the backdrop for the claim in 2:28.

Contemporary Judaism would have had no major quarrel with 2:27 as a statement that the sabbath was God's created gift for "man" = Israel. She would simply desire to go further and know how one was to use the sabbath as part of God's created order. But contemporary Judaism would have had serious objections to the implications of the sequel in 2:28 where the "Son of man" = "a man" or "I" (= Jesus) is declared to be lord over the sabbath. Therefore, 2:28 combined with 2:27 answers the Pharisees' question and explains the disciples' conduct based not on the principle of freedom in 2:27 but on the authority claimed for the "Son of man" in 2:28. Concomitantly, 2:27–28 would then correlate with the response in 2:25–26. The "Son of man" = Jesus has the authority to permit his disciples to do what was unlawful on the sabbath (2:27–28), just as David had the authority to do with his own (2:25–26).

Both responses (2:25–26, 27–28) point to Jesus as the basis for the disciples' actions. Yet it is difficult to know the precise reason why he permitted his disciples to transgress the sabbath. Neither Jesus' nor his disciples' lifestyle, as best we can tell, indicate a penchant for abrogating the Law nor does the sabbath practice of the primitive Church, limited though our knowledge be, indicate a cavalier approach to the sabbath (Rordorf, *Sunday,* 80–138; Kuhn, *Sammlungen,* 77–80). Consequently, we do not have any basis for considering Jesus to have annulled in principle the sabbath law for himself or his followers.

A clue might lie in the other sabbath controversies. All others involve Jesus whose healing ministry creates an issue with his opponents (3:1–5 // Matt 12:9–14 // Luke 6:6–11; Luke 13:10–17; 14:1–6; John 5:1–16; 9:1–38). Jesus' ministry takes precedence over the sabbath law (see 3:1–5). Similarly, Jesus as David's counterpart claims authority over the sabbath in 2:25–26 and 2:27–28. Matt 12:5–7 argues the same way in comparing the sabbath work of the priests and Jesus' ministry. Thus, Manson may be correct in suggesting that the disciples were journeying with Jesus from one place to another in "the missionary work of the Kingdom" and not just on a "quiet sabbath afternoon stroll" (*Sayings,* 190). As one authorized for a special ministry, Jesus claimed the authority to permit his disciples, who had left all to follow him in his ministry (Matt 19:27), to pick wheat on the sabbath, which was made for man's benefit, in order to satisfy their hunger.

"Also" (καί) for some combines this saying with the Son of man saying in 2:10 (e.g., Kuhn, *Sammlungen,* 73). For Pesch (1:185) "also of the sabbath" refers to the dominion given to "man" at creation over not only the previous days of creation but even the last day including the sabbath. If, however, we take 2:27–28 to have been originally a wordplay in Aramaic, then the καί would reinforce the "so that." Just as "the sabbath" was made for "man," so the "Son of man" was "lord also of the sabbath."

Explanation

This pericope along with the two preceding ones (2:15–17, 18–22) belonged to a traditional complex of three conflict stories involving Jesus, his disciples, and the Pharisees over conduct having to do in one way or another with eating. In each case the Pharisees raised questions about inappropriate, if not illegal, conduct that placed the nature and validity of his ministry in doubt. Consequently, Jesus responds in all three by focusing on himself and the nature of his ministry (2:17, 19, 25–26, 28).

It is doubtful that an ascending scale of culpability underlies the thematic shift from eating with sinners to not fasting, to the transgression of the sabbath. But certainly the desecration of the sabbath set Jesus in direct confrontation with the Law. This issue in particular took on even greater proportions because of the special significance accorded the sabbath as a distinctively Jewish day by contemporary Judaism. Jesus' conduct seems out of line with this concern, since, as far as the gospel tradition goes, the one recurring charge against him was his transgression of the sabbath.

The Pharisees' question makes clear that the disciples' behavior was illegal. They were breaking the sabbath by reaping, one of the thirty-nine specifically proscribed tasks in the Mishnah for the sabbath (Šabb. 7:2). As in the previous conflict narratives, Jesus does not deny the accusation but responds as though accepting their charge. This does not come down to an argument over "scribal interpretation" of the Law. It has to do with the sabbath law regardless of who is interpreting it. For this reason, Jesus' response does not fit the categories of rabbinical debate, as though he were one rabbi setting his view of the Law over against a competing interpretation.

In this story, Jesus gives two responses to the question. The first addresses the question of illegal behavior by referring to David's eating the shewbread (2:25-26). The second deals with the sabbath law specifically by placing the "Son of man" over the "sabbath" (2:27-28).

In the first response, the point of comparison lies between David and Jesus at the level of their respective roles rather than in their conduct. The story as told in 2:25-26 has little in common with the details of 1 Sam 21. David emerges as the primary figure who sets the pace, while the priest, whose name does not even coincide with that in 1 Sam 21, recedes into the setting. David's men also come into prominence in conjunction with David's actions (implied at best in 1 Sam 21). This change in focus and details from 1 Sam 21 corresponds to the setting of Jesus and his disciples, making the response in actuality a typology. What David in view of his calling and position did with and for his own, so Jesus in view of his calling and position could do for his own.

In this way, the story has Jesus claim for himself the prerogative to provide for those who had left all to accompany him in his work, even when as with David this activity went beyond the limits of the Law. Why and how he compared himself to David and his prerogatives remains unstated. Yet his making the claim, veiled though it be, indicates his awareness of a unique authority in his role and ministry. Naturally, this David/Jesus typology takes on clear messianic tones in the Christology of the early Church, and its obliqueness rather than direct messianic overtones most likely indicates a setting in the more veiled context of Jesus' ministry. But it was just such a setting that most likely provided the roots for the later, developed messianic Christology. Thus, the answer to the Pharisees' question in 2:25-26 as in 2:17 and 2:19a lies in the person and ministry of Jesus. Allegiance to him and his ministry, discipleship, took precedence over the Law (so 2:15-17; 2:18-22, see 3:1-5).

Despite the numerous attempts to interpret the responses in 2:27-28 independently, they must be viewed together as one answer. Furthermore, 2:27-28, though perhaps added later to complement the first of 2:25-26, gives essentially the same response as 2:25–26. Both respond by explaining the disciples' behavior in light of Jesus' authority. But whereas 2:25–26 uses a typology drawn from David's life and work, 2:27–28 use a play on words and the doctrine of creation to make the point.

Jesus first sets the sabbath law in the perspective of Gen 1 and the order of creation. The sabbath was created for the benefit and welfare of the human creature. The sabbath was to serve humanity, not humanity to serve the sabbath (2:27). Taken in isolation, this response offers a basis but no directives for how the sabbath was to benefit humanity as a gift of creation. That lies in 2:28.

The Son of man saying has also been taken in isolation. It ascribes to Jesus as the Son of man the authority to set aside sabbath regulations. Though often read as foundational to the early Church's sabbath practice, had the early Church used Jesus' authority over the Law to guide or justify their sabbath practice would not the tradition have preserved specific directives from Jesus to clarify this matter? Unless one were to argue that Jesus simply abrogated the sabbath law (a view without support either in the tradition or the early Church's practice), picking grain and healing the sick are the only "examples" of questionable conduct in the tradition. These "examples" hardly represent a broad rejection of the sabbath law or distinctive issues between the early Church's behavior and Jewish critics. Thus the saying of 2:28 more likely has its place in Jesus' ministry and in combination with 2:27 as the opening conjunction, "so that," indicates.

If 2:27–28 are taken as a unit, "Son of man" cannot function as a Christological title. The authority of a messianic "Son of man" over the sabbath does not flow from the creation of the sabbath for man. "Son of man," however, taken in conjunction with "man" to form an original play on words does follow by virtue of the ambiguity of the underlying Aramaic expression for "son of man" in 2:28 which can be synonymous with "man" = "humanity" in 2:27 or "I" expressed in the third person. By referring to the order of creation in 2:27, Jesus affirms the value of both "man" and the "sabbath" in light of creation but places the sabbath in the service of humanity. In 2:28 by virtue of this order in creation ("so"), he, the "Son of man," claims the authority over the sabbath not for humanity in general ("son of man" meaning "man") but for himself ("Son of man" meaning "I").

Jesus makes a similar appeal to creation as the basis for his demands regarding marriage in contrast to the Law in 10:2–9. One must not confuse, however, Jesus' authority over the sabbath and his demands for marriage with a romantic "back to nature" or an attempt to reconstruct the "original, divine intent" behind the Law, neither of which characterizes Jesus' ministry. Rather the reference to creation must be seen in view of his eschatological message of the Kingdom. Creation is but the paradigm of the new order of salvation, especially as depicted by Isaiah (see *Comment* on 1:12–13). Therefore, in the light of Gen 1 and the order of creation, Jesus claimed the authority to do God's work of the age of salvation (see 3:1–5) and to provide for his own (2:23–26) in conjunction with his ministry even when such actions came into conflict with the sabbath law. He was not annulling the sabbath law in principle, rather he was interpreting the sabbath law in the light of his ministry.

This was precisely the claim behind the typology of David and his followers in Jesus' response of 2:25–26. And this claim informs Matthew's additional comparison of the priests in the service of the temple and the followers of one who is greater than the temple (Matt 12:5–6). This pericope, therefore, found its place alongside of 2:15–17 and 2:18–22 in the tradition because it too bore witness to who Jesus was and why his ministry met opposition with the religious authorities. The focus centered in Jesus' claim to "call sinners" (2:17), to be the "bridegroom" (2:19), to be David's counterpart (2:25–26), the one in whom God was doing a new thing in human history (2:27–28). The implicit authority behind each of these claims set Jesus at odds with the religious "authorities" and their perception of God's will and activity.

Mark's redactional activity within the pericope seems quite limited. Yet the story continues several themes important to his portrait. Jesus' authority that explains the disciples' behavior on the sabbath corresponds with Jesus' authority as introduced in 1:21–27 and in 2:1–12. At the same time, the nature of this authority remained veiled, even in the use of the ambiguous designation "Son of man." The implied authority did not lie in his being the messianic "Son of man" but in Jesus' words and actions. Thus the "Son of man" in 2:10, 28 carried no greater specification of the nature of his authority than his use of "I" in 2:17 or the "bridegroom" in 2:19 when addressing his opponents. For Mark, "Son of man" was but another way of Jesus' referring to himself.

Jesus' authority, however, not only differed from that of the scribes in regard to Jesus' teaching (1:22, 27) but in regard to his and his disciples' conduct (2:15–28). And this difference led to an ultimate conflict between him and the "authorities." By choosing to place the conflict narratives of 2:15–28 at this juncture in his Gospel, the evangelist clearly wants this aspect of Jesus' ministry evident from the outset. The addition of 2:1–12 with the culpable charge of blasphemy (2:7) at the beginning of this section finds its counterpart in Mark's adding a second sabbath conflict story that culminates in a counsel of death (3:1–6) at the end of this section.

K. A Sabbath Healing   (3:1–6)

Bibliography

Abrahams, I. *Studies in Pharisaism and the Gospels.* First Series. Cambridge: CUP, 1917. **Albertz, M.** *Die synoptischen Streitgespräche: Ein Beitrag zur Formgeschichte des Urchristentum.* Berlin: Trowitzsch, 1921. **Banks, R.** *Jesus and the Law in the Synoptic Tradition.* SNTSMS 28. Cambridge: CUP, 1975. **Bennet, W. J.** "The Herodians of Mark's Gospel." *NovT* 17 (1975) 9–14. **Daniel, C.** "Nouveaux arguments en faveur de l'identification des Hérodiens et des Esséniens." *RevQ* 27 (1970) 397–402. **Dewey, J.** "The Literary Structure of the Controversy Stories in Mark 2:1–3:6." *JBL* 92 (1973) 394–401. ———. *Markan Public Debate: Literary Technique, Concentric Structure, and Theology in Mark 2:1–3:6.* SBLDS 48. Chico, CA: Scholars Press, 1977. **Dietzfelbinger, C.** "Vom Sinn der Sabbatheilungen Jesu." *EvT* 38 (1978) 281–98. **Dunn, J. D. G.** "Mark 2.1–3.6: A

Bridge between Jesus and Paul on the Question of the Law." *NTS* 30 (1984) 395–415. **Goppelt, L.** *Theology of the New Testament,* I. Grand Rapids: Eerdmans, 1981. **Hoehner, H. W.** *Herod Antipas.* SNTSMS 17. Cambridge: Cambridge UP, 1972. **Hübner, H.** *Das Gesetz in der synoptischen Tradition.* Witten: Luther Verlag, 1973. **Hultgren, A.** *Jesus and His Adversaries: The Form and Function of the Conflict Stories in the Synoptic Tradition.* Minneapolis: Augsburg, 1979. **Kertelge, K.** *Die Wunder Jesu in Markusevangelium.* 1970. **Kiilunen, J.** *Die Vollmacht in Widerstreit: Untersuchungen zum Werdegang von Mk 2,1–3,6.* Helsinki: Suomalainen Tiedeakatemia, 1985. **Koch, D. A.** *Die Bedeutung der Wundererzählungen für die Christologie des Markusevangeliums.* 1975. **Kuhn, H. W.** *Ältere Sammlungen im Markusevangelium.* 1971. **Lohse, E.** "Jesu Worte über den Sabbat." In *Judentum, Urchristentum und Kirche,* FS J. Jeremias, ed. W. Eltester. BZNW 26. Berlin: Töpelmann, 1960. 79–89. **Lührmann, D.** "Die Pharisäer und die Schriftgelehrten im Markusevangelium." *ZNW* 78 (1987) 169–85. **Pyrke, E. J.** *Redactional Style in the Marcan Gospel.* 1978. **Roloff, J.** *Das Kerygma und der irdische Jesus.* 1970. **Rordorf, W.** *Sunday.* London: SCM, 1968. **Rowley, H. H.** "The Herodians in the Gospels." *JTS* 41 (1940) 14–27. **Schenke, L.** *Die Wundererzählungen des Markusevangeliums.* 1974. **Sibinga, J. S.** "Text and Literary Art in Mark 3,1–6." In *Studies in New Testament Language and Text,* FS G. D. Kilpatrick, ed. J. K. Elliot. *NTS* 44, Leiden: Brill, 1976. 357–65. **Theissen, G.** *The Miracle Stories of the Early Christian Tradition.* 1983.

Translation

[1] *And he entered again into a* [a] *synagogue. And a man was there who had a withered hand.* [2] *And they were watching him closely to see if he might heal him on the sabbath, in order to charge him.* [3] *And he said to the man having the withered hand, "Stand here in the middle!"* [4] *And he said to them, "Is it legal on the sabbath to do good or to do evil, to save a life or to kill?" But they remained silent.* [5] *And looking around at them with anger, deeply grieved at the hardness of their heart, he said to the man, "Extend your hand." He extended it and his hand was restored.* [6] *And the Pharisees departed immediately and began taking counsel* [b] *with the Herodians against him on how they might destroy him.*

Notes

[a] Only B ℵ support an anarthrous construction (cf. Matt 12:9; Luke 6:6), but it is the more difficult reading (Sibinga, *Studies,* 357–61).

[b] συμβούλιον ἐδίδουν has no parallel in Greek. Cf. Latin *consilium capere* and συμβούλιον ἔλαβον of Matt 12:14 and *consilium facere* with συμβούλιον ποιεῖν of Mark 15:1 and variant ποιεῖν here: ℵ A D C Θ W.

Form / Structure / Setting

The story fails to fit neatly into any of the form critical categories. It contains a mixture of controversy (3:2,4), healing (3:1,3,5) and biographical (3:5a,6) narratives. Thus Roloff has argued on the basis of form that this pericope reflects a narrative shaped to a great extent by the memory of an encounter between Jesus and his opponents (*Kerygma,* 64). To see how an unstylized narrative becomes tailored to a given form (controversy narrative), one need only compare Matt 12:9–14 with Mark 3:1–6.

Although Roloff's evidence may not necessarily imply a historical reminiscence, there seems to be no solid evidence for disputing the historical roots of this story in Jesus' ministry (Lohse, *Judentum*, 85; cf. Dietzfelbinger, *EvT* 38 [1978] 287). The failure to identify the subjects (Jesus and his opponents) at the outset and the truncated setting (time and place) may be the result of Mark's redactional combination of the story with the previous sabbath pericope (Schenke, *Wundererzählungen*, 162–63). Since Albertz (*Streitgespräche*, 5–6) this pericope has commonly been viewed as the concluding segment of five controversy narratives found by Mark as a traditional complex. Pesch (1:187) has even argued that it belonged together with the sabbath conflict of 2:23–28 before these were gathered into a pre-Markan controversy complex. But we have noted that the traditional core more than likely consisted of three conflict stories (2:15–28) with a common cast (Jesus, disciples, Pharisees), theme (eating), and form (a controversy story with an extended response to a direct question). Furthermore, the opening (2:1–12) and concluding (3:1–6) pericopes have more in common with each other in form and content than with any of the other three stories. Both have a mixed form of healing and controversy stories whose initial question is unstated; both involve Jesus and a cripple (paralytic and withered hand) without any mention of the disciples; both healings serve a paradigmatic purpose related to Jesus' counter question (2:9–10; 2:4–5); and both imply capital consequences (cf. 2:5, blasphemy; 3:6, a counsel of death). Consequently, several scholars have more recently questioned the assigning of this pericope to a pre-Markan complex of controversy narratives (Kuhn, *Sammlungen*, 88; Roloff, *Kerygma*, 63; Schenke, *Wundererzählungen*, 161–63; Gnilka, 1:131–32).

Apart from indications of Mark's redaction in 3:5 (see *Comment*), numerous writers have assigned the concluding verse to Mark's redaction (Bultmann, 52; Schweizer, 74; Kuhn, *Sammlungen*, 19–21; Koch, *Wundererzählungen*, 50–52; Gnilka, 1:126; Lührmann, 66). The grounds usually given (see esp. Kuhn, *Sammlungen*, 19–21) are formal (an uncommon "biographical" element in a controversy narrative and the identification of the opponents at the end), stylistic (Markan use of καὶ ἐξέρχεσθαι and the similarity to 11:18), and thematic (Mark's emphasis on Jesus' death, cf. 11:18; 12:12; 14:1; the "Herodians" in 12:13, cf. 8:15; the direction of the larger context of 2:15–3:5).

These arguments, however, are not convincing (see esp. Schenke, *Wundererzählungen*, 164–65; Taylor, 220–21; Lohmeyer, 69; Roloff, *Kerygma*, 64; Kertelge, *Wunder*, 83; Pesch, 1:188). First, the failure of this pericope to fit neatly into any formal category precludes the use of form critical grounds for eliminating 3:6. Second, Mark does favor the use of καὶ ἐξέρχεσθαι, but this is an inadequate basis for concluding that the entire verse must be redactional. This becomes even more questionable when the supposed parallel with 11:18 reveals key differences (συμβούλιον ἐδίδουν/ἐζήτουν, cf. 14:1; and ὅπως only here, cf. πῶς in 11:18; 14:1). Third, Mark's thematic emphasis on Jesus' death might have led him to use a tradition with 3:6 not only here but to form the concluding segment of the larger context. Thus, the remaining arguments obtain to the identification of the opponents (see *Comment* on 3:6). Structurally, this story, as 2:1–12, consists of two elements, a healing and a controversy that grows out of the healing. Whereas 2:1–12 has a healing story (2:1–5,11–12) surrounding a discrete controversy element (2:6–10), 3:1–

6 has a controversy (3:1a, 2,4–5a, 6) interwoven (not a "ring construction," cf. Dewey, *Debate,* 104) with a healing story (3:1b,3,5b). In each case the healing story could stand alone (2:1–5,11–12; 3:1,3,5b), but the controversy depends on the miracle story for the issue (2:5; 3:2) and the response (2:10–11; 3:4–5). Furthermore, the controversy element provides the focus of the two pericopes, as the controversial tone of 2:1–3:6 indicates. Therefore, 3:1–0 shares more in common structurally with 2:1–12 than with any of the intervening pericopes. Yet their own mutual, structural differences are great enough to indicate that both came to Mark as traditional units which he has adapted for their present setting.

Without doubt 3:1–6 concludes the series of conflict stories from 2:1–3:6. If, as has been maintained, Mark is responsible for placing the opening (2:1–12) and concluding (3:1–6) pericopes in their present context, one cannot avoid the implication of these stories for Mark's narrative. Jesus' authority underlying each pericope in 2:1–3:6 comes into mortal conflict here and in 2:1–12 with the religious authorities over the right to forgive sin and the use of the sabbath, two issues that have to do with God's prerogatives alone. The capital punishment implicit in the charge of blasphemy in 2:7 becomes explicit in the counsel to destroy Jesus in 3:6. Therefore, much more was at stake for Mark in the stories of 2:15–28 than a difference with the religious authorities over the interpretation of the Law. The root of the conflict goes to Jesus' claim of authority. According to Mark, that claim of authority throughout 1:16–3:6 had its ultimate roots in the "beginning" of 1:1–15, the announcement of the time of fulfillment. Consequently, Jesus' authority represented a fundamental challenge to the Jewish religious authorities.

Comment

1 "He entered again into a synagogue" (καὶ εἰσῆλθεν πάλιν εἰς συναγωγήν). This opening statement contains several clues of Mark's redactional insertion of an independent, traditional unit into the context of 2:15–28. The main verb εἰσῆλθεν ("entered") in the singular with no reference to any companions (cf. 2:15,23) last appeared in 2:1–12 and 13, traditional units most likely added by Mark to 2:15–23. "Again" (πάλιν) also appears in the redactional seams of 2:1 (see *Comment* on 2:1 and 13). While it could be a reminder of Jesus' first entrance into the synagogue of Capernaum in 1:21 (Gnilka, 1:126), "again" redactionally underscores a shift of setting (2:1, Capernaum; 2:13, the sea; 3:1, a synagogue). There is little evidence of "again" signalling Jesus' habitual practice of attending the synagogue (Grundmann, 95), though that feature is not to be denied. Finally, the absence of Jesus' name, the time, and place of the synagogue at the outset may reflect Mark's adaptation of this unit to its present context, especially 2:23–28.

"A man was there who had a withered hand" (ἦν ἐκεῖ ἄνθρωπος ἐξηραμμένην ἔχων τὴν χεῖρα, cf. 1:23) sets the stage for the conflict and healing scenes that follow. Unlike the possessed man, whose presence dominated the synagogue scene in 1:21–28, this crippled man plays more a supporting role in the conflict between Jesus and his opponents.

2 "They were watching him closely" (παρετήρουν αὐτόν) introduces the

opponents without specifying who "they" were. Their identity, now supplied from the context of 2:23–28 (cf. 3:6), may have been dropped from the opening of the traditional unit or its context. "Watching" (παρετήρουν) can have the more malicious connotation of "to lie in wait for" (BGD, s.v.). Their intention to catch Jesus in the act of a transgression and charge him would support this stronger rendering. The opponents' anticipation suggests their knowledge of similar healings on the sabbath (cf. Luke 13:14).

"If he would heal him" (εἰ τοῖς σάββασιν θεραπεύσει αὐτόν) provides the opponents' unstated question of the conflict story. Whereas the question was posed in 2:16,18,24, the question went unstated here and in 2:6–7. In fact, one could argue that the question was moot in these two pericopes, since in 2:7 the opponents accuse Jesus of blasphemy and their intention here is to "charge him" (κατηγορήσωσιν αὐτοῦ) with breaking the sabbath law. Their response is now a calculated one.

3 "Stand in the middle!" (ἔγειρε εἰς τὸ μέσον). Those attending a synagogue sat on stone benches around the walls or squatted on mats on the floor. With this command, Jesus had the crippled man arise (ἔγειρε) for all to see. This direct action of placing the man at the center prior to posing his own question (3:4) or restoring the hand (3:5) has led many to see this as a provocative gesture. The fact that neither the man himself nor a friend came to Jesus for his healing underscores at least the demonstrative character of the action. Jesus' statement of forgiveness in 2:5 prior to the healing in 2:11 had the same effect, especially as seen in the rhetorical questions of 2:9–10.

The opponents' "watching closely" (3:2) and Jesus' placing the man in "the center" of attention (3:3) graphically draw the lines of conflict. But does the nature of this conflict lie in differing views of the Law or in a much more fundamental claim by Jesus for his ministry? The answer lies in the significance of his counter-question.

4 "Is it legal (ἔξεστιν) on the sabbath?" introduces Jesus' question (cf. 2:24) by using the technical language of scribal legal discussions (so Lohse, Judentum, 86). Concern for the sabbath had led to extensive discussion in Judaism about what was legal on the sabbath (see Comment on 2:24). Jesus appears to enter into that discussion. Pesch (1:191) suggests that this expression shows Jesus' desire to act in obedience to the Law. But as the question develops, it implies either that Jesus was over his head in the debate or that something other than casuistic scribal debate was at issue.

"To do good or to do evil" (ἀγαθὸν ποιῆσαι ἢ κακοποιῆσαι) is the first of two antithetical parallelisms that complete the question. Taken by itself, this alternative begs the question, since keeping the sabbath law was the "good," unless a greater "good" called for actions that otherwise would have desecrated the sabbath. The real question then becomes, what standard determines the greater good that would permit one to transgress the sabbath? The criterion for "doing good" and, conversely for "doing evil," comes in the second antithetical parallelism. And the second parallelism stands in synonymous parallelism with the first.

"To save a life or to kill" (ψυχὴν σῶσαι ἢ ἀποκτεῖναι) leaves us with a life or death situation, which appears to have been the one constant principle in all the Jewish debates over the Law (e.g., m. Yoma 8:6; Str-B, 1:623–29;

Abrahams, *Studies,* 129–35). Thus Jesus' opponents would have found no fault with a definition of doing good based on the saving of a life. Even more certain is the illegality of the antithesis, to kill (ἀποκτεῖναι), which defines doing evil.

Consequently, this question of 3:4, expressed in synonymous parallelism, really leaves no choice. Not only was it legal to save a life on the sabbath, but it was illegal to kill, according to the Law, seven days a week! There was only one answer. The opponents' reaction, however, makes clear that much more was involved than scribal casuistry. They remained silent (3:4) and later took counsel to destroy him (3:6). What led to their response?

Many have sought the answer in Jesus' apparent attack on a calloused system of legalism that had lost the sense of human worth (Kertelge, *Wunder,* 85; Gnilka, 1:127; Dietzfelbinger, *EvT* 38 [1978] 294). As Schweizer has put it (75): "There is no escape, nor is there any justification for a legalism which merely for the sake of orthodoxy fails to do the good and therefore produces evil." But if it were merely a question of doing good on the sabbath and prohibiting doing evil, what makes the sabbath so special, when the same would hold for any day of the week? This principle, in effect, would actually set aside the sabbath law (Nineham, 109). Furthermore, if that were the intent of the question, as some would indeed argue, why does Jesus' response narrow or define "doing good" and "doing evil" to "saving life" and "taking life?" The former set of alternatives must be read in light of the latter.

Yet the question of saving a life or taking a life makes the opponents' silence the more surprising. On the one hand, the Jewish authorities would have concurred that saving a life was a legal possibility. "The established general rule was that the sabbatical regulations might be, nay must be, waived in order to save life . . . ." (Abrahams, *Studies,* 1:132). This principle finds its expression in *m. Yoma* 8:6: "Any case in which there is a possibility that life is in danger thrusts aside the sabbath law." On the other hand, the opponents could easily have dismissed the case in question, by countering that the man's crippled hand was hardly a life threatening situation. The strict Jewish-Christian apocryphal *Gospel According to the Hebrews* appears to work within this casuistry by having the man inform Jesus that he needed his right hand as a stone mason to earn his living. But no such need appears either here or in the parallels of Matthew and Luke. Therefore, the ruler of the synagogue's exhortation in Luke 13:14 to limit healing to the six work days with a request that Jesus wait until sunset would have been an appropriate response.

Consequently, removing Jesus' question from its context and using it as a general rule for sabbath conduct would leave us with essentially the same governing principle found in Judaism regarding the sabbath. Yet the question obviously does not function in this manner in 3:1–6. Why not? Because the healing of the man with a crippled hand qualifies Jesus' meaning of "doing good" and "saving a life." That is also why the healing story and the controversy narrative cannot be separated. By defining "to do good" and "to save a life" in terms of healing a crippled man, Jesus alters the Jewish understanding of saving a life in terms of mortal danger. How does healing a crippled hand equal "saving a life"?

Jesus' question and the opponents' response only become intelligible when set against the broader scope of Jesus' ministry as summarized in 1:14–15 and the implicit claim in the previous controversies. "To do good" and "to save a life" takes on the eschatological ring of the coming of the day of salvation, the fulfillment of God's promised activity in history (cf. Matt 11:5// Luke 7:22; see *Comment* on 7:37), which Jesus came to announce and effect. In other words, "God's redemptive rule is realized in the making whole of a person" (Dietzfelbinger, *EvT* 38 [1978] 297). To this extent every healing was "clearly a question of life or death" for the one whose moment had come in his encounter with Jesus (Rordorf, *Sunday*, 70). Much more was at stake than the restoration of a crippled hand. This one was brought into a new life relationship with God through Jesus' healing. A similar claim underlies the healing of 2:1–12 and Jesus' fellowship with sinners in 2:13–17.

Read in this manner, the alternatives posed by 3:4 take on personal dimensions. Instead of abstract alternatives ("doing good"/"doing evil" and "saving life"/"taking life"), these refer concretely to what is transpiring in this scene. Thus many have ascribed the "doing of evil"/"taking a life" to the opponents' "lying in wait" and their "taking counsel to destroy" Jesus (Taylor, 222; Lohmeyer, 68; Grundmann, 96; Roloff, *Kerygma*, 95; Pesch, 1:192; Gnilka, 1:127). This reading, however, does not follow from the text. First, the opponents do not kill and only take action that could lead to Jesus' death after the healing (3:6). Second, if "doing good" and "saving a life" has a pregnant meaning in reference to Jesus' ministry of the new age, "doing evil" and "taking life," the antithetical parallelism, must share that meaning and refer to actions that negate the work of the Kingdom. At most "doing evil"/"taking life" would refer to the opponents' hindering of the work of the Kingdom (cf. Matt 23:13//Luke 11:52) even in the name of the Law. Third, and most important, Jesus' conduct is in question, not that of his opponents. Therefore, the alternative is Jesus' alternative, either to heal or not to heal. If "to do good"/"to save a life" meant to heal, then "to do evil"/"to take a life" meant not to heal and thus deprive this one of the benefits of God's restoring power.

In terms of 2:23–28, Jesus' healing on the sabbath shows him to be indeed the "Lord of the sabbath" (2:28). In this story, by healing the man, Jesus claims the authority to take action that would have been viewed as illegal by his opponents (Luke 13:14). But this action was anchored in the nature of his work and ministry (2:25–26). To the degree that he brings wholeness to this crippled man by restoring his hand and his relationship with God, he brings to reality God's promised intent at creation. This corresponds with God's gift of the sabbath for the benefit of the human creature (2:27).

Therefore, Jesus' question and subsequent action had far more at stake than simply a protest or provocative challenge of a rigid legalism that placed the good of keeping the sabbath against the good of healing a crippled hand (Cranfield, 125; Lohse, *Judentum*, 86; Schweizer, 75–76; Gnilka, 1:127; Dietzfelbinger, *EvT* 38 [1978] 294). Nor was Jesus' question intended primarily to set forth the real meaning of the sabbath as God's day for the benefit of humanity, especially as experienced in God's saving rule (Dietzfelbinger, *EvT* 38 [1978] 297–98; cf. Pesch, 1:193 and Ernst, 106), since such an understanding would hardly be limited to the sabbath. Rather than a casuistic justification for healing on the sabbath or a programmatic annulment or reinterpretation of the sabbath law, Jesus' question called for a decision regarding his person and ministry. Once again the focus of the pericope was ultimately Christological (Banks, *Jesus,* 125; Roloff, *Kerygma,* 66; Goppelt, *Theology,* 1:92–95).

"But they remained silent" (οἱ δὲ ἐσιώπων) gives the initial response by the opponents. This silence, however, does not reflect the casuistic persuasiveness of Jesus' answer. On the surface, from the opponents' perspective the answer was clear, but the question was irrelevant to this situation. Their silence and subsequent response (3:6) show their perception of a much deeper issue that challenged far more than their interpretation of the Law. Thus, the following verse describes this silence as a "hardness of heart."

5 "Looking around at them with anger" (περιβλεψάμενος αὐτοὺς μετ᾽ ὀργῆς) is the first of two asyndetic participial phrases that precede the main verb. "Looking around" (περιβλέπεσθαι) is a characteristic verb in Mark (6x, Matt has none, Luke has only the parallel here), which may indicate that it is Markan redaction (Pryke, *Style,* 122; Schenke, *Wundererzählungen,* 166–67; Gnilka, 1:126). Perhaps an underlying expression of irritation by the healer toward the one in need (cf. 1:41) was altered to focus on the opponents.

"Deeply grieved at the hardness of their heart" (συλλυπούμενος ἐπὶ τῇ πωρώσει τῆς καρδίας) follows without a conjunction. This too has been attributed to Mark's redaction (Koch, *Wundererzählungen,* 51–52; Schenke, *Wundererzählungen,* 166–67; Gnilka, 1:126), because he alone makes use of the term *hardness* (πώρωσις) of heart and in similar miracle situations (cf. 6:52; 8:17).

Whether Mark or his tradition formulated one or both of these phrases, the meaning remains the same. Jesus perceives their silence to be culpable. Their response is described in language reminiscent of Israel's response to the prophets' message (e.g., Jer 3:17; 7:24; 9:13; 11:18; 13:10; 16:12; Ps 81:13; Deut 29:18). Thus, Jesus' reaction to their response gives additional support to the veiled Christological claim behind his question in 3:4.

"He said to the man" (λέγει τῷ ἀνθρώπῳ) turns the attention back to the man standing in the middle of this scene. This time Jesus commands him to extend his hand. When he does so, it is "restored" (ἀπεκατεστάθη). This verb occurs rarely in the NT and twice in an explicitly eschatological context (9:12//Matt 17:11; Acts 1:6). It occurs again in a healing narrative to refer to the complete restoration of sight (8:25).

Jesus has acted according to the opponents' expectation (3:2) but in terms of his own ministry (3:4). Nothing further is said about the man or his healing.

6 "The Pharisees departed" (ἐξελθόντες οἱ Φαρισαῖοι). The contrast between Jesus "entering" (εἰσέρχεσθαι) a synagogue at the outset (3:1) and the Pharisees "departing" (ἐξέρχεσθαι) may be coincidental but it accents the difference in direction between Jesus and his opponents. The mention of the "Pharisees" at this juncture rather than at the beginning does seem strange. The reader might assume their identity from the larger context of 2:15–28. But the mention of them now may reflect a Markan theme, since they appear again with the "Herodians" in a redactional setting in 12:13; cf. 8:15.

"Took counsel (συμβούλιον ἐδίδουν) against him" is most unusual. In 15:1 we have a similar expression with the more common Latin style (συμβούλιον ποιεῖν, cf. *consilium facere*). This expression in contrast to the related motif in

11:18 and 14:1 (ἐζήτουν πῶς . . .) supports a non-Markan tradition behind
3:6 (cf. Kiilunen, *Vollmacht*, 231–32).

"With the Herodians" (μετὰ τῶν Ἡρῳδιανῶν). The identity of the "Herodians" has been the occasion for much conjecture. Rowley identified eleven
different possibilities (*JTS* 41 [1940] 14–27). Daniel added at least a twelfth
by identifying them with the Essenes (*RevQ* 27 [1970] 397–402).

Hoehner (*Herod*, 331–42) identified them with the Boethusians, a subgroup
of the Sadducees, but leaves unanswered why Mark specifically refers to them
as "Herodians" and not "Boethusians." More recently, Hultgren (*Adversaries*,
154–56) has revived Bacon's thesis (*JBL* 39 [1920] 102–112) based on Epiphanius' (died A.D. 403) reference to the "Herodians" as a group who believed
that Herod Agrippa was the Messiah. Herod, the grandson of Herod the
Great and his Jewish wife, Mariamne and thus considered Jewish, reunited
Galilee and Judea under Emperor Claudius in A.D. 40–41. He was known
to be friendly with the Pharisees and an enemy of the early Church (cf.
Acts 12:1–3,11). Since, however, he only ruled until A.D. 44, this reference
to the "Herodians" would mean it came into the story after A.D. 41 and not
much after A.D. 44. One could hardly have referred to the "Herodians" before
they existed or long after their "Messiah" had died.

Apart from the fact that the reference would be anachronistic for Mark
and his readers as well as for Jesus' own ministry, this view has other problems.
First, Epiphanius' exclusive reference comes over three centuries after this
event. Second, the only biblical reference to the "Herodians" occurs here
and in 12:13 (par Matt 22:16) along with a reference to the "leaven of the
Pharisees and Herod" in 8:15. Josephus refers to them once (*War* 1.319)
and mentions "those thinking like Herod" (*Ant.* 14.15.10). Both references
come in context of violent death. This evidence has led most to reject the
possibility they represented a political party or religious group within Judaism.
Most follow Rowley's suggestion that they were a mixed group of influential
aristocrats who were pro-"Herod."

The lack of other references to this "group" and their presence here and
in 12:13 in conjunction with the Pharisees and the warning about the leaven
of the Pharisees and Herod suggests a Markan motif. Bennet has sought to
trace this motif to the Baptist's role as forerunner in Mark (*NovT* 17 [1975]
9–14). Since the Baptist's death came at the hands of Herod Antipas, the
"Herodians" become the link between the Baptist's death as the "forerunner"
and Jesus' death. But if this were Mark's motif, why are the "Herodians"
never mentioned elsewhere in connection with Jesus' death, especially within
the passion narrative? The one reference in 12:13 has to do with the religious
and political issue of taxes to Caesar (see *Comment* on 12:1). Instead, we
find the "chief priests" and "scribes" collaborating against Jesus (e.g., 11:18;
14:1; 15:1).

Perhaps, as Pesch has indicated, the "Herodians" refers to the politically
influential aristocracy under Herod Antipas' jurisdiction of Galilee (1:195)
and their presence in Jerusalem in 12:13 was at the request of the Jerusalem
authorities (Pesch, 2:225). Their political counterpart in Jerusalem would
be the "chief priests" with whom the "scribes" (representing the Pharisees
for Mark? cf. 2:6,16,24; 3:6) join rank.

In any event, the "Herodians" represent for Mark the political powers (Lührmann, *ZNW* 78 [1987] 171) of Herod Antipas (8:15) and Rome (12:13), which explains the Pharisees' strange cooperation with them here in seeking Jesus' death. According to Mark's passion narrative, it is just this cooperation by the religious authorities with the Roman political powers that eventuates in Jesus' death.

This correspondence may give us the clue about the identification of Jesus' opponents at the end of a traditional unit. Whereas the traditional pericope most likely ended with the unnamed opponents leaving to take counsel against Jesus (3:2,6), Mark adapts the opponents' actions to the political realities of that time by identifying them as the "Pharisees" from the larger context of 2:15–28 and the "Herodians" from 12:13 (Lohmeyer, 67; Schenke, *Wundererzählungen*, 164–66; Kiilunen, *Vollmacht*, 225–30). In so doing, Mark sets the stage for the eventual collusion that does result in Jesus' death.

"How they might destroy him" (ὅπως αὐτὸν ἀπολέσωσιν) recurs in 11:18 with chief priests and scribes as the opponents but the phrase is introduced by πῶς instead of ὅπως, which only occurs here in Mark. Later in 14:1 the chief priests and scribes again seek a way (πῶς) to "kill" (ἀποκτείνωσιν) him. Finally, 15:1 notes that the chief priests, elders and scribes hold counsel on delivering Jesus to Pilate, the Roman, political authority.

With this action the opponents give their ultimate response to Jesus' question, indeed to Jesus' ministry. The irony of the pericope cannot be avoided. Whereas Jesus confronted by a "life"/"death" situation of restoring a crippled hand and life, chooses to act by giving wholeness and life as a gift of the age of salvation, his opponents use his action as the occasion to arrange to have him killed. By bringing the new life of God's rule to bear, Jesus risks losing his own life. This is the irony not only of these controversy narratives but also of Mark's Gospel.

Explanation

Many have argued that the sabbath law became the most important law for the Jews in terms of their sense of identity. This day had been given to them by God and their observance of it set them off from the Gentiles. As it was one of the Ten Commandments, no one questioned its importance or its validity. The only question was how rigorous should one be in making certain that this day was not desecrated. Scribal casuistry sought to clarify and protect the sabbath, not to circumvent its demands. Therefore, Jesus' activity on the sabbath brings about a deliberate confrontation with his opponents who are waiting to charge him with breaking the sabbath.

Many have interpreted this pericope as Jesus' challenge of a scribal casuistry which so legalistically controlled sabbath conduct that it denied even a person's worth. Jesus' question supposedly uncovers the fallacy of this legalism. "Doing good" for his opponents meant keeping the sabbath, and keeping the sabbath meant not healing this cripple. Thus, "doing good" means keeping the sabbath regulations that prevent one from healing which would be "doing evil." In other words, the sabbath was more important than the well-being of a person. By healing this man, Jesus placed himself on the side of human worth against a depersonalized legalism. The picture becomes even more grotesque when the law declares Jesus' healing as "evil," yet the opponents' use of the Law to destroy Jesus is considered "good." Jesus certainly had little time for scribal casuistry (see 7:1–13), but such a reading misses the point of this story. The issue of "doing good" and "doing evil" is further qualified by "saving life" or "taking life" which stands in synonymous parallelism with "doing good"/ "doing evil." Saving a life was the fundamental standard used by the Jews to determine "good" and "evil" conduct on the sabbath. Thus Jesus did not programmatically set aside the sabbath law for the general "good" of humanity or even in terms of the Love commandment, which does not enter the discussion. He appears to concur with the Jewish view of the sabbath. One wonders then how some could argue on the basis of Jesus' question that Jesus was actually getting back to the real meaning of the sabbath.

The opponents' response of complete silence, and Jesus' action of healing the man demonstrate that more was at stake than Jesus' challenge of the sabbath law. If the matter had concerned the interpretation of the Law, the opponents had no cause for silence. They not only agreed in principle but could have applied that principle to the situation (Luke 13:14). They did not. Jesus did. And therein lies the difference.

By healing the man in response to his own question (3:5), Jesus laid claim to "saving a life." Not to have done so would have meant to "take a life." But how could healing a crippled hand, when neither the setting nor illness implied a sense of urgency, be "saving a life"? The answer lies in the implicit claim of Jesus' ministry as depicted in the previous controversy narratives. Healing the sick, forgiving the sinner, sharing a table with toll collectors and sinners, feasting rather than fasting, and his authority over the sabbath— all point to an implicit claim of something special in his work. This claim is summarized in 1:14–15. Jesus was announcing the coming of God's sovereign rule in history, the "fulfillment of time," the dawn of the day of salvation as promised in the scriptures (cf. 1:1–3). Jesus was not only healing a crippled hand, he was bringing wholeness and a new life in relationship with God befitting the age of salvation. In this sense, he was "saving a life."

Therefore, the narrative declares that God's redemptive work knew no constraints, not even the sabbath law. Just as Jesus claimed the authority to supply the needs of his own who had left all to accompany him in his ministry without the constraints of the sabbath law in 2:23–28, so he lays claim here to be doing God's work of making a person whole. Ultimately, Jesus' confrontation with his critics lay in the claim of his ministry and not in a different interpretation of the sabbath law.

The opponents' silence and their subsequent actions indicate they rejected the claim of Jesus' ministry. Instead of arguing the point of legality, they found his claim to be a fundamental threat to their understanding of how God worked and would work in history. This motif underlies each of the controversy narratives in this section and later in 10:2–31 and 11:27–12:44. As a transgressor of the Law, Jesus could have been classed with toll collectors and sinners and left for the day of judgment. But as one who called into question the very premises of their understanding of God's action in history by his own claims and ministry, he represented an ultimate threat. He could neither be tolerated nor easily dismissed. They sought to remove him from the scene.

Mark takes this pericope that captures the poignancy of the conflict and uses it to conclude the series of controversies which began with 2:1–12. He apparently recognizes the subtle implications of this story by describing Jesus' reaction of anger and grief at their "hardness of heart" (3:5). As Israel with the prophets of old, the opponents refused to perceive the message from God in this ministry. Their actions give first indication of the ultimate character of this conflict. By following up Jesus' opening ministry of 1:21–45 with this series of conflict stories, Mark gives the reader an early clue of where and how the story will end. He even notes the combination of religious and political forces, by identifying the Pharisees and the Herodians, that will eventually come together in order to accomplish the final destruction of Jesus. Yet each controversy makes plain that the conflict grew out of Jesus' authority that led him to do and allow that which burst the old wineskins.

L. Summary of Jesus' Healing Ministry (3:7–12)

Bibliography

Best, E. *Following Jesus.* 1981. **Burkill, T. A.** "Mark 3,7–12 and the Alleged Dualism in the Evangelist's Miracle Material." *JBL* 87 (1968) 409–17. **Daube, D.** *The New Testament and Rabbinic Judaism.* London: Athlone Press, l956. **Egger, W.** *Frohbotschaft und Lehre.* 1976. **Hedrick, C. W.** "The Role of 'Summary statements' in the Composition of the Gospel of Mark: A Dialogue with Karl Schmidt and Norman Perrin." *NovT* 26 (1984) 289–311. **Hill, D.** *Greek Words and Hebrew Meanings: Studies in the Semantics of Soteriological Terms.* SNTSMS 5, Cambridge: CUP, 1967. **Kazmierski, C. F.** *Jesus, the Son of God. A Study of the Markan Tradition and its Redaction by the Evangelist.* Forschung zur Bibel 33. Würzburg: Echter Verlag, l979. **Keck, L.** "The Introduction to Mark's Gospel." *NTS* 12 (1965–66) 352–70. ———. "Mk 3,7–12 and Mark's Christology." *JBL* 84 (1965) 341–58. **Kee, H. C.** "The Terminology of Mark's Exorcism Stories." *NTS* 14 (1967–68) 232–46. **Kertelge, K.** *Die Wunder Jesu im Markusevangelium.* 1970. **Kingsbury, J. D.** "The 'Divine Man' as the Key to Mark's Christology—The End of an Era?" *Int* 35 (1981) 24–57. **Koch, D. A.** *Die Bedeutung des Wundererzählungen für die Christologie des Markusevangeliums.* 1975. **Luz, U.** "Die Geheimnismotiv und die markinische Christologie." *ZNW* 56 (1965) 9–30. **Marxsen, W.** *Mark The Evangelist.* 1969. **Perrin, N.** *The New Testament: An Introduction.* New York: Harcourt, Brace Jovanovich, l974, 145–47. **Reploh, K. G.** *Markus—Lehrer der Gemeinde.* 1969. **Schweizer, E.** "Neuere Markusforschung in USA," *ET* 33 [1973] 533–37. **Snoy, T.** "Les miracles dans l'évangile de Marc. Examen de quelques études recentes." *RTL* 3 (1972) 449–66; 4 (1973) 58–101. **Theissen, G.** *The Miracle Stories of the Early Christian Tradition.* 1983.

Translation

⁷*And Jesus withdrew to the sea with his disciples and a large crowd*[a] *followed from Galilee.*[b] ⁸*And a large crowd from Judea, Jerusalem, Idumea, the Trans-Jordan, Tyre and Sidon, having heard all what he was*[c] *doing, came to him.*

⁹*And he told his disciples to*ᵈ *prepare a small boat for him on account of the crowd, lest they should press upon him.* ¹⁰*For he had healed many, so that they eagerly fell upon him in order that all those who were suffering might touch him.* ¹¹*And the unclean spirits, whenever they saw him, would fall before him and cry out, saying: "You are the Son of God."* ¹²*He silenced them many times,*ᵉ *lest they should make him known.*

Notes

ᵃπλῆθος used only here and in 3:8 in Mark. Taylor (226) follows variant πολὺς ὄχλος of D lat (syˢ).

ᵇTexts have differing order, suggesting different punctuation. Some place verb after "Judea" (א C *pc* [vg]). Text supported by B L 565 *pc*.

ᶜποιεῖ B L 892; ἐποίει has greater text support א A C D W Θ 0133 1235 *f*¹·¹³ lat syʰ boᵖᵗ.

ᵈἵνα introduces the content of a command (Cranfield, 125; Moule, *Idiom-Book*, 145–46).

ᵉAdverbial use of πολλά; cf. 5:10,23,38,43; 6:20; 9:26.

Form / Structure / Setting

This material comes in the form of a summary report (cf. 1:14–15,32–34,35–39). As with the previous summaries, the extent of tradition and redaction have been disputed. While Pesch (1:198) has assigned all of 3:7–12 to pre-Markan tradition that originally introduced a cycle of miracle stories (4:35–5:43; 6:32–52; 6:53–56), Keck (*JBL* 84 [1965] 346–47; similarly Schweizer, 79) has argued for a traditional core consisting of 3:7a,b,9–10. This core and redactional reworking accounts for the disjointed nature of the material, the "dualism" in the unusual words for Mark (πλῆθος in 3:7,8 and ἐπιπίπτειν, προσπίπτειν in 3:10,11), the *hapax legomenon* (ἀνεχώρησεν, 3:7) and the two crowds of 3:7c–8 (from Galilee and from other areas). Furthermore, Keck finds a boat and θεῖος ἀνήρ or "divine man" motif that link this core to the cycle of pre-Markan miracle stories noted above. Burkill (*JBL* 87 [1968] 409–17) has brought a major critique of Keck's thesis, both on literary and Christological grounds. Others after an extensive analysis of 3:7–12 have joined him in rejecting a traditional core behind this summary (Egger, *Frohbotschaft*, 95–101; Snoy, *RTL* 4 [1973] 73–78; Kazmierski, *Son of God*, 77–103). The question of style becomes moot in view of Mark's clumsy constructions, and the unusual vocabulary is either left unexplained (Egger, *Frohbotschaft*, 101) or attributed to our limited knowledge of the extent of Mark's vocabulary (Snoy, *RTL* 4 [1973] 69–70; Kazmierski, *Son of God*, 82–83). Others have likewise attributed this material to Mark's redaction (Klostermann, 33; Taylor, 225; Cranfield, 124; Reploh, *Markus*, 37; Koch, *Wundererzählungen*, 167; Gnilka, 1:133; Best, *Jesus*, 36–37).

The question of tradition or redaction cannot ignore the fact that five significant terms in 3:7,9–10 are *hapax legomena* (ἀναχωρεῖν, πλοιάριον, προσκαρτερεῖν, θλίβειν, ἐπιπίπτειν) and several terms are found elsewhere in the pre-Markan tradition (ἅπτεσθαι—1:41; 5:27,28,30,31; 7:33; 8:22; 10:13, μάστιξ—5:29,34, πνεῦμα ἀκάθαρτον—1:23,26,27; 5:2,8,13; 7:25; 9:25; θεωρεῖν —5:15,38; 12:41; 15:40,47; 16:4; προσπίπτειν—5:33; 7:25; ἐπιτιμᾶν —1:25; 4:39; 8:30,32,33; 9:25; 10:13,48. This proportionately high number of *hapax legomena* within a brief passage containing several "traditional" terms would suggest at least a traditional basis for this material. This possibility becomes even clearer when we note (see *Comment*) the close connection between terms and concepts in 3:7–12 and the hypothetical miracle cycle.

For example, 3:7 has one *hapax legomenon* (ἀνεχώρησεν) and one word that only occurs again in the next verse (πλῆθος), while including references to the "disciples" and the "sea," which play a prominent role in the miracle cycle. The same is true for 3:9–10 with four *hapax legomena* (πλοιάριον, προσκαρτερεῖν, θλίβειν, ἐπιπίπτειν) and several related terms in the miracle cycle (cf. πλοιάριον/πλοῖον, θλίβειν/συνθλίβειν, ἅπτεσθαι, μάστιξ).

By contrast, the linking of the anonymous crowds with the areas of Palestine (3:7c–8) may well reflect Mark's redactional interest in describing the vast impact of Jesus' ministry and the positive response in contrast to the reaction of the religious and political establishment in 3:1–6. Furthermore, the shift in tone and the distinctive use of terminology (πνεύματα ἀκάθαρτα, ἐπιτιμᾶν) related to 1:21–28 and 5:1–20 in keeping with the redactional thrust of 1:34 and the Christological title "Son of God" suggests Mark's redaction behind 3:11–12.

Thus, Keck's traditional core of 3:7,9–10 seems to accord best with the verbal and thematic considerations. This view gains even greater support, if the summary originally introduced a traditional "cycle" of miracles stories, as argued by Pesch, 1:198, that concluded with a parallel summary in 6:53–56.

Structurally, the disjunctive character of this pericope has led to several proposals. Egger (*Frohbotschaft*, 92–93) has divided the pericope syntactically into three sections: (a) an introductory statement (3:7a,b); (b) an *inclusio* between 3:7c and 3:8; and (c) a block of statements held together by a series of conjunctions (3:9–12, ἵνα, ἵνα μή, γάρ, ὥστε, ἵνα, ὅταν, ὅτι, ἵνα μή). While this division may help prove his point that the account is not a summary of "healings and exorcisms," this syntactical analysis is neither clear nor helpful in bringing order to this account, especially 3:9–12.

Koch (*Wundererzählungen*, 167–68) has divided the materials into two parallel expressions of a revelation/concealment theme. The first expression is seen in Jesus' withdrawal set in tension with the press of the crowd in 3:7–8 and repeated in 3:9–10. The second expression is the unclean spirits' confession set in tension with Jesus' command to silence (3:11–12). Both expressions for Koch represent the tension in Mark's "secret" about who Jesus is. Unfortunately, Koch's thesis suffers the unfounded assumption that Jesus' attempt to withdraw parallels in any way his silencing the unclean spirits. In fact, it assumes that Jesus' withdrawal meant leaving the crowds, which in fact does not take place either in 3:7–8 or 3:9–10.

Reploh's suggestion (*Lehrer*, 36–43; cf. Kazmierski, *Son of God*, 92,95–96) seems to account most adequately for the materials: (a) Jesus' withdrawal to the sea in the company of his disciples (3:7a,b); (b) the thronging of the crowds from Galilee (3:7c) and areas beyond (3:8), underscored by his ordering of a boat to be on hand, in quest of his healing (3:9–10); (c) the behavior of the unclean spirits and Jesus' response (3:11–12), which form a climax to the summary.

Most have viewed this summary as a break with what has gone before and an introduction to the material that follows (Taylor, 225; Cranfield, 124; Lane, 126; Schweizer, 78; Kertelge, *Wunder*, 34; Egger, *Frohbotschaft*, 93; Pesch, 1:201–2). The shift in tone from the controversy narratives in 2:1–3:6 to 3:7–12 seems to confirm the beginning of a new section. Yet this perspective gives too much prominence to the controversy unit as an entity in itself, overlooks the thrust of 1:21–45, and fails to see how 3:7–12 functions to bring together Mark's portrait of Jesus' ministry from 1:16 to 3:6. Furthermore, the absence of any reference to Jesus as teacher, a Markan motif (cf. 1:21–28), seems to offer a strange prelude for a section beginning with the call of the Twelve and including Jesus' teaching about the "mystery of the Kingdom."

Mark has expanded one traditional core to introduce Jesus' ministry in and around Capernaum (1:16–45) and another traditional core to portray the conflict inherent in that ministry (2:1–3:6). But these are not two discrete sections. Together they offer the first glimpse of Jesus' ministry. And 3:7–12, regardless of the issue of tradition and/or redaction, draws together the materials of 1:16–3:6 by resuming in summary fashion the crowds' response to Jesus' ministry (1:21–45) which stands in stark contrast with his opponents' response (2:1–3:6, esp. 3:6). Furthermore, Mark also gathers up the theme of the "unclean spirits" with which he opened Jesus' ministry in Capernaum (1:23) and has them announce, though silenced (cf. 1:34), Jesus' true identity as the Son of God. Even the disciples of 1:16–20 familiar with boats and the sea come into the picture here. In other words, Jesus' ministry as depicted in 1:16–3:12 reaches its zenith in the graphic portrait of 3:7–12 when set against the backdrop of 1:21–3:6 (Keck, *JBL* 84 [1965] 344–45; Gnilka, 1:135; Kazmierski, *Son of God*, 84–85, 95). We found a similar situation in the summary of 1:14–15 that brought to a climax 1:1–15.

The numerous motifs in this summary that reappear in subsequent passages (see Egger, *Frohbotschaft*, 95–106 and *Comment* below) most likely stem from a traditional connection of 3:7–12 with a pre-Markan block of miracle material scattered throughout Mark 4–6. Thus, the lexical and thematic similarity with what follows should not come as a surprise. Consequently, 3:7–12 refers, on the one hand, to what has come before (1:21–3:6) through Mark's redactional location and modification of a traditional summary and, on the other hand, anticipates what follows as a result of the traditional connection especially with 4:35–5:43 (so Egger, *Frohbotschaft*, 108–9). But Mark's choice to use the "summary" at this juncture in his outline, clearly encapsulates Jesus' ministry as depicted in 1:21–3:6.

Comment

7 "Jesus" (ὁ Ἰησοῦς). The last time Jesus was identified by name at the beginning of a pericope occurred in 1:14, the beginning of the summary statement in 1:14–15. "The disciples" (τῶν μαθητῶν) enter the scene again, after not being mentioned in 3:1–6. They were an important part of the controversy narratives in 2:15–28. They also play an important role in the miracle stories of 4:35–41, 5:24–34, 6:32–44, 45–52.

"Withdrew to the sea" (ἀνεχώρησεν πρὸς τὴν θάλασσαν). "To withdraw" (ἀναχωρεῖν) does not appear again in Mark. Set against 3:6, some have taken the verb in the sense of "to flee" from the authorities (Marxsen, *Mark,* 63; Pesch, 1:199). Yet the pursuing crowds make clear that Jesus was hardly escaping in Mark's narrative. More than likely the meaning here corresponds for Mark with the scenes in 1:35,45 and 2:13 where Jesus seeks to get away, to retire from the scene of activity. Therefore, to "withdraw with his disciples" merely indicates a change in venue.

This is the third reference to Jesus around the sea (cf. 1:16; 2:13). In 1:16–20 he called four disciples. In 2:13 he taught the crowds who came to him. Here he accompanies the disciples to the sea and will heal the sick. No pattern appears to have emerged so far. We have no evidence indicating the sea to be "the sphere of the demonic" (Lane, 128). The presence of the "unclean spirits" (3:11–12) at the sea seems little different from their presence in 1:34,39; cf. 1:21–28. The "sea" ($\theta\dot{\alpha}\lambda\alpha\sigma\sigma\alpha$) does play a role in the miracles of 4:35–41 and 6:45–52 and provides the setting for the miracles in 5:1–20,21; 6:31–32 and the teaching in 4:1.

"A large crowd followed" ($\pi o\lambda\dot{\upsilon}\ \pi\lambda\tilde{\eta}\theta os\ \ldots\ \dot{\eta}\kappa o\lambda o\dot{\upsilon}\theta\eta\sigma\epsilon\nu$). This demonstrates the eager response of the crowds to Jesus' ministry (1:37,45; 2:13) and the resultant futility of Jesus' attempt to withdraw. Mark has already sketched a similar response in 1:35–37,45 and 2:13, especially in contrast to the opponents' response (2:13 cf. 2:5–7; 3:7–10 cf. 3:6).

Two unusual expressions for Mark occur in this clause. First, instead of Mark's common word for "crowd" ($\ddot{o}\chi\lambda os$, 38x; cf. 3:9), we have one of the two usages of $\pi\lambda\tilde{\eta}\theta os$ (cf. 3:8). Kazmierski's suggestion that Mark had a specific reference to the "Christian community" (*Son of God,* 91) in mind with the choice of this term (so Acts 15:30; 19:9; 21:22 *v.l.,* cf. 4:32; 6:5; 15:12) has no support in Mark and only contextual support in Acts (cf. Acts 14:1; 17:4; 21:36).

"Followed" ($\dot{\eta}\kappa o\lambda o\dot{\upsilon}\theta\eta\sigma\epsilon\nu$) frequently has the more technical meaning of discipleship in Mark (cf. 1:18; 2:14; 8:34; 9:38; 10:21,28), but it also has the more general meaning of "following behind" (5:24; 10:32; 11:9; 14:13,54; cf. 6:1; 10:52; 15:41; see *Note* d, 2:16).

"From Galilee" ($\dot{\alpha}\pi\dot{o}\ \tau\tilde{\eta}s\ \Gamma\alpha\lambda\iota\lambda\alpha\dot{\iota}\alpha s$). Several have attributed this geographical note and those of 3:8 to Mark's redaction (e.g., Marxsen, *Mark,* 63; Keck, *JBL* 84 [1965] 346). Accordingly, this geographical reference reflects Mark's particular interest in Galilee as a special place of revelation (Lohmeyer, 71), the meeting place for the Church at the parousia (Marxsen, *Mark,* 62–66), or the land of the Gentiles (Best, *Jesus,* 37).

Yet these suggestions may be a little too subtle. The distinction, if intended, between Galilee and the rest of the areas may simply reflect the location of Jesus' ministry in Galilee in 1:16–3:6 where he attracted a crowd who simply "followed" him to the sea. The other crowds "came" ($\ddot{\eta}\lambda\theta o\nu$, 3:8) to Jesus from surrounding areas on the basis of his reputation. Materially, therefore, the text makes little distinction between those "following behind" ($\dot{\eta}\kappa o\lambda o\dot{\upsilon}\theta\eta\sigma\epsilon\nu$) Jesus and those who "come to him" ($\ddot{\eta}\lambda\theta o\nu\ \pi\rho\dot{o}s\ \alpha\dot{\upsilon}\tau\dot{o}\nu$). The one group has had the advantage of the presence of his ministry; the other group has had only the report of that ministry. Jesus' response in 3:10 does not distinguish between the groups.

As to the question of tradition or redaction, Mark's propensity for $\dot{\epsilon}\xi\dot{\epsilon}\rho\chi\epsilon\sigma\theta\alpha\iota$

(cf. ἀναχωρεῖν), ὄχλος (cf. πλῆθος) and perhaps the more technical use of ἀκολουθεῖν suggests that these unusual terms may indeed have come to him from a prior tradition (Keck, *JBL* 84 [1965] 346–47; Pesch, 1:198).

8 A list of seven areas from which the crowds came to Jesus concludes with a second reference to a "large crowd" (πλῆθος πολύ; cf. πολὺ πλῆθος of 3:7) and forms an *inclusio* with the first. The punctuation of 3:7 has been disputed and the manuscript tradition is quite mixed (cf. *Note* b), but the presence of two large groups presents no internal difficulties within the summary. The first group included Galilee. The second group is listed from the perspective of Galilee.

"Judea" represents the region with "Jerusalem" being a particular city within the area. "Idumea" lay southeast of Judea, then came the "Trans-Jordan" or "Perea" to the east and northeast of Judea or southeast of Galilee. Finally, the area north to northwest of Galilee, "Tyre and Sidon," rounds out the list. Noticeably absent are Samaria, and the area of the Decapolis.

Much speculation has gone into decoding the significance of this list. Schmidt (106; similarly Lane, 129) considered it to cover the areas of Jesus' ministry depicted in the Gospel (although we have no reference otherwise to Idumea and the Decapolis is missing). Klostermann (33) noted that these areas were either Jewish or had large Jewish populations. This observation concurs with the omission of Samaria and the Decapolis. But most have attributed the list, either to the existence of churches in this area during the stage of the development of the summary (Pesch, 1:200; Ernst, 110) or to the time of the evangelist (Lohmeyer, 71; Marxsen, *Mark*, 64; Grundmann, 99). Unfortunately, we have no solid evidence for such an assumption (Gnilka, 1:134). In any case, the effect of this listing underscores the attraction of the crowds to Jesus from almost all of Palestine (Egger, *Frohbotschaft*, 102; Gnilka, 1:134). Whether intended as a contrast or not, the expanse of Jesus' ministry far exceeded that of his predecessor, John the Baptist (cf. 1:5, "Judea and Jerusalem").

This emphasis on the success of Jesus' ministry in attracting popular interest and the resultant pressure of the crowds corresponds to Mark's emphasis in 1:21–3:6. This correspondence may suggest that the evangelist was responsible for expanding a tradition that mentioned the crowds (πλῆθος, 3:7) to include crowds from Galilee and from the Jewish regions (3:7c–8). This portrait of Jesus' ministry to the Jews does not deny his ministering on occasion to Gentiles (cf. 7:24–30) but shows how the Jewish populace, in contrast to their authorities (2:1–3:6), responded to Jesus' ministry.

"Heard all what he was doing" (ἀκούοντες ὅσα ἐποίει) explains why the crowds from beyond Galilee came to Jesus. If Mark was responsible for this listing and the location of this summary at this juncture in Jesus' ministry, both the selection of "Jewish" areas and the cause of the crowds' interest (report rather than personal appearance) would reflect a sensitivity by the evangelist for the "historical" situation in Jesus' ministry as he was portraying it, since Jesus to this point in Mark's story line has had no contact with either this area or the Gentiles.

9 "To the disciples" (τοῖς μαθηταῖς) mentions the disciples a second time in this summary (3:7). Their association with Jesus and a boat form the focus

of several of the following miracle stories (4:35–41; 5:1–20; 6:31–32; 45–52). This too may point to a pre-Markan traditional core for this material as a part of a collection of miracle stories.

"To prepare a boat" contains two *hapax legomena* ("to prepare" [προσκαρτερῇ] and "little boat" [πλοιάριον]). Mark's tendency to use diminutives (e.g., 5:23, 39,41; 6:9; 7:25,27,28; 8:7; 14:47) has been noted as an explanation for the appearance of πλοιαριον here (Cranfield, 125; Grundmann, 99; Kazmierski, *Son of God*, 92). But it should be noted that the diminutive terms elsewhere usually occur within traditional material. This does not support the redactional nature of "boat" here. Furthermore, the related term for "boat" (πλοῖον) occurs several times in the miracles of 4:35–5:43,6:32–52 (4:36,37; 5:2,18,21; 6:32,45,47,51). In each instance the boat serves as a means of transportation, as it would have here (cf. 4:1–2). In 6:32 it even provides a means of getting away from the crowds, although the attempt was futile.

"On account of the crowd (διὰ τὸν ὄχλον), lest they should press upon him." "To press" (θλίβωσιν) is another Markan *hapax legomenon*, but it too has a related term in the miracle stories that follow (συνθλίβειν, 5:24,31). The grounds given for preparing a boat underscore the eager press of the crowd (Grundmann, 99–100; Reploh, *Lehrer*, 38–39; Ernst, 110; Kazmierski, *Son of God*, 92; Schmithals, 1:203). The boat is there to provide transportation away from the crowd if needed, but not a means to leave the crowd as such as in 6:32 (cf. Koch, *Wundererzählungen*, 168; Egger, *Frohbotschaft*, 94,104). In 4:1 Jesus uses a boat to get space from which he could teach those gathered on the shore. Thus, 3:9 may have offered Mark the redactional setting for 4:1 (see *Comment* on 4:1 and 4:36).

10 "For he healed many" (πολλοὺς γὰρ ἐθεράπευσεν) introduces an explanatory statement for the great crowds in 3:9. Whereas, the "crowds" (πλῆθος) in 3:8 had come from all over because they had heard of Jesus, the "crowd" (ὄχλος) in 3:9 threatened to overwhelm Jesus in eager response to his having healed many of them. Their eagerness is conveyed by the fifth *hapax legomenon* of this passage, their "falling upon him" (ἐπιπίπτειν αὐτῷ).

"In order to touch him" (ἵνα αὐτοῦ ἅψωνται) represents for some at least a hellenistic tone (e.g., Gnilka, 1:135) and for others a Θεῖος ἀνήρ Christology (Keck, *JBL* 84 [1965] 348–51; Weeden, 57). By desiring to "touch" (ἅπτειν) him, the crowds ascribed to Jesus a healing power with which they needed to come into contact. This motif also appears in the healing story of the woman with a hemorrhage (5:27–28) and the summary in 6:56 (Keck, (*JBL* 84 [1965] 341–58). In the miracles of 1:40–45; 7:31–37; 8:22–26 Jesus heals a leper, a mute and a blind man by touching them. Whereas 3:10; 5:27–28 and 6:56 share in common an action by the afflicted, the other accounts share in common an action by the healer. According to Theissen, however, the significance remains the same (*Miracle Stories*, 62–63).

Several have questioned the basis for assigning this and the other occurrences of healing by touching the healer to a Θεῖος ἀνήρ Christology (Burkill, *JBL* 87 [1968] 414–16; Kazmierski, *Son of God*, 94–95). In fact, the idea of a developed and clearly defined Θεῖος ἀνήρ concept in the background of the Gospel tradition has come into serious question (e.g., D. Tiede, *The Charismatic*

Figure as Miracle Worker, SBLDS 1, [Missoula: Scholars Press, 1972]; O. Betz, "The Concept of the So-called 'Divine Man.'" *Studies in New Testament and Early Christian Literature*, FS A. P. Wikgren, ed. D. Aune. [Leiden: Brill, 1972], 229–40; and J. Kingsbury, *Int* 35 [1981] 243–57).

Furthermore, Daube (*Rabbinic Judaism*, 228–29, 235) has argued against ascribing these healings to any hellenistic setting in view of OT parallels (2 Kgs 13:21; 1 Kgs 17:21//2 Kgs 4:34). More importantly within this context the healing is directly ascribed to Jesus' action ("he healed many") and in 5:34 Jesus describes the woman's desire to touch his robe as an act of faith that "saved" (σέσωκεν, cf. 3:4) her (Egger, *Frohbotschaft*, 105; Schmithals, 1:202).

"Were suffering" translates εἶχον μάστιγας that technically means "scourging" or "lashes." Since it often came from punishment, it can connote divine affliction, or the affliction of a sinner (Cranfield, 125; Grundmann, 100). Yet the context supports a more general concept of "suffering." The only other occurrence of this term is in the miracle story of the woman with a hemorrhage in 5:29,34.

11 "The unclean spirits" (τὰ πνεύματα τὰ ἀκάθαρτα). See *Comment* on 1:23.

"Whenever they saw him, would fall before him" sets a different tone from the rushing crowds of 3:7–10. The imperfect tense of the verbs, the indefinite temporal conjunction "whenever," and the position of prostration contrast with the previous aorist tenses, the press of the crowds to touch Jesus and the ordering of a boat in case the press became too intense in 3:7–10. This shift in tone may reflect the difference between tradition (3:7,9–10) and redaction (3:11–12). The combination of healing and exorcism was present in 1:32–34 but only healings are mentioned in the summary of 6:53–56, the possible counterpart to this summary of 3:7–12 in the pre-Markan miracle cycle. Thus Mark may have introduced this reference to the unclean spirits in 3:11–12 by drawing on material from 1:23–28 and 5:1–20, just as he added the summary about exorcisms in 1:39.

"Fall before him" (προσέπιπτον αὐτῷ) picks up the root of the *hapax legomenon* προσπίπτειν ("to fall upon") in 3:10. Some have interpreted this as an apotropaic gesture by the unclean spirits to avoid the exorcist's power (Grundmann, 100; Gnilka, 1:135). But the use of it in 5:33 and 7:25 with reference to individuals indicates rather the gesture of humble recognition, a meaning appropriate to this context, as will be seen.

"You are the Son of God" (σὺ εἶ ὁ υἱὸς τοῦ ὁαέῦ) has also been taken as an apotropaic gesture (see *Comment* on 1:24) identical to the unclean spirit's address of "Son of the Most High God" in 5:7. "Son of God" represents without a doubt Mark's Christological designation for Jesus (1:1,11; 9:7; 15:39). But apart from God himself (1:11; 9:7), the demons are the only ones to refer to Jesus by this title before the centurion in 15:39. They do so correctly for Mark (cf. "they knew who he was," 1:34).

12 "Many times he subdued them" (πολλὰ ἐπετίμα αὐτοῖς) uses ἐπιτιμᾶν as a technical expression for an action by which God establishes control over evil powers (Kee, *NTS* 14 [1967–68] 232–46; see *Comment* on 1:25). Accordingly, Jesus appears in 3:11–12 to have power over the unclean spirits as seen in their prostration and recognition of him. They had no power against Jesus as seen in the exorcisms (cf. 1:27–28,34,39). Unfortunately, the view which takes the silencing of 3:11–12 in terms of an exorcism (e.g., Lane,

130; Grundmann, 100; Gnilka, 1:135) fails to accord with 3:12b which gives a specific reason for Jesus' "subduing" the unclean spirits.

"Lest they should make him known" (ἵνα μὴ αὐτὸν φανερὸν ποιήσωσιν) corresponds to the same reason given for Jesus' not permitting the demons to speak in 1:34 *after* they had been exorcised. Taken literally, Jesus' action in 3:12 also comes somewhat late in the sequence. The unclean spirits would have already made public his identity as the Son of God. Consequently, Kazmierski has suggested that "the cries of the evil spirits in 3:11 are actually not heard at the seashore" (*Son of God*, 102–3) but were intended by Mark for his Gentile Christian readers. This attempt at smoothing out the logical inconsistency places too much weight on the generalized tone of 3:11–12 and fails to see how Mark has stylized the exorcisms for his purposes. In other words, Mark has changed a technical exorcism formula (ἐπιτιμᾶν) for subduing the evil forces to serve his own purposes of silencing the demonic spirits.

On the one hand, the unclean spirits have the correct knowledge of who Jesus is. Thus, their cries correctly identify Jesus as the Son of God and the designation forms the climax of Jesus' ministry as depicted in 1:16–3:6 and summarized in 3:7–12 (Reploh, *Lehrer* 39). The crowds have come to Jesus because they responded to his ministry, especially his ministry of healing. The demons by virtue of their supernatural knowledge recognize who Jesus is as seen by their prostration and their statements. Thus, Mark uses the opportunity in such a summary setting to identify again for the reader who Jesus is, namely, the Son of God. Though not intended as a Christological confession by the unclean spirits, their cry is Christologically correct for Mark.

On the other hand, the unclean spirits are subdued or forbidden to speak (1:34; 3:12), lest they, who know (1:34), make known who Jesus is (3:12). But why does Mark have them cry out who Jesus is, only to have Jesus prevent them from speaking or making him known? This is the evangelist's way of signalling the inappropriateness of the unclean spirits' cry. But why inappropriate? The answer can hardly lie with their being, as evil spirits, inappropriate witnesses (e.g., Taylor, 228; Lane, 130–31; Grundmann, 100). Mark himself has made them the witnesses in 3:11 ("You are the Son of God," cf. 1:24; 5:7). Nor can their cries convey an incorrect identification of Jesus for Mark (e.g., Ernst, 110; Gnilka, 1:135; Weeden, 56–57), since as supernatural beings they recognize Jesus and Mark has placed on their lips the correct identity of Jesus as "Son of God." We are left then with the possibility that their statement of who Jesus is came at an inappropriate time. Though the demons knew and understood who Jesus was, others could not. In fact, this understanding can only come in view of the cross and resurrection (cf. 9:9; 15:39). Thus, we have a solid clue that Mark's own "messianic secret" has to do with the timing and thus meaning of the proclamation of Jesus as Son of God (Luz, *ZNW* 56 [1965] 18–20; Reploh, *Lehrer*, 41–42; Egger, *Frohbotschaft*, 106–7).

Explanation

Mark has used a summary account in 3:7–12, drawn for the most part from the tradition, to bring his introduction of Jesus' ministry to a climactic conclusion. The first part of this material reads more like a day at a busy seashore with the press of the crowds for healing. By contrast, the passage concludes with a much more generalized description of the reaction of the "unclean spirits" whenever they met Jesus (3:11), and Jesus' response to their identifying him as the Son of God (3:12).

Three elements stand out in this complex. First, Jesus withdraws with his disciples to the sea. This theme of withdrawal has appeared in 1:35 for prayer, in 1:37 for mission, and in 1:45 because of a veiled threat awaiting him in the cities. Then in 2:13 with no reason given Jesus leaves the city for the sea where he teaches the crowds. In the immediate context of 3:1–6, he leaves the scene of conflict with his opponents (cf. 2:1–3:6). Thus some have viewed this move to be an attempt to escape the authorities who were planning how to destroy him. The presence, however, of the pursuing crowds makes this explanation unlikely. Since, as in 2:13, no reason is given, we may have here simply a change of venue.

Second, Jesus is met and surrounded by crowds. The crowds come seeking him in 1:36 and find him in 1:45; 2:1–3 and 2:13. This same scene is repeated and intensified in 3:7–10. Standing in stark contrast to Jesus' opponents whose rejection of Jesus ultimately takes the form of planning his destruction (2:1–3:6), the crowds pursue him (1:45) not only from Galilee but from all the Jewish centers of Palestine. Their response to his ministry, which many have only heard about, is so positive that he finds himself endangered by the press of the crowd. So in an action that graphically depicts the intensity of the crowd's response, Jesus orders a boat to be available as a safety measure. The focus of his ministry here is his healing (cf. 1:32–34; 6:53–56). Third, the "unclean spirits" enter the scene and prostrate themselves in recognition of Jesus. Mark uses formal material from other exorcism stories to have these unclean spirits declare Jesus to be the Son of God. Since, according to Mark (1:34), the demons knew who Jesus was, this title identifies who Jesus is. The voice from heaven has made the same declaration in 1:11 and will again in 9:7. Mark affirms this in his introduction of the Gospel about "Jesus, Messiah, Son of God" (1:1) and on the lips of the centurion at the cross (15:39). Therefore, the unclean spirits bring to the climax this initial portrait of Jesus' ministry in 1:16–3:12 by revealing who Jesus actually is. That authority which has attracted disciples, crowds, sick, and sinners and threatens the demons finds its basis in Jesus, the Son of God.

Yet Mark does not let their identification stand unchallenged. In 3:12 Jesus subdues the unclean spirits by silencing them (cf. 1:34) "lest they should make him known." We have here one of Mark's primary theological motifs and a clue to the so-called "messianic secret." Jesus does not avoid the crowds who come for his teaching or for his healing. He affirms their pursuit of him by teaching them (2:1–3, 13) and healing them (1:29–31, 32–34, 40–45: 2:1–12; 3:9–10). He even responds to his critics with a claim of authority (2:10, 17, 19, 25–26, 28). And Jesus does not deny the evil spirits' identification of him (1:24, 34). But, according to Mark, Jesus counters the demons by silencing them. The disciples', crowd's and opponents' knowledge of Jesus was incomplete, not necessarily wrong. More had to be known about Jesus' ministry in light of the cross and resurrection (9:9). Thus, the cries of the unclean spirits, whose knowledge was accurate and complete, had to be stifled. Only Jesus' ministry as seen in 1:16–3:12 and including the cross and resurrection could ultimately reveal him to be the Son of God. That was the "gospel of Jesus Messiah, Son of God" for Mark.

But why does Mark choose to portray the events in this manner? Does he seek to repudiate or warn against a false Christology in his community that affirms Jesus to be the glorified Son of God, the great miracle worker whose wondrous works display his deity, but denies the pain and ignominy of the cross? Apart from the fundamental question of any historical basis for such a Christology, we have found little in the portrait of Jesus in either the miracle stories or the summaries of 1:21–3:6 that reflects such a distinctive Christology.

Is Mark simply trying to balance a Jesus tradition that focused on Jesus' teaching, exorcism and healings as eschatological signs of the Kingdom with a kerygma of the cross? If so, the expected language of the Kingdom and related concepts are unexplainably sparse in 1:21–3:6.

Is Mark in proclaiming the gospel in narrative form reflecting a sensitivity to the historical context of this message? Does he preserve and enhance the tension between Jesus' self-revelation and concealment embedded in a tradition with roots in Jesus' ministry? The fact that Mark has used tradition (1:23–28, 40–45; 2:1–12; 3:1–6) to supplement blocks of tradition (1:29–38; 2:15–28) and the presence of these themes in the various traditions suggest that Mark's "secret" belongs at the heart of the gospel about Jesus Messiah, Son of God.

III. *The Mystery of the Kingdom of God (3:13–6:6)*

Introduction

Mark 3:13–6:6 comprises the second major section of the first half of the Gospel. It too begins with a pericope about the disciples (3:13–19; cf. 1:16–20 and 6:7–13) and concludes with a summary statement about Jesus' ministry (6:6b; cf. 3:7–12 and 8:22–26). Jesus stands at center stage throughout this material but always in the company of the disciples.

After focusing on the startling authority of Jesus that called disciples (1:16–20), confounded the crowds (1:21–45), and confronted the "authorities" (2:1–3:6), Mark expands on the nature of Jesus' ministry, the "mystery of the Kingdom of God." The theme of discipleship sounded initially at the call of four fishermen (1:16–20) and echoed in the call of Levi (2:13–17) is developed by the appointing of the Twelve to be "with him" and to participate in that ministry (3:13–19) as well as by a new definition of "family" (3:20–21, 31–35). Jesus' authority over the "unclean spirits" (1:21–28, 34; 3:11–12) gains further development in the discussion about his exorcisms (3:22–30), hinted at in the stilling of the storm (4:35–41) and is elaborately illustrated by the story of the Gerasene demoniac (5:1–20). And the healings that marked the opening section (1:29–31, 32–34, 40–45; 2:1–12; 3:1–6, 7–12) continue with the healing of the woman with a hemorrhage and the raising of Jairus' daughter (5:21–43).

Yet this section also develops some elements of Jesus' ministry that were latent in the first section. First, though his "teaching" in the Capernaum synagogue caused astonishment in the opening section (1:21–28), we now find him teaching those "around him" in a house (3:31–35), crowds on the seashore (4:1–34), friends and family in the synagogue of his home town (6:1–6a) and in surrounding towns and villages (6:6b). Furthermore, in 4:1–34 we gain insight into the content of this teaching through a series of parables concerning the Kingdom of God, a motif central to Jesus' preaching in the summary of 1:15.

Second, the foreboding resistance from the religious and political authorities continues in the question by the "scribes from Jerusalem" in 3:22 but spreads to encompass Jesus' friends and family (3:21; 6:1–6a). Lines appear to be drawn more clearly between "insiders" and "outsiders" (3:31–35; 4:10–12). Those on the "inside" have been given the "mystery of the Kingdom of God" (4:11). Having responded to his call (3:13–19), they are "around him" seeking to "do the will of God" (3:31–35; 4:10–11) and are open to his help (5:1–43). To them Jesus "explains all things" (4:13–20, 33–34) and ministers his healing, life-giving presence (4:35–5:43). The "outsiders" include those who have rejected Jesus considering him to have become insane (3:21) or in league with Satan (3:22). Their lack of faith precludes his ministering to them and working among them (6:1–6). For them, Jesus, his teaching and ministry are at best "riddles."

A new motif appears as well in this section. Even the "insiders," the disciples, show a lack of understanding (4:10) and an awestruck consternation (4:41). They are warned to listen attentively (4:24–25) and rebuked by Jesus' questioning of their response (4:13, 40). Obviously, their gift of the "mystery of the Kingdom" (4:11) included neither esoteric "inside information" nor a clear grasp of who Jesus was. Yet the gift of the "mystery of the Kingdom" was integral to Jesus and his ministry as seen in the special privileges of their relationship to him (3:13–19, 31, 35) and their private instruction by him (4:13–20, 33–34) as well as in the faith displayed by those seeking his help (5:25–34, 35–43; cf. 6:1–6a).

Mark seems to have constructed the center of this section from two blocks of traditional material. First, the evangelist appears to have used a collection of parables (4:3–20, 26–34) to which he has added other tradition (4:21–25) and a setting (4:1–2). Second, he appears to have used a portion of a miracle collection in 4:35–5:43 for four miracles set on or around the sea of Galilee (4:35–41; 5:1–20; 5:21–24, 35–43; 5:24–35; cf. 3:7–12). He breaks into the miracle collection by shifting to Jesus' rejection in Nazareth (6:1–6a) and concludes with a brief summary statement about Jesus' teaching in the surrounding villages (6:6b). All this is prefaced by the call of the Twelve (3:13–19) and a story about true family (3:21, 31–35) containing an intercalation of an encounter with the "scribes from Jerusalem" in 3:22–30.

A. The Calling of the Twelve (3:13–19)

Bibliography

Best, E. "Mark's use of the Twelve." *ZNW* 69 (1978) 11–35 = *Disciples and Discipleship: Studies in the Gospel According to Mark.* T.& T. Clark, 1986. 131–61. ———. "The Role of the Disciples in Mark." *NTS* 23 (1976–77) 377–401 = *Disciples and Discipleship: Studies in the Gospel According to Mark.* T.& T. Clark, 1986. 98–130. **Betz, O.** "Donnersöhne, Menschenfischer und der davidische Messias." *RevQ* 3 (1961) 41–70. **Brown, R. E., Donfried, K. P.,** and **Reumann, J.** eds. *Peter in the New Testament.* Minneapolis/New York: Augsburg/Paulist Press, 1973. **Buth, R.** "Mark 3:17 ΒΟΝΕΡΓΕΣ and Popular Etymology." *JSNT* 10 (1981) 29–33. **Cullmann, O.** *Peter: Disciple, Apostle, Martyr.* New York: World, 1958. ———. "Der Zwölfte Apostel." In *Vorträge und Aufsätze 1925–1962.* Tübingen: Mohr, 1966. 214–22. **Fitzmyer, J. A.** "Aramaic *Kepha* and Peter's Name in the New Testament." In *To Advance the Gospel: New Testament Studies.* New York: Crossroad, 1981. 112–24 = *Text and Interpretation.* FS Matthew Black, ed. E. Best and R. M. Wilson. Cambridge: UP, 1979. 121–32. ———. "The Name Simon." In *Essays in the Semitic Background of the New Testament.* London: Chapman, 1971. 105–12. **Gärtner, B.** *Iscariot.* Philadelphia: Fortress, 1971. **Horsley, R. A.** and **Hanson, J. S.** *Bandits, Prophets, and Messiahs: Popular Movements at the Time of Jesus.* Minneapolis: Winston, 1985. **Jeremias, J.** *New Testament Theology.* 1971. **Klein, G.** *Die Zwölf Apostel.* FRLANT 77. Göttingen: Vandenhoeck & Ruprecht, 1961. **Lampe, P.** "Das Spiel mit dem Petrus-Namen—Matt. xvi. 18." *NTS* 25 (1978–79) 227–45. **Meye, R. P.** *Jesus and the Twelve.* 1968. **Meyer, E.** *Ursprung und Anfänge des Christentums,* I, Stuttgart/Berlin: Cotta, 1921. **Pesch, R.** "The Position and Significance of Peter in the Church

of the New Testament: A Survey of Current Research." *Concil* 7 (1971) 21–35.
———. *Simon Petrus: Geschichte und geschichtliche Bedeutung des ersten Jungers Jesu Christi.* Stuttgart: Katholisches Bibelwerk, 1980. **Popkes, W.** *Christus Traditus: Ein Untersuchung zum Begriff der Dahingabe im Neuen Testament.* Zürich: Zwingli, 1967. **Reploh, K. G.** *Markus—Lehrer der Gemeinde.* 1969. **Rigaux, B.** "Die 'Zwölf' in Geschichte und Kerygma." In *Der historische Jesus und der kerygmatische Christus,* ed. H. Ristow and K. Matthiae. Berlin: Evangelische Verlaganstalt, 1964. 468–86. **Roloff, J.** *Apostolat-Verkündigung-Kirche: Ursprung, Inhalt und Funktion des kirchlichen Apostelamtes nach Paulus, Lukas und der Pastoralbriefen.* Gütersloh: Mohn, 1965. **Rook, J. T.** "'Boanerges, Sons of Thunder' (Mk 3:17)." *JBL* 100 (1981) 94–95. **Schmahl, G.** *Die Zwölf im Markusevangelium.* TTS 30, Trier: Paulinus, 1974. **Schmithals, W.** *The Office of Apostle in the Early Church,* tr. J. E. Steely. Nashville: Abingdon, 1969. **Stock, K.** *Boten aus dem Mit-Ihm-Sein: Das Verhältnis zwischen Jesus und den Zwölf nach Markus.* Analecta Biblica 70, Rome: Pontifical Institute, 1975. **Torrey, C. C.** "The name 'Iscariot.'" *HTR* 36 [1943] 52–56.

Translation

[13] *And he went up the mountain and called those whom he himself wanted. And they came to him.* [14] *He appointed twelve, whom[a] he also named apostles, that they might be with him and that he might send them to preach* [15] *and have authority to cast out demons.* [16] *He appointed the Twelve:[b] Simon[c] to whom he gave the name Peter,* [17] *James the son of Zebedee and John the brother of James to whom he gave the name Boanerges, which means Sons of Thunder,* [18] *Andrew, Philip, Bartholomew, Matthew, Thomas, James the son of Alphaeus, Thaddaeus, Simon the Zealot,* [19] *and Judas Iscariot, who also betrayed him.*

Notes

[a]Clause omitted by A, C[2,] (D), L, 0133, *f*[1], Majority text, lat, sy but read by א. B, (C*), Θ, *f*[13], 28 *pc*. Since the MS evidence reflects numerous attempts to harmonize this pericope with Matt 10:1–4 and Luke 6:12–16, this clause may reflect a later alignment of the text with Luke 6:13. Yet the parallel reference to the twelve "apostles" in Matt 10:2, the only use of "apostle" in Matthew, and the reference to the "apostles" in Mark 6:30 suggest the good possibility of this reading here, especially in view of the rather strong external evidence (see Metzger, 80; Haenchen, 138–39).

[b]Clause omitted by A, C[2,] D, L, Θ 0133,0134, Majority text, lat, sy, bo and read by א. B, C* Δ 565, *pc*. It is often viewed as a dittography of 3:14. But the clause resumes the thought after the parenthesis of 3:14b–15 (see Metzger, 81) and either it or a similar clause controlled the accusative form of the names in the list that follows.

[c]Literally, "he gave the name Peter to Simon." The translation smoothes the awkward syntax of 3:16b in keeping with the listing of the other names in the accusative case controlled by "appointed" (ἐποίησεν).

Form / Structure / Setting

Formally, this pericope defies all attempts at neat classification. The material opens with an apparent calling narrative without a commission (3:13) and concludes with a catalog or listing of the names of the Twelve (3:16–19).

This formally composite character of the material has generally been attributed to the evangelist's redaction. For some the evangelist combined two traditions, the one pertaining to the call of disciples and the other a listing of the Twelve (Meyer, *Ursprung,* 136; Klostermann, 34; Grundmann, 101; Reploh, *Lehrer,* 43–44; Gnilka, 1:137). For others the evangelist took a catalog of the Twelve (3:16–19) and gave it a redactional setting (Taylor, 329; Stock, *Boten,* 50–52; Schmahl, *Zwölf,* 46–49; Pesch, 1:202–03; Ernst, 111–12).

With few exceptions (e.g., Klein [*Apostel,* 60–61] and Schmithals [*Office,* 68–71]; cf. 1:205–06), the common consensus accepts the appointment of the Twelve (3:16–19) as a pre-Markan tradition. The Semitism behind "to appoint" (ἐποίησεν), the names of many who never appear again in Mark, the use of patronyms and surnames like Peter, Boanerges and Iscariot, and the presence of similar lists in Matt 10:2–4; Luke 6:14–16; and Acts 1:13 support this consensus.

The extent of Mark's redaction in 3:13–15, however, is more debatable. Despite those who assign this material to Mark's composition because of style (parataxis, the historical present) and content, the evidence does point to an underlying tradition. First, the substance of 3:13 (ascending a mountain, calling, coming out to him) represent neither Markan motifs nor a parallel with 1:16–20 (cf. *Comment*). Second, the awkward juxtaposition of the infinitive clause in 3:15 with the second purpose clause in 3:14 would make more sense if the second infinitive clause (3:15) were seen as a Markan expansion of a tradition by adding a motif which anticipates the mission of 6:7 (Gnilka, 1:137). Finally, Mark 5:18–20 offers an interesting traditional parallel to the content of 3:14–15 in which "being with Jesus" is denied one who is then sent to preach about Jesus' work of exorcism.

Mark, therefore, found 3:13–14, 16b–19 as a unit in the tradition. At some point in the pre-Markan tradition, a catalog of the names of the Twelve came to be introduced by a story of their appointment. Mark's redactional expansion of 3:15 necessitated his repeating the statement of appointment (3:14a) in 3:16a. The evangelist may also have added the explanation in 3:17c (cf. similar expression in 7:11, 34; 12:42; 15:16, 34, 42) and the statement about Judas in 3:19b.

Structurally, the section opens with Jesus calling those he wants and their response (3:13). Then he appoints twelve for two purposes, to be with him and to be sent in mission with two tasks (3:14–15). Finally, the section concludes with a listing of the appointed Twelve. Taken together, we have a story of the calling and appointment of the Twelve with 3:14–15 serving as the pivot for the account.

As to setting, many have taken this pericope in conjunction with the previous summary of 3:7–12. Accordingly, Jesus' ascending a mountain and calling those he wanted offers a stark contrast to the press of the crowds by the seaside of the previous summary (3:7–12). Yet we have seen how 3:7–12 functions in Mark's portrait to bring to a fitting summary the initial thrust of 1:21–3:12 which is material that began with Jesus' call of four disciples (1:16–20). At the same time, no significant point is made here or elsewhere in Mark by the contrast between seaside and mountain or between the press of the crowds for healing and his calling of the Twelve. In other words, 3:13–19 does not function as a contrasting element to what precedes in 3:7–12 but rather it functions for its own sake to highlight the calling and appointment of the Twelve.

What follows in 3:20–6:6 does involve the disciples (including the Twelve for Mark) in a contrast. By virtue of context, the disciples' response contrasts to that of Jesus' relatives (3:20–21,31–35), whose reaction was not all that different from his opponents (3:22–30). The disciples then provide a contrast to the great crowds who gather around him in 4:1–2, since the former are given the "mystery of the Kingdom" (4:10–12,33–34). Finally, the disciples follow him to his home town where the residents reject his ministry (6:1–6). Thus, the calling and appointing of the Twelve to accompany Jesus and participate in his ministry in 3:13–19 sets the stage for the contrasting response of his family (3:20–21,31–35), his opponents (3:22–30), the crowds (4:1–2,11–12,33–34), the Gerasenes (5:14–17), and the people of Nazareth (6:1–6).

Furthermore, as noted before (p. 4), Mark appears to have used traditional units on discipleship to begin each of the three sections in the first half of his portrait of Jesus' ministry. He began his initial depiction of Jesus' ministry in 1:21–3:12 with the calling of the four fishermen (1:16–20). He now opens his depiction of the critical response to Jesus' ministry in 3:20–6:6 with the calling and appointing of the Twelve who accompany and share in his ministry. We shall see how he continues this pattern by beginning the third part of his portrait of Jesus' ministry leading to the turning point at Caesarea Philippi with the sending of the disciples into mission in 6:7–13.

Comment

13 "The mountain" (τὸ ὄρος) sets the scene for Jesus' calling and appointing the Twelve. Many view it to have more theological than geographical significance for Mark. Therefore, against its OT context "the mountain" represents a place of divine revelation, a place near to God (Grundmann, 101; Lane, 132; Schweizer, 81; Pesch, 1:204; Ernst, 101). More precisely, the events here represent a Sinai typology with Exod 19:3–6 (Lohmeyer, 74; Nineham, 115). By contrast, Schmahl (Zwölf, 51; similarly, Pesch, 1:204) locates the theological significance in Mark's usage of "the mountain" as a place of secret events which corresponds to the evangelist's contrast between the hidden and public character of Jesus and his ministry (cf. the seaside in 3:7–12 and the mountain in 3:13–19).

Yet neither the OT background nor Mark's use of "mountain" elsewhere offers sufficient grounds for ascribing such theological weight to the usage here. What follows in 3:13–15 is hardly a divine revelation. Even if one read this pericope as the establishing of the new people of God, Exod 19:3–6 does not provide the typological counterpart. Furthermore, "the mountain" does not consistently represent "secret events" in Mark (cf. 5:5,11) any more than a "house" always represents a place of private instruction for the disciples (7:17; 9:28,33; 10:10 cf. 2:1–2; 3:29). The other ten occurrences of "mountain" in Mark are traditional and refer to a mountain or the hill country (5:5,11; 6:46; 9:2,9; 11:1,23; 13:3,14; 14:26) with the last five referring specifically to the Mount of Olives. Therefore, we have no reason for taking this occurrence to be redactional or less "geographical" because we cannot give "the mountain" a precise location. It may stem from a local tradition or connote the more general, less populated "hill country" north of the Sea of Galilee (Lagrange, 63; Taylor, 129; Cranfield, 126; Rigaux, "Die 'Zwölf'," 474; Stock, *Boten*, 10–11). For Mark, therefore, "the mountain" simply offers a locale for the calling of the Twelve.

"Called whom he himself wanted." The verb for "called" (προσκαλεῖται) occurs nine times, eight of which offer almost a formulaic "summons" of the disciples, the crowds, or a centurion for teaching or instruction (3:23; 6:7; 7:14; 8:1,34; 10:42; 12:43; 15:44). The usage here, however, has more the sense of "to call" or "to select" as used in Acts 2:39; 13:2; 16:10 (cf. Luke 6:13). This too points to the traditional character of 3:13. The object and basis of this calling follow in the relative clause, "whom he himself wanted" (Reploh, *Lehrer*, 44). The use of the intensive pronoun αὐτός clearly accents that the choice was Jesus' alone based on his own desire. One cannot help but hear a faint echo of the OT references to God's sovereign call or selection of his own.

How those called in 3:13 relates to the Twelve who are appointed (3:14a) remains unclear (Cranfield, 126), as the difference in Matthew and Luke attests. Some take the former to be a larger group (cf. 2:15–17) from whom the Twelve are appointed (so Luke 6:13; Taylor, 230; Klostermann, 33; Lohmeyer, 74–75; Ernst, 113). Others take the group to be synonymous with the Twelve (so Matt 10:1; Grundmann, 101; Meye, *Jesus*, 147; Pesch, 1:204). When 3:13–19 is taken as a whole, however, the content of 3:14–15 and the listing of names in 3:16–19 appears to specify the significance of Jesus' "calling whom he wanted" and their response in 3:13.

"They came to him." The verb (ἀπῆλθον) occurs in a comparable setting in 1:20 where it is used in parallel (1:18) with "to follow" (ἀκολουθεῖν). Literally, it means "to come away," "to depart" and connotes one's leaving one's former way of life (Lagrange, 63; Gnilka, 1:139; Schmahl, *Zwölf*, 53). Here it expresses "unreserved discipleship" (Nineham, 116). Coming "to (πρός) Jesus" means that he became their new, single goal in life (Lohmeyer, 74; Schmahl, *Zwölf*, 53–54).

14 In 3:14–15 the calling of those whom Jesus wanted is explicated. These two verses consist of a complex syntactical construction. The main verb (ἐποίησεν) is followed by two purpose clauses, the last of which has two infinitive clauses. The verb "he made" (ἐποίησεν) most likely represents a Semitism (Taylor, 235; Cranfield, 127; Rigaux, 475; Schweizer, 81; Gnilka, 1:139) with parallels in the LXX (1 Kgs 13:33; 2 Chron. 2:17; 1 Sam 17:6; cf. Heb 3:2; Rev 5:10) that suggest the meaning of "he appointed." Some have additionally taken "made" in the sense of "he created" and found here a subtle allusion to a divine creative act (Lohmeyer, 74; Grundmann, 101; Schmahl, *Zwölf*, 55; Pesch, 1:204; Ernst, 113).

This difference in rendering between "he made" or "he appointed" is not without significance. Taking the verb with the force of "he made" or "created" accents the Twelve and implies the coming into being of something new. It follows that the "making" of the Twelve is viewed accordingly as the creation of the new people of God. Taking the verb with the LXX force of "he appointed," however, maintains the Twelve in the foreground but deflects the thrust of the statement from accenting the coming into being of the Twelve to the purpose clauses that declare for what reasons they were appointed (Stock, *Boten*, 16–17). The latter alternative seems the more natural reading of the syntax.

"Twelve" (δώδεκα). "The Twelve" becomes a common designation in Mark (3:16; 4:10; 6:7; 9:35; 10:32; 11:11; 14:10,17,20,43). Most of these may reflect the evangelist's redaction (Reploh, *Lehrer*, 47–49). Despite Schmithals' argument for a post-Easter development of this concept and Mark's redactional responsibility for it in his Gospel (1:208), most trace the existence of the Twelve to Jesus' own ministry. Obviously, the number twelve relates to Israel, historically a nation of twelve tribes. But how? The Twelve could hardly have served as representatives of historic Israel (cf. Num 1:4–17; 13:1–10). And since in Jesus' day Israel consisted of only two and a half tribes, the Twelve were hardly chosen as representative of contemporary Israel. Thus, they have often been viewed as the "new Israel," the "new People of God" (e.g., Grundmann, 101; Cranfield, 127; Schweizer, 81). This terminology, however, risks mistaking the "new People of God" as a replacement for a rejected "old People of God" and fails to do justice to the contemporary Jewish expectation of Jesus' day. Israel's hope, based on the prophets' word, was for the restoration of Israel, *all* (twelve tribes) Israel (Sir 36:10; 48:10; Isa 49:6; Ezek 45:8; *Ps Sol* 17:26–32). Consequently, the appointing of Twelve offered a sign of the expected eschatological restoration of *all* God's People.

To the degree that the Twelve represented a discontinuity with historic Israel, they indeed represented the new People of God, the redeemed community of the eschaton. To the degree that they were the Twelve, they represented a continuity of God's redemptive activity on behalf of historic Israel, his covenant people. Therefore, the appointing of the Twelve represents a powerful indication of Jesus' sense of his mission and would be commensurate with his announcement of the "fulfillment of time" and his proclaiming the coming of the Kingdom (1:15).

"Whom he also named apostles" (οὓς καὶ ἀποστόλους ὠνόμασεν) most likely reflects the early Church's terminology rather than Jesus' own action of naming the twelve "apostles." It comes as a parenthetic comment, perhaps added by Mark, that breaks the flow of the sentence. By equating the "apostles" with the "Twelve," this comment tends to accent Jesus' appointing of the Twelve (3:14a) more than their role as spelled out in the purpose clauses (3:14b,c, 15). This emphasis appears in 3:16a where 3:14a is repeated without purpose clauses and may well be why the clause came to be omitted from the text (see *Note* a).

"In order that" (ἵνα) introduces two subordinate clauses that state the intention of the main verb, the intention behind the appointment of the Twelve. First, Jesus appointed the Twelve to "be with him" (ὦσιν μετ' αὐτοῦ). This expression (εἶναι μετ' αὐτοῦ/ὤν, cf. 1:13; 2:19; 3:14; 4:36; 5:18; 14:67) always includes being in the physical presence or in the company of someone or something (Stock, *Boten*, 17–18). Its special tone may be seen in Jesus' denial of the Gerasene demoniac's request to accompany him personally in 5:18 and in the young woman's charge that Peter had been "with the Nazarene, Jesus" in 14:67. The Twelve, therefore, were given a special personal relationship with Jesus whereby they shared in his life and ministry (cf. Best, *ZNW* 69 [1978], 34).

Second, Jesus appointed twelve to "send out" (ἀποστέλλῃ). Since Meyer (*Ursprung*, 136), numerous scholars have found this second purpose clause to stand in tension with the first (Klostermann, 34; Lohmeyer, 74; Grundmann, 101; Schweizer, 81). How could one be appointed to "be with Jesus" when he "sends them out"? For some this tension has found its resolution in the assignment of the clauses to different periods in the life of the Twelve, before and after Easter. Prior to Easter they found themselves in the company of Jesus; after Easter they became his missioners (Schweizer, 81; cf. Cranfield, 128; Reploh, *Lehrer*, 46; Ernst, 113).

Yet many have found these two purpose clauses as complementary, especially in view of the sending of the disciples in 6:7. Their being in the company of Jesus provided the Twelve with the basis for their mission, to proclaim what was transpiring in the person of Jesus. Furthermore, they went as his messengers to declare his message as participants in his ministry and with his authorization. Thus the Twelve were not only emblematic of the eschatological community; they were the organ through which this community was being announced.

"To preach" (κηρύσσειν) brings the first of two infinitive clauses that set forth the task of their mission. This verb describes the work of John the Baptist (1:4, 7), Jesus (1:14, 38–39), a healed (1:45) and cleansed man (5:20), the Twelve (3:14; 6:12) and by implication the early Church (13:10; 14:9). The Baptist preaches a repentance baptism and the coming one; the healed proclaim what has happened to them; the early Church preaches "the gospel," and in 1:14 Jesus preaches "the good news of God" which follows in 1:15. Only Jesus and the Twelve are said to preach without any delineation of what was preached (1:38, 39; 3:14; 6:12). Yet since the Twelve are preaching as Jesus' messengers, one can assume that the unspecified content of both his and their preaching is his message given in summary form in 1:14–15, the message of the Kingdom.

15 "To have authority to cast out demons" (ἔχειν ἐξουσίαν ἐκβάλλειν τὰ δαιμόνια). This clause stands out for its awkwardness in style and content (Lagrange, 64; Lohmeyer, 74; Reploh, *Lehrer*, 46). As the second infinitive clause to explain the nature of the mission, simply "to cast out demons" (ἐκβάλλειν τὰ δαιμόνια) in parallel construction with "to preach" (κηρύσσειν) would have been smoother. "To have authority" (ἔχειν ἐξουσίαν) not only complicates the style but it makes no sense with the verb "to send" (Lohmeyer, 74). One is sent (ἀποστέλλειν) to perform an action not to have an ability (Matt 21:34; 22:3; Luke 1:19; 4:18; 9:2; 1 Cor 1:17; so Stock, *Boten*, 23).

Many have accounted for this awkwardness in style and content by assigning 3:15 to Mark's redaction (Reploh, *Lehrer*, 46; Schmahl, *Zwölf*, 58–59; Pesch, 1:202; Gnilka, 1:138). This suggestion gains support from an analysis of the clause. First, "casting out demons" is used almost like a fixed expression in 1:34, 39; 3:15, 22; and 6:13. In each of these cases "demons" rather than "unclean spirits," for example, are "cast out." In fact, "demons" (δαιμόνια) only occurs in Mark in the phrase or context (cf. 7:29–30) of "to cast out demons" (see *Comment* on 1:34). Second, this expression accompanies Jesus' "preaching" in the summary of 1:39, here in 3:15 and in the summary of the Twelve's ministry in 6:12. Third, when speaking of "authority," Jesus' "authority" in 1:27 pertains to "unclean spirits," and he "gives" the Twelve "authority over the unclean spirits" in the commissioning of 6:7. "To have authority" (ἔχειν ἐξουσίαν) in 3:15 implies the possession of the "authority over unclean spirits" given (ἐδίδου) in 6:7 (cf. Matt 10:1). Thus the commissioning of 6:7 may have influenced Mark's awkward shaping of 3:14c, 15 (Stock, *Boten*, 23–24). He combined a formulaic expression ("to cast out demons") with the idea of authorization ("to have authority") to round out the summary of the Twelve's mission ("to preach" and "to cast out demons").

16 "He appointed the Twelve" repeats the statement of 3:14a but without the qualifying clauses. Though this reading has been questioned on grounds of dittography (see *Note* b), the accusative case of the following names requires this or a comparable clause. Mark may have inserted it after the extended parenthesis of 3:14b–15 to resume the thought of 3:14a. Furthermore, the meaning here differs slightly from the use in 3:14a where the "appointment" of the Twelve is qualified by the dual role "to be with him" and "to be sent out" in mission. Here "he appointed the Twelve" expresses the end in itself and accents more the note of status or position. Thus the action of "appointing" focuses on the Twelve as a discrete entity or group.

"Simon to whom he gave the name Peter" (καὶ ἐπέθηκεν ὄνομα τῷ Σίμωνι Πέτρον) raises several questions. First, the self-contained statement is out of alignment with the following eleven names given in the accusative case and standing in apposition to "the Twelve." It takes the place of the actual listing of Simon. Thus a few MSS (*f*[13] *pc*) resolve the problem by inserting "first Simon" (πρῶτον Σίμων), most likely a later harmonization with Matt 10:2. The absence of Simon's name at the head of the list may presume the obvious, namely, the prominence of Simon and his primary status among the Twelve as seen in his being listed first in all the other lists (Matt 10:2; Luke 6:13; Acts 1:13). Consequently, Jesus' giving to Simon the name Peter assumes his being listed first but accentuates Jesus' act of giving the new name.

Second, this self-contained statement could hardly have been Mark's redactional addition (Reploh, *Lehrer*, 46; Schmahl, *Zwölf*, 61), since the list would then have had no reference to Simon. But it is conceivable that Mark dropped the name Simon from his tradition to underscore the change in names from Simon to Peter. This change in name is reflected in Mark's use of "Simon" prior to 3:16 (1:16,29,36,) and "Peter" consistently from this point on (19x) with only one exception (14:37).

Third, if this statement belongs to Mark's tradition, it is impossible to determine whether the statement is intended to date or merely to note the event of the naming. In John 1:42 the naming accompanies the calling; in Matt 16:18 the naming follows Peter's confession at Caesarea Philippi; 3:16 could be taken to indicate that the naming accompanied the appointment of the Twelve. While these differences can be harmonized, the precise occasion for this naming appears to have been lost in the tradition (Cullmann, *Peter*, 21). For Mark, however, since the appointment of the Twelve marks such a noticeable change in his own use of "Simon" and "Peter" and since the naming actually stands in the place of the listing of Simon's name in 3:16, we can conclude that Mark associated this change in names with the appointment of the Twelve.

Some interpreters have suggested that this shift in the Gospels of the setting of Jesus' giving Simon this name and the fact that Jesus consistently uses "Simon" in addressing Peter (cf. Mark 14:37) indicates that Jesus did not personally give Simon the name "Peter (Cephas)." Rather the name began originally as a nickname of honor in the post-Easter community and gradually replaced "Simon" in the Church's usage. This shift in name was then attributed to Jesus and read back into his ministry (e.g., Pesch, *Concil* 7 [1971] 26–27). But why the need to assign this change in names to Jesus, particularly since only Matt 16:18, hardly the earliest tradition regarding the name Cephas/ Peter, has Jesus assigning any significance to this change in names? Is it not more likely that Jesus gave Simon the nickname at some point, the occasion and significance of which was either not preserved or lost, without necessarily intending to rename him? Matt 16:18 would then be only an example of the early Church's reflection on the occasion and significance of this nickname.

The pre-Markan text, however, may indicate its own theological reflection on the fact of Jesus' nicknaming Simon rather than on the occasion or the significance of the name. The expression, "gave him the name . . ." (ἐπιτιθῆναι αὐτῷ ὄνομα), occurs only here (3:16–17) in the NT. It does have a parallel in the LXX (Judg 8:31; 2 Kgs 24:17; Neh 9:7 [2 Esdr 19:7]; Dan 1:7) where in each case an individual was either given a name or renamed. Read against this LXX background, "Peter," though a translation of "Cephas" (Stock, *Boten*, 29–30; cf. O. Cullmann, *TDNT*, 6 [1968] 101) would have been perceived in this listing to be a proper name and not simply a nickname. Thus, this listing declares that Jesus actually gave Simon a new name, a name which the Church came to use with regularity in place of or along side of Simon (cf. "Simon Peter" in John 1:41; 6:8,68; 13:6,9,24,36, etc.), and not merely a nickname. Thus what may have begun as a nickname given by Jesus (Lampe, *NTS* 25 [1979] 227–45; cf. Jesus' consistent use "Simon" in the Gospel tradition) is now perceived as a new name.

Finally, "Simon" (Hebrew, Simeon) is the most frequently attested Jewish name for the period of the Roman domination, a fact in itself that may have fostered the use of a nickname or patronym (Fitzmyer, "Simon," 106,110). But the use of "Peter" doubtless goes beyond a question of identification, and has led to much discussion about the significance of this name. "Peter" (Πέτρος), a translation of the Aramaic כיפא, *kēpāʾ* (Κηφᾶς in John 1:42; 1 Cor 1:12; 3:22; 9:5; 15:5; Gal 1:18; 2:9,11,14), means primarily "stone" rather than "rock" (Lampe, *NTS* 25 [1979] 227–45). The Greek rendering (Πέτρος) has not yet been attested in pre-Christian usage as a proper name (Lampe, *NTS* 25 [1979] 228–31; Fitzmyer, "*Kepha*," 119–20), while כפיא, *kēpāʾ*, apparently appears as an Aramaic name in a fifth century B.C. text (Fitzmyer, "*Kepha*," 115–18; cf. Lampe, *NTS* 25 [1979] 228–31). This nickname which soon became Simon's name in the tradition has spawned numerous explanations. Matt 16:18 is obviously the earliest. For Mark, however, "Peter" is simply a name. He makes no attempt at explaining it or its significance apart from assigning its origins to Jesus.

17 "James the son of Zebedee and John the brother of James" are identified in the same manner 1:19 (cf. 10:35). Their position as second and third in this listing (so Acts 1:13) may reflect the special relationship accorded "Peter,

James and John" with Jesus (cf. 5:37; 9:2; 14:33). Therefore, the position of Peter, James and John at the top of this list (cf. Matt 10:2; Luke 6:14; Acts 1:13) may indicate their relative importance in the early Church. It may also be noteworthy that Jesus gives a name to only these three among the Twelve.

"Boanerges" (Βοανηργές). The same expression for giving a name (ἐπέθηκεν ὄνομα) occurs here as in 3:16 where we saw it implied a renaming rather than simply a nickname. But here this implication presents its own difficulties. First, the name (ὄνομα, singular) is given to both James and John as a pair. Yet they continue to be named individually in Mark and elsewhere. Second, in contrast to Peter/Simon, this name not only fails to replace "James and John" in the tradition but it never appears again in the Gospel tradition. Thus we are left with an anomaly of a tradition behind 3:17 that ascribes a name change for which the broader tradition of the early Church offers no evidence.

The name itself poses unresolvable problems of derivation and significance. Considered to be a Greek rendition of an underlying Hebrew/Aramaic phrase, Βοανηργές fails, on the one hand, to follow the rules of transliteration (Βοαν from בני, běnê) and, on the other hand, to indicate clearly the underlying Hebrew/Aramaic root. Buth's suggestion (*JSNT* 10 [1981] 29–33) of the Greek βοαν from βοᾶν = "to shout" suffers the same fate of an unexplained uncontracted οα. At least four Hebrew/Aramaic words have been suggested: (a) רגש, *rēgeš* = "commotion" (Betz, *RevQ* 3 [1961] 41–52; Cranfield, 131); (b) רגז, *rōgez* = "excitement" or "agitation" (Taylor, 232, "rumbling of the sea," cf. Job 37:2); (c) רעש, *ra‘aš* = "quaking" (Rook, *JBL* 100 [1981] 94–95); (d) רעם, *ra‘am* = "thunder" (Buth, *JSNT* 10 [1981] 32–33).

Mark's translation, "Sons of Thunder," offers little help, since the word for "thunder" (רעם, *ra‘am*) does not correspond to the transliteration, even granting a ע for γ equivalency (Rook, *JBL* 100 [1981] 94–95). Thus either Mark's translation offers a traditional meaning of the underlying Semitic phrase that is lost to us or it simply represents an attempt to clarify an obscure, if not corrupted, Βοανηργές. Thus, even given the name, "Sons of Thunder," we remain at a loss to explain its occasion and significance, a situation not unlike that with "Peter" above.

18–19 "Andrew" appears fourth on the list (so Acts 1:13), despite his being called together with Simon in 1:16–18 and his place of prominence in John 1:40–42,44 (cf. Matt 10:2; Luke 6:14). This may have resulted from the grouping of Peter, James and John (Acts 1:13) that places Andrew just outside that circle as in 13:3 (cf. 1:29).

"Philip" along with Andrew has a Greek name. Though not mentioned again in Mark, he appears several times in John (6:5; 12:21; 14:8), where we learn that he comes from Bethsaida, the town of Peter and Andrew (1:44). Clement of Alexander (*Stromateis* 3.4.25) identifies him as the second disciple in Matt 8:21–22//Luke 9:59–60.

"Bartholomew" is a patronym, "Son of Talmai" (cf. 2 Sam 3:3; 8:37). His place following Philip (cf. Acts 1:13) has led some to identify him with Nathanael of John 1:45.

"Matthew" is an abbreviation for the OT Mattathias. Matt 10:3 identifies this one as "the toll collector" of Matt 9:9, who is "Levi, the toll collector" in

Mark 2:14. Mark simply has Matthew and makes no adjustment in the listing to accommodate Levi among the Twelve.

"Thomas," who precedes Matthew in Matt 10:3 and Bartholomew in Acts 1:13, renders the Aramaic name תּאוֹמָא, *tĕʾōmāʾ*, which means "Twin." Not mentioned again in Mark, he plays an important role in John (11:16; 14:5; 20:24,26–29; 21:2).

"James the son of Alphaeus" is sometimes equated with James the Younger (15:40) and possibly the brother of Levi who was also a "son of Alphaeus" (2:14). This qualification helped to distinguish the two disciples, each with the name James.

"Thaddaeus" is listed here and in Matt 10:3, but Luke has Judas the son of James (6:16; Acts 1:13). Jeremias (*Theology*, 232–33) suggests that Luke preserved the correct name, while Matthew and Mark use Judas' second name, the name preferred in the early Church after the traitor besmirched the name Judas. The patronym, Judas son of James, however, should have been enough to ensure the distinction (cf. John 14:22).

"Simon the Zealot" is often cited as Simon the Cananaean which risks one's mistaking the nickname as a place name (e.g., Cana or Canaan). "Cananaean" renders a Greek transliteration (Καναναῖον) of the Aramaic קַנְאָנָא, *qanʾānāʾ*, meaning "zeal" or Zealot (Klostermann, 35). Therefore, Luke appropriately has "Simon the Zealot" (Luke 6:15; Acts 1:13).

"Judas Iscariot" comes at the end of the list for obvious reasons. But the origin and significance of "Iscariot" remain in doubt. The most common reading takes "Iscariot" to mean "Man from Kerioth" (אִישׁ קְרִיּוֹת, *ʾîš qĕrîyōt*), a town mentioned in Josh 15:25 (near Hebron) and in Jer 48:24 (in Moab). A parallel name Ishtobos (אִישׁ טוֹב, *ʾîš ṭob*) in Josephus (*Ant.* 7.6.1), the apparent ascription of this name to Judas' father, Simon Iscariot, in John 6:71 and 13:26 and the variant reading ἀπὸ Καρυώτου in John 6:71 give strong support to this position. But Torrey questioned the existence of such a town and the possibility of a name arising using the Hebrew "man" (אִישׁ, *ʾîš*) in an Aramaic setting (*HTR* 36 [1943] 52–56).

Gärtner (*Iscariot*, 6–7) has followed Torrey in suggesting an Aramaic term (סָכָר, *sakar*) meaning "liar," "fraud" or "false one," a name applied to Judas after his act of betrayal. Naturally, John 6:71 and 13:26 would then be a mistranslation of the Aramaic phrase with Iscariot belonging to Judas and not Simon. But Cullmann rightly questions how the meaning of a name developed so late could have been forgotten so quickly (*Aufsätze*, 219). Agreeing with Torrey's objection to the popular etymology of Iscariot = "man of Kerioth" because of lack of support for Kerioth as a town, Cullmann opts for *sicarius* = "assassin" as the underlying Latin word that has been Semitized from "sicarius" to "iskarioth" (*Aufsätze*, 219). This would place Judas along with Simon among the radicals or Zealots. The variant reading of Σκαριώθ in 3:19; Matt 10:3; Luke 6:16 (D, it, vg,) appears to support this position. But one wonders where and how in the tradition a term so technical as *sicarius* could be so misunderstood as to be "Semitized" to the point of total distortion, assuming to begin with that it was not anachronistic (see Horsley and Hanson, *Bandits*, 200–19). Therefore, Judas, "Man of Kerioth" appears to offer the least difficulty.

"Who also betrayed him" is most likely a Markan redaction that anticipates the scenes in 14:10–11, 18, 20–21, 41–44 (see *Comment* on 1:14). Even the appointing of the Twelve has its foreboding moment for Mark as Judas harbingers the coming passion. At the same time, this comment and the inclusion of Judas in the listing of the Twelve provides compelling evidence for setting the appointment of the Twelve in Jesus' ministry.

Explanation

Mark begins the second major section of Jesus' ministry (3:13–6:6) in a fashion similar to the first (1:16–3:12) and third (6:7–8:26) with a pericope involving the disciples (cf. 1:16–20 and 6:7–13). Here we have the calling and appointing of the Twelve.

This material most likely came to the evangelist as a traditional unit consisting of a listing or catalog of the Twelve (3:16–19) introduced by a calling narrative (3:13–14). The list, with minor exceptions, corresponds to the lists in Matt 10:2–4, Luke 6:14–16, and Acts 1:13. The calling narrative, missing in Matthew and Acts, has a different focus from that in Luke 6:13 which accents the selection of twelve from a larger group of disciples to be "apostles." Mark's account gives the purpose of their calling and sets the stage for the listing of the names.

The account opens with Jesus' calling "those whom he himself wanted" (3:13a). This succinct statement places the focus solely on Jesus' activity, just as in the calling of the four disciples in 1:16–20 and Levi in 2:14. Therefore, Jesus' call to discipleship contains at least an oblique analogy to God's sovereign electing and calling role in Israel's history. Accordingly, discipleship has more the character of response than decision. This response appears to entail a "departure," a break with the past, as seen in 1:16–20 and 2:15. Here the rather pregnant expression "came to him" (3:13b) indicates a similar break or departure from former, unspecified contexts and goals in life in exchange for making Jesus the new context and single purpose in life.

The appointment of the Twelve (3:14) is set against this calling backdrop. For Mark's account the emphasis lies more on the reasons for which they were appointed than on their appointment as such (cf. Luke 6:13). The purpose of this appointment was two-fold. First, the Twelve were appointed in order to be in the company of Jesus, to participate as companions in his life and work. While this personal association may seem implied from other calling or discipleship passages, its distinctiveness becomes apparent when a verbatim request for this privilege was denied the Gerasene demoniac in 5:18–19. Consequently, this personal association with Jesus was special to the Twelve.

Second, the Twelve were appointed in order to be sent in mission. The relationship of these two tasks is neither contradictory nor chronological but complementary. To participate in Jesus' life and ministry did not preclude the sending of the Twelve to share in that ministry, as the mission in 6:7–13 shows. And despite the formative role often assumed for the Twelve in the developing Church's mission after Easter, our sources refer to individuals, most of whom were unrelated to the Twelve, rather than the Twelve as having principal roles in the mission after Easter. Therefore, to be sent in mission referred to the role given the Twelve as participants in Jesus' earthly ministry, a necessary corollary to their being "with him."

Thus, the appointment of the Twelve finds its significance in the calling together of twelve men to share indirectly and directly in Jesus' ministry. By sharing in his company and in his mission, the Twelve become an integral part of his ministry. To this extent they stand apart from all others who respond positively and negatively to Jesus' ministry.

"The Twelve," consequently, take on even greater significance as being indicative of God's action in history through Jesus on behalf of his people. By calling and appointing "Twelve" to become integral to his ministry, Jesus sets his ministry of the Kingdom within the context of God's promise to restore all Israel, and the appointing of the Twelve stands in continuity with God's activity for historic Israel. At the same time, the Twelve are called and appointed with no physical ties to the twelve tribes of Israel. As such, they represent the eschatological discontinuity of the new people of God from historic Israel (cf. Rev. 21:12,14).

The listing of the Twelve in 3:16–19 reflects the perspective of the post-Easter community. Peter heads the list followed by James and John with Judas mentioned last. Yet this perspective need not be relegated solely to the Church after Easter, since we find Peter, James and John forming an inner circle around Jesus elsewhere in the Gospel tradition (e.g., 5:37; 9:2; 14:33).

Mark uses this traditional unit (3:13–19) to introduce a section (3:13–6:6) in his Gospel that depicts Jesus' ministry under severe question by his family (20–21,31–35), his religious opponents (3:22–30), and the people of his home town, Nazareth (6:1–6). Even the crowds stand in contrast to the disciples in 4:1–34, the former cannot perceive what is given to the disciples (4:11,33–34). Nevertheless, though choosing to place the calling and appointing of the Twelve at the outset of this section, Mark does not modify what follows in terms of this pericope. The Twelve only appear explicitly in 4:10 and then in the company of other disciples (see *Comment* on 4:10). Otherwise Jesus' constant companions are the "disciples" (3:34; 4:34,35; 5:31; 6:1; cf. 3:20,34), who most likely include the Twelve for Mark (5:31; cf. 5:37).

The relationship then of this pericope to what follows has no more structural or thematic ties to the following accounts than the calling of the four fishermen (1:16–20) to its respective section (1:16–3:12). It plays a more formal role of beginning a new section by depicting this integral character of the disciples (1:16–20: 3:13–19) to Jesus' ministry (1:21–3:12; 3:20–6:6).

Mark's redactional activity in adding the authorization for exorcism (3:15) to complement the mission of preaching underscores the integral relationship of the disciples to Jesus' mission. In 1:21–28 the evangelist opens Jesus' ministry with an exorcism, notes his healing and exorcisms in 1:34 and 3:10–12 and sums up Jesus' ministry by referring to his preaching and exorcisms (1:39). Accordingly, Jesus sends the Twelve in mission to preach and to exorcise demons in 6:7. Thus, Mark adds the exorcism motif to demonstrate the full participation of the Twelve in Jesus' total ministry.

Finally, apart from Mark's emphasis on Jesus' renaming Simon as Peter, a change reflected consistently from this point on in Mark, and the explanation of "Boanerges" to mean "Sons of Thunder," the evangelist's addition of the comment to Judas' name (3:19b) has special significance. Most of the comments accompanying the names serve to distinguish them from others. Judas Iscariot needs no further limitation. His name and his infamy marked him. By adding "who betrayed him," Mark subtly reminds the reader of what is to come, even in an account that accents the participation of the Twelve in Jesus' ministry. One can hardly miss the irony.

B. Jesus and His Family   (3:20–35)

Bibliography

Becker, J. *Das Heil Gottes. Heils- und Sündenbegriffe in den Qumrantexten und im Neuen Testament.* SUNT 3, Göttingen: Vandenhoeck& Ruprecht, 1964. **Berger, K.** *Die Amen-Worte.* BZNW 39. Berlin: de Gruyter, 1970. ———. *"Zur Geschichte der Einleitungsformel 'Amen, ich sage euch.'"* ZNW 63 (1972) 45–75. **Best, E.** "Mark iii. 20,21,31–35." *NTS* 22 (1975–76) 309–19 = *Disciples and Discipleship: Studies in the Gospel according to Mark.* Edinburgh: T.& T. Clark, 1986. 49–63. ———. *The Temptation and the Passion: The Markan Soteriology.* SNTSMS 2. Cambridge: Cambridge UP, 1965. **Black, M.** *An Aramaic Approach to the Gospels and Acts.* 1967. **Blinzler, J.** *Die Bruder und Schwester Jesu.* SBS 21. Stuttgart: Katholisches Bibelwerk, 1967. **Boring, M. E.** "How May We Identify Oracles of Christian Prophets in the Synoptic Tradition? Mark 3,28–29 as a Test Case." *JBL* 19 (1972) 501–21. ———. "The Unforgivable Sin Logion, Mark iii 28–29/Matt xii 31–32/Luke xii 10: Formal Analysis and History of the Tradition." *NovT* 18 (1976) 258–79. **Colpe, C.** "Der Spruch von der Lästerung des Geistes." In *Der Ruf Jesu und die Antwort der Gemeinde,* FS J. Jeremias, ed. E. Lohse. Göttingen: Vandenhoeck & Ruprecht, 1970. 65–79. **Crossan, J. D.** "Mark and the Relatives of Jesus." *NovT* 15 (1973) 81–113. **Donahue, J. R.** *Are You the Christ? The Trial Narrative in the Gospel of Mark.* SBLDS 10. Missoula: Scholars Press, 1973. **Evans, O. E.** "The Unforgivable Sin." *ExpTim* 68 (1956–57) 240–44. **Fuchs, A.** *Die traditionsgeschichtliche und redaktionsgeschichtliche Entwicklung der Beelzebulkontroverse Mk 3,22–27 und Parallelen, verbunden mit der Rückfrage nach Jesus.* Freistadt: Plöchl, 1979. **Gaston, L.** "Beelzebul." *TZ* 18 (1962) 247–55. **Hasler, V.** *Amen: Redaktionsgeschichtliche Untersuchung zur Einführungsformel der Herrenworte 'Wahrlich, ich sage euch.'* Zürich: Theologischer Verlag, 1969. **Higgins, A. J. B.** *Jesus and the Son of Man.* Philadelphia: Fortress, 1964. ———. *The Son of Man in the Teaching of Jesus.* SNTSMS 39. London: Cambridge UP, 1980. **Jeremias, J.** *ABBA: Studien zur neutestamentlichen Theologie und Zeitgeschichte.* Göttingen: Vandenhoeck & Ruprecht, 1966. 145–52. ———. *Theology of the New Testament.* 1971. ———. "Zum nicht-responsorischen Amen." *ZNW* 64 (1973) 122–23. **Koch, D.-A.** *Die Bedeutung der Wundererzählungen für die Christologie des Markusevangeliums.* **Kruse, H.** "Die 'dialektische Negation' als semitisches Idiom." *VT* 4 (1954) 385–400. ———. "Das Reich Satans." *Bib* 58 (1977) 29–61. **Kuschke, A.** "Das Idiom der 'relativen Negation' im Neuen Testament." *ZNW* 43 (1950–51) 263. **Lambrecht, J.** "The Relatives of Jesus in Mark." *NovT* 16 (1974) 241–58. **Limbeck, M.** "Beelzebul—eine ursprüngliche Bezeichnung für Jesus?" In *Wort Gottes in der Zeit,* FS H. Schelkle. Düsseldorf: Patmos, 1973. 31–42. **Lövestam, E.** *Spiritus Blasphemia: Eine Studia zu Mk 3,28f //Mt 12,31f, Lk 12,10.* Lund: Gleerup, 1968. **Meye, R. P.** *Jesus and the Twelve.* 1968. **Pryke, E. J.** *Redactional Style in the Marcan Gospel.* 1978. **Robinson, J. M.** *The Problem of History in Mark and Other Marcan Studies.* SBT 21. 1957. **Schippers, R.** "The Son of Man in Matt. xii.32 = Lk. xii.10, compared with Mk. iii.28." In *Studia Evangelica IV,* ed. F. L. Cross. Berlin: Töpelmann, 1968. 231–35. **Scroggs, R.** "The Exaltation of the Spirit by Some Early Christians." *JBL* 84 (1965) 359–73. **Tödt, H. E.** *The Son of Man in the Synoptic Tradition.* Philadelphia: Westminster, 1965. **Trocmé, E.** *The Formation of the Gospel According to Mark.* Philadelphia: Westminster, 1975. 132–37. **Wansbrough, H.** "Mark 3,21—Was Jesus out of His Mind?" *NTS* 18 (1972) 233–35. **Wenham, D.** "The Meaning of Mark iii.21." *NTS* 21 (1974–75) 295–300. **Williams, J. G.** "A Note on the 'Unforgivable Sin' Logion." *NTS* 12 (1965–66) 75–77.

Translation

[20] Jesus[a] went[b] to his house. And again the crowd gathered so he[c] and the Twelve were not even able to eat[d] a meal. [21] When his people heard[e], they set out to take him into their custody. For they said, "He was out of his mind."

[22] The scribes from Jerusalem came down and said, "He is possessed by Beelzebul"[f] and "He casts out demons by the prince of demons." [23] After summoning them, Jesus[a] said to them in parables, "How is Satan able to cast out Satan? [24] If a kingdom is divided against itself that kingdom is not able to stand. [25] And if a home is divided against itself that home is not able to stand. [26] If Satan had risen up against himself and been divided, he would not be able to stand but have met his end. [27] Nor is anyone able when entering a strong man's house to plunder his possessions, unless one first bind the strong man and then plunder his house. [28] I assure you, all things shall be forgiven every human being, all sinful behavior and all blasphemies that[g] they utter. [29] But whoever blasphemes against the Holy Spirit will never[h] have forgiveness but is guilty of an eternal sin."[i] [30] For they said, "He has an unclean spirit."

[31] Then his mother and his brothers came, and, standing[j] outside, they sent a message to him to summon him. [32] A crowd sat around him and they said to him, "Your mother and your brothers[k] seek you outside." [33] And he answered[l] them, "Who is my mother and my brothers?" [34] After scanning those seated around him in a circle, he said, "These are my mother and my brothers. [35] For[m] whoever does the will of God, this one is my brother, sister, and mother."

Notes

[a] Romanized words added from context.

[b] אֲ2 A C L Θ 0133 0134 f[1.13] lat sy[p,h] read ἔρχονται (cf. εἰσέρχονται in D) to align explicitly the subject of the main and subordinate clauses. The more difficult reading (ἔρχεται) is found in א* B W Γ 1241 pc b sy[s] bo[pt].

[c] Literally, "they" (αὐτούς), but "Jesus and the Twelve" are the antecedents for αὐτούς in the context of 3:13–19.

[d] ἄρτον φαγεῖν, literally "to eat bread," is a Semitism (אכל לחם, ʾākal leḥem) meaning "to eat a meal."

[e] This clause replaced in D W it with ἀκούσαντες (ἤκουσαν—D) περὶ αὐτοῦ οἱ γραμματεῖς καὶ οἱ λοιποί to set the stage for 3:22 and remove any question about Jesus' relatives.

[f] Read βεελζεβούλ with א A C D L W Θ f[1.3] Majority text rather than βεεζεβούλ with B and א B in Matt and Luke parallels. The latter most likely is a result of the awkward Greek combination λζ (Taylor, 238). The Vulgate and Syriac versions without Greek parallel read "Beelzebub" (MT בעל זבוב, baʿal zebûb = "lord of the flies"; LXX βααλ μυῖαν), the god of Ekron, under the influence of 2 Kgs 1:2.

[g] ὅσα for ὅσας has been variously explained as a "Semitism" (Lohmeyer, 80, n. 1; cf. Deut 4:2; 5:28 [31]), as a "cognate accusative" after βλασφημεῖν without any antecedent (Gould, 65) or similarly the neuter accusative *ad sensum* (Lagrange, 74; Taylor, 243).

h Wellhausen (27) omits εἰς τὸν αἰῶνα with D W Θ λ and the old Latin texts. But this reading most likely reflects the awkwardness and redundancy of the phrase in the context of the following clause.

i κρίσεως in A C² 074 0134 f¹ sy p,h bo pt because of awkwardness of this expression. Cf. κολάσεως 348 1216 and ἁμαρτίας C* vid D W f¹³.

j ἑστήκοντες present from perfect stem of ἵστημι that emerges in the hellenistic period. It is used here and in 11:25. It is read in B C* Δ 28 but changed to more common ἑστῶτες in A D W Θ 074 0134 f¹³. Only present participle of ἵστημι used by Mark.

k καὶ αἱ ἀδελφαί σου read by A D Γ 700 1010 it vg mss sy hmg possibly assimilated with 3:35 and/ or 6:3. But why not also in 3:31,33? Thus the reading with brackets in Nestle²⁶ and GNT. But shorter text has better manuscript support (א B C W Θ f¹.¹³ vg) and gains further support if 3:31a is redactionally constructed from content of 3:32–34 (see below).

l Literally, "answering he said to them" (ἀποκριθεὶς αὐτοῖς λέγει) the first Markan use of this Semitism common in the LXX (Taylor, 246).

m Read γάρ with majority of witnesses (א A B D L W Θ 074 f¹.¹³ lat sy sa bo mss) against omission in B (W) b e bo.

Form / Structure / Setting

This section contains several literary forms. We find at least two pronounce-ment stories, one a controversy narrative (3:22–26) and the other a teaching narrative or a biographical apothegm (3:31–35), with 3:20–21 being either the remains of a biographical apothegm or the first part of the second pro-nouncement story, a parabolic saying (3:27) and a sentence of holy law (3:28–29). This mixture of forms suggests what an analysis of source and content supports, namely, that 3:20–35 consists of a collection of originally discrete traditions. That leaves us with the questions about when these traditions were combined and what role, if any, did the evangelist have in bringing together and modifying the material.

An apparent parallel in Luke 11:14–28 that begins with an exorcism (11:14// Matt 12:22–23), Beelzebul controversy (11:15–23//Matt 12:24–30), return of more demons (11:24–26//Matt 12:43–45) and reference to Jesus' mother and doing "the word of God" (Luke 11:27–28) has led some to see varying degrees of Q-influence on Mark (e.g., Wenham, NTS 21 [1974–75] 299–300; Lambrecht, NovT 16 [1974] 247–52; Schmithals, 1:220–21). Yet the differences in vocabulary, omissions, and narrative flow warn against positing Mark's use of Q as a source (e.g., Schmithals), as the basis for his redactional composition (e.g., Lambrecht) or even as a determining influence (e.g., Wen-ham). Furthermore, the apparent sequential correspondence between Mark and Q assumes that Mark has dropped an initial exorcism and that the refer-ence to Jesus' mother in Luke 11:27–28 concluded the Q complex (cf. 3:31–35). Both assumptions are possible but not necessary as Mark's use of 3:22–30 without an exorcism and Matthew's omission of the latter indicates. Even should the reference to Jesus' mother in Luke 11:27–28 have been a part of Q, its beatitude form and its content so remote from the theme of 3:31–35 makes a traditional or redactional connection speculative at best. Therefore, Mark 3:20–35 can best be treated as traditional materials independent from the apparent parallels in Q.

Some have viewed this complex as consisting of three traditional units (3:20–21; 3:22–30; 3:31–35) modified and combined redactionally by the evangelist (e.g., Schmidt, 122–23; Taylor, 235). Others (e.g., Pesch 1:209–10; Boring, JBL 91 [1972] 519, n. 59) have taken the first two (3:20–21,22–

30) as a pre-Markan combination with Mark adding the third (3:31–35). Still others have found the second and third (3:22–30,31–35) to be pre-Markan combinations with 3:20–21 being essentially Mark's redactional creation (e.g., Dibelius, 47; Lambrecht, *NovT* 16 [1974] 242; Gnilka, 1:144–45). Dibelius' point of view represents the rejection of any traditional connection between the first and third units (3:20–21,31–35) because of: (a) two supposedly different introductions for 3:32–35 (3.21 and 3.31), (b) the difference in subjects (3:21, "his people" [οἱ παρ' αὐτοῦ] cf. 3:31, "his mother and his brothers" [ἡ μήτηρ αὐτοῦ καὶ οἱ ἀδελφοί]), and (c) the thematic difference between 3:21 and 3:31–35 (Dibelius, 47).

Yet the analyses that preclude the traditional connection of 3:21 with 32–35 overlook one of Mark's distinctive redactional characteristics, his "sandwiching" or intercalating of traditions (Donahue, *Trial*, 58–63). In 6:7–13/30–32; 9:37/41; 11:12–14/20–26; 14:1–2/10–11; 14:54/66–72 the evangelist interrupts traditional material by inserting another traditional unit which allows time for the first action to come to fruition. In each instance, the evangelist interrupts a traditional unit rather than using two or more traditional units to frame a central unit for his sandwich. This redactional style suggests that the story of Jesus' family (3:21,31–35) was the traditional unit which the controversy with the scribes from Jerusalem (3:22–30) interrupts. Furthermore, the redactional adjustments necessary to accommodate the inserted tradition accounts for the differences between 3:21 and 3:31–35 noted by Dibelius. The separation of 3:32–35 from 3:21 would require a second introduction (3:31) of the subjects. The difference in subjects is one of detail and may stem from the redactional formation of 3:31 from the comment in 3:32. Lastly, the difference in tone and content between 3:21 and 3:32–35 disappears, if the charge of 3:21b is itself a redactional change (see *Comment* on 3:21,22) to set the stage for the inserted tradition of 3:22–30. The family's objective in 3:21 is hardly blunted by their behavior in 3:31b, since one can take another "into custody" without using force. It seems, therefore, that Mark has modified a traditional unit underlying 3:21,31–35 by inserting 3:22–30 (Bultmann, 13; Grundmann, 106–7; Gnilka, 1:144–45; Haenchen, 139–40; Koch, *Wundererzählungen*, 145–46; Schmithals, 1:211; Best, *NTS* 22 [1975–76] 313–14). But to what extent did the evangelist rework or combine traditions within the two units of 3:20–21,32–34 and 3:22–30?

The opinion regarding the extent of the tradition and redaction in the opening scene (3:20–21) runs the spectrum from essentially traditional (Pesch, 1:209–10; Schmithals, 1:211) to essentially redactional (Gnilka, 1:144–45, Schweizer, 83–84; Crossan, *NovT* 15 [1973] 83–87; Lambrecht, *NovT* 16 [1974] 251). The answer may well lie between these two extremes. In 3:20 content and stylistic indications point to a probable Markan redaction. This verse has familiar Markan motifs: (a) the house (1:29,32–33; 2:1), (b) the press of the gathered crowds (1:33,37,45; 2:2,4,13; 3:7–9), even (c) to the extent of preventing an action (2:2–4; esp. 6:31). Furthermore, the mention of "a crowd" with the family "outside" in 3:32 may have contributed to the redactional development of this setting in 3:20. Stylistically, the historical present (ἔρχεται), the use of "again" (πάλιν), and the result clause (ὥστε) with accusative and infinitive (Pryke, *Style*, 96,117) also fit Mark's redactional pattern.

By contrast, 3:21a contains almost no Markan redactional traits in style or content. Indeed the presence of the ambiguous "his people" (οἱ παρ' αὐτοῦ) in contrast to their precise identity in 3:31, the content (cf. "set out" [ἐξῆλθον], 3:21; "came" [ἔρχονται], 3:31), and Mark's redactional "sandwich" structure of 3:21,31–25 make a strong case for at least an underlying tradition behind 3:21 (Best, *NTS* 22 [1975–76] 314). The severity of the charge in 3:21b (Taylor, 325) and the untypical Markan use of ἐξίστημι (cf. 2:12; 5:42; 6:51) might also indicate pre-Markan tradition, but the use of "for" (γάρ) in explanatory clauses and the similar form and content of the "scribes'" charge in 3:22b may well indicate Markan redaction to simplify the insertion of the Beelzebul controversy (see *Comment* on 3:21).

In 3:31–35, apart from Lambrecht, who hints that Mark might have creatively "elaborated" the traditional saying in 3:35 into the scene of 3:32–34 (*NovT* 16 [1974] 250–51), and Crossan, who takes 3:31–34 to be traditional and 3:35 Mark's redactional composition (*NovT* 15 [1973] 97–98), most have concluded that the evangelist has simply taken over tradition with little redactional change, apart from 3:31. If, as suggested above, this traditional unit began originally with a tradition underlying 3:20–21 and was interrupted by the insertion of 3:22–30, then 3:31a with the arrival and identification of οἱ παρ' αὐτοῦ as Jesus' "mother and brothers" would represent the evangelist's bridge between 3:21 and 31b.

In 3:22–30, a traditional unit doubtless underlies the Beelzebul controversy of 3:22–26, and most concur in assigning to the pre-Markan Beelzebul tradition the related but once independent parable of the strong man (3:27; cf. Luke 11:21–22 and *Gos. Thom. 35*). The presence of a thematically related combination in Q (Luke 11:15–18,21–21; Matt 12:24–26, cf. 12:29) supports this conclusion. The more difficult and perhaps unresolvable question pertains to the introduction of the "unpardonable sin" saying in 3:28–29. The difference from 3:22–27 in subject ("forgiveness" rather than "exorcism"; "Holy Spirit" introduced without explanation), form (a "sentence of holy law" in contrast to "parables" [3:23]; an introductory ἀμήν-formula to set off 3:28–29), Luke's location of the saying (12:10), and a parallel in *Did.* 11:7 and in *Gos. Thom.* 44 without similar context have led most interpreters to view this material as having once existed as an independent logion (cf. Cranfield, 139). Was Mark then responsible for introducing the saying into this context (Taylor, 241; Grundmann, 110; Schmithals, 223; Crossan, *NovT* 15 [1973] 92–93; Lambrecht, *NovT* 16 [1974] 248; Best, *NTS* 22 [1975–76], 316)? Or did he find it already combined with the exorcism materials (Pesch, 1:209–10; Gnilka, 1:146; Boring, *NovT* 18 [1976] 279)? Both the Jesus tradition (e.g., Matt 12:28//Luke 11:20) and Mark (see *Comment* on 1:14–15,21–27) directly correlate Jesus' ministry of exorcism with Jesus' ministry of the Kingdom of God. This alignment of themes certainly lies implicit to the flow of 3:22–29 and could point to either Mark's redaction or his tradition.

The thematic combination, however, of Jesus' exorcism with the eschatological work of God present in the Q-parallel to Mark 3:22–27 (Luke 11:15–20// Matt 12:24–28), the more natural use of 3:28–29, apart from the explanation in 3:30, to counter the charge of collaborating with Satan (3:22c) instead of demonic possession, and the likely probability that 3:22b ("He has Beelzebul") and 3:30 ("He has an unclean spirit") form simply Mark's redactional inclusion around a traditional unit (3:22–29) suggest the probability that Mark found 3:28–29 as part of one complex traditional unit (3:22–29) which he inserted into the traditional unit of 3:20–21,31–35. This would also correspond to the other cases of "sandwiching," since the evangelist always inserts a given traditional unit into another traditional unit (6:7–13 [14–29] 30–32; 14:1–2 [3–9] 10–11; cf. 5:21–24 [25–34] 35–43).

Within the Beelzebul material (3:22–26) the evangelist's redactional hand comes to light most likely in 3:22ab. The charge of "having Beelzebul" (3:22b) is not only missing in the Q parallels but is missing a counterargument in Jesus' response (3:23–26 [27]; cf. 3:30). The thematic and formal similarity to "his people's" charge in 3:21b aligns the "scribes'" charge with what has preceded and makes the transition to the controversy that follows. Mark's redaction here most likely includes the summons in 3:23a.

Few distinctive Markan stylistic or theological traits occur in the parable of the "strong man" in 3:27 or the saying about the "unpardonable sin" in 3:28–29. Only the explanatory statement of 3:30 which forms an inclusion with the "scribes'" charge in 3:22 and "explains" the thrust of 3:28–29 for the immediate context reflects Markan redaction (see *Comment* on 3:30).

Structurally, many have noted that 3:20–35 presents us with the first of Mark's characteristic "sandwiches" (e.g., Best, *NTS* 26 [1975–76] 314). Opening with a scene portraying the popular response to Jesus (3:20) and the notice of "his people's" intent to take him into custody because of their concern about his sanity (3:21), the scene is "interrupted" and Jesus' opposition is heightened by the "scribes" related but more pointed charge of demon possession and being in league with the prince of demons (3:22). The severity of the scribes' charge finds its counterpoint in the warning against the unforgivable sin (3:28–30); the severity of the family's charge finds its counterpoint in a new definition of "family" (3:34–35).

Yet the internal structure of this section suffers the consequences of its thematic relatedness but traditional disparity. Not only does the "sandwich" approach divide the family's concern into two parts (3:20–21,31–35), but the diverse traditions that compose the scribes' charge and Jesus' response in 3:22–30 break the structural flow of the parts into discrete units (3:22c–26,27,28–29) bound together by Mark's redactional inclusion of 3:22ab and 3:30. Lambrecht has also found a chiastic pattern in 3:23b–26 (Beelzebub controversy) and 3:28–29 ("unpardonable sin," similarly, Boring, *NovT* 18 [1976] 267–70) set around the pivotal "binding" saying in 3:27. Lambrecht also posits a thematic chiasm for the whole of 3:20–35 (*NovT* 16 [1974] 241–58):

a. Jesus at home and the initiative of the relatives (3:20–21)
b. The scribes' accusation (3:22)
c. Jesus' apology (3:23b–29)
b'. Scribes' accusation repeated (3:30)
a'. Arrival of relatives and declaration of true kinship (3:31–35)

The setting of this material immediately following the call and catalog of the Twelve disciples sharpens the contrast between the disciples and the crowds who follow on the one hand and his family and the scribes on the other hand. Our first clear hint of opposition to Jesus came in 3:6 when the Pharisees and Herodians took counsel to destroy Jesus. We now find that ironically his own family and the scribes of Jerusalem, whom one would most likely have expected to understand, have failed to understand and support his ministry. In fact, they express opposition to him and his ministry.

Comment

20 "To his house" (εἰς οἶκον) may be translated simply as "home" (Pesch, 1:211). We have already had mention of the home of Peter's mother-in-law in 1:29,32–33. The redactional use of "a house" in 2:2 may refer to the same place and have similar implications for this reference. In the flow of the narrative, Jesus goes from the mountain where he has called the Twelve to a house.

The crowd's gathering "again" (πάλιν) may refer to 3:7–9 but "again" generally signals a redactional shift in setting to a previously mentioned locale (see *Comment* on 3:1). Jesus' popular appeal is a repeated motif running through the narrative from 1:33,37,45; 2:2,4,13; 3:7–10 and 4:1. The situation is graphically intensified this time by the result that neither Jesus nor his companions (see *Note* c), the Twelve in view of the context (3:13–19, esp. 3:14), were able to eat (cf. 2:2–4; 3:7–9 and 4:1–2; 6:31). Naturally, this motif emphasizes the popular success of Jesus' ministry, and simultaneously sets the reaction of Jesus' family and the scribes from Jerusalem in bold contrast.

21 "His people" renders an ambiguous Greek construction (οἱ παρ᾽ αὐτοῦ) which generally means "envoys" or "adherents" but on occasion can mean "relatives" (e.g., LXX Prov 31:21; Taylor, 236). Wansbrough (*NTS* 18 [1971–72] 234–35; similarly Wenham, *NTS* 21 [1974–75] 296–97) has recently argued for "adherents," meaning the Twelve, to be the more natural reading. Accordingly, Jesus' disciples go outside to control the excited crowd. This reading, however, fails to take several factors into consideration, not least of which being the evangelist's "sandwich" structure of 3:20–21 and 3:31–35 around 3:22–30. Mark 3:31 makes clear that Jesus' "family" is the subject of 3:21.

"Heard" (ἀκούσαντες) obviously has something in 3:20 for its object. We have no indication of any commotion or disturbance which the disciples needed to quiet (cf. Wansbrough, *NTS* 18 [1971–72] 235). Nor need we think that Jesus' family heard of his inability to eat and came out of their concern for his needs (cf. Lagrange, 70; Lane, 139). Such a dire situation and its report requires a greater time sequence than implied by 3:20–21. More likely "heard" refers to Jesus' being "in a house" or "at home" (cf. 2:1). Having heard where Jesus was located, the family "set out" (ἐξῆλθον) to take him into custody.

"To take him into their custody" (κρατῆσαι αὐτόν) renders a strong verb occurring several times in Mark with the meaning "to arrest" (e.g., 6:17; 12:12; 14:1,44,46,49,51). We have no attestation of the meaning "to calm down" suggested by Wansbrough (*NTS* 18 [1971–72] 235). Even Lagrange, who views the action as stemming from affection, has to qualify the verb by adding "violent affection" (70). The pronoun (αὐτόν) cannot refer to "the crowd," (ὁ ὄχλος) in spite of its being the nearest masculine antecedent (Wans-brough, *NTS* 18 [1971–72] 234), because "crowd" is a collective noun for Mark and always takes a plural pronoun (Meye, *Jesus*, 150; Best, *NTS* 22 [1975–76] 311). Jesus as the unnamed subject of this section supplies the masculine antecedent as indicated by "*his* people" (οἱ παρ' αὐτοῦ).

"For" introduces an explanatory γάρ-clause which often indicates Mark's redaction (Pryke, *Style*, 126–35). The possibility of this clause being redactional, despite its severe content (cf. Taylor, 235), gains support from the fact that Mark has the same ἔλεγεν γάρ construction explaining the arrest (κρατεῖν) of the Baptist (6:18) and Jesus (14:2) and from the related and parallel con-structed charge by the scribes in 3:22b. By explaining "his people's" behavior with this charge, the evangelist sets the stage for the first of two charges by the "scribes" in form and content and smoothes the way for inserting the Beelzebul controversy (3:22–30). Though 3:21b may be redactional, we have ample evidence from the early Church that such a charge related to Jesus' being possessed existed (e.g., John 10:20; 7:20; 8:48,52; 10:20; R. E. Brown, *The Gospel according to John*. I. AB 29, [Garden City, NY: Doubleday, 1966], 312,358,387). Whereas Mark may have formulated the charge in 3:21b and its corollary in 3:22b, the charge certainly did not originate with Mark.

"They said" (ἔλεγον) most likely implies "his people" as the subject (Taylor, 236), although Mark often uses impersonal plural verbs (Lagrange, 70). The impersonal verb would remove some of the onus from Jesus' family by attribut-ing the charge to others rather than the relatives. Yet Mark does not seem to protect the family in 3:31–35, and they would still be culpable for their intended actions in 3:21. Furthermore, the theme of the family's unbelief or lack of understanding appears elsewhere in the tradition (cf. Luke 2:48; John 2:3–4; 7:3–5).

"Out of his mind" renders a verb (ἐξέστη) that expresses astonishment in its three other occurrences in Mark (2:12; 5:42; 6:51). Wansbrough's (*NTS* 18 [1971–72] 234–35) insistence on a similar meaning here with the crowd as the subject cannot be sustained. He ignores this verb's otherwise well attested meaning of "to be out of one's mind" and the absence of any astonishing event which always provokes the reaction of astonishment in the other contexts. Furthermore, the lack of parallels in Matthew and Luke as well as the variant textual readings point to the more severe meaning.

22 At this point the story breaks off and the "scribes from Jerusalem" (οἱ γραμματεῖς οἱ ἀπὸ Ἱεροσολύμων) enter the scene. Nothing is done to change the setting. The controversy that follows over Jesus' exorcisms seems to be without provocation. So some have suggested that the evangelist abbreviated his tradition that began, as it does in Matt 12:22; 9:33; and Luke 11:14, with an exorcism (Bultmann, 13). As the text now stands, the reader finds the occasion for the ensuing charge in the previous references to Jesus' exor-cisms that have consistently played an important role in his ministry (1:21–28,34,39; 3:11,15). Instead of a specific exorcism, this controversy centers on a major component of Jesus' ministry and that of the Twelve as seen so far in the narrative.

The "scribes from Jerusalem" (cf. "the Pharisees" in Matt; "some of the crowd" in Luke) shifts the focus from "his people." Most likely reflecting

Mark's redaction, this phrase strikes an ominous note. The "scribes," the first named opponents of Jesus (2:6, similarly 7:1), always appear in confrontation scenes (see *Comment* on 1:22). Whereas "Jerusalem" as the center of Jewish legal authority (Lane, 141; Pesch, 1:213) may give weight to the delegation, it clearly represents in Mark a place of hostility for Jesus, the place of his death and itself destined for destruction. These considerations along with the contextually related motifs of "custody" (κρατεῖν) in 3:21 and the capital crime of blasphemy in 3:28–29 may be a harbinger of things to come and the evangelist's focus on the passion (cf. 2:6–8; 3:6). There is little evidence that the "scribes from Jerusalem" represent opposing forces from the Jerusalem Church for Mark's audience (cf. Crossan, *NovT* 15 [1973] 113).

"He is possessed by Beelzebul" (Βεελζεβοὺλ ἔχει), literally, "He has Beelzebul," but ἔχειν in similar contexts is a common expression for being "possessed" (cf. 3:30; 5:15; 7:25; 9:17). This first of two charges made by the "scribes" does not occur in the Q-material and has no direct counter in either the traditional unit of 3:22c–26 or in the related parabolic saying in 3:27. Even the "unpardonable sin" saying (3:28–29) fails to respond directly to the charge, apart from its explanation in 3:30. Therefore, the presence of the charge makes the most sense when taken as Mark's redactional bridge from his inserted material regarding Jesus' ministry of exorcism (3:22c–29) to the previous context of 3:20–21 by linking "his people's" charge in 3:21b with that of the "scribes." The evangelist then returns to this charge by forming an inclusion in his explanatory statement for 3:28–29 in 3:30. John 10:20 illustrates how interchangeable insanity and demon possession were in the popular mind. Mark's narrative, therefore, heightens "his peoples'" charge of being out of his mind by the "scribes" thematically related and formally parallel charge of Jesus' being possessed.

"Beelzebul" (βεελζεβούλ) defies precise definition. The term does not occur in extant Jewish literature. Most interpreters take the Greek word to be a transliteration of a Hebrew expression, either בעל זבל, *baʿal zĕbûl*, meaning "lord of the dwelling" (cf. οἰκοδεσπότης in Matt 10:25) or בעל זיבול, *baʿal zibûl*, meaning "lord of dung." Gaston has disputed these renderings as oversimplified (Gaston, *TZ* 18 [1962] 245–51). First, בעל זיבול, *baʿal zibûl*, would be more accurately transliterated as Βεελζεβούλ, and, further, זיבול *zibûl* = "dung" does not exist (cf. זבל, *zebel*) except in the context of and as a play on words for זיבוח, *zibûaḥ*, meaning "sacrifice" (Gaston, 251). Second, although more likely a transliteration of בעל זבל, *baʿal zĕbûl*, זבל, *zĕbûl*, does not etymologically mean "dwelling" as such but only in the context of the temple and/or heaven as God's dwelling (Gaston, 248–50, 252; Limbeck, *Wort Gottes*, 39. n. 1).

But why would Satan be known as "Lord of the (heavenly) dwelling"? Gaston notes that Yahweh's "chief rival" during the hellenistic period was known in Greek as Ζεὺς Ὀλύμπιος and in Aramaic as בעל שמין, *bĕʿel šĕmayin*, or "Lord of heaven" (Gaston, 252). Israel countered with a מרי שמיא, *mārē šĕmayyā* ("Lord of heaven," cf. Dan 5:23) as Yahweh's name. Since ample evidence in Judaism and the NT shows that pagan gods were thought to be demons, Gaston suggests that בעל זבל, *baʿal zĕbûl* = "lord of the (heavenly) dwelling" was "coined specifically for this situation" in which Jesus is linked with the prince of demons and represents a transparent play on words with בַּעַל שָׁמַיִן, *bĕʿel šĕmayin,* = "lord of heaven" (Gaston, 523).

"By the prince of demons" (ἐν τῷ ἄρχοντι τῶν δαιμωνίων) introduces a second charge against Jesus, the charge of collaborating with Satan that is countered in 3:23–27 (28–29). This charge found in the Q-material of Matthew and Luke directly addresses the question of Jesus' exorcisms. The "prince of demons" is specifically called "Beelzebul" in the Q-materials. Mark, however, leaves the prince's identity with Beelzebul unclear, since 3:30 identifies Beelzebul with "an unclean spirit." This ambiguity may be more the result of Mark's redactional development of the first charge and its counter in 3:30 than an attempt to distinguish between "Beelzebul" and the "prince of demons."

Inherent to the charge and Jesus' counter lies the assumption of a hierarchical structure among the demons, which at one time was considered atypical of Judaism (Lohmeyer, 78). But the evidence for such a concept in Judaism exists for example in 1QS 3:20–21; *T. Sal.* 2:9; 3:5; 6:1 where mention is made of the "prince of demons" (see Becker, *Heil,* 208–13, esp. 210).

23 "After summoning them" (προσκαλεσάμενος αὐτούς) seems to be a Markan phrase (cf. 6:7; 7:14; 8:1,34; 10:42; 12:43; Pesch, 1:214). The ones summoned most naturally in this context would be the "scribes from Jerusalem" of 3:22. "His people" of 3:21 have not yet arrived and the crowd has not been immediately involved in this scene.

"In parables" (ἐν παραβολαῖς) includes many forms of speaking such as riddles, metaphors, similes, and other figures of speech, even at times allegory (see pp. 188–89). This word carries much more theological weight for Mark than the term often connotes for us (see *Comment* on 4:11). Jesus speaks in "parables" for the crowds and his opponents. Only those prepared to follow Jesus receive an interpretation of them. Therefore, for Mark these sayings or "riddles" represent a form of judgment directed at the opponents rather than an exchange of viewpoints (Gnilka, 1:149). As Schweizer has noted (85–86), one's understanding of parables, metaphors and figures of speech assumes a certain relationship between the speaker and listener, a relationship rejected by the "scribes from Jerusalem."

"How can Satan . . ?" (Πῶς δύναται Σατανᾶς;) identifies the "prince of demons" as Satan and poses the essential question that exposes the "scribes'" charge of collaboration with Satan to be a contradiction in terms. One would assume that the response to Jesus' question would be negative. From the viewpoint of the narrator and the reader who know that Jesus is not working in collaboration with Satan, Satan is not casting out Satan. Yet the argument that follows operates *reductio ad absurdum* with this premise to show that Satan has indeed "met his end" (3:26).

Recognizing the tact used in the argument still leaves us with the logical possibility that Jesus' counter can be refuted. First, one must start with the assumption of the tight, hierarchical structure of the demonic world assumed by the answer of 3:24–26, a starting point the "scribes" need not have shared. Second, both the OT (e.g., Exod 7:11; 8:7) and NT (e.g., 2 Thess 2:9; Rev 13:13) know of miracles worked by evil powers, so it would not be beyond "Satan," the "father of lies," to work deceptively. But instead of faulting the argument (so Haenchen, 146), the fact that it assumes what is not true, namely,

Satan's self-destruction through Jesus' exorcisms, and the fact that one can dismiss it on other grounds gives Jesus' response its "parabolic" character. It leaves the hearer with the choice of either dismissing Jesus' claim or accepting it. The decision ultimately reflects one's relationship with Jesus.

24–25 The parallel constructed illustrations, consisting of two conditional sentences, makes use of macro-("kingdom") and micro-("household") political and social units. The common experience of civil war and domestic conflict serves as familiar material for the argument.

26 The conclusion shifts from the hypothetically conditional sentences (ἐάν + subjunctive) to the condition assumed contrary to fact (εἰ + augmented tenses of indicative). In other words, the argument shifts from the hypothetical to the assumption that Satan has indeed not risen up against himself. Were it so, then the result would mean Satan's fall, his "end." "Met his end" (τέλος ἔχει) specifies "not able to stand" (οὐ δυνήσεται σταθῆναι) by speaking of Satan's personal demise in hellenistic terms for "end of life" (Heb 7:3, so Lohmeyer, 79; Gnilka, 1:158). The idea corresponds materially to the graphic portrait of Satan's demise in Luke 10:18 as "lightning falling from heaven."

Therefore, Jesus responds to the "scribes'" charge of collaborating with the "prince of demons" by arguing that given their assumption it would mean Satan has "met his end" through Jesus' ministry of exorcism.

27 This conclusion becomes more explicit in the parabolic saying whose existence as an independent logion seems confirmed by its variant form in Q and *Gos. Thom.* 35 (cf. 21). Thematically, it corresponds with 3:22–26 and the catchwords "house" (οἰκία) and "able" (δύνεσθαι) make its combination with 3:25–26 very logical.

Few would question the applicability of this parable to Jesus' preaching of the Kingdom. Many would trace it back to Jesus himself (e.g., Grundmann, 111; Schweizer, 86; Gnilka, 1:150; Schmithals, 1:223; Ernst, 120). Set against Jesus' ministry and Isa 49:24–25 (cf. 3:12), the details become transparent. Clearly the "strong man" (ἰσχυρός) stands for Satan; his "possessions" (σκεύη) represents those possessed; the "binding" (δήσῃ) of the "strong man" takes place in Jesus' ministry; and the "plundering" (διαρπάσει) bespeaks Jesus' own exorcisms of those "possessed." Consequently, this saying makes clear the ultimate or eschatological character of Jesus' ministry of exorcism that has accompanied his preaching and teaching (1:21–27,34; 3:11–12) as being a consequence of Satan's being "bound" or having "met his end."

Can one determine even more precisely when the binding of the strong man took place for Mark? Robinson has taken 3:22–27 together with the temptation scene (1:12–13) to be interpretive of Jesus' exorcisms as the "cosmic struggle between the Spirit and Satan begun in the temptation" so that the "single event of the temptation becomes in the exorcisms an extended history of redemptive significance" (Robinson, *History*, 83,78). The "when" becomes, therefore, a continuous process or "cosmic struggle" in history. Best also has taken 3:22–30 in light of the temptation scene but argues that the defeat of Satan in the temptation (1:12–13) represents the "when." The exorcisms are but the plundering or "making real of a victory already accomplished" at the "very beginning of the ministry of Jesus" (*Temptation*, 15).

Both alternatives appear to go beyond the text of Satan's defeat at the temptation and the limits of the parable here. Although Mark notes Jesus' temptation by Satan, he adds little to underscore Satan's "defeat" or a "cosmic struggle" (see *Comment* on 1:12–13). Similarly, it is unclear how either the narrator would imply or the reader infer a connection between the controversy narrative here and the temptation scene. At issue is Jesus' ministry of exorcism. To be sure, the logic of the parable requires the "binding" before the "plundering," but must the parable be taken so allegorically that we must identify a similar sequence for Mark in Jesus' ministry? It may be enough to say that 3:22–27 declares Jesus' ministry, without specifying the "when," to reflect the eschatological defeat of Satan as seen in his exorcisms.

28–29 Mark ends Jesus' response to the "scribes'" charge with the warning about the "unpardonable sin." This saying in slightly different form appears in another context in Q (cf. Luke 12:10) and in *Gos. Thom.* 44. Despite the attempts of many to determine a linear literary relationship between Mark and the Q-saying, recent studies of the history of the tradition have denied any such linear development between the traditions and have handled the Mark and Q sayings as two independent traditional developments from an earlier tradition as seen by the differences in form and content (Schippers, *SE* IV, 231–35; Colpe, *Ruf*, 65, and Boring, *NovT* 18 [1976] 258–79).

28 "I assure you" (ἀμὴν λέγω ὑμῖν) is the first of several such introductory formulas in Mark. This formula of assurance points to a revelatory moment analogous to the authoritative declaration by the prophet, "Thus says the Lord" (Jeremias, *Abba*, 149; *Theology*, 35). The common liturgical use of a responsive "amen" (ἀμήν) meaning "so be it" in Judaism and the early Church needs no additional comment. But the shift of a response formula to an introductory formula stands out, particularly since this introductory ἀμήν combined with "I say to you" occurs only on the lips of Jesus in the New Testament. We only have one possible parallel to such usage in Jewish/Christian literature (*T. Abraham*, 8,20). Therefore, Jeremias has interpreted this formula as a possible sign of an *ipsissima vox Jesu* (*Abba*, 148–51).

Hasler (*Amen*) and Berger (*Amen-Worte*) have disputed Jeremias' conclusion. The former assigned these ἀμήν formulas to the prophetic utterances of the words of the risen Lord in hellenistic Christian worship services. The latter has traced these to a hellenistic Jewish apocalyptic milieu in which the visionaries used the formula as legitimation for their messages. Such a pattern was then transferred to the Jesus' tradition by placing these formulas on lips of the earthly Jesus. Neither Hasler, however, nor Berger accounts for why this unparalleled formula came to be exclusively on Jesus' lips or where the early "hellenistic Christian" prophets found it. Even Berger's attempt to find traditional parallels in hellenistic Judaism with apocalyptic overtones fails to uncover any actual use of this formula (Berger, *Amen*, 4–6; Jeremias, *ZNW* 64 [1973] 122–23). Jeremias, therefore, with good reason has stood by his earlier conclusions (*Theology*, 35–36).

The absence of a comparable formula in the Q-parallel to 3:29 of Luke 12:10 and the apparent replacement of ἀμήν with διὰ τοῦτο in the Matthew parallel (12:31) together with the tendency by some to see these formulas more at home in early Christian prophecy than in Jesus' ministry (Käsemann, *Questions*, 102–3; Scroggs, *JBL* 84 [1965] 359–65; Boring, *JBL* 92 [1972]

515; *NovT* 18 [1976] 273–74, 276–77) has led to the assigning both the formula and the saying to the early Church. Yet the questionable assignment of these formulas to early Christian prophets (D. E. Aune, *Prophecy in Early Christianity and the Ancient Mediterranean World* [Grand Rapids: Eerdmans, 1983], 240–42), the unprecedented scope of forgiveness expressed in what follows, and its correlation in Jesus' ministry to "sinners" give strong support for the authenticity of the formula here.

"All things shall be forgiven" (πάντα ἀφεθήσεται) emphasizes the startling and unparalleled declaration of total forgiveness by bringing forward at the beginning of the sentence the sweeping, inclusive subject, "all things" (πάντα). This subject is then resumed and specified at the end of the sentence. The divine passive expresses God's role as the forgiver and the future tense points to God's ultimate actions at the final judgment.

"Every human being," literally, "the sons of men" (τοῖς υἱοῖς τῶν ἀνθρώπων), a Semitic idiom meaning all humanity (cf. τοῖς ἀνθρώποις in Matt 12:31), stands in contrast to "the Son of man" (τὸν υἱὸν τοῦ ἀνθρώπου) in Luke 12:10//Matt 12:32. Mark's phrase renders with plural nouns the generic singular of the Aramaic בַּר נָשָׁא, *bar nāšā*, whereas the Q-form refers to Jesus as a self-designation.

This difference has occasioned much debate over whether Mark's phrase (Bultmann, 131; Lövestam, *Blasphemia*, 68, n. 46; Higgins, *Teaching*, 127–32; Schweizer, 84) or Q's phrase (Tödt, *Son of Man*, 314–18; Crossan, *NovT* 15 [1973] 92–93; Schulz, *Spruchquelle*, 247; Schmithals, 1:223) was the earlier. Both alternatives assume a linear development from either one or the other text and ignore further disparity between Mark and Q in form and content. Mark has "the sons of men" as the recipients of divine forgiveness in a chiastic construction; Q has "the Son of man" as the object of the "blasphemy" in the form of an antithetical parallelism. So several have recently argued that these sayings reflect variant traditions whose roots lie in a common Aramaic saying but whose histories of tradition differ (Schippers, *SE*, 231–35; Colpe, *Ruf*, 63–69; Boring, *NovT* 18 [1976] 258–79; Higgins, *Son of Man*, 89–92). One cannot, therefore, explain either Mark or Q as a "redactional" derivative of the other.

Mark's plural "the sons of men" represents an attempt in the pre-Markan tradition to capture in Greek the idiom of the Aramaic generic singular (so Wellhausen, 26–27, long ago; see *Comment* on 2:10) rather than a redactional attempt by the evangelist either to remove the Christological difficulty of distinguishing between the work of Jesus, Son of man, and the work of the Holy Spirit (Crossan, *NovT* 15 [1973] 92–93) or to remove the redemptive historical distinction between pre- and post-Easter (Schweizer, 84). For the possible development of the generic "son of man" to Q's "the Son of man" referring to Jesus see the extended discussion by Colpe (*Ruf,* 65–69) or Higgins (*Son of Man,* 89–90, 116–17). In any event, "the sons of men" underscores the all-inclusive character of God's forgiveness that not only encompasses all things but "every human being."

"All sinful behavior" (ἁμαρτήματα, only here in Mark; cf. Rom 3:25; 1 Cor 6:18) refers more specifically to sinful acts than to sin in general (cf. the more common ἁμαρτία, Lagrange, 74; Lohmeyer, 80; Taylor, 243). This expression may have sins against other human beings as its focus, particularly when combined with "all blasphemies," which has God as the primary object (Schlatter, 91; Grundmann, 112; Pesch, 217). "Blasphemy" in Greek (βλασφημία) renders several Hebrew expressions in LXX that refer to words spoken directly or indirectly against God (see H. W. Beyer, *TDNT* 1 [1964] 621–22), normally a capital offense in Judaism (Lev 24:16, cf. *S. Num.* 112; *b. Pesah.* 93b; *m. Sanh.* 7,5). This saying, therefore, speaks forgiveness to all humanity for all sins committed against God and other human beings. One could not imagine a more universal or comprehensive expression of forgiveness.

29 This saying with its exception stands in apparent contradiction to 3:28, which has just categorically declared that "all sins and blasphemies" would be forgiven. So some have attributed the substance of 3:28 to Jesus' ministry and 3:29 to early Christian prophecy in the primitive Church's polemic with the Jews who rejected Jesus (e.g., Ernst 120; cf. Gnilka 1:150) or to the struggle within the early Church over the role of prophets (Boring, *JBL* 19 [1972] 501–21). But this combination of 3:28–29 represents a biblical idiom in which a general statement is followed by a specific exception (e.g., Gen 2:16–17; Exod 12:10; Matt 15:24–32; cf. Kuschke's "relative Negation," *ZNW* 43 [1950–51] 263; Colpe, *Ruf*, 72 and *TDNT*, 8 [1972] 449, n. 349, or Kruse's, "dialectical negation," *VT* 4 [1954] 385–400, see *Comment* on 2:17]). The force of the general statement adds special gravity to the exception. Therefore, rather than primarily accenting God's forgiveness for "all sins and blasphemies," the expression of general amnesty in 3:28 makes the denial of forgiveness for the exception of "blasphemy against the Holy Spirit" in 3:29 even weightier. Without denying the content of 3:28, the focus lies on 3:29, the second half of this double saying.

"Blasphemes against the Holy Spirit" (βλασφημήσῃ εἰς τὸ πνεῦμα τὸ ἅγιον) may well reflect more the language of the early Church, since the verb "to blaspheme" in Aramaic and in classical Greek generally appears as intransitive without any direct object (cf. Colpe, *Ruf*, 69, n. 31). By the time of NT usage the verb had become more transitive in force by taking simply a direct object (cf. 3:28). The parallel, therefore, in Matt 12:32; Luke 12:10 with "speak against" ([λέγειν] κατά εἰς) may more literally render the earlier tradition (Tödt, *Son of Man*, 315–17; cf. Colpe, *Ruf*, 74, n. 45).

"Will never have forgiveness," literally, "does not have forgiveness into the age" (οὐκ ἔχει ἄφεσιν εἰς τὸν αἰῶνα). Although the phrase εἰς τὸν αἰῶνα can mean "this age" (so Mark 11:14), here it includes both "this age" and "the age to come" (cf. Matt 12:32) in the sense of "never" (Lagrange, 75; Taylor, 243).

"Guilty of an eternal sin" translates the Greek phrase (ἔνοχός ἐστιν αἰωνίου ἁμαρτήματος) literally. Cranfield (141) notes three functions of ἔνοχος with the genitive: (a) "in the power of" (Heb 2:5); (b) "guilty of" (2 Macc 13:6 and classical usage); and (c) "liable to" (Mark 14:64). The second and third suggestions distinguish between an indictment ("guilty of") and a sentence ("liable to"). The context must determine the usage. If we take ἁμαρτήματος in 3:29 as in 3:28 to mean a "sinful deed," then one is indicted for or "guilty of" committing "an eternal ("permanent," Gould, 66) sinful act." Since, however, this expression can at most mean, a sinful act with "eternal consequences" (see *Note* h), several have sought an explanation in an underlying Aramaic expression (Black, *Approach*, 140, n. 3; Cranfield, 141; Colpe, 70, n. 33). The Aramaic חוב, *ḥūb*, can mean "sinful act" (ἁμάρτημα, as in 3:28) or "condemnation" (κατάκριμα). The latter would make the more sense, "liable to eternal condemnation," as an explication of preceding statement, while the former may reflect the wordplay with ἁμάρτημα in 3:28.

The meaning of this verse has given rise through the centuries to much debate and great concern by some about just what is the "unpardonable sin." This issue was even a part of Jewish discussion (G. F. Moore, *Judaism in the First Centuries of the Christian Era: The Age of the Tannaim*, II. [Cambridge, MA: Harvard, 1962], 108–09). What does it mean to "blaspheme against the Holy Spirit"?

The answer generally comes either from the consequence as stated in 3:29b or from the context of 3:22–30. In the first instance, the focus lies on the individual's culpable rejection of or refusal to recognize God's redemptive activity. Grundmann (112), who compares this statement with the warning in Exod 23:30–31, defines this action as the rejection of God's comprehensive offer of amnesty and forgiveness. Lövestam (*Blasphemia*, 62) more precisely calls blasphemy against the Spirit the "opposition to God as seen in his eschatological, redemptive activity wherein the gift of forgiveness of sin has its basis and its starting point." One is culpably refusing God's offer and thus sealing one's own eternal judgment by committing the sin for which by definition there can be no forgiveness.

Such an understanding focusing more generally on the individual's culpable response to God's redemptive activity may well account for the meaning of the saying in the pre-Markan tradition (cf. Matt 12:32; Luke 12:10) and perhaps in Jesus' own ministry, but the double saying has a more specific Christological focus in Mark. Instead of seeking to understand the meaning of this warning simply from the consequence of 3:29b, we must also read the double saying of 3:28–29 according to Mark's context.

30 "For they said, 'He has an unclean spirit'" expresses the evangelist's redactional explanation of 3:28–29 and forms a redactional inclusion with the charge in 3:22a of Jesus' being possessed by Beelzebul. In this way, Mark points the finger directly at those who attribute God's redemptive work through the Spirit in Jesus to the work of Satan. Whereas Jesus' use of parables in 3:24–27 answered the "scribes'" charge of his working in league with Satan (3:22b), this explanation in 3:30 directs Jesus' response in 3:28–29 specifically to the redactional charge of demon possession in 3:22a. In other words, to attribute the work of the Spirit through Jesus to demonic forces is the ultimate calumny for which there is no forgiveness. In so doing, Mark clarifies the seriousness of the charge in 3:22a through the warning of 3:28–29, but stops short of pronouncing final judgment on the scribes. Therefore, for Mark Jesus is clearly the bearer of the Spirit and the issue is about Jesus' earthly ministry rather than the exalted Lord (Gnilka 1:151).

31 This verse resumes for Mark the interrupted scene of 3:20–21 where Jesus' "people" (οἱ παρ' αὐτοῦ) had set out to take him into their custody. This introduction may well have been constructed by Mark from the following statement in 3:32 where we not only find the first of four references to "mother and brothers" but also their "seeking him outside."

"His mother and his brothers came" (ἔρχεται ἡ μήτηρ αὐτοῦ καὶ οἱ ἀδελφοὶ αὐτοῦ). Most commentators assume that the absence of "father" here signals Joseph's early death (cf. the wording, "Jesus, son of Mary" in 6:3). The suggestion (Pesch, 1:224; Ernst, 122; Best, *NTS* 22 [1975–76] 318) that this results from theological concerns, such as the Christian recognition of God alone as "father" (cf. Matt 23:9), overlooks the movement from literal, distinct members of a family ("mother and brothers," 3:31) to a figurative use of family members ("brother, sister and mother") as an expression for family as a whole (3:34b, 35) for which a "father" would be a natural part (cf. John 6:42).

The presence of Jesus' "brothers" (ἀδελφοί) has raised the issue of whether Jesus had any brothers and, if so, whether Mary was their physical mother. Most Catholic commentators, doubtless in part a reflection of the view of Mary's perpetual virginity, have taken this passage appropriately but more exclusively in terms of its theological thrust (3:34–35). According to Ernst, for example, the scene in 3:31–35 reflects a catechetically reworked text that means "relatives in the broader sense" (e.g., Ernst, 122). Yet in the light of 6:3 one cannot totally avoid the question, even if this scene has primarily "catechetical" concerns. Nor can one ignore Mark's use of the tradition behind 3:32–35 that identifies "his people" (3:21) as "his mother and his brothers" (3:31a). The question, therefore, remains. And despite the attempts to identify the ἀδελφοί with Joseph's sons of another marriage (Epiphanius) or as cousins, the sons of Mary's sister (Jerome), the more natural and persuasive answer points to Mary's sons (see *Comment* on 6:3 and Pesch, 1:322–35).

"Standing outside" (ἔξω στήκοντες) appears to offer an important contrast to those "seated around him" (ἐκάθητο περὶ αὐτὸν) somewhat in keeping with 4:10–11 (Pesch, 1:222; Ernst 121; Best, *NTS* 22 [1975–76] 317, see *Comment* on 4:10). Certainly, the contrast becomes clear in the comments that follow between the "mother and brothers" outside and the "mother and brothers" around Jesus inside (3:31–32, 33–34). Furthermore, the proximity of this pericope to what follows in 4:1–12 makes the "insider"/"outsider" comparison inevitable.

Yet we must not overlook the story line in 3:20–35. The scene has been set with a house so filled by the crowd that Jesus and his disciples could not even eat (3:20). The press of the crowd would doubtless have prevented the family from directly approaching Jesus (cf. 2:4) and their "standing outside" would have been a logical predicament for the story, especially if their being "outside" was already noted in the tradition of 3:32. Consequently, the logic of this story may actually have given rise to the "insider"/"outsider" language of 4:10–11 rather than vice versa (see *Comment* on 4:10–11). The family show themselves to be "outsiders" similar to the "scribes from Jerusalem" (3:22–30) more by their designs and words (3:21) than by their location. Therefore, "outside" here means, above all, "outside the house" (so 3:32).

"They sent to call him" (ἀπέστειλαν πρὸς αὐτὸν καλοῦντες αὐτόν) has frequently been placed in tension with the family's designs in 3:21 as though it implied simply a family visit (Pesch, 1:222; Gnilka, 1:115). But nothing in Mark's wording or context need imply a change of plans from 3:21 (cf. Matt 12:46;

Luke 8:20). Because of the "crowd" (3:20,32), the family sent word for him to come outside where they could carry out their intentions (cf. 6:17).

32 "A crowd sat around him" (ἐκάθητο περὶ αὐτόν ὄχλος) may have served as the traditional source for "the crowd" in Mark's redactional development of 3:20. At any rate, there appears to be no grounds for distinguishing between this group as an "inner circle" of friends and disciples and "the crowd" (simply because one is articular and the other anarthrous) in 3:20 (cf. Swete, 69; Pesch, 1:222). The "crowd seated around him" here and "those seated around him in a circle" in 3:34 refers to the same group, the crowd who had gathered around Jesus to hear his teaching.

"They said to him" (λέγουσιν αὐτῷ) follows Mark's consistent pattern of using the singular "crowd" (ὄχλος) as a plural subject. The "crowd" becomes the intermediary that passes the message to Jesus that his family "seeks" him "outside."

The verb "to seek" (ζητοῦσιν, cf. Matt 12:47; and Luke 8:20, ἰδεῖν θέλοντές σε) receives an ominous tone from the context of the family's intention given in 3:21. "Outside" (ἔξω) not only describes the situation but may have provided the redactional setting for 3:31b. It clearly accents the separation between Jesus, the crowd around him and his "mother and brothers."

33 Jesus' response in the form of a question forms the structural pivot for this section. He turns their call and the crowd's message (3:31–32) into a question about who is his family (3:33) and thereby sets the stage for his answer (3:34–35).

34 Jesus' answer to his own question comes through his action and his word. First, he "looks around" (περιβλεψάμενος) at those seated "around him" (περὶ αὐτόν) "in a circle" (κύκλῳ). Mark may have heightened the tone of this phrase by using περιβλέπεσθαι (cf. 3:5; 10:23), but a similar verb of seeing or looking must have been in the tradition (Best, *NTS* 22 [1975–76] 314–15). This almost redundant expression of proximity "around him" offers a "visual" contrast to those "standing outside." One cannot avoid the emphasis on a "circle" or the possible suggestion of a certain "circle." But the identity of this visual circle comes from 3:32, "a crowd sat around him," and in the context of 3:20–21, 31–35 and 3:13–19 this "crowd" includes the Twelve but is certainly larger than the Twelve (cf. Meye, *Jesus,* 148–52). Second, he "says" (λέγει) and verbally identifies this visually delineated group "around him" to be "my mother and my brothers" (ἴδε ἡ μήτηρ μου καὶ οἱ ἀδελφοί μου).

Jesus identifies his family on the basis of the response to him rather than on natural kinship. The response of his natural family who sought to take him into their custody reflected their rejection of his ministry regardless of their motivation, which in Mark is given as concern for his mental stability. The response of the crowd who sought his presence and gathered around him, doubtless to hear his teaching, reflected their acceptance of him. We find here a redefinition of family akin to Jesus' teaching on discipleship in Mark 10:29 and may be latent to James' and John's leaving of their father in 1:20. Therefore, this pericope serves as a concrete illustration from the Master's experience that sets the tone for the disciple, a discipleship motif that recurs throughout Mark.

Both Matthew and Luke specify more narrowly than Mark 3:32–34 who

Jesus' "family" is. Matt 12:46 refers to "the disciples" rather than to "those seated around him." Luke 8:21 identifies Jesus' "mother and brothers" on the basis of those who "hear and do the word of God." It may well be that similar desire for precision led to the addition of 3:35 to sharpen Mark's focus.

35 This saying has been viewed from the one extreme, a traditional saying that spawned the "ideal scene" of 3:31–34 (Bultmann, 29–30; Lambrecht, *NovT* 16 [1974] 249–50), to the other, Mark's redactional conclusion of 3:31–34 (Crossan, *NovT* 15 [1973] 97–98; cf. Dibelius, 57,63–64, a "sermonic saying"). Apart from Schmithals (1:218–19), who takes this saying to have been part of this unit from the beginning, most interpreters have taken 3:35 to have been an independent logion appended in the pre-Markan tradition to 3:31–34. The change in order, the introduction of "sister," the absence of the personal pronouns, the change in content from an absolute to a conditional statement and the possible traditional variants in Luke 11:28; 2 Clem 9:11 and *Gos. Thom.* 99, all point to an earlier independent saying (Best, *NTS* 22 [1975–76] 315).

The lack of Markan characteristics supports the view of its being a traditional logion, though the use of γάρ might indicate the evangelist's hand in combining this saying with 3:32–34 (see *Comment* on 3:21). Furthermore, the narrowing or qualifying of "the crowd" (cf. 3:20,32) to those "doing the will of God" (3:35) corresponds to Mark's distinction between "the crowds" as a more neutral designation in contrast to the disciples, on the one hand, and the religious leaders, on the other. Here the "crowd" becomes synonymous with "those around him" (cf. 4:10).

"Whoever does the will of God" (ὃς ἂν ποιήσῃ τὸ θέλημα τοῦ Θεοῦ) introduces a further answer to Jesus' own question of 3:33. But instead of including all those "around him," this answer appears, on the one hand, to limit further those who qualify as Jesus' family to those who hear (cf. 3:32,34) *and* do (ποιήσῃ) the "will of God." On the other hand, this saying appears to soften the harsh contrast between Jesus' natural family and those whom he identifies "around him" as his family (3:33–34) by opening the possibility that even his own natural family could become his "brother, sister, and mother" by doing the will of God.

Yet neither the tendency to moralize nor the desire to soften the statement about family must of necessity lie behind the combination of 3:35 to 3:31–34. Matthew and Luke accomplish both of these ends by their handling of the material. Mark, however, heightens the contrast between Jesus and his family by his modification of 3:21 and by linking them with the "scribes of Jerusalem" by the insertion of a parallel and even more culpable charge in 3:22–30. Furthermore, the introductory "For" (γάρ) suggests that 3:35 explains Jesus' answer in 3:34. So "doing the will of God," a phrase that does not occur elsewhere in Mark (cf. Matt 6:10; 7:21; 12:50; 13:14; 26:52; Luke 11:2; 22:42) explains the significance of the conduct displayed by the crowd seated around Jesus, namely, the acceptance of Jesus as the one in whom God's will is at work (cf. 14:36).

Despite the tendency of some to find an inner Church polemic against Jesus' family and especially James' leadership in the Jerusalem Church

(Schweizer, 87; Trocmé, *Formation*, 136; Pesch, 1:224; Crossan, *NovT* 15 [1973] 112–13), the thrust of this passage corresponds more with Mark's dual concern to show both the varying response to Jesus' ministry in 3:13–6:6 and the cost of doing the will of God or of discipleship that underlies the whole Gospel (1:16–20; 3:14; 8:34–38; 10:29). Jesus' way was in obedience to the will of God (cf. 8:34 and 14:36). Therefore, Jesus' own experience of rejection by his family serves as a model for a discipleship that may well have cost others their family ties (cf. 1:20; 10:29). On the other hand, it may be going too far to say with Best (*NTS* 22 [1975–76] 317–18) that Mark uses this material "homiletically" to encourage his readers who find themselves victims of a similar family situation as Jesus, since "his family came to believe in him, so may theirs." For Mark, one's "hope" lies more in one's new family status (3:34–35; 10:29–30) than in the salvation of one's "former" family.

Explanation

Mark 3:20–35 consists of two pre-Markan traditional units. The first, 3:21/ 32–35, uses a confrontation between Jesus and his family to redefine the meaning of "family." The second, 3:22–29, uses a confrontation between Jesus and his religious opponents to describe the nature of Jesus' exorcistic ministry and warn against the culpable rejection of that ministry.

The family material contains two elements characteristic of Jesus' ministry, opposition on the home front and a fundamental realignment of relationships. Although we can no longer reconstruct the specific circumstances surrounding his family's actions in 3:21/32–35, their alien relationship with him emerges in the statement of their intention (3:21), their position "outside" the house in contrast with the circle around him, and in his own identification of those "around him" as his "mother and his brothers" (3:32–34). Mark's tradition may well reflect the situation in Jesus' ministry in which his family, initially at least, did not belong to those who responded positively to his work and teaching. This experience may in part have contributed to Jesus' own redefinition of family in light of his ministry.

The new definition of family is based on the differing response between his natural family, whose conduct reflected serious question, if not rejection (3:21,32), and those gathered around him (3:34–35), whose conduct reflected acceptance of him and his ministry (3:35). This redefinition in terms of one's response to Jesus' ministry and to doing the will of God corresponds to the cost of discipleship set forth in 10:29–30 and suggested in the behavior of the sons of Zebedee in 1:20 (cf. Matt 8:21–22//Luke 9:59–60; Matt 10:35// Luke 12:53). The dimension of discipleship that costs one life's most natural and valued relationship of family had more bite in a context where one's commitment to Christ and to doing "the will of God" sets one at odds with one's family (see *Comment* on 10:29–30). Yet we are not to distort this passage or those thematically consonant with it by suggesting that Jesus himself repudiated or called others to repudiate one's ties and responsibilities for the family (see 7:8–13; 10:19). One's separation from family can only come as a consequence of discipleship, not as a condition for discipleship.

By identifying those around him as "mother and brothers" in this pericope,

Jesus expresses his experience of new relationships befitting his ministry of the Kingdom (1:14–15). "Those around him" had become his "mother and brothers," his family, in view of their new and bonding relationship of "doing the will of God" (cf. 10:29–30). Accordingly, God was calling one to a new allegiance that could lead to the disavowal of the demands of one's natural family which failed to take into account "the will of God." Jesus' allegiance and loyalty belongs to the new "family of God" rather than to those who do not even recognize that "family."

In the traditional unit concerning Jesus' exorcisms, two aspects of Jesus' ministry come together: the charge of the religious opposition and Jesus' parabolic claim for his ministry. First, we have the charge made by the religious opponents of being in league with Satan (3:22c; similarly Q, Matt 12:24 [9:34]; Luke 11:15) that may well reflect one of the responses to Jesus' ministry by some of the authorities and may also reflect the perhaps later but related charge among the Jews of Jesus' use of forbidden magic. Second, we have Jesus' response that his ministry, to the contrary, involves the destruction of Satan (3:23b–27) accomplished by the Holy Spirit's work through his ministry of exorcism (3:28–29). Furthermore, one's view of Jesus' ministry had ultimate consequence for one's eternal standing before God.

Jesus' initial response demonstrates the logical fallacy of the charge, assuming one shares the same view of the hierarchical structure of demonic authority (3:23b–26). Should the opponents be correct in their charge, then Satan would be self-destructing. Indeed, he would already have met his end (24–26). Then the same point is made by the parabolic saying of 3:27 in which Jesus notes that one can only plunder a strong man's house when the strong man has been bound. Finally, Jesus warns his opponents that God will hold eternally accountable those who speak against the Holy Spirit as seen, at least implicitly, at work in Jesus' ministry of exorcism (cf. Matt 12:28; Luke 11:20).

Throughout the ages many within the Church have struggled with the question of the "unpardonable sin." This warning, often coupled with the "sin unto death" in 1 John 5:15–17, has left many with the question of whether they themselves had slipped past the point of no return. But one must take this verse in context and note the nature of the warning. As a part of 3:22–29, this saying in 3:28–29 pertains to those who have aligned Jesus' ministry with the work of Satan. In other words, Jesus' opponents were attributing to Satan God's redemptive activity in Jesus through the work of the Spirit. In so doing, they not only were rejecting Jesus but also God's offer of redemptive activity in history. One commits the "unpardonable sin," therefore, by rejecting God's redemptive overture for humanity in Jesus Christ. God leaves the decision with us. God does not force the issue or his forgiveness upon those who deny God's redemptive activity. At the same time, the first half of this double saying (3:28) assures whoever seeks God's forgiveness that God's comprehensive amnesty includes all sins committed against others as well as against God (3:28).

The evangelist sandwiches the Beelzebul pericope and the saying on the unpardonable sin into the tradition (3:22–30) allowing time for the action of 3:21 to take place. But his adaptation of this tradition at the seam (3:22) also colors the surrounding tradition. First, Mark identifies the opponents as "scribes from Jerusalem" (3:22a) with the ominous ring from 2:6 (cf. 2:16) where they charge Jesus with blasphemy (cf. 3:29!). Then he expands their charge of being in league with Satan (3:22c) to accuse Jesus of being possessed by Beelzebul (3:22b), a charge parallel in form and content with the family's in 3:21b (cf. John 10:20). Therefore, Jesus' family and the scribes from Jerusalem are linked by their similar rejection of Jesus. Yet these are precisely the two groups one would most expect to have recognized and accepted Jesus, especially in contrast to the Twelve and the anonymous crowd.

Mark's primary concern lies with the contrast, on the one hand, between the response of the crowd and those with Jesus (3:20) to his ministry and, on the other hand, the response of Jesus' family and the scribes from Jerusalem who reject his ministry. This becomes apparent in his redactional combination of the traditions (3:21/32–35 and 3:22–29) and in his redactional work with the charges in 3:21b, 22b. It becomes even more apparent in his redactional location of 3:20–35 between the call and response of the Twelve, including Jesus' empowering the Twelve to cast out demons (see *Comment* on 3:15), and Jesus' teaching in "parables" to the crowds and explaining them to the "disciples" which immediately follows in 4:1–34.

Therefore, this material accents varying responses to Jesus' ministry. On the one hand, Jesus' family and the scribes from Jerusalem misunderstand and discredit Jesus' ministry. The family seeks to take him "into custody," while the authorities from Jerusalem charge him with being in consort with Satan. The slight but ominous tone of Jesus' ultimate rejection in Jerusalem can be heard here. On the other hand, the calling and response of the Twelve in 3:13–19, the crowds around him in 3:20, 32–34, and Jesus' "private" instruction to his disciples in Mark 4 indicate the positive response to him and his ministry. Those "around him" become the new "family," the core of a new fellowship, of those who do the will of God. The response of the disciples and the crowd around Jesus in contrast to Jesus' family and the religious leaders and the identification of the former as Jesus' "mother and brothers" show how radical the break with family and religious tradition is for Jesus' disciples. Jesus' experience here prefigures the experience of the disciple (10:29–30; cf. 1:20; 3:13).

C. The Parable of the Seeds   (4:1–9)

Bibliography

Black, M. *An Aramaic Approach to the Gospels and Acts.* 1967. **Boobyer, G. H.** "The Redaction of Mk 4,1–34." *NTS* 8 (1961–62) 59–70. **Boucher, M.** *The Mysterious Parable: A Literary Study.* CBQMS 6. Washington, DC: Catholic Biblical Association, 1977. **Carlston, C. E.** *The Parables of the Triple Tradition.* Philadelphia: Fortress, 1975. **Crossan, J. D.** "The Seed Parables of Jesus." *JBL* 92 (1973) 244–66. ————. *In Parables: The Challenge of the Historical Jesus.* New York: Harper & Row, 1973. **Dahl, N. A.** "The

Parables of Growth." *ST* 5 (1951) 132–66 = *Jesus in the Memory of the Early Church.* Minneapolis: Augsburg, 1976, 141–66. **Dalman, G.** *Arbeit und Sitte in Palästina.* 3. Gütersloh: Bertelsmann Verlag, 1933. ———. "Viererlei Acker." *PJ* 22 (1926) 120–32. **Dietzfelbinger, C.** "Das Gleichnis vom ausgestreuten Samen." In *Der Ruf Jesu und die Antwort der Gemeinde,* ed. E. Lohse. Göttingen: Vandenhoeck & Ruprecht, 1970. 80–93. **Dodd, C. H.** *The Parables of the Kingdom.* **Egger, W.** *Frohbotschaft und Lehre.* 1976. **Frankemölle, H.** "Hat Jesus sich selbst verkündigt? Christologische Implikationen in den vormarkinischen Parabelen." *BibLeb* 13 (1972) 184–207. **Geischer, H.-J.** "Verschwenderische Güte. Versuch über Markus 4,3–9." *EvT* 38 (1978) 418–27. **Gerhardsson, B.** "The Parable of the Sower and Its Interpretation." *NTS* 14 (1967–68) 165–93. **Gnilka, J.** *Die Verstockung Israels. Isaias 6:9–10 in der Theologie der Synoptiker.* Munich: Kösel, 1961. **Hahn, F.** "Das Gleichnis von der ausgestreuten Saat und seine Deutung (Mk iv. 3–8, 14–20)." In *Text and Interpretation,* ed. E. Best and R. McL. Wilson. Cambridge: Cambridge UP, 1979, 133–42. **Harris, J. R.** "An Unnoticed Aramaism in St. Mark." *ExpTim* 26 (1914–15) 248–50. **Hegermann, H.** "Bethsaida und Gennesar: Eine traditions- und redaktionsgeschichtliche Studie zu Mc 4–8." In *Judentum, Urchristentum, Kirche,* ed. W. Eltester. BZNW 26. Berlin: Töpelmann, 1960. 130–40. **Horman, J.** "The Source of the Version of the Parable of the Sower in the Gospel of Thomas." *NovT* 21 (1979) 326–43. **Jeremias, J.** "Palästinakundliches zum Gleichnis vom Sämann." *NTS* 13 (1966–67) 48–53. ———. *The Parables of Jesus.* 1963. **Jülicher, A.** *Die Gleichnisreden Jesu.* 1–2. 2d ed. Tübingen: Mohr, 1910. **Kelber, W.** *The Kingdom in Mark.* 1974. **Klauck, H.-J.** *Allegorie und Allegorese in synoptischen Gleichnistexten.* NTA 13. Münster: Aschendorff, 1978. **Kuhn, H.-W.** *Ältere Sammlungen im Markusevangelium.* 1971. **Lemcio, E. E.** "External Evidence for the Structure and Function of Mark iv. 1–20, vii. 14–23 and viii. 14–21." *JTS* 29 (1978) 323–38. **Linnemann, E.** *Jesus of the Parables: Introduction and Exposition.* New York: Harper & Row, 1966. **Malbon, E. S.** *Narrative Space and Mythic Meaning in Mark.* San Francisco: Harper & Row, 1986. **Maloney, E. C.** *Semitic Interference in Marcan Syntax.* 1981. **Marcus, J.** *The Mystery of the Kingdom of God.* SBLDS 90. Atlanta: Scholars Press, 1986. **Marxsen, W.** "Redaktionsgeschichtliche Erklärung der sogenannten Parabeltheorie des Markus." *ZTK* 52 (1955) 255–71 = *Der Exeget als Theologe: Vorträge zum Neuen Testament.* Gütersloh: Mohn, 1968. 13–28. **Payne, P. B.** "The Order of Sowing and Ploughing in the Parable of the Sower." *NTS* 25 (1978–79) 123–29. **Petersen, N.** "The Composition of Mark 4:1–8:26." *HTR* 73 (1980) 185–217. **Räisänen, H.** *Die Parabeltheorie im Markusevangelium.* Schriften der finnischen exegetischen Gesellschaft 26. Helsinki: Finnish Exegetical Society, 1973. **Weeden, T. J.** "Recovering the Parabolic Intent in the Parable of the Sower." *JAAR* 47 (1979) 97–120. **Wenham, D.** "The Synoptic Problem Revisited: Some New Suggestions about the Composition of Mark 4:1–34." *TB* 23 (1972) 3–38. **White, K. W.** "The Parable of the Sower." *JTS* n.s. 15 (1964) 300–7. **Wilder, A. N.** *Early Christian Rhetoric.* New York: Harper & Row, 1964. ———. "The Parable of the Sower: Naiveté and Method in Interpretation." *Semeia* 2 (1974) 134–51.

Translation

[1] *Again Jesus[a] began to teach by the sea. And a very large crowd gathered to him, so that, getting into a boat, he sat on the sea. The whole crowd was on land near the sea.* [2] *And he began teaching them many things with parables.*

He said to them in the course of his teaching: [3] *"Listen! See, a sower went out to sow.* [4] *And while he was sowing, it happened that[b] a seed fell on the path, and the birds came and devoured it.* [5] *Another seed fell on rocky ground where it did not have much soil. It immediately sprouted, because it did not have deep soil.*

⁶*When the sun rose, it was burned up, and, because it had no root, it withered.*
⁷*Another seed fell into the thistles. And the thistles rose up and choked it, and it
did not give fruit.*ᶜ ⁸*Other seeds*ᵈ *fell into good soil and gave fruit, coming up
and increasing*ᵉ, *they bore thirty, sixty and a hundredfold*ᶠ *respectively."*
   ⁹*And he said, "Whoever has ears, let that one hear."*

Notes

ᵃRomanized words added from context.
ᵇSemitic idiom behind καὶ ἐγένετο with finite verb following temporal clause to express a
past event. See *Notes* on 1:9.
ᶜκαρπὸν ἔδωκεν may render Hebrew פרי נתן (*natān pĕrî*, cf. Ps 1:3).
ᵈRead ἄλλα (B C L W Θ 28 33 892 *pc*) which shifts from ἄλλο in 4:5, 7. ἄλλο (ℵ* A D *f*¹·¹³
lat) represents a harmonizing tendency with 4:5, 7.
ᵉRead αὐξανόμενα (ℵ B *pc* sa) in agreement with ἄλλα rather than αὐξανόμενον (A D L W Δ
892 *pc* bo) influenced either by καρπόν (cf. ἀναίνοντα) or the variant ἄλλο.
ᶠThe text raises two questions: (a) which of several readings should one choose and (b) is
εἰς/ἐν a preposition or a numeral? The εἰς, ἐν, ἐν (B) makes no contextual sense as a numeral
with shift in gender and little sense as a shift in prepositions. Most texts read ἐν, ἐν, ἐν (A C² D
Θ *f*¹³ *pc* lat syᵖ; cf. ℵ C* Δ 28 700 *pc* with εἰς, εἰς, εἰς), which in the unmarked uncials could be
either the preposition ἐν or the neuter numeral ἕν. Greek uses ἐν with dative meaning "amounting
to" (Taylor, 254) but always with a "particular unit or measure," such as drachmas, acres, or
bushels (Maloney, *Interference*, 150–51). Since the unit or measure is missing here, the construction
most likely renders an idiom found only in Aramaic (e.g., Dan 3:19), the number "one" (חד,
ḥad) followed by a cardinal to express a multiplicative numeral which Greek normally expressed
by adding -πλασιως to the cardinal (e.g., Luke 8:8; Mark 10:30; Maloney, *Interference*, 150–52).

Form / Structure / Setting

   Since the classic work of Jülicher, "parables" have been grouped form-
critically into four categories: (a) similitudes, (b) parables proper (c) illustrations
or examples, and (d) allegories (e.g., Linnemann, *Parables,* 3–8; a practice
disavowed by Jeremias, *Parables,* 20; cf. discussion by Boucher, *Parable,* 11–
25). Accordingly, "similitude" applies to a story told in the present tense
about a *typical,* everyday situation or event drawn from general human experience; "parable proper" applies to a story told in the past tense about an
atypical situation or event drawn from a particular occasion in human experience (Bultmann, 174; Linnemann, *Parables,* 3–4). "Illustrations" by contrast
make their point by way of direct example rather than by use of analogy.
And "allegories" say something other than what they mean by placing "pictures" in front of the "reality" (Taylor, 249; Linnemann, *Parables,* 5–7). To
understand the allegory on its own terms (i.e., the "pictures" or metaphors)
one must also know to what the pictures or metaphors refer (the "reality").
Therefore, similitudes, parables proper and illustration enhance understanding; allegory presupposes understanding.
   Yet these categories follow more closely the narrower, more technical terminology used in Greek rhetoric to classify a developed comparison, such as a
developed simile or metaphor (F. Hauck, *TDNT* 5 [1967] 745; Haenchen,
162; cf. Aristotle, *Rhet.* 1.20.2–4). Παραβολή in the Gospels, and certainly in
Mark, takes its significance from the LXX rendering of the Hebrew משל,
māšāl (Jeremias, *Parables,* 20; Hauck, *TDNT* 5 [1967] 747–54). The variety

of forms a "parable" in this sense can take is hardly exaggerated by Hauck's statement, "משל is used for all expressions which contain a comparison," (*TDNT* 5 [1967] 747; similarly, Jeremias, *Parables*, 20; Boobyer, *NTS* 8 [1961–62] 61–64; Wilder, *Rhetoric*, 71–77; Boucher, *Parables*, 12–13, 87–89; Crossan, *Parables*, 7–8). Therefore, ἐν παραβολαῖς aptly includes the two similitudes of 4:26–32, the allegorized interpretation in 4:13–20 (cf. 3:26, 27), the "riddles" of 4:10–12 (cf. 7:17), the aphoristic sayings in 4:21–22 (cf. 3:24–25, 27; 7:15) and the prophetic sayings of 4:24–25 (cf. 3:28–29).

Most interpreters have viewed 4:3–8 as being in the form of a "parable proper." Frankemölle has argued this case on formal bases by noting the absence of an introductory comparison formula, the developed narrative style, the use of the aorist or past tense and the persuasive moment being in the telling of the story rather than in a pointed conclusion (*BibLeb* 13 [1972] 189–90). Kuhn, on the other hand, grants that formally the story approximates the parable proper but argues that the typical, everyday-life character of the content makes it a similitude. Form and content must both be taken into consideration (*Sammlungen*, 121; similarly, Pesch 1:229; Ernst, 126; Marcus, *Mystery*, 41). Perhaps Linnemann finds herself caught in this quandary of form and content, since she refers to this story as a "parable" in her discussion of it (*Parables*, 114–19) and as a "similitude" in her analysis of similitudes (*Parables*, 8–9). It may well be a classic illustration of Bultmann's (174) caveat with Jülicher's distinction when he notes that the "boundaries fluctuate." Certainly this case exposes the artificiality of the classical classifications, since the form (introduction and tense) points to a "parable proper," while the content (as will be seen in *Comment*) indicates a "similitude" drawn from everyday life.

None would question that Mark found this story in the tradition, and most would assign it to Jesus' ministry (cf. Carlston, *Parables*, 146). The *Gos. Thom.* 9 offers a parallel which may in part represent a pre-Markan tradition (Crossan, *JBL* 92 [1973] 248–50; Horman, *NovT* 21 [1979] 326–43). At issue in the discussion, however, is whether Mark found the story and its interpretation (4:14–20) in a larger "parable source" that included at least the "seed" parables of 4:26–29, 30–32 or whether Mark simply drew this story and the other materials of 4:1–34 at random from the Jesus tradition. The isolated appearance of this parable without its interpretation (4:14–20) in *Gos. Thom.* 9 may suggest the latter. But a closer examination of the other units in 4:1–34 suggests that he found it in combination with at least 4:14–20 and 4:26–29, 30–33.

Mark's redactional hand appears beyond doubt in the setting of 4:1 (Gnilka, *Verstockung*, 57; Kuhn, *Sammlungen*, 137–38; Egger, *Frohbotschaft*, 111–13; Pesch 1:230). Vocabulary (πάλιν, cf. 2:1, 13; 3:1, 20; παρὰ τὴν θάλασσαν, cf. 1:16; 2:13; cf. 3:7), content (Jesus' teaching, cf. 1:21–27; gathered crowds, cf. 2:2; 3:9, 20), and style (ἤρξα[ν]το plus infinitive, cf. 1:45; consecutive clause, cf. 1:45) all point to Mark's hand. The same is likely to be true of 4:2, though Mark may have reworked a traditional introductory statement (see *Comment* on 4:26) that prefaced the telling of the parable. Therefore, Mark redactionally constructed a setting not only for the first parable but for Jesus' teaching "with parables" that concludes again with a similar statement in 4:33–34.

Structurally, one can divide this pericope into two parts: general introduction (4:1–2), which introduces the entire section of 4:1–34 and parable (4:3–
8). The parable itself opens and closes with a summons to hear (4:3a, 9)
and follows the common folkloric pattern (Wilder, *Semeia*, 138–40) of threes—
two sets of three seeds (4:4–7, 8) under three adverse conditions (path, rocky
ground, thistles) contrasted with three degrees of productivity from the seeds
sown in good conditions (thirty, sixty and a hundredfold). Apart from the
opening statement and incipit (4:3–4a), each strophe also consists of a pattern
of verbal triads (planting, event, consequence) that is disrupted in 4:5–6 and
4:8 by apparently secondary modifications (see *Comment*). Yet the story line
does not follow a typical story of sowing and harvesting. Unexpectedly, the
failure of three seeds to mature and produce fruit is described with three
statements, while the three productive seeds are described with one statement.
Despite the reference to a successful harvest in the concluding statement,
this structure places the emphasis throughout the parable on the seeds.

Mark shifts the setting in his narrative from a house with "those around
him" (3:20–35) to the sea where a great crowd has gathered (similarly 2:13;
3:7–12). In 3:13–35 the evangelist has just underscored the distinction between
the Twelve (3:13–19) along with "those around" Jesus who did the will of
the Father (3:20, 34–35) from the Jerusalem scribes (3:22–30) and even his
own family (3:21, 31–35). What follows initially appears to include the crowds
in Jesus' teaching (4:1–2; cf. 4:33) but 4:10 sets off the Twelve and those
with them from "those outside" by the use of "parables" (4:2, 10–12; cf. 4:34).

Comment

1 This verse betrays numerous traces of Mark's redaction. Stylistically, it
has a resumptive use of "again" (πάλιν) and ἄρξασθαι with the infinitive. These
features together with the crowds and Jesus by the sea and the presence of
a boat could not help but remind the reader of the similar scene in 3:7–12.
The triple mention of Jesus' teaching in this opening scene also corresponds
to Mark's introduction of Jesus' public ministry in terms of his "teaching"
(1:21–22, 27). "By the sea" (παρὰ τὴν θάλασσαν) not only introduces the first
of three references to the "sea" in 4:1–2, but Jesus' teaching of crowds by
the sea is reminiscent of a similar redactional seam in 2:13. Nevertheless,
despite the redactional character of this material, Mark does not appear to
attach any special theological significance to Jesus' teaching of great crowds
by the sea (cf. Marxsen, *Exeget*, 27; Malbon, *Space*, 99–100). He simply uses
motifs found in his tradition (cf. 3:7–12; 4:35–5:43; 6:32–56) to develop a
setting for 4:3–34.

"A very large crowd." The superlative (ὄχλος πλεῖστος) followed by "the
whole crowd" (πᾶς ὁ ὄχλος) may suggest a climax in Jesus' popular ministry
(Ernst, 148; Grundmann, 118). Yet Mark's use of ὄχλος πλεῖστος here hardly
suggests a crowd significantly greater than his πολὺς ὄχλος (cf. πολὺ πλῆθος,
3:7, 9) in 5:21 or 6:34, where a "large crowd" included five thousand "men."
Consequently, the superlative ὄχλος πλεῖστος along with the πολὺ πλῆθος in
3:7, 9 may simply underscore an increase in the crowds following Jesus (cf.
Marcus, *Mystery*, 15).

"So that, getting into a boat, he sat on the sea." For Mark's use of ὥστε with infinitive see *Comment* on 1:45. The evangelist has previously accented the adverse consequence (2:2; 3:9, 20) of a "gathered" (συνάγεται) crowd. The awkwardness of "sat" (καθῆσθαι ἐν τῇ θαλάσσῃ) rather than the more natural "embarked" (ἐμβάντα) in the complementary infinitive of the result clause (ὥστε, i.e., Jesus "sat on the sea" rather than "embarked into a boat" as a result of the great crowd) may reflect an Aramaism in the combination of the two verbs (ἐμβάντα . . . καθῆσθαι) to mean simply "go aboard" (Harris, *ExpTim* 26 [1914–15] 248–50; Taylor, 251; Pesch 1:230, n. 5). Read in this way, Mark would have Jesus boarding the boat because of the "great crowd."

This reading, however, is not the only option. In contrast to the other occurrences of the boat motif with the crowds, the boat is not used here to escape the press of the crowd (cf. 3:9; 4:36; 6:45) but as a vantage point from which to teach. Jesus' being seated (the normal position for a teacher) might also reflect Mark's attempt to call attention to the importance of Jesus' teaching in keeping with the evangelist's previous emphasis on Jesus' authoritative teaching (1:21–27) and the repeated reference to Jesus teaching in 4:1–2. Taken in this manner, the boat serves more as a podium than a means of escape. If the boat motif found in 3:7–12 belonged to a traditional summary (see *Comment* on 3:9) originally linked directly to an earlier collection of miracle stories containing a boat motif (cf. 4:36; 5:2, 18, 21; 6:32, 45, 54), then the evangelist might well have taken the "boat" (πλοῖον) from the larger context to serve here as Jesus' "seat" and as a thematic bridge to the miracle material beginning with 4:35–41. This would further support the boat's primary function as the "seat" for Jesus' teaching instead of a ready means of escape from the crowd, a role the boat consistently plays in the pre-Markan tradition (cf. 3:9; 4:36; 6:45).

2 "And he was teaching them many things with parables." This statement has often been attributed to Mark's redactional setting (cf. 6:34 without a reference to parables). "Many things" (πολλά) may imply that Mark understood Jesus' teaching to be more comprehensive, less tied to any one subject. Yet the evangelist's focus on Jesus' preaching of the Kingdom (1:14–15) and the prominence given to the Kingdom in 4:10–12, 26–29, 30–32 suggest that the "many things" had their basis for Mark in Jesus' preaching and teaching of the Kingdom.

"With parables" (ἐν παραβολαῖς) indicates the vehicle used by Jesus for his teaching (cf. 3:23). Whether Mark meant for what follows in 4:3–32 to be a sampler of Jesus' teaching "with parables" (cf. 4:33) or whether he meant to label Jesus' actual teaching in 4:3–32 as "parabolic" (4:12), the term "parables" aptly describes the variety of literary forms in 4:3–32 (see Boucher, *Parable*, 11–25).

"And he said to them in the course of his teaching" has been assigned to Mark's redaction because of the characteristic καὶ ἔλεγεν αὐτοῖς and the emphasis on Jesus' teaching (Grundmann, 118; Gnilka, 1:156; Kuhn, *Sammlungen*, 131). But others have found behind this rather redundant statement a remnant, though reworked, of the traditional introduction for a parable(s) collection (Pesch, 1:230; Ernst, 127; see *Comment* on 4:26). Taylor correctly captures the force of ἐν τῇ διδαχῇ αὐτοῦ with "in the course of his teaching" (252).

3 The parable begins with an awkward combination of two introductory imperatives, "Listen!" (ἀκούετε) and "See!" (ἰδού), neither of which introduces a parable elsewhere (cf. Judg 9:7; Isa 28:23; Ezek 20:47). Though probably coincidental, this unique parable opening corresponds to the "seeing" and "hearing" found in Isa 6:9–10 that is cited at the end of the discussion in 4:10–12. Together these imperatives call for "attentive listening" (Cranfield, 149). Furthermore, a summons to hear in 4:9 forms a framework with 4:3a around the parable whose interpretation (4:14–20) focuses on hearing, a note that obliquely reappears at the end of the section (4:33b). Therefore, this awkward combination of introductory imperatives may well reflect a stage in the developing pre-Markan tradition when the interpretation (4:14–20) and related parables (4:26–29, 30–32) were combined (Marxsen, *Exeget*, 17; Kuhn, *Sammlungen*, 135, n. 61; Pesch, 1:229; Gnilka, 1:146).

In any event, this specific call to "attentive listening" in conjunction with Jesus' teaching in parables suggests that "parables" involved something more than simply transparent stories obvious to all (Taylor, 252). The command to "listen" (4:3, ἀκούετε) implied "ears to hear" (4:9) or the ability to "hear" (4:33), an issue that is addressed in 4:10–12. The thematic use of "hearing" in 4:1–34 makes any connection of 4:3a with the *Shema* (Deut 6:4) highly dubious both for the pre-Markan tradition as well as for Mark (cf. Gerhardsson, *NTS* 14 [1967–68] 165–93; Boucher, *Parable*, 45).

"The sower" (ὁ σπείρων) has become for many the focal point of the parable and given rise to the title, the Parable of the Sower (e.g., Dodd, *Parables*, 145–47; Jeremias, *Parables*, 11–12; Frankemölle, *BibLeb* 13 [1972] 184–207; Gnilka 1:155). As such, the parable speaks about the success, despite setbacks and opposition, of Jesus' ministry either in terms of the Kingdom of God specifically (Dodd, *Parables*, 146; Jeremias, *Parables*, 150) or of his ministry in general (Frankemölle, *BibLeb* 13 [1972] 195; Gnilka 1:161). Yet the fact remains that "the sower" appears only at the outset of the parable, never to be mentioned again. Rather than central to the story, this figure simply sets the story in motion (Linnemann, *Parables*, 115, n. 2; Pesch 1:231; Boucher, *Parable*, 49; cf. Marcus, *Mystery*, 21). This narrative feature, a feature that does not change in the parable's earliest interpretation (4:14–20), ought to warn against a primarily Christological reading of the parable (Weeden, *JAAR* 47 [1979] 97–120).

Marcus (*Mystery*, 37–39) has made a strong case for the Markan reader identifying the "sower" with Jesus. The "going out" (ἐξῆλθεν) may be reminiscent of 1:38; 2:13 and 2:17. Certainly, within the context of Mark 4, Jesus is the one "teaching" the "word" (cf. 4:14–20) "with parables." Within the larger context of the Gospel, Jesus' "sowing" meets and/or anticipates the same fate as the "sower" in the parable. Yet this identification remains at best latent in both the parable and the interpretation of 4:13–20 where the "sower" plays even a smaller role.

4 The parable itself lacks any direct word for "seed" (cf. σπορά, σπόρος [4:27], or σπέρμα [4:31] used commonly for plants). Most commentators have taken the subject ὁ μέν with the meaning of "a part of (the seed)" and the following ἄλλο, ἄλλο in 4:5, 7 as "another portion (of the seed)" (e.g., Taylor, 252). This rendering appears at first glance to be supported by Luke 8:5–8 where the neuter ὁ μέν, ἕτερον, ἕτερον, ἕτερον cannot refer to the previous masculine σπόρον (8:5) as its antecedent.

Hahn, however, has convincingly argued that Mark's shift from the singular subjects in 4:4–7 to the plural ἄλλα in 4:8 is best rendered by "a/another seed" in 4:4–7 and "other seeds" in 4:8 ("Gleichnis," 134–36; cf. Marcus, *Mystery*, 42, n. 98). This rendering would allow for the same antecedent behind ὁ μέν, ἄλλο, ἄλλο and ἄλλα (e.g., σπέρμα, σπέρματα or τὸ σπειρόμενον, τὰ σπειρόμενα; cf. ὄν in 4:31b). This also avoids the difficulty of changing subjects unnecessarily (cf. "a/another part/portion [of the seed]" in 4:4–7 and "other seeds" in 4:8) when the shift in Greek is merely from singular ἄλλο to plural ἄλλα (cf. Taylor, 253).

A comparison of the parallels supports this reading. Matthew's rendering of Mark's text by the plural throughout (ἃ μέν, ἄλλα, ἄλλα, ἄλλα; Matt 13:4–8) suggests his reading of "seed/seeds" behind Mark's construction (cf. plural in the interpretation of Mark 4:14–20). Luke, instead of using ὁ μέν, ἕτερον, ἕτερον with the abstract meaning of "a part/another part," as suggested above, may rather have taken Mark's neuter in terms of an understood antecedent (e.g., τὸ σπειρόμενον) and also have had a "seed" in mind. Just as Matthew consistently uses the plural, Luke uses the singular, even in the last example of the seed falling on "good ground" (8:8). Consequently, when Luke gives the results of the harvest, the "other seed" produces fruit "a hundred-fold" (ἑκατονταπλασίονα).

"On the path" (παρὰ τὴν ὁδόν) may render the ambiguous Aramaic preposition על, ʿal (Black, *Approach*, 162) with the meaning of "by the path" or "on the path" (Jeremias, *Parables*, 12, n. 4). The parallel in Luke 8:5 where the seed is "trampled" (κατεπατήθη) and the general point of the story support the rendering "on the path." The path may have led through the field (cf. 2:23, διὰ τῶν σπορίμων) or around the borders of the field. Jeremias opts for the former, trodden by people after the previous harvest had ended, and emphasizes the ancient order of sowing and then plowing to account for sowing on the path (*Parables*, 11–12; *NTS*, 13 [1966–67] 48–53; G. Dalman, *PJ* 22 [1926] 120–32; cf. Payne, *NTS* 25 [1978–79] 123–29). But this and the other details seems moot, since the fact that the birds ate it before the seed could take root implies that the path was left unplowed. But this and the other details (sprouting over night, 4:5; sown among thistles, 4:7) stem more from a stylized and truncated perspective in the telling of the story than from an attempt by the teller to correspond to reality (Klauck, *Allegorie*, 190; cf. Geischer, *EvT* 38 [1978] 418–27).

5–6 The description of the seed sown on "rocky ground" (πετρῶδες) contrasts sharply in its length and redundancy from the simple statements of 4:4, 7. Twice in 4:5 we learn that the topsoil is thin which explains that "rocky ground" means ground where the substratum limestone is covered in places by only a thin layer of soil. And in 4:6 we learn that the young plant withers for lack of root, again implying shallow soil. Furthermore, the plant is "burned up (ἐκαυματίσθη) by the sun" and "withers (ἐξηράνθη) because it has no root" (4:6). This redundancy hints at a later embellishment (Lagrange, 95; Klostermann, 40; Taylor, 252).

If the parable's symmetry or structure can serve as a guide (Crossan, *JBL*

92 [1973] 244–66; Weeden, *JAAR* 47 [1979] 97–120), the triadic pattern in
4:4 (ἔπεσεν, ἦλθεν, κατέφαγεν), 4:7 (ἔπεσεν, ἀνέβησαν, συνέπνιξαν) and 4:8 (ἔπεσεν,
ἐδίδου, ἔφερεν) and the "terse, paratactic style" of this section do indeed indicate
a development of the tradition. But where and by whom? The answer may
lie in the parable's interpretation (4:16–17) where the *lack* of root makes
the "hearers" vulnerable to persecution. This emphasis on rootlessness corresponds to the sudden springing up of the seeds (εὐθὺς ἐξανέτειλεν διὰ τὸ μὴ
ἔχειν βάθος γῆς) in 4:5b and to its withering without roots (διὰ τὸ μὴ ἔχειν
ῥίζαν ἐξηράνθη) in 4:6b. By removing these statements as secondary, we would
have syntactic and thematic parallels in 4:5a–6a with 4:4 and 4:7 remaining.
And this remaining verbal triad (ἔπεσεν, ἀνέτειλεν, ἐκαυματίσθη) corresponds
thematically with the "seed" that "falls" on various types of soil and is *violently*
destroyed ("devoured" [κατέφαγεν], "burned up" [ἐκαυματίσθη], and "choked"
[συνέπνιξαν]) in all three instances.

Naturally, Jesus or the early Church could easily have told a structurally
asymmetrical parable with "pointers" that led directly to the allegorizing interpretation (cf. Pesch 1:232–33). And the presence or absence of these sentences
in 4:5b, 6b have no immediate bearing on the overall meaning of the parable.
But the more symmetrical parallel in the *Gos. Thom.* 9, though different in
content, may support an earlier, less developed form of this parable in the
tradition which was then expanded at the time and from the standpoint of
the interpretation (Crossan, *JBL* 92 [1973] 244–66; Weeden, *JAAR,* 47 [1979]
28–103; Marcus, *Mystery,* 32–33; cf. Crossan, *Parables,* 40–41).

7 This example also follows the triadic verbal pattern: (a) a seed is sown
(ἔπεσεν), (b) a destroying agent appears (ἀνέβησαν αἱ ἄκανθαι) and (c) causes
violent destruction (συνέπνιξαν αὐτό). The verse, however, has an additional
statement about not "giving fruit" (καρπὸν οὐκ ἔδωκεν) that appears to break
again the symmetry of the triadic, paratactic style of this story. If, according
to some commentators (e.g., Pesch 1:233; Crossan, *JBL* 92 [1973] 246), this
concluding statement offers a summary for the three previous examples (4:4–
7a) rather than for only the seed sown among the thistles, the problem of
asymmetry is resolved by dividing the parable into the contrast between nonproductive seed (4:4–7) and productive seed (4:8). Yet no basis syntactically
or structurally exists to support this reading. Furthermore, the absence of
this statement in Matt 13:7 and Luke 8:7 should caution against assigning it
such a pivotal role in Mark.

Weeden has assigned this "interpolation" along with 4:5b, 6b discussed
above to the stage in the tradition when the parable was being interpreted
(4:14–20). Whereas it plays an integral role in the logic of the interpretation
(4:19—the "word" remains "fruitless"), it, like 4:5b, 6b, is redundant in the
parable. It serves only to set up the interpretation that is to come (Weeden,
JAAR 47 [1979] 103). Nevertheless, one must take note of the unusual construction (see *Note* b) and note that the idea but not the construction is carried
over into the interpretation, which may indicate its presence in the earlier
tradition. In this instance, the tradition may have influenced the interpretation,
rather than vice versa. We would then have to accept the asymmetry of 4:7b
but might find 4:7b more tolerable as a statement of transition (Gnilka 1:159)

to 4:8 where the focus shifts from seed "destroyed" (4:4, 6a, 7a) to seed "giving fruit" (4:8).

8 The same triadic structure apparently lies behind 4:8 as noted in 4:4–7. But again the pattern is interrupted. Two participles emphasizing growth (ἀναβαίνοντα καὶ αὐξανόμενα), a motif found only in the "additions" of 4:5b and 6b, appear which are awkwardly anachronistic, since they follow the statement of "giving fruit" (ἐδίδου καρπόν). This disruption in symmetry and theme has led Weeden to assign their insertion to the time of the pre-Markan combination of this parable with the related parables of "growth" in 4:26–29, 30–32 (*JAAR* 47 [1979], 104). Whether an awkward part of the earliest tradition or a later addition, these participles play no role in the meaning of the parable and, unlike 4:5b, 6b, they play no further role in the parable's interpretation in 4:14–20. At most, they function now in Mark's text as pointers to the "growth" parables at the end of this collection.

"Other seeds" (ἄλλα), often taken as a reference to "individual seeds" (e.g., Taylor, 253), stand in contrast to the singular "a/another seed" in 4:4, 5, 7 in number and result. Hahn sees a correlation between the plural "other seeds" and the triadic result which specifies the product of the "other seeds." In other words, one of the "other seeds" produces "thirty," another "sixty" and another a "hundredfold" (so Matt 13:8). This reading accounts for the triad of results found in Mark and Matthew (cf. Luke 8:8, consistent with Luke's singular throughout) and also maintains the triadic pattern found at the heart of the parable and the primary focus on the "seeds."

Taken in this manner, the parable contrasts three seeds sown which do not bear fruit (4:4–7) with three seeds sown (4:8) that bear an increasing abundance of fruit. Mark's parable thus forms a balanced 3:3 comparison (Hahn, "Gleichnis," 134–36). This reading demonstrates the inadequacy of referring to the parable as the Parable of the Four Soils (the more common title in German works, particularly since Jülicher, *Gleichnisreden*, 2:514), since that would leave us an unbalanced 3:1 comparison (cf. 4:14–20). The narrative focus of the parable on the fate or ultimate outcome of the "seeds sown" means that the parable should be called the Parable of the Seeds (Haenchen, 163; Dietzfelbinger, "Gleichnis," 80–93; Hahn, "Gleichnis," 133–42; cf. Weeden, *JAAR* 47 [1979] 120).

By taking the harvest to refer to the *seeds'* productivity, the point frequently made about the *field's* "abnormally" large productivity (e.g., Jeremias, *Parables*, 150), in view of Dalman's observation that a good harvest fell between a 7.5 and 10 percent increase (*Arbeit*, 153–65; so Jeremias, *Parables*, 84), becomes moot. Dalman also noted that individual grains were known to produce an ear with thirty-five kernels on the average, with sixty not out of the ordinary and some even producing a hundred (Dalman, *PJ* 22 [1926] 128). Therefore, our parable concludes with a harvest that is above average but not so extraordinary as to strain the credibility of the story as drawn from the common experiences of life (cf. Gen 26:12).

9 This exhortation in conjunction with the opening imperative in 4.3 (ἀκούετε) encloses the parable in a framework calling for attentive hearing. The saying itself parodies a negative form of an expression in Jer 5:21 and

Ezek 12:2 (so Mark 8:18) that is thematically related to Isa 6:9 (cf. Mark 4:12). We find it again in 4:23; Matt 11:15; 13:43; Luke 14:35 and Rev 2:7, 11, 17, 29; 3:6, 13, 22; 13:9 (cf. *Gos. Thom.* 8, 21, 24, 63, 65, 96). Yet the atypically Markan introductory καὶ ἔλεγεν, appearing only here and in 4:26, 30 (Jeremias, *Parables*, 14, n. 8; Kuhn, *Sammlungen*, 131), suggests the presence of this summons in the pre-Markan tradition (see *Comment* on 4:26), a suggestion that gains further support from the function of 4:9 in its context.

The saying removed from its context has a dual implication. First, it may imply that not everyone (cf. τις, 4:23) has "ears to hear" (ὦτα ἀκούειν) or the ability to hear. Second, it may imply that those who do, do not always use their ears or "hear" (cf. 8:18). When taken in the context of the opening summons to listen or hear (4:3a), 4:9 calls for responsible hearing, and the accent falls on the second implication. Taken in conjunction with 4:10–12 and 4:33, 4:9 suggests that the parable is not for just anyone to hear but for those "with ears" who have the ability to hear. The accent then falls on the first implication (cf. 4:33).

Since a summons to hear introduces the parable (4:3a) and since "hearing" finds specific development in the interpretation of 4:14–20, both 4:3a and 4:9 were most likely added to the parable at a time when the interpretation (4:14–20) was added. Perhaps this coincided with the collection of the parables in 4:26–29 and 30–32, which also open with the same non-Markan introductory formula (καὶ ἔλεγεν) as 4:9a. We have seen other indications of this stage in the development of the tradition within the parable itself (cf. 4:6–7, 8).

Mark's present text, however, separates the parable and the interpretation with a private conversation between Jesus and his disciples (4:10–12) about who "has ears" or who can hear so that 4:9, understood in the first sense of implying that not everyone could "hear" the parables, builds an appropriate transition. Therefore, though 4:9 may have functioned to call one to attentive hearing in one context of the pre-Markan tradition, its present context points to the distinction between those who have and those who do not have the ability to hear (4:11) and sets the stage for the discussion of this question in terms of the thematically related Isa 6:9, 10 (4:12).

Explanation

This parable introduces a series of parables in 4:1–34. Evidence in the parable's framework (4:3a, 9) and within the narrative structure (4:5b, 6b, 8b) points to an earlier development in the pre-Markan tradition that aligns the parable with its interpretation in 4:14–20. Therefore, we have at least three potentially different settings for this parable that might have bearing on its meaning.

Two common misnomers for this parable reflect a failure to pursue the real point of comparison. When it is labeled the Parable of the Sower (cf. Matt 13:18), the point of comparison has been misconstrued by the title's failing to recognize that the sower appears only in the opening line rather than at the heart of the narrative. When it is labeled the Parable of the Soils, the point of comparison stems at best from the parable's interpretation in 4:14–20 rather than from the story's narrative structure. The focal point of the parable lies clearly on the seed that has been sown. Thus, the Parable of the Seeds comes closest to signalling the parable's content in the earliest tradition and even in the *Gos. Thom.* 9. But what did it mean?

Since the parable's original context in Jesus' ministry is lost to us and since the parable itself does not begin with an explicit comparison, one might be tempted to abandon as futile speculation any explanation of the parable in Jesus' ministry. Yet the correlation between the use of agriculture as an eschatological metaphor in Judaism and the eschatological nature of Jesus' ministry certainly sets parameters within which one might offer an explanation.

Starting with the parable itself, we observe that the accent falls on the scattered seeds. Some are destroyed before producing fruit; others produce an abundant harvest. Assuming here, as elsewhere, that Jesus tells the parable in keeping with the thrust of his ministry, we readily see that it makes a statement about God's eschatological activity or more specifically about the outcome of God's eschatological activity in history, an outcome that is more complex than the common Jewish expectation of a final harvest. God's eschatological activity does not consist in one grand harvest of deliverance and/or judgment. Rather God's eschatological activity, be it the more specifically defined "Kingdom of God" of Jesus' preaching/teaching or the more general "ministry of Jesus," like scattered seed, encounters opposition and failure but also produces an abundant harvest. Unfortunately, lack of a specific context within Jesus' ministry makes further precision impossible. Yet this break with the common Jewish expectation of God's ultimate radical, irresistible and overpowering act of deliverance and/or judgment coheres with Jesus' parabolic claim elsewhere about the vulnerable nature of God's eschatological activity (see 4:26–29; 30–32).

We shall return to the interpretation of this parable (4:14–20) within the identifiable levels of the early Church, but the opening summons and concluding exhortation to "hear" (4:3a, 9) appears to combine the parable (4:3–8) more closely with the interpretation (4:14–20). This framework calls the reader/hearer to "hear." And this motif gains significance in the parable's interpretation (4:14–20) where "hearing" becomes even more prominent when the "seed," the focal point of the parable, is identified as "the ones hearing" (see *Explanation* of 4:14–20). When, however, 4:10–12 was inserted between the parable (4:3–9) and its interpretation (4:14–20), the thrust of 4:9 shifted from an admonition for responsible listening to a statement implying a distinction between those who could and could not hear with understanding, a distinction explained by 4:11–12. Since "hearing" involved the "word," the parable most likely applied to the mission situation at this stage in the tradition.

Mark's use of this parable gives little indication of any break with the tradition. Finding the parable in combination with at least 4:14–20 and, most likely, 4:26–29, 30–32, 33, he introduces it as Jesus' teaching, specifically, Jesus' public teaching "with parables" (4:1–2). Naturally, this redactional setting underscores Jesus' summons in 4:3ab, 9 to "hear." Its meaning for the reader is now qualified by the following discussion in 4:10–12 and the parable's interpretation in 4:14–20, a thrust that the evangelist develops in 4:21–23, 24–25.

D. The Mystery of the Kingdom   (4:10–12)

Bibliography

Ambrozic, A. M. *The Hidden Kingdom: A Redaction Critical Study of the References to the Kingdom in Mark's Gospel.* CBQMS 2. Washington: Catholic Biblical Association, 1972. ————. "Mark's Concept of Parable." *CBQ* 29 (1967) 220–27. **Best, E.** "Mark's Use of the Twelve." *ZNW* 69 (1978) 11–39 = *Disciples and Discipleship: Studies in the Gospel According to Mark.* T.& T. Clark, 1986. 131–61. **Black, M.** *An Aramaic Approach to the Gospels and Acts.* 1967. **Boobyer, G. H.** "The Redaction of Mk 4,1–34." *NTS* 8 (1961–62) 59–70. ————. "The Secrecy Motif in St Mark's Gospel." *NTS* 6 (1959–60) 225–35. **Boucher, M.** *The Mysterious Parable: A Literary Study.* CBQMS 6. Washington: Catholic Biblical Association, 1977. **Bowker, J. W.** "Mystery and Parable: Mark iv. 1–20." *JTS* 25 (1974) 300–17. **Brown, R. E.** *The Semitic Background of the Term "Mystery" in the New Testament.* Philadelphia: Fortress, 1968. **Brown, S.** "The Secret of the Kingdom of God (Mark 4,11)." *JBL* 92 (1973) 60–74. **Burkill, T. A.** *Mysterious Revelation.* Ithaca: Cornell UP, 1963. **Chilton, B.** *A Galilean Rabbi and his Bible.* GNS 8. Wilmington, DE: Michael Glazier, 1984. **Coutts, J.** "'Those Outside' (Mark 4,10–12)." *SE* 2 (1964) 155–57. **Crossan, J. D.** "The Seed Parables of Jesus." *JBL* 92 (1973) 244–66. **Dahl, N. A.** "The Parables of Growth." *ST* 5 (1951) 132–66 = *Jesus in the Memory of the Early Church.* Minneapolis: Augsburg, 1976. 141–66. **Daube, D.** *The New Testament and Rabbinic Judaism.* London: Athlone, 1956. 141–50 = "Public Pronouncement and Private Explanation in the Gospels." *ExpTim* 57 (1946) 175–77. **Egger, W.** *Frohbotschaft und Lehre.* 1976. 115–18. **Evans, C. A.** "A Note on the Function of Isaiah vi, 9–10 in Mark iv." *RB* 88 (1981) 234–35. ————. "The Function of Isaiah 6:9–10 in Mark and John." *NovT* 24 (1982) 124–28. **Gnilka, J.** *Die Verstockung Israels. Isaias 6:9–10 in der Theologie der Synoptiker.* Munich: Kösel, 1961. **Haacker, K.** "Erwägungen zu Mc IV 11." *NovT* 14 (1977) 219–25. **Haufe, G.** "Erwägungen zum Ursprung der sogennanten Parabeltheorie des Markus 4,11–12." *EvT* 32 (1972) 413–21. **Jeremias, J.** *The Parables of Jesus.* 1972. **Kelber, W.** *The Kingdom in Mark.* 1974. **Kermode, F.** *The Genesis of Secrecy.* Cambridge, MA: Harvard UP, 1979. **Kirkland, J. R.** "The Earliest Understanding of Jesus' Use of Parables: Mark IV 10–12 in Context." *NovT* 19 (1977) 1–21. **Klauck, H.-J.** *Allegorie und Allegorese in synoptischen Gleichnistexten.* NA 13, Münster: Aschendorf, 1978. **Kuhn, H.-W.** *Ältere Sammlungen im Markusevangelium.* 1971. **Lampe, P.** "Die markinische Deutung des Gleichnisses vom Sämann, Markus 4, 10–12." *ZNW* 65 (1974) 140–50. **Lemcio, E. E.** "External Evidence for the Structure and Function of Mark iv. 1–20, vii. 14–23 and viii. 14–21." *JTS* 29 (1978) 323–38. **Malbon, C. S.** *Narrative Space and Mythic Meaning in Mark.* San Francisco: Harper & Row, 1986. **Maloney, E. C.** *Semitic Interference in Marcan Syntax.* 1981. **Manson, T. W.** *The Teaching of Jesus: Studies of the Form and Content.* Cambridge: Cambridge UP, 1943. **Manson, W.** "The Purpose of the Parables: A Re-Examination of St Mark iv. 10–12." *ExpTim* 68 (1956–57) 132–35. **Marcus, J.** *The Mystery of the Kingdom of God.* SBLDS 90. Atlanta: Scholars Press, 1986. **Marxsen, W.** "Redaktionsgeschichtliche Erklärung der sogenannten Parabeltheorie des Markus." *ZTK* 52 (1955) 255–71 = *Der Exeget als Theologe: Vorträge zum Neuen Testament.* Gütersloh: Mohn, 1968. 13–28. **Masson, C.** *Les paraboles de Marc IV.* Neuchatel-Paris: Delachaux and Niestlé, 1945. **Meye, R. P.** "Those about him with the Twelve." *SE* 2 (1964) 211–18. **Minette de Tillesse, G.** *Le secret messianique dans L'Evangile de Marc.* LD 47. Paris: Cerf, 1968. **Moule, C. F. D.** "Mark v, 1–20 Yet Once More." In *Neotestamentica et Semitica,* FS M. Black, ed. E. E. Ellis and M. Wilcox. Edinburgh: T. and T. Clark, 1969. 95–113. **Peisker, C. H.** "Konsekutives ἵνα in Markus IV, 12." *ZNW* 59 (1968) 126–27. **Pryor, J. W.** "Markan Parable Theology: An Inquiry into Mark's Principles of Redaction." *ExpTim* 83 (1972) 242–45. **Räisänen, H.** *Das 'Messiasgeheimnis' im Markusevangelium.* Helsinki: Finnish Exegetical Society, 1976. ———. *Die Parabeltheorie im Markusevangelium.* Schriften der finnischen exegetischen Gesellschaft 25. Helsinki: Finnish Exegetical Society, 1973. **Reploh, K.-G.** *Markus—Lehrer der Gemeinde.* 1969. **Schweizer, E.** "Zur Frage des Messiasgeheimnisses bei Markus." *ZNW* 56 (1965) 1–8. **Sjöberg, E.** *Der verborgene Menschensohn in den Evangelien.* Lund: Gleerup, 1955. **Suhl, A.** *Die Funktion der alttestamentlichen Zitaten und Anspielungen im Markusevangelium.* Gütersloh: Mohn, 1965. **Trocmé, E.** "Why Parables? A Study of Mark IV." *BJRL* 59 (1977) 458–71. **Weeden, T. J.** *Mark: Traditions in Conflict.* 1971. **Wenham, D.** "The Synoptic Problem Revisited: Some New Suggestions about the Composition of Mark 4:1–34." *TB* 23 (1972) 3–38. **Windisch, H.** "Die Verstockungsidee in Mk 4:12 und das kausale ἵνα in der späteren Koine." *ZNW* 26 (1927) 203–09. **Wrede, W.** *The Messianic Secret.* 1971. **Zerwick, M.** *Untersuchungen zum Markus-Stil: Ein Beitrag zur stilistischen Durcharbeitung des Neuen Testaments.* Rome: Pontifical Biblical Institute, 1937.

Translation

[10] *And when he was alone, those around him with the Twelve asked him about the parables.* [11] *He said to them, "To you the mystery of the kingdom of God has been given, but to those outside all things come in riddles,* [12] *that is, 'seeing they see but do not perceive and hearing they hear but do not understand. If they did, they would repent and be forgiven.[a]'"*

Notes

[a] Greek has impersonal, ἀφεθῇ αὐτοῖς. Some texts read a specifying τὰ ἁμαρτήματα (A D Θ *f*[13] Majority text lat sy bo[pt]).

Form / Structure / Setting

This passage sits awkwardly at best in its present context. It introduces a change of setting and audience from 4:1–2 that appears to have been forgotten in the concluding summary of 4:33–34 and the opening scene in 4:35–36. Although Jesus has just completed one parable (4:3–9), the disciples question him about "parables" (4:10) and thus interrupt the sequence of parable (4:3–8) and interpretation (4:14–20) by interjecting the broader topic of "parables." It employs παραβολή (4:11b), meaning "riddles," in a chapter that consistently uses παραβολή with the more general meaning of "parables" (4:2, 10, 13, 30, 33). And its implication that Jesus teaches in "riddles" to keep "outsiders" in confusion seems contrary to the tone of the setting in 4:1–2, the reproach directed at the "disciples" in 4:13 and the statement in 4:33. Consequently, with few exceptions (e.g., Lane, 156–58; Trocmé, *BJRL* 59 [1977] 464–65; Haacker, 423–24), 4:10–12 has been viewed as a later insertion into its present context.

This conclusion raises numerous literary questions, especially the question about source. Many have ascribed at least 4:11–12 to Mark's insertion of traditional material (e.g., Taylor, 254–55; Jeremias, *Parables*, 14; Marxsen,

Exeget, 16–19; Gnilka, *Verstockung,* 23–24; Pesch, 1:236; Marcus, *Mystery,* 29, 80–87). Others have argued for the presence of 4:10–12 in the pre-Markan parable collection (Moule, *Neotestamentica,* 95–113; Schweizer, 92–94; Trocmé, *Formation,* 161, n. 2; Haacker, *NovT* 14 [1972] 219–25; Pryor, *ExpTim* 83 [1972] 242–45; Räisänen, *Parabeltheorie,* 27–47; Ernst, 130). And some have assigned part (4:10—Minette de Tillese, *Secret,* 173–79; Ambrozic, *Kingdom,* 52–53; 4:12—Suhl, *Zitaten,* 150–51; Lampe, *ZNW* 65 [1974] 147–48; Klauck, *Allegorie,* 249–53) or all (Bultmann, 199, 325, n. 1; cf. *Ergänzungsheft,* 325; Lambrecht, *Marc,* 277–85; Schmithals, 1:239–40) to Mark's own redaction. The answer to this question has major implications for the function and significance of this text for Mark. Should he have composed it or even inserted it, the material takes on primary importance. Should he have found it in place, the focus moves to what, if anything, he has done to qualify it or apply it for his purposes. In either case, to grasp the significance of 4:10–12 in context one cannot avoid the question of tradition and redaction.

Apart from minor modifications in 4:10 (see *Comment*), language (κατὰ μόνας, οἱ περὶ αὐτὸν σὺν τοῖς δώδεκα, ἠρώτων, μυστήριον, τοῖς ἔξω, γίνεται ἐν), style (divine passive, redundant demonstrative pronoun, antithetical parallelism) and content (similarity of 4:12 to *Tg. Isaiah,* clear and ultimate dichotomy between disciples and crowd) point to a pre-Markan tradition rather than a redactional composition. But if 4:10–12 represents a pre-Markan unit, where did 4:10–12 come from and what did it mean?

Jeremias (*Parables,* 15), following and expanding on Manson's lead (*Teaching,* 76–80), traced this material, based on several Semitisms, back to Jesus' ministry where devoid of any "parable" context the sayings referred to Jesus' ministry in general and how it had been perceived by "outsiders" (similarly, Taylor, 257; Marxsen, *Exeget,* 27; Gnilka, *Verstockung,* 24). Others, however, have traced its roots to the primitive Church's struggle with their mission experience, especially with the rejection by Judaism (Haufe, *EvT* 32 [1972] 415–18; Lampe, *ZNW* 64 [1974] 147–148; Pesch 1:238; Gnilka, 1:167; Räisänen, *Parabeltheorie,* 115–20). Certainly, the Greek rendering of 4:12 (see *Comment* on 4:12) in potentially harsher tones than the more ambiguous Aramaic suggests a more separatistic, if not sectarian, exclusiveness comparable to motifs in John (6:44, 64–65; 10:26; 16:25–26), Acts (28:17–29), Romans (9–11, esp. 11:25), and Qumran (1QS 3:13–4:14).

The second alternative which focuses on the early Church situation need not exclude an original setting in Jesus' ministry. There is nothing inherently improbable about the suggestion of the Aramaic background of 4:11–12 or of its roots extending into Jesus' ministry. We find a similar motif in Luke 10:21 // Matt 11:25–26 and Luke 12:23–24 // Matt 13:16–17 (cf. Grundmann, 124; Nineham, 137). The Greek text, however, may reflect the early Church's use of this tradition as partial support or explanation for the realities of the Christian mission. This is the form we meet in 4:11–12 and most likely represents the form, in contrast to an Aramaic tradition, that Mark found in his tradition.

Did Mark insert an independent traditional unit into its present context, or did he find the material in place within the parable collection? An examination of form, material, and context shows that he found it already in place.

Formally, the argument that the introductory καὶ ἔλεγεν αὐτοῖς in 4:11

represents "one of Mark's typical link-phrases" (Jeremias, *Parables,* 14) by which the evangelist consistently inserts traditional material into a section in progress (Zerwick, *Markus-Stil,* 60–61; 67–70; Marxsen, *Exeget,* 16; Gnilka, *Verstockung,* 23–24; Kuhn, *Sammlungen,* 131; Ambrozic, *Kingdom,* 50–51) has presented the most formidable argument for Markan redaction. But Räisänen's close analysis (*Parabeltheorie,* 93–102) has called this evidence into question. He argues that the phrase in 2:27; 6:10 and 7:9 could just as easily have been pre-Markan, whereas 2:24a and 7:27 have the same formula with a different subject and indirect object respectively in clearly traditional settings.

Materially, the content of 4:11–12 fails to mesh with Mark's perspective evident in its immediate and broader context.

First, many interpreters have noted the awkward use of παραβολή = "riddles" (4:11) in a chapter on "parables" (see *Comment* on 4:11). Second, the content of 4:11–12 is also at odds with the evangelist's treatment of "the crowds" and "the disciples" in the rest of his Gospel. Mark 4:10–11 categorically distinguishes between "disciples" to whom the "mystery of the Kingdom" has been given and "outsiders" to whom all things come in befuddling "riddles" (cf. 4:12). But whereas the evangelist does set off the disciples in his Gospel, this particular delineation claiming special revelation exclusively for the "disciples" and confounding riddles for the "outsiders" fails to cohere either with his larger portrait of the disciples (cf. 7:14–18; 10:10–12; 12:1–12) or the crowds (4:1–2; 6:34; 7:14, Ambrozic, *Kingdom,* 56–66; cf. Jeremias, *Parables,* 18). Third, most incongruous with the thrust of 4:11–12 is Mark's use in 8:14–21 of Jer 5:21. There Mark redactionally uses Jer 5:21 closely related in content to Isa 6:9–10, which is cited in 4:12 with reference to "outsiders," to describe the disciples' lack of understanding (see *Comment* on 8:17–21). Fourth, the note in 12:12 that Jesus' opponents "knew" he had spoken the "parable against them" indicates even "outsiders" had understanding. The same appears to be assumed in the discussion of 3:22–29 and appears to be assumed for the crowd in 7:14.

From the standpoint of the literary context, the immediate setting illustrates even more the incongruity in Mark's supposed redactional depiction of the disciples and the crowd. On the one hand, the evangelist redactionally develops a setting with a large crowd (ὄχλος πλεῖστος) in 4:1–2 whom Jesus teaches "many things with parables" (see *Comment* on 4:2). On the other hand, immediately following Mark's supposed redactional insertion of 4:11–12 that declares the disciples to have been given the "mystery of the Kingdom" while "outsiders" receive everything in "riddles," Jesus has to explain the "parable" to the "insiders" (4:14–20) and even reproaches them for not understanding the "parable" (see *Comment* on 4:13).

In 4:1–2 Mark has apparently created the setting of Jesus teaching the crowd while sitting in a boat, a setting that obtains through 4:35–36. Yet 4:10 assumes a private setting. Therefore, if we take 4:11–12 to have been redactionally added to this context by Mark, we have at best an evangelist who is working very clumsily, if not inconsistently, with his materials. This has certainly not been our impression from Mark's deft use of tradition up to this point in his Gospel. The introduction of 4:11–12 into this literary context fits more smoothly when regarded as a pre-Markan stage in the development of the traditional complex behind 4:3–33. The complex of parable and interpretation (4:3–8, 14–20) with its focus on the different responses offered a thematic context for a pronouncement on both privileged information and failure in perception (4:11–12). The original question about the parable of 4:3–9 that underlies 4:10 and led into the interpretation of 4:14–20 provided a natural setting into which to introduce a scene of private instruction. Mark 4:11–12, therefore, offers a further, more theological interpretation of the parable (4:3–8), the statement on hearing in 4:9, and the interpretation (4:14–20). Furthermore, if the "Kingdom" parables of 4:26–32 were already part of a parable collection (4:3–9, 10b, 13a, 14–20, 26–32, 33), 4:11–12 would have verbal links to the broader context through a play on words with παραβολή (4:11; cf. 4:10b, 30, 33) and the "Kingdom of God" (4:11; cf. 4:26, 30).

The evangelist's redactional activity in 4:10–12 seems limited to the use of "those around him" in 4:10 (Best, *Disciples*, 137–40). His choice to place a series of parables at this juncture within his narrative in the larger context of the contrasts drawn in 3:13–35 between "insiders" and "outsiders" and, as will be noted in 4:13, his addition of at least one reproachful question pointing to the disciples' lack of knowledge do qualify the thrust of 4:11–12.

Structurally, Daube has posited a rabbinic pattern behind 4:1–20; 7:14–23 and 10:1–12 consisting of a fourfold structure: (a) an opponent's question, (b) a public but opaque response, (c) a disciple's request for clarification, (d) which is given then in a smaller, private circle (*Rabbinic Judaism*, 141–50). Unfortunately, 4:10–12 represents only the third and part of the fourth elements. The first two are missing (Gnilka, *Verstockung*, 43, n. 76). Therefore, while the pattern may hold more for 7:14–23 and 10:1–12, it offers little toward our understanding of the presence or function of 4:10–12 in this context.

Lemcio has also found a common, four part pattern behind 4:1–20; 7:14–23; and 8:14–21 rooted in OT (e.g., Ezek 17:1–24; Zech 14:2–10, 11–14) and apocalyptic writings (e.g., *1 Enoch* 24:1–25:5; *2 Apoc. Bar.* 13:1–15:8): (a) ambiguity (4:3–8), (b) incomprehension (4:10), (c) surprise/critical rejoinder (4:13a), (d) explanation (4:14–20). Yet should one assume such a "traditional" structure, it fails to account for 4:11–12. The more natural flow would have been from 4:10 directly to 4:13–20. Consequently, the structure might have obtained for an earlier stage in the tradition prior to the addition of 4:11–12 and would suggest that at least one of the critical questions (4:13) as in (c) belonged to the tradition behind 4:13.

The immediate setting finds 4:10–12 wedged between the parable in 4:3–9 and its interpretation in 4:14–20. A query, most likely about the meaning of the preceding parable (4:10b), has been changed into a question and response about "parables" or "riddles" (4:10–11). The focus on the parable returns in 4:13a where it is interpreted (4:14–20). Thus, on the one hand, the parable and the interpretation graphically illustrate the "riddle" character of Jesus' teaching (4:11b) through the failure of the seed; on the other hand, the interpretation (4:14–20) given privately to a select few (4:10a) illustrates the giving of the "mystery" (4:11a).

In the larger setting of Mark's Gospel, the language of 4:10–12 may have provided the catalyst for the evangelist's introduction of his parable materials at this juncture in his narrative. Though he shifts the scene redactionally to the seaside in 4:1–2 from a house in 3:20–35 and makes no further mention about the scribes from Jerusalem or Jesus' family, the two "audiences" of 4:10–12 do correspond with the language used to describe the two audiences of 3:31–35: those "around him" (4:10—περὶ αὐτόν; cf. 3:32, 34) and those "outside" (4:11—ἔξω; cf. 3:31, 32). Furthermore, the thrust in 4:11–12 parallels that of 3:31–35 which distinguishes the disciples from those who reject Jesus and his ministry. At the same time, 4:11–12 must be read in the broader context of the evangelist's portrait of the disciples in which he maintains a tension between their special relationship with Jesus, including special instruction (e.g., 3:31–35; 4:33–34; 7:17; 9:2; 10:10–12; 13:3), and their lack of understanding (e.g., 4:13, 40–41; 6:51–52; 7:18; 8:17–21; 9:32). This tension is very apparent in the reproachful questions directed at the same group in 4:13 that had been set in contrast with the "outsiders" as those given the "mystery of the Kingdom of God" in 4:11a.

Comment

10 "When he was alone" (κατὰ μόνας) shifts the scene without explanation from the public setting of the seaside and strikes a note of private instruction characteristic of Mark's Gospel (e.g., 4:34; 9:28; 13:3; cf. 10:10). While Mark does use this motif and would certainly resonate with its use here, his preference for κατ᾽ ἰδίαν used adverbially in similar situations (cf. 4:34; 6:31, 32; 7:33; 9:28 and 13:3) suggests he found κατὰ μόνας in his tradition (cf. Boobyer, *NTS* 8 [1961–62] 64–66; Minette de Tillesse, *Secret*, 173–79; Ambrozic, *Kingdom*, 52–53). Luke 9:18, the other occurrence of κατὰ μόνας in the Gospels, indicates its currency in the tradition.

This change in scene creates a dilemma of locale and audience. First, the setting of 4:1–2 leaves problematic how Jesus, who was seated in a boat, could be approached while "alone" by "those around him," a problem that Lane (155–56) resolves without further evidence by positing a time "later." But Jesus is still in the boat and on the sea in 4:35–36 (cf. 4:1–2). Second, this shift creates an inconsistency in audience within 4:1–34. Beginning with a public setting of Jesus teaching large crowds (4:1–2) and moving to a private setting with the disciples (4:10a), the passage gives no indication of Jesus' return to the public teaching implied by 4:33.

Mark has frequently been held accountable for both dilemmas. Yet the inconsistency in audience stems more likely from the tradition. The shift from a public (4:3–8) to a private audience (4:10) probably set the stage in the pre-Markan tradition for the interpretation in 4:14–20. This shift then provided an occasion later for the insertion of the more esoteric theme of 4:11–12 between 4:3–8 and 14–20 and for adding the appropriate conclusion in 4:34. The resultant inconsistency between the private (4:10a) and the public audience (4:33–34a) becomes of no greater consequence than the presence of two other parables (4:26–32) without an interpretation (cf. 4:34). Mark, finding a tradition already containing the inconsistency between the private and public instruction of 4:10a and 4:33, left his tradition intact and constructed the redactional public setting of 4:1–2 primarily with 4:33–36 in mind. The shift from a public to a private audience (4:10a) now intensified by the emphasis on the crowds in 4:1–2 would hardly have disturbed him and may have even given impetus to his own use of this device later in his Gospel (6:31, 32; 7:33; 9:28; 13:3; cf. 7:17; 10:10, see *Comment* on 4:34).

The evangelist's choice of a sea setting in 4:1–2 from 4:35–36 does create the unresolved dilemma of locale between 4:1–2 and 4:10a. Located in a boat, Jesus is no more "alone" in 4:10 than in 4:1–2 or 4:35–36. Obviously, Mark's concern to have Jesus teaching by the sea outweighed his concern for consistency of locale.

"Those around him with the Twelve" most likely began simply as "those around him" (οἱ περὶ αὐτόν) or those in close proximity to Jesus who asked about the parable and to whom the interpretation (4:14–20) was given (Best, *Disciples*, 137–40). In the context of the introduction now for 4:11–12, this group is the "you" to whom the mystery has been given in 4:11a and sets "those around him" off as a special group, the productive seed of the parable, in contrast to "those outside," the seeds that fail to come to fruition. These are the "believers," those who had positively responded to Jesus, who formed an inner circle (cf. τοῖς ἰδίοις μαθηταῖς—4:34).

In Mark's literary context "those around him" (οἱ περὶ αὐτόν) offers a clear reminiscence of 3:31–35 where a similar description occurs twice and refers to the crowd seated "around him" as Jesus' true family, those who "do the will of the God" (3:34–35; cf. Marcus, *Mystery*, 81). Though scene and audience have changed, the motif remains and may have contributed in part to the evangelist's placing the parable chapter in this context. Those "around him" not only have a special relationship ("family") to Jesus, they, in contrast to "those outside," have been given the "mystery of the Kingdom of God."

"With the Twelve" (σὺν τοῖς δώδεκα) has frequently been assigned to the evangelist in keeping with his emphasis on the Twelve (see *Comment* on 3:14). Best (*Disciples*, 139; similarly, Marcus, *Mystery*, 80–81) has argued for its presence in the tradition on the basis that "he was alone with the Twelve" accounts for the singular ἐγένετο. In either case, the evangelist does not limit the inquirers to the circle of the Twelve (so Meye, *SE* 2 [1964] 211–18; Ambrozic, *Kingdom*, 70–71), as the phrase "with the Twelve" (σὺν τοῖς δώδεκα) and the larger context of 3:31–35 indicates (cf. "his own disciples" in 4:34b). The specific reference to "the Twelve" does tie 4:1–34 to the calling of "the Twelve" in 3:13–19. At the same time it places them in an anomalous situation characteristic of the evangelist's handling of members of the Twelve. Called to be "with him" (3:14), privileged to have a special relationship, given special instruction and even a share in Jesus' mission (6:7–13), they lack understanding (see *Comment* on 4:13 and 8:17–21). In 4:10–11 they are set apart from "those outside" for whom all things come in riddles, but in 4:13bc they are reproached for their lack of knowledge requiring the explanation that follows (cf 7:17–18).

"Ask him about the parables" (ἠρώτων αὐτόν . . . τὰς παραβολάς) contains further evidence of pre-Markan tradition. Instead of the simple ἐρωτᾶν (cf. 7:26; 8:5), Mark prefers the compound ἐπερωτᾶν (25x; cf. esp. 7:17; 8:27; 9:11, 28, 32; 10:10; 13:3). Initially, this question set the stage for the interpretation in 4:14–20 and most likely asked about the preceding παραβολήν (4:3–8). When 4:10 was later adapted as the setting for 4:11–12, the question shifted from the singular παραβολήν to the plural παραβολάς and focused on the use of "parables" or more precisely the use of "riddles" (cf. 4:11b). If, as suggested, 4:11–12 was inserted into an existing parable collection (4:3–9, 14–20, 26–33), "the parables" or "riddles" may have referred directly to the collection (Pesch 1:237), but more probably it questions the use of parables or "riddles" as a means of discourse (Gnilka, 1:162).

When Mark, however, placed Jesus' teaching "with parables" in the public setting (4:1–2), he returned to the collection's original nuance of παραβολή referring more generally to Jesus' parabolic form of teaching (Ambrozic, *Kingdom,* 72) by which he spoke the "word" (4:33) rather than the narrower "riddles" (see *Comment* on 4:11). The use of "parables" in the larger context of 4:30, 33–34 makes a reference to the figurative components of 4:3–8 most unlikely either for Mark or the pre-Markan tradition (cf. Trocmé, *Formation,* 463; Boobyer, *NTS* 8 [1961–62] 59–70; Lampe, *ZNW* 65 [1974] 147; Marcus, *Mystery,* 44, n. 107).

11 "And he said to them" (καὶ ἔλεγεν αὐτοῖς) has been labelled a distinctive Markan "link-phrase" by which he inserts material into a block of tradition (Jeremias, *Parables,* 14; Marxsen, *Exeget,* 16; Zerwick, *Markus-Stil,* 60–61). It differs from the introductory phrase in 4:9, 21, 25 and 14:36 (καὶ ἔλεγεν) by specifying an audience (αὐτοῖς, see *Comment* on 4:26) and from the much more common phrase (27x) in 4:13 (καὶ λέγει αὐτοῖς) by the use of the imperfect rather than present tense. Perhaps *how* these formulas are used has greater significance than *where* they are used. Our formula occurs nearly a dozen times in Mark and only rarely to pose a question (8:21) or give a command (6:10). It, along with καὶ ἔλεγεν, generally introduces a saying or statement. By contrast, the more frequent καὶ λέγει αὐτοῖς generally gives a command (13x) or poses a question (11x; cf. 4:13) and only rarely introduces a saying or statement (9:35; 10:11–12). This pattern consistently followed in 4:1–34 supports Räisänen's caution about arbitrarily assigning passages to tradition or redaction simply on the basis of the formula used (*Parabeltheorie,* 93–102).

This verse consists of an antithetical parallelism whose accent falls on the contrast between two different groups, as seen by the primary position of "to you" (ὑμῖν) and "to those outside" (ἐκείνοις τοῖς ἔξω). The "you," whose identity originally lay in the setting of the direct address and in the contrast with "those outside," gains further identity from the setting in 4:10 as "those around Jesus with the Twelve" asking for more explanation.

"Have been given the mystery of the Kingdom of God" sets the one group in contrast to the other, who by implication have not received this gift. The divine passive (δέδοται), a Semitism (Jeremias, *Parables,* 15), attributes this action to God, a motif closely related to Luke 10:21 // Matt 11:25 (cf. Luke 10:23–24 // Matt 13:16–17) and the beatitude to Peter in Matt 16:17. Accordingly, one does not obtain the "mystery of the Kingdom" strictly by one's own reading of the signs or the empirical evidence but as a gift from God. In the context of 4:3–8, 14–20, those receiving the seed as good soil and bearing fruit represent the ones to whom God has given the mystery of the Kingdom.

But what is the "mystery of the Kingdom of God" (τὸ μυστήριον τῆς βασιλείας τοῦ Θεοῦ)? Although connections have been made in the past between the initiatory rites of the hellenistic mystery religions and this esoteric disclosure of the "mystery" (μυστήριον) of the Kingdom, most recognize the distinctive place and function of μυστήριον in contemporary Judaism, particularly in the apocalyptic writings (G. Bornkamm, *TDNT* 4 [1967] 814–17). The term itself first occurs in the LXX as a translation of the Aramaic רז, (*rāz*) in Dan 2:18–19, which may lie behind μυστήριον here, though μυστήριον itself appears in transliteration (מסטירין, *mstyryn*) in rabbinic texts. Our word "mystery," or "secret," fails to carry the full freight of this technical term. Rather than referring to something hidden, unknown or mysterious, the μυστήριον itself, generally of eschatological and cosmic concern, is disclosed in the revelation (G. Bornkamm, *TDNT* 4 [1967] 820–21; Brown, *"Mystery"*). Thus μυστήριον functions as a part of the language of revelation.

Taken as an independent saying devoid of context, "the mystery of the Kingdom of God" lacks further definition. The genitive τῆς βασιλείας τοῦ Θεοῦ merely delimits "mystery" as pertaining to the Kingdom of God. It does not tell us what the disclosure of the "mystery" of the Kingdom of God actually is. Assuming that one can trace the roots of this saying to Jesus' ministry (see *Comment* on 1:14–15), we are still unable to specify the content of the "mystery of the Kingdom," since the content must come from the context of the saying and that context in Jesus' ministry is lost to us. One might, however, assume that the saying involved in some way Jesus' ministry, which had gathered those addressed by "to you," and its relation to the Kingdom of God, since "those outside" found "all things" (done and taught by Jesus?) as "riddles." The key here lies in the contrasting "all things" (τὰ πάντα, see below).

In the context of 4:3–9, 13–20, no explicit reference to the Kingdom of God occurs. But in the broader context, the two parables of 4:26–32 do pertain to the Kingdom. It is reasonable to assume that by virtue of the insertion of this statement about the Kingdom of God into the context of the parable (4:3–9) and its interpretation (4:14–20) this parable also becomes a "Kingdom" parable. Thus all three parables would then pertain to the "mystery of the Kingdom."

If the "mystery of the Kingdom" in its present context pertains to the parables of the Kingdom, what does this context offer about the content of the "mystery of the Kingdom"? Since none of these parables focuses directly on Jesus, we hardly have a "messianic secret" (cf. Wrede, *Secret*, 56–57; Burkill, *Revelation*, 98–99, 115). Rather the three seed parables illustrate various aspects of the Kingdom of God by depicting God's sovereign rule at work in the present but in a way unexpected in Judaism (cf. Jeremias, *Parables*, 146–53). As Dahl has noted, this and other "growth parables" preach "the presence of salvation and the activity of the powers of the Kingdom in spite of all facts which seem to point to the contrary" (*Memory*, 163). Therefore, the mystery of the Kingdom that God has given to "those around him" has to do in this context with the presence of God's eschatological rule now, though in a limited, vulnerable way (4:3–8, 26–29, 30–32; cf. Crossan, *JBL* 92 [1973] 265–66).

According to the pre-Markan redactor who introduced 4:11–12 into the context of 4:3–34, this divine disclosure of the "mystery" came through Jesus' private instruction, his interpretation of the παραβολάς (so 4:14–20; cf. 4:34b), for "those around him" (4:10a). In this way a sharp line was divinely drawn between the "you" and "those outside." The parable collection as a whole (4:3–9, 14–20, 26–34) and the explanation that follows (4:14–20) provide an example of such special instruction. Brown (*JBL* 92 [1973] 60–74) correctly recognizes this point but wrongly attributes it to Mark's redaction.

Mark, who introduced Jesus' ministry as that of proclaiming the coming of the Kingdom of God (1:14–15), beginning with the call of disciples (1:16–20) and marked by his authoritative teaching, exorcisms and healing that created conflict with the religious authorities (1:21–3:6), would stand in full agreement with the tradition that God has disclosed the "mystery of the Kingdom" through Jesus' ministry and does so here in his teaching in parables. The evangelist has even been pointing more and more to a distinction in the response to Jesus' ministry from the negative responses in 2:6–8 and 3:7 to the positive response of the Twelve in 3:13–19 and the definition of his true family in 3:20–35. Therefore, this declaration that God had given the mystery of the Kingdom to "those around Jesus with the Twelve" accords with Mark's portrait of the Twelve and those "around Jesus" in the previous narratives.

Mark does, however, qualify the force of 4:10–12 by the reproachful questions of 4:13 (see *Comment* on 4:13). These questions indicate that he, in contrast to the tradition behind 4:10–12, does not draw as sharp a line between "insiders" and "outsiders." Even "insiders" (4:10a) find the "parable" to be enigmatic. The questions in 4:13 also indicate a different perception of what it means to have received the "mystery of the Kingdom." This concept of the "mystery of the Kingdom" has to do with the accepting, though not unquestioning, response to Jesus and his ministry, as seen in the contrast between "the ones around him with the Twelve" and "those outside" (Moule, *Neotestamentica*, 99–104). It certainly is not synonymous for Mark with any esoteric knowledge that led the "insiders" to complete understanding of a "messianic secret" (Wrede, *Secret*, 56–60) or even a "Kingdom secret" (Brown, *JBL* 60–74), as 4:13 and numerous related episodes that follow indicate.

"But to those who are outside" (ἐκείνοις τοῖς ἔξω) may also contain a Semitism in the redundant demonstrative ἐκείνοις (so Jeremias, *Parables*, 15). This construction, however, does appear in hellenistic literature (Maloney, *Interference*, 125–26). Whether "those outside" ever spatially identified a group as "those outside," for example, a house (Lohmeyer, 83) or a circle of disciples (Cranfield, 154), is lost along with the original context of this saying. Gnilka has taken this phrase and the reference in 4:12 to Isa 6:9–10 as referring specifically to Israel (*Verstockung*, 83–34; similarly, Boucher, *Parable*, 44, 82), since Isa 6:9–10 provided the early Christian mission with a theological explanation for Israel's failure to respond to the mission (John 12:40; Acts 28:26–27; Rom 11:8). But while "those outside" may have referred to Israel at some stage in the development of this tradition, such a categorical judgment of Israel is certainly too broad for Jesus' ministry and hardly Mark's concern.

Perhaps a broader usage of "those outside" found in Judaism (Str-B, 2:7) to refer both to Gentiles and to unbelieving Jews offers the setting in the early Christian mission from which this designation was applied to those who did not believe in God's work seen in Jesus' ministry. Most take "those outside" in its present context just in this way (cf. 1 Cor 5:12; Col 4:5; 1 Thess 4:12) to refer to non-Christians or "unbelievers" including both Jews and Gentiles (Grundmann, 122–24; Pesch, 1:239; Ernst, 131–32). And this more general reference fits the mission context reflected in the response to "the word" in the interpretation of 4:14–20.

For Mark's text, however, "those outside" (ἐκείνοις τοῖς ἔξω) which does not occur elsewhere in his Gospel, inevitably picks up the double reference in 3:31, 32 to his family that was "outside" in contrast to the crowd "around him" in the house. It may be going too far to designate "outsiders" as Jesus' "enemies" for Mark (Ambrozic, *Kingdom* 66), but the context of 3:20–35 makes possible a reference to a group who has specifically rejected Jesus' ministry (see Malbon, *Space*, 129–31). In 3:22–30 the "scribes from Jerusalem" to whom Jesus responded in "parables" charge him with being in league with Satan, and in 3:20–21, 31–35 his family accuses him of being out of his mind. Furthermore, Mark's use of the "crowds" in the setting of Jesus' ministry (1:22, 27; 2:13; 6:2, 6, 34; 10:1; 11:17; 12:35; 14:49—Ambrozic, *Kingdom*, 58–59) and especially his redactional setting in 4:1–2 make it unlikely that "those outside" referred to "the crowds" in contrast to the disciples. For Mark, therefore, as with his tradition "those outside" meant those who had rejected Jesus' ministry, the seed/word sown that did not bear fruit for various reasons.

"All things . . . in riddles" (ἐν παραβολαῖς τὰ πάντα) stands in antithesis to "the mystery of the Kingdom" but gains no further definition from this juxtaposition. The antithesis lies in the contrast between the two groups ("insiders," "outsiders") and in the verbs ("given," "comes") rather than the subjects ("mystery," "all things"—so Sjöberg, *Menschensohn*, 224; Ambrozic, *Kingdom*, 79).

To what then does "all things" (τὰ πάντα) refer? If this saying has its roots in Jesus' ministry, "all things" must have referred to Jesus' ministry in general, his words and his works (Cranfield, 154–55; Grundmann, 123; Ernst, 131). In the later context of the Christian mission, the phrase involves the proclamation of "the word," as illustrated by the parable and its interpretation (4:3–8, 14–20; cf. *Comment* on 2:2). For Mark "all things" certainly includes the proclamation of all that Jesus has taught and done so far in 1:14–3:35 and the pattern continues until it reaches its climax in Jesus' execution.

"In riddles" contextually renders ἐν παραβολαῖς and again betrays the Semitic background of this saying. "Riddle" as a meaning of מָשָׁל (māšāl) has several parallels in the OT (Ezek 17:2; Hab 2:6; Pss 49:5; 78:2; Prov 1:6; Sir 47:17; 4 Ezra 4:3; Jeremias, *Parables*, 16, n. 22), and the context makes that meaning most natural here. Yet our English *riddle* misses the play on words with *parables* in 4:10, not to mention 4:2, 13bc, 30, 33–34, and our English *parable* is too narrow to cover *riddle*. If, however, we remember that מָשָׁל (māšāl) and its Greek translation, παραβολή, could mean either "parable" or "riddle" as well as other forms of figurative speech, we can see how this reference to παραβολάς meaning "riddles" may originally have had no connection with Jesus' teaching in "parables" *per se* (Jeremias, *Parables*, 17–18; Kelber, *Kingdom*, 32–33). The τὰ πάντα with its broader reference to Jesus' ministry in general rather than to his teaching "in parables" supports this conclusion. This more general reference to Jesus' ministry may also account for the reversal of the order of seeing and hearing in 4:12 as compared with Isa 6:9–10. Consequently, these verses most likely had little to say originally about any so-called *parable* theory.

The situation appears to change, however, when 4:11–12 is introduced into its present "parable" context of 4:3–9, 14–20, if not the parable collection (4:3–8, 14–20, 26–33). The interpretation of the "parable" of 4:3–8 in 4:14–20 to "those around him" (4:10), the "you" of 4:11a, suggests that it too was a "riddle" in need of interpretation. Thus, the introduction of 4:11 into the pre-Markan collection colored the existing reference to "parable" in 4:10a, 4:30 and 4:33, 34. So one could accurately render παραβολή throughout as "riddle" synonymous with ἐν παραβολαῖς in 4:11. The reference in 4:34a points specifically to Jesus' *teaching* in contrast to the more encompassing τὰ πάντα of 4:11.

Since Mark has taken over this tradition, one might argue that he simply follows suit and thus offers a "parable theory" by which he distinguishes the "insiders" to whom special revelation has been given from "outsiders" who receive Jesus' deeds and teaching as riddles and whose eyes and ears have been divinely closed. A quick glance at a parallel passage in 7:17 appears to support this conclusion. As in 4:13–20, the disciples receive private instruction that explains a παραβολή given earlier to the "crowd" (cf. 13:28–30). But it is very questionable whether Mark takes παραβολή as meaning "riddle" even in 4:2–34 (cf. Kelber, *Kingdom*, 32–33). In 7:14, Jesus prefaces his παραβολή addressed to the "crowd" with a summons to "hear" (ἀκούετε) and "understand" (σύνετε). This charge implies intelligibility or "parable" rather than "riddle." We have a similar situation in 4:1–9 with the admonition to "hear" opening (4:3a) and closing (4:9) the parable. Neither 4:1–2 nor 7:14 suggest that Jesus is teasing or taunting his audience. Furthermore, Mark uses parables at times without explanation with disciples (cf. 4:26–32; 13:34) and, on at least one occasion, even with opponents, "those outside," who seem to understand (ἔγνωσαν) "parables" aimed at them (12:1–12). Consequently, there is no reason why ἐν παραβολαῖς should not connote the broader "parables" in 4:2 and thus in 4:10, 13bc, 33–34 for Mark (Räisänen, *Parabeltheorie*, 22–30).

By introducing this discourse in 4:2 as Jesus' "teaching with parables" and by qualifying 4:11 by the reproachful questions of 4:13 addressed to the disciples rather than "outsiders," Mark does not pursue the "riddle" motif behind the tradition of 4:10–12 (cf. Wrede, *Secret*, 56–57; Burkill, *Revelation*, 115). On the other hand, in contrast to our popular usage, "parable" hardly reflected the opposite of "riddle" for Mark. The difference lies in the degree of opacity. While not as cryptic as "riddle," "parable" still maintained an enigmatic character (4:13; 7:17; 8:14–18) that called for responsible and attentive hearing by the disciples (4:9, 24–25, 33b; cf. 7:17–18; see Boucher, *Parable*, 11–25, for discussion of the double meaning of parables that leads to their "mysteriousness").

12 This verse expounds on 4:11. On the surface, the introductory ἵνα and μήποτε appear to give the purpose for the "riddles" of 4:11b. Jesus apparently says that he deliberately uses riddles in order that "outsiders" may not perceive and understand lest they be forgiven. The struggle to reconcile such a harsh statement unique to the Jesus tradition with Jesus' ministry has left its traces as early as Matthew and Luke's parallels. Matt 13:13 assigns the responsibility to the audience by changing ἵνα to ὅτι = "because" and introducing this statement with a causal clause. Luke 8:10 follows Mark in the first part but drops the μήποτε statement that appears to eliminate hope for forgiveness.

T. W. Manson (*Teaching*, 77–78), followed by Jeremias (*Parables*, 15) and others, has noted several differences between this verse and the Hebrew or Greek text of Isa 6:9–10, differences that correspond instead to the Aramaic *Tg. Isaiah* (see Chilton, *Rabbi*, 91–98). For example, both the Hebrew and Greek text conclude with the reference to being healed; Mark 4:12 and the Targum refer to forgiveness. The Hebrew and Greek texts have the verbs in the second person; Mark and the Targum have the third person. And only the Targum has the participial equivalents of βλέποντες and ἀκούοντες. Taken with the Semitisms noted in 4:11, this similarity of 4:12 with the Aramaic Targum gives strong indication of an early, underlying Aramaic tradition (cf. Suhl, *Zitaten*, 149–51).

This parallel with the Targum led Manson (*Teaching*, 77–79) and Jeremias (*Parables*, 15–17) to focus on the Aramaic form of this saying and the use of Isa 6:9–10 in the rabbinic literature as the controlling factor in the interpretation of 4:12. Consequently, the ἵνα that opens the statement and the μήποτε that rounds it off lose their function as introductory formulas for final clauses. The Aramaic terms behind both words are ambiguous. In the Targum, this material is introduced by ד (dě), which can be rendered in Greek as a relative pronoun (οἵ = "who" or "that") or as a final clause (ἵνα). Manson (*Teaching*, 78) faulted Mark's version as being a mistranslation of a relative clause. Similarly, דלמא (dilema) introduces the last clause and can mean (a) "in order that . . . not," (b) "perhaps," (c) "unless," and (d) "lest" in the sense of "if they did." Manson opted for (d) with (b) a possibility, because this statement is not directly linked to the first one in Isa 6:10 (Manson, *Teaching*, 78–79). Jeremias chose (c) "unless" under the influence of the rabbinic use of this text as a promise of salvation rather than judgment (Jeremias, *Parables*, 17). In other words, by appealing to an underlying Aramaic tradition, the troublesome final clauses are removed and one is left with material more appropriate to Jesus' ministry.

But what about 4:12 as it stands now? Black (*Approach*, 213) quite rightly states the obvious: "Nothing is more certain than that Mark wrote and intended ἵνα . . . μήποτε." But must this rendering be laid at Mark's door? Such a use of Isa 6:9–10 might well reflect a particularistic stage in the developing tradition, a more sectarian setting corresponding to the private instruction of "those around Jesus" (4:10a). Accordingly, ἵνα would express the purpose of the "riddles" in 4:11b and μήποτε would give the purpose of the blindness and deafness. Whether this use of Isaiah in 4:11–12 ever had Israel specifically as its narrower target in either an earlier Aramaic rendering or a later Greek rendering of the tradition or whether "those outside" included unbelieving Jews and Gentiles is no longer possible to say. But the use of Isa 6:9–10 elsewhere in the Church's struggle to explain Israel's rejection of the gospel (Rom 11:3; Acts 28:27 and John 12:40) indicates this to have been a possibility at some point in the developing tradition.

The evangelist, however, betrays no such particularism or sectarian tendency. The redactional setting of the crowds in 4:1–2 as well as Jesus' and the disciples' public ministry of teaching, healing and exorcising that follows makes clear that the evangelist did not read 4:12 as a judgment on Israel. At most, "those outside" (4:11) who do not see or understand (4:12) refers to those who have deliberately rejected or will reject Jesus' ministry, the unbelievers who hear and fail to bring forth fruit, not only during Jesus' ministry but also in the mission of the Church.

Mark does not depict Jesus' ministry as being in riddles *for* the purpose of preventing either his audience or the disciples from responding, *with* the result that neither his audience nor the disciples will perceive, understand and be forgiven, or *because* his audience and/or his disciples did not respond. Each of these possible meanings of ἵνα have been suggested: (a) ἵνα-final (most common, e.g., Taylor, 256–57; Cranfield, 156; Black, *Approach*, 212–14; Ambrozic, *Kingdom*, 67–68); (b) ἵνα-result (e.g., Peisker, 126–27; Suhl, *Zitaten*, 149–50; Kirkland, 6–7); and (c) ἵνα-causal (e.g., Lohmeyer, 84).

Jeremias has gained numerous supporters for a variation on ἵνα-final as a formula introduction for a Scripture citation. In this case it functions as ἵνα πληρωθῇ, "that it might be fulfilled." In other words, all things come in riddles to those outside in keeping with the prophecy of Isa 6:9–10 (*Parables*, 17; Lagrange, 99; Marxsen, *Exeget*, 25; Gnilka, *Verstockung*, 45–48; Ernst, 131). But apart from the fact that ἵνα represents the first word of the citation rather than an introductory formula, Suhl has shown that ἵνα never functions this way in Mark. More importantly, he has shown that the evangelist uses the OT primarily to characterize or to interpret rather than in a promise-fulfillment pattern. Consequently, he takes the ἵνα to be a "qualifying consecutive relative clause" (*Zitaten*, 66, 94, 149–51).

Lampe (*ZNW* 65 [1974] 141, so Pesch, 1:239) has suggested an epexegetic function of ἵνα that captures the thrust of Suhl's point and has a parallel elsewhere in Mark. In other words, 4:12 qualifies or interprets 4:11b by giving an explication using an OT citation: "To those outside, all things come to them in riddles, *that* is . . . ." This reading also gains significant support from 9:12 where ἵνα again functions epexegetically with reference to the Scriptures. Furthermore, Mark later employs Jer 5:21 in just this manner to characterize the disciples (8:18) without any promise-fulfillment motif. Therefore, even if Mark was faithfully preserving a traditional reading in 4:12, in contrast to Matthew and Luke, he could certainly have read it other than as a ἵνα-final which would leave us with a statement for which we have no other evidence in Mark.

But what about the μήποτε-clause? It too most naturally expresses purpose, in a negative sense. The Hebrew of Isa 6:10 is equally clear with פֶּן (*pen*), and the Aramaic דִּלְמָא (*dilema*), though more ambiguous, can have this meaning. One of the strongest arguments for its function as a final particle here has been its apparent relationship with the preceding ἵνα-clause (Black, *Approach*, 213–14). If, however, the ἵνα-clause had an epexegetic function, then this clause becomes logically coordinate rather than subordinate to the first and open to more than one reading.

The range of meanings is really limited to two. It can introduce an indirect question with the meaning of "perhaps," or it can introduce a negative purpose or final clause. "Lest" can render each of these, depending on how it is used. Despite the possibility of אלמד (*dilema*) meaning "unless" (Jeremias, *Parables*, 17), μήποτε does not and thus can hardly be translated in this way. The indirect question, expressed by "if they had" (Manson, *Teaching*, 78; Suhl, *Zitaten*, 150, 152; Lampe, *ZNW* 65 [1974] 143), fits both the Greek and Aramaic terms. It also leaves open the possibility for forgiveness, a motif common to the rabbinic understanding of Isa 6:9–10 (Gnilka, *Verstockung*, 48–49; Str-B, 1:662–63).

If 4:11–12 went through a more sectarian stage at a later point in the developing tradition, as seems likely, μήποτε would have introduced a statement that gave the ultimate purpose for the use of "riddles." It would have helped delineate the difference between two mutually exclusive responses. To those "around Jesus" was given the "mystery of the Kingdom," salvation; to those "outside" all things came in "riddles" in order that they might not repent and be forgiven. As noted above, this narrow understanding of 4:11–12 may reflect the view in some sectors of the early Church in an attempt to account for the positive and negative response to the mission.

This sharp bifurcation into two distinct groups finds little correspondence with Mark's portrait and makes it unlikely that the evangelist read μήποτε as a final clause. That the evangelist read μήποτε in the sense of an indirect question rather than as an expression of divine judgment seems clear from his previous treatment of "those outside" in 3:21–35 as well as from his subsequent use of Jer 5:21 in a thematically related passage (8:14–21) to describe the *disciples*.

Jesus' warning to his opponents in 3:24–29 and his identification of his true family in 3:31–35 stopped short of pronouncing the scribes guilty of blasphemy and of renouncing totally his family (see *Comment* on 3:30, 35). Furthermore, the evangelist employs Jer 5:21 in 8:14–21 to interpret the disciples' inability to "see" and "hear" his parabolic reference to the leaven of the Pharisees and Herodians. But the blindness, deafness and hardness of heart does not reflect a divine judgment that precludes forgiveness for "those around him" in 8:14–21 any more or less than the "outsiders" in 3:20–35. The "disciples" of all people in Mark's Gospel are to be included among the "forgiven." Therefore, though "all things" come as "parables" to the "outsiders" for Mark, if they "perceived" and "understood," they would repent and be forgiven.

Explanation

This passage stands as one of the most controversial of Mark's Gospel. Historically, it has given rise to some fundamental questions about Jesus' ministry, his use of parables, the "mystery" of the Kingdom, and the "messianic secret." More recently, the passage has provoked debate about the "original" setting for this material, about its function in the various, posited traditional layers and about the evangelist's use of this vignette. Most recently, the play on words between "parable" and "riddle" as well as the distinction between "insiders" and "outsiders" has contributed to a more literary-critical discussion of "parable" as metaphor in terms of Jesus' ministry as such. The average reader, however, simply struggles with what appears to be a rather arbitrary, if not capricious, statement about Jesus' teaching with parables and its consequence.

Our study has isolated three contexts in which this pericope can be viewed: (a) an earlier Semitic or Aramaic tradition whose roots might well extend to Jesus' ministry; (b) a development in the tradition as used by the early Church that is reflected in the Greek rendering, particularly as seen in the combination of this material with the parable collection underlying 4:1–34; (c) Mark's own reading of these sayings. Unfortunately, a failure to note at least these three discrete contexts has led to an ignoring or a distorting of Mark's text. Therefore, a look at each should clarify the meaning and role of our text in its Markan context.

Numerous indicators point to an underlying Semitic tradition. This tradition most likely included 4:11–12, but its context in Jesus' ministry or in the intervening tradition is lost to speculation. Assuming that we can trace the roots of these sayings to Jesus' ministry, we can make some general observations. First, these sayings indicate a distinction drawn between two groups along the lines of perceiving and not perceiving God's redemptive activity, the "Kingdom of God." The one group is gathered around Jesus and addressed by him. This suggests that the disclosure of the "mystery of the Kingdom" had a point of contact with Jesus' ministry and involved one's response to that ministry. When we recognize that the Kingdom of God lay at the heart of Jesus' ministry, 4:11a declares the "you" to have experienced God's disclosure of God's sovereign rule through Jesus. Unfortunately, this saying makes no further statements about the nature of the "mystery of the Kingdom" that has been disclosed.

On the other hand, the second group consists of those "outside" to whom "all things" come in "riddles." The "all things" most likely makes general reference to Jesus' ministry, including both his words and his works. This saying gives no evidence of originally having dealt with "parables" or Jesus' use of them. Nor does this saying speak abstractly about the "parabolic" or "metaphorical" nature of Jesus' ministry as depicted in the Gospels. It merely declares that a group fails to perceive Jesus' ministry clearly. "All things" come to them in "riddles."

The use of Isa 6:9–10 in 4:12 elaborates upon this theme. This text could explain *why* all things are "in riddles" in terms of divine judgment. But the similarity of 4:12 to the Aramaic *Targum of Isaiah* with its hope for salvation rather than to the LXX or the Hebrew text suggests that 4:12 originally illustrated instead of explained 4:11b. In other words, 4:11b and 4:12 describe those who had not responded positively to Jesus' ministry about the Kingdom of God, those who had found "all things" to be in "riddles," to have seen without perception and heard without understanding (4:12ab). Had it been otherwise, they would have repented and been forgiven (4:12c).

Despite the assignment by many of the present location of this material to Mark's redaction, our analysis has found more evidence to support a pre-Markan adaptation of this passage to a collection of parables. Without doubt, 4:10–12 interrupts the complex of 4:3–9, 14–20. If the interpretation of the parable (4:14–20) immediately followed the parable (4:3–9) in some earlier stage in the tradition, the interpretation in 4:14–20 may have given occasion for the use of 4:11–12 in a more sectarian manner to explain why some responded (4:11a, received divine gift) and others did not (4:11b, 12 read with final clauses, i.e., divine rejection). This saying might also have explained how the disciples "understood" the "parables," when the parables had become more and more like "riddles" for later ears temporally and spatially removed from Jesus' ministry.

At this stage in the development of the pre-Markan tradition the lines were sharply drawn between "those around him" and "those outside." But this distinction is no longer based on the perceiving or not perceiving of "all things." Both groups receive Jesus' teachings as "riddles" (4:10b, 11b, 33–34a). The distinction is based on the divine decision to give or disclose the mystery to some (4:11a, e.g., the interpretation in 4:14–20) and withhold it from others (4:12). In other words, the distinction between the two groups is seen in Jesus' private instruction of the one rather than the other (cf. 4:33, 34a). To be "given the mystery" is to have it disclosed or revealed. And since the interpretation (4:14–20) of the parable (4:3–9) reveals the "mystery of the Kingdom," it turns the parable of the seed into a "Kingdom" parable.

Mark, the evangelist, both accepts and modifies the thrust of this composite traditional block. First, he maintains the contrast between two groups present in 4:11 and implicit in the productive and nonproductive seeds of the surrounding parable and its interpretation. In fact, by choosing to use the parable collection at this point in his story, he continues the contrast present in the preceding narratives where the Twelve have been called apart (3:13–19) and given the special privilege of being with Jesus and where the "crowd around him" (3:20–35, 32) has been set in contrast to the "scribes from Jerusalem" and Jesus' own family who stood "outside." The evangelist actually strengthens these ties within the narrative, despite the change in setting of 4:1–2. For Mark, "those around Jesus *with* the Twelve" had clearly been given the "mystery of the Kingdom." They had heard and their response to Jesus indicated their position. By contrast, the "scribes from Jerusalem" (3:22) and Jesus' own family (3:21, 30–34) had failed to perceive the "riddles" of his ministry. They had seen but not perceived; heard but not understood, as indicated by their response to his ministry (3:21, 22).

Unlike his tradition, however, Mark does not view the line of distinction between those "around him with the Twelve" and "those outside" to have been drawn ultimately. The evangelist's handling of both the scribes (3:28–29) and Jesus' family (3:35), which left open the question of their ultimate response, indicates that he took the citation of Isa 6:9–10 in 4:12 as epexegetic to, rather than as the purpose for, the enigmatic character of Jesus' teaching. Accordingly, instead of pronouncing judgment, the Isaiah text underscores in another way the fact that the "outsiders" fail to perceive the real moment in Jesus' ministry. If they did, they not only would recognize the dawning of God's sovereign rule (the "Kingdom of God," cf. 3:23–27) but would also repent and be forgiven; in other words, they would do the "will of God" (3:35). Consequently, Jesus does not cease teaching the crowds (e.g., 4:1–2; 6:34; 7:14; 8:2–3) nor does he play games with the Jewish rulers in the following narrative (e.g., 4:22, 36; 12:28, 34).

Mark also qualifies the gift or disclosure of the "mystery of the Kingdom" to "those around him with the Twelve" by his addition of the reproachful questions that follow in 4:13. Instead of letting the interpretation (4:14–20) illustrate, as in the pre-Markan tradition, how they had been "given the mystery of the Kingdom," Mark prefaces the interpretation with two questions that show the disciples to be culpably ignorant of the parable's (4:3–9) meaning or for that matter of all the parables. But it is precisely this rather paradoxical trait of depicting the disciples as being privileged people, given a special relationship with Jesus (1:16–20; 3:13; 4:35; 6:31–32; 9:2) and even receiving special instruction (4:34b; 7:17; 8:31; 10:10) only to fail in their understanding of Jesus that characterizes Mark's depiction of the "you," the disciples (cf. 4:40–41; 6:52; 7:18; 8:14–21, 32–33; 9:5–6, 32; 10:24; 14:40).

Consequently, to have been given the "mystery of the Kingdom" did not mean to have received clear perception or enlightened understanding. The "insider's" response to Jesus had not resulted from any special "knowledge" given to them. The disciples' continued lack of understanding makes this clear. Yet their positive though confused response to Jesus meant that the "mystery of the Kingdom" had been given to them. They recognized something new and special in Jesus. Through their response to and share in his ministry they were participating in the disclosure of the "mystery of the Kingdom" as it was transpiring in Jesus' ministry.

E. Interpretation of the Seeds (4:13–20)

Bibliography

Best, E. *Following Jesus.* 1981. ———. *Mark: The Gospel as Story.* London: SPCK, 1983. ———. "The Role of the Disciples in Mark." *NTS* 23 (1976–77) 377–401 = *Disciples and Discipleship: Studies in the Gospel According to Mark.* Edinburgh: T. & T. Clark, 1986. 98–130. **Boucher, M.** *The Mysterious Parable: A Literary Study.* CBQMS 6. Washington, DC: Catholic Biblical Association, 1977. **Brown, R. E.** "Parable and Allegory Reconsidered." *NovT* 5 (1962) 36–45 = *New Testament Essays.* Garden City, NY: Image/Double-day, 1968. 321–33. **Carlston, C. E.** *The Parables of the Triple Tradition.* Philadelphia: Fortress, 1975. **Cranfield, C. E. B.** "St Mark iv. 1–34." *SJT* 4 (1951) 398–414; 5 (1952) 49–66. **Crossan, J. D.** *In Parables: The Challenge of the Historical Jesus.* New York: Harper & Row, 1973. ———. "The Seed Parables of Jesus." *JBL* 92 (1973) 244–66. **Dahl, N. A.** "The Parables of Growth." *ST* 5 (1951) 132–66 = *Jesus in the Memory of the Early Church.* Minneapolis: Augsburg, 1976. 141–66. **Daube, D.** "Public Pronouncement and Private Explanation in the Gospels." *ExpTim* 57 (175–77) = *The New Testament and Rabbinic Judaism.* London: Athlone, 1956. 141–50. **Dodd, C. H.** *The Parables of the Kingdom.* 1961. **Drury, J.** "The Sower, the Vineyard, and the Place of Allegory in the Interpretation of Mark's Parables." *JTS* 24 (1973) 367–79. **Gerhards-son, B.** "The Parable of the Sower and Its Interpretation." *NTS* 14 (1967–68) 165–93. **Hahn, F.** "Das Gleichnis von der ausgestreuten Saat und seine Deutung (Mk. iv. 3–8, 14–20)." In *Text and Interpretation,* FS M. Black, ed. E. Best and R. McL. Wilson. Cambridge: Cambridge UP, 1979. 133–42. **Jeremias, J.** *The Parables of Jesus.* 1972. **Jülicher, A.** *Die Gleichnisreden Jesu* I-II. 2d ed. Tübingen: Mohr, 1899. **Kelber, W.** *The Kingdom in Mark.* 1974. **Klauck, H.-J.** *Allegorie und Allegorese in synoptischen Gleichnis-*

texten. NA 13, Münster: Aschendorff, 1978. **Kuhn, H.-W.** *Ältere Sammlungen im Markusevangelium.* 1971. **Lemcio, E. E.** "External Evidence for the Structure and Function of Mark iv. 1–20, vii. 14–23 and viii. 14–21." *JTS* 29 (1978) 323–38. **Linnemann, E.** *Jesus of the Parables.* New York: Harper & Row, 1966. **Marcus, J.** *The Mystery of the Kingdom of God.* SBLDS 90. Atlanta: Scholars Press, 1986. **Marxsen, W.** "Redaktionsgeschichtliche Erklärung der sogenannten Parabeltheorie des Markus." *ZTK* 52 (1955) 255–71 = *Der Exeget als Theologe: Vorträge zum Neuen Testament.* Gütersloh: Mohn, 1968. 13–28. **Moule, C. F. D.** "Mark 4, 1–20 Yet Once More." In *Neotestamentica et Semitica,* FS M. Black, ed. E. Ellis and M. Wilcox. Edinburgh: T. & T. Clark, 1969. 95–113. **Neirynck, F.** *Duality in Mark.* 1972. **Payne, P. B.** "The Authenticity of the Parable of the Sower and Its Interpretation." In *Gospel Perspectives* I, ed. R. T. France and D. Wenham. Sheffield: JSOT Press, 1980. 163–207. ———. "The Seeming Inconsistency of the Interpretation of the Parable of the Sower." *NTS* 26 (1979–80) 564–68. **Pryor, J. W.** "Markan Parable Theology: An Inquiry into Mark's Principles of Redaction." *ExpTim* 83 (1972) 242–45. **Pryke, E. J.** *Redactional Style in the Marcan Gospel.* 1978. **Räisänen, H.** *Das 'Messiasgeheimnis' im Markusevangelium.* Helsinki: Finnish Exegetical Society, 1976. ———. *Die Parabeltheorie im Markusevangelium.* Schriften der finnischen exegetischen Gesellschaft 25. Helsinki: Finnish Exegetical Socieity, 1973. **Schweizer, E.** "Zur Frage des Messiasgeheimnisses bei Markus." *ZNW* 56 (1965) 1–8 = "The Question of the Messianic Secret in Mark," in *The Messianic Secret,* ed. C. Tuckett. London/Philadelphia: SPCK/Fortress, 1983. 65–74. **Sider, J. W.** "Proportional Analogy in the Gospel Parables." *NTS* 31 (1985) 1–23. **Trocmé, E.** "Why Parables? A Study of Mark IV." *BJRL* 59 (1977) 458–71. **Tyson, J. B.** "The Blindness of the Disciples in Mark." *JBL* 80 (1961) 261–68 = *The Messianic Secret,* ed. C. Tuckett. Philadelphia: Fortress, 1983. 35–43. **Weeden, T. J.** "Recovering the Parabolic Intent in the Parable of the Sower." *JAAR* 47 (1979) 97–120. ———. *Mark: Traditions in Conflict.* 1971. **Wenham, D.** "The Interpretation of the Parable of the Sower." *NTS* 20 (1973–74) 299–319. **Wrede, W.** *The Messianic Secret.* 1971. **Zerwick, M.** *Untersuchungen zum Markus-Stil: Ein Beitrag zur stilistischen Durcharbeitung des Neuen Testaments.* Rome: Pontifical Biblical Institute, 1937.

Translation

[13] And he said to them, *"Do you not grasp this parable? How will you understand all the parables?* [14] *The sower sows the word.* [15] *These are the ones on the path where the word is sown. Whenever they hear, immediately Satan comes and takes away the word that has been sown in them.*[a] [16] *Similarly, these are the ones sown on rocky ground who, whenever they hear the word, immediately receive it with joy.* [17] *They do not have a root in themselves and last for a short time. Then when affliction and persecution on account of the word come, they immediately fall away.* [18] *Others are the ones sown among the thistles. These are they who hear the word,* [19] *but the anxieties of this age, the deceit of wealth and the desires for other things come and choke the word and it is unfruitful.* [20] *And those are the ones sown on the good soil who hear the word and receive it and bear fruit thirty, sixty and a hundredfold."*[b]

Notes

[a] Read εἰς αὐτούς with B W *f*[13] 28 rather than ἐν ταῖς καρδίαις αὐτῶν with D Θ 0133 Majority text lat sy or ἀπὸ τῆς καρδίας αὐτῶν with A that represent a harmonization with Matt 13:19; Luke 8:12.

Form / Structure / Setting

Many have viewed this interpretation to be an "allegory" or an allegorization of the parable in 4:3–8 by identifying its various components in a one-to-one correspondence. Since Jülicher's study that carefully distinguished between a "parable" (an extended simile) and an "allegory" (an extended metaphor) and attributed the former to Jesus and dismissed the latter as a later development, "allegory" has become a loaded term, a second-class citizen, in parable studies (e.g., Dodd, *Parables,* 1–7; Jeremias, *Parables,* 12–13).

More recent studies of "parables" in the OT, Jewish and rabbinic writings as well as the Jesus tradition reject the often fanciful allegorical method of interpreting the parables in the history of the Church but also recognize the sharp distinction between "parable" and "allegory" to be at best artificial (Klauck, *Allegorie;* Sider, *NTS* 31 [1985] 1–23; Boucher, *Parable,* 17–25; cf. Crossan, *Parables,* 8–15). "In the OT, the apocrypha, and the rabbinic writings, משל covers parable and allegory and a host of other literary devices (riddle, fable, proverb, etc). Therefore, there is no reason to believe that Jesus of Nazareth in his *meshalim* ever made a distinction between parable and allegory" (Brown, *NovT* 56 [1962] 36–45; similarly, Moule, *Neotestamentica,* 109–110; Drury, *JTS* 24 [1973] 367–79).

Sider (*NTS* 31 [1985] 1–23) has even argued that simile ("parable") and metaphor ("allegory") represent different forms of statement but not different forms of thought (cf. Klauck, *Allegorie,* 139–45). Whereas the former makes an explicit comparison by the linking words "is like" ("he is like a bear"), the latter makes an implicit comparison through an identification by a one-to-one correspondence ("he is a bear today"). Both use a comparison as the basis for conveying the same rational content in the different statements. Both are משלים (*mĕšālîm*) or παραβολαί and both forms of statement occur in the Jesus-tradition. Thus, the difference between the parable of 4:3–8 and the interpretation in 4:14–20 is one of expression rather than kind. The parable makes an elliptical or unstated comparison by leaving the comparison without a direct referent for the hearer or reader; the interpretation makes an explicit comparison by identifying some of the parable's details.

With rare exception (Trocmé, *BJRL* 59 [1977] 466), 4:14–20 has been assigned to pre-Markan tradition (see *Comment* on 4:13). The absence of distinctive Markan stylistic and verbal traits along with the presence of eight Markan *hapax legomena* (Klauck, *Allegorie,* 200, n. 77) support this assessment. But does the interpretation, like the parable, have its ultimate roots in Jesus' ministry or does it reflect a later application of the parable in the life of the early Church?

Two approaches have marked the debate over authenticity. One approach under the influence of Jülicher's work has argued on the basis of principle or definition for the secondary nature of this interpretation. By definition "parables" function to clarify and thus have little need for explanation. And by definition "parables" radically differ from "allegories." Another approach, often combined with the former, has argued from language, style and content for the secondary nature of the interpretation. (See Taylor, 258; Cranfield, 158–161; Brown, *NovT* 56 [1962] 36–45, and Payne, *Gospel Perspectives*, 169, for a listing of arguments.)

As to the approach in principle or by definition, 4:13–20 "explains" the Parable of the Seeds by means of "allegory." As noted above, however, the sharp distinction between "parable" and "allegory" holds neither for משל (*māšāl*) nor from a literary-critical perspective. Furthermore, the interpretation of parables in the OT, Jewish literature, and by the rabbis demonstrates the fallacy of denying the authenticity of 4:13–20 in principle. In other words, we have no reason "in principle" or "by definition" for denying the authenticity of the interpretation.

As to the approach from language, style and content, several scholars have shown that the argument from language (so persuasive for Jeremias, *Parables*, 77–79) is hardly beyond question (Cranfield, 158–61; Brown, *NovT* 56 [1962] 42–45; Moule, *Neotestamentica*, 111–12). Granting that the language has its place in the early Christian mission setting, these and others have shown at least the likely possibility that these words could have had their place in Jesus' ministry. As to the difference in content, the slippery character of this criterion becomes evident when we see the variety of contents or meanings given the parable itself. Is the difference one of degree or one of kind? For those who see it as authentic, the answer is one of degree; but for those who see it as a later composition, it is often a difference in kind.

Perhaps the most persuasive evidence for the secondary nature of the interpretation comes from the change in the parable's basic structure. Rather than a balanced 3:3 comparison of seeds, the interpretation makes a 3:1 comparison of "hearers." Three ("these") groups of "hearers" who do not bear fruit for various reasons stand in contrast with one ("those") group of "hearers" that does. This shift from a balanced to an unbalanced comparison changes the parable's focus to accentuate the unproductive "hearers." Furthermore, the structurally disruptive elements found in the parable (4:5–6) play a pivotal role in the interpretation (see *Comment* on 4:16–17).

This change in structure and focus, the presence of language that bespeaks the early Church's struggle in its mission and the absence of the Semitisms prevalent in the parable strongly indicate an application of the parable in the life of the early Church. We have no basis for denying a priori that Jesus interpreted this or any other parable. In fact, the rarity of such interpretations in the Jesus tradition could speak for an underlying traditional interpretation of this parable in Jesus' ministry (e.g., Brown, *NovT* 56 [1962] 42). But the interpretation as we now have it appears to have extended the comparisons of the parable in a way that makes the reconstruction of that interpretation impossible and the issue moot.

After an opening double question by Jesus in 4:13, the basic structure of 4:14–20 follows and identifies the components of the parable. Many have noted the interpretation's identification of the seed as both "the word" and the "hearers." The incipit (4:14) identifies the seed as "the word," while the seed that "falls" on various soils is identified as those who "hear the word," though even the latter motif follows no syntactical pattern (subjunctive—4:15, 17; participle—4:18; indicative—4:20).

The earlier setting of 4:14–20 immediately following the parable has been disrupted by the insertion of the discussion regarding parables in general in 4:11–12. At the time of the insertion of 4:11–12, the interpretation (4:14–20) most likely illustrated how the "insiders" were given the "mystery of the Kingdom" by means of Jesus' special teaching. This reading of the interpretation, however, is now precluded by the opening questions of 4:13 which point out the disciples' surprising lack of understanding despite having been given the "mystery of the Kingdom." Mark also appears to have added a group of sayings immediately following this interpretation (4:21–25) that paraenetically underscores the disciples' privilege and responsibility as those to whom "the word" or the "mystery of the Kingdom" has been given.

Comment

13 "And he said to them" (καὶ λέγει αὐτοῖς) has been cited as a pre-Markan formula (Marxsen, *Exeget*, 16–17; Kuhn, *Sammlungen*, 131, n. 39; Pesch, 1:241; Gnilka, 1:173). But Kuhn's recognition that some occurrences of this phrase are redactional (e.g., 9:35) and Räisänen's detailed analysis (*Parabeltheorie*, 102–06) caution us about hasty assumptions. In this case, the formula may have originally introduced the response in 4:14, or it may be Mark's way of moving to the double question in 4:13b (similarly 7:18; 8:17).

"Do you not grasp this parable?" (οὐκ οἴδατε τὴν παραβολὴν ταύτην) poses the first of two questions that belittle the disciples for failing to comprehend. Did Mark find these questions in his tradition (Gnilka, *Verstockung*, 33; Pesch, 1:243) or add them (Reploh, *Lehrer*, 78; Grundmann, 125; Schweizer, *ZNW* 56 [1965] 6–7)?

The argument for their presence in the pre-Markan tradition appears to be lexical (Pesch, 1:243, n. 1) and structural (Lemcio, *JTS* 29 [1978] 323–38). While Mark exhibits little aversion to using either οἴδατε (21x) or γινώσκειν (12x), γινώσκειν never occurs in similar contexts and οἴδατε appears in the very passages that Reploh (*Lehrer*, 79, n. 19) assigns to the pre-Markan tradition (9:6; 10:40). By contrast, the evangelist consistently uses ἀσύνετος and συνιέναι in similar contexts (e.g., 6:52; 7:18; 8:17, 21). Lemcio has found a common pattern behind 4:1–20; 7:14–23; and 8:14–21 rooted in OT (e.g., Ezek 17:1–24; Zech 14:2–10, 11–14) and apocalyptic writings (e.g., *1 Enoch* 24:1–25:5; *2 Apoc. Bar.* 13:1–15:8) consisting of four parts: (a) ambiguity (4:3–8), (b) incomprehension (4:10), (c) surprise or critical rejoinder (4:13a), and (d) explanation (4:14–20) which he assigns to the pre-Markan tradition. Yet the parallels in 7:14–23 and 8:14–21 come from passages in which (c) surprise or critical rejoinder was almost certainly formed by Markan redaction, a factor which supports the redactional rather than traditional character of the rejoinder here.

This argument is countered by the weightier arguments of style and content. Zerwick (*Markus-Stil*, 24–25) has noted Mark's propensity for rhetorical questions and Neirynck (*Duality*, 57–58) has pointed to Mark's use of the double question (e.g., 7:18; 8:17). The matter of content is even more telling. These questions that underscore the inquirers' ignorance by implying they should have "grasped" the meaning of the parable stand in open tension with the previous statement (4:11) that as "insiders" they have received the "mystery of the Kingdom." What purpose would 4:11–12 have served had it been inserted into a pre-Markan tradition in which 4:13 opened the interpretation or disclosure with questions that placed the inquirers, the "insiders," on the same footing with the "outsiders?" Yet this anomalous picture of disciples as "recipients of special knowledge" and "lacking in spiritual insight and hard of understanding" (Weeden, *Traditions*, 26–32; Best, *Jesus*, 235) corresponds to Mark's portrait of the disciples throughout his Gospel, particularly from this point on (e.g., 4:40–41; 6:52; 7:18; 8:14–21; 9:5–6; 10:24; 14:40; cf. 8:32–33; 9:32).

So characteristic of Mark's Gospel is the tension between 4:11 and 4:13 that we are left with the choice that he either added 4:11–12 to accent the special privilege of the "insiders" to heighten their lack of understanding in 4:13 or he added the questions of 4:13 to accent the disciples' lack of understanding. We have argued above (see pp. 200–202) for the pre-Markan addition of 4:11–12 into a context that originally illustrated how the "insiders" were given the mystery of the Kingdom by special instruction (4:14–20) and a context which in turn gained an additional theological explanation of why many who heard, like the various unproductive seeds, remained "outsiders."

This leaves the option of attributing the questions of 4:13 to Markan redaction, a redaction that redirects the thrust of 4:11–12 in combination with 4:14–20. Instead of 4:14–20 illustrating 4:11 by showing how Jesus gave the "insiders" the mystery of the Kingdom through special instruction, these questions in 4:13 serve to accent the failure of the disciples to grasp Jesus' meaning of this parable, despite their special position ("around him") and privilege (recipients of the mystery of the Kingdom).

Why does Mark play up the motif of the disciples' failure to understand Jesus, a motif doubtless drawn from the tradition but highlighted by Mark (Best, *NTS* 23 [1976–77] 383–90)? Wrede (*Secret*, 101–14) viewed this to be part of Mark's "messianic secret" by which the evangelist deliberately portrayed the disciples as ignorant of who Jesus was prior to Easter. Tyson (*JBL* 80 [1961] 261–68) sees Mark's use of the disciples' "blindness" as an attempt to indicate they misunderstood Jesus' death and the nature of his messiahship. Weeden (*Traditions*, 27–69) sees the "disciples" portrayed as representatives of a current, θεῖος ἀνήρ (divine man) Christological heresy. But Best, after an extensive review of the disciples' role in Mark, seems closest to the point when he concludes that Mark is not (a) "attacking the reputation of the historical disciples," (b) using them as a representative group of "heretics" of his day, or (c) setting them off as special "ministers" of the early church. Rather the role of the disciples was to be "examples to the community. Not examples by which their own worth or failure is shown, but examples through whom teaching is given to the community and the love and power of God made known" (*NTS* 23 [1976–77] 399–401; similarly Reploh, *Lehrer*, 81–86; Räisänen, 'Messiasgeheimnis,' 119–21). The disciples "weakness and failure to understand gives Mark the opportunity of teaching what true discipleship is" (Best, *Mark*, 47).

The second question, "How will you understand all the parables" (πῶς πάσας τὰς παραβολὰς γνώσεσθε) indicates the significance of this parable for understanding the others. By tying 4:3–8 in this way more closely to the "Kingdom" parables (4:26–32) in the parable collection, the one parable that does not specifically refer to the Kingdom becomes more clearly a parable of the Kingdom. Furthermore, this linking of the parable in 4:3–8 with 4:26–32 through 4:13 would indicate that the interpretation itself (4:14–20) had maintained for Mark its eschatological thrust (cf. Jeremias, *Parables*, 79). Paraenesis had not eclipsed eschatology in the interpretation.

14 "The sower sows the word" (ὁ σπείρων τὸν λόγον σπείρει) serves as the incipit for the interpretation. Nothing further is made of the "sower's" identity. But whereas the parable opened with simply a statement of a sower going out to sow, this incipit identifies what is sown as "the word" (ὁ λόγος). This identification of the seed sown (cf. Luke 8:11) repeated in 4:15a stands in tension with the further identification of the parable's seeds sown on the path, rocky ground, among thistles and on good soil as "those who hear the word."

"The word" (τὸν λόγον) used absolutely occurs elsewhere in Mark (1:45; 2:2; 4:33; 8:32), but this is the only occurrence on Jesus' lips in the Synoptics. Brown (*NovT* 56 [1962] 42) and others have rightly noted that the "prophet's employment of דבר, *dābār* / λόγος for the divine message entrusted to them" could well have served as precedent for Jesus' use of this or a similar Semitic expression behind ὁ λόγος to refer to his preaching of the Kingdom (see *Comment* on 2:2). The strong evidence that ὁ λόγος became a technical term synonymous with the Christian gospel in the language of the early Church (Taylor, 193; Jeremias, *Parables*, 77, n. 8; Pesch, 1:243) should in no way preclude a similar usage by Jesus.

However, Jeremias has also shown that not only "the word" corresponds to the language of the early Church, but the very expressions pertaining to "the word" in 4:13–20 are at home in the early Christian mission (Jeremias, *Parables*, 77–78). For example, the word is "received" (4:16, cf. Acts 17:11; 1 Thess 1:6; 2:13; 2 Cor 11:4; James 1:21) "with joy" (4:16; cf. 1 Thess 1:6); persecution comes "because of the word" (4:17, cf. 1 Thess 1:6; 2 Tim 1:8; 1:9); the word causes offense (4:17; cf. 1 Pet 2:8) and it brings forth fruit (4:20; cf. Col 1:6, 10). This material, along with Mark's four other uses of "the word," certainly indicates that "the word" was very much a part of the technical language of the early Church. If it is not inappropriate to attribute this language to Jesus, it is even less inappropriate to attribute it to the early Church.

15 "These are the ones on the path, where the word is sown" poses quite clearly the dilemma of having two different "seeds" sown. First, the parable's seed (4:5) that "fell on the path" is here identified as "the ones . . . when they hear the word." Yet, as in 4:14, "the word" (ὁ λόγος) is also the seed sown and thus a second seed is introduced which obtains for the rest of this verse when Satan comes and takes "the word" away (αἴρει τὸν λόγον τὸν ἐσπαρμένον), not "the ones on the path" (οἱ παρὰ τὴν ὁδόν).

Many interpreters have noted a similar shift in a seed metaphor in 4 Ezra where in 8:41–44 people are represented by seed sown, not all of which takes root or will be saved. In 4 Ezra 9:31 the seed represents the Law that is sown in God's people that will bring forth fruit. Yet this example merely illustrates the possible uses of seed as a metaphor and hardly explains the present dilemma of shifting between metaphors within the same parable. The attempt by Moule (*Neotestamentica*, 112) and Payne (*Perspectives*, 172–77; *NTS* 26 [1979–80] 564–68) to ameliorate this awkward shifting between seeds by noting that "sown" can refer both to seed sown ("the word") and fields or soil that is sown (the various types of soil) unfortunately misses the point at issue. The interpretation does not shift between "seed" sown and "soils" sown but between two different "seeds." The one seed is extraneous to the details of the parable and identified as "the word." The other seed is indigenous to the parable and identified as the various "hearers of the word."

The interpretation identifies the "birds" with "Satan," an identification that finds a parallel in *Jub* 11:11 (cf. *Apoc. Abr.* 13:3–7) and explains the seed's fate by Satan's opposition rather than in the failure of the seed (Pesch, 1:243; Ernst, 136). Paul also uses this motif in the mission setting of 1 Thess 2:18; 3:5 and 2 Cor 11:3. The "path" remains an unidentified detail of the parable.

16–17 The explanation of the seed sown on rocky ground (4:5–6) shifts back to the "hearers" as the seed sown, and it develops the very elements in 4:5–6 that disrupt the parable's symmetrical structure (see *Comment* on 4:5–6). Furthermore, the "seed" remains the subject of the verbs rather than giving way to the destructive agent (birds, sun, thistles) of the parable, a change in focus beginning to show in the disruptive expansion of the parable in 4:6–7. These changes give further indication of a later shift in focus in the interpretation and its carry over into the parable itself (see *Comment* on 4:5–6).

The sudden emergence of the seed (ἐξανέτειλεν, 4:5a) is identified as "suddenly receiving the word with joy." This description sets the hearers off from the first analogy where the seed was snatched away before a response was possible. The lack of root (μὴ ἔχειν ῥίζαν) makes the reception very "temporary" (πρόσκαιροι). And this sets it off from the following analogy where the seed evidently grows until it is eventually choked before producing fruit. These seeds do not last long because the parable's "sun" is here identified as "affliction" (θλίψις) and "persecution because of the word" (διωγμοῦ διὰ τὸν λόγον), again terms associated with the early Christian mission (Rom 8:35; 2 Cor 4:8–9; 2 Thess 1:4). And the result is a "falling away" (σκανδαλίζονται), a term meaning to be trapped or snared but used in biblical Greek to describe apostasy or a falling away (G. Stählin, *TDNT* 7 [1971] 349).

18–19 Again we have the mixing of the seed metaphors, the "hearers" and "the word." The seed that falls among thistles (4:7) is identified as the ones "hearing the word" (τὸν λόγον ἀκούσαντες), but it is "the word" itself that is "choked" (συμπνίγουσιν τὸν λόγον). The focus falls on the "thistles" which receive an expanded interpretation as the "anxieties of this age, the deceit of wealth, and the desires for other things" (αἱ μέριμναι τοῦ αἰῶνος, ἡ ἀπάτη τοῦ πλούτου, αἱ ἐπιθυμίαι). As with most of the identifying terms in the interpretation, these too are rare in the Synoptics. The first appears only in Luke 21:34; the second only here; and the third is omitted in Matt 13:22 and Luke 8:14. Pesch (1:244) has noted the movement from those who never receive the word before Satan snatches it away, to those who receive it but succumb to adverse, external pressures, to those who receive it and have it ultimately choked out by concerns and attractions from within themselves. The parable's interpretation, therefore, addresses the full range of the mission situation from the proclamation of the word to life as part of the community of faith.

20 The final analogy returns to the "hearers" as the seed. They not only receive the word but produce fruit corresponding to the triple response found in the parable (4:8). Rather than a distributive description of three respective seeds, as in the parable, the interpretation uses this triad to characterize the harvest in general.

A more subtle form of comparison between the last analogy and the previous three lies in the shift of tenses used in reference to the "hearing." In each of the previous expressions, the aorist tense in the oblique mood (subjunctive, participle) indicating punctiliar action has described the situation; here the present tense in the indicative mood characterizes the continuing reality of hearing the word. This may correspond to the exhortations to hear in 4:3 and 4:9 that enclose the parable as well as the exhortations in 4:23–24a.

Explanation

We have in 4:13–20 a later application of the Parable of the Seeds to the mission context of the early Church. Perhaps the presence of this rare explanation of a parable by Jesus in the tradition indicates its ultimate roots along with the parable in Jesus' ministry. In any case, the interpretation as it now stands goes beyond the limits of the parable in detail and structure. The language, though not necessarily exclusively that of the early Church, certainly has its place there and most likely reflects a later stage in the development of the tradition than that of the parable itself. But has the interpretation significantly altered the thrust of the parable?

Many have responded in the affirmative and read the interpretation as a paraenetic warning to the "hearers." The parable's opening imperative (4:3a) and closing exhortation (4:9) to "hear" appear to set the stage for such a reading. Accordingly, the interpretation explains the parable as a warning against "hearing" in the first three categories of respondents and an admonition for all "hearers" to be like the fourth category that "bears fruit."

This reading of 4:13–20 from the standpoint of the introductory and concluding imperatives surrounding the parable may accurately identify "hearing" as the connecting link used to bind more tightly the interpretation with its clear emphasis on "hearing the word" to the parable. But this reading takes imperatives that most likely have been added at a later stage in the development of the tradition to explain the interpretation (4:13–20) rather than letting the interpretation explain itself. Consequently, 4:3a, 9 have become the basis for distorting the thrust of the interpretation.

Our analysis of 4:14–20 gives no basis for taking its meaning so differently in kind from that of the parable. The subject throughout has been "the seed(s)." In fact, the major difficulty in rendering the interpretation has been the shift in subject from "hearers" as the seed planted to "the word" as the planted seed, not a shift from the seeds sown to the soils sown. At no point do the "soils" themselves become central to the interpretation. All four soils remain unidentified. This gives even more basis for rejecting any title or explanation built on the popular misconception of the role of the "soils." Thus we have neither a summons to be "good soil" nor a warning against being "a path," "rocky soil" or "thistles." The thrust throughout remains, as it was in the parable itself, on the fate of the seed(s) sown.

When we concentrate on the fate of the seed(s), it becomes clear that the seed(s) are more victims than culpable for their demise. Satan and the evil forces of this age are the subjects; the sown seeds are the objects of destruction. The "word" itself is the victim in two of the three examples (4:15, 18–19), and it could hardly be held accountable or responsive to a paraenetic admonition. In the one negative example where the "hearers" are the subject, their fate is expressed in the passive (4:17). The only possible exception is the fourth example (4:20), but even there the "hearers" do nothing more commendable than those in the second example (4:16). Each "hears and receives" the word. The major distinction between the fourth and the first three is in the maturing to produce fruit, a quality inherent in the seed rather than something to be demanded. Thus the thrust of 4:13–19 is more descriptive than prescriptive.

If, then, the interpretation functions more descriptively than prescriptively, what purpose does it serve? In one sense, it serves the same purpose as the parable itself, namely, to address the realities of both Jesus' ministry and that of the Church's mission. The parable and its interpretation climax in a statement of an abundant harvest. Only cosmetic verbal changes distinguish the latter from the former. The interpretation extends the figure of the parable simply by identifying the seed as "hearers" who "receive the word and bear fruit." The "fruit" is the same and produced in the same proportions, though described collectively rather than individually. The parable's eschatological thrust has not been altered.

At the same time, evidence of opposition and failure precedes this climax in both the parable and its interpretation. Yet in this regard, the interpretation does alter the parable's emphasis. No longer comparing three seeds that meet differing ends with three that produce a varied harvest, the interpretation sets three examples of failure against one of productivity. This shifts the balance toward the negative. Furthermore, the developed identification of the forces of opposition highlights this portion of the parable and indicate the shift in emphasis between the parable set in Jesus' ministry and its interpretation set in the mission of the early Church.

Whereas the parable expressed the good news of Jesus' message about God's vulnerable but redemptive activity in the world, the interpretation expressed a keen awareness of opposition and defeat of "the word" of God's redemptive activity through Jesus Christ without losing sight of the "hearers" that produce abundant fruit. Whereas the parable set forth God's activity as seen in the harvest despite the adversity seen in the unproductive seed, the interpretation explained the realities of adversity without losing sight of the reality of the harvest. This shift in emphasis may indicate the use of the parable to offer assurance and encouragement for the mission in the face of the experience of opposition and failure.

If the focus on "hearing the word" that dominates the interpretation influenced the introduction of the summons to "hear" surrounding the parable (4:3a, 9), we must read these imperatives from the standpoint of the interpretation. Since all four examples identified the seed as those who "hear the word" and since the interpretation gives little indication in itself of a paraenesis pertaining to responsible hearing, these imperatives most likely functioned more as a thematically related call to attention (cf. "See," 4:3a) and an invitation for those who could (4:9) to hear with understanding (4:33), an invitation that set the stage for the interpretation whose focal point was "hearing the word."

At the stage in the pre-Markan tradition when 4:10–12 was inserted, this interpretation functioned as an example of how the "mystery of the Kingdom" was given through special instruction to those "around" Jesus. They in contrast to "those outside" would identify with the seed that produced fruit. For them, the Kingdom of God had come to fruition through "the word" in their life. "Those outside" would refer to the ones who heard "the word" but failed to produce fruit for various reasons.

In the interpretation of the parable, the failure to produce fruit or the destruction of the seed was attributed to outside forces. In 4:11b, 12, Isa 6:9–10 provides the theological explanation for the failure. These explanations are not incompatible, since divine judgment can take place through the forces of evil (e.g., "The god of this world has blinded the minds of unbelievers," 2 Cor 4:4). But the line between productive and nonproductive seeds appears to have been sharply drawn, a situation that may well reflect the mission experience of the early Church.

For Mark this interpretation illustrates both the "mystery of the Kingdom," which is not only represented by Jesus and his ministry but also by the "gospel," the "word" of good news (cf. 1:14–15; 10:29). To proclaim "the word" (1:45; 4:33) was but another way of announcing the "gospel" about God's activity through Jesus in bringing the Kingdom. Therefore, the interpretation corresponds with the parable in pointing to Jesus' message, the gospel of the Kingdom, as taught by Jesus (4:3–8, 26–33) and proclaimed as the word (4:14–20).

At the same time, by introducing this interpretation with two questions critical of the disciples' lack of understanding, Mark indicates to his readers that "insiders" or believers may also lack understanding. While this may offer comfort to his audience in that even "the Twelve" lacked understanding, the tone of rebuke in 4:13 comes as a warning and an encouragement to grasp the meaning of Jesus' ministry. The fact that Jesus proceeds to give them an explanation (4:14–20; cf. 4:34b) shows that they not only needed instruction but also the opportunity to learn. At stake here, as throughout Mark's Gospel beginning with 1:14–15, is the heart of the gospel, "the word," i.e., the Kingdom of God. This becomes apparent in 4:11a and the fact that this parable is the "key" to all the parables, especially 4:26–32 (so 4:13b).

F. Summons to Hear   (4:21–25)

Bibliography

Ambrozic, A. H. *The Hidden Kingdom: A Redaction Critical Study of the References to the Kingdom in Mark's Gospel.* CBQMS 2. Washington, DC: Catholic Biblical Association, 1972. **Carlston, C. E.** *The Parables of the Triple Tradition.* Philadelphia: Fortress, 1975. **Chilton, B.** *A Galilean Rabbi and His Bible.* GNS 8. Wilmington, DE: Michael Glazier, 1984. **Dodd, C. H.** *The Parables of the Kingdom.* 1961. **Gnilka, J.** *Die Verstockung Israels: Isaias 6,9–10 in der Theologie der Synoptiker.* Munich: Kösel, 1961. **Jeremias, J.** "Die Lampe unter dem Scheffel." *ZNW* 39 [1940] 237–40 = *Abba: Studien zur neutestamentlichen Theologie und Zeitgeschichte.* Göttingen: Vandenhoeck & Ruprecht, 1966. ————. *The Parables of Jesus.* 1972. **Kelber, W.** *The Kingdom in Mark.* 1974. **Klauck, H.-J.** *Allegorie und Allegorese in synoptischen Gleichnistexten.* NA 13, Münster: Aschendorff, 1978. **Marcus, J.** *The Mystery of the Kingdom of God.* SBLDS 90. Atlanta: Scholars Press, 1986. **Marxsen, W.** "Redaktionsgeschichtliche Erklärung der sogennanten Parabeltheorie des Markus." *ZTK* 52 (1955) 255–71 = *Der Exeget als Theologe: Vorträge zum Neuen Testament.* Gütersloh: Mohn, 1968. 13–28. **Neuhäusler, E.** "Mit welchem Masstab misst Gott die Menschen? Deutung zweier Jesusspruche." *BibLeb* 11 (1970) 104–113. **Räisänen, H.** *Die Parabeltheorie im Markusevangelium.* Schriften der finnischen exegetischen Gesellschaft 25. Helsinki: Finnish Exegetical Society, 1973. **Reploh, K.-G.** *Markus— Lehrer der Gemeinde.* 1969. **Schneider, G.** "Das Bildwort von der Lampe." *ZNW* 61 (1970) 83–209.

Translation

21 And he said to them: "A lamp is not brought in [a] to be placed under a bushel [b] or a bed, is it? Is it not brought in [c] to be placed on a lampstand? 22 For nothing is hidden except that it might be revealed; nor has anything become secret but that it might come into the open. 23 If anyone has ears to hear, let that one hear."

24 And he said to them: "Pay attention to what you hear. By what measure you measure it will be measured to you and given additionally to you. [d] 25 For those who have, it shall be given to them. And those that do not have, even what they have will be taken."

Notes

[a] The text reads ἔρχεται, which may be a Semitism (Jeremias, ABBA, 100), though a similar use of ἔρχεσθαι with inanimate subjects occurs in Greek (J. Behm, TDNT 2 [1964] 667). ἅπτεται (D [W f13] it samss bopt) is a later attempt to smooth the text (cf. Luke 11:33).

[b] "Bushel" (μόδιος) is a Latinism (modius) and primarily a measure (ca. two gallons dry measure, Taylor, 263) but, like the English, "bushel" can be used in the sense of a container.

[c] This clause supplies an ellipsis in the Greek text.

[d] Hauck-Greeven reads τοῖς ἀκούουσιν with A Θ 0107 0133 0167 f1.13 in keeping with context of 4:23, 24a and 4:9, 14–20. The phrase is omitted by א B C L Δ 700 892 lat, though perhaps the omission is assimilated to Matt 7:2 // Luke 6:40.

Form / Structure / Setting

This section consists of four sayings at the heart of which lie two exhortations to hear (4:23, 24b). Each of the four sayings belongs to the broad category of wisdom sayings in that they reflect observations drawn from everyday experience. Jeremias (*Parables,* 90) has classified this material as a double parable in which two metaphors (4:21b, 24b) have attracted two explanatory sayings (4:22, 25) to form parables ("lamp," "measure") combined around the theme of measure ("bushel" and "measure").

Each of the four sayings appears in Matthew and Luke but in different contexts. Luke follows Mark 4:21–22, 25 in 8:16–18 but also has Q-parallels in 6:38 (cf. Mark 4:24c); 11:33 (cf. Mark 4:21); 12:2 (cf. Mark 4:22); and 19:26 (cf. Mark 4:25). Matthew only follows Mark 4:25 in 13:12 but has Q-parallels in 5:15 (cf. Mark 4:21); 7:2 (cf. Mark 4:24c); 10:26 (cf. Mark 4:22). Since these sayings appear in different contexts throughout the Synoptics, it is clear that they circulated as independent sayings. Each may have had its roots in Jesus' ministry, but the original context so important for determining their meaning in that setting has been lost to us.

More debatable is whether Mark found these sayings grouped together in his tradition (Taylor, 262; Jeremias, *Parables,* 91; Pesch, 1:247; Ambrozic, *Kingdom,* 103; Ernst, 138) or first combined them himself (Reploh, *Lehrer,* 61–62; Schweizer, 195; Grundmann, 127; Gnilka, 1:179–80, 182; Schmithals, 1:242; Marcus, *Mystery,* 130). The use of the ἵνα-clause in 4:22 and the influence of 4:25 on 4:24c may tip the scales in favor of Mark's redactional hand (see *Comment*).

A vast consensus attributes the present location of this material to Mark's redaction. If we eliminate the redactional introductions along with the exhortations to hear (4:23, 24a), we are left with two sayings followed by explanatory statements (4:21b–22, 4:24c–25) whose only possible logical connection could be the use of a measure (μόδιος) in the first (4:21b) and the reference to measure (μέτρῳ) in the second (4:24c) (so Bultmann, 325, n. 1; Jeremias, *Parables,* 91). Even this connection seems improbable, because μόδιος is used more as a container than a unit of measure in 4:21b. As we shall see, the two groups of sayings now relate to each other through their relation to the larger context of Mark 4.

Mark's redactional hand within the sayings has been found by some in the use of ἔρχεται, the interrogative form, and the reference to a "couch" in 4:21. Similarly, Mark appears to have adapted 4:22 to its present context by the use of the ἵνα-clauses instead of the smoother relative clauses. And προστεθήσεται in 4:24 breaks the rhythm and symmetry of 4:24c which may indicate the influence of 4:25 on this saying. Structurally, the section consists of two groups of sayings, each opening with the introductory formula καὶ ἔλεγεν αὐτοῖς (4:21a, 24a). The first group concludes with an exhortation to hear (4:23) and the second begins with a similar warning (4:24b). These exhortations form the heart of the complex by rounding off the one saying followed by an explanatory statement (4:21b–22) and introducing the second saying followed by an explanatory statement (4:24c–25). This accent corresponds to the emphasis on "hearing" found in the previous parable (4:3a,9), discussion (4:11–12) and interpretation (4:14–20).

As to setting, Mark inserts this material between the interpretation of the Parable of the Seeds (4:14–20) and the seed parables of 4:26–32. It continues the motif of "hearing" from 4:3–20, and the motif of concealment and becoming publicly apparent (4:21–22) corresponds to a similar theme in 4:11–12 and in the parables of 4:26–32. Furthermore, the motif of special privilege and accountability in 4:24–25 connects with the thrust of 4:11a and the hard questions in 4:13. This contextual setting in Mark 4 greatly influences how one then reads these generalized sayings.

Comment

21 This saying differs from the parallels in Luke 8:16 and Matt 5:15 // Luke 11:33 and the *Gos. Thom.* 33 in form and syntactical structure. Whereas Mark poses a double question with two ἵνα-purpose clauses forming an antithetical parallelism (μήτι, οὐχ), the parallels make a statement that concludes with an expression of the lamp's intended function, namely, to give light. This differ-ence may reflect variations in the oral tradition. Matt 5:15 has generally been considered to reflect the earliest form of the saying (Jeremias, *Abba*, 99–100; Schneider, *ZNW* 61 [1970] 184–95). The absence, however, in Mark of this type of double question forming a negative (μήτι)/positive (οὐκ) antithe-sis, his lack of negative questions in general (cf. 2:19 and 14:19, each tradi-tional), and the evidence supporting a tendency in traditional development to move from the interrogative to the declarative form (Schneider, *ZNW* 61 [1970] 187) contradict the suggestion that Mark has redactionally reshaped this tradition (cf. Schneider, *ZNW* 61 [1970] 197–99; Klauck, *Allegorie*, 228; Marcus, *Mystery*, 130–33).

"And he said to them" (καὶ ἔλεγεν αὐτοῖς) introduces 4:21–23 and 4:24–25 into this context (see *Comment* on 4:11). Contextually, "them" could refer to the private audience of 4:10–20 (cf. 4:11) or to the public crowds in 4:1–2 and 4:36 (cf. 4:2b). The exhortation, however, in 4:24–25 fits more closely Mark's portrait of the disciples' struggle (4:13) to comprehend fully the "mystery of the Kingdom" given to them (4:11). Therefore, the content of 4:24–25 may well suggest that the evangelist had in mind the narrower audi-ence, the representatives of his own readers (see *Comment* on 4:13) to whom the "mystery of the Kingdom" had been given (Marcus, *Mystery*, 140).

"A lamp is not brought in" or literally "the lamp does not come" (μήτι ἔρχεται ὁ λύχνος) contrasts with the parallels which speak of a "burning lamp" (καίειν—Matt 5:15) or "lighting a lamp" (ἅπτειν—Luke 8:16; 11:33, cf. *Gos. Thom.* 33). The use of the definite article here has no more significance than the use of the definite article throughout the saying (τὸν μόδιον, τὴν κλίνην, τὴν λυχνίαν; cf. Luke 8:16). And since ἔρχεται occurs with inanimate subjects in both Semitic and Greek sources (see *Note* a), this construction provides no solid evidence of an earlier Aramaism. Yet Mark most likely found this construction in his tradition. To link the choice of this verb even remotely to Jesus' "coming" (Grundmann, 128; Gnilka, 1:180; Klauck, *Allegorie*, 234; Marcus, *Mystery*, 131) or even the Kingdom's "coming" (Lohmeyer, 86; Schneider, *ZNW* 61 [1970] 195) not only allegorizes this parable in a way atypical for Mark but it ignores the fact that Mark uses this traditional motif (cf. 2:17 and 10:42; 13:26 and 14:62; 9:1 and 11:9) but goes to no extra lengths elsewhere to emphasize either Jesus' or the Kingdom's "coming."

Although the evangelist himself most likely did not allegorize this parable by altering the verb, the location of the saying with this construction in the context of the "mystery of the Kingdom" in 4:11 and the parables of the Kingdom in 4:26–32 does make this reference to a "coming" all the more appropriate. The idea of a "Kingdom that comes" was certainly at home in Judaism as seen in their common prayers (e.g., second petition of the Kaddish; eleventh of the Eighteen Benedictions) and the early Church (e.g., "Thy Kingdom come," Matt 6:10; cf. 9:1; 11:9).

"Under a bushel" (ὑπὸ τὸν μόδιον) offers one of two illogical locations for a lamp introduced by ἵνα. Despite Jeremias' frequently cited references to the use of a bushel to extinguish a lamp in emergency situations on the Sabbath and other holy days according to the Rabbis and his own surmising that such practice was an everyday means of extinguishing a lamp to avoid unpleasant smoke and smell (*Abba*, 100–102), this reference to a "bushel" most likely has nothing to do with extinguishing the lamp. Klauck (*Allegorie*, 230) has raised questions about Jeremias' meager evidence and certainly his unsupported assumption about everyday practice. Schneider (*ZNW* 61 [1970] 189–90) has noted that the rabbinic texts speak of placing something over a lamp to extinguish it rather than setting a lamp under a container. The closest analogy appears to be Gideon's instruction to his men in Judg 7:16 (Klauck, *Allegorie*, 230, n. 219).

"Under a couch" (ὑπὸ τὴν κλίνην) disrupts the symmetry between a balanced alternative of "under a bushel" or "on a lampstand." This consideration together with the absence of "under a couch" in Matt 5:15, Luke 11:33 and *Gos. Thom.* 33 has led many (cf. Pesch, 1:249) to view this phrase as a later expansion either in the pre-Markan tradition (Gnilka, 1:179) or by Mark himself (Jeremias, *Abba*, 99–100; Schneider, *ZNW* 61 [1970], 191; Klauck, *Allegorie*, 228). Since one does not place a lamp under a couch to extinguish it, this phrase and the explanatory saying in 4:22 make clear that the thrust of the Markan parable lies in the contrast between a lamp hidden or covered and a lamp apparent or visible rather than between lighting and extinguishing a lamp. The repudiation of the former and the affirmation of the latter is heightened by the formal use of a question expecting a negative reply in the one (μήτι) instance and a positive reply in the other (οὐκ). At issue is the proper or expected function of a lamp.

What then was the point of the parable? "Lamp" serves as a metaphor in a number of ways in the OT and Judaism (for God—2 Sam 22:29; David—2 Sam 21:17; Messiah—Zech 4:2; Torah—Ps 119:105; Israel, Jerusalem, Temple—cf. Wis 18:4). The different contexts for this saying in the Gospels (Matt 5:15—applied to disciples; Luke 11:33—with other sayings about light and darkness and the *Gos. Thom.* 33) indicate that it circulated in the early Church as an isolated saying, so we can only speculate about its setting and consequent meaning in Jesus' ministry. Dodd (*Parables*, 114) attributed it to Jesus' charge against the Jewish leaders for their interference in his ministry (cf. Matt 23:13; Luke 11:52). Jeremias (*Parables*, 121) has taken the parable as a reference to Jesus' rejection of the warning to protect himself against danger by extinguishing the light of his ministry. A more fitting interpretation places this parable originally in the context of Jesus' parabolic teaching about the Kingdom (Klauck, *Allegorie*, 233).

In its present Markan context three considerations qualify the saying's meaning. First, 4:22 now conditions the parable (cf. γάρ). Second, the evangelist has followed this material with two other sayings (4:24b–25) and separated these by two exhortations to "hear" (4:23, 24a). Third, and most importantly, the evangelist has set this material into a context between the interpretation of the first parable (4:14–20) and two other parables (4:26–32). Some would add a fourth consideration, namely, the evangelist's apparent addition of 4:11–12 to the larger context. But this begins with the assumption that Mark has redactionally added both 4:11–12 and 4:21–25. Before pursuing the significance of the parable in Mark, we must consider the "explanation" given in 4:22.

22 This saying comes in the form of a synonymous parallelism. Luke 8:17 follows Mark 4:22 and a similar saying appears in Matt 10:26 and Luke 12:2 in differing contexts as well as the *Gos. Thom.* 5 and *P. Oxyr.* 654, 4. Again the absence of a common context indicates that this saying too circulated as an isolated tradition in the early Church. Here we find it combined with 4:21 by γάρ. "Nothing is hidden . . . nor has anything become secret" (οὐ γὰρ ἐστιν κρυπτόν . . . οὐδὲ ἐγένετο ἀπόκρυφον) begin the parallel statements and on first impression seem to concur with the negative (μήτι) question of 4:21 about placing a lamp under something. But this correspondence breaks down when we discover that these statements speak in fact exclusively of things that *have been* hidden and *are* secret. Consequently, 4:22 stands in tension with the negative question of 4:21. Whereas the latter denies that one would bring a lamp to cover it, 4:22 assumes that something is covered. In this way, 4:22 modifies 4:21 by suggesting that the lamp has indeed been covered, though contrary to the expectations for a lamp.

"Except in order to be revealed . . . but in order that it might come into the open" (ἐὰν μὴ ἵνα φανερωθῇ . . . ἀλλ' ἵνα ἔλθη εἰς φανερόν) conclude and qualify the respective opening statements. Strictly speaking, these statements are self-contradictory (Klostermann, 48; Grundmann, 128). One does not hide something in order to make it known.

The other occurrences of this saying, including the parallel in Luke 8:17, avoid this difficulty by employing a relative clause rather than Mark's ἵνα-clauses. Instead of giving disclosure as the reason for the concealment, the parallels simply make a general observation that everything hidden will eventually be revealed. Some have traced the difference in syntax between a relative pronoun and a ἵνα construction to a misreading in Mark's text of the ambiguous Aramaic ٦, *dĕ,* (see Taylor, 264) which can be rendered as introducing either a relative or a purpose clause (see *Comment* on 4:12). This explanation, however, accounts for Mark's different syntax without resolving the problem of Mark's meaning. The ἵνα-clauses must be rendered here as purpose clauses.

Although this saying removed from a context makes little sense, placed in the narrower context of 4:21 (γάρ) and the broader context of Mark 4 the saying with its ἵνα-clauses does come into focus. Each of the parallel statements corresponds to the positive (οὐκ) question in 4:21. The purpose of concealing something is that it might be seen or visible (4:22a, b); the purpose of the lamp is that it might be apparent or placed on a lampstand rather than hidden or covered by either a bushel or a bed (4:21b).

Therefore, this saying "explains" the parable in 4:21 by implying that the lamp or its referent, despite its expected purpose or function, was indeed covered (4:21a), but this unnatural or unexpected "covering" was intentional or deliberate "in order that" it might be revealed or be "placed on a lampstand" to carry out its expected purpose. Therefore, the shift from the earlier relative clauses to the purpose clauses most likely took place when this saying was combined with the parable of 4:21 as its "explanation" either by Mark or earlier in the development of the tradition. The appropriateness of this combination (4:21–22) for Mark's immediate context as well as the unusually high number of ἵνα-clauses in Mark (Mark—64x, cf. Matt—39x; Luke—46x) points to Mark's redactional reworking of this traditional saying and his linking the two sayings by γάρ.

The key to understanding both 4:21 and 4:22 lies in determining the referent of the "lamp" and that which was "hidden" (κρυπτόν) or a "secret" (ἀπόκρυον). Since Wrede (*Secret*, 70–71), many scholars have found the referent in the "mystery" (μυστήριον) and the concealment motif of 4:11 (*Secret*, 70–71). "Almost everyone seems to think that 4:21–22 speak of the provisional reign of the secret which is, for a time, entrusted to a few but is destined to be manifest to all very soon" (Ambrozic, *Kingdom*, 103). Accordingly, for Mark these verses set the record straight by summoning his community to their missionary activity and responsibility of making known what had been concealed from the "outsiders" but entrusted to the disciples by Jesus during his ministry. These verses speak of the disclosure of the "messianic" (Wrede, *Secret*, 70–71) or "Kingdom" secret (Brown, *JBL* 92 [1973] 60–94) after Easter.

This interpretation not only places far too much weight on a clue that first appears in 9:9 (rather belated, if it is such an important clue for the reader; so Räisänen, *Parabeltheorie*, 79–80) but it runs afoul of the broader context of Mark 4, not least in the use of μυστήριον itself in 4:11. We noted in 4:13 that though the disciples had been "given the mystery of the Kingdom" they themselves did not understand the Parable of the Seeds (4:3–8) and thus could not know the meaning of "all the parables." "All the parables" certainly included for Mark the explicit "Kingdom" parables of 4:26–32. By virtue of this association of understanding or not understanding the Parable of the Seeds with understanding the "Kingdom" parables of the Seed Growing Secretly and the Mustard Seed, the Parable of the Seeds also becomes a "Kingdom" parable (see *Comment* on 4:13). Therefore, the contextual referent for the "lamp" (4:21) and that which was "hidden" only to become visible (4:22) is the "Kingdom of God" itself, the subject of the parables. Mark, therefore, has added the sayings of 4:21–22 as another "Kingdom parable."

As noted in 4:11 (see *Comment*), "mystery" (μυστήριον), biblically and technically understood, connotes revelation rather than concealment (G. Bornkamm, *TDNT* 4 [1967] 818–19). In other words, the disciples had received the "Kingdom of God" through the same "all things" that remained "riddles" for "those outside" (4:11b). And it was precisely the reception of this "revelation of the Kingdom of God" that made their lack of understanding of the Parable of the Seeds all the more surprising, if not culpable (4:13). But what was this "mystery"/"revelation" that they had received, if not the experience of the presence of the "Kingdom of God" itself?

This is the message of the parables in Mark 4, namely, that the Kingdom is above all present. But it is present in an unexpected manner and form. The Parable of the Seeds (4:3–8, 14–20) depicts the Kingdom as present though unexpectedly vulnerable and resistible. The parables of the Seed Growing Secretly and the Mustard Seed (4:26–32) underscore the enigma of the Kingdom's unexpected presence in seed rather than mature form. Consequently, the Kingdom's presence can be overlooked. It appears as though it has come "under a bushel" or "hidden" from public view. At the same time, the parables of 4:26–29 and 30–32 also indicate a future dimension of the Kingdom much more in keeping with the expectation that God's rule will be completely revealed and supreme, a time when the "lamp" will be placed on a stand and what is now "hidden" will be made public for all to see.

Read against this broader context of Mark 4, 4:21–22 represents another parable of the Kingdom which speaks of the Kingdom's enigmatic present as well as its ultimate future. The fact that the Kingdom's coming has not been made irrefutably and publicly known means neither that it has not come nor that it will not be revealed as a lamp on a lampstand to give light for all. Rather these sayings explicitly point to the ultimate purpose of the lamp, namely, that though it is concealed, it will be placed in public.

For Mark and his readers the time of the Kingdom's being made public, the lamp's ultimate purpose, is still future (Ernst, 139). It was not marked by the cross and resurrection (Wrede, *Secret*, 70–71; Cranfield, 164–65; Gnilka, 1:181; Carlston, *Parables*, 155; cf. Marcus, *Mystery*, 150–151). Consequently, the point of the Kingdom's present and its future still needs to be made for Mark's audience, who like the disciples had been given the "mystery of the Kingdom," the experience of the Kingdom present, but struggle to understand the enigma of the Kingdom's presence (cf. 4:13).

23 This struggle gives rise to the exhortation, "If anyone has ears to hear, let that one hear!" an adaptation of the exhortation in 4:9 to summon Mark's readers to attentive listening to Jesus' message.

24 "Pay attention to what you hear" (βλέπετε τί ἀκούετε), similar to the double imperative preceding the parable in 4:3 (ἀκούετε, ἰδού), underscores the evangelist's concern that his audience mark well what is said. These two exhortations to hear (4:23, 24b) form the heart of 4:21–25. Yet this alignment is more a coincidental result of the typical use of these exhortations than an editorial design (cf. Schmithals, 1:242). The first exhortation (4:23) consistently concludes a sayings complex (e.g., 4:9; Matt 11:15; 13:43; Luke 14:35; Rev 2:7, 11, 17, 29, etc.; *Gos. Thom.* 8, 21, 24, 63, 65, 96); the second exhortation functions as an introductory formula (e.g., 4:3; 7:14 // Matt 15:10). Consequently, they come together at the center of 4:21–25 as a concluding (4:23) and introductory (4:24a) formula of exhortation.

"By what measure you measure" (ἐν ᾧ μέτρῳ μετρεῖτε) appears as a saying in the Sermon tradition of Matt 7:2 and Luke 6:38 where it refers to the final judgment. Chilton (*Rabbi*, 123–25) has noted the presence of this proverbial saying in the *Tg. Isaiah* and the Talmud. Of interest is the use of the second person form in the Gospels and the Targum as compared to the third person form in the Talmud.

Mark has most likely inserted the sayings of 4:24b–25 into the context of the parable in 4:21–22. But the use of a second introductory formula, "And he said to them" (καὶ ἔλεγεν αὐτοῖς), along with the introductory exhortation also suggests that these sayings, though introduced coincidentally with 4:21–23, were not intended to be a continuation of the parable in 4:21–22. At most, they pick up the theme of the exhortation to hear in 4:23 (cf. 4:3, 9; 4:14–20).

"Given additionally to you" (προστεθήσεται ὑμῖν) goes beyond the saying in Matt 7:2 and Luke 6:38. This clause breaks the saying's structural rhythm and symmetry as well as the equivalency correspondence between what one does and what one receives. One receives even more than what one would expect. Its meaning and perhaps its presence is explained by the following saying.

25 This gnomic saying also appears in a common context at the end of the Parable of the Talents/Pounds in Matt 25:29 and Luke 19:26, where the saying explains the gain of one servant at the expense of another. It corresponds to the proverbial "The rich get richer; the poor get poorer." Here it serves as the "explanation" of 4:24c (γάρ). Consequently, the accent falls on the first half, the receiving (cf. δοθήσεται, προστεθήσεται), rather than the taking (ἀρθήσεται). This should alert us against taking Mark's saying primarily as a warning. It functions more as a promise than a threat.

But to what do these sayings refer? Many see these sayings to be an expansion on the theme of 4:14–20, a theme keynoted again in the opening exhortation to "hear" and in the variant "to those who hear" (Cranfield, 167; Gnilka, 1:181–82; cf. Kelber, *Kingdom,* 38–39). As such, these sayings reinforce the call to a proper hearing illustrated by the seed that falls on the good soil in contrast to the other seeds. But this reading is forced at best. First, this understanding of 4:24–25 would mean that Mark took the parable and its interpretation in 4:3–8, 14–20 as primarily a paraenetic call to proper hearing rather than a statement about the enigmatic nature of the Kingdom (see *Explanation* on 4:14–20). Second, when read against the backdrop of 4:14–20, the warning motif (4:25b), which is secondary here, becomes primary as a warning against losing the word and experiencing the fate of the first three seeds. What "more" (4:24c, 25a) could the productive seed (4:20) receive? Finally, 4:24c–25 places the responsibility on the reader, whereas 4:14–20 describes the ultimate outcome of the various seeds rather than their culpable or meritorious "hearing."

Others have interpreted these verses with reference to 4:21–23, whose supposed thrust is a mission challenge to make public the secret reign of God (Pesch, 1:253; Reploh, *Lehrer,* 70–71; Ambrozic, *Kingdom,* 104). Accordingly, these sayings call for an active engagement in the mission of making public the "mystery of the Kingdom" that had been imparted exclusively for a period of time to a few. The promised reward surpasses the effort (4:24c, 25a), but the warning remains for those who fail to take their part in the mission (4:25b). To that extent, the interpretation of 4:14–20 illustrates their fate. Either they produce for the harvest (4:20) or, like the three seeds that fail to produce, they will end up with a loss (4:14–19). The weakness of this interpretation lies in the assumption that 4:21–22 speaks of the Church's present mission to make public what had been hidden during Jesus' ministry (see *Comment* on 4:21–22).

Since the evangelist has most likely added 4:24–25 to the underlying tradition behind Mark 4, we need to weigh these verses in terms of Mark's other contributions to this chapter. The evangelist added the reproachful questions in 4:13 to form a tension between 4:11 and 4:13 that highlights the lack of understanding by those "given the mystery of the Kingdom." The evangelist has also added the parable and explanation in 4:21–22 to the three other parables in Mark 4 which have the enigmatic present/future Kingdom of God as their subject or referent. Furthermore, the evangelist concludes his parable in 4:21–22 with an exhortation to hear (4:23) and introduces 4:24c–25 with a direct challenge that the audience take note of what they hear. All this suggests that the sayings in 4:24c–25, like the questions in 4:13, point to the need for the audience who have responded to Jesus to grasp more fully the import of his teaching about the coming of the Kingdom, especially its present and future dimensions as seen in the parable of 4:21–22 and illustrated further in 4:26–29, 30–32.

Therefore, unlike the interpretation of 4:14–20, 4:24–25 does have a paraenetic function not unlike the questions of 4:13 to summon the reader/"hearers" typified by Jesus' audience to "pay attention to what they hear" (4:24b). These sayings support the summons to listen attentively with the promise of an abundant understanding and a greater experience of the Kingdom than what they already have (4:24c, 25a).

"The one who does not have" (ὅς οὐκ ἔχει). To whom does this refer? To the disciples, as an ominous threat (e.g., Gnilka, *Verstockung*, 40; 1:181) or to "those outside" to whom the "mystery of the Kingdom" has not been given, the unproductive seeds of 4:14–20 (Marcus, *Mystery*, 156–58)? The distinction may well be moot for Mark. The contrast in 4:25 does not lie between those who have ("disciples") and those who do not have ("outsiders"). Rather the ultimate contrast lies in whether they receive more or lose what they have.

The difference between "having" and "not having" is one of orientation. Seen from the perspective of the parable, all the sown seed "had it" at the outset. Only at the end can one determine who the "haves" and "have nots" really are. The distinction for Mark lies in how one responds to the "word." Attentive listening points to the productive "haves" who are blessed with more. Failure to respond exposes the "have nots" to the destructive forces that take away what they have. Since "haves" can become "have nots," this exhortation comes with a promise and a warning. Therefore, Jesus' challenge to the disciples and in turn for Mark's readers is more than a rhetorical device to set the stage for Jesus' further teaching. It comes as a warning that supports the exhortation to attentive listening.

Explanation

Mark 4:21–25 can be easily divided into two triads, each introduced by the formula, "And he said to them." The first triad accents the difference between something hidden and something visible (4:21–22); the second the abundance of reward (4:24b–25). The concluding summons to hear in 4:23 sets the stage for the introductory call to listen attentively in 4:24b. Four of these wisdom sayings circulated independently in the early Christian tradition as seen by their unrelated appearances in different contexts in Matthew and Luke. Mark may well have been the first to bring them into the combination as they now stand here. This means that we can only speculate about their context and consequent meaning in Jesus' ministry as well as in the early Church's usage.

The parabolic saying in Mark about a lamp (4:21b) gains some of its meaning from the imagery used and the antithetical structure of the saying. One does not bring a lamp into a room to place it under either a bushel or a couch but rather on a lampstand. The contrast points to the expected, normal function of a lamp to give light rather than to have the light covered. This proverbial saying also gains some of its meaning from the broader context in which it is placed, a context of three parables pertaining implicitly (4:3–20) and explicitly (4:26–29, 30–32) to the Kingdom. When taken as another "Kingdom parable," the metaphor indicates that the Kingdom, like a lamp, brings with it certain expectations. The parallel even runs through the imagery used, since the Kingdom, like a lamp, was expected to come in a public manner, visible for all to see.

This parabolic saying, however, gains its particular significance in Mark from a second explanatory saying (4:22) that follows and directly qualifies the former. By itself 4:22 appears self-contradictory. No one conceals something for the sole purpose of making it public. Yet compared with the Matthean and Lukan parallels of the saying, Mark's distinctive formulation of 4:22 becomes evident when taken in conjunction with 4:21. The function of a lamp to shine visibly (4:21) finds a correlate in the making public of everything hidden (4:22). Set against the background of the Kingdom expectation, both sayings refer to a public display of the Kingdom for all to see.

The purpose clauses of 4:22 indicate that a certain intended hiddenness or covert element preceded the manifestation. Therefore, though the function of the lamp was to give light, by implication from 4:22 it has indeed been placed under a bushel or couch, hidden from public view. In other words, 4:21–22 form a parable stating that the Kingdom has come in an unexpected manner, a manner uncharacteristic of its true character, but that such an unexpected appearance is only temporary. One can still expect its full, public revelation. Thus, 4:21–22 offer a parable of the Kingdom that focuses on its unexpected, hidden presence and points to its future appearance for all to see. These themes are also present in the subsequent parables of this collection.

Mark concludes the first group of sayings by summoning anyone who has ears, to hear. Those to whom God has given the "mystery of the Kingdom," the experience of the Kingdom, "hidden" though it may be, are exhorted to hear and grasp this message. Mark's Gospel reflects the disciples' difficulty in comprehending the coming of the Kingdom in a way different from their expectations. While this misunderstanding doubtless has its roots in the disciples' experience during Jesus' ministry, the issue most likely continued to burn in a community for whom the gospel of Jesus, Messiah, Son of God, was also proclaimed in terms of the "Kingdom of God" (1:1, 14–15), especially after Easter. Thus, Mark's readers like the disciples struggled to comprehend more fully the veiled presence and future manifestation of the Kingdom. It was as though one had brought a lamp to place it under a bushel! The community had to be reminded that the Kingdom had indeed come according to God's design and the future would make it clear, revealing it for all to see.

The evangelist begins the second group of sayings with a command to pay attention to what is heard (4:24b) that reinforces the preceding summons to hear (4:23) and strikes the key for the thrust of the two sayings that follow. Despite using the same introductory formula, "And he said to them," as in 4:21a, the evangelist does not use this group of sayings as another parable of the Kingdom. Nor does the evangelist use this group of sayings to expound directly upon the interpretation of 4:14–20 that describes four different types of hearing. Rather he uses these sayings to pick up the theme of the need for those given the "mystery of the Kingdom," those for whom the Kingdom is present in an unexpected or veiled manner, to hear and understand more fully the nature and scope of the Kingdom's coming (cf. 4:13).

Thus these sayings function in relation to the parable in 4:21–23 much as the evangelist's introductory questions in 4:13 function for the interpretation (4:14–20) of the parable in 4:3–8. Just as the reproachful questions (4:13) were directed at those given the "mystery of the Kingdom" to summon them implicitly to understand the parable in 4:3–8 by grasping its interpretation (4:14–20), this summons to pay attention to what they hear explained further by the promises of 4:24c–25 calls the disciples to a greater understanding of the coming of the Kingdom set forth in the parable of 4:21–23 and in the coming parables of 4:26–29, 30–32.

By taking an independent saying about one's receiving in measure for one's own efforts (4:24c; cf. Matt 7:2 // Luke 6:38) and expanding it in terms of the following saying (4:25), the evangelist breaks the equivalency principle of a tit for tat by adding that one will receive even "additionally." With the saying set in this context, Mark assures the reader/hearer who attentively hears Jesus' message of the Kingdom taught in the parables that the hearer will not only experience the Kingdom but receive an even greater grasp of the Kingdom's coming.

This promise gains support from an explanatory saying (4:25) which declares that the one who has will be given more. In other words, those who have been given the "mystery of the Kingdom" but lack in understanding what this entails will gain even more by "hearing" Jesus' teaching regarding the Kingdom in these parables. On the other hand, those who "have not," those who have not experienced the Kingdom in Jesus' ministry, find even his parabolic teaching to be "riddles." To those who have experienced and responded to the veiled presence of the Kingdom in and through Jesus' ministry with attentive listening, a greater understanding of what is and will be happening comes to them through Jesus' teaching. For those, however, who have not experienced or responded to Jesus' ministry with continued attentive listening, there is the risk of losing what they have known. Therefore, the challenge of 4:24-.25 is not so much to experience the Kingdom, which is a given (4:11; 24c, 25a), nor to be engaged in the mission of making the Kingdom known, to which neither 4:24b nor 4:24c–25 pertain thematically, but to comprehend more completely Jesus' message about the coming of the Kingdom.

G. The Parable of the Seed's Growth   (4:26–29)

Bibliography

Ambrozic, A. M. *The Hidden Kingdom: A Redaction Critical Study of the References to the Kingdom in Mark's Gospel.* CBQMS 2. Washington: Catholic Biblical Association, 1972. **Baltensweiler, H.** "Der Gleichnis von der selbstwachsenden Saat (Mk 4, 26–29) und die theologische Konzeption des Markusevangelisten." In *Oikonomia: Heilsgeschichte als Thema der Theologie,* FS O. Cullmann, ed. F. Christ. Hamburg-Bergstadt: H. Reich, 1967. 69–75. **Black, M.** *An Aramaic Approach to the Gospels and Acts.* 1967. **Crossan, J. D.** "The Seed Parables of Jesus." *JBL* 92 (1973) 244–66. ———. *In Parables: The Challenge of the Historical Jesus.* New York: Harper and Row, 1973. **Dahl, N. A.** "The Parables of Growth." *ST* 5 (1951) 132–66 = *Jesus in the Memory of the Early Church.* Minneapolis: Augsburg, 1976. 141–66. **Dodd, C. H.** *The Parables of the Kingdom.* 1961. **Dupont, J.** "La parabole de la semence qui pousse toute seule (Mc 4,26–29)." *RSR* 55 (1967) 367–92. **Jeremias, J.** *The Parables of Jesus.* 1972. **Kelber, W.** *The Kingdom in Mark.* 1974. **Klauck, H.-J.** *Allegorie und Allegorese in synoptischen Gleichnistexten.* NA 13. Münster: Aschendorff, 1978. **Kuhn, H.-W.** *Ältere Sammlungen im Markusevangelium.* 1971. **Kümmel, W. G.** "Noch Einmal: Das Gleichnis von der selbstwachsenden Saat." In *Orientierung an Jesus,* FS J. Schmid, ed. P. Hoffmann, N. Brox, and W. Pesch. Freiburg: Herder, 1973. 226–37. **Ladd, G. E.** "The Life-Setting of the Parables of the Kingdom." *JBR* 31 (1963) 193–99. **Maloney, E. C.** *Semitic Interference in Marcan Syntax.* 1981. **Manson, T. W.** "A Note on Mark 4, 28f." *JTS* 38 (1937) 399–400. **Marxsen, W.** "Redaktionsgeschichtliche Erklärung der sogenannten Parabeltheorie des Markus." *ZTK* 52 (1955) 255–71 = *Der Exeget als Theologe: Vorträge zum Neuen Testament.* Gütersloh: Mohn, 1968. 13–28. **Räisänen, H.** *Die Parabeltheorie im Markusevangelium.* Schriften der finnischen exegetischen Gesellschaft 25. Helsinki: Finnish Exegetical Society, 1973. **Reploh, K.-G.** *Markus—Lehrer der Gemeinde.* 1969. **Stuhlmann, R.** "Beobachtungen und Ueberlegungen zu Markus IV, 26–29." *NTS* 19 (1972–73) 153–62. **Suhl, A.** *Die Funktion der alttestamentlichen Zitaten und Anspielungen im Markusevangelium.* Gütersloh: Mohn, 1965.

Translation

[26] *And he said: "The kingdom of God is*[a] *as if*[b] *a man should cast*[c] *seed on the ground* [27] *then sleep and rise night and day. The seed sprouts*[d] *and grows, but he does not know how.* [28] *Without visible cause the earth produces a crop; first the blade, then*[e] *the head, then*[e] *the whole grain*[f] *in the head.* [29] *But when the crop permits,*[g] *he immediately puts in*[h] *the sickle, because the harvest is ready."*

Notes

[a] Literally, "So (οὕτως) is the Kingdom of God, as (ὡς). . . ." This awkward parable introduction has no parallel in the other Synoptic parables.

ᵇRenders the meaning, though best attested text reads simply ὡς—א B D L Δ 33, 892*. Variants smooth this construction (ὡς ἄνθρωπος ὅταν—W f¹ saᵐˢˢ boᵐˢˢ; ὡς [ἐ]ὰν ἄνθρωπος—A C 0107 0133; ὥσπερ ἄνθρωπος Θ f¹³ 28 565 700).

ᶜMoule (Idiom-Book, 23) calls βάλῃ a "parabolic subjunctive."

ᵈβλαστᾷ, a subjunctive form of βλαστᾶν, a variation of βλαστάνω (cf. Matt 13:26; Heb 9:4).

ᵉεἶτα. The Ionic form of εἶτεν is read in א* B* L Δ.

ᶠRead πλήρης σῖτον with C*ᵛⁱᵈ 28, since, as Taylor (267) suggests, this best explains the other readings (πλῆρες σῖτος—B; πλήρης ὁ σῖτος D W; πλήρη σῖτον—א A C² L Θ f¹.¹³).

ᵍπαραδοῖ, a variant subjunctive form of παραδίδωμι (cf. δοῖ—8:37; γνοῖ—5:43), has the rare but attested meaning in Classical Greek of "to allow" or "to permit." Manson (JTS 38 [1937] 399–400) and Black (Approach, 164–65) suggest that the unusual choice of παραδίδωμι reflects the influence of an underlying Aramaic expression meaning "to yield (fruit)."

ʰLiterally, "sends" (ἀποστέλλει).

Form / Structure / Setting

Form-critically, the choice of an everyday experience and the predominance of the present tense make this story a similitude. At the same time, the idealized depiction of both the farmer and the seed diverges from common experience. We read nothing about the farmer's normal tasks of plowing, fertilizing, and tilling. Nor do we read anything about the essentials for the seed's growth like sun or rain. And what about the various destructive forces like wind, hail, weeds, and drought that at least threaten the seed's maturation (cf. the Parable of the Seeds!)? This noticeable absence of the obvious warns us against seeking the parable's meaning in what is missing.

Few question that this story has its roots in Jesus' ministry. Less certain is whether Mark found this similitude combined with the "seed" parables that precede (4:3–9) and follow (4:30–32) or personally introduced it into this context. Since this is the only section in Mark's entire Gospel without a parallel in either Matthew or Luke, Baltensweiler (Oikonomia, 69–70) has maintained that the evangelist added it to underscore the disciples lack of knowledge (4:10–13; cf. 4:27b) after the Gospel was used by Matthew and Luke. This hypothesis lacks textual support, begs the question of the parable's absence in Matthew and Luke, and unduly accents the ignorance motif in 4:27b.

Kelber (Kingdom, 29–32) has argued that Mark's interest in the Kingdom motif led him to combine the "Kingdom" parables (4:26–29, 30–32) with other units to form a speech about the Kingdom (4:11–32). Yet neither the introductory formulas (καὶ ἔλεγεν) nor the introductions to the parables, awkward though they be, give any evidence of Markan redaction. To the contrary, the rare καὶ ἔλεγεν (4:9, 26, 30; cf. 12:35, 38) has generally been taken (Jeremias, Parables, 14, n. 8; Marxsen, Exeget, 16; Kuhn, Sammlungen, 131; cf. Räisänen, Parabeltheorie, 108–09) as sufficient evidence to support a pre-Markan combination of the two "Kingdom" parables (4:26–29, 30–32) with the "seed" parable (4:3–8) and its interpretation (4:14–20). This possibility becomes even more likely, if 4:11–12, which introduces the concept of the Kingdom of God into the Parable of the Seeds, belongs to this earlier collection rather than Mark's redactional efforts.

The similitude's complexity has raised questions about its integrity. Kuhn (Sammlungen, 105–11), rigorously applying the principle that a parable has only one main point, has pared it to an earlier form (4:26, 28b, 29) by eliminating the secondary motif of the farmer's inactivity and ignorance (4:27–28a). Similarly, Crossan (*JBL* 92 [1973] 252) has eliminated 4:28 for structural and thematic reasons that correspond to the secondary expansions accenting growth and development in 4:5–6 and lexically related to 4:20 (καρποφορεῖν). He also finds the divine judgment in 4:29 incompatible with the flow of the parable (similarly, Suhl, *Zitaten*, 154–57), especially the note of ignorance in 4:27b. Both suggestions, however, unduly narrow the thrust of the similitude and solve the problem of interpretation by eliminating it. Parable interpretation has moved beyond the rigorous application of one point of comparison, and the details of 4:28, at home here, might themselves have led to the subsequent expansions in 4:5–6.

Structurally, this similitude can be divided into three parts (Dupont, *RSR* 55 [1967] 376–88): (a) sowing (4:26b), (b) growth (4:27b, 28), and (c) harvest (4:29). But this division appears arbitrary, since the subject of the story moves back and forth between the seed and the farmer, who unlike the farmer in the Parable of the Seeds remains central to the story. In fact the subjects move somewhat symmetrically from the farmer twice (4:26, 27a) to the seed (4:27b) to the farmer again (4:27c) in the first half and from the earth and crop ("seed"—4:28, 29a) to the farmer (4:29b) to the harvest ("seed"—4:29c) in the second half. Rather than simplify the parable by highlighting either the role of the farmer or the seed, this shifting of subjects indicates the importance of both the farmer and the seed and argues for the importance of 4:29 as a part of the story's flow (Gnilka, 1:183).

The setting of this parable between two other seed parables and its reference to the Kingdom of God gives us a specific context from which to interpret it. If Mark inserted 4:21–25, which accents both the enigma of the Kingdom's coming and the exhortation for the disciples to grasp its significance, between this parable and the interpretation in 4:14–20, he inevitably highlights the same motifs found in 4:27c, 28a.

Comment

26 "And he said" (καὶ ἔλεγεν) appears four times in Mark, three in this chapter (4:9, 26, 30; cf. 14:36). Expanded forms appear in 12:35 (καὶ ἀποκριθεὶς ὁ Ἰησοῦς ἔλεγεν) and 12:38 (καὶ ἐν τῇ διδαχῇ αὐτοῦ ἔλεγεν), but these give every indication of being traditional formulas which Mark may well have expanded (see *Comment* on 12:35, 38). It is quite likely, therefore, that the formulas point to a pre-Markan combination of this and the following seed parable with the Parable of the Seeds in 4:3–8, 14–20.

The absence of an indirect object may indicate a collection of parables without a particular audience in mind. By contrast, the presence of the indirect object (αὐτοῖς) in 4:2, 11, 13, 21 and 24 may indicate the evangelist's appropriation of a general audience to the specific audience of either "the great crowd" (cf. 4:2b, 21a, 24a) or "those around him with the Twelve" (4:11a, 13a, 21a, 24a; cf. 4:11a). The same καὶ ἔλεγεν may have originally introduced the Parable of the Seeds in the pre-Markan parable collection (cf. 4:9a). If so, Mark has preempted and expanded it (4:2b, καὶ ἔλεγεν αὐτοῖς ἐν τῇ διδαχῇ αὐτοῦ; cf. 12:38, but without a specific audience) in line with his development of the setting for this discourse in 4:1–2a. "The Kingdom of God" (ἡ βασιλεία τοῦ Θεοῦ) makes this an explicit "Kingdom" parable, though the uniqueness of this parable introduction suggests that the introduction was added to the parable at some point in its transmission (see *Note* a). But since nothing apart from the Kingdom reference in the introduction is particularly Markan, we can assume that Mark found it in the tradition (cf. Kelber, *Kingdom*, 29–30). This and the following "Kingdom" parable may have given rise to the addition of the saying on the "mystery of the Kingdom" in 4:11–12 which, sandwiched between the Parable of the Seeds and its interpretation, now makes the first parable into a "Kingdom" parable.

Mark himself reinforces the connection of the first with the following parables by adding the question in 4:13 that assumes understanding the first parable has implications for understanding "all the parables," a reference which must certainly include these "Kingdom" parables. This emphasis on the Kingdom in Mark corresponds with Ambrozic's (*Kingdom*) and Kelber's (*Kingdom*) findings that make clear how central Jesus' message of the Kingdom was for Mark's Gospel. Not only does the evangelist summarize Jesus' preaching as proclaiming the "gospel of God," the coming of the Kingdom (1:14–15), but he uses a collection of "Kingdom" parables in his one extended example of Jesus' teaching apart from the Olivet Discourse.

But to what is the "Kingdom of God" compared? The answer to this question determines how the parable is interpreted. For example, if the farmer provides the basis of comparison, then we might have the Parable of the Patient Farmer (e.g., Dahl, *Memory*, 157; Jeremias, *Parables*, 151), the Unbelieving Farmer (Baltensweiler, *Oikonomia*, 69–75) or the Reaper (Crossan, *Parables*, 85). If the seed provides the basis, we could have the Parable of the Seed Growing Secretly or the Parable of the Harvest.

Several factors point to the seed as the parable's primary motif. First, the seed motif remains consistent from sowing to harvest. By contrast, an inconsistency exists in the roles played by the farmer. The divine reaper of 4:29 could hardly be the same uninvolved and uninformed farmer of 4:27. Second, even the concluding role of the farmer depends upon the crop's allowance (4:29a) and the harvest's readiness (4:29c). Third, this parable was surrounded in the collection by two "seed" parables, indicating that this too was understood to be a "seed" parable.

At the same time, we cannot ignore the important role(s) played by the farmer in this story. The structure of the parable weaves back and forth between the farmer and the seed and has led some to find the point of comparison in the story as a whole rather than in either the seed or the farmer (Gnilka, 1:184; Ernst, 142; cf. Kümmel, *Orientierung*, 232–33). But this solution makes a virtue of complexity and fails to distinguish the main (seed) from the supporting character (farmer).

"Cast the seed on the ground" (βάλῃ τὸν σπόρον) is an unusual way of describing the act of sowing but not so novel (cf. Luke 13:19) as to connote a careless act of simply tossing out the seed (so Lohmeyer, 86; Baltensweiler, *Oikonomia*, 72). Yet the expression may describe the farmer's action of literally casting seed on the ground in a way that disassociates the seed from the farmer and eliminates any hint of his contributing to the seed's germination.

The aorist subjunctive in contrast to the subsequent present subjunctives reflects the difference in activities. The seed is cast only once upon the ground; the other activities are continuous.

27 "He sleeps and rises night and day" (καθεύδη καὶ ἐγείρηται νύκτα καὶ ἡμέραν) describes the farmer's passing of time. In other words, it is life as usual day after day. The reversal of sleeping and rising, night and day, reflects the oriental understanding of a "day" beginning at sundown. This description, however, of the farmer's activity does disassociate him further from any direct involvement in the life of the seed, a motif underscored in the following sentence. The "seed sprouts and grows," and the farmer "does not know how it does so." "How" (ὡς) most likely introduces an indirect question ("how it grows") that is answered by the next statement in 4:28a (Ambrozic, *Kingdom*, 115–16).

The mystery of germination and growth has often served as the main point of the parable so that it frequently is known as the Parable of the Seed Growing Secretly. The meaning has been applied either to the Kingdom's "secret" growth, the organic development from its "planting" by Jesus to its maturity when full grown, or to the Church's irresistible growth in the world. This title and subsequent interpretation focuses too narrowly on one element in the complex story.

The farmer's lack of understanding, doubtless integral to the story from the beginning, gains further significance in the present context of 4:13 and 4:21–23 that implies a lack of understanding about the Kingdom on the part of the disciples. Thus, the certainty of the seed's growth offers assurance to the disciples or readers of the presence and work of the Kingdom despite its enigmatic character. Just as the seed "sprouts and grows" apart from the understanding of the farmer, the Kingdom is present even though the disciples, who have been given the mystery of the Kingdom, fail to understand how or fully comprehend it.

28 "Without visible cause, the earth produces a crop" (αὐτομάτη ἡ γῆ καρποφορεῖ) changes the subject to "the earth" (γῆ) but continues to underscore the disassociation of the efforts of the farmer from the growth of the seed. Several have followed Jeremias' suggestion (*Parables*, 149, 151–52) that this theme expressed a common perception at that time of germination being God's miraculous activity in contrast to human activity (e.g., Grundmann, 131; Pesch, 1:256; Ernst, 142). Stuhlmann in particular has argued that "without visible cause" (αὐτομάτη) used with plants actually means "by God" rather than "without human effort" (*NTS* 19 [1972–73] 154–56). Consequently, the parable's point of comparison would lie in God's role behind the seed's growth that points to God's role in effecting his Kingdom and, thus, giving assurance that God would bring it all to "harvest" apart from any human efforts (Cranfield, 167; Grundmann, 131; Pesch, 1:256; Ernst, 142; Marcus, *Mystery*, 172–73).

Yet a closer examination of the passage shows little evidence for taking αὐτομάτη to be synonymous with "by God." While Scripture does identify the fruit of the earth as God's blessing (Gen 8:22), Dahl (*Memory*, 149) questions whether a farmer in antiquity who looked over his fields sprouting with grain actually saw "miracle upon miracle, nothing less than resurrection from the dead" (so Jeremias, *Parables*, 149). Furthermore, Klauck (*Allegorie*, 221) has shown that Stuhlmann failed to do justice to the biblical and extrabiblical data for αὐτομάτη (Acts 12:10; Josh 6:15 are divine miracles but unrelated to plants growing; Lev 25:5, 11 involves seed growing spontaneously during a sabbath or jubilee year in a context that accents no human activity rather than divine activity). Even the immediate context of 4:28a emphasizes the seed's growth independent of both the farmer's efforts *and* understanding. So contextually "without visible cause" has to include "without human efforts."

Indeed nothing either implicitly or explicitly makes this a "contrast parable" differentiating between human and divine activity (cf. Jeremias, *Parables*, 151). To be sure, the "earth (not the farmer) produces the fruit." But the farmer initiates the harvest indicative of the consummation, a task which metaphorically belongs to God alone. Therefore, though the parable does accent the independence of the seed's growth from the efforts of the farmer, its design does not repudiate human effort in favor of divine action.

"First the blade, then the stalk" (πρῶτον χόρτον εἶτα στάχυν) describes the normal process of coming to maturity, a process that spells out what is implied in the statement: "The earth produces a crop." This series has the same function as the reference to the farmer's sleeping and rising night and day. Both details sketch "life as usual" respectively without intending to accent any "delay" between seedtime and harvest or emphasizing an interval of time.

29 "But when the crop allows" (παραδοῖ) begins with an expression of contrast, "but" (δέ), that brings the similitude to its climax (Taylor, 268). Two points stand out in this verse. First, the introductory temporal clause and the concluding causal clause highlight the climactic fullness of time in comparison to what has gone before. Even the main clause accents this climactic note by beginning with the adverb, *immediately* (εὐθύς). This imagery certainly points to the culmination of all things, both in terms of the seed's growth (4:28b) and the Kingdom (4:26). Second, the farmer again enters the scene as the subject of the main verb. Initially, we met the farmer as he was broadcasting the seed. The story continued by separating his activity from that of the seed until this point. Now he becomes involved again with the seed as the initiator of the harvest whose time has come. Yet the focus on the seed is not totally eclipsed, since the appointed time of the harvest is determined by the seed ("crop"/"harvest") in both the introductory temporal and concluding explanatory clause.

"Puts in the sickle" (ἀποστέλλει τὸ δρέπανον) clearly echoes Joel 4:13 (MT). The language stands closer to the MT and the Aramaic Targum than the LXX (Stuhlmann, *NTS* 19 [1972–73] 161–62). For example, Mark has the singular of sickle (δρέπανον; cf. מגל, *maggāl* [MT] and חרבא, *ḥrb⁾* [Targum with article]; cf. δρέπανα [LXX]) and the usual word for grain harvest (θερισμός; cf. קציר, *qāṣîr*, [MT]), whereas the LXX uses the term often used for grape harvest (τρύγητος; cf. בציר, *bāṣîr*) appropriate to Joel's immediate context.

The reference to Joel has been viewed by some interpreters to be a later accretion to the parable (e.g., Suhl, *Zitaten*, 154–57; Pesch, 1:257; Crossan, *JBL* 92 [1973] 253). But if this allusion to Joel represents a later conclusion to the parable, the language suggests it must have been added quite early in the tradition, and there is no compelling reason for denying that Jesus himself might have made use of a scriptural reference to conclude the parable.

Crossan has found the shift of imagery from an unknowing and uninvolved farmer to the divine judge too inconsistent (cf. Crossan, *JBL* 92 [1973] 253). In fact, the very inconsistency in the farmer's roles as one who first lacks direct involvement and is uncomprehending of the seed's growth and then as one who is the divine reaper indicates the farmer's place to be secondary to that of the seed in the story.

Taken simply as a figure in the story without any symbolic significance, the farmer does play a consistent supporting role. He initiates the action by sowing the seed (4:26). He illustrates the inherent power of the earth and seed to grow inexorably to maturity (4:28) by his contrasting behavior and lack of understanding (4:27). Then when the time is right, he concludes the action and brings the seed to its ultimate purpose by harvesting the grain. His crucial role at the climax of the story taken on this level has led to the title of the Patient Farmer or Husbandman. Accordingly, the parable gives the audience assurance that God will accomplish his sovereign purposes. In other words, the consummation of the Kingdom is certain.

Unfortunately, this reading of the farmer does not obtain for the parable's figurative or indirect meaning. First, we have here a "Kingdom" parable, a parable that refers in its indirect meaning to the Kingdom (4:26). Second, when read as a Kingdom parable, Crossan is correct in finding an inconsistency in the farmer's roles and a consequent tension in his identity. This inconsistency is intensified by setting the harvest against the backdrop of Joel 4:13 (MT). In such a setting the "harvest," a common metaphor in Judaism for the last judgment, must involve God implicitly and the reference to Joel only insures such a connection. Thus the divine reaper of 4:29 hardly corresponds to the uninvolved and uninformed farmer of 4:27.

Marcus (*Mystery*, 177–85) has sought to resolve this tension by identifying the farmer with Jesus. The seed represents the "word" of the Kingdom. The farmer's "sleeping" refers to Jesus' apparent lack of concern or detachment from even critical events both during his ministry (cf. 4:35–41) and certainly during the time of Mark's readers. The farmer's failure to understand the growth also points to Jesus' lack of understanding about what is taking place or will take place (e.g., his continued popularity despite his plans otherwise— 1:44–45; 6:32–33; 7:24; his lack of knowledge—5:30; 6:6; 13:32). And the role of "reaper" or "judge" clearly belongs to one aspect of the Son of man (8:38; cf. Rev 14:15) as God's designated agent.

This attempt to combine the various statements about the farmer by identifying the farmer with Jesus remains forced at best. Not only does Marcus have to reach for material supporting Jesus' lack of understanding, but the evidence used hardly suggests Jesus' ignorance about the nature of the Kingdom and how it is at work. Furthermore, the emphasis on "sleeping" ignores the setting in which "sleeping and rising" merely connote the normal process of passing time. The farmer has no more involvement with the growth process when he rises than when he sleeps. It is even more difficult to imagine that the parable's emphasis on the farmer's disassociation with the process could represent either for Jesus or for Mark a similar detachment between Jesus and the dynamic of the Kingdom.

Read as a "Kingdom" parable, we have one of two alternatives. Either we concur with Crossan and remove the tension by assigning the Joel reference to a later addition (cf. *Gos. Thom.* 21), or we take this inconsistency to be inherent in the story-line itself. If we accept the first alternative, we have a story that simply focuses on the growth of seed from seeding to maturity. Nothing is said about a harvest. But this solution ignores the parable's structure reflected precisely in the shifting complexity of the subjects. Even Crossan recognizes the need for a harvest but assumes that it has been replaced by the eschatological reaper of Joel 4:13 (*JBL* 92 [1973] 253). If, however, a harvest was indeed the climax of the story involving a farmer (cf. *Gos. Thom.* 21) and if/when the parable had the Kingdom as its point of reference, it is hard to imagine how the farmer/reaper, with or without an allusion to Joel, could have had any other referent but God because of the common metaphorical understanding of harvest in such an eschatological setting. Therefore, the farmer's shift in roles stems from his changing role within the parable itself. Initially, the farmer served as a foil for the seed to enhance the emphasis on its inherent, unassisted and climactic growth. Then the farmer works in concert with the seed to bring it to its culmination as the reaper who harvests the seed. This shift in roles that defies consistent identification of the "man" with either a "disciple," "God" or even "Jesus" should signal the reader that no such consistent identification was ever intended.

The allusion to Joel has led some to interpret the harvest as the final judgment in keeping with Joel's usage (e.g., Schweizer, 102; Pesch, 1:258). We find the same judgment motif in Rev 14:17–20 and in the Parable of the Wheat and the Tares in Matt 13:24–30, which many take to be Matthew's expansion of the Markan parable. But in the immediate context of the seed's growth to maturity (4:28b, 29a), along with the similar reference in the larger context of 4:8, 20, the "harvest" most likely connotes the final stage in the story of the seed from sowing to harvest. This more positive ending overshadows the judgment theme inherent in the reference to the sickle (Gnilka, 1:184; Ernst, 142).

Explanation

The complexity of the parable's story line has led to many interpretations. Some have followed the role of the farmer; some have followed the seed; and some, eschewing either the farmer or the seed as the key, have followed the "story." One could further divide the interpretations according to which aspect of the farmer's role or the seed's role has stood out for the interpreter. When taken as a whole, the story appears to offer the interpreter a broad range of meanings corresponding to the many quirks the story itself seems to contain. Our analysis, however, has found the seed to be central, leaving us with the question of how this story about seed illustrates the Kingdom.

Following the story line of the seed, it begins with sowing (4:26b), continues with sprouting and growing (4:27b) described by stages until maturity (4:28), and culminates in the production of a crop for harvest (4:29a,c). Nothing is said about positive (e.g., sunshine or rain) or negative (e.g., hail, drought, insects) factors. The seed appears to grow inexorably and irresistibly to its fullness, as though it were perfectly natural or "automatic" to do so. This rather idealized description of the seed's process stands in stark contrast to the much more common experience of the seed in 4:3–8. Therefore, the unrelenting, successful process of the seed's coming to its intended purpose apart from any visible cause must hold at least one key to this parable.

The farmer's role supports this motif. First, by describing his sowing as "casting" the seed on the ground (4:26), the story disassociates the farmer from any involvement with the seed's germination. Next the story describes the farmer as passing the time, day after day, in the normal manner of sleeping and rising (4:27). Nothing is said about any connection between his "normal" activities and the growth of the seed. In fact, the disassociation extends even to his incomprehension of how the seed grows. Only at the end of the process does the farmer interact again with the seed, when he puts in the sickle at the harvest to bring the crop to its culmination (4:29). Thus, the farmer's role enhances the role of the seed in the parable.

But how does this parable illustrate Jesus' teaching about the Kingdom? Two features stand out in the story and both are related to the seed—the growth of the seed and the harvest. First, the seed grows on its own apart from any visible, external causes. Applied to the Kingdom, the Kingdom germinates, grows and matures of its own accord without any enhancement from visible, external forces. This may have originally addressed the question about the Kingdom's presence despite the absence of the expected, visible enhancements either from Jesus' ministry or from those who heard and followed him. So understood, the parable would assure those who were finding it difficult to comprehend how the Kingdom might be present and at work in a manner contrary to their expectations. The parable may also have addressed any false assumptions that certain actions by Jesus' followers or by those who sought to usher in the Kingdom for Israel by force could enhance the work of the Kingdom.

Since the parable comes to us removed from its original context in Jesus' ministry, we must leave the options open for that setting. For Mark, however, the context of 4:13, 21–25 and the theme of the parable chapter as a whole indicate that this parable also illustrated the presence and work of the Kingdom despite the disciples' lack of understanding and the absence of visible enhancements. If this was true for the disciples during Jesus' ministry, the need of assurance only increased for those after Easter who found the enigma of the Kingdom all the more puzzling in view of the response from "outsiders" and especially in view of the failure of "insiders" who had "heard the word" (e.g., 4:14–19). The parable, therefore, assured the reader that God's Kingdom, like the seed, had a life of its own.

The second feature lies in the climactic conclusion of the parable. Both the introductory and concluding clause point to the fullness of time—"when the crop allows" and "because the harvest is ready." With these clauses surrounding the statement reintroducing the farmer who puts in the sickle, one cannot escape the sense of an appointed time. Yet little is made of the interval between seedtime and harvest other than what was necessary to describe the inexorable process of moving from the one to the other through natural stages. Consequently, this parable has little to say about growth or the length of the time between seedtime and harvest. But the accent on the harvest does affirm a time when all will be brought to its final end, the ripe grain will be harvested. The allusion to Joel 4:13 (MT) leaves no doubt about this culmination being God's harvest, the consummation of God's rule which is now at work, enigmatic though it be, in the world.

This assurance of harvest made more intelligible the presence of God's rule by assuring the hearers that God was acting, though enigmatically, through the presence of the Kingdom in the present and would act at the appropriate time in the future to consummate the Kingdom in a manner more in keeping with their expectation. The future, however, is related to the present just as the harvest is related to the growth of the seed. The Kingdom is present, though unexpectedly vulnerable (4:3–8,14–20), hidden (4:21) and small (4:31) with a power of its own (4:27–28). Its consummation, the harvest, is still future.

H. The Parable of the Mustard Seed   (4:30–32)

Bibliography

Ambrozic, A. M. *The Hidden Kingdom: A Redaction Critical Study of the References to the Kingdom in Mark's Gospel.* CBQMS 2. Washington: Catholic Biblical Association, 1972. **Bartsch, H.-W.** "Eine bisher übersehene Zitierung der LXX in Mk 4,30." *TZ* 15 (1959) 126–28. **Black, M.** *An Aramaic Approach to the Gospels and Acts.* 1967. **Carlston, C. E.** *The Parables of the Triple Tradition.* Philadelphia: Fortress, 1975. **Crossan, J. D.** "The Seed Parables of Jesus." *JBL* 92 (1973) 244–66. **Dahl, N. A.** "The Parables of Growth." *ST* 5 (1951) 132–66 = *Jesus in the Memory of the Early Church.* Minneapolis: Augsburg, 1976. 141–66. **Dodd, C. H.** *The Parables of the Kingdom.* 1961. **Donahue, J. R.** *Are You the Christ? The Trial Narrative in the Gospel of Mark.* SBLDS 10. Missoula: Scholars Press, 1973. **Frankmölle, H.** "Hat Jesus sich selbst verkündigt? Christologische Implikationen in den vormarkinischen Parabelen." *BibLeb* 13 (1972) 185–91. **Funk, R. W.** "The Looking-glass Tree Is for the Birds; Ezekiel 17:22–24; Mark 4:30–32." *Int* 27 (1973) 3–9. **Kelber, W.** *The Kingdom in Mark.* 1974. **Klauck, H.-J.** *Allegorie und Allegorese in synoptischen Gleichnistexten.* NA 13. Münster: Aschendorff, 1978. **Kuhn, H.-W.** *Ältere Sammlungen im Markusevangelium.* 1971. **Kümmel, W. G.** *Promise and Fulfillment: The Eschatological Message of Jesus.* 2d ed. SBT 23. London: SCM, 1961. **McArthur, H. K.** "The Parable of the Mustard Seed." *CBQ* 33 (1971) 198–210. **Marcus, J.** *The Mystery of the Kingdom of God.* SBLDS 90. Atlanta: Scholars Press, 1986. **Mussner, F.** "1Q Hodajoth und das Gleichnis vom Senfkorn." *BZ* 4 (1960) 128–32. **Wenham, D.** "The Synoptic Problem Revisited: Some New Suggestions about the Composition of Mark 4:1–34." *TB* 23 (1972) 3–38.

Translation

[30] And he said, "How shall we compare the Kingdom of God, or by what parable shall we present it? [31] It is as with a mustard seed,[a] which, when sown in the ground, is[b] the smallest[c] of all seeds of the earth. [32] And when it is sown, it comes up and becomes the largest[c] of all herbs, and produces great branches, so that the birds of heaven are able to nest in its shade."

Notes

ᵃRead κόκκῳ with ℵ B Cᵛⁱᵈ D Δ(*) most likely reflecting an Aramaic ל (*l*) underlying the ὡς κόκκῳ construction (Jeremias, *Parables*, 101, 146). κόκκον in A L W Θ 0107 0133 *f*¹·¹³ takes the accusative from the previous verb θῶμεν.

ᵇVery awkward syntax. The relative ὅς has κόκκος as its antecedent; ὅν, neuter, nominative participle rendered "is," takes its antecedent from σπερμάτων. Literally: "which, when planted in the earth, being the smallest of all seeds on earth. . . ." The relative clause remains without a verb. This awkwardness has led several to take the participial phrase through the repeated καὶ ὅταν σπαρῇ (4:32a) as added by Mark or a later redactor (Dodd, *Parables*, 153, n. 1; Taylor, 270; Lane, 171).

ᶜRenders idiomatically the comparative (μικρότερον ὄν πάντων τῶν σπερμάτων . . . μεῖζον πάντων τῶν λαχάνων) used superlatively in Koine Greek (Taylor, 270).

Form/Structure/Setting

Form-critically, Mark's story has the classic form of a similitude. It describes a typical scene in the present tense. Luke's parallel (13:18–19), however, takes the form of a parable proper set as a narrative about an event told in the past tense. This formal difference in the same parable illustrates how immaterial the distinctions between similitudes and parables proper can be (so Jeremias, *Parables*, 20; cf. Frankemölle, *BibLeb* 13 [1972] 185–91, and Kuhn, *Sammlungen*, 101–02).

We have numerous indications that Mark and Luke employ separate traditional versions of the same parable. The difference in form, the verbal agreements of Matthew and Luke against Mark, Luke's combining this parable with the Parable of the Leaven (Matt 13:31–33 // Luke 13:18–21) and his use of the parable in another context, the apparent conflation by Matthew of Mark and Q along with Luke's eschewing of dealing with two traditions (McArthur, *CBQ* 33 [1971] 198, and Klauck, *Allegorie*, 210), all indicate separate traditions. On the other hand, the striking agreements between Mark, Luke and *Gos. Thom.* 20 are too extensive to suggest two separate parables (cf. Lohmeyer, 88). Therefore, the differences reflect variations that developed during the oral transmission of a parable whose roots extend to Jesus' ministry.

If we accept the introductory formula καὶ ἔλεγεν to be a clue of a pre-Markan collection of parables (see *Comment* on 4:26), then Mark found this parable in a collection of "seed" parables with 4:3–8 (14–20) and 4:26–29 which spoke about the Kingdom of God (4:26, 30; cf. 4:11). Mark's redactional contribution appears limited to 4:31, 32a, where we find an awkward repetition of ὅς ὅταν σπαρῇ . . . καὶ ὅταν σπαρῇ. Several scholars have taken this material to be secondary (e.g., Dodd, *Parables*, 153, n. 1; Taylor, 270; Lane, 171; Kuhn, *Sammlungen*, 100, n. 8) either to clarify the choice of a mustard seed or to emphasize the contrast. Crossan (*JBL* 92 [1973] 256–57) following Donahue's clue about Markan "insertions" (*Christ*, 77–83) argues that the intervening reference to the "smallest of seeds" (μικρότερον ὄν πάντων τῶν σπερμάτων τῶν ἐπὶ τῆς γῆς) as well as the resumptive statement of sowing (ὅταν σπαρῇ) comes from Mark's characteristic style of inserting his material and then repeating the previous traditional thought to return to the tradition (see *Comment* on 2:7–8). From a structural standpoint, Crossan has also argued that Mark added the parallel reference to greatness (cf. Crossan, *JBL* 92 [1973] 257;

cf. Ambrozic, *Kingdom*, 252; Klauck, *Allegorie*, 212). It should, however, be noted that the contrast in size was implicit in the selection of the mustard seed and explicit in *Gos. Thom.* 20 as well.

Structurally, this similitude opens with a double question (4:30). The answer comes in the form of an antithetical parallelism contrasting the comparatively small size of the seed (4:31) and the comparatively large size of the mature plant (4:32ab). An OT allusion illustrates the plant's size (4:32c) and concludes, as 4:29 does for 4:26–28, the parable. Yet the antithetical parallelism lacks symmetry. The repetition of the statement about sowing (4:32a) and the two statements about largeness, one explicit (γίνεται μεῖζον πάντων τῶν λαχάνων—4:32b) and the other implicit (ποιεῖ κλάδους μεγάλους, ὥστε . . . κατασκηνοῦν—4:32c), disturb the balance in the contrasting parts of the story. Should we remove the statements about smallness and sowing (4:31b–32a), the parable would consist of a triad of verbs (cf. 4:3–7; 4:28!): "comes up" (ἀναβαίνει), "becomes" (γίνεται), and "produces" (ποιεῖ).

This story is the third "seed" parable (4:3–8, 26–29) and like the second (4:26) explicitly identifies the Kingdom of God as the point of comparison. But the setting is probably secondary. Luke's use of a traditional variant of this parable (Q) combined with the thematically related Parable of the Leaven in a different context (13:18–19) and Matthew's conflation of this Q parable with Mark's parable in the Markan context shows Mark's setting to be a later, thematic grouping of once independently transmitted "seed" parables in the pre-Markan tradition. Mark himself has done little to affect the narrower setting found in his tradition. But his addition of the sayings in 4:21–23 speaking of the Kingdom as "hidden" and "under a bushel" to be made public for all to see corresponds with the contrast in the size of the seed and the plant and may aid our understanding of his reading of this parable as well as the sayings in 4:21–22.

Comment

30 See *Comment* on 4:26 for discussion of the introductory formula, "And he said" (καὶ ἔλεγεν). The parable begins with a double question, a construction characteristic of Mark (see *Comment* on 4:13). But this method of introduction is also typical of both biblical (Isa 40:18; cf. Bartsch, *TZ* 15 [1959] 126–28) and rabbinic style (e.g., *Pirqe 'Abot* 3:18). A similar introduction in the Q parable (Luke 13:18; cf. *Gos. Thom.* 20) makes this introduction almost certainly traditional, and the reference to the "Kingdom of God" (see *Comment* on 4:26) in Luke 13:18 (Q) and *Gos. Thom.* 20 indicates its presence in the pre-Markan tradition (cf. Kelber, *Kingdom*, 29–30; Marcus, *Mystery*, 206–07).

How is "parable" (παραβολή) used here? The answer depends on which layer of the tradition we have in mind. Neither Luke 13:18 nor *Gos. Thom.* 20 uses παραβολή here, and Matt 13:31 (cf. 13:24) uses it to connect this story with the previous one. This suggests its presence in Mark is secondary. Thus παραβολή may have entered the tradition as a modification of the second question, since the question itself does not parallel the usual form of such introductory questions (cf. Str-B, 2:7–8; Luke 13:18, "To what shall we compare it?"). This modification does set the stage for the following summary about Jesus' use of "parables" (4:33) and might well have been made at the time the "seed" parables were brought together into a collection or grouping. In that setting, "parable" seems the most natural meaning.

If, as has been suggested above (see 4:10–12), the pre-Markan collection, which included 4:10a, 14–20, was modified at a later stage in the pre-Markan tradition by the insertion of the dialogue in 4:11–12, the παραβολή behind 4:10a, here and in the conclusion of 4:33, would then have acquired more the sense of "riddle" under the influence of παραβολαῖς in 4:11b (see *Comment* on 4:11). This rendering would reflect an understanding of the parable collection to be intelligible only to those to whom God had given the "mystery of the Kingdom," an understanding that would explain, perhaps in the mission situation, the failure of "those outside" to understand and respond to the "parables" that come to them as "riddles." Mark, however, by placing Jesus and his teaching in the positive public setting of crowds in 4:1–2 returns to the collection's original use of παραβολή as "parable" (see *Comment* on 4:11) by which Jesus spoke "the word" (4:34).

31 The "mustard seed" (κόκκῳ σινάπεως) stood proverbially in Jewish folklore for the smallest seed (H. Hunzinger, *TDNT* 7 [1971] 288). As a symbol of smallness (Str-B, 1:669), it generally had a negative, minimal ring to it (cf. "faith as a mustard seed," Matt 17:20; Luke 17:6). Therefore, the subject of this parable included inherently the idea of smallness.

"When sown in the ground" (ὅταν σπαρῇ ἐπὶ τῆς γῆς). According to the Mishnah (*Kil.* 3:2), this herb, cultivated for both its grain and its leaves, was grown in a field (cf. ἀγρός—Matt 13:31) rather than a garden (cf. κῆπος—Luke 13:19). Mark (similarly, *Gos. Thom.* 20) uses the more neutral γῆ (cf. 4:5, 8, 20, 27).

"Smallest of all seeds" (μικρότερον ὂν πάντων τῶν σπερμάτων). Our botanical knowledge legitimately disputes this claim, but "precision (is) hardly to be expected in gnomic sayings, esp. in botanical matters" (Carlston, *Parables*, 158, n. 8). This phrase antithetically parallels the statement of largeness in 4:32, "largest of all herbs" (μεῖζον πάντων τῶν λαχάνων). Yet the first element fits neither syntactically (see *Note* b) nor structurally (Black, *Approach*, 165; Crossan, *JBL* 92 [1973] 256–57).

Two solutions have been proposed. Black (*Approach*, 165) attributes the awkwardness to a mistranslation of an Aramaic play on words. By taking the second "is sown" (σπαρῇ; cf. זְרִיעַ, *zĕrî*ᶜ) as a mistranslation of the noun "seed" (זַרְעָא, *zar*ᶜ*a*), he eliminates the redundancy and leaves an antithetical parallelism with a play on words: "Which, when it is sown in the earth, is less than all seeds that be in the earth, but *when the seed is grown* it becomes greater than all herbs." Unfortunately, while removing the structural difficulties, this explanation does not resolve the syntactical or textual problem ("which" [ὅς] . . . "is" [μικρότερον ὂν] or ἀναβαίνει for αὐξάνει). Crossan (*JBL* 92 [1973] 256–57) has convincingly assigned this material to Mark as an "insertion," a distinctively Markan redactional technique of inserting his material (4:31b) into a traditional unit and repeating the last traditional phrase (e.g., ὅταν σπαρῇ, 4:32a; cf. 31a).

If Mark has added this material, he has merely made explicit what lay implicit in the proverbial use of a "mustard seed" (cf. Dodd, *Parables*, 153).

The presence of a similar qualification in *Gos. Thom.* 20 ("which is the smallest of all seeds") may indicate Markan influence but more likely indicates the need to clarify for certain audiences the symbolic value of the "mustard seed." Mark's parallel construction, however, accenting largeness in 4:32b, missing in *Gos. Thom.* 20, suggests more a desire to accent the contrast than to clarify the parable's choice of metaphor. In any case, this antithetical parallelism does underline the contrast by taking nothing for granted.

32 "Comes up" (ἀναβαίνει) may be a relatively rare verb (cf. αὐξηθῇ—Matt 13:32; ηὔξησεν—Luke 13:19) in this setting (Taylor, 270), but other parallels (5:7; Gen 41:5; Deut 29:22; Isa 5:6 LXX) caution against assigning this to Mark (cf. Crossan, *JBL* 92 [1973] 257; Ambrozic, *Kingdom*, 126). The appearance of ἀναβαίνοντα καὶ αὐξανόμενα in 4:8 has little to add to the source of ἀναβαίνει in 4:32. Their presence in 4:8 is syntactically awkward and materially redundant (see *Comment* on 4:8). Ἀναβαίνει offers a natural transition between the sowing (4:31a) and "producing great branches," if the second member of the parallelism (4:32b) is also secondary, or if not, it forms a triad of verbs with γίνεται and ποιεῖ for the now verbless relative pronoun in 4:31a (cf. 4:28b).

"Becomes the largest of all herbs" supplies the second member of the parallelism. This statement is missing in Luke 13:19 and *Gos. Thom.* 20. Crossan (*JBL* 92 [1973] 257; Kuhn, *Sammlungen*, 100, n. 8) has also assigned it to Mark's redaction. The continuation of the neuter adjective μεῖζον (cf. μικρότερον) to modify σπέρμα (4:31b) instead of κόκκος (4:31a) seems to support this suggestion. The weakness, however, lies in the strength of Crossan's argument for the first "insertion" in 4:31b. If Mark used his "insertion" technique to add the first member of the parallelism, why does the second member lie outside the bounds of that "insertion," especially if Mark is also responsible for the verbs ἀναβαίνει and γίνεται? How is the resumptive function of ὅταν σπαρῇ characteristic of Mark's "insertion" technique, if the evangelist continues with more redaction? Could it be that "largest" (μεῖζον) took its neuter antecedent from λαχάνων and gave rise to the "insertion" of 4:31b with its "neuter" syntax drawn from σπερμάτων to form the parallelism (so Ambrozic, *Kingdom*, 256; Klauck, *Allegorie*, 212)?

Whereas the first qualification (4:31b) merely accented the proverbial, this qualification adds to the metaphorical role of the "mustard seed." We have no parallels pointing either to the contrast in size between the seed and the fully grown plant or to the size of the mustard plant. Yet Luke 13:19 // Matt 13:32 also accents the plant's size by referring to it as a "tree" (δένδρον), a designation that seems at least hyperbolic for a plant that generally grew to a height of eight to ten feet (Jeremias, *Parables*, 148). Furthermore, *Gos. Thom.* 20 maintains the same contrast by setting a "great branch" against the "smallest seed." Therefore, whether this particular qualification in 4:32 was added by Mark or at some point earlier in the tradition, it merely highlights the novel contrast drawn in the parable itself between the seed and the plant. "Produces great branches" (ποιεῖ κλάδους μεγάλους) differs from Luke's "becomes a tree" (ἐγένετο εἰς δένδρον). *Gos. Thom.* 20 ("produces a great branch") stands much closer to Mark. The statement may reflect a variation in the tradition precipitated by the subsequent OT allusion. Should one assume that it originally provided the main verb for the relative pronoun (ὅς) in 4:31, the basic parable would compare the Kingdom to a "mustard seed, which, when planted, produced great branches" (cf. *Gos. Thom.* 20). This represents the basic ingredients of the parable. The other elements simply amplify the contrast between the "smallest seed" and its producing "great branches."

"Birds of heaven might nest in its shade." Finding here an OT allusion, some have assigned this conclusion to a later development of the parable (e.g., Schweizer, 103–04; Crossan, *JBL* 92 [1973] 259). *Gos. Thom.* 20 does not have it, and Mark differs from Luke in how it is worded. Yet this conclusion seems arbitrary. While *Gos. Thom.* 20 does not have the extensive allusion of Mark and Luke, "it becomes a shelter (σκέπη) for the birds of heaven" along with the reference to a "great branch" may well be a reminiscence of such an allusion. We also need to remember the tendency of the *Gospel of Thomas* to avoid scriptural references. Furthermore, the difference between Mark and Luke's wording most probably stems from the general nature of the allusion. No one OT text stands clearly behind either version.

"Nest in its shade" (ὑπὸ τὴν σκιὰν αὐτοῦ . . . κατασκηνοῦν). Some prefer "rest" to "nest" in view of the location—literally, "under its shadow" (Taylor, 270; Kümmel, *Promise*, 130). The same verb (κατασκηνεῖν) in Luke 13:19, however, has been consistently rendered "to nest" because the birds are in the "branches" of the "tree." Either rendering is possible. The translation depends on the extent of influence granted to the OT texts purportedly behind this allusion, since all speak of the birds "nesting." For example, Ezek 17:23 describes Israel's future as a "stately cedar" where "in the shade of its branches birds of every sort will nest" (cf. 31:6 pertaining to Assyria). Dan 4:12, 21 describes Nebuchadnezzar's dream of a huge tree where the "beasts of the field found shade under it" and the "birds of the air dwelt in its branches." Mark 4:32 comes closer to Ezek 17:23. Since the OT texts all speak of the birds "nesting" in the tree or its shade, that meaning seems as logical for Mark as for Luke.

This concluding OT allusion serves two purposes. First, it enhances the idea of the plant's size. The branches are large enough for the birds to nest in its shade, a statement that strengthens the contrast between the "smallest" seed and the grown plant. Second, this OT imagery brings with it an implicit meaning of an immense kingdom (cf. Israel, Assyria, Babylon) which encompasses the nations. Applied to the Kingdom of God, it depicts the greatness of the Kingdom. It is not clear, however, that the "birds of heaven" refer to the Gentiles (e.g., Dodd, *Parables*, 154; Jeremias, *Parables*, 147).

Explanation

This concluding parable in Mark 4 stands out as having the least disputed meaning of the three "seed" parables. Unlike the other parables in this collection, it has been consistently known by one title, the Parable of the Mustard Seed.

Yet the parable, whose introduction explicitly compares the Kingdom of God to a mustard seed, takes a couple of curious turns. First, the proverbial use of this seed connotes smallness, bare minimum. And it usually carries a negative tone like "least possible" with it. Such a metaphor seems surprisingly out of place for the majestic Kingdom of God. Second, the parable concludes by describing the greatness of the mustard plant, a plant with branches so large that birds can nest in its shade. But this focus on the plant catches the reader by surprise, since the mustard plant itself had no such symbolic value. If a large "tree" were to symbolize the Kingdom, would not a mighty oak or at least the stately cedar (Ezek 17:23) seem more appropriate?

These two ironies give us the clue about the parable's meaning. The subject controls the parable. We are dealing with a mustard seed, not an acorn. So the very selection of the analogy raises the issue of "smallness." But the conclusion of the parable does qualify the analogy by adding an element that expands the analogy from simply the "seed" to include the fully grown plant. Consequently, we have two foci whose implicit and explicit descriptions stand in contrast to each other. Whereas the "seed" stands for smallness, the fully grown plant stands for greatness as seen by the concluding OT allusions. Without doubt, therefore, the point of comparison lies in the contrast.

In Jesus' ministry, this parable set forth his teaching about two dimensions of the Kingdom. The one dimension was present in and through his ministry. The choice of the mustard seed appropriately described the almost infinitesimal presence of God's rule relative to the popular expectation of the times. At the same time, this dimension did not represent the total picture. A second dimension included the coming of the Kingdom in its greatness. The contrast gives instruction about both dimensions but offers little about the interval in between or the growth process. Despite the loss of the original setting in Jesus' ministry that would help determine just how this teaching was used, the message of this parable coheres with the lessons of the previous parables, both those of the tradition (4:3–8, 26–29) and those of Mark (4:21–23) regarding the surprising presence of the Kingdom and its future manifestation.

We have no clear indications of the early Church's use of this parable. A comparison with Luke 13:18–19 and *Gos. Thom.* 20 does suggest development in the second half of Mark's parable. But granting this development, the comment about the mustard plant's comparative largeness (4:32b) missing in the parallels simply makes explicit the implicit contrast between the seed's beginning and the end product. The different wording between Mark's and Luke's OT allusion reflects the tendency to align the general allusion to Ezek 17:23 in Mark and to Dan 4:12, 21 in Luke. In both cases, the development accents the greatness of the Kingdom in its future manifestation. Perhaps the unusual choice of a mustard plant instead of a tree necessitated these enhancements.

The evangelist, by contrast, appears to have focused on the first half of the parable. At least, his accenting the smallness of the mustard seed (4:31b) balances in antithetical parallelism the second half. This emphasis on the enigmatic presence of the Kingdom corresponds with his addition of the parabolic sayings about the lamp and bushel (4:21) and things hidden and revealed (4:22). These all speak about the contrasting dimensions of the Kingdom present and future.

Mark's concern here as in the previous parables appears directed at a confusion about the present. This chapter setting forth Jesus' "teaching" (4:2) about the "Kingdom of God" (4:11, 13, 26, 30) wrestles with the disciples' lack of understanding (4:13) and need for "attentive listening" (4:23–25; cf. 4:3a, 9). But where is the confusion? Familiar with the Scriptures as well as being followers of Jesus, the disciples could hardly have been confused about the future manifestation of God's rule in history, the fully grown plant. Rather the questions had arisen because of its surprisingly vulnerable (4:3–8, 14–20), hidden (4:21–22), small presence (4:31) without visible cause (4:28).

The struggles with the presence of the Kingdom displayed by the disciples during Jesus' ministry doubtless continued as intensely in the mission after Easter (cf. 4:14–20). These parables, therefore, remind the reader that Jesus proclaimed the "gospel of God," the coming of the Kingdom, (1:14–15) in two, contrasting dimensions. The Parable of the Mustard Seed calls the reader to faith in Jesus and in God's rule present and future.

I. Summary (4:33–34)

Bibliography

Ambrozic, A. M. *The Hidden Kingdom: A Redaction Critical Study of the References to the Kingdom in Mark's Gospel.* CBQMS 2. Washington: Catholic Biblical Association, 1972. **Egger, W.** *Frohbotschaft und Lehre.* 1976. **Gnilka, J.** *Die Verstockung Israels: Isaias 6,9– 10 in der Theologie der Synoptiker.* Munich: Kösel, 1961. **Kelber, W.** *The Kingdom in Mark.* 1974. **Klauck, H.-J.** *Allegorie und Allegorese in synoptischen Gleichnistexten.* NA 13. Münster: Aschendorff, 1978. **Kuhn, H.-W.** *Ältere Sammlungen im Markusevangelium.* 1971. **Lambrecht, J.** "Redaction and Theology in Mk., IV." In *L'évangile selon Marc: Tradition et Rédaction,* ed. M. Sabbe. BETL 34. Gembloux: Duculot, 1974. 269–307. **Marcus, J.** *The Mystery of the Kingdom of God.* SBLDS 90. Atlanta: Scholars Press, 1986. **Marxsen, W.** "Redaktionsgeschichtliche Erklärung der sogenannten Parabeltheorie des Markus." *ZTK* 52 (1955) 255–71 = *Der Exeget als Theologe: Vorträge zum Neuen Testament.* Gütersloh: Mohn, 1968. 13–28. **Minette de Tillesse, G.** *Le secret messianique dans l'évangile de Marc.* LD 47. Paris: Cerf, 1968. **Moule, C. F. D.** "Mark v, 1–20 Yet Once More." In *Neotestamentica et Semitica,* FS M. Black, ed. E. E. Ellis and M. Wilcox. Edinburgh: T. and T. Clark, 1969. 95–113. **Neirynck, F.** *Duality in Mark.* 1972. **Pryor, J. W.** "Markan Parable Theology: An Inquiry into Mark's Principles of Redaction." *ExpTim* 83 (1972) 242–45. **Räisänen, H.** *Die Parabeltheorie im Markusevangelium.* Schriften der finnischen exegetischen Gesellschaft 25. Helsinki: Finnish Exegetical Society, 1973. **Reploh, K.-G.** *Markus—Lehrer der Gemeinde.* 1969. **Wenham, D.** "The Synoptic Problem Revisited: Some New Suggestions about the Composition of Mark 4:1–34." *TB* 23 (1972) 3–38.

Translation

³³*And with many such parables he spoke to them to the extent they were able to hear it.* ³⁴*He did not speak to them apart from parables. But privately he explained all things to his own disciples.*

Form / Structure / Setting

These verses form a concluding summary for Jesus' teaching in parables (4:3–32). Their source or sources, however, is much disputed. Some attribute both verses to the pre-Markan traditional collection (e.g., Gnilka, *Verstockung,* 60; cf. 1:190; Pryor, *ExpTim* 83 [1972] 244; Räisänen, *Parabeltheorie,* 48–64; Klauck, *Allegorie,* 255–56). Others attribute both verses to Mark's redaction (e.g., Schweizer, 105–06; Reploh, *Lehrer,* 62–63; Lambrecht, *Marc,* 273–77; Kelber, *Kingdom,* 33–34). And some find both traditional and Markan elements, assigning 4:33 to the tradition and 4:34 to Mark (e.g., Minette de Tillesse, *Secret,* 181–82; Kuhn, *Sammlungen,* 132–34; Egger, *Frohbotschaft,* 118; Pesch, 1:265). Still others take the verses themselves to be composites of pre-Markan tradition (e.g., 4:33a, 34a—Wenham, *TB* 23 [1972] 35–36; 4:33b, 34b—Marxsen, *Exeget,* 20) and Markan redaction (e.g., 4:33a, 34a—Marxsen, *Exeget,* 20; 4:33b, 34b—Wenham, *TB* 23 [1972] 35–36). Since these verses hold a major clue to Mark's understanding of Jesus' use of parables, the discussion is far from academic.

The lexical argument has played a key role in the discussion. On the one hand, 4:34 has three *hapax legomena* in Mark (χωρίς, τοῖς ἰδίοις μαθηταῖς, ἐπέλυεν) and two occurrences of δέ rather than Mark's characteristic use of καί. These data suggest a pre-Markan tradition (Gnilka, *Verstockung,* 60; 1:190; Klauck, *Allegorie,* 255). But this creates a material problem for some, since 4:34 reflects the same view of "parables" or "riddles" found in the supposedly redactionally inserted 4:11 (Gnilka, *Verstockung,* 23–24; Kuhn, *Sammlungen,* 132; Egger, *Frohbotschaft,* 116; Pesch, 1:265–66).

On the other hand, the vocabulary of 4:33 fits Mark (παραβολαῖς, πολλαῖς, ἐλάλει τὸν λόγον, ἠδύναντο) and could point to Mark's redaction (Lambrecht, *Marc,* 274–75; Kelber, *Kingdom,* 33–34). Yet the content of 4:33 stands in tension with the supposedly redactional 4:11–12 and certainly 4:34, unless we translate καθώς in a restrictive sense (e.g., "to the extent that") uncharacteristic of Mark. Therefore, assuming 4:11–12 to be a redactional insertion and thus representative of Mark's "parable theory," the lexical data of 4:33–34 pose a dilemma by suggesting the opposite regarding tradition and redaction of what one would expect to find based on the content of 4:33–34.

One can escape this dilemma by discounting the force of the lexical argument (e.g., Minette de Tillesse, *Secret,* 181–85; Lambrecht, *Marc,* 274–75). After all, the *hapax legomena* of 4:34 do not disprove Markan redaction, since there is no rule against Mark using an expression only once. And despite the compatibility of the terms in 4:33 with Mark's vocabulary, they could just as easily reflect the language of the mission tradition (Kuhn, *Sammlungen,* 133–34; Pesch, 1:264–65). Consequently, we need more than the lexical argument to decide the question of source and redaction.

Style and content are more decisive factors, especially when combined with the lexical argument. The content of 4:33 corresponds with the use of "parables" in 4:3–8, 26–29, 30–32 as a teaching device and with the reference to the "word" coupled with the response based on "hearing" in the interpretation of the Parable of the Seeds (4:14–20). So 4:33 might well have been the concluding statement of an earlier parable "collection" involving 4:3–

8, 9, 10a, 14–20, 26–29, 30–32. The distinctive use of παραβολαῖς and καθὼς and the mission terminology (ἐλάλει τὸν λόγον) supports this alignment with the pre-Markan tradition (see *Comment*).

The content of 4:34 corresponds specifically to 4:10–12. It considerably narrows the thrust of 4:33 by using παραβολῆς as "riddle" (4:11b) requiring special interpretation (4:10a, 11) for the disciples (e.g., 4:14–20). Therefore, the traditional or redactional character of 4:34 depends to a great extent on whether 4:11–12 is interpreted as traditional or redactional. We have argued that Mark found 4:10–12 in his tradition. Certainly, the unusual use of δέ and the lexical argument support the pre-Markan character of 4:34 (see *Comment*). If true, 4:34 would then represent an additional conclusion to the pre-Markan parable collection. This narrower statement qualifying the more general statement of 4:33 would then reflect an adaptation of the parable "collection" at some point in the pre-Markan tradition to a more restrictive viewpoint expressed in 4:10–12 and illustrated in 4:14–20.

Structurally, these two statements stand in antithetical parallelism. Mark 4:34a counters 4:33a and 4:34b counters 4:33b. This structure suggests a clarifying role for 4:34. In terms of the larger context, 4:33–34 rounds off the parable discourse introduced by an expanded setting in 4:1–2. The noticeable absence of lexical (e.g., διδάσκειν; cf. λαλεῖν) and stylistic (ἐν παραβολαῖς; cf. παραβολαῖς) correspondence between the setting and the summary gives further evidence for the pre-Markan character of 4:33–34. Had the summary (4:33–34) like the setting (4:1–2) been Mark's redactional product, we could have expected greater correlation between the two. The lack of correspondence indicates the evangelist's development of the setting (4:1–2) from the content (cf. ἐν παραβολαῖς) of the parable collection and the sea setting of the subsequent miracle stories (cf. 4:35–5:43). Consequently, the setting (4:1–2) instead of the summary (4:33–34) of the miracle discourse provides the transition to the miracle stories that follow.

Indeed the implication that Jesus used "parables" to confuse the public stands in tension with the clearly redactional setting of 4:1–2 for this material. Mark depicts Jesus as teaching publicly "with parables" (4:1–2) without a hint of anything cryptic in the setting. Furthermore, the scene shifts from a public to a private audience in 4:10 and back to a public audience in 4:33–34a with no indication of when or where. Since Mark has redactionally created the public setting in 4:1–2 and since he found the shift to a private setting in his tradition (see *Comment* on 4:10), his failure to mark the shift from a private back to the public setting in 4:33–34 would make him, if he was also redactionally responsible for 4:33–34a, a clumsy writer at best.

If, however, Mark created the public scene in 4:1–2 based on the assumed public setting in a traditional 4:33–34a and the sea setting of 4:35–5:43, the inconsistency in audiences between 4:10 and 4:33 would have already been in the tradition which the evangelist simply took over intact. Rather than developing a consistent narrative, Mark let the tension stand because of his greater interest in both the ministry of Jesus Messiah who proclaimed the Kingdom to the crowds through parables (4:1–2, 33; cf. 1:14–15) and the disciples' lack of understanding (4:13, 27b) that required further instruction (4:14–20, 34b) and attentive hearing (4:24–25; cf. 4:9). Consequently, Mark's intention was not so much to set the disciples off from the crowd as a privileged group with esoteric knowledge (so 4:11–12 in the pre-Markan tradition) as to show their lack of understanding and need for responsible hearing of what Jesus taught.

Comment

33 "With many such parables" (τοιαύταις παραβολαῖς πολλαῖς) appears to resume the introductory statement—"He taught them many things with parables"—and forms a redactional inclusion around the intervening material (Lambrecht, *Marc,* 277). But appearances deceive. First, the Markan theme of teaching (cf. 4:1–2) is missing here. Second, πολλαῖς has an adjectival rather than the typically Markan substantival function ("many things" [πολλά]; cf. 4:2; 6:34; 7:13). And third, the dative construction παραβολαῖς differs from Mark's characteristic ἐν παραβολαῖς (e.g., 3:23; 4:2; 12:1—Kuhn, *Sammlungen,* 134). These stylistic differences outweigh the strictly lexical arguments for Markan redaction.

"Spoke the word to them" (ἐλάλει αὐτοῖς τὸν λόγον) has a verbatim parallel in what may well be a redactional introduction in 2:2 (see *Comment* on 2:2). But the common use of this phrase in the mission setting as synonymous with the "gospel" (e.g., Acts 4:29, 31; 8:25; 11:19; Phil 1:14; Heb 13:7; cf. John 12:48; 15:3) prevents us from assigning it exclusively to Mark's redaction, particularly since it also picks up the pre-Markan theme of the "word" in 4:14–20.

"To the extent they were able to hear it" (καθὼς ἠδύναντο ἀκούειν). καθὼς means either "as" without limitations or "to the degree that" implying limitations (see Bauer, καθώς, *s.v.* 2). Taken in the second sense, καθὼς states that Jesus spoke the word in parables "to the degree that" or "as far as" his audience could hear it. Taken in the first sense, καθὼς states that Jesus spoke the word in parables "in a way" his audience could hear it (Lambrecht, *Marc,* 276, n. 31). Since either is lexically possible, only the context determines the more appropriate.

Mark does use καθὼς eight times; three with εἶπεν (11:6; 14:16; 16:7) and three with γέγραπται (1:2; 9:13; 14:21). Mark 15:8 offers the only parallel but is little help for our rendering of καθὼς in 4:33b. In any case, 4:33b must be understood first in terms of the mission language of 4:33a—"to speak the word." In this setting, varying degrees of hearing the word do not exist. Either one hears the gospel or one does not (Räisänen, *Parabeltheorie,* 53–54). Even the interpretation of 4:14–20 assumes that all four categories "heard" the word.

Read in the broader context of 4:3–8 and 4:14–20 as well as perhaps 4:26–32, this summary describes Jesus as proclaiming "the word" with "many parables" of which 4:3–8, 14–20 and most likely 4:26–29, 30–32 represented a selection (cf. "such parables" [τοιαύταις παραβολαῖς]). Thus, 4:33 most likely concluded an early stage of a parable collection (4:3–8 [9] 10a, 14–20, [26–29, 39–32]) where the qualifying clause, "as they were able to hear," had more than a tautological function of saying the obvious or a cryptic way of denying hearing (cf. 4:12). "Hearing the word" meant hearing and responding to the message, even though that hearing and response were vulnerable to various destructive threats, as 4:14–20 illustrates.

When, however, we read 4:33b with its antithetical parallel in 4:34b, then the restrictive sense of καθώς is required. If Jesus had to explain the parables privately to his own disciples (4:34b), the extent of the crowd's hearing would clearly be limited to the superficial (cf. 4:12—"hearing they hear but do not understand"). By contrast, "his own" hear, are intrigued, and desire to move beyond the superficial (e.g., Gnilka, *Verstockung,* 63; Moule, *Neotestamentica,* 98–99). Thus 4:34 provides a later qualification of 4:33.

34 "Apart from parables" (lit., "without a parable," χωρὶς δὲ παραβολῆς). "Without" (χωρίς) is the first of three *hapax legomena* in this verse, a fact which may have little significance, since Mark may simply have lacked the occasion to use at least two words (χωρίς, ἐπέλυεν) or their synonyms elsewhere (Minette de Tillesse, *Secret,* 183–85; Räisänen, *Parabeltheorie,* 57). Yet these *hapax legomena* occur in clauses whose thrust differs from Mark's in comparable settings. Lexically, the appearance twice of δέ instead of the typically Markan καί also provides support for a pre-Markan tradition.

On the surface, 4:34a declares negatively what 4:33a has stated positively. But more is at stake. Whereas the positive statement in 4:33a leaves open the possibility of Jesus "speaking the word" in more ways than "with such parables," this negative statement declares that Jesus spoke exclusively with "parables." Furthermore, 4:34b indicates that "parable" (παραβολῆς) in 4:34a and by association in 4:33a is more precisely rendered "riddle." Consequently, 4:34a definitely narrows the scope and means of Jesus' teaching implicit to 4:33a in keeping with 4:11b that declares that "all things" (τὰ πάντα—4:11b; cf. πάντα—4:34b) come as "riddles."

"But privately he interpreted all things to his own disciples" has often been attributed to Mark's redactional interest in the disciples' private instruction. But despite the "Markan" κατ' ἰδίαν (6:31–32; 7:33; 9:2, 28; 13:3), the two *hapax legomena,* τοῖς ἰδίοις μαθηταῖς and ἐπέλυεν, should caution us against assigning this clause too readily to Mark. Rather than οἱ ἴδιοι μαθηταί Mark has his own favorite phrase, οἱ μαθηταὶ αὐτοῦ (over 30x) and never uses ἴδιος adjectivally elsewhere in contrast to Matthew (9:1; 22:5; 25:14, 15) and Luke (6:41, 44; 10:34; Acts 1:7, 19, 25; 2:6, etc.). And while the "duality" of κατ' ἰδίαν, τοῖς ἰδίοις may look distinctively Markan (Neirynck, *Duality,* 101–06; Lambrecht, *Marc,* 274, n. 20), τοῖς ἰδίοις may have led to the adding of the more characteristic κατ' ἰδίαν rather than vice versa. If so, Mark would simply have been responsible for adding the privacy motif found in 4:10a (cf. 7:17; 10:10a).

Furthermore, ἐπέλυεν in the context of 4:34a,b suggests a use of parables different from Mark's more obvious redactional settings (3:23; 12:1). Gnilka (*Verstockung,* 62–63), after tracing this verb and noun in the NT (1 Pet 1:20), the LXX/Aquila (Gen 40:8; cf. 41:8, 12 Aquila) and extrabiblical texts, especially Hermas' frequent and analogous use with "parables" (cf. *Sim.* 5.3.1– 2), has demonstrated that ἐπιλύειν means "to interpret" a difficult saying or discourse not readily understandable.

Therefore, in this context ἐπέλυεν not only explicitly states that Jesus "interpreted" the unintelligible "all things" (πάντα) but implies that the "parables"

(4:33a, 34b) remained "riddles" to "those outside" and thus qualifies the καθώς of 4:33b. Instead of the positive meaning "in a way that" (καθώς) of 4:33b taken by itself and as an earlier conclusion to the parable collection, καθώς must now be read restrictively, "(only) to the extent," in light of the later 4:34. "Hearing" they could not understand apart from an interpretation.

This motif concurs with the "riddle" character of "all things" (τὰ πάντα) in 4:11b (cf. πάντα in 4:34b). Consequently, this conclusion (4:34) was added to qualify the original summary (4:33) of the pre-Markan parable collection by limiting its thrust in terms of the understanding of "parables" or "riddles" in terms of 4:11–12. This qualification most likely came about at the stage in the tradition when 4:11–12 was inserted into the parable collection.

Despite the tendency to ascribe this adaptation to Mark, we have already seen that 4:34 can hardly be attributed to Mark on the basis of vocabulary and style. More importantly 4:34 stands in material tension with Mark's understanding of Jesus' teaching with "parables" as seen in his clearly redactional settings elsewhere. Not only does the evangelist go out of his way to create a setting of Jesus' teaching the crowds in "parables" in 4:1–2 and has Jesus summon the crowds to "hear" and "understand" the "parable" in 7:14 but he introduces "parables," assuming their intelligibility, into settings even with "outsiders" (cf. 3:23; 12:1, 12).

Why then did Mark retain a motif that apparently ran at cross purposes to his own understanding of Jesus' use of parables? Because this summary corresponds with Mark's depiction of the disciples as also lacking in understanding (see *Comment* on 4:13). This would be reason enough for leaving 4:34 intact with the accent on 4:34b and perhaps even for adding the privacy motif κατ᾿ ἰδίαν. At the same time, his redactional setting in 4:1–2 corresponding to his use elsewhere of "parables" indicates his failure to subscribe to the "riddle" motif of the tradition.

Explanation

This two-verse summary has played a pivotal role along with 4:10–12 in determining Mark's understanding of Jesus' use of parables. Both passages imply Jesus taught in "riddles," and both distinguish between two groups of "hearers." The one group, "those outside" (4:11), only hears Jesus' teaching as "riddles." The other, "those around him with the Twelve" (4:10), "his own disciples" (4:34), has "all things" given or explained to them (4:11a, 14–20, 34b). By assigning the presence of these passages, especially 4:11–12 and 4:34 to Mark's redaction, many exegetes have attributed this distinctive view of Jesus' use of "parables" to Mark.

Our analysis, however, of 4:10–12 and 4:3–34 has shown little evidence lexically, stylistically, or materially to support any such Markan "parable theory." In fact, 4:33 and 34 stand in a tension with each other that reflects different stages in the development of the pre-Markan tradition. Whereas 4:33 speaks in summary of Jesus publicly speaking the word in parables in a way that his audience could hear, 4:34 limits Jesus' public speaking exclusively to the use of "riddle," a device that limited "hearing" (4:33b) and required interpretation (4:34b).

Therefore, 4:33 originally concluded an earlier collection of parables that included at least 4:3–9, (10) 14–20, and likely 4:26–29, 30–32. The statement views "parables" as a device by which Jesus "spoke the word." And although the parable collection doubtless contained the interpretation of 4:14–20, the question behind 4:10 and the explanation of 4:14–20 did not necessarily imply a cryptic note behind the use of "parables," a fact that becomes particularly clear if the uninterpreted parables of 4:26–29 and 4:30–32 belonged to that earlier collection.

The addition, however, of 4:11–12 changed the thrust of the collection from "parables" by which Jesus set forth "the word" to a collection of "riddles" that divided the hearers into "insiders," the recipients of special interpretation (e.g., 4:14–20) from Jesus, and "outsiders" for whom all things remained enigmatic. This change required a different conclusion from 4:33 to correspond with the new thrust of the materials and led to constructing 4:34 in parallel with 4:33. The adaptation most likely took place in the mission situation which struggled not only with the loss of "hearers" (e.g., 4:14–20) but more specifically with the apparent inability of the audience even to hear. By contrast, those who did hear were viewed as having been given the "mystery of the Kingdom," that is, they were given understanding of the "riddles" about the Kingdom through Jesus' teaching.

Mark took over at least portions of this parable collection including the complex summary. But he altered the enigmatic thrust of the tradition by adding an extended introduction depicting Jesus teaching a great crowd by the sea "with parables." This same setting carries over to the beginning of the next section (4:35–36) involving Jesus' miracles and eclipses the summary of 4:33–34 as the transitional bridge. Consequently, 4:33–34 simply expresses in passing a general summary of Jesus' teaching, a function served originally by 4:33 from which the evangelist most likely developed the theme of Jesus' teaching with parables in 4:2.

At the same time, Mark develops the motif of Jesus' private instruction for his disciples by underscoring their failure to understand despite their having received the "mystery of the Kingdom" by adding the sharp questions of 4:13 and the summons to hear ("understand") in 4:21–25. He may have even highlighted this motif in 4:34b by adding the private setting (cf. 6:31–32; 9:2, 28; 13:3). In this way, Mark portrays Jesus as a teacher whose concern is the Kingdom of God and the disciples to whom the mystery of the Kingdom had been given. Yet they are struggling to comprehend what it all meant. Therefore, this parable "discourse" presents us with a portrait of Jesus' ministry to the crowds, his teaching them with parables (4:33–34a) and his disciples' need for understanding (4:34b), as appropriately summarized by 4:33–34.

J. The Stilling of the Storm (4:35–41)

Bibliography

Achtemeier, P. "Gospel Tradition and the Divine Man." *Int* 26 (1972) 174–97.
———. "The Origin and Function of the Pre-Markan Miracle Catenae." *JBL* 91 (1972)

198–221. ———. "Person and Deed. Jesus and the Storm-Tossed Sea." *Int* 16 (1962) 169–76. ———. "Toward the Isolation of Pre-Markan Miracle Catenae." *JBL* 89 (1970) 265–91. **Annen, F.** *Heil für die Heiden: Zur Bedeutung und Geschichte der Tradition vom besessenen Gerasener (Mk 5,1–20 par.).* FTS 20. Frankfurt: J. Knecht, 1976. **Best, E.** "The Miracles in Mark." *RevExp* 75 (1978) 539–54 = *Disciples and Discipleship: Studies in the Gospel according to Mark.* Edinburgh: T. & T. Clark, 1986. 177–96. **Betz, O.** "The Concept of the So-called 'Divine Man' in Mark's Christology." In *Studies in New Testament and Early Christian Literature,* FS A. P. Wikgren, ed. D. E. Aune. NTS 33. Leiden: Brill, 1972. 229–40. **Fisher, K. M.** and **von Wahlde, V. C.** "The Miracles of Mark 4:35–5:43: Their Meaning and Function in the Gospel Framework." *BTB* 11 (1981) 13–16. **Hilgert, E.** "Symbolismus und Heilsgeschichte in den Evangelien: Ein Beitrag zu den Seesturm- und Gerasenererzählungen (Mk 4,35–5,20 par)." In *Oikonomia,* FS O. Cullmann, ed. F. Christ. Hamburg: Reich, 1967. 51–56. **Iersel, B. M. F. van** and **Linmans, A. J. M.** "The Storm on the Lake. Mk iv 35–41 and Mt viii 18–27 in the Light of Form Criticism, 'Redaktionsgeschichte' and Structural Analysis." In *Miscellanea Neotestamentica,* ed. T. Baarda, A. F. J. Klijn, and W. C. van Unnik. NTS 48. Leiden: Brill, 1978. 17–48. **Kee, H. C.** *Community of the New Age: Studies in Mark's Gospel.* Philadelphia: Westminster, 1977. ———. "Aretalogy and Gospel." *JBL* 92 (1973) 402–22. **Kertelge, K.** *Die Wunder Jesu im Markusevangelium.* 1970. **Kingsbury, J. D.** "The 'Divine Man' as the Key to Mark's Christology—The End of an Era?" *Int* 35 (1981) 243–257. **Koch, D.-A.** *Die Bedeutung der Wundererzählungen für die Christologie des Markusevangeliums.* 1975. **Kuhn, H.-W.** *Ältere Sammlungen im Markusevangelium.* 1971. **Liefeld, W. L.** "The Hellenistic 'Divine Man' and the Figure of Jesus in the Gospels." *JETS* 16 (1973) 195–205. **Loos, H. van der.** *The Miracles of Jesus.* NTS 8. Leiden: Brill, 1965. **Maloney, E. C.** *Semitic Interference in Marcan Syntax.* 1981. **Meye, R.** "Psalm 107 as 'Horizon' for Interpreting the Miracle Stories of Mark 4:35–8:26." In *Unity and Diversity in New Testament Theology,* FS G. E. Ladd, ed. R. A. Guelich. Grand Rapids: Eerdmans, 1978. 1–13. **Neirynck, F.** *Duality in Mark.* 1972. **Petzke, G.** "Die historische Frage nach den Wundertaten Jesu." *NTS* 22 (1975–76) 180–204. **Robbins, V. K.** "*Dynameis* and *Semeia* in Mark." *BR* 18 (1973) 5–20. **Roloff, J.** *Das Kerygma und der irdische Jesus.* 1970. **Schenke, L.** *Die Wundererzählungen im Markusevangelium.* 1974. **Schille, G.** "Die Seesturmerzählungen Markus 4,35–51 als Beispiel neutestamentlicher Actualisierung." *ZNW* 56 (1965) 30–40. **Smith, M.** "Prolegomena to a Discussion of Aretalogies, Divine Men, the Gospels and Jesus." *JBL* 90 (1971) 174–99. **Synge, F. C.** "A Matter of Tenses—Fingerprints of an Annotator in Mark." *ExpTim* 88 (1977) 168–71. **Theissen, G.** *The Miracle Stories of the Early Christian Tradition.* 1983. **Tiede, D. L.** *The Charismatic Figure as Miracle Worker.* SBLDS 1. Missoula: Scholars Press, 1972. **Weeden, T. J.** *Mark: Traditions in Conflict.* 1971.

Translation

     [35]*And he said to them on that day when evening had come, "Let us go* [a] *to the other side."* [36]*Leaving the crowd, they took him as he was in the boat, and other boats were with him.* [37]*And a great windstorm came up and the waves beat against the boat so that the boat was being swamped.* [38]*And he was in the stern asleep on the cushion.* [b] *They aroused him and said, "Master, do you not care that we perish?"* [39]*Aroused, he rebuked the wind and said to the sea, "Be still! Remain quiet!"* [c] *And the wind abated, and a great calm settled in.* [40]*And he said to them, "Why were you frightened?* [d] *Do you not yet* [e] *have faith?"* [41]*And they were awestruck and said to one another, "Who indeed is this that even the wind and the sea obey him?"*

Notes

ᵃLiterally, "go through" (διέρχεσθαι), more appropriate to a land journey. But Luke, who frequently uses διέρχεσθαι (31x in Luke-Acts), follows Mark (8:22) and has a similar use in Acts 18:27.

ᵇπροσκεφάλαιον may mean "pillow" or "cushion." The setting suggests the use of a rower's cushion. The definite article may be "deictic" (Maloney, *Syntax*, 105), referring to something assumed present in the mind of the speaker (e.g., the usual rower's or passenger's cushion on board).

ᶜThe unusual perfect imperative πεφίμωσο is more emphatic than the aorist imperative.

ᵈThe texts vary between omitting οὕτως (א B D L Δ Θ 565 700 lat) and placing it before (p⁴⁵ f¹·¹³) or after ἐστε (A C majority text).

ᵉA οὕτως originally after ἐστε may have influenced the change of οὔπω ἔχετε to πῶς οὐκ ἔχετε (so A C Majority text sy⁽ᵖ⁾ʰ), a reading that softens Jesus' rebuke, οὔπω ἔχετε πίστιν (א B D L Δ Θ 565 700 lat).

Form / Structure / Setting

Form-critically, this pericope fails to fit neatly into a formal category. Most have taken it to be an epiphany story (Dibelius, 93–94) set in the form of a miracle story. The difference of opinion involves the specific kind of miracle story. Is it a "nature miracle," as the stilling of the winds and waves might suggest (Bultmann, 215; Schmithals, 1:255)? Does the use of exorcistic language make it an "exorcism" (e.g., Grundmann, 137; Ernst, 149) or simply a miracle story with exorcistic language (Gnilka, 1:194)? Or does the content make it a "rescue miracle" (Theissen, *Miracle Stories*, 99–103; Pesch, 1:268; see p. 346)? Each answer reflects a decision about the focal point of the story.

A closer look at the components of this story raises important questions about the "form" of the text as it now stands. Though many have found here the basic pattern of a miracle story, Mark's story contains significant breaks with this pattern. For example, the request for help is at best implicit (4:38) and Jesus rebukes his disciples prior to the response (cf. 4:40–41). Consequently, Gnilka (1:194; similarly van Iersel and Linmans, *Miscellanea*, 22–23) finds Mark to have modified the form to give us a "disciple story" (*Jüngergeschichte*). But as will be seen, ecclesiology does not eclipse Christology; the "disciples" play an important but not the predominant role in the story.

As to source, with rare exception (e.g., Lane, 173–74; Schenke, *Wundererzählungen*, 17–22) the vast majority of scholars consider Mark to have found this story in a collection with at least the three subsequent stories in 5:1–43. Achtemeier (*JBL* 89 [1970] 265–91) has argued for a larger collection (4:35–5:43; 6:34–44) that formed one of two pre-Markan cycles ("catenae") of miracle stories (4:35–5:43; 6:34–44 and 6:45–56; 8:22–26; 7:24–8:10), and Kuhn (*Sammlungen*, 191–213, similarly, Keck, *JBL* 84 [1965] 341–58) has assigned this to a traditional collection of six miracle stories (4:35–5:43; 6:32–52). Others consider Mark to have found this story combined not only with what follows (4:35–5:43) but with the parables of 4:1–9 (Kertelge, *Wunder*, 91) or 4:1–34 (Ernst, 147).

Our earlier analysis of 3:7, 9–10 concurred with Keck's conclusion (*JBL* 84 [1965] 346–47, similarly, Pesch, 1:198) that 3:7, 9–10 originally introduced an earlier collection of miracle stories that included 4:35–5:43, 6:32–56. We also have seen in our analysis of 4:1–2 that the evangelist constructed the setting for Jesus' teaching in 4:1–34 from the introductory summary now in 3:7–12 and with a view toward 4:35–41. This traditional background would explain the temporal and local connection of 4:1–2 with 4:35–36 as well as the thematic similarity to 3:7, 9–10.

The story's origin has been variously assigned to a "Petrine" or personal reminiscence, on the one hand, based on the vividness of details (Taylor, 272; Cranfield, 172; Lane, 173–4; Ernst, 147) or to the early Christian mission, on the other hand, as a "free narrative," based on Jonah 1 and Ps 107:23–25, that reflects the Church's mission and Christology rather than an experience of the historical Jesus (Pesch, 1:276; Koch, *Wundererzählungen*, 94). The listing of numerous Semitisms by van Iersel and Linmans (*Miscellanea*, 21, e.g., paratactic sentences, numerous impersonal plurals, unrelated imperatives in 4:39, interrogative pronoun in 4:40, and ἐφοβήθησαν with cognate accusative in 4:41) appears to locate the original story at least in the early traditions of an Aramaic-speaking community rather than a Greek-speaking Jewish Christian community (cf. Kuhn, *Sammlungen*, 191–99, and Schenke, *Wundererzählungen*, 22–23).

Mark's redactional contribution comes for many interpreters in 4:35–36, 38c, 40. Much of 4:35–36 supposedly comes from Mark's hand in an attempt to align what follows with 4:1–34 (Grundmann, 136; Schenke, *Wundererzählungen*, 23–33; Gnilka, 1:193). We shall see in the *Comment* that, though relatively inconsequential, this is far from certain. Of greater consequence is the portrait of the disciples that emerges from the apparent reworking of a formal request for help into an accusing question in 4:38c. This portrait is sustained through Jesus' rebuke of the disciples illogically located in 4:40 *after* calming the sea but *before* the disciples respond in keeping with his charge.

And if Mark developed the setting in 4:1–2 from a tradition containing at least 3:7, 9–10 and 4:35–41, he is, therefore, responsible for bringing 4:35–41 into the context of 4:1–34. Consequently, the evangelist would also be responsible for identifying Jesus' anonymous companions in 4:35–41 as the disciples, since their identity now comes from the context of 4:1–2, 10 and 34b. If, however, Mark originally found 4:35–41 in the context of 3:7, 9–10 and at least 5:1–43, the identity of Jesus' companions as the "disciples" now drawn from the setting of 4:10, 34b would coincide with that of the traditional collection (cf. 3:9; 5:31). Therefore, Mark's identification of Jesus' anonymous shipmates as the disciples would have actually had its roots in his tradition.

By way of structure, numerous attempts have been made to divide this story into strophes. Lohmeyer (89) described it as a six-verse ballad with a 2, 2, 3, 2, 2, 3-line arrangement. Schille (*ZNW* 56 [1965] 32) finds a hymnic structure of 4 strophes with three lines each (4:37, 38, 39, 41a), and Pesch (1:269) has five strophes with three lines each. The failure of any two approaches to agree argues against such a structure. The story line follows the general pattern of such narratives with two major exceptions. Instead of the usual request for help or deliverance we find an accusing question directed at Jesus (4:38c). His response and help follow but we are again surprised by Jesus' unexpected rebuke of the disciples after calming the sea but prior to their response. This surprise element stands out the more when the disciples react in 4:41 in consternation. These breaks in the expected flow of the narrative most likely hold an important key for understanding the story's message.

The setting of this story in the pre-Markan tradition appears attributable to the thematic combination of a series of miracle stories around the sea of Galilee. Naturally, the role this story plays in that collection depends on the extent of the collection, at least as far as we can identify it. For example, if it is the first story in a cycle of stories which Mark follows with a second cycle in 6:45–8:26, each cycle would begin with stories of Jesus' calming the sea (Achtemeier, *JBL* 89 [1970] 265–91). If the collection ended with 5:43, we might find here an ascending hierarchy of miracles showing Jesus' power over nature (4:35–41), demons (5:1–20), and sickness and death (5:21–43). Most likely, however, Mark found this as the first of six miracle stories with the sixth (6:45–52) forming an inclusion by offering a sequel with an epiphanic self-disclosure of Jesus on the sea that specifically answers the disciples' concluding question of 4:41.

In Mark's Gospel this miracle story now introduces a series of four miracle stories (4:35–5:43). The connection with what precedes (4:1–34) lies in the temporal and local ties between 4:1–2 and 4:35–36, a connection arising from Mark's use of the miracle collection (3:7, 9–10 and 4:35–41) to develop the setting (4:1–2) for what has just preceded (4:3–34). The reader, however, finds a broader context. It includes the special call of the Twelve (3:13–19) and Jesus' identification of his true "family" as "insiders" in contrast to the "outsiders" (3:20–35), a theme that carries through Jesus' teaching in 4:1–34 (4:10–12, 33–34).

By placing the parable collection temporally (4:35) and locally (4:36) in conjunction with Jesus' miraculous activity (4:35–5:43), Mark portrays Jesus through his authoritative teaching and actions (4:1–5:43; 6:1–6), a portrait that corresponds to Matthew's opening portrait of Jesus as Messiah of word (5–7) and deed (8–9). That Jesus' words and deeds belong together for Mark has been seen from the beginning (1:21–28) where Jesus' exorcism was declared to be a "new teaching with authority" (1:27; cf. 1:21–22). This combination of teaching and miracle working as an expression of Jesus' authority has implications for the θεῖος ἀνήρ debate, since Tiede's work has shown the combination of teaching and miraculous activity in one figure to be "remarkable . . . for the first century A. D." (*Charismatic Figure*, 253) in view of the previously discrete nature of the two traditions in the Hellenistic world.

Comment

35 "And he said to them" (καὶ λέγει αὐτοῖς) occurs as an introductory formula sixteen times in Mark (Matt 5x; Luke 0) and provides van Iersel and Linmans (*Miscellanea,* 18) with a statistical argument for Markan redaction. The context also appears to support their conclusion. An introductory statement leaving both speaker and audience unnamed could hardly have opened an independent traditional story in which they remain anonymous. Since the subject and audience now receive their identity from the previous context

(4:1–34), a context which Mark has most likely created by combining the miracle stories of 4:35–5:43 with the parables of 4:1–34, the evangelist could logically have used this introductory formula to bridge between 4:1–2 and 4:35.

The statistical preponderance, however, of this formula in Mark over Matthew and Luke does not necessarily demonstrate Mark's redactional thumbprint. On many occasions, in contrast to Matthew and Luke, Mark may simply have chosen to preserve a formula found in his tradition (see 1:35, 41, 44; 2:25; 4:13). The fact that the evangelist never uses καὶ λέγει αὐτοῖς in any other redactional seam to open a narrative unit should caution us against assigning this one to his style. More importantly, if 3:7, 9–10 originally preceded 4:35–41 in Mark's tradition, that setting would have provided even more clearly the identity of the subject ("Jesus"—3:7) and audience ("the disciples"—3:7, 9) for the introductory formula of 4:35. This means that the identity of the subject and the audience in 4:35 now drawn from 4:1–2, 10, 34 resulting from Mark's combination of 4:35–41 with 4:1–34 merely corresponds with the identity of Jesus' companions found by Mark in his tradition. Consequently, Mark did not introduce the disciples into a narrative with a previously unnamed audience to make it a "disciple story" (cf. Gnilka, 1:194). This had already taken place in his tradition.

"On that day when evening had come" (ἐν ἐκείνῃ τῇ ἡμέρᾳ ὀψίας γενομένης) represents a Markan "progressive two step expression" of time in which the latter gives precision to the former (Neirynck, Duality, 46: e.g., 1:32, 35; 2:20; 4:35; 10:30). Four of the ten occurrences involve "when evening had come" (ὀψίας γενομένης, 1:32; 4:35; 14:12; 15:42), three of which explain the significance of its being "evening" for Jewish cultic practice, perhaps for a non-Jewish audience (1:32—sabbath, 14:12 and 15:42—Passover). In this case, Mark may have added "on that day" (ἐν ἐκείνῃ τῇ ἡμέρᾳ) to tie 4:35 more closely with the events of 4:1–2 (Kertelge, Wunder, 91; Schenke, Wundererzählungen, 25; Gnilka, 1:193; cf. Cranfield, 172; Pesch, 1:269). "That day" has an apocalyptic overtone in 13:19, 24, 32; 14:25, but here it simply specifies time (cf. 2:20).

"When it was evening" stands in tension with 5:1 where the story continues as though it were daytime. This has led some to assign this expression too to Mark's redaction (Gnilka, 1:193; similarly van Iersel and Linmans, Miscellanea, 19). But this view assumes too close a chronological association of 4:35–41 with 5:1–20. Even if viewed as sequential events, nothing in 5:1 excludes a time elapse between 4:41 and 5:1. More importantly, this view ignores the integrity of the topos of nightfall with the storm-tossed sea in the story itself as an intensification of the chaos motif (Schenke, Wundererzählungen, 27; cf. 6:47). For Mark, however, "When it was evening" serves a temporal purpose of concluding "that day" of Jesus' teaching in 4:1–34. There is little need for using the reference to time to explain Jesus' sleeping (Bultmann, 215; Kertelge, Wunder, 91).

"To the other side" (εἰς τὸ πέραν) sets the stage for the storm on the lake by suggesting a destination away from where Jesus had been sitting off shore (4:2; cf. 3:9–10). In 5:1 this crossing ends with the arrival on "the other side." Nothing further is said about the trip except for the stilling of the storm (4:35–41).

36 "Leaving the crowd" (ἀφέντες τὸν ὄχλον) along with the temporal expressions of 4:35 further aligns 4:35–41 with 4:1–2. Consequently, some have assigned this phrase to Mark's redaction (Koch, *Wundererzählungen,* 95, Gnilka, 1:193; Schenke, *Wundererzählungen,* 30). In 1:35–36, 45; and 6:46 Jesus leaves the crowds for a time and place alone. In 6:30–31 he sends the disciples away for the same reason after the completion of their mission. But here and in 8:10 they depart for another destination. If, as has been suggested, this story was preceded by 3:7, 9–10 in Mark's tradition, this particular phrase occurring only here in Mark may have referred originally to "the crowd" (ὄχλον) of 3:9–10 which with this reference in 4:36 may have provided Mark with the audience of 4:1. By "leaving the crowd," the events of this story focus solely on Jesus and his disciples.

"They took him in a boat" (παραλαμβάνουσι ἐν τῷ πλοίῳ). This verb appears with similar meaning in 5:40; 9:2; 10:32; and 14:33. The shift of subjects from Jesus in 4:35 to the disciples in 4:36 has led many to take this verb as belonging to the traditional story (Klostermann, 46; Gnilka, 1:193; Schenke, *Wundererzählungen,* 30–31; van Iersel and Linmans, *Miscellanea,* 19). The shift in subjects, however, corresponds to the continued shift in subjects throughout the story and may well reflect the traditional connection of 4:35–41 with 3:7, 9–10 where Jesus has initiated the action by asking for a boat. It follows that "when evening had come" he should ask the disciples to depart with him to the "other side" (4:35). The disciples respond by "leaving the crowd" and taking "him as he was in a boat." Although the boat motif in these miracle stories has often been attributed to the evangelist (e.g., Annen, *Heil,* 40–44, 64, 70, 211–14), the reference to the "boat" in 4:37 is integral to the story and the redundancy of the "other boats" makes a reference in the tradition to Jesus' "boat" most likely. Meanwhile, Mark has used this traditional material to develop the setting of Jesus teaching from a "boat" in 4:1–2. And he ties it all together with "as he was."

"As he was" (ὡς ἦν) may mean "immediately" or "without going ashore" (Lohmeyer, 90; Taylor, 273). But it most likely was added by Mark to remind the reader of the setting in 4:2 where Jesus was teaching seated in a boat.

"Other boats were with him" is doubtless a "traditional splinter" (Pesch, 1:270), which Taylor views as a "genuine reminiscence" (274). Why this note was originally made has given rise to much speculation. Schille (*ZNW* 56 [1965] 31) takes it to reflect an originally larger group of witnesses to the event (cf. Matt 8:27, similarly, Schweizer, 107; Schenke, *Wundererzählungen,* 32). According to Taylor (274), the loss of these ships points to the severity of the storm (so Theissen, *Miracle Stories,* 102). And Lohmeyer (90) resolves their enigmatic presence by removing them through the addition of a missing οὐκ with the verb.

The story now focuses exclusively on Jesus, the disciples and their boat, as it apparently did in the pre-Markan tradition at the time when this story was combined with 3:7, 9–10 and the subsequent stories in 5:1–43. But it is not inconceivable that the story originally involved more than one boat, especially, if, as some have claimed, the little fishing boats of the sea of Galilee were much too small to hold Jesus and the disciples in one boat (Lohmeyer, 90). The request of 4:38 could have been made by those in Jesus' boat, but the response registered in 4:41 might have included all involved in the storm and the subsequent miracle. It must be admitted, however, that Mark and his tradition thought of Jesus and his disciples crossing the lake in one boat (cf. 5:1; 6:30–32; 8:10). Consequently, this comment has no relevance to the story as it now stands.

37 "A great windstorm" (λαῖλαψ μεγάλη ἀνέμου) describes the predicament in language reminiscent of Jonah 1:4. The Hebrew word for storm (סער־גדול, saʿar-gādô) in Jonah 1:4 (LXX—κλύδων μέγας) is actually rendered λαῖλαψ μεγάλη in Jer 32:32 LXX (= MT 25:32) and in Jonah stands in combination with רוח־גדולה, rûaḥ gĕdôlāh, which may account for the presence of ἀνέμου = "wind" in this context (cf. Ps 107:25—רוח סערה, rûaḥ sĕʿārāh). A story about "Jacob's ship," symbolic of Israel, with language equally similar to that of the Jonah story in T. Naph. 6.3–9, may suggest the influence of the Jonah story in shaping this narrative in the tradition. The catastrophic proportions of the storm can be felt as each wave crashes over the boat threatening to swamp it at any moment.

38 Meanwhile, Jesus lies asleep in the stern of the boat. The graphic description of Jesus asleep (καθεύδων) on "the cushion" (τὸ προσκεφάλαιον) in the stern (πρύμνη) of the boat offers a stark contrast to the description of the raging storm. At the same time, the parallel with Jonah's sleep during a life-threatening storm is hardly avoidable. Some have attributed Jesus' sleep to the topos of rescue stories in which the savior is present but unknown (e.g., Pesch, 1:271; cf. Acts 27:13–44). Taylor (276) ascribes Jesus' peaceful sleep to his own faith in the Father's care, while Gnilka (1:195) sees it as a sign of Jesus' sovereignty and security.

Jesus' subsequent actions (4:39) and the disciples' response (4:41) seem to support Gnilka's suggestion. To this extent, Jesus' sleep in the storm indicating his sovereignty and security in the face of death differs from Jonah's sleep during his attempt to escape from his mission. The difference between Jonah and Jesus begins to emerge even more clearly at the point of their initial response to the storm.

The Jonah parallel, however, continues a bit further. Jonah's captain arouses him with a charge of dereliction of duty, sleeping when all was about to be lost (Jonah 1:6). Jesus' companions arouse him (ἐγείρουσιν) with the charge that he does not care about their survival (οὐ μέλει σοι ὅτι ἀπολλύμεθα—cf. Jonah 1:6b). Their question comes as an accusation rather than the typical request for help one would expect in this kind of a story (cf. Matt 8:25). Several have attributed the change from request to cry of despair and doubt to Mark's redactional portrait of the disciples (Koch, Wundererzählungen, 96–97; Gnilka, 1:194, n. 7; Schmithals, 1:260). Others, however, take it to be more an indirect request for help (Kertelge, Wunder, 95; Pesch, 1:272; van Iersel and Linmans, Miscellanea, 20–21; cf. Luke 8:24).

It is difficult to know to what extent, if any, the disciples' cry has been altered. The captain's rebuke of Jonah was followed by a request that he pray to his God for help (Jonah 1:6). The disciples' rebuke may too have at least implied a "Do something!" in an earlier form of the story. Perhaps they simply wanted him to share in their concern or help them by prayer in keeping with the Jonah story and similar rescue stories in Judaism (Str-B, 1:489–90). In any case, the resulting awe and question in 4:41 do indicate that Jesus acted contrary to their expectations. And as the story now stands, the disciples' cry sets the stage for Jesus' rebuke of their fear and lack of faith in 4:40. Their cry, therefore, does not come as a request but as an expression of despair and anger aimed at their "Master" (διδάσκαλε) who apparently cared little about them. Jesus' rebuke in 4:40 now sets the tone of the disciples' cry in 4:38.

39 Jesus responds by stilling the storm and calming the sea. Van der Loos (*Miracles,* 641–44) gives numerous examples from Greek and Hebrew literature for such "weather miracles." But the language here closely parallels the exorcism of the demon in 1:25. Jesus "rebukes" (ἐπιτίμησεν) the wind and "silences" (πεφίμωσο) the "sea" (see *Comment* on 1:25). By having Jesus address the elements as though they were demonic, a theme that appears in Judaism (e.g., *2 Enoch* 40:9; 43:1–3; 69:22; *4 Ezra* 6:41–42; *Jub.* 2:2), the story underscores the nature of the struggle (Achtemeier, *Int* 16 [1962] 169–76).

Jesus' actions actually answer the question posed in 4:41b—"Who indeed is this that the wind and sea obey him?" The answer has two dimensions. First, the parallel with Jonah shows him to be greater than Jonah (cf. Matt 12:41; Luke 11:32). Instead of praying to God, he personally addressed the wind and the sea. Second, Jesus accomplished what in the OT only God could do in overcoming the chaotic powers of evil as numerous OT passages indicate (e.g., Gen 8:1; Pss 74:13–14; 104:4–9; 107:25–30). God was uniquely at work in Jesus. The awed response in 4:41 appropriately confirms this point.

40 Before we come to the formal response in 4:41, Jesus turns to his companions and rebukes them with two incriminating questions. This hitch in the flow of the story has led some to assign it to Mark's redaction (Koch, *Wundererzählungen,* 97; Pesch, 1:268; Gnilka, 1:193; Ernst, 149) and others to relocate the initial question (4:40a) to a position prior to Jesus' actions in 4:39 (e.g., Schenke, *Wundererzählungen,* 41; van Iersel and Linmans, *Miscellanea,* 19). In support of a traditional element behind 4:40a, Mark does not seem redactionally disposed to begin a saying with καὶ εἶπεν αὐτῷ (αὐτοῖς) (e.g., 1:17; 2:19; 7:29; 9:29; 10:21, 52; cf. 3:9; 4:39) and he only employs δειλοί here (cf. 6:49–52). And though logically and formally this expression fits more naturally between 4:38–39, no pause in the narrative gives any hint of its having been relocated after 4:39. Therefore, nothing except strictly formal concerns precludes the present location of this question in the story's sequence. The real issue lies in the second question.

"Do you not yet have faith?" (οὔπω ἔχετε πίστιν) is the second half of a Markan "double question" (see *Comment* on 4:13) and most likely expands the first question. Their "fear" (δειλοί) of the storm's danger exposed their lack of faith. But what does "faith" mean here? Dibelius (79) defines this faith as "belief in the power of the miracle-worker." This rendering would assume that 4:40 belonged originally to the tradition, since this use of "faith" is one of the earmarks of this collection of "tales," according to Dibelius, in 4:35–5:43. The thrust of this and the following stories would then be to display Jesus as the "great miracle-worker" who "excelled all other thaumaturges" (Dibelius, 71). Yet most today take at least this second question in 4:40 to have been Mark's redactional addition, and Mark hardly had defined "faith" for the disciples as "belief in the power of the miracle-worker."

If we, however, take it to mean trust in "God's helping power present and active in Jesus" (Cranfield, 175; similarly Lane, 177), the question suggests the disciples' fear of the storm's threat came from their failure ultimately to believe in God (Taylor, 276). Thus the disciples' response that follows in 4:41 actually answers Jesus' question in the negative. Their failure to recognize who Jesus was meant at least their failure to recognize that God was at work in him.

But this reading not only paints a picture of the disciples too bleak for even Mark but also misconstrues the thrust of 4:41 in view of Mark's previous depiction of the disciples and fails to do justice to the "not yet" (οὔπω) that opens the question. "Not yet" suggests something is lacking that could or should have been expected (cf. 8:17, 21). And the basis for this expectation lies in Mark's previous reference to the disciples in contexts that set them apart through their relationship to Jesus (e.g., 1:16–20; 2:13–14; 3:14–15, 34–35; 4:10–12, 34b). Yet Mark begins in 4:13 (see *Comment*) a series of questions that show a serious lack in the disciples' response to Jesus' ministry (cf. 4:40; 7:18; 8:17, 21). For the most part, this lack is described as a failure to comprehend, to understand, Jesus' teaching in parables (4:13; 7:18) and his miracles (οὔπω twice; cf. 6:52). But here Jesus questions their "faith."

The difference, however, between Jesus' question here and in 4:13, the one focusing on faith and the other on understanding, may be more apparent than real. First, the disciples' failure to understand in 6:52 and 8:17 was attributed not to the thickness of their heads but to the "hardness of their hearts" so that having eyes they fail to see and having ears they fail to hear (8:18; cf. 4:11–12). And secondly, this miracle story illustrates the very issue of the previous parables (4:3–32), namely, the presence of God's sovereign rule, the "kingdom of God," in Jesus' person and ministry despite appearances to the contrary. Consequently, the disciples' behavior in this story illustrates their failure to understand the parables (4:13) even after Jesus has "explained all things to them privately" (4:34b).

Their fear of the storm overwhelmed their commitment to Jesus and their confidence that he did care for them (4:38), a reflection of their lack of faith that God could be at work in Jesus to protect them even during the threat of a raging storm. Jesus' questions imply their fear was unfounded, since their faith should have assured them of their safety, though not necessarily of a miracle (cf. Dibelius, 71). Such assurance was reflected in Jesus' own serenity during the storm.

This tension in Mark's portrait of the disciples between a group of followers given a special calling, a relationship to Jesus, and even special instruction that sets them apart and at the same time a group who culpably fail to comprehend and even trust themselves at times to Jesus in no way suggests that Mark considered the disciples to be "unbelievers" who rejected Jesus and his ministry. Yet they do at times respond to Jesus like the "outsiders," when they too failed to recognize how it was that God was working in Jesus (4:13, 40; 8:17–21).

Rather than being the creator of this complex portrait of the disciples, as is often assumed, Mark seems to have enhanced its lines as found in his tradition. We noted in 4:13 how Jesus' incriminating questions make explicit what is implicit behind the traditional question underlying 4:10a, the disciples' need for further explanation of the parable. Here Mark may well have developed the question about the disciples' "fear" (4:40a) by raising the question of their "faith" based on their response in 4:41. And if, as has been suggested, the scene in 3:7, 9–10 preceded this story, the *disciples'*, not an anonymous group's, failure to recognize Jesus (4:41) was already in the tradition. By adding this question about their faith, Mark again makes explicit what lies implicit in his tradition.

Mark most likely highlights this rather negative side of the disciples' response to address the struggles of his own community to understand the hidden presence of God's sovereign rule (Pesch, 1:276). One can only speculate about whether Mark was addressing his own "disciples" in this way because they were struggling with the absence of their Lord after Easter (Koch, *Wundererzählungen*, 98), the delayed Parousia (Schenke, *Wundererzählungen*, 78) or experiencing the apocalyptic woes of suffering (Kertelge, *Wunder*, 98). But Mark's emphasis on the way of the cross, the cost of discipleship (8:27–10:52), may point to his community's struggle to comprehend how God could have been and still be at work in the world through the Christ whom they followed in view of appearances to the contrary. Thus their fear betrays their lack of faith.

41 This verse concludes the story with an expression of astonishment and a choral ending. "They were awestruck" renders Mark's only cognate accusative (φοβήθησαν φόβον), a construction that is more Semitic than Greek (Maloney, *Semitic Interference*, 189–90). Jonah 1:10 [LXX] employs the same expression to describe the reaction of Jonah's companions to his reference to God. And a similar expression in Jonah 1:16 describes their response to the calming of the sea after Jonah had been thrown overboard, a response that led to sacrifice and prayers.

This "fear" (φόβον), consequently, differs from that of 4:40 (δειλοί). Δειλός arose from their anxiety about the storm; φόβος refers to a "reverential awe" (Taylor, 277). The one expressed a lack of faith; the other a sense of awe in the presence of God. This response clearly corresponds to the experience of an epiphany (Dibelius, 94; Pesch, 1:273; Gnilka, 1:197), and points to the presence of God at work in Jesus. The Semitic setting, however, negates any hellenistic θεῖος ἀνήρ motif and places it, as the Jonah parallels indicate, within an OT context.

The story ends with a question set as a choral ending. This has led some to regard it as a secondary ending to align the miracle story formally with other such endings (Schille, *ZNW* 56 [1965] 34; Roloff, *Kerygma*, 165, n. 215; Schmithals, 1:256–57). Others argue on form-critical grounds for its authenticity as the "natural" ending (Gnilka, 1:194; Schenke, *Wundererzählungen*, 34). In either case, one must understand the question in light of the comment about reverential awe. Taken from its immediate context, the question could express confusion and doubt about who Jesus was. But in the context of 4:41a and the story itself, the question takes on a rhetorical force. The answer lies at hand in the story itself. Jesus has just shown himself to be greater than Jonah by his actions. He spoke and the wind and waves obeyed. He accomplishes God's work of stilling the storm and calming the sea (e.g., Ps 107:28–29).

Nevertheless, this response to Jesus' ministry does come somewhat as a surprise. The question seems out of place on the lips of disciples who seldom reflect such astonishment at Jesus' miracles (see 6:45–52). The story may originally have had a more general audience, a remnant of which may lie behind the reference to the other boats in 4:36 (see *Comment*). But even should we posit such an audience behind the response of 4:41, the reaction and comment still point to an epiphany.

The thrust of this response does not change. Mark simply develops the surprise element by raising the question about the disciples' lack of faith (4:40b) reflected in their fear of the storm (4:40a) and their cry of despair (4:38).

In the pre-Markan miracle collection, the final question sets the stage for Jesus' epiphany and self-disclosure in the concluding miracle, the second sea story, of 6:45–52. Jesus' statement in 6:50 provides the answer to the question of 4:41. As the story now stands in Mark, however, the evangelist leaves the concluding question for the reader to answer on the basis of the story. Rather than pose a question to be answered later either after Easter (Ernst, 151) or at Caesarea Philippi by Peter (Gnilka, 197), Mark preserves the rhetorical force of the question. It forces the reader to respond in view of the OT setting of the story as well as the reader's knowledge of the larger story. A greater than Jonah is here; one in whom God's power is indeed at work (Jonah 1:4–16; Pss 74:12–17; 89:9; 104:5–9; 107:28–29). At the same time, Mark blunts Jesus' answer in 6:50 by underlining there the disciples' lack of understanding (see *Comment* on 6:52).

Explanation

This story begins a series of miracle stories found most likely by the evangelist in a collection introduced by the summary of 3:7, 9–10. Between these two elements, Mark has placed a section on the disciples (3:13–35) and Jesus' discourse of "Kingdom" parables (4:1–34). The discourse also contains the motif of the disciples' special privilege (4:10–11, 23–24, 34b), a theme clearly related to the calling of the Twelve to be with Jesus in 3:13–19 and the reference to his true family in 3:20–35. At the same time, 4:1–34 introduces the disciples' failure to understand Jesus' teaching about the Kingdom in the question underlying 4:10, Jesus' questions of the disciples in 4:13, his interpretation of the parable in 4:14–20, the admonition to hear illustrated by the parabolic saying in 4:23–24 and the need for explicit instruction implicit in the privilege of 4:34b. The Stilling of the Storm continues the Kingdom motif seen in Jesus' "rebuke" of the wind and the waves as well as in the implied answer to the rhetorical question in 4:41, and it also continues the theme of the disciples' struggle by underscoring their surprising behavior in response to the storm (4:38, 40) and the miracle (4:41). Mark underscores this latter point (4:40b) and may even have reworked the disciples' cry of despair (4:38b) accordingly. In so doing, he does not alter the story's focus on Jesus but continues the theme of the disciples' struggle with the apparent anomaly between the coming of the Kingdom and the almost overwhelming indications to the contrary, a point illustrated by the parables in 4:3–32. He does this by accenting their fear and lack of faith (4:40) in the one through whom God is at work in the world. The serenity of Jesus' sleep in the face of disaster (4:38a), the authority with which he rebuked the chaotic powers of nature (4:39; cf. Ps 107:28–29) and the reverential awe engendered in the disciples (4:41a; cf. Jonah 1:10, 16) testify to the reader of one greater than Jonah, an epiphany of God's power and presence in Jesus and his ministry.

Mark most likely underscores this struggle in order to call his own community of "disciples" to account for their own lack of faith in view of the storms that threaten their lives. At the same time, this story assures Mark's readers through the concluding question (4:41b) that in Jesus they have one in whom God was and is at work, one whom the "wind and the waves" do obey, even when it appears the storms may overwhelm them.

K. The Gerasene Demoniac (5:1–20)

Bibliography

Annen, F. *Heil für die Heiden: Zur Bedeutung und Geschichte der Tradition vom besessenen Gerasener (Mk 5,1–20 par.).* FTS 20. Frankfurt: J. Knecht, 1976. **Baarda, T.** "Gadarenes, Gerasenes, Gergesenes and the 'Diatesseron' Tradition." *Neotestamentica et Semitica.* FS M. Black, ed. E. Ellis and M. Wilcox. Edinburgh: T. & T. Clark, 1969. 181–97. **Bächli, O.** "'Was habe ich mit dir zu schaffen?' Eine formalhafte Frage im Alten Testament und Neuen Testament." *TZ* 33 (1977) 69–80. **Bauernfeind, O.** *Die Worte der Daimonen im Markusevangelium.* BWANT 44. Stuttgart: Kohlhammer, 1927. **Bonner, C.** "The Technique of Exorcism." *HTR* 36 (1943) 39–49. **Burkill, T. A.** "Concerning Mk 5,7 and 5,18–20." In *Mysterious Revelation: An Examination of the Philosophy of St. Mark's Gospel.* Ithaca: Cornell University Press, 1963 = *ST* 11 (1957) 159–66. **Cave, C. H.** "The Obedience of the Unclean Spirits." *NTS* 11 (1964) 93–97. **Craghan, J. F.** "The Gerasene Demoniac." *CBQ* 30 (1968) 522–36. **Dalman, G.** *Sacred Sites and Ways: Studies in the Topography of the Gospels.* Tr. P. P. Levertoff. New York: Macmillan, 1935. **Derrett, J. D. M.** "Contributions to the Study of the Gerasene Demoniac." *JSNT* 3 (1979) 2–17. ———. "Legend and Event: The Gerasene Demoniac: An Inquest into History and Liturgical Projection (Mk 5,1–20)." In *Studia Biblica 1978* II, ed. E. H. Livingstone. JSNTSup 2. Sheffield: University of Sheffield Press, 1980. 63–73. **Fowler, R. M.** *Loaves and Fishes.* SBLDS 54. Chico, CA: Scholars, 1981. **Kertelge, K.** *Die Wunder Jesu im Markusevangelium.* 1970. **Koch, D.-A.** *Die Bedeutung der Wundererzählungen für die Christologie des Markusevangeliums.* 1975. **Luz, U.** "Das Geheimnismotiv und die markinische Christologie." *ZNW* 56 (1965) 9–30 = "The Secrecy Motif and Marcan Theology." Tr. R. Morgan. In *The Messianic Secret,* ed. C. Tuckett. London/ Philadelphia: SPCK/Fortress, 1983. 75–96. **Minette de Tillesse, G.** *Le secret messianique dans l'évangile de Marc.* LD 47. Paris: Cerf, 1968. **Parker, S. T.** "The Decapolis Reviewed." *JBL* 94 (1975) 437–41. **Pesch, R.** "The Markan Version of the Healing of the Gerasene Demoniac." *EcumRev* 23 (1971) 349–76. **Robinson, J. M.** *The Problem of History in Mark.* SBT 21. London: SCM, 1957. **Sahlin, H.** "Die Perikope vom gerasenischen Besessenen und der Plan des Markusevangeliums." *ST* 18 (1964) 159–72. **Schenke, L.** *Die Wundererzählungen im Markusevangelium.* 1974. **Schwarz, G.** "'Aus der Gegend' (Mk v. 10b)." *NTS* 22 (1975–76) 215–16.

Translation

^{1} *And they* ^{a} *came to the other side of the sea into the region of the Gerasenes.* ^{b} ^{2} *When Jesus* ^{c} *had come out of the boat,* ^{d} *a man from the tombs with an unclean spirit immediately met him.* ^{3} *The man* ^{c} *lived* ^{e} *among the tombs, and none could bind him any longer even with chains,* ^{4} *because he had often been bound by shackles and chains but the chains had been torn apart and the shackles smashed in pieces by him. No one was able to subdue him.* ^{5} *All night and day he screamed in the tombs and mountains and beat himself with stones.*

^{6} *Seeing Jesus at a distance, he ran and bowed before him,* ^{7} *and screaming with a loud voice said, "What do we have in common, Jesus, Son of the Most High God? I adjure you by God, do not torment me."* ^{8} *For he had said,* ^{f} *"You unclean spirit, come out of the man!"* ^{9} *And Jesus* ^{c} *asked him, "What is your name?" And he said to him, "Legion is my name, for we are many."* ^{10} *And he appealed to him many times that he not send them out of the region.*

^{11} *Now a large herd of swine was feeding there near the mountain,* ^{12} *and the* unclean spirits ^{c} *continued appealing to him saying, "Send us to the swine that we might enter them."* ^{13} *He gave them permission. And the unclean spirits, after departing, entered the swine and the herd rushed down the steep bank into the sea, about 2000 of them, and were drowned in the sea.*

^{14} *Those tending them fled and announced it in the city and on the farms. And the* inhabitants ^{c} *came to see what had happened.* ^{15} *They came to Jesus and saw the demon possessed man, the one who had the legion, sitting, clothed and in his right mind, and they were afraid.* ^{16} *And those who had seen it told them how it had happened to the demon possessed man and about the swine.* ^{17} *And the* inhabitants ^{c} *began to appeal to him to depart from their territory.*

^{18} *When Jesus* ^{c} *was getting into the boat, the man who had been demon possessed appealed to him that he might be with him.* ^{19} *Jesus* ^{c} *did not permit him but said to him, "Go to your home and to your people and announce to them how much the Lord has done for you and how He has been merciful to you."* ^{20} *He departed and began to proclaim in the Decapolis how much Jesus had done for him, and all were amazed.*

Notes

^{a} Several mss read ἦλθεν (ℵ^{cvid} C L Δ Θ f^{13} 28 700 892 sy bo), a secondary alignment with the focus on Jesus in v 2 and throughout the story.

^{b} Γερασηνῶν should be read here based on better manuscript evidence (ℵ* B D 28 33 525 *al* it vg cop^{sa}). Γαδαρηνῶν (A C K f^{13} Majority text syr^{ph}) is probably a later alignment with Matt 8:28, and Γεργεσηνῶν (ℵ^2 L X Θ f^1 cop^{bo}) represents a correction that is first witnessed, if not suggested, by Origen (see Metzger, *Textual Commentary*, 23–24; Baarda, *Neotestamentica*, 181–97).

^{c} Romanized words supplied from context.

^{d} Genitive absolute.

^{e} Literally, "had his dwelling" (τὴν κατοίκησιν εἶχεν).

^{f} Imperfect rendered as a pluperfect (Taylor, 281).

Form/Structure/Setting

Form-critically, several commentators have taken this pericope as an exorcism story (e.g., Bultmann, 210; Koch, *Wundererzählungen*, 55–56), but most recognize that it breaks down at several points with the typical exorcism pattern. Apart from its vivid detail, which led Dibelius (71–72) followed by Grundmann (140) and Schmithals (1:266) to view it as a tale (*Novelle*), the use of the adjuration formula by the demon rather than the exorcist (5:7), the awkward position of the expulsion command (ἀποπομπή, 5:8), the unusual banishment (ἐπιπομπή, 5:13), and the "unevenness of the narrative" (Taylor, 277; similarly Pesch, 1:284) indicate the story to be more than a simple exorcism.

Consequently, many scholars explain this complex story to be a combination or development of traditions that began with an original exorcism story and became a mission story (Craghan, *CBQ* 30 [1968] 524; Kertelge, *Wunder*, 103; Schenke, *Wundererzählungen*, 190–92; Gnilka, 1:202, 208). In any case, like the previous pericope (4:35–41), this one fails to fit any neat formal category, and our analysis will question whether the pericope at any stage in the tradition narrowly fit the normal pattern of the typical exorcism story.

As to Mark's source, with the exception of Gnilka (1:200–02) most concur with Bultmann's (210) judgment that Mark has taken over the material "essentially intact." Yet few would question that Mark's traditional story itself reflects a development in the tradition (cf. Bultmann, 210; Schmithals, 1:266). Apart from formal considerations that show the story to outstrip the usual categories of an exorcism story, other factors have led to a positing of multiple stages in the development of the tradition such as: (a) tensions within the story (e.g., the proximity of Gerasa to the sea implied by 5:1, 13 and 18; the two different encounters in 5:2, 6; the location of the exorcism command in 5:8; the apparent redundancy or afterthought of 5:16 or at least 5:16b); (b) differing vocabulary (e.g., μνημείων, μνήμα in 5:2, 3–5; πνεῦμα ἀκάθαρτον, δαιμονιζόμενος in 5:2, 8, 13, 15, 18); and (c) midrashic motifs behind 5:3–5. This evidence has led to the positing of at least three stages (so Craghan, *CBQ* 30 [1968] 522–36; Pesch, *EcumRev* 23 [1971] 349–76; Ernst, 153–54; cf. Kertelge, *Wunder*, 102–03; Cave, *NTS* 11 [1964] 93–97; Derrett, *Studia*, 63–73). The original exorcism story represents the first stage. The story then underwent midrashic development for mission purposes. Then came the redactional adjustments made at the time of the combining the miracle stories into a pre-Markan collection of miracle stories. Our analysis below will show that the original story consisted of an opening scene in Gerasa behind 5:1–2, exorcism behind 5:7–8, and response and demonstration in 5:14–15, 17, 19. The story was next embellished with midrashic references especially to Isa 65 to underscore the man's predicament (5:3–6, 9). When the story was added to the collection of miracle stories around the sea (4:35–5:43; 6:32–56), this led to a changing in the setting (5:1–2, 18) and made possible the drowning of the swine (5:10, 12–13, 16).

For most interpreters Mark's redaction, if any, has been limited to 5:8 (Bultmann, 210; Klostermann, 49; Taylor, 272; Koch, *Wundererzählungen*, 63; Schmithals, 1:265). By contrast, Gnilka (1:200–02) attributes most of the expansion of the original story to Mark's redaction (5:1–2a, 8, 16, 18a, 20). Schenke (*Wundererzählungen*, 173–75) concurs with him regarding 5:1–2, 16, 18a and Luz (*ZNW* 56 [1965] 18), Kertelge (*Wunder*, 101) and Schweizer (112) regarding 5:20. Craghan (*CBQ* 30 [1968] 524) and Schenke (*Wundererzähl-ungen*, 177) assign both 5:19–20 to Mark's redaction and Schenke only 5:19a,

20. Our examination below will suggest that only 5:20 may have come from Mark's redaction.

Structurally, Taylor (277) finds the rudiments of a four-act drama in the scenes depicting Jesus and the demoniac (5:1–10), the swine (5:11–13), the townspeople (5:14–17) and the freed man (5:18–20). Pesch (1:282) divides it along the lines of the setting and description of the illness (5:1–5), Jesus and the demon(s) (5:6–13), the witnesses (5:14–17) and the healed man (5:18–20). Our translation opens with the setting (5:1–5) followed by Jesus and the demon(s) (5:6–10), the swine (5:11–13), the witnesses (5:14–17) and the healed man's response (5:18–20). Yet no structure adequately divides the story into discrete segments, since 5:2 describes the demoniac's initial encounter with Jesus that is resumed in 5:6, whereas the swine enter the story in 5:11 because of the demons' request for a domicile in 5:10b (cf. 5:12).

The setting for this story in Mark's Gospel as the second in a series of four miracles provides the destination ("to the other side") for the boat trip, which was the occasion of the first miracle, mentioned in 4:35. It also provides the occasion (5:17) for Jesus leaving "the other side" to cross again (5:21) where he heals the woman with a hemorrhage (5:25–34) and raises the daughter of Jairus, a "ruler of the synagogue" (5:21–24, 35–43). At the same time, these stories share a thematic and perhaps ironic connection in that Jesus delivers his disciples from death in 4:35–41 by "rebuking" (ἐπετίμησεν) and "silencing" (πεφίμωσο) the wind and the sea, language associated with the exorcisms (see *Comment* on 1:25; 3:12; 4:39 and 9:25, though missing in 5:1–20!). Yet he delivers a demon possessed man in 5:1–20 whose deliverance concludes with the demons drowning a herd of swine in the same sea (5:13) from which the disciples had been delivered. Jesus' power over the evil forces of nature becomes even clearer in this story which from the outset shows him to be superior to the demon(s).

The setting of 4:35–41, however, raises a chronological and geographical question (see *Comment* on 5:1, 2) that suggests the two stories (4:35–41; 5:1–20) existed as independent traditions before being connected to each other. Their present association may have been precipitated by the thematic similarity that led to the more contrived temporal and geographical setting in an attempt to bind them together. Most likely, the combination took place at an earlier stage in the pre-Markan tradition.

In the larger setting of Mark's Gospel, this story repeats previous events familiar to the reader. In 1:24 and 3:11 the "unclean spirits" had correctly identified Jesus as the "Holy One of God," the "Son of God," because "they knew who he was" (1:34). Here they address him as the "Son of the Most High" (5:7). Furthermore, the spirits acknowledge his superiority in 1:24, fall before him when they see him in 3:11, just as they do in 5:6–10. Thus the evil spirits clearly recognize Jesus to be their superior and this note rings consistently through these stories.

This story also introduces Jesus' ministry in the Decapolis (5:20) most likely connoting a Gentile environment. Mark repeats this theme again in 7:24–34 in the story of the Syrophoenecian woman and in his summary of Jesus' expansive ministry that includes the areas of Tyre and Sidon, the region around the Sea of Galilee, and the district of the Decapolis (7:31; cf. 38), which in the latter case is certainly anticipated by the man's proclamation in 5:20.

Comment

1 "They came to the other side." Though some mss read "he came" (ἦλθεν—C L D Θ *f*¹³), this reading most likely stems from the alignment of 5:1 with the singular genitive absolute (ἐξελθόντος αὐτοῦ) in 5:2a or with Matt 8:28 (ἐλθόντος αὐτοῦ εἰς τὸ πέραν) rather than from a vestigial singular in the tradition changed into a plural by the redactor who combined 5:1–20 with 4:35–41 (e.g., "Mark," so Schenke, *Wundererzählungen*, 174; Gnilka, 1:200). "The other side" ties this story to the previous one by indicating the arrival at the destination given in 4:35 for the boat trip. This phrase provides a common thread running through the miracle stories of 4:35; 5:1, 25; 6:45 and does not connote any specific "side" of the sea (cf. 4:35/5:1 and 5:21) but serves as a "nondescript expression used to shift the stage scenery" (Fowler, *Loaves*, 59–60). But the specification of "the other side" geographically as "the region of the Gerasenes" does indicate that here the "other side" means the east side of the sea.

"The region of the Gerasenes" (εἰς τὴν χώραν τῶν Γερασηνῶν) specifies where Jesus and the disciples had landed on "the other side." Despite textual variants pointing to Gadara (so Matt 8:28) and Gergesa (so Luke 8:26), the superior witnesses support the reading of "Gerasenes" (see *Note* b). This reading, however, creates a dilemma.

"Gerasa" (Γερασηνῶν), Jerash today, was one of the prominent cities of the Decapolis, a fact which squares with the notice in 5:20. But it was situated thirty miles or a two-day journey from the sea and the events of the story imply that the action took place near the sea. Not only does the demoniac meet Jesus "immediately" after the latter had left the boat (5:2b), but the swine rush down a steep bank into the sea and drown (5:13). One cannot avoid the dilemma by accenting "region" (χώραν) rather than "Gerasenes" (Kertelge, *Wunder*, 104), because the swineherders run to "the city" (τὴν πόλιν) to announce the events and the curious respond by going to Jesus and the man as though it all happened at least on the same day (5:14–17).

One of the earliest resolutions of this dilemma denies Gerasa to have been the correct place and posits another. Matt 8:28 has "Gadara," another city of the Decapolis which was located much closer to the sea. But it still was five miles away and across the Jarmuk River with no steep embankment in the vicinity.

A variant reading behind Matt 8:28; Mark 5:1 and Luke 8:26 offers another alternative, the "Gergesenes" from "Gergesa," a town unknown to us now (see *Note* b). Dalman (*Sites*, 177) has suggested that the ruin of Kursa (Kursi) or Kersa near Wadi es-Samak with a hill nearby might have been the ancient town and the original "Gergesa" of the story (so Taylor, 279; Cranfield, 176; Lane, 180; Gnilka, 1:201). Even assuming the correctness of Dalman's site, it leaves us with the further dilemma of explaining how Mark's better attested reading of Γερασηνῶν replaced the original Γεργεσηνῶν.

Logically, one can imagine the exchange of the better known "Gerasa" for the lesser known "Gergesa." But by whom? If it was done by Mark (so Gnilka, 1:201) or in the pre-Markan tradition (implied by Taylor, 279; Cranfield, 176; Lane, 180) as the superior manuscript evidence suggests, how did "Gergesa" survive? Or if Mark originally had "Gergesa," as some manuscripts suggest, why did Matthew change it to "Gadara," assuming that "Gadara" was an attempt to set the story in proximity to the sea? Furthermore, Baarda (*Neotestamentica*, 181–97) demonstrates the likely possibility based on manuscript evidence that Γεργεσηνῶν first entered the text as Origen's attempt to solve the problem of Γερασηνῶν. In other words, by finding a setting near the sea, we exchange the geographical problems within the story and its larger context for the textual problem of explaining the Γαδαρηνῶν of Matt 8:28 and the strong manuscript evidence behind Γερασηνῶν of Mark 5:1.

A second solution explains the dilemma by assigning the place name, Γερασηνῶν, to Mark's mistaken redaction of a story originally without a specific location (e.g., Klostermann, 47; Lohmeyer, 94; Schenke, *Wundererzähl-ungen*, 174; Schmithals, 1:265). Accordingly, Mark added the locale associated with Gerasa, a prominent city of the Decapolis, which he thought to be in the vicinity of the sea. Consequently, the geographical tension within the story simply reflects the evangelist's ignorance of the area (e.g., Schenke, *Wundererzählungen*, 174). And since Mark's text underlies Matthew's and Luke's account, Matthew's "Gadarenes" represents an attempt to "correct" Mark's faulty geography, an attempt doubtless reflected in the variant reading of "Gergesenes" regardless of when it was first introduced. This explanation takes seriously the manuscript evidence but does not resolve the tension within the story. It merely explains how the confusion might have come about by attributing it to Mark. Its major weakness, however, lies in explaining why Mark, given his supposed geographical ignorance, picked Gerasa of the Decapolis. It was hardly the most prominent city of the Decapolis.

A third explanation accepts the textual evidence supporting Γερασηνῶν and also accepts its presence in the original story as referring to the actual place of the exorcism (Grundmann, 142; Pesch, 1:282; Ernst, 154). And the presence of this locale in the original story best explains why it was there despite the later "corrections." By moving the exorcism to Gerasa, one does not relax the geographical tension within the story. But this tension coincides with the formal tension in the story itself and may indicate a stage in the story's development when it was combined with the miracle of 4:35–41 and placed in the sea setting.

If originally set around Gerasa, the references to the sea in 5:1–2a, 13 and 18a would come from later developments. Mark 5:1–2a and 5:18 are related to Jesus' mode of travel, i.e., a boat, which connects the miracle collection (4:35–5:43; 6:32–56) and were likely added when these stories were combined. Only the drowning in 5:13 connects the sea with the exorcism per se, and it might, one could argue, have given rise to the sea setting of 5:1–2a and 5:18. But actually, the opposite seems more likely. Mark 5:13 is verbally related to the framework of 5:1–2a through its connection with 5:10. In 5:10 the unclean spirit(s) ask that Jesus not send them out of the "region" (χώρας). In 5:13 Jesus complies with their request allowing them to enter the swine who then rush into the sea indicating that the "region" in question included the area around the sea, the very area implied by Jesus' arrival in the "*region* (χώραν) of the Gerasenes" in 5:1.

Thus the accommodation of the original exorcism story at Gerasa, some distance from the sea, to the collection of miracles set around the Sea of Galilee maintained continuity with the "Gerasa" tradition by adding the "region" (χώραν) to an original reference to the "Gerasenes" in 5:1 and 5:10. By so doing, the area of Gerasa was extended to the sea in keeping with the setting of 4:35–41 and 5:21. The accommodation, however, shifts the story's focus to the sea and creates an unresolved tension implicit in the reference to the city of Gerasa in 5:14. It also opens up the possibility of introducing the sea as a factor into the story itself (see *Comment* on 5:12–13)

2 "When (Jesus) had come out of the boat" (ἐξελθόντος αὐτοῦ ἐκ τοῦ πλοίου) signals the arrival of Jesus and his party on land. Many interpreters have noted the chronological tension between this story, which transpires during the day, and the previous one, which occurs during the night. Since a crossing would hardly take more than a couple of hours, considerable time had elapsed between the "evening" in 4:35 and the arrival in 5:1–2. But this time gap simply exposes a less than smooth temporal seam created by the combination of two stories that once had existed as unrelated traditional units.

"Immediately met him" (εὐθὺς ὑπήντησεν αὐτῷ) relates the first of two encounters (cf. 5:6). Such an encounter between the possessed and the exorcist typifies an exorcism story. The man is described as coming from the "tombs" (μνημείων) and having "an unclean spirit" (πνεύματι ἀκαθάρτῳ). The sense of uncleanness accompanies not only the evil spirit but also the man's point of departure, the "tombs." And if, as has been suggested, Gerasa was the original place, this gentile setting also connoted ritual impurity as illustrated above all by the presence of the herd of swine (5:11).

3–5 These verses, distinctive to Mark's account, break with the normal pattern of an exorcism story by detailing the man's condition. This formal break coupled with the repeated but varied references to the man's dwelling (cf. ἐκ τῶν μνημείων—5:2, and τὴν κατοίκησιν . . . ἐν τοῖς μνήμασιν—5:3) and the presence of five *hapax legomena* (κατοίκησις, ἅλυσις, πέδη, διασπᾶν, δαμάζειν) may support the thesis that the verses represent a midrashic development of the tradition based on Isa 65:4–6 and Ps 67:7[LXX] (Cave, *NTS* 11 [1964] 96; Craghan, *CBQ* 30 [1968] 529; Grundmann, 142; Pesch, 1:285). The reference to the tombs in 5:2 and the swine in 5:11 could have provided the key words leading to a midrashic use of these texts.

"He lived" freely renders τὴν κατοίκησιν εἶχεν, one of the *hapax legomena* (cf. Ps 67:7b LXX). This statement makes explicit the implication of 5:2 (cf. "from the tombs" [ἐκ τοῦ μνημείων]) that the man actually lived among the tombs. The imperfect tense (εἶχεν) here and in 5:5 vividly describes his previous condition as though recalled by those who knew him (Taylor, 280; Cranfield, 177). But the vivid style may simply correspond to the style of the "midrash."

"Among the tombs" (ἐν τοῖς μνήμασιν) changes the previous word for "tomb" (μνημείων) in 5:2. Mark uses the latter seven times (5:2; 6:29; 15:46; 16:2, 3, 5, 8) and the former four times, twice here and once each in the same context with μνημεῖον (15:46; 16:2). The change here may reflect a later development of 5:2 under the influence of Isa 65:4[LXX] (Cave, *NTS* 11 [1964] 96; Craghan, *CBQ* 30 [1968] 530; Grundmann, 142). The man's "home" among the tombs bespeaks his ostracism from society and corresponds to his possession by an unclean spirit, a being often thought to dwell among the tombs.

3b–4 These verses describe the futility of all attempts to constrain the man's wildness. Even chains and shackles could not hold him. This display of uncontrollable strength may reflect his possession by "Legion" (5:9). In any case, these verses describe a man whom no one could tame.

5 This verse graphically describes the terrible state of the man's mind through the use of the imperfect periphrastic (ἦν κράζων καὶ κατακόπτων). His screams accompanied by his self-destructive behavior (κατακόπτων ἑαυτὸν λίθοις) rang through the tombs and the hills day and night. Taken together these three verses contain the four characteristics of insanity in Judaism (Str-B, 1:421): (a) running about at night (5:5); (b) spending the night in a cemetery (5:3); (c) tearing one's garments (cf. διεσπάσθαι, 5:4); and (d) destroying what one has been given (cf. συντετρῖφθαι, 5:4). At the same time, the thematic development of Isa 65:3–4 seen here in the "demons" (δαιμονίοις, 65:3), spending the night in the "tombs" (ἐν τοῖς μνημάσιν . . . κοιμῶνται, 65:4), and the eating of "swine flesh" (κρέα ὕεια, 65:4) implied later by the presence of the herd of swine in 5:11 show this story to involve more than Jesus' restoring an insane man to his senses. Though Isa 65:3–4 was addressed originally to Israel, Isaiah's words become the more biting because the behavior was so characteristic of gentile practice. The use of Isa 65 here to refer to the condition of a gentile man parallels Paul's application of Isa 65:1 in Rom 10:21 to the Gentiles and leaves little basis for viewing this man as a "nominal" Jew along the lines of the "prodigal" in Luke 15:15 (cf. Derrett, *JSNT* 3 [1979] 6).

6 Seeing Jesus "at a distance" (καὶ ἰδὼν . . . ἀπὸ μακρόθεν), he "ran" (ἔδραμεν) and "bowed" (προσεκύνησεν) before him. This verse resumes the action of 5:2 by describing in greater detail the encounter between Jesus and the possessed man. Yet this encounter hardly sets the stage for conflict or a struggle (cf. Robinson, *Problem*, 83–86). The man not only takes the initiative but does so as though urgently drawn by Jesus (cf. 1:23). Certainly, his "bowing," though most likely not an act of "devotion" (so Lohmeyer, 95), betrays his recognition and acknowledgement of Jesus as his superior (cf. 3:11). And this submissive gesture of recognition stands in stark contrast to the previous description of one totally uncontrollable (5:3–4) and accents Jesus' power to do what none before had accomplished.

This description of the encounter became necessary after the expansion of the opening scene (5:2) by 5:3–5. As 5:3–5 developed the description of the man in 5:2b, 5:6 develops the initial encounter of 5:2a by employing the recognition motifs found in the demoniac's response to Jesus in 5:7. Therefore, rather than being a Markan redactional expansion (Schenke, *Wundererzählungen,* 175), this encounter was likely added in the pre-Markan tradition along with the expansion in 5:3–5 along midrashic lines to underscore Jesus' redemptive power in an otherwise futile situation and to set the stage for 5:7 (Pesch, 1:286).

7 The possessed man screaming with a loud voice (κράξας φωνῇ μεγάλῃ) begins with a formulaic question, "What do we have in common?" (τί ἐμοὶ καὶ σοί), that expresses his disadvantage and seeks to set some distance between him and Jesus (see *Comment* on 1:24). Then, reminiscent of the demoniac in 1:24 and those possessed by unclean spirits in 3:11, the man reveals his knowledge of who Jesus is by addressing him as "Jesus, the Son of the Most High God" (Ἰησοῦ υἱὲ τοῦ Θεοῦ τοῦ ὑψίστου; cf. 1:24). Rather than serve as an apotropaic device for gaining power over the exorcist (so Bauernfeind, *Worte*, 56–57, 73–93; Grundmann, 143; Pesch, 1:287; Robinson, *Problem*, 85; cf. Burkill, *ST* 11 [1957] 161), an interpretation without literary parallel in exorcisms (Koch, *Wundererzählungen*, 59), this address demonstrates the demoniac's actual recognition of who Jesus is (see *Comment* on 1:24 and cf. 3:11). Furthermore, the specific name, "the Most High God," has particular relevance for this "gentile" setting, since it almost always occurs in the LXX (cf. עֶלְיוֹן, *ᶜelyon*) on the lips or in the context of Gentiles (e.g., Gen 14:18–20; Num 24:16; Isa 14:14; Dan 3:26, 42) and, apart from here and a comparable setting in Acts 16:17, only appears in the NT as a reference from an OT passage. Therefore, the selection of this name for God underlines the gentile setting for the story.

After acknowledging Jesus' superiority by way of question and address, the demoniac betrays his clear awareness of his inferior position and the futility of his situation (Gnilka, 1:204) by desperately "adjuring" Jesus not to "torture" him (μή με βασανίσῃς). In so doing a double irony arises. First, adjuration formulas generally appear on the lips of the exorcist and accompany the exorcism proper rather than being uttered by the one possessed (Koch, *Wundererzählungen*, 58). This cry obviously parodies the usual adjuration formula by putting Jesus in a subservient position to the demon, a position clearly denied by the man's actions in 5:6 and his words in 5:7b (Pesch, 1:287; cf. Bultmann, 210, n. 5). Second, the demoniac adjures Jesus by the God whom he has just recognized to be Jesus' father! Thus, the man's response to Jesus further demonstrates the unclean spirit's confused desperation before Jesus. The "demon" has abandoned all attempts to use his own power to gain control. Instead we have an "encounter" where the one recognizes at the outset (cf. 5:6 and 5:7) that he has met his match and simply desires to negotiate a settlement.

Finally, Jesus' superiority over the unclean spirit is expressed by the demoniac's fear of "torture" (βασανίσῃς). Many find here a latent reference to an apocalyptic expectation of the final judgment as in Matt 8:30 (so Lohmeyer, 95; Taylor, 280; Grundmann, 144). Others find simply a fear of "punishment" or banishment from the spirit's "home," as supported by the context (e.g., 5:10–13, Haenchen, 193; Gnilka, 1:205). The latter most likely expressed the thrust of the exorcism story (cf. a similar fear expressed in 1:24 and note the destruction in 5:13), but Mark's use of the Strong Man parable in 3:27 to explain Jesus' exorcisms in 3:23–30 suggests that both their destruction and the eschatological character of that destruction are combined for Mark and his readers. Jesus' power over the "Strong Man" (in this case one too strong for any to bind or control) becomes evident from the beginning, so that the demoniac's "adjuration" merely makes Jesus' ultimate power the more obvious.

8 This verse reads like an afterthought. Mark's tendency to use explanatory γάρ-clauses has led several to attribute this awkward verse to his redaction (Klostermann, 49; Taylor, 281; Koch, *Wundererzählungen,* 63–64). The reason for its addition supposedly stems from the absence of the typical, explicit command for the demon to come out (e.g., Klostermann, 49). Thus Mark or an earlier redactor simply supplied a missing component to an exorcism story (Lohmeyer, 95; Grundmann, 144; Schweizer, 112). Koch (*Wundererzählungen,* 63–64) notes that the silence command typical of an exorcism story is missing, simply because it has no appropriate place in this story (so Minette de Tillesse, *Secret,* 85, n. 1; Burkill, *ST* 11 [1957] 161–62), and suggests that Mark adds this comment to take its place. Pesch (1:288) simply views this comment as setting the stage for the dialogue in 5:9–10.

Without doubt, the comment stands in awkward tension with what has gone before by implying a previous ineffectual command for the unclean spirit to come out of the man. This implication stands at odds, however, with the story's repeated emphasis on the servile position of the unclean spirit toward Jesus. Thus, Haenchen (192–93) attributes this to a redactor's misunderstanding of 5:2–7. Failing to recognize that Jesus has been in control from the beginning (5:2–7), the one who added 5:8 read the story more as a traditional exorcism and sought to add a missing but essential component of such a story. And if one reads 5:8 with what precedes it, that seems the most logical explanation.

If, however, we take this explanatory comment specifically with the adjuration of 5:7b, it explains why the unclean spirit feared "torture" and what the "torture" was. The unclean spirit had been ordered out of its present habitat. This explanation also sets the stage for the dialogue in 5:9–10, 12 which develops both the concern of "torture" by expulsion (5:7b, 8) and sets up the actual banishment of 5:13 in keeping with the demon(s)' request in 5:10, 12.

Furthermore, since the destruction of the swine in 5:13 carries out the expulsion of 5:8 according to the request of 5:10 and 12, it seems most likely that the explanatory 5:8 was added at the stage in the story's development when 5:10, 12–13 expanded the original exorcism story to include the drowning of the swine. And since this material (5:10, 12–13) involved the "sea" (5:13; cf. 5:1) and the "region" (5:10; cf. 5:2), 5:8 too may have been added or modified when the exorcism story was adapted to the sea setting of 4:35–41 and 5:21–43 rather than as a redactional afterthought by Mark. If so, 5:8 without the explanatory conjunction "for" (γάρ) and with a different tense of λέγειν may well have expressed the original exorcism order per se by having Jesus, who disregards the adjuration of 5:7b, simply order the unclean spirit out.

9 In the present form of the story, however, the exorcism continues along a different tack. Jesus asks the name of the unclean spirit. Typically, this request for the name represents a ploy used by the exorcist in gaining control over the spirit (Bonner, *HTR* 36 [1943] 39–49; K. Thraede, *RAC* 7 [1969] 51, 56). But abdication of control by the unclean spirit from the beginning of this story and the spirit's ready response implies a different function for this question here. Furthermore, if Jesus needed to know the unclean spirit's identity, it would have meant Jesus' lack of knowledge had put him at a disadvantage against the unclean spirit's knowledge of Jesus' identity. Here as before, the story diverges from the formal pattern of an exorcism story.

Instead of granting Jesus control over the demon(s), the question and response reveal the extent of the man's domination. On the one hand, this verse explains his uncontrollable behavior in 5:3–4 in terms of the power of "legion" (Haenchen, 190). On the other hand, the ready submission of the man to Jesus in 5:6 accents Jesus' power over this extensive force of the demonic. Consequently, this part of the story may also have been added with the expansion of 5:3–6 that elaborated on the man's extreme predicament. Accordingly, the subject begins to vacillate between the singular "I" and the plural "we" from this point on. "Legion" appears as a Latin loan word in Greek and Aramaic texts which indicates how pervasive the concept was in the ancient world. A military term, it designates a unit or brigade in the Roman army including infantry and cavalry. The number varied between 4000 and 6000, but by Jesus' day and during the time of the empire the number appears fixed at approximately 6000 men of whom nearly 5800 were infantry.

Whether "Legion" actually represented a name (Klostermann, 49; Pesch, 1:288) or simply a collective noun (Grundmann, 144; Haenchen, 190) is disputed but somewhat moot. On the one hand, taken as the answer to the question, "What is your name?" (τί ὄνομά σοι;), "Legion" favors the former. On the other hand, the lack of evidence for the name "Legion" elsewhere and the reference in 5:15 to the man as the one having "the legion" (τὸν λεγιῶνα) favors the latter. Should one take it as a name, the spirit(s)' immediate explanation, "For we are many" (ὅτι πολλοί ἐσμεν), makes clear that the "name" primarily connoted a vast number rather than an identity by which the exorcist might gain control over the unclean spirit.

10 The unclean spirit(s)' subservient role comes through again in the repeated request for a concession from Jesus. The repetition is accented by the imperfect tense and the adverbial use of πολλά (παρεκάλει αὐτὸν πολλά). This request that Jesus not send them "out of the region" continues and specifies the content of the spirit's adjuration in 5:7b. Some have found traces of an ancient folktale behind this request that expresses the demon's fear of being displaced or sent back to the place of origin (Klostermann, 49; Lohmeyer, 96; Taylor, 282; Kertelge, *Wunder,* 102). But this request may well have been a later addition coordinated with the later setting of 5:2 that adapted an earlier exorcism story set at Gerasa to its present setting by the sea. This request not to be sent from the "region" (χώρας) refers to a geographical area and uses the very term, "region" (χώρα), of 5:2a that expanded the boundaries of the Gerasenes to include the sea (cf. Luke 8:31, ἄβυσσον).

11 The reference to a "large herd of swine" feeding on a hill underscores the tone of uncleanness struck at the outset by the man "from the tombs" with an "unclean spirit" (5:2b). Consequently, it likely belongs to the original story set in the "unclean" land of the Gentiles. Mishnaic law strictly forbade the Jews from raising pigs (*m. B. Qam.* 7:7). The large herd of swine obviously implies the use of pigs for food and/or commercial purposes, and this implication may also have influenced the employment of Isa 65:5 ("who eat swine flesh") in the midrashic expansion of the story in 5:3–4.

12 The mention of the swine in 5:11 gives occasion again for the unclean spirit(s)' to repeat the earlier request for a concession by specifying their choice of a destination. Such a banishment of demons into other areas or objects has its parallel in ancient literature but such action never comes as a concession to the demons (Pesch, 1:290). Consequently, some have read this request as the stage setting for the main point of an original "tricked devil" story (e.g., Bultmann, 210) in light of the consequence of their request (5:13). Others have attributed this verse to a later expansion attempting to soften Jesus' responsibility for the subsequent destruction of the swine (e.g., Schenke, *Wundererzählungen*, 185).

But this specification belongs to the same stage in the development of the tradition as the request in 5:10, which it specifies and which in turn corresponds to the adjuration of 5:7b. This secondary material pertains to the fate of the demons and the nearby herd of swine that underscores Jesus' work not only of cleansing the man of the unclean spirit but the unclean land of their unclean animals.

13 "He gave them permission" (ἐπέτρεψεν αὐτοῖς) now has the function of an exorcism command. The expulsion command (*apopompe*) typical of exorcisms (cf. 5:8) has become a banishment (*epipompe*) by permission. But instead of giving an order (ἔξελθε; cf. 5:8; 1:25; 9:25), he delivers the man by granting the unclean spirit(s)' request. Jesus' ultimate authority over the unclean spirit remains in force. He grants the permission.

But why this change of pattern from the other exorcism stories in the Gospels? It is dubious whether this change in pattern stems from a later attempt to soften Jesus' role in the destruction of the swine by placing the onus on the unclean spirits (cf. Schenke, *Wundererzählungen*, 185). More likely, the story now reflects the secondary development of the adjuration in 5:7b. The adjuration not to be tormented became the request for a concession in 5:10 that is now specified in 5:12. Once the adjuration was developed into a request, the change in the story line from command to permission was set without loss of Jesus' authority over the unclean spirit(s). Consequently, the underlying expulsion command behind such a story became the parenthetic clarification in 5:8 of the adjuration of 5:7b and the requests of 5:10, 12.

The suggestion that this material belonged to the expansion of an earlier exorcism story gains more support by what happens. The drowning of the swine in the sea (ἐπνίγοντο ἐν τῇ θαλάσσῃ) had to enter the tradition when the original reference to the "Gerasenes" was changed to the present "*region of the Gerasenes*" (5:2a, 10) because of the sea setting in 5:1–2 and here in 5:13 (see *Comment* on 5:2). The number of swine, 2000 (missing in Matt 8:32; Luke 8:33), corresponds to the "name" of Legion which the spirit gives in 5:9 without necessarily implying a one to one ratio between the unclean spirits and the pigs. Like the description of the unmanageable man in 5:3–4, whose behavior "Legion" helps explain, 2000 uncontrollable swine demonstrate the immense power of the forces that had taken control of their victim. Furthermore, the death of the swine vividly depicts the destructive nature of these evil forces. From the beginning, however, these unclean spirits had recognized and submitted themselves to Jesus' authority.

This apparent disregard for others' property has caused many to question the morality of this story. Some have explained it as a "Jewish" story originally (cf. Dibelius, 101; Craghan, *CBQ* 30 [1968] 531), as though this unintended slur made it more palatable for "Christian" readers. If, as has been suggested, this part of the story stems from a later expansion of an earlier exorcism story set in Gerasa, we only ignore the question by arguing that Jesus did not actually destroy someone's herd of swine. But to raise the question of whether to do so with or without recompense was moral or not misses the point of the story, since these verses develop a purity or cleanliness theme inherent in the original story.

Jesus encounters a man "from the tombs" with an "unclean spirit" in the area of the "Gerasenes" whose gentile orientation and uncleanness is illustrated by the presence of a herd of swine. Thus, one can hardly miss the repeated emphasis on uncleanness or impurity found in the original story. The destruction of the herd of swine is now the extension of the healing of the man through the banishment of the unclean spirit(s) into unclean animals and illustrated by the man's behavior in 5:15, 18–19 and the pigs' destruction in 5:13. The story of the deliverance of a man becomes the story of the deliverance of a land. Consequently, the destruction of the herd of swine extends the expulsion of the unclean spirit to signify Jesus' authoritative deliverance in the land of the Gentiles. This thrust of the expanded tradition most likely comes from a mission setting with a view to the gentile mission (e.g., Kertelge, *Wunder*, 107; Pesch, 1:282; Gnilka, 1:207). It anticipates Mark's own emphasis on the scope of Jesus' ministry by his use of tradition in 7:24–8:9.

The story's resultant tension in portraying the unclean spirit's awareness, on the one hand, of Jesus' identity and threat to the spirit's existence, and the spirit's ignorance, on the other hand, in requesting to escape "torment" by entering the herd of swine only to be destroyed anyway stems more from the growth of the narrative than from a folkloric "tricked demon" motif. The story consistently focuses on Jesus and his ministry, not on the unclean spirit, except to the degree the latter contributes to highlighting the former. Therefore, the destruction of the unclean spirit(s) not only illustrates Jesus' authority over Satan and his forces by delivering a man possessed by an unclean spirit, it also removes the swine, the symbols of gentile impurity.

14–17 The development of these verses is disputed. Pesch (1:292) finds an underlying tradition involving only the swineherders who, aroused by the exorcism, came to see what had happened (5:14) and seeing Jesus and the healed man (5:15) responded with awe (5:15). This supposedly concluded the original exorcism story (Pesch, 1:292; similarly, Kertelge, *Wunder*, 103). The rest of the details along with the concluding scene in 5:18–20 come from the later expansion of the exorcism into a mission story when it was adapted to the collection of miracle stories. Such a development in the tradition would account for the change in vocabulary (δαιμονιζόμενος, δαιμονισθείς, 5:15, 16, 18; cf. 5:2) and the description of the man (τὸν ἐσχηκότα τὸν λεγιῶνα, 5:15; cf. 5:9). Others, however, take these verses as integral to the original story with the possible exception of the redundant 5:16 and take 5:17 as having originally concluded the story (e.g., Dibelius, 101; Schenke, *Wunder-erzählungen*, 182).

The key lies in whether the loss of the swine (5:13) belonged to the original story. As the story now stands, the swineherders apparently rush to the city and hamlets to report the loss of the swine (5:14). When the inhabitants come to see what happened, they find Jesus and the man healed and react with "awe" or "fear" (5:15, ἐφοβήθησαν can mean either). Then (5:16) the eyewitnesses tell the crowd what happened to the man and about the swine (περὶ τῶν χοίρων) either retelling the story or telling it in greater detail. The inhabitants then respond by asking Jesus to leave their territory (5:17), which implies that what may initially have been "awe" (5:15) turned to "fear" of what Jesus might do next.

If, however, the unclean spirit's request of 5:10, 12 and its granting in 5:13 are expansions along with 5:8–9 of the original story, as discussed above, the events of 5:14–17 would have read differently in the original story. First, the swine herders' reaction would have come from the exorcism itself which they announced to the surrounding area (5:14a). Their consternation at the deliverance of this man was shared by others who came to see for themselves (5:14b). Second, the reaction of the herders and the inhabitants (5:15, 17) indicated the extent of the man's reputation and the severity of his situation, a point that is now developed in 5:3–4, 9. Third, when the townspeople found Jesus and the man, they responded with "fear" (cf. 4:41) and asked Jesus to leave their "territory" (5:17—ὁρίων; cf. χώρα in 5:2, 10). This "fear" (ἐφοβήθησαν) reflects their perception of Jesus' awesome power rather than any feeling of "reverential awe" (cf. epiphanic language, ἐφοβήθησαν φόβον μέγαν, of 4:41), as their request for Jesus to leave the area indicates.

After the addition of 5:10, 12–13, however, these verses maintain the emphasis on Jesus' astounding power by underscoring the demonic character of the man (δαιμονιζόμενος, the man who "had a legion") and his deliverance seen in his "sitting, clothed and in his right mind" (5:15; cf. 5:3–4) and by having the eyewitnesses retell "how it had happened" in 5:15–16. But these verses also report the loss of the swine, implicitly by 5:14 set now in the context of 5:13 and explicitly by the eyewitnesses in 5:16b. Consequently, the addition of the swine's fate makes the townspeople's request appear to come from their material loss rather than their fear of Jesus.

18 "When (Jesus) was getting into the boat" describes Jesus' departure from the setting of 5:1–2, 13 in the larger sea/boat setting of the miracle story collection (see *Comment* on 5:1–2). The inhabitants' request in 5:17 gave occasion for this transition. Haenchen (195) notes that Jesus leaves because his work is completed, not because he has been defeated by either the demons, whose last act makes him *persona non grata* (Bauernfeind, *Worte*, 43), or by the people's rejection of his ministry (5:17). "That he might be with him" (ἵνα μετ' αὐτοῦ ᾖ) has two functions. First, this request offers a stark contrast to that of the inhabitants in 5:17. The one rejected Jesus out of fear; the other wanted to share his company. Second, the wording of this request corresponds to one of Jesus' purposes for calling the Twelve in 3:14, namely, "to be with him" (ἵνα ὦσιν μετ' αὐτοῦ). Thus it might appear that the man wanted to become one of Jesus' disciples, and this would make Jesus' denial of the request seem curious, if not unfair. If, however, "to be with him" is limited in the tradition specifically to the close personal relationship shared exclusively by the Twelve (see *Comment* on 3:14), then Jesus' response merely indicates the special place accorded to the Twelve whom he specifically called to "be with him." To this extent, Jesus' denial of the request simply means the man is not called and does not belong to the circle of the Twelve.

Some scholars have attributed this material (5:18–20) to Mark's redaction (e.g., Schweizer, 113; Craghan, *CBQ* 30 [1968] 534; Schenke, *Wundererzählungen*, 176). But there is nothing distinctively Markan about this phrase or view of discipleship. In fact, not being one of the Twelve does not preclude one from being a disciple for Mark (see *Comment* on 2:15). On the contrary, one of the disciples' primary tasks, including the Twelve, is to "preach" (cf. *Comment* on 3:15), a task which the man carries out with great success in 5:20. Furthermore, the use of δαιμονισθείς (cf. 5:15, 16) in the context of the "boat" indicates at least a pre-Markan reworking of this material at the time of the adaptation of this story into the miracle story collection and its present sea setting. Whether the man's request belonged to the original story is no longer clear. But it does turn the focus back to the man and his healing and sets the stage for Jesus' final instruction to him (5:19).

19 "Go to your home" (ὕπαγε εἰς τὸν οἶκον) rounds off the story in the "style of a dismissal conclusion" (Theissen, *Miracle Stories*, 147) and may have been the original ending of the story that gives further indication of the man's healing. The one ostracized to the tombs for his behavior, since his untameable wildness had made him unfit for any social contact, can now return home. He has indeed been domesticated by one who could do what no one or nothing else had been able to do. These instructions demonstrate that his healing was not simply a momentary lapse into sanity or behavior controlled by the presence of one superior. The man was free to be his own person and reenter normal human relations. He had been delivered.

"To your people" (πρὸς τοὺς σούς), unique to the NT, has been taken narrowly by some to mean "your family" (e.g., Wrede, *Secret*, 140; Gnilka, 1:206). But most take this to refer more broadly to "the people of your area" (Lohmeyer, 97; Taylor, 284; Ernst, 157). Pesch (1:294) renders it to your own "milieu" (e.g., the Gentiles). The following command makes the broader reading more likely (cf. 5:14).

"Announce to them" (ἀπάγγειλον αὐτοῖς) has a parallel in the early Christian mission terminology (e.g., Acts 15:27; 26:20). Furthermore, the content of his announcement, "how much that the Lord has done and how merciful He has been," reinforces this apparently technical usage. But this hardly provides sufficient basis for making this man the first missionary to the Gentiles and his task a product of the early Christian mission (e.g., Pesch, 1:2:93–94). Nor does the fact that no other healing or exorcism story contains such an explicit commission necessarily imply that the task comes from a later development. If indeed this story has its roots in a Gerasene exorcism, such an "explanation" would be commensurate with the man's healing in a gentile setting where Jesus' ministry was unknown. The reference to "the Lord's" (κύριος = "God") work and mercy rather than to "Jesus'" gives credence to its roots in Jesus' ministry rather than the early Church's mission. In either case, this commission even taken neutrally (cf. ἀπήγγειλαν, 5:14) hardly contains a command to silence or secrecy (e.g., Wrede, *Secret*, 140; Gnilka, 1:207). Theissen's (*Miracle Stories*, 146–47) appeal to Mark's understanding of "home" as a place of "secrecy" (e.g., 7:17; 7:24; 9:28; 10:10) ignores the force of ἀπάγγειλον, the reference to "your people" (πρὸς τοὺς σούς) in 5:19, and Mark's other uses of οἶκος, οἰκία without the motif of secrecy or privacy (e.g., 1:29–34; 2:1–2, 15–16; 3:20–34; 14:3; cf. esp. 8:26). More importantly, all of Theissen's references to Mark's particular usage of "home" implying secrecy, with the exception of 10:10, explicitly make the point of privacy which indicates that it is not necessarily implicit in the location itself. And regardless of the use of ἀπάγγειλον in a technical or a general way, it can hardly have meant "to give thanks for his cure" (Miracle Stories, 147; cf. 5:14).

20 This verse states what eventually happened and does so in a way that suggests Mark's redactional hand (Schweizer, 113; Luz, ZNW 56 [1965] 18; Schenke, Wundererzählungen, 176; Theissen, Miracle Stories, 146–47). Luz (ZNW 56 [1965] 18) lists several terms that are used elsewhere redactionally by Mark: ἄρξεσθαι (see Comment on 1:45; cf. 4:1; 6:2, 34; 8:31; 10:32; 12:1), ὅσος (cf. 3:8, 10; 6:30, 56; 9:13) and θυμάζειν (cf. 6:6; 15:44). The evangelist employs κηρύσσειν as one of the essential tasks of a disciple (e.g., 3:14; 6:12; cf. 1:45). Here it clarifies the nature of the commission (ἀπάγγειλον) in 5:19 (cf. 1:4, 7, 14, 38, 39, 45; 7:36; 13:10; 14:9).

Materially, this verse has several Markan traits. The message about what "the Lord" had done in 5:19 becomes what "Jesus" had done. But this is hardly a "correction" by Mark (Luz, ZNW 56 [1965] 18). For Mark the proclamation (κηρύσσειν) of the "good news of God" (1:14; cf. 5:19) was the proclamation of the "good news about Jesus Messiah, Son of God" (see Comment on 1:1). And Mark alone makes use of the "Decapolis" in this story. The earliest literary reference to the Decapolis comes in the Gospels. Josephus mentions it four times (Life, 65; 74; War, 3.9.7), but Pliny (Nat. Hist. 5.74) gives us our earliest list of the ten cities (Damascus, Philadelphia, Rapana, Scythopolis, Gadara, Hippo [=Hippos], Dion, Pella, Galasa [= Gerasa], Cantha). Later nine other names are added to the list in Ptolemy's Geography (5.14.22). Though often conceived as a league of cities in close political and economic cooperation, Parker has argued that our sources, literary and archeological, suggest that "Decapolis" refers more to a geographical region "composed of territories of member cities" than to a "league" or "confederation" of cities (JBL 94 [1975] 439–40). This understanding certainly corresponds to the usage here and in 7:31 where Mark returns to it as the setting for Jesus' healing of the deaf mute and the feeding of the four thousand.

If, therefore, as seems likely, Mark has added this concluding verse to the story, he adds it not to counter or correct the commission of 5:19 by making it serve his secrecy motif (Wrede, Secret, 141; Klostermann, 50; Luz, ZNW 56 [1965] 18; Gnilka, 1:207; Theissen, Miracle Stories, 146–47) nor to show that the demons failed to get the last laugh by having Jesus run out of town (Grundmann, 146) but simply to note the outcome of Jesus' commission and set the stage for the Gospel among the Gentiles. Therefore, according to Mark, Jesus not only made inroads into gentile territory to heal this man but the impact of the man's witness spreads throughout the Decapolis and prepares for Jesus' further ministry there in 7:31–8:9. Consequently, "all were amazed" (5:20b) describes the response to the man's preaching rather than to the miracle.

The ending of this story stands in contrast to other healing and exorcism stories in Mark in which Jesus orders the event be kept quiet (e.g., 1:44; 5:43; 7:36; 8:26). The contention by some that Mark reworked the commission of 5:19 into a command to return home "secretly" by adding the broader 5:20 ignores significant aspects of the commission. Furthermore, the supposed silence or secrecy command in 5:19 would have been far too subtle in view of the explicit demands for silence in the other accounts. And the suggestion that Mark treated this pericope differently from the others because of its location in gentile territory does not square with the evidence of a later story (7:31–37) set in the Decapolis which also concludes with an explicit command of silence (see 7:36).

Two of the four stories containing Jesus' "secrecy" admonition conclude with the persons involved actually doing the opposite (1:45; 7:36–37). To that extent, the man's action in 5:20 parallels these accounts, especially 1:45. After Jesus healed the leper (1:41–45), the latter's "preaching many things" generated such a response in Galilee that Jesus found it difficult to enter the cities because of the crowds (1:45b). Here the man's "preaching . . . how much Jesus had done for him" generates a great response throughout the Decapolis (5:20b). By contrast, nothing is said to the contrary following Jesus' command to silence in 5:43 and 8:26. We are left with the impression that his wishes were carried out in these cases. Why this apparent inconsistency in Mark's stories? On the one hand, Jesus prohibits people from telling anything about his healing activities in some accounts but commissions another to announce boldly what had happened. On the other hand, some accounts end with the people disregarding Jesus' prohibition, while others let it stand.

Rather than seek the answer in some overarching theological motif that resolves this obvious inconsistency, could not the answer simply lie in Mark's use of a traditional motif as a literary device? Whenever the setting called for large crowds, the silence commands were ignored and the subsequent "preaching" created large crowds (e.g., 1:45–2:2; 5:20 [cf. 7:31–37]; 7:36 [cf. 8:1–9]; cf. 6:7–13, 30 [6:32–44]). Whenever a change of venue was in order, the injunction was apparently followed allowing Jesus the opportunity to move on (e.g., 5:43 [cf. 6:1–6a]; 8:26 [cf. 8:27–30]). See *Comment* on 8:36.

Here in 5:20 Mark merely expands the commission found in his tradition (5:19) by putting it into his "kerygmatic" terminology and magnifying its scope throughout the Decapolis. Therefore, Mark's consistency appears to lie in accenting the "kerygmatic" element of the tradition and the response. He shows little interest in either adding or developing the silence motif per se of the tradition.

Explanation

This story comes as the second of four miracle stories (4:35–5:43) and is thematically related to the previous one (4:35–41). In 4:35–41, Jesus miraculously delivers the disciples from drowning in the sea by stilling a storm and calming the waves with exorcistic formulas. In this story Jesus actually exorcises unclean spirits (without exorcistic formulas!) who apparently, along with a herd of swine, drown in the sea. In both stories, Jesus' awesome power stands out. The thematic link most likely led to the present geographical link between the two stories.

From the outset, the story depicted Jesus' power and control over one tormented and controlled by the forces of evil. The man's reaction to Jesus' presence (5:2b), the unclean spirit's recognition of Jesus (5:7), and the response of the local inhabitants (5:14–17) and the healed man (5:18–19) to Jesus, all bear witness to his power. At the same time, the scene accentuates the man's condition. Defiled by living among the tombs (5:2b), himself inhabited by an "unclean spirit" (5:2), he lived in a gentile land marked by its herd of swine (5:11).

As the story developed, each of these themes became more pronounced. The man's uncontrollable nature, his incredible strength to shatter all attempts to chain him, his tormented mind and his self-destructive behavior all point to the superhuman forces and their number (5:3–5, 9). At the same time, the man's description makes all the more remarkable his and/or the unclean spirit(s)' servile response to Jesus when he "runs" and "bows" before him (5:6). Jesus clearly controls the situation. Not only does the unclean spirit recognize that Jesus is "the son of the Most High God" from whom he seeks to keep his distance and seeks through an adjuration to avoid the inevitable but the spirit(s) obediently reveal their identity at Jesus' request (5:7, 9). Furthermore, acknowledging their vulnerability, the unclean spirits appeal to Jesus for a concession. They ask him to banish rather than simply to expel them (5:10, 12). Then the townspeople, frightened by Jesus' mysterious power that can domesticate such a wild man and create such a disturbance with their herd of swine, ask Jesus to leave their vicinity (5:14–17).

The evangelist does little to alter this story. At most he adds a summary of what the man did in 5:20 to carry out Jesus' commission of 5:19. To that extent, the story concludes like the story of the leper (1:41–45). Both men proclaim ("preach") what Jesus had done for them. Here the man goes throughout the Decapolis, and his message receives a great response—"all were amazed." In this way, though denied the right to accompany Jesus with the Twelve (5:19), he becomes part of the mission and carries out one of the essential tasks of a disciple, i.e., to proclaim or preach the "good news" about Jesus (cf. 14:9).

What then is the thrust of this story? From the beginning, the story clearly pointed to Jesus' power over the forces of evil. Of all the exorcism stories, none does it as graphically as this. The picture of one seated, clothed, and in his right mind starkly contrasts with a wild, uncontrollable man totally possessed by "Legion." Jesus not only has the power and authority to subdue the chaotic forces of nature, as seen in the previous story, but he has power as the "Son of the Most High God" over the demonic forces that defy all human control.

At the same time, an "unclean" or "gentile" motif stands out. We have a man defiled by his habitat, himself inhabited by an unclean spirit, in a gentile land marked by a herd of swine. Even the name of God, "Most High God," occurs elsewhere in the Scriptures as a gentile expression for God. Therefore, though likely rooted in an event in Jesus' ministry, the story's details play a role in the early Christian setting of the gentile mission. One can only speculate as to where or how it was used, but one cannot miss its affirmation of Jesus' redemptive ministry to a Gentile in gentile territory.

For Mark, the story has to be read as the "gospel of Jesus Messiah, Son of God" (1:1). Once again (cf. 1:24, 34; 3:12) the demonic world accurately recognizes who Jesus is, "the Son of the Most High God" (5:7). Even the man himself becomes a preacher of "what Jesus had done" (5:20), which was but another way of expressing the "good news" of the coming of God's sovereign rule (1:14–15), or "how much the Lord had done" (5:19).

Furthermore, in the flow of Mark's narrative, this story must be read against the backdrop of the dispute between Jesus and the scribes over his exorcisms in 3:22–27. It vividly describes Jesus as the one in whom "the Most High God's" sovereign rule was being established through the binding of the "strong man" (3:27) who through Legion had so powerfully controlled a man that no one else could successfully bind with human fetters (5:3–5).

Mark does not ignore the significance of the gentile setting. He accents this by having the man carry out Jesus' commission (5:19) as a faithful disciple through his preaching about Jesus throughout the Decapolis (5:20). This ameliorates in a way the negative response of the Gerasenes in 5:17, especially when "all were amazed" (5:20b) at his preaching of what Jesus had done. Mark will follow this motif further in chapter 7 where he develops Jesus' "gentile journey" that specifically includes the Decapolis.

L. The Raising of Jairus' Daughter and the Healing of the Woman with a Hemorrhage (Mark 5:21–43)

Bibliography

Achtemeier, P. "Toward the Isolation of Pre-Markan Miracle Catenae." *JBL* 89 (1970) 265–91. **Donahue, J. R.** *Are You the Christ? The Trial Narrative in the Gospel of Mark.* SBLDS 10. Missoula: Scholars Press, 1973. **Kertelge, K.** *Die Wunder Jesu im Markusevangelium.* 1970. **Koch, D.-A.** *Die Bedeutung der Wundererzählungen für die Christ-ologie des Markusevangeliums.* 1975. **Kuhn, H.-W.** *Ältere Sammlungen im Markusevange-lium.* 1971. **Loos, H. van der.** *The Miracles of Jesus.* NTS 8. Leiden: Brill, 1965. **Luz, U.** "Das Geheimnismotiv und die markinische Christologie." *ZNW* 56 (1965) 9–30 = "The Secrecy Motif and Marcan Theology." Tr. R. Morgan. In *The Messianic Secret,* ed. C. Tuckett. London/Philadelphia: SPCK/Fortress, 1983. 75–96. **Moule, C. F. D.** *Idiom-Book of New Testament Greek.* 1959. **Neusner, J.** "The Idea of Purity in Ancient Judaism." *JAAR* 43 (1975) 15–26. **Pesch, R.** "Jairus (Mk 5,22/Lk 8,41)." *BZ* 14 (1970) 252–56. **Pryke, E. J.** *Redactional Style in the Markan Gospel.* 1978. **Robbins. V. K.** "*Dyna-meis* and *Semeia* in Mark." *BR* 18 (1973) 5–20. **Schenke, L.** *Die Wundererzählungen im Markusevangelium.* 1974. **Schmahl, G.** *Die Zwölf im Markusevangelium: Eine redaktionsge-schichtliche Untersuchung.* TTS 30. Trier: Paulinus, 1974. **Tagawa, K.** *Miracles et Evangile: La pensée personelle de l'évangeliste Marc.* Paris: Presses Universitaires de France, 1966. **Theissen, G.** *The Miracle Stories of the Early Christian Tradition.* 1983. **Wrede, W.** *The Messianic Secret.* 1971.

Translation

21 When Jesus had crossed in the boat again[a] to the other side, a large crowd gathered around him, and he was by the sea. 22 One[b] of the presidents of the synagogue by the name of Jairus[c] came and, seeing him, fell at his feet. 23 And Jairus[d] repeatedly[e] appealed to him, saying, "My little daughter is near death.[f] Come and lay[g] hands on her that she might be made well and live." 24 Jesus[d] went with him, and a large crowd followed him and pressed against him.

25 And a woman, who had a hemorrhage for twelve years and 26 had suffered much from many physicians and spent all she had to no avail only to become worse, 27 when she heard about Jesus, she came from behind in the crowd and touched[h] his clothing. 28 For she had said[i], "If I might touch his clothes, I shall be made well." 29 And immediately the well of her blood was dried up, and she knew in her body that she had been healed from suffering.

30 And Jesus,[d] immediately perceiving in himself that the power proceeding from him[j] had gone out, turned around in the crowd and said, "Who touched my clothes?" 31 And his disciples said to him, "Look at the crowd pressing against you and you say, 'Who touched me?'" 32 And he looked around to see who had done this.

33 Then the woman afraid and trembling, knowing what had happened to her, came and fell down before him and told him the whole truth. 34 But he said to her, "Daughter, your faith has made you well. Go in peace[k] and be healed from your suffering."

35 While he was speaking, they came from the synagogue president's house and said, "Your daughter is dead. Why bother the teacher?" 36 But Jesus, ignoring[l] what was said, said to the synagogue president, "Do not be afraid; only believe!"

37 And he did not permit anyone except Peter, James, and John, the brother of James, to follow with him. 38 They came to the synagogue president's house and found a commotion with much weeping and wailing. 39 Entering, Jesus[d] said to them, "Why are you making such a commotion and weeping? The child is not dead. She is sleeping." 40 And they began ridiculing him. But after putting them all out, he took the father of the child and her mother and those with him and went in to where the child was.

41 Taking hold of the child's hand, he said to her, "Talitha koum!"[m] which means, "Little girl, I say to you arise!" 42 And immediately the little girl stood up and began walking around. For she was twelve years old. And they were immediately[n] and utterly amazed.[o] 43 And Jesus[d] strictly ordered them that no one should know this and said that something should be given her to eat.

Notes

[a] ἐν τῷ πλοίῳ is missing from P45 D Θ f1 28 565 700 pc it sys and precedes τοῦ Ἰησοῦ in W, leading some to assign it to a later scribal insertion (e.g., Taylor, 286). But strong Alexandrian and other witnesses (א A [B] C L O132 O134 f13 Majority text vg syp,h bo) suggest the omission resulted from assimilation to Luke 8:40 (Metzger, Textual Commentary, 84). Similarly א* D 565 700 it syp P45 place πάλιν before συνήχθη (so Taylor, 286) resuming the thought of 4:1, 34.

[b] εἷς used as τις (Moule, Idiom-Book, 125; BDG, s.v. 3).

[c] ὀνόματι Ἰάϊρος is missing in D itvar leading Taylor (287) to take it as a scribal interpolation on the basis of its Lukan dative form and its absence in Matt 9:18. Luke 8:41, however, has ᾧ ὄνομα Ἰάϊρος rather than dative construction and Matthew has an abbreviated story, if dependent

on Mark. The extensive textual support argues in favor of the phrase (p[45] ℵ A B C L N Δ Π Σ Φ most minuscules vg syr and it[var]). See Metzger, *Textual Commentary*, 85–85.

d Romanized words added from context.

e Adverbial use of πολλά.

f Renders ἐσχάτως ἔχει.

g Imperatival use of ἵνα (Moule, *Idiom-Book*, 144).

h The main and only finite verb in this sentence. All others render seven participles.

i See *Note* f on 5:8 for ἔλεγεν γάρ, perfect force of imperfect tense.

j Note the construction τὴν ἐξ αὐτοῦ δύναμιν with the prepositional phrase between the article and the noun, which it modifies, rather than following the noun and accompanying the participle (e.g., τὴν δύναμιν ἐξ αὐτοῦ ἐξελθοῦσαν).

k εἰς εἰρήνην is most likely a Semitism (לכי לשלם, *lēkî lĕšālōm*); cf. Judg 18:6; 1 Sam 1:17; 2 Sam 15:9 [LXX].

l παρακούσας can supposedly be rendered (a) "to overhear" or (b) "to ignore" (BGD, *s.v.*). But all seven LXX usages and the only other NT (Matt 18:17) usage has the force of "to ignore." Contextually, "to overhear" would fit here. But the issue is moot, since Jesus' words to the ruler indicate he "ignored," if he did "overhear," the thrust of what was said.

m A D Δ Θ Π Φ f[13] most minuscules it vg syr read κουμι, a rendering of the Aramaic feminine imperative קומי (*qûmî*). ℵ B C L M N Σ f[1] 33 892 support the masculine imperative קום, used at times without reference to sex. ταβιθα in W 28 245 349 and some OL and Vg MSS is an assimilation to Acts 9:40. See Metzger, *Textual Commentary*, 87.

n The textual evidence for εὐθύς is very mixed. p[45] A W Θ 0133 f[1,13] Majority text lat sy bo omit it, while ℵ B C L Δ 33 892 have it. Mark's propensity for using it and its awkwardness speak more for its later omission than for its addition.

o The cognate construction ἐξέστησαν . . . ἐκστάσει is most likely a "Septuagintalism" (Taylor, 297) rendering the Hebrew infinitive absolute (cf. Gen 2:17 [LXX]; Moule, *Idiom-Book*, 177–78).

Form / Structure / Setting

Form-critically, 5:21–43 consists of two healing stories, the one (5:25–34) found within the other (5:21–43). Technically, the story of Jairus' daughter involves a raising from the dead, but the formal elements remain the same as other healing miracles (Theissen, *Miracle Stories*, 90, n. 25). Death itself represents the extreme form of illness (Pesch, 1:297).

The combination of two healing miracles gives us an opportunity to compare two closely related stories and see just how flexible the formal elements of the miracle/healing stories really are. Though tightly interwoven, the two stories share in common only the broadest categories of setting, miracle, and conclusion in common.

They differ extensively in their formal characteristics. As to setting, Jairus' need is expressed in the form of a repeated request for healing; the woman's need comes to light in the description of her predicament and the request implied in her actions. Jairus' request is heightened by a further development in the story; the woman's condition finds elaboration through a reference to years of suffering and her great expenditure on ineffective physicians. Regarding the miracle itself, the woman's healing takes place without Jesus' initial consent by her touching his clothes; Jairus' daughter is raised after Jesus deliberately assures Jairus, expels the skeptical public, then takes the girl by the hand and commands her to arise. Whereas the woman "knows" that she has been immediately healed, Jairus' daughter demonstrates the miracle by immediately walking about and being fed. Finally, Jesus publicly calls attention to the woman's healing through a conversation focusing on her faith and concludes with a dismissal; Jesus conceals the miracle of Jairus' daughter by removing the public at the outset and prohibiting even the small circle of witnesses from making the miracle known. But despite the lack of formal parallels between these two pericopes, each formal characteristic within them has parallels in ancient miracle stories within and without the NT.

Regarding source, most take this complex to be the result of the combination of two originally independent stories (cf. Schmidt, 148; Taylor, 288). The stylistic differences in the two stories (Jairus' story with short, paratactic sentences in the historical present; the woman's story in long, participle-filled sentences in the aorist tense), the integrity of each story as a unit in itself, and the apparent influence of 5:25–34 on the setting of 5:22–24, 35–43 through the introduction of the crowds, which otherwise play no role in the Jairus story, support this conclusion (Achtemeier, *JBL* 89 [1970] 277; Kertelge, *Wunder*, 111). Most commentators also assign these stories to the same pre-Markan collection of miracle stories as 4:35–5:20 (cf. Schenke, *Wundererzählungen*, 196–97; Gnilka, 1:223, 273–34). Whether Mark found these stories as presently intercalated or himself inserted 5:24–34 into the Jairus story from the same source or elsewhere is more debated.

Generally speaking, those supporting a pre-Markan miracle collection view the combination to have occurred at some point in the pre-Markan tradition, perhaps at the time of the collection (Kertelge, *Wunder*, 110–11; Grundmann, 148; Pesch, 1:295; Ernst, 160; cf. Achtemeier, *JBL* 89 [1970] 278–79; Kuhn, *Sammlungen*, 200–03). This view finds support in that thematically 5:21 connects these stories with what has preceded and also sets the stage with the introduction of the crowds for the healing of the woman rather than for Jairus' request.

Nevertheless, several have assigned the insertion to Mark on the basis of Mark's tendency to use intercalation to "fill time lapses" (e.g., Schweizer, 116). Other commentators concur and assign 5:21 to Mark based on "Markan" stylistic (genitive absolute) and lexical (διαπερᾶν, πλοῖον, πάλιν, ὄχλος πολύς, εἰς τὴν πέραν) considerations (Koch, *Wundererzählungen*, 65; Kuhn, *Sammlungen*, 201–02; Schenke, *Wundererzählungen*, 196–97; Gnilka, 1:210).

In spite of a current trend in assigning the combination to the evangelist, the evidence remains disputable. Unlike Mark's redactional intercalations elsewhere (see p. 169), the healing of the woman does not "fill a time lapse" nor does it have to do, as otherwise, with narratives on discipleship (cf. Donahue, *Trial*, 59, n. 3). It does create a delay in the Jairus story but not for the critical arrival of the messenger in 5:35 (cf. Luke 8:40–56). Rather the insertion dramatically heightens the suspense in the Jairus story and accents the call to faith in 5:36 (Kertelge, 110; Grundmann, 148). Furthermore, the stylistic and lexical arguments cut both ways, since one could also argue these to be characteristic of the one putting together the miracle collection (see *Comment* on 5:21, 25–27).

Apart from the question of intercalation and the related setting in 5:21, 24, several have assigned the selection of the three disciples in 5:37 to Mark's hand (Pesch, 1:307; Gnilka, 1:210; Schenke, *Wundererzählungen*, 205). And with few exceptions (e.g., E. Lohmeyer, 104; K. Tagawa, *Miracles*, 167; Pesch, 1:295, 320–11), most commentators assign the injunction to silence in 5:43 to Mark's redaction based on his "messianic secret" (Wrede, *Secret*, 35; Klostermann, 53–54; Schweizer, 116; Grundmann, 148; Kertelge, *Wunder*, 119–20; Gnilka, 1:211; Ernst, 160) as well as stylistic and lexical considerations (Koch, *Wundererzählungen*, 67; Schenke, *Wundererzählungen*, 204). Yet our analysis below concurs with Achtemeier's conclusion that these stories along with those of 4:35–5:20 "show remarkably few evidences of redactional activity, appearing apparently in substantially the form in which Mark got them" (*JBL* 89 [1970] 279).

As to structure, the Jairus story offers the basic framework for the present narrative which has four scenes (Lohmeyer, 104). It opens with Jesus' return to "the other side" of the sea where a large crowd and Jairus meet him "by the sea" (5:21–23). Then Jesus, followed by the crowd, accompanies Jairus "on the way" (5:24–37). Eventually leaving the crowd behind, Jairus, Jesus and three disciples next enter into "the house" (5:38–40a) and finally, Jesus, his three disciples and the parents enter "where the girl lay" (5:40b–43).

A series of events, however, breaks into the directional flow of the story from the sea to where the little girl lay. First, the story of the woman's healing (5:25–34) and then the announcement of the girl's death (5:35) while on the way enhance the narrative (5:36). At the house the mourners give pause for comment and countercomment (5:38–40a) that also heighten the suspense. Finally, the narrative reaches its climax in the miracle of 5:41 followed by the demonstration and response in 5:42–43.

Viewed separately each story concludes with a slight twist. In the story of the woman's healing the miracle actually occurs immediately and is confirmed by her awareness in 5:29. Yet the next five verses focus on the miracle, first from Jesus' side (5:30–31) then the woman's side (5:32–33). The story finally concludes with a dismissal (5:34a) followed by a word of healing (5:34b) even though the healing had already taken place in 5:29. The story of Jairus' daughter concludes with a demonstration (her walking about, 5:42a), wonder (absolute astonishment, 5:42b), injunction to secrecy (5:43a) and then surprisingly a second demonstration in the order to feed her (5:43b). As often the case, these quirks in structure offer important clues about the history of the tradition and the significance of these stories.

The setting of these miracles in conjunction with those of 4:35–5:20 exhibits several points of connection. This complex story corresponds to the sea setting of the previous miracles in 4:35–5:20 as seen in the reappearance of several terms: "boat" (5:21; cf. 4:36, 37; 5:2, 18), the "other side" (5:21; cf. 4:35; 5:1), the "sea" (5:21; cf. 4:39, 41; 5:1, 13). At the same time, motifs within this story correspond with motifs from the previous one. For example, the issue of impurity so prominent in 5:1–20 relates to both the woman's condition which made her and any she should touch impure (Lev 15:25) and also Jesus' physical contact with the corpse of the dead child (Neusner, *JAAR* 43 [1975] 21). The woman's response of "fear and trembling" (5:33) and Jesus' assurance of Jairus to "fear not" (5:36) remind us of the inhabitants' "fear" in 5:15 and the disciples' "fear" in 4:41. The description of the length of the woman's illness and the futility of the physicians to heal her as well as the messenger's hopeless advice to Jairus to cease troubling the teacher because it was too late remind us of the uncontrollable state of the demoniac in 5:3–5 and the dire straits of the disciples in 4:37–38.

This complex story shows Jesus' power to heal an incurable illness and even to raise one from the dead, the ultimate result of illness. Therefore, set along side of 4:35–5:20, the focus of these miracles has moved from Jesus' power over the forces of nature, to his power over the demonic forces, to his power over sickness and death itself. For the setting in Mark's Gospel, the miracles and the double reference to "faith" (5:34, 36; cf. 4:40) prepare for Jesus' startling rejection in Nazareth (6:1–6).

Comment

21 This verse clearly connects what follows to what has preceded by providing a setting. Who made this connection? Many have assigned it to a pre-Markan redactor who brought the collection of miracle stories together. Some, however, have attributed it to Mark's own redaction on the basis of style and vocabulary.

Stylistically, the verse opens with a genitive absolute, "When Jesus had crossed" (διαπεράσαντος τοῦ Ἰησοῦ). Pryke (*Style*, 62) lists this construction as characteristically Markan (29x, 24 redactional). Yet to this point in Mark's Gospel all the genitive absolutes, except for the almost formulaic ὀψίας γενομένης in 1:32 (cf. 4:35; 6:21, 35, 47; 15:42; cf. 6:2, 21), have occurred in these four miracle stories (4:35; 5:2, 18, 21, 35). This example also appears in a transitional seam appropriate to the collection of these miracle stories. Since Mark has not used a genitive absolute in any transitional "seams" prior to 4:35 and since, by contrast, a genitive absolute occurs in every transitional seam in these miracle stories (4:35; 5:1–2, 18; 5:21, 35), it seems more appropriate to assign these to the hand of a pre-Markan redactor who collected and connected these stories together.

As to vocabulary, Koch (*Wundererzählungen*, 65), Kuhn (*Sammlungen*, 202) and Schenke (*Wundererzählungen*, 196) have recently found most of the words in 5:21 to be characteristically Markan. But this view is difficult to substantiate. In 6:53 Mark again uses διαπερᾶν in what may be a redactional seam (see *Comment* on 6:53), but *one* example hardly ensures exclusive Markan preference. The argument from the reference to a boat (πλοῖον) is circular, since the boat occurs primarily in the context of these miracles (4:36; 5:2, 18, 21; 6:32, 45, 47, 51, 54; cf. 8:10, 14). It clearly ties the miracles in 4:35–5:43 together (4:36; 5:2, 18; 5:21) without implying that Mark rather than an earlier redactor used this device (see *Comment* on 4:36). The same can be said about "the other side" (εἰς τὸ πέραν; cf. 4:35; 5:1; 5:21; 6:45). The expression "large crowd" (ὄχλος πολύς) occurs twice in this story (5:21, 24) and in the immediate context of the Feeding Miracle in 6:34. Only 9:14 stands outside this miracle complex, a rate of occurrence that hardly looks "Markan" in light of Mark's frequent use of ὄχλος (38x). Finally, Mark does appear to have an affinity for Jesus' ministry near the sea (θάλασσα, see *Comment* on 2:13). But the sea has also been the setting for Jesus' boat crossings connecting these miracles. And one can hardly question the traditional character of θάλασσα in the first of these stories (4:39, 41) which may have provided the locus for 5:1–2 (see *Comment* on 5:1) as well as here.

"The other side" used with the Jordan (τὸ πέραν τοῦ Ἰορδάνου) always refers to the area east of the Jordan. Consequently, some have read the implied τὸ πέραν τῆς θαλάσσης in the same manner and posited a place on the eastern or northeastern side of the sea (e.g., Schmidt, 146; Schenke, *Wundererzählungen,* 196). Yet the use of "again" (πάλιν) and the presence of a "large crowd" takes the reader back to the setting of Jesus' initial departure in 4:35.

Since the gathering of a large crowd by the sea plays no role in the Jairus story, the one developing this seam may have taken it from an earlier setting for the woman's healing (cf. 5:24). The added note "by the sea" (καὶ ἦν παρὰ τὴν θάλασσαν) could have the "large crowd" as the subject (cf. Luke 8:40; so Klostermann, 51) but most likely refers to Jesus. Its awkwardness may point to Mark's tendency to place Jesus in the vicinity of the sea, or it may come from an earlier setting for the Jairus story (Lohmeyer, 100; Achtemeier, *JBL* 89 [1970] 278).

22 "One of the presidents of the synagogue" gives both the identity (5:35, 36, 38) and title of the one seeking Jesus' help. The "president of the synagogue" (ἀρχισυνάγωγος) was an elected position of esteem in the Jewish community. This leader had responsibilities for arranging the synagogue services and overseeing the building concerns. The construction "*one* of the presidents of the synagogue" (see *Note* b) may refer in general to the office of president (as in 5:35, 36, 38), but Acts 13:15 indicates a synagogue could have more than one president (Schrage, *TDNT* 7 [1971] 846–47).

"By the name of Jairus" (ὀνόματι Ἰάϊρος) stands out since most healing stories are anonymous. Matthew does not give a name. The tendency is to add names later to the tradition. For example, the woman in 5:25–34 becomes Veronica (*Gos. Nicodemus* 7) or Bernice (*Acta Pilati* 7). Consequently, Bultmann (215) assigns this name to a secondary stage in the pre-Markan tradition (see *Note* c). The absence of the name in the rest of the story supposedly supports this point (Schmidt, 147). Yet the textually uncontested name Bartimaeus in 10:46 shows that miracle stories can have circulated with a name, even when the name only occurs at the outset and is omitted in the parallel accounts. Pesch (*BZ* 14 [1970] 252–56) argues for its originality and traces its import to symbolism (similarly, Grundmann, 150). "Jairus" transliterates יָאִיר, *ya'îr* = "he enlightens" (Num 32:41; Judg 10:3–4; Esth 2:5) and יעיר, *ya'îr* = "he awakes" (1 Chron 20:5). Such a symbolic use is subtle at best, especially when Jesus' call for faith (5:36) is supposedly understood as faith in the "promise expressed in the name, 'He will awaken'" (Pesch, *BZ* 14 [1970] 255).

"Fell at his feet" (πίπτει πρὸς τοὺς πόδας). In a similar manner the demoniac (5:6) "bowed" (προσεκύνησεν) and the unclean spirits (3:11) fell before him (προσέπιπτον) in awesome recognition of his authority (cf. 5:33). Though awe is missing here, one can hardly miss the urgency displayed in this action by a synagogue president. This gesture may also contain some irony in the context of Mark's Gospel, since the only other specific Markan reference to falling at Jesus' "feet" (πρὸς τοὺς πόδας) occurs in the story of the gentile, Syrophoenician woman (7:25).

23 "Lay hands on her" (ἐπιθῇς τὰς χεῖρας). This expression, at times accompanying a blessing or ordination, does not occur in connection with healing in the Hebrew OT. It does appear in the LXX account of Naaman's healing by Elisha (2 Kgs 5:11). Theissen (*Miracle Stories,* 92), who cites parallels from

the non-Christian world, notes in connection with healings that it implies
the transmission of a healing power by touch, either by the touch of the
one in need or by the laying on of hands. The sandwiched story in 5:25–34
clearly illustrates this point (5:30; so 3:10; 6:56) and indicates a thematic
connection between the two stories. Jesus does not actually follow through
with Jairus' request, since the nature of the request itself changes in 5:35,
but he does heal by laying on hands in 6:5; 7:32; and 8:23, 25.

"Made well and live" ($\sigma\omega\theta\tilde{\eta}$ $\kappa\alpha\iota$ $\zeta\dot{\eta}\sigma\eta$) could refer to two distinct ideas (Taylor,
288). Yet since these two verbs render the Aramaic חיה, ḥayâh, some have
taken them to be a hendiadys, two expressions for the same thing (Black,
Approach, 71, n. 1; Klostermann, 51). The use in Mark tends to support this
reading. In 3:4; 8:35; 13:20; 15:30 $\sigma\dot{\omega}\zeta\epsilon\iota\nu$ has to do with "saving one's life"
or "living." In 5:28, 34; 6:56; 10:52 it refers specifically to "healing" or "making
well." But in 3:4 and in the derisive cries from the crowd of 15:30, 31 "saving
life" is synonymous with "healing" or "making well." In this case, in view of
the story's ending, "making well" actually means "making live," so "that she
might live" ($\zeta\dot{\eta}\sigma\eta$) takes on specific content for the reader who knows the
story. At the same time, "that she be made well" ($\sigma\omega\theta\tilde{\eta}$) offers a verbal connecting link to the sandwiched story in 5:25–34 (cf. 5:28, 34).

24 "A large crowd followed him and pressed against him" provides a
scene quite similar to the general summary in 3:7, 9–10, which may originally
have introduced the pre-Markan miracle collection of 4:35–5:43, 6:32–56
(see pp. 142–49). In fact, Pesch (1:301) has conjectured that the pre-Markan
redactor of the miracle collection constructed the summary in 3:7–12 from
this setting for the story of the woman which began with Jesus by the sea
(5:21c) followed and pressed by a large crowd (cf. 3:7–9). In any case, this
reference to the pressing crowd picks up the gathered crowd motif from
5:21b and sets the stage for the woman's entry and dramatic healing through
contact with Jesus. Rather than a redactional bridge to the inserted story of
5:25–34 (Schenke, *Wundererzählungen,* 199), this verse most likely provided
the traditional setting for the story. The earlier mention of the $\dot{o}\chi\lambda o\varsigma$ $\pi o\lambda\dot{\upsilon}\varsigma$
in 5:21b may well have been drawn from, and introduced in anticipation
of, this setting. If so, the redactor of the miracle collection, who constructed
the redactional seam in 5:21 between 5:22–43 and 5:1–20, would have intercalated these two stories.

25–27 These verses graphically describe the woman's plight with a series
of seven participles in a pattern untypical of Mark's style (cf. Lohmeyer,
101). The list begins by generally describing her ailment as a hemorrhage.
Though unspecified, her problem has been associated by implication with a
ritually defiling bleeding (Lev 12:1–8; 15:19–30). Lev 15:25 LXX describes
such a condition with similar terms ($\dot{\rho}\dot{\epsilon}\eta$ $\dot{\rho}\dot{\upsilon}\sigma\epsilon\iota$ $\alpha\dot{\iota}\mu\alpha\tau o\varsigma$; cf. $o\dot{\upsilon}\sigma\alpha$ $\dot{\epsilon}\nu$ $\dot{\rho}\dot{\upsilon}\sigma\epsilon\iota$). Consequently, the purity question so integral to the previous story (5:1–20) comes
immediately to the surface. This woman was not only defiled, she defiled
anything and anyone she touched. Her illness had left her personally, socially
and spiritually cut off.

The severity of her problem comes to light in both the length of the
illness and the futile measures she had undertaken. She had suffered for
"twelve years," another perhaps less than coincidental point of contact with

the Jairus story where the daughter was "twelve years" old (5:42). At the same time, her suffering had only intensified at the hands of the physicians, a motif not uncommon in healing stories (Tob 2:10; Sir 38:15; *b. Qidd.* 4:14). It had cost her all she had (δαπανήσασα τὰ παρ' αὐτῆς πάντα) only to become worse. Thus like the Gerasene demoniac in 5:1–20, this woman appeared beyond all hope and help. Nothing had worked for her.

She, however, had "heard about Jesus" (ἀκούσασα περὶ τοῦ Ἰησοῦ). This statement implies hearing about Jesus' power to heal. Coming from the rear of the crowd, the appropriate place for the defiled, she risked defiling others by approaching and deliberately touching Jesus' clothes. Such action could appear at best irresponsible except for the fact that she had heard that Jesus could heal her and thus remove the cause of her impurity. The explanation of 5:28 makes this explicit.

28 We have noted Mark's redactional propensity for γάρ-explanatory (e.g., 1:16, 22, 34; 2:15; 3:10; Pryke, *Style*, 126–35), which has led some (Schenke, *Wundererzählungen*, 200; Gnilka, 1:213) to assign this verse to Mark. But this verse has much in common with the γάρ-clause in 5:8. Like the statement in 5:8 (see *Comment*) and unlike the ἔλεγεν γάρ construction in 3:21; 6:18; 14:2 (see *Comment* on 3:21), this explanatory digression reads like an awkward afterthought that adds little except background to the story. It does exonerate the woman's questionable public behavior by explaining her intention in the same language found in the summaries of 3:10 (see *Comment* on 3:10) and 6:56. Consequently, this explanation of the woman's unusual behavior in 5:27 as well as the explanation (5:8) of the demoniac's unusual adjuration in 5:7b may well have come from the hand of the pre-Markan redactor who brought this collection of miracles together.

29 "The well of her blood" (ἡ πηγὴ τοῦ αἵματος αὐτῆς) corresponds verbatim to the LXX of Lev 12:7 (ἀπὸ τῆς πηγῆς τοῦ αἵματος αὐτῆς) that declares the woman clean through the rite of purification. Might this wordplay with Lev 12 subtly address the underlying purity question of how Jesus could be touched by a defiled person without personal consequence? His power to remove the defilement (ἡ πηγὴ τοῦ αἵματος αὐτῆς) makes the issue moot. The same would apply to his touching the leper (see *Comment* on 1:41).

The demonstration of the miracle takes place through the woman's recognition of immediate healing. She "knew in her body" that she had been healed (ἴαται). The miracle clearly accompanies her touching of Jesus' clothes. She had been healed from her "suffering" (μάστιγος), an expression occurring only in this story and in the possibly related summary in 3:10!

On form-critical grounds some would end the original story at this point. What follows appears to be an explanation or even a correction of the miracle story. But nothing in the story as it now stands supports such a theory. The narrative continues in the same style of participles and past tenses that differ from the short, paratactic sentences in the historical present of the surrounding Jairus story.

30 The narrative shifts to a dialogue which becomes the actual focal point of the story. The transition comes through Jesus' "perceiving" that "the power proceeding from him had gone out" when someone touched his clothes. Jesus' perception of what had happened corresponds to the woman's expectation that healing takes place through contact with the healer (so 3:10; 6:56). This same motif appears in Acts where Peter's shadow (5:15) and Paul's contact with handkerchiefs and aprons (19:12) transmit healing power.

Some have attributed this "hellenistic" view associating "touch" and "power" in Mark to a distinctive early Christian Christology that presented Jesus as a θεῖος ἀνήρ (Kertelge, *Wunder*, 114; Kuhn, *Sammlungen*, 192–200; Koch, *Wundererzählungen*, 136–37). But apart from the dubious existence of such a definitive figure in the ancient world (see *Comment* on 3:10), the thrust of the following dialogue explains the efficacious nature of the "touch" here and in the related summaries of 3:10 and 6:56. These summaries, as part of the pre-Markan miracle cycle, clearly had this story as their point of reference, if not their actual starting point in the tradition.

This is the first occurrence of δύναμις in Mark's account. In 6:2, 5 and 9:39 it refers to an act of power or a mighty work. But here and in 6:14, "power" (δύναμις) is the force which effects the mighty works. It is something that goes out from Jesus (ἡ ἐξ αὐτοῦ δύναμις), whose absence can be perceived (ἐπιγνοὺς . . . τὴν . . . δύναμιν ἐξελθοῦσαν). The nature of the power remains unspecified (cf. Taylor, 291; Gnilka, 1:215). Yet the reader could hardly miss its supernatural character in view of the immediate context. The stories of 4:35–5:20 have born witness to Jesus' awesome (4:41) and frightening (5:15) control over the humanly uncontrollable forces of nature and the demonic. The questions in Nazareth about his "mighty works" (δυνάμεις, 6:2) and the reference in 6:14–15 to the Baptist's coming back from the dead as Herod's explanation for this power (cf. 12:24) certainly point in that direction.

31 The "disciples" (οἱ μαθηταὶ αὐτοῦ), as an expression, last occurred in the redactional note of 4:34. Their presence was only assumed in 4:35–41 and 5:1. The last mention of them in Mark's tradition came in 3:7, 9, the summary which may well have originally opened the pre-Markan collection of miracle stories and supplied the subjects for 4:35–41 (see *Comment* on 4:35). Their mention here adds a further tie between 3:7–12 and these miracle stories.

The disciples counter Jesus' question with an obvious response in view of the situation. By doing so, they heighten the point of Jesus' query, "Who touched my clothes?" The press of the crowd (τὸν ὄχλον συνθλίβοντά σε; cf. 5:24) made contact with him unavoidable and his question ridiculous. Yet Jesus knew someone had done more than simply touch him in passing; more was involved in the action than merely physical contact. This becomes the point of the dialogue.

33 "Afraid and trembling" (φοβηθεῖσα καὶ τρέμουσα). This reaction hardly reflects a sense of guilt either because she had acted surreptitiously without permission (cf. διὸ πεποιήκει λάθρᾳ, a variant reading in D [Θ] 28 565 [700] it; Taylor, 292) or because she had acted irresponsibly according to the law by touching Jesus (Grundmann, 151). Nor does this reaction express fear of being misunderstood as having had less than honorable intentions (Theissen, *Miracle Stories*, 133). Rather, in view of similar responses in 4:41 and 5:15 to the miraculous deed, this description expresses her reaction of awe at what had happened to her (εἰδυῖα ὃ γέγονεν αὐτῇ).

Consequently, she bows (προσέπεσεν; cf. 5:22) before Jesus in obvious wonder and respect and tells him "the whole truth" (πᾶσαν τὴν ἀλήθειαν), which included at least her actions in seeking Jesus' help, as seen by his comments in 5:34.

34 Jesus addresses her affectionately as "daughter" (θυγάτηρ), a term that offers another connecting link to the Jairus story (cf. 5:23, 35), and then declares that her "faith has made her well" (ἡ πίστις σου σέσωκέν σε). This statement carries the weight of the entire story (see *Comment* on 2:5). It certainly brings the dialogue to its climax.

Some view this statement and thus the dialogue to be a correction of any magical misconceptions underlying the miracle story itself and expressed in 5:28 (Kertelge, *Wunder*, 115; Koch, *Wundererzählungen*, 137; Gnilka, 1:213). By attributing her becoming well to her faith, Jesus apparently reinterprets the actual means of her healing. But this bifurcation of the story into tradition and interpretation fails to take seriously the integral nature of its content. When Jesus attributes her healing to her faith, he does not repudiate the actions described in 5:25–29 or even the stated intention and hope of 5:28. In fact, repeated references to her touching Jesus run through the miracle and the dialogue (cf. 5:27, 28, 30, 31). More was involved from the outset than simply physical contact. This becomes clear in her statement of hope (5:28) and in Jesus' question about someone touching him, which is parodied by the disciples' response (5:30, 31).

Furthermore, the same verb (σῴζειν) used to express her hope for healing by touching Jesus is used here to describe what has come through her faith. The future tense of 5:28 (σωθήσομαι) becomes the perfect tense here (σέσωκεν) denoting action already *completed* whose results continue into the present. By using the perfect tense, this statement recognizes that she has indeed been "made well." Though σῴζειν can mean "to save" as well as "to make well," the parallel use in 5:28 and the related use in 5:22 as well as the perfect tense pointing to a past event leave little doubt that "has made you well" is the primary rendering here.

According to the story, the woman became well when she touched Jesus' clothes. Therefore, Jesus' statement does not correct what happened earlier but sets what happened in the perspective of her faith that brought her to him and led her to take a public risk to touch his clothes in view of what she had heard about him (5:27).

Since the summary statements referring to the sick being healed by touching Jesus in 3:10 and 6:56 most likely stood in the pre-Markan context of this story, this account provides the basis for understanding the other passages (see *Comment* on 3:10; 6:56). In other words, for the reader of Mark's Gospel as well as the pre-Markan collection of miracle stories, healing that came through one's touching Jesus came about through an act of faith rather than through some "magic touch." The nature and significance of this faith for Jesus' work becomes even clearer in the following story of his rejection in Nazareth (see *Comment* on 6:5).

"Go in peace" (see *Note* k) expresses a common Semitic farewell. But it represents more than simply a dismissal formula here. Together with the following imperative, it sets forth the full meaning of the previous declaration, "Your faith has made you well!" Going in peace means to go as one "restored to a proper relationship with God" (Schweizer, 118). Her healing, though certainly including her physical illness as the next statement indicates, involved more than simply the physical dimension of her existence (cf. 2:5–11).

"Be healed from your suffering" (ἴσθι ὑγιὴς τῆς μάστιγός σου) concludes this story. Some have found this command to be in tension with the events described in 5:29. But such a reading places more weight than is necessary on this command and overlooks the crucial preceding statement that her faith had made her well. As coordinate with the previous command, this imperative reiterates rather than replaces the primary thrust of the opening declaration of healing that had already happened (5:34a). As Haenchen (207) suggests, Jesus merely sanctions what has transpired with the word of assurance. In this case, the healing took place through her faith expressed in her touching Jesus' clothes. The word ratifies what has already happened (Cranfield, 185).

35 "While he was speaking" (ἔτι αὐτοῦ λαλοῦντος) forms a bridge back to the Jairus story. Jesus is obviously still speaking to the woman when messengers arrive. Many have assumed this genitive absolute originally connected 5:35 with 5:22–24a. If so, Jairus would have been the subject before the insertion of 5:25–34. The consistent use, however, of the genitive absolute in the pre-Markan seams of the miracle collection (see *Comment* on 5:21) suggests this too came from the redactor who intercalated these stories to make the transition more natural.

"Your daughter is dead" (ἀπέθανεν) heightens the drama. Jairus came with his daughter at the point of death to ask for Jesus' help (5:23). That would now appear to be too late. At least, the advice of the messengers implies as much. Now that the girl has died, no further reason exists for "bothering" (σκύλλεις) the teacher (διδάσκαλον). Once again we have a situation beyond human hope that has marked these miracles (4:37–38; 5:3–5; 25–26).

36 Jesus "ignored" (παρακούσας; cf. *Note* l) what had been announced by the messengers and encouraged the synagogue president not to fear (μὴ φοβοῦ), but to have faith (μόνον πίστευε). Although some take this command to be typical language of a theophany or an epiphany (Lohmeyer, 105; Grundmann, 152), the immediate setting is hardly theophanic or epiphanic. Assuming the story had an independent existence in the early tradition, Jesus' assurance summoned Jairus to maintain his faith that Jesus could help his daughter even when the situation appeared absolutely hopeless. He was not to lose heart because of his fears in the face of death. Set in the present context of the woman's faith in 5:25–34, Jesus' words place the emphasis all the more on Jairus' faith in one who had just ignored a death announcement. By contrast, the following story in Nazareth demonstrates what happens when such faith is missing.

37 Jesus excludes all followers from this point on, except the three disciples whom he selects. In the present setting, this action excludes the large crowd of 5:21, 24, 27, 32.

Peter, James and John stand out in the list of the Twelve in 3:16–17, accompany Jesus at the Transfiguration (9:2), trigger along with Andrew (cf. 1:29) the Olivet Discourse (13:3), and are separated from the other disciples in Gethsemane (14:33). But does Mark introduce them into this scene (so Grundmann, 152; Schmahl, *Zwölf*, 129–30; Pesch, 1:307; Schenke, *Wunderer-*

zählungen, 205; Gnilka, 1:217)? Since the prominence of these three disciples antedates Mark's Gospel as seen in their calling (1:16–20), their place in the listing of the Twelve (see *Comment* on 5:16–17) and their role in the Transfiguration story (see *Comment* on 9:2), we have no clear reason for assigning their presence here to Mark's redaction rather than to their place of prominence in the tradition (Ernst, 160).

The exclusion of the public is a recurring motif in miracle stories (e.g., 7:33; 8:23; Acts 9:40; 1 Kgs 17:19; 2 Kgs 4:4, 33; Theissen, *Miracle Stories,* 60–61). This appears to be the primary thrust of the statement here. In 5:40 Jesus expels the mourners from Jairus' house but as an indication of the inappropriateness of their presence and a response to their mockery (see 5:40). Therefore, the exclusion of the rest of the public gives prominence to the selection of the three disciples.

Does the selection of the three disciples give special significance to this story? Does their presence make this the "greatest" of Jesus' miracles (Pesch, 1:307; cf. 1:29)? Since they are present for special revelations (9:2–9; 13:3–37), does this mean they witness here a special revelation of God's power (Gnilka, 1:217; cf. 14:33)? Does it mean they are privy to special insight about the resurrection of the dead which they cannot fully comprehend until after Easter (Grundmann, 152)?

Each suggestion has some merit based on Mark's Gospel. But each risks making more of this miracle than the story itself does. While raising the dead may be the greatest miracle from our perspective, this miracle comes in a series of miracles involving absolutely hopeless situations. Furthermore, we must not overlook the distinction between raising the dead as the ultimate healing miracle, resuscitation, and the resurrection of the dead as the eschatological event. The early Church never confused the raising of one of their dead with the resurrection. Therefore, the choosing of the three disciples represents, as does their selection in Gethsemane (14:33), more of a statement about their special privilege of accompanying Jesus than about the miracle itself.

38 The presence of the mourners supports the earlier message of the girl's death. Even the poorer families had mourners that usually included two flute players, a woman to lead in antiphonal singing or chanting accompanied by hand clapping and percussion instruments. Given the social status of a synagogue president, the size of the group and the resultant commotion would be appropriate.

39 Jesus questions their reason for creating the commotion and weeping by announcing that the girl is not dead, only asleep (τὸ παιδίον οὐκ ἀπέθανεν ἀλλὰ καθεύδει). How could Jesus say the girl was not dead? Some would answer quite literally, meaning she was only apparently dead (Taylor, 295). But this solution does violence to the story's flow by ignoring the messengers' report in 5:35 and the presence of the mourners in 5:38, not to mention the fact that Jesus had yet to see the child. Consequently, others have taken this statement euphemistically. "Sleep" can be a euphemism for death in the OT as well as the NT (e.g., Dan 12:7 LXX; Ps 87:6 LXX; 1 Thess 5:10) but hardly in a statement explicitly denying death (οὐκ ἀπέθανεν).

Most today take her "sleep" as a qualification of rather than an antithesis to her "death." Thus several interpret Jesus' comment as speaking from God's perspective who sees all death transformed by the resurrection (Lohmeyer, 106; Grundmann, 153; Schweizer, 119; Gnilka, 1:217). Jesus' reply to the Sadducees in 12:27 that God is "not the God of the dead, but of the living" and a relatively late (AD 250) rabbinical saying expressing a similar sentiment ("Thou shalt sleep, but thou shalt not die," *Gen. Rab.* 96 [60c]; Taylor, 295) supposedly provide supporting evidence. Unfortunately, this reading ignores Jesus' rebuke of the mourners and confuses what follows with the resurrection.

Jesus' reference to the girl's sleeping corresponds with his word that summons her to "arise" or "wake up" (see *Comment* on 5:41). Therefore, the statement to the mourners explaining his question about their commotion is of the same cloth as Jesus' earlier assurance to Jairus to have no fear but merely have faith (5:36). Jesus viewed her death, which was real, in light of the approaching miracle (Klostermann, 53; Lane, 197). In other words, "though she is dead . . , her death will be no more permanent than a sleep" (Cranfield, 189) in view of what Jesus was about to do.

40 The mourners "ridiculed" (κατεγέλων) him. They took him literally and missed the point of his statement. Like the messengers in 5:35, they thought death to be the final barrier. Their ridicule expressed their unbelief, their skepticism, a motif that also occurs repeatedly in miracle stories (e.g., 9:22; John 11:39; 2 Kgs 5:11; Theissen, *Miracle Stories*, 56). Their presence no longer pertinent, Jesus "put them out" (ἐκβαλὼν πάντας). Though often taken as part of Mark's messianic secret motif and/or a typical trait of removing the public from the scene (see *Comment* on 5:37), their dismissal stems from the inappropriateness of their presence as mourners in view of Jesus' comment in 5:39. By contrast (δέ), he takes the girl's father and mother and "those with him" (τοὺς μετ' αὐτοῦ), obviously the three disciples of 5:37, into where she lay.

41 "Taking hold of the child's hand" (κρατήσας τῆς χειρός) puts Jesus in "touch" with her. This gesture corresponds to a degree with the woman's touch in 5:25–34. And it again involves the purity question, inherent in the woman's illness, by placing Jesus in direct contact with a corpse (see Neusner, *JAAR* 43 [1975] 21). But the miracle makes the issue moot by removing the cause of the defilement (e.g., 1:41–45; 5:25–34). Yet Jesus' word, not his touch (cf. 1:31; 8:22), conveys the healing here.

The healing word is spoken in Aramaic (see *Note* m), leading some to take it as a ῥῆσις βαρβαρική (Klostermann, 53). Such foreign words had the function of magical incantations by which the healer mysteriously performed the cure (Theissen, *Miracle Stories*, 64). The accompanying translation, however, and the repeated use of Aramaic expressions in Mark (e.g., 3:17; 7:11, 34; 11:9–10; 14:36; 15:22, 34), with only 7:34 in a healing setting, suggest Jesus' word of healing was preserved but not as a magic formula. Rather the healing power lay with the speaker as seen in the freely rendered, "I say to you" (σοὶ λέγω), missing in the Aramaic. Jesus commands her to "arise" (1:31; 2:10; cf. 9:27) or, corresponding to his earlier comment about being asleep (5:39), to "wake up" (cf. 4:27, 38; 14:41–42).

The miracle of raising the dead appears elsewhere in the Gospel tradition (e.g., Luke 7:11–17 [L]; Matt 11:4–6 // Luke 7:22–23 [Q]; John 11:1–46).

Acts 9:40 attributes the same miracle to Peter and possibly 20:9–12 to Paul. By contrast, the NT apocryphal literature makes numerous references to such miracles by the apostles (see van der Loos, *Miracles,* 526–63). The power to raise the dead is not unknown outside the Christian literature, since Apollonius of Tyana (Philostratus, *Vita Apoll.* 4.45) and *Asclepiades* (Pliny, *Nat. Hist.* 7.37.124; cf. Apuleius, *Florida,* 4.19) are said to have exercised this power in the hellenistic world. And Str-B (1:560) lists rabbinical texts of a much later date that mention rabbis with this power.

The most immediate backdrop for this miracle lies in the stories of Elijah (1 Kgs 17:17–23) and Elisha (2 Kgs 4:18–37) and may be seen by the identification of Jesus as Elijah in 6:15. Both Elijah and Elisha isolated themselves with the dead child, prayed for God's help and stretched themselves over the child. Yet Jesus' taking the parents with him to the child, grasping her hand and directly commanding her to arise belies any direct influence of the OT stories on this account.

42 The girl immediately "stood up" (ἀνέστη) and "began walking around" (περιεπάτει). This action formally serves as a demonstration of the miracle. "For she was twelve years old" not only informs the reader that she was old enough to walk on her own but also offers another point of contact with the story of the woman who had suffered for twelve years (5:25).

Those present were "utterly amazed" (ἐξέστησαν ἐκστάσει μεγάλῃ, see *Note* o). This expression of wonder accompanies the healing of the paralytic in 2:12 and the calming of the winds in 6:51. Its Semitic construction here (infinitive absolute) and the use of the Aramaic command before may indicate an underlying Aramaic tradition (Lohmeyer, 104).

43 Jesus then gives two further commands, a command to secrecy and instructions to feed her. The secrecy command has often been assigned to Mark's redaction (Klostermann, 53–54; Grundmann, 148; Kertelge, *Wunder,* 119; Gnilka, 1:213; Ernst, 165). A similar command forms part of the conclusion of the story of the leper in 1:41–45 (44) and the story of the hearing and speech impaired man in 7:31–37 (36). It may also be implicit in the dismissal instructions in 8:26.

Theissen (*Miracle Stories,* 68–69, 140–44), however, has assigned the secrecy commands on formal grounds to the miracle stories as a recurrent motif analogous to the prohibition of the dissemination of magical formulas in the magical papyri (see *Comment* on 1:44). He notes, as in 5:42, that these injunctions come in the context of wonder and acclamations. Pesch (1:311) also assigns this injunction to the pre-Markan tradition on stylistic grounds, i.e., the adverbial use of πολλά, the use of διαστέλλειν in warnings and the optative γνοῖ. The almost exclusive use of an adverbial πολλά in 5:10, 23, 38, 43 does carry some weight, though Mark could have simply adopted this usage from his immediate tradition (cf. 3:12). Second, the use of διαστέλλειν in secrecy commands (5:43; 7:36; 9:9) and once in a warning (8:15) and the optative mood (γνοῖ—5:43; 7:24) are distinctive but they constitute a circular argument, since the other occurrences could also be redactional.

Perhaps the strongest argument for the presence of this command in the pre-Markan story lies along formal lines. First, the secrecy motif corresponds to the exclusion of the public in 5:40. Second, the story ends very awkwardly with a second demonstration in the form of Jesus' command to give her something to eat (δοθῆναι αὐτῇ φαγεῖν). Not only is this demonstration formally redundant (cf. 5:42), but it comes after the wonder/acclamation which the secrecy command logically follows (cf. 7:35–37). Therefore, if Mark were redactionally responsible for the secrecy command, why would he not have given it more prominence by using it to round off the story after, if not in place of, the second demonstration? This would seem all the more logical, since this is the one healing in which the explicit secrecy command is not broken (cf. 1:44–45; 7:36!).

Perhaps the combination of this story into a larger miracle collection best explains the anomaly of 5:43. The secrecy command following the wonder or acclamation would have concluded the original miracle story. The redundant demonstration that now ends the story (5:43b) could well have been added by the collector of the miracle stories to prepare for the next miracle, the Feeding of the Five Thousand (6:35–52; Achtemeier, *JBL* 89 [1970] 279). If so, the concluding command to feed the girl corresponds to Jesus' command to his disciples to feed the crowds (5:43b; cf. 6:37) providing a natural transition to the next story. This connection is now lost in view of Mark's interruption of the collection by the insertion of 6:1–30.

Explanation

This narrative includes two miracles, the one sandwiched by the other. But unlike other examples of this Markan literary technique (e.g., 3:22–30 [20–35]; 6:14–29 [7–31]), this intercalation combines thematically related stories and enhances the drama of the Jairus story.

Both stories involve women, "daughters," beyond all apparent human help, one twelve years old and the other having suffered for twelve years, who come into defiling contact with Jesus. Yet the thrust of each story is faith. The woman's healing faith provides the climax in 5:34 and the backdrop against which Jesus' assurance to Jairus, "only believe" (5:36), gains an added dimension.

By raising Jairus' daughter, Jesus hardly prefigures the miracle to top all miracles, the resurrection, any more than did Elijah (1 Kgs 17:17–24) or Elisha (2 Kgs 4:32–37) who performed a similar miracle. While the distinction between resuscitation and resurrection may be modern, there is no evidence that the story or the early Church confused what transpired in this account with the resurrection which connoted a categorically different kind of life. Jairus' daughter simply returned to life as usual with her family as seen by her walking about and eating (5:42–43).

Like Elijah and Elisha, whose similar miracles could hardly be overlooked by one familiar with the OT, Jesus does show himself to be a man of God. Yet he shows himself to be greater than Elijah by raising the child with his authoritative word. This perception of Jesus corresponds with the Gerasene demoniac's recognition of him as the "Son of the Most High" (5:7) and the disciples' awestruck response to his epiphanic deliverance (4:41; cf. 6:49–50).

For Mark these two stories stand out by virtue of what follows next. He uses the explicit reference to Jesus' power (5:30), implicit in the previous two stories (4:35–5:20), to connect the following Nazareth episode in which reference is made to Jesus' power displayed in his "mighty works" (6:2). Yet we find Jesus' "power" limited in Nazareth by the absence of faith (6:1–6a).

Faith involved more than simply believing Jesus could perform miracles. No one questioned that in Nazareth. They questioned how he could do what he was doing because of who they "knew" him to be. By implication, therefore, healing faith for Mark in these two stories means more than faith in a miracle worker. Both Jairus and the woman displayed faith that God was somehow at work in Jesus. Therefore, the evangelist uses these stories to underscore the role of faith and its corollary, the person of Jesus as seen in his ministry that highlights the role of faith in these stories.

M. Jesus in Nazareth (Mark 6:1–6a)

Bibliography

Achtemeier, P. "Toward the Isolation of Pre-Markan Miracle Catenae." *JBL* 89 (1970) 265–91. **Betz, O.** "Jesus in Nazareth." *Israel hat dennoch Gott zum Trost.* In FS Schalom Ben-Chorin, ed. G. Müller. Trier: Paulinus, 1978. 44–60. **Blinzler, J.** *Die Brüder und Schwestern Jesu.* SBS 21. Stuttgart: Katholisches Bibelwerk, 1967. **Crossan, J. D.** "Mark and the Relatives of Jesus." *NovT* 15 (1973) 81–113. **Grässer, E.** "Jesus in Nazareth (Mark VI.1–6a): Notes on the Redaction and Theology of St. Mark." *NTS* 16 (1969–70) 1–23. **Haenchen, E.** *Gesammelte Aufsätze,* II. Tübingen: Mohr, 1968. **Huston, H. W.** "Mark 6 and 11 in P45 and in the Caesarean Text." *JBL* 74 (1955) 262–71. **Kertelge, K.** *Die Wunder Jesu im Markusevangelium.* 1970. **Koch, D.-A.** *Die Bedeutung der Wundererzählungen für die Christologie des Markusevangeliums.* 1975. **McArthur, H. K.** "Son of Mary." *NovT* 15 (1973) 38–58. **Mayer, B.** "Ueberlieferungs- und redaktionsgeschichtliche Ueberlegungen zu Mk 6, 1–6a." *BZ* 22 (1978) 187–98. **Robbins, V. K.** *"Dynameis* and *Semeia* in Mark." *BR* 18 (1973) 5–20. **Roloff, J.** *Das Kerygma und der irdische Jesus.* 1970. **Schmahl, G.** *Die Zwölf im Markusevangelium: Eine redaktionsgeschichtliche Untersuchung.* TTS 30. Trier: Paulinus, 1974. **Schulz, S.** *Die Stunde der Botschaft.* Hamburg: Furche, 1967. **Stauffer, E.** "Jeschua ben Mirjam (Mk 6,3)." In *Neotestamentica et Semitica,* FS M. Black, ed. E. Ellis and M. Wilcox. Edinburgh: T. & T. Clark, 1969. 119–28. **Sturch, R. L.** "The ΠΑΤΡΙΣ of Jesus." *JTS* 28 (1977) 94–96.

Translation

[1] *And Jesus[a] departed from there and came to his hometown. And his disciples followed him.* [2] *It being the sabbath, he began to teach in the synagogue. And when all[b] had heard, they were overwhelmed, saying, "Where does this man get these things? What wisdom has been given this man? How do such mighty works happen through him?* [3] *Is this man not the carpenter,[c] the son of Mary, the brother of James, Joses, Jude and Simon? And are not his sisters here with us?" And they refused to believe in him.[d]* [4] *And Jesus said to them, "A prophet is not without honor except in his own hometown, among his relatives and in his own house."*

⁵*And he was not able to do any mighty work there, except that he laid his hands on a few sickly ones and healed them.* ⁶*And he was amazed at their unbelief.*

Notes

ᵃRomanized words added from context.

ᵇThe anarthrous πολλοί has the stronger MSS evidence—ℵ A C W 0133 *f*¹ Majority text; οἱ πολλοί in B L 28 *f*¹³. In either case, it likely carries the inclusive sense of "all" (J. Jeremias, *TDNT* 6 [1968] 540–41; cf. Taylor, 299).

ᶜThe overwhelming MSS evidence favors ὁ τέκτων over ὁ τοῦ τέκτονος υἱός (p⁴⁵ᵛⁱᵈ *f*¹³ it boᵐˢˢ), an apparent assimilation to Matt 13:55. Klostermann (55) prefers the latter as less influenced by the doctrine of the virgin birth. Taylor (300) prefers it because of the unusual "Son of Mary" that follows.

ᵈἐσκανδαλίζοντο carries a more technical force than simply "to be offended." In this and similar Gospel contexts this verb connotes a "deep religious offence" at the preaching of Jesus which "causes the denial and rejection of Jesus" (G. Stählin, *TDNT* 7 [1971] 350; similarly, Grässer, *NTS* 16 [1969–70] 16).

Form / Structure / Setting

Form-critically, Bultmann (31) called this a "typical example (*Musterbeispiel*) of how an imaginary situation (*Idealszene*) is constructed from an independent saying" to form a biographical apothegm (so Koch, *Wundererzählungen*, 149). By contrast, Pesch (1:316) refers to this story as a "report" that is more informational than reflective in nature. Despite these extremes, form-critical considerations highlight a fundamental question for the story. What is its point? Strictly speaking, an apophthegm climaxes with a concluding saying, in which case the point of this story would be Jesus' rejection in his hometown (6:4). But the story now ends (6:5–6) with Jesus' inability to work miracles and his amazement at their lack of faith. This accents the relationship between faith and miracles (Koch, *Wundererzählungen*, 147).

The question of source is not much clearer. The occurrence of the saying behind Mark 6:4 in Luke 4:24; John 4:44; *Gos. Thom.* 31 and P. Oxy 1:5 certainly demonstrates its circulation as an independent unit of tradition. With reference to its usage here, the views run the gamut from Mark's own composition of this story as a setting for the saying by assembling some undefined traditional data (e.g., Grässer, *NTS* [1969–70] 7–8) to Mark's finding the story virtually intact in the tradition (e.g., Pesch, 1:316). The issue becomes one of tradition and redaction.

A review of the many analyses shows that no two writers agree completely on what parts belonged to Mark's tradition or stem from his redaction. Yet since Grässer's analysis that essentially attributed the story to Mark's composition (*NTS* [1969–70] 7–9), most interpreters have concluded that at least 6:2b–6a provided a traditional core which the evangelist may have modified at points (6:2b, 4bc, 5b). At the same time, most commentators have assigned the opening scene (6:1–2a) to Mark's redaction, primarily because of its similarity to 1:21–22. We shall take a closer look at this question in the *Comment*, particularly where the issue has bearing on the passage's significance for Mark.

The story lacks formal structure, but one can divide it into four parts.

First, it opens with Jesus teaching in the synagogue (6:1–2a). The astounded audience responds with a series of questions about Jesus (6:2a–3). He responds with a proverbial saying about lack of honor (6:4), and the story concludes with a couple of comments about the impact of the response on Jesus' ministry (6:5–6a).

At the same time, the narrative contains some inherent tensions. For example, Jesus is described as teaching but the audience also questions his "mighty deeds." Initially "overwhelmed" by him, they take offense and refuse to believe in him (6:2, 3). Though referring to his "hometown" in 6:1–3, the saying in 6:4 introduces his "relatives" and "house." The second part of 6:5 implies Jesus healed some people, when the first part declares that he could not do any mighty deeds there. Finally, the concluding remark in 6:6a underscores Jesus' amazement at their lack of faith, even though he himself had expressed the rule regarding the absence of honor in one's own hometown. Most have resolved these tensions by attributing them to the composite nature of this material (Schmidt, 155; Grässer, *NTS* 16 [1969–70] 4–9; Koch, *Wundererzählung- en*, 150–52; Mayer, *BZ* 22 [1978] 187–98).

As to setting, Mark interrupts a series of miracles (cf. 4:35–5:43; 6:32– 52) with this story about Jesus' rejection in Nazareth. Luke has a similar story which he used programmatically at the outset of his Gospel (4:16–30), while Matthew chose to place the story at the conclusion of Jesus' parable discourse in 13:53–58. In other words, each evangelist has used the story for his own purposes.

Mark makes two points of contact with the preceding narrative. First, the emphasis on the woman's faith in 5:25–34 and Jairus' faith in 5:35–43 offers a startling contrast to the absence of faith (ἀπιστία) among Jesus' own people. Second, the explicit reference to "power" (δύναμιν) in 5:30 provides the concep- tual foreground for the use of δύναμις as "mighty deed" in 6:2, 5.

At the same time, this story provides at least a partial transition for what follows. By bringing the disciples to Nazareth to experience his rejection and limited healing activities, Jesus prepares them for their own mission with its varied response (6:7–13). Furthermore, the question regarding his "mighty deeds" (6:2, 5), including implicitly his identity, connects with the varied responses by the people to Jesus' ministry and in particular Herod's question about Jesus' identitification with John the Baptist in light of his "mighty deeds" in 6:14–16.

In the broader context, this pericope comes toward the end and interprets a section in Mark's Gospel that has focused on Jesus' words (3:20–4:34) and work (4:35–5:43). The villagers question his "wisdom," based on his synagogue teaching, and his "mighty deeds," of which they had presumably heard. They, including specifically his family, reject him and refuse to have faith in him (6:3, 6a), in a scene reminiscent of his family's response in 3:20–21, 31–35 (not unlike that of the "scribes from Jerusalem," 3:22–30) after Jesus had called the Twelve (3:13–19) to "be with him" and "to send them" in mission.

By connecting this pericope with the miracles that immediately preceded (cf. "such mighty deeds" [αἱ δυνάμεις τοιαῦται], 6:2), Mark shows that Jesus' works per se made no more sense to "those outside" than his teaching (4:11– 12). In fact, as the subsuming of an exorcism under teaching in 1:21–27 and the deliberate setting of synagogue teaching here indicate, Mark does not sharply distinguish Jesus' miracles from his teaching. The former belong to the broader category of the latter for the eye of faith. In themselves, neither Jesus' teaching nor his miracles makes clear who he is. That is why "faith," as this story illustrates, belongs so integrally with miracle (5:30–34; 6:5–6a). This will become even clearer in the disciples' role in Mark's next major section (6:7–8:26).

Comment

1 "Jesus departed from there" (ἐξῆλθεν ἐκεῖθεν) is Mark's redactional bridge from Jairus' house to the scene in Nazareth. "From there" (ἐκεῖθεν) plays a similar role in 7:24; 9:30; and 10:1.

"Hometown" (πατρίδα), one's native place, may have come originally from 6:4 (Grässer, *NTS* 16 [1969–70] 10; Gnilka, 1:228). Mark takes for granted his readers' knowledge that Nazareth was Jesus' hometown based on 1:9, 24, if not otherwise. Matthew's and Luke's account of Jesus' birth in Bethlehem do not contradict this inference, since Nazareth also becomes his hometown in those Gospels.

"His disciples followed him" (ἀκολουθοῦσιν αὐτῷ οἱ μαθηταί) is an added note by Mark. The disciples play no role in the story except to accompany Jesus. Yet the mention of their presence corresponds to their call to be "with him" (3:13) and their implied presence throughout 3:13–6:6a. It also prepares for Jesus' sending them in mission in 6:7–13. Their experience of the negative aspect of Jesus' own mission as well as the positive side (cf. 3:20–5:43) may anticipate the two responses of their own mission (cf. 6:10–11).

2 Jesus' teaching in the synagogue on the sabbath closely parallels the scene in Capernaum in 1:21. This similarity and the Markan characteristic ἤρξατο with the infinitive (especially διδάσκειν—4:1; 6:34) suggests the evangelist's hand in this setting. This is the last mention in Mark of Jesus' teaching or even his presence in a synagogue. The previous reference (3:1–6) ended in Jesus' sharp rejection by the religious authorities. Thus the synagogue becomes the place of rejection by both the religious leaders and those who knew him best, a feature that parallels the Markan story about his family and the "scribes from Jerusalem" at the outset of this section (3:20–35).

"Were overwhelmed" renders a verb (ἐκπλήσσειν) that expresses positive surprise (7:37; 11:18) as well as incredulity (10:26) in Mark. The following questions reflecting the audience's perplexity suggest the latter here. We have no grounds for assuming an initial positive response (Grässer, *NTS* 16 [1969–70] 5–6, 12–14) or a positive response by "many" with a dissenting undercurrent eventually taking over (see *Note* b; cf. Taylor, 299). The audience simply found his teaching more than they could comprehend in view of their knowledge about him (cf. 10:25–26).

The reason for their reaction comes to light in a series of five questions, three aimed at Jesus' ministry and two at him personally. A detached, almost disparaging, tone rings through the repeated use of the demonstrative "this man" (τούτῳ . . . τούτῳ . . . οὗτός). The second question concerning his wisdom and the third about his mighty deeds specify the general question, "Where did he get these things?" Where (πόθεν) did such wisdom and work come from—from "heaven or from human resources" (11:30) or from "Satan" (3:22)?

Some have taken these comments to echo the awe inspired by a hellenistic θεῖος ἀνήρ (Grässer, *NTS* 16 [1969–70] 13). But these questions have their roots in the OT idea of God granting divine wisdom and power through a designated person (cf. Job 12:13). Perhaps we even have a subtle reference, at least for the reader, to the hope of Isa 11:1–3 which spoke of God's anointed redeemer, the "branch" (נצֶר, *nēṣer*, cf. a Jesus from "Nazareth"—Betz, *Israel*, 55) from the shoot of Jesse, upon whom God's Spirit of wisdom (חכמה, *ḥākmâh*) and power (בינה, *bînâh*) would rest (see *Comment* on 1:9–11). In any case, both the question about his wisdom and his power offered the alternative that God had given him this wisdom (δοθεῖσα, a *divinum passivum*) and was at work "through" (διὰ τῶν χειρῶν) him performing redemptive and beneficial works for the people.

The crowd's response to Jesus' "wisdom" (ἡ σοφία), a word occurring only here in Mark, arises logically from their having heard him teach. But the story provides little basis here or later for their astonishment at "such mighty works." The lack of an antecedent in the story for the demonstrative (τοιαῦται) means that the miracles of the preceding context (4:35–5:43) come into play. Certainly, Mark intended the reader to make the connection, but the question on the lips of the crowd implies that they had heard of his "mighty deeds."

Mark has δύναμις, the common Greek term for "miracle," five times (5:30; 6:2, 5, 14; 9:39) in reference to miracles. Each comes as a part of his tradition. Three times the word refers to "miracles," or "mighty works" (6:2, 5; 9:39); twice it refers to the power or powers effecting the "mighty deed" (5:30; 6:14). The latter usage comes close to the hellenistic meaning of a miracle-working power that performs wonders. But this context makes clear the OT background of God's "mighty works." The Semitism, "happen through his hands" (διὰ τῶν χειρῶν αὐτοῦ γινόμεναι), shows Jesus to be the agent through whom God is at work (Kertelge, *Wunder*, 120–124).

The "mighty works" are "events" that proclaim God's acts on behalf of God's people (Kertelge, *Wunder*, 124). Therefore, Jesus' "teaching" and his "work" lay a claim on his audience to recognize that God was at work in him in a new way inaugurating God's sovereign reign in the lives of those who would respond (cf. 6:6a). But the townspeople reject this claim because they knew who Jesus "really" was.

3 "Is this not the carpenter, the son of Mary?" The variant readings for this passage (see *Note* c) reflect a concern about the awkward "son of Mary," a rare way of identifying someone. Matt 13:55 has "the son of the carpenter" and his mother's name, Mary. Mark's text has received various explanations: (a) theologically motivated by the virgin birth (Klostermann, 55), (b) a reference to Jesus as being illegitimate (Stauffer, *Neotestamentica*, 121–22), (c) Mary was a widow (e.g., Schweizer, 124), or simply (d) Mark was not "interested" in Jesus' father whom he never mentions (Crossan, *NovT* 15 [1973] 102).

McArthur examines the various alternatives by seeking parallels in the OT and Judaism and concludes that none can be supported by the evidence (*NovT* 15 [1973] 55). Thus, he concludes that "son of Mary" represents an "informal descriptive" rather than a "formal genealogical" way of identifying Jesus by his well-known mother, since his father was "presumably long since dead" (*NovT* 15 [1973] 55). He supports this usage by OT and NT examples (Judg 11:1–2; 1 Kgs 17:17; Luke 7:12; Acts 16:1; 23:16; Gal 4:21–31). Whatever the answer, "son of Mary" need not be a cruel insult. Neither the reference to his trade nor his brothers and sisters connotes anything pejorative.

A "carpenter" (τέκτων) renders a term used for manual labor with stone, metal or wood and suggests that Jesus grew up and learned a trade like everyone else in Nazareth. Justin (*Dial.* 88) notes that Jesus made plows, yokes and other farm instruments, though this tradition is admittedly from the late second century. By contrast, Origen (*Against Celsus* 6.36) defended Jesus against the charge that he was merely an ordinary carpenter (the same charge leveled here!) by stating that no text of the Gospels supports it, an indication that Origen might not have been aware of our present text in Mark (cf. *v.l.* and Matt 13:55).

The naming of Jesus' four brothers, only two of whom are known elsewhere in the NT (James, Jude), and the reference to his sisters round out the questions about his personal life. These questions point to his being a local son, a common, ordinary man with a trade and a family known to all. This common knowledge of who Jesus "really" was led the townspeople to reject the alternative that God might be using him in any special way.

"They refused to believe in him" carries the freight in this context of σκανδαλίζειν. Their "taking offense" connoted more than an insult to their intelligence (see *Note* d). It meant a rejection of the claim his teaching and work, his "wisdom" and "mighty works," made on them. They refused to accept him for who he was as seen by his words and work in lieu of who he was as known by them. In other words, both Jesus' words and his works were "riddles" (παραβολαί) for those without the ears or eyes of faith (cf. 4:11). This gives even more significance to the faith previously displayed by the hemorrhaging woman (5:25–34) and Jairus (5:36) when contrasted with the people of Nazareth (6:5–6).

4 Jesus employs an aphoristic rule of thumb that accounts for their response, a saying about a prophet without honor that circulated independently (see Luke 4:24; John 4:44; *Gos. Thom.* 31; P. Oxy 1:5 [I, 31–36]). The introductory "And Jesus said to them" (καὶ ἔλεγεν αὐτοῖς) suggests a greater possibility of this saying having been added to an earlier story about Jesus' ministry in Nazareth (Gnilka, 1:229) than for it to have spawned the surrounding scene (e.g., Bultmann, 31; Schulz, *Botschaft*, 30–31; Koch, *Wundererzählungen*, 149–50).

The extracanonical form has two parts: (a) a prophet is not accepted in his own home area, and (b) a physician is not able to heal those who know him (*Gos. Thom.* 31; P. Oxy. 1:5). Some have taken this version to be earlier with Mark citing the first half about the prophet and incorporating the second half about the physician in the following statement about Jesus' healing in Nazareth (Bultmann, 31; Achtemeier, *JBL* 89 [1970] 267; cf. Crossan, *NovT* 15 [1973] 103). Most, however, follow Haenchen's lead (*Aufsätze*, 160, n. 10) in rejecting the originality of the extracanonical saying as a later combination of two sayings by the *Gospel of Thomas* which reflects a penchant for expanding single proverbs by adding parallels (Lohmeyer, 111–12; Grässer, *NTS* 16 [1969–70] 8; Pesch, 1:320; Koch, *Wundererzählungen*, 148; Gnilka, 1:228–29).

Although it is not clear whether Mark added this saying to an earlier story (Gnilka, 1:128–29), his saying does show signs of redaction. None of the other sayings about the "prophet" contains any mention of "relatives" (συγγενεῦσιν). In fact, this concept injects a personal motif into an otherwise impersonal "native area" (πατρίς) or "home" (οἰκίᾳ). And except for Matt 13:57, no other parallel even mentions "home" (οἰκία).

Mark has already singled out Jesus' family in a similar story in 3:20–21, 31–35. The addition of "house" further specifies the irony of being rejected at "home." Not only in one's "hometown" but even in one's very "home." Thus, by adding these terms, Mark turns a general saying about lack of honor in one's "hometown" (πατρίς) into a statement that includes even Jesus' very family and home (cf. John 7:1–5). In doing so, the evangelist accents Jesus' rejection not only by those who knew him but even by those who knew him best, his family.

One takes the aphorism far too literally should one deduce from it that Jesus saw himself as a "prophet." To be sure, his ministry certainly led some of the public at least to view him this way as seen in 6:14–15. His authoritative ministry in word and his mighty works did share much in common with that of the prophets. But his "teaching" and his "mighty works" show him to be "more than a prophet," even more than the "eschatological prophet," to those of faith (4:11). He was gifted by God's Spirit with "wisdom" and "might" as the "branch from the root of Jesse" (Isa 11:1–2).

5 Jesus' inability to do any "mighty work" (δύναμιν) points to the nature of his ministry. Their unbelieving response (6:6a) precluded his working among them, since his work was a "redemptive event" (Gnilka, 1:233). Jesus did not come as a magician or a miracle worker to display and dazzle his audience. His "words" and his "work" were from God (cf. 6:2). Those who rejected this inherent claim in his ministry could not experience God's redemptive work on their behalf. Therefore, while faith does not represent the necessary cause for the effect of a miracle, miracles do not take place in the absence of faith (Ernst, 170).

"Except" (εἰ μή) introduces an apparent softening, if not correction, of the opening statement (cf. Matt 13:58). Many interpreters have assigned it to Mark (Pesch, 1:321; Gnilka, 1:229), but neither the style nor vocabulary betray distinctive Markan traits (Koch, *Wundererzählungen*, 151; Mayer, *BZ* 22 [1978] 196). Naturally, an "except"-clause qualifies a statement. But how? Ernst (170) takes it as a correction demonstrating Jesus' mercy despite the absence of faith. Others have taken it along with the initial response in 6:2 as a Markan softening of the story's treatment of the people of Nazareth in contrast to his highlighting of Jesus' family and home (Gnilka, 1:233; Crossan, *NovT* 15 [1973] 104–05). But neither of these squares with the text. Not only is "faith," or more accurately the lack of faith, the very point of this story, but we found no evidence in 6:2 of any positive or even neutral response by the people (see *Comment* on 6:2).

We had best take this statement to be another way of saying that Jesus did only a few miracles there (cf. Matt 13:57; Betz, *Israel*, 58; Taylor, 301; cf. 8:14). By having the categorical statement of "not any" at the beginning, the statement accentuates the lack of faith expressed in the audience's response of 6:2b–3 and in the response of Jesus' own family (6:4). The qualifying "except"-clause does not imply that he arbitrarily worked a few miracles based on mercy rather than faith (cf. Ernst, 170) nor that he accomplished a few "insignificant" miracles even when he could not do "mighty works," a distinction with no basis (Betz, *Israel*, 58). Rather, in line with the thrust of the story, these exceptions also reflect exceptions to the general response. Despite the general lack of faith, some did believe and were healed (Grundmann, 158).

6a Jesus' amazement at the general lack of faith need not come as a surprise in view of the saying in 6:4. A proverbial saying can appropriately describe a situation but not necessarily make it any more acceptable. Faced with the general rejection of himself and his ministry by those who knew him so well, Jesus' amazement expresses his humanness, the very issue that had blinded those who knew him best! His puzzlement reflects personal and compassionate pain. Their lack of faith meant not only their personal rejection of him (6:2b–3) but precluded his offering to them what God was doing through him (6:5a).

Explanation

Mark apparently interrupts the series of miracles found in his collection by introducing this story of Jesus' experience in Nazareth. It offers a commentary on what has preceded since the call of the Twelve (3:13–5:43) and adds the significant tone of rejection to a section that has highlighted Jesus' teaching (3:20–4:1–34) and mighty deeds (4:35–5:43), the very elements of his ministry that confound those of his hometown (6:2).

We found a similar note of rejection by the religious authorities near the conclusion of the previous section (3:1–6 in 1:16–3:12). And whereas that rejection ended with a threat to Jesus' life (3:6), this story stands in the shadow of the ominous and foreboding account of the Baptist's death (6:14–29; cf. 9:12–13). Thus the evangelist subtly reminds the reader of Jesus' ultimate destiny while depicting his ministry of word and work, a point that becomes the primary concern of the second half of Mark's narrative (8:27–16:8).

As a commentary on 3:13–5:43 this story of Jesus' rejection in his hometown and even in his own house first picks up a theme introduced in 3:21, 31–32. Neither his family nor his acquaintances could combine what he was doing with who they knew him to be. Nonplussed by his words of wisdom and his mighty works, they viewed him as simply Mary's son, the carpenter, whose brothers were known by name and whose sisters lived among them (6:3). They show themselves to be "outsiders" for whom all things are in "riddles" (4:11), and their lack of faith precludes his working among them (6:5).

Second, the absence of faith in this episode accentuates the role of faith in the previous story of the woman with a hemorrhage (5:34) and Jairus' daughter (5:36). Faith represented the critical link in one's relationship with

Jesus. Jesus was not a wandering thaumaturge, a miracle worker, whose words of wisdom and mighty acts in themselves led to faith.

Although Mark does not actually define "faith," this story shows it meant much more than being impressed with Jesus' words and deeds in view of his modest family background. Staying with the known (6:3) meant that his hometown and family who knew him best could not grasp who had given him such wisdom and was working through his hands (6:2). Ultimately, the lack of faith meant their failure to recognize that God was at work in Jesus.

By contrast, the disciples had committed themselves to him in faith and to them the "mystery of the kingdom" had been given (4:11) and his message in "parables" had been explained (4:13–20, 33–34). To those who came to him in faith seeking his help (2:5; 5:34, 36), he responded by meeting their need. Since the outset, the reader too has been informed about who Jesus is (1:1, 11, 14–15, 24; 2:10, 28; 5:7). His role proclaiming the "good news of God," namely, the fulfillment of time and the coming of the kingdom (1:14–15), has been evident in his teaching and his miracles, the stuff of Mark's Gospel, but only to those of faith. To those "outside" his teaching and miracles have only generated repudiating questions rather than faith (cf. 3:6, 21, 30–31, 22–29; 6:1–6).

N. Summary Report *(Mark 6:6b)*

Bibliography

Best, E. *Following Jesus.* 1981. **Egger, W.** *Frohbotschaft und Lehre.* 1974. **Hedrick, C.** "The Role of 'Summary Statements' in the Composition of the Gospel of Mark." *NovT* 26 (1984) 289–311. **Kertelge, K.** *Die Wunder Jesu im Markusevangelium.* 1970. **Perrin, N.** "Towards an Interpretation of the Gospel of Mark." *Christology and a Modern Pilgrimage: A Discussion with Norman Perrin.* Ed. H. D. Betz. Claremont, 1971. **Reploh, K. G.** *Markus—Lehrer der Gemeinde.* 1969. **Stock, K.** *Boten aus dem Mit-Ihm-Sein: Das Verhältnis zwischen Jesus und den Zwölf nach Markus.* AnBib 70. Rome: Biblical Institute Press, 1975.

Translation

⁶*He went around the villages nearby teaching.*

Form / Structure / Setting

This brief statement has the distinct form of a summary report (Egger, *Frohbotschaft,* 141). It is one of several that emphasize Jesus' teaching activity (1:21–22; 2:1–2; 2:13; 4:1–2; 6:6b; 6:30–34; 10:1) and belongs to the larger category of summary accounts found in Mark (Egger, *Frohbotschaft,* 27–31; Schmidt, 320). But in what sense is this a summary report?

Hedrick has correctly argued that these statements do not provide a literary summary of what has happened before. Instead they give a "brief summary description of some aspect of Jesus' ministry" (*NovT* 26 [1984] 294, 303–

04). In fact, three of these short statements use the imperfect tense and a participial construction to describe Jesus' activity over a period of time (2:13; 6:6b: 10:1). Therefore, despite their brevity, they cover even a longer period of time than the stories that surround them. For example, barely a sentence long, this summary report covers a much more extended period of time than the longer, preceding story of Jesus' rejection in Nazareth (6:1–6a).

What role do the summaries play in Mark? Perrin following Schmidt's lead takes the summaries that coincide with a geographical shift to play a structural role marking a transition in the narrative (Perrin, *Christology*, 3–6). Accordingly, 1:14–15; 3:7–12; and 6:6b provide such structural markers. Hedrick (*NovT* 26 [1984] 293–304) rejects this thesis by correctly challenging the assumptions of Perrin's methodology by noting other geographical shifts and summaries that play no such role in Mark even for Perrin. Some summaries, however, 6:6b being one, may indeed play just such a role, though for other reasons.

With rare exception (Schmidt, 158–60; Lagrange, 150; Schmithals, 1:307; Stock, *Boten*, 83), the commentators, after duly noting the possibility that it might belong to the Nazareth story, nevertheless take this statement as the backdrop for Jesus' sending of the disciples in 6:7–13. But 6:6b must be viewed carefully in its literary context.

First, by reading 6:6b with 6:7–13 we have no reference point for κύκλῳ that describes the villages. In 3:34 and 6:36 the context provides a locus for "nearby" or "surrounding." If we read 6:6b against 6:1–6a, Jesus' πατρίς makes clear what "nearby" or "surrounding" towns means. Second, the use of προσκαλεῖται and ἤξατο with the infinitive in 6:7 signal the start of something significant in itself. Third, the only possible connection between 6:6b and what follows comes in 6:30 where the Twelve report what they did and "taught" (ἐδίδαξαν, Reploh, *Lehrer*, 51). Yet this correspondence between the Twelve and Jesus' "teaching" ministry most likely stems from the evangelist's general tendency to describe Jesus' ministry, which the Twelve now share, in terms of teaching (cf. 1:21–27 and 6:1–2). Therefore, 6:6b does not serve as the setting for 6:7–13.

Yet a pattern does emerge in Mark's Gospel viewed to this point. And this pattern supports a structural role for this and two other summaries. Jesus calls the four disciples in 1:16–20 after a summary of his preaching (1:14–15). He calls the Twelve in 3:13–19 after an extended summary account of his healing ministry (3:7–12). And again he calls and commissions the Twelve in 6:7–13 after a brief summary of his teaching ministry (6:6b). Furthermore, a note of rejection precedes each summary statement (1:14a [implicit]; 3:1–6; 6:1–6a) suggesting that the statement about his ministry directly counters the rejection. Each calling of the disciples begins a new tack in Jesus' ministry (1:16–3:12; 3:13–6:6; 6:7–8:26), which means that these summary statements offer a concluding statement about Jesus' ministry and also provide a positive transition to the next series of episodes in the narrative.

Comment

6 "Went around" (περιῆγεν) only occurs here in Mark. This plus the rarely used κύκλῳ (3:34; 6:36) led Schmidt (158–60; similarly, Pesch, 1:327) to assign this summary report to Mark's tradition. Whether or not Mark found this summary in place (Schmidt, 158–59; Schmithals, 1:307), took it from another traditional block (Pesch, 1:327) or composed it himself (Best, *Following Jesus*, 190; Reploh, *Lehrer*, 51; Gnilka, 1:236), the statement fits Mark's use of a general statement to describe positively Jesus' ministry after the note of rejection in Nazareth.

The use of the imperfect tense and the present participle describes a period of time in which Jesus was moving about the villages around Nazareth in his teaching ministry. Yet "teaching" (διδάσκων), as used by Mark, cannot be construed too narrowly (e.g., Hedrick, *NovT* 26 [1984] 296–97). Jesus' "teaching" has served as a general heading that included an exorcism (see *Comment* on 1:27). Furthermore, teaching and miracles come together in 6:1–6a in Mark's handling of the Nazareth story (Kertelge, *Wunder*, 125–26). We find the same combination in the healings of 2:1–12, 3:1–6 and 6:34–44.

Therefore, this brief summary of Jesus' "teaching" ministry appropriately concludes a section of the Gospel that began exclusively with teaching (3:20–4:34) and ended with a series of Jesus' mighty deeds (4:35–6:6a), just as the summary of Jesus' "healing" ministry (3:7–12) concluded a section that began with many healings (1:21–2:12) and ended with conflict stories accenting Jesus' teaching (2:13–3:6).

Explanation

This summary statement captures Mark's portrait of Jesus' ministry as moving about from town to town "teaching." Jesus' "teaching" identified him, on the one hand, as an authority like a rabbi who with his disciples came to teach. On the other hand, Jesus' "teaching" set him off from all others (cf. 1:21–22) and led to his rejection by the religious authorities (2:1–12; 3:6, 22–30) and his family (3:20–21, 31–35) and hometown (6:1–6a). His teaching reflected his person and mission as one in whom God was at work through his words and his deeds establishing his redemptive rule in the lives of those who in faith would hear and respond (1:14–15; 1:21–3:6; 4:1–34; 4:35–5:43).

IV. "Do You Not Yet Understand?"
(6:7–8:26)

Introduction

After the "beginning of the gospel" in 1:1–15, the first half of Mark's Gospel falls rather neatly into three major sections (1:16–3:12; 3:13–6:6; 6:7–8:26). Each section opens with a story about the disciples (1:16–20; 3:1–19; and 6:7–13). Each section winds down with a story about the negative response generated by Jesus' ministry (3:1–6; 6:1–6a; 8:14–21). And each section concludes with a summary statement that recalls for the reader the nature of Jesus' ministry (3:7–12; 6:6b; 8:22–26).

Structurally, the opening story of the disciples depicts Jesus sending the Twelve in mission according to the explicit purpose of their calling found at the outset of the previous section and implicit in the calling to be "fishers of men" at the outset of the first section (6:7–13, cf. 3:13–19; 1:16–20). The closing story of Jesus' warning about the "leaven of the Pharisees and Herod" (8:14–21; cf. 8:10–13) shows that the disciples' (cf. religious leaders in 3:6, family and friends in 6:1–6a) lack of understanding is perilously close to the prophetic charge of "seeing but not seeing" and "hearing but not hearing" leveled at those "outside" in 4:11–12.

Whereas the previous sections concluded with a transitional summary statement that left the reader aware of the nature of Jesus' ministry despite the rejection (3:7–12; 6:6b), this section concludes with a healing miracle that functions in the same manner. The healing of the blind man in phases sums up Jesus' ministry with reference to the disciples and serves as the transition to that same theme underlying the second half of the Gospel. The disciples in contrast to the opponents, family, and "outsiders" have been given partial sight. This accounts for their response so far and will explain their response to Jesus' specific ministry to them in 8:27–10:52 and their response to his death in 11:1–16:8. But the story assures the reader that Jesus' work ultimately brings total sight.

This section also continues themes from the previous sections. Jesus remains the central figure, and the disciples are "with him" with the exception of their special mission in 6:7–13. The crowds also pursue him to listen to his teaching and to seek his healing power. He casts out demons (7:24–30), heals the sick (6:53–56; 7:31–37; 8:22–26), and miraculously provides for human needs (6:34–44; 45–52; 8:1–9). Though in a more restrained form, we also find the conflict over authority in the purity questions of 7:1–13, 14–23 and in the Pharisees' request for a "sign" (8:10–13). And the ominous horizon of 3:6 (2:18–22) draws closer in the story of the Baptist's tragic death (6:17–29) that harbingers things to come.

At the same time, the evangelist develops with broader strokes other themes which have been previously introduced. Without doubt, one of the major themes of this section is the role of the disciples. Their mission in keeping with their calling and their authorization to share in Jesus' ministry underscores their special place and privilege of call (6:7–13, cf. 1:16–20; 3:13–19) as does their role in the Feedings and their presence with Jesus along the way. But standing in stark contrast to their mission and its great success (6:7–13, 30) that leads to the story of Herod and the Baptist (6:14–29) and the crowds for the Feeding of the Five Thousand (6:31–44), we find an inability to see clearly to the heart of who Jesus really is and what he is about (cf. 4:10a, 13, 41). This emerges subtly in the dialogue of the two Feedings (6:34–44; 8:1–9) and is highlighted by the evangelist's own commentary about their lack of understanding of these Feedings in 6:52 and 8:19–20. Their myopia also prevents them from grasping the epiphanic character of Jesus' presence on the water in 6:45–51 that provides the answer to their previous question about who this was (4:41). Their failure to understand the parabolic statement about clean and unclean (7:15) corresponds to their need to have the parables explained (7:17–18; cf. 4:10a, 13, 34). And Jesus warning them about the "leaven" of the Pharisees and Herod, each of whom had culpably failed to recognize Jesus (6:14–16; 8:10–13), makes their lack of understanding explicit in 8:14–21.

The evangelist also develops the motif of Jesus' work in gentile territory (see *Comment* on 5:1–20). In Mark's story line the Gerasene demoniac and his preaching (5:1–20) may have set the stage for Jesus' healing of the Deaf Mute (7:31–37) and a second Feeding (8:1–9) in the area of the Decapolis preceded by a journey through Tyre (7:24–30) and Sidon (7:31; cf. 3:8) that clearly put Jesus in touch with Gentiles (cf. 7:26, a "Greek"; 8:3, "from afar"). These stories all follow a critical discussion (7:1–13; 14–23) about the nature of the purity laws, the social boundaries that set off Jew from Jew and not least Jew from Gentile.

Although Mark does not highlight the shift, Jesus essentially concludes in this section his active public ministry in Galilee with the Feeding of the Five Thousand in 6:34–44 and the summary account in 6:53–56. The audience narrows down quite perceptively in the second half of the Gospel to Jesus' ministry to the disciples. And, though perhaps too subtle to have been intended, the shift in focus of Jesus' work from the public in Galilee to the public beyond Galilee may reflect the movement of the mission from primarily among the Jews to the Gentiles and gentile lands.

As in the previous sections, the evangelist made use of different traditions in composing this part of the narrative. He returns to the collection of miracle stories underlying 4:35–5:43 centered around the Sea of Galilee and uses the Feeding Story (6:32–44), its accompanying epiphanic story of Jesus Walking on the Sea (6:45–51), and the concluding summary of the cycle in 6:53–56. But before returning to the miracle collection, Mark brings the disciples and their work onto center stage (6:7–13, 30; cf. 6:14–29). He then integrates the crossing in 6:45–52 more closely with the Feeding to accent the disciples' failure to understand Jesus (6:52), a motif that becomes paramount in this section.

To prepare for a shift in Jesus' ministry to gentile territory, the evangelist takes a complex tradition dealing with purity issues and the traditional law and separates it into two stories (7:1–13, 14–23). As a result, the question of the "tradition of the elders" is de-emphasized; the issue of purity, especially pertaining to foods, becomes central. By addressing this critical social boundary between Jews and Gentiles, Mark sets the stage for Jesus' ministry in gentile territory.

Perhaps Mark drew from isolated traditions to fill out the journey of Jesus outside of Galilee: the Syrophoenician Woman (7:24–30), the Healing of the Deaf Mute in the Decapolis (7:31–37), the Feeding of the Four Thousand (8:1–9) and the blind Man of Bethsaida (8:22–26). Yet the formal, lexical and structural similarities between the two healings suggest that they may have been previously transmitted as a pair. The Feeding of the Four Thousand appears to have thumbprints of a more "hellenistic" community.

To this point in the story, the evangelist's redaction has been limited mostly to bringing together materials and shaping them for their context. In this section, however, he not only continues to do as he has done but appears to take a more active role in developing something that may well have its extended roots in the tradition into a unit for his story. This redactional work becomes evident in the Sending of the Twelve (6:7–13), the structuring of an extended journey by Jesus outside of Galilee (7:30–8:26), and the development of the Warning Against the Leaven (8:14–21)—all stories having to do particularly with the two themes of discipleship and ministry among the Gentiles highlighted in this section.

A. *The Mission of the Twelve*   (*Mark 6:7–13*)

Bibliography

Best, E. *Following Jesus.* 1981. **Caird, G. B.** "Uncomfortable Words 11: Shake off the Dust from Your Feet." *ExpTim* 81 (1969) 40–47. **Hahn, F.** *Mission in the New Testament.* SBT 47. London: SCM, 1965. **Hengel, M.** *The Charismatic Leader and His Followers.* Tr. J. Greig. New York: Crossroad, 1981. **Hoffmann, P.** *Studien zur Theologie der Logienquelle.* NTA 8. Münster: Aschendorff, 1971. **Jeremias, J.** "Paarweise Sendung im Neuen Testament." In *Abba: Studien zur neutestamentlichen Theologie und Zeitgeschichte.* Göttingen: Vandenhoeck und Ruprecht, 1966. **Manson, T. W.** *The Sayings of Jesus.* London: SCM, 1957. **Meye, R.** *Jesus and the Twelve.* 1968. **Neusner, J.** "'First Cleanse the Inside.'" *NTS* 22 (1976) 486–95. **Reploh, K.-G.** *Markus—Lehrer der Gemeinde.* 1969. **Schmahl, G.** *Die Zwölf im Markusevangelium.* TTS 30. Trier: Paulinus, 1974. **Stock, K.** *Boten aus dem Mit-Ihm-Sein.* AnBib 70. Rome: Biblical Institute, 1975. **Theissen, G.** "Wanderradikalismus: Literatursoziologische Aspekte der Ueberlieferung vom Worten Jesu im Urchristentum." *ZTK* 70 (1973) 245–71.

Translation

[7] *And he called the Twelve and began to send them out in pairs.*[a] *And he gave*[b] *them authority over unclean spirits.* [8] *He instructed them to take nothing for the journey except simply a staff and sandals strapped on;*[c] *no bread, no bag, no money*[d] *in their belt,* [9] *and he instructed them,*[e] *"Do not wear*[f] *two coats."* [10] *And he said to them, "Wherever you enter a home, stay there until you leave that place.* [11] *And*

any place that does not receive you or they do not listen to you, when you leave there, shake off the dust from under your feet as a witness against them." [12] Departing, they preached that people should repent, [13] and they cast out many demons. They anointed many sick with oil and healed them.

Notes

[a] Literally, "two by two" (δύο δύο) instead of the usual distributive use of κατά or ἀνά. The doubled cardinal is "known to vulgar Greek" but generally viewed as a translation of a Semitic idiom (BDF, 248, 1).

[b] This phrase usually takes the aorist ἔδωκεν ἐξουσίαν (Mark 11:28; 13:34; Matt 9:8; 10:1; 28:18; John 1:12; 5:27; 17:12). Imperfect ἐδίδου may suggest a granting of authority to each individual or to each pair (Stock, *Boten*, 87; cf. Taylor, 303).

[c] The exception of sandals actually begins 6:9.

[d] Literally, "no copper coin" (χαλκόν); cf. "silver coin" (ἀργύριον) in Luke 9:3.

[e] Romanized words supplied from context.

[f] Read ἐνδύσασθε with B* 33 *pc*, since the unusual construction of μὴ with aorist imperative led to corrections of ἐνδύσασθαι (B² S Π* Ω 892 *pc*), ἐνδέδυσθαι (L N 1424 *al*), ἐνδύσησθε (א C Θ Π *pc*) or ἐνδύθησθαι (A D W Δ 28 118).

Form / Structure / Setting

With few exceptions (Lohmeyer, 113; Hahn, *Mission*, 41–46; Pesch, 1:326; Ernst, 174–75), the commentators today see this narrative in Taylor's words to have been "put together by the evangelist himself" (302). And those who take it as one of two "sending" traditions treat it as a composite narrative constructed by a pre-Markan redactor of the tradition (e.g., Pesch, 1:326; Ernst, 175). Nevertheless, few would so arbitrarily declare such an event to contain "no historical tradition" (so Wellhausen, 44), even if Manson's comment that the "mission of the disciples is one of the best-attested facts in the life of Jesus" (*Sayings*, 73) risks overstatement.

This pericope consists of a narrative framework (6:7, 12–13) around three sayings (6:8–11) that have a rough parallel in Q (Matt 9:37–42 // Luke 10:1–16). The sayings obviously form the heart of this unit, but even these appear to have been selected from a larger group and adapted. For example, the opening instruction (6:8) begins in indirect address (παρήγγειλεν with ἵνα + subjunctive) and shifts midway (6:9) to direct address (μὴ + imperative). Then the instructions in 6:10–11 are formally introduced by "and he said to them" (6:10a). Slight differences from the Q-material also exist in the instructions themselves (see *Comment* below).

The evangelist's hand becomes most evident, however, in the framework of these sayings. Vocabulary, style and content point to Mark's own redaction based to a large extent on the calling of the Twelve in 3:13–19 (Reploh, *Lehrer*, 52–53; Schmahl, *Zwölf*, 74–76; see *Comment*). In this way, Mark develops a scene in which the disciples are sent out (ἀποστέλλειν, 3:14; 6:7) to preach (κηρύσσειν, 3:14; 6:12) and have authority to cast out demons (ἔχειν ἐξουσίαν, 3:15; 6:7, 12) as one of the two purposes for which they were called (προσκαλεῖται, 3:13; 6:7). Their implicit and explicit presence "with him" throughout the intervening stories, as well as those to follow, fulfills their other purpose of 3:14. For Mark, their ministry was obviously an extension of Jesus' ministry, as the summary (6:30) referring to all they *did* (ἐποίησαν) and *taught* (ἐδίδαξαν) indicates.

To say that Mark has created this scene, however, does not mean that Jesus never sent his disciples in mission during his ministry. The multiple attestation of instructions for such mission activity in the gospel tradition (Manson's point referring to Q, Mk, M and L passages; *Sayings,* 73–74) requires such mission activity. "That Jesus did send forth the disciples can hardly be doubted in principle, even if it is no longer possible to reconstruct the circumstances in detail" (Hengel, *Leader,* 74).

In other words, Mark's account did not create *de novo* the idea of such a sending. Nor did the evangelist create the materials from which he constructed this scene. He used a traditional motif whose roots doubtless lay in Jesus' own ministry. As a construct by the evangelist, this story does not answer the detailed what-or-when questions of such a mission. It simply declares *that* it happened. Ours is to question *why* it happened in terms of Mark's narrative.

Part of the answer to that question lies in Mark's setting for the story. In the immediate context, it follows a brief summary report of Jesus' teaching in the towns surrounding Nazareth (6:6b) after he is rejected by his own hometown (6:1–6a). Looking in the other direction, this mission story is actually interrupted in that its conclusion comes in the summary statement of 6:30, when the missioners return and report all they had done and taught. Between these two parts of the story, we learn the details of the Baptist's death (6:17–29).

That story, however, is precipitated by Herod's hearing about Jesus and his mighty deeds that have given the "king" pause to think the Baptist had been raised from the dead (6:16). A public stir so great as to get Herod's attention immediately following the sending of the Twelve may be attributed to their mission in Mark's sequence (Reploh, *Lehrer,* 56). Though we have a brief report of the disciples' activities in 6:12–13, Herod hears about Jesus' "name," which might have come from the activities of the Twelve ministering in Jesus' name. This is inherent in the specific mission of authorized agents (cf. 6:30, ἀπόστολοι). Even the "powers" (δυνάμεις) at work in Jesus need not preclude the work of the Twelve (cf. Best, *Jesus,* 192), since the Twelve most likely would have worked in Jesus' name (cf. 9:38–41).

In the broader context, the location of this story corresponds to a related calling of disciples in two previous segments of Mark's narrative (1:16–20; 3:13–19). Each calling begins the respective segment by following a summary statement about Jesus' ministry (1:14–15; 3:7–12) that concludes a section (1:1–13; 1:21–3:6) after a note of rejection (1:14a; 3:1–6). So far, the calling of the disciples has only meant their presence with Jesus throughout the subsequent section which indicates that "being with Jesus" was one of the distinguishing marks of the Twelve (3:14; cf. *Comment* on 5:18–19). But Jesus had also called the first four "to be fishers of men" and the Twelve "to be sent" in mission (3:14–15).

Having accompanied Jesus, heard him teach, and watched him perform mighty deeds, they now are given a part in that ministry as his authorized representatives. This work leads to the feeding miracle where it becomes increasingly clear (6:35–8:26) that, despite fulfilling their calling as the Twelve, their own understanding of Jesus and his ministry is seriously deficient (cf. 4:11, 13, 41; 6:52). In fact, the story of the Baptist's death that interrupts this successful mission scene anticipates at least part of the missing element in their understanding of Jesus. This element, the suffering Son of man, becomes the main motif of Jesus' instruction for his disciples in 8:27–10:52.

Comment

7 "Called the Twelve" (προσκαλεῖται τοὺς δώδεκα) is reminiscent of the calling of the Twelve in 3:13. Mark frequently uses the participial form of προσκαλεῖσθαι to introduce a pronouncement by Jesus or to set a new scene (e.g., 3:23; 7:14; 8:1, 34; 10:42; 12:43). But the present indicative form occurs only here and in 3:14 (Reploh, *Lehrer*, 54; Schmahl, *Zwölf*, 74) and suggests that what follows is inherent in the "calling" of the Twelve. This gains support from Jesus' move to "send them out" (ἀποστέλλειν), one of the two purposes given for their call in 3:13–14. For Mark this sending of the Twelve implemented one aspect of their call.

Little is said about the specifics of this mission other than that they were to go in pairs, "two by two" (δύο δύο), and that they were given "authority over unclean spirits." Only in the brief summary in 6:12–13 do we learn that it included preaching and healing. In light of the one "sending" them, the nature of their mission is assumed. The verb related to "apostle" (ἀποστέλλειν) can have the more technical meaning of sending an authorized representative or agent to act in one's stead in a Jewish setting (see *Comment* on 6:30). Therefore, Jesus' "sending" implies that the Twelve will go in his place to carry out his mission with all that it involves.

The sending in pairs corresponds to the early Christian mission practice as frequently illustrated in Acts (e.g., Acts 13:1–3). A similar pairing appears in the sending of the Seventy (Luke 10:1) and in the listing of the Twelve in Matt 10:2–4 (cf. Acts 1:13). Jeremias lists numerous illustrations of similar use of pairs in Judaism, though missing from the OT, as well as in the NT (*Abba*, 133–34). The background may lie in Jewish legal practice where two witnesses established the evidence (Deut 17:6; 19:15; cf. Matt 18:16; John 8:17; 2 Cor 13:1; 1 Tim 5:19). But it also may reflect the travel conditions and the need for personal and moral support (Jeremias, *Abba*, 135).

"Gave to them authority" (ἐδίδου) in the imperfect tense may mean he gave to each successive pair the authority over unclean spirits (Taylor, 303). The task of casting out unclean spirits is the only specific task mentioned at the outset. It reappears in the brief summary in 6:13, which indicates the importance that Mark attached to this part of the mission. It also shows how integral the mission of the Twelve was to Jesus' own ministry, since Mark introduced Jesus' public ministry with an exorcism (1:21–27) and adds exorcisms to several earlier summaries (1:39; 3:11; cf. 3:22–29).

8–9 Jesus then "instructed" (παρήγγειλεν) the Twelve on what they were to take by way of travel provisions. The indirect address with a ἵνα-clause introducing the content, a common feature in Mark (e.g., 3:9; 5:18, 43; 7:26, 32, 36; 8:22, 30; 9:9, 12, 18; 10:48; 13:34; 14:35), subordinates the instructions to the framework. The mission has primary importance for Mark; the instructions add to its character (Hoffmann, *Studien,* 238).

Actually, Jesus instructs the Twelve more about what not to take than what to take. With the exception of a staff and sandals, which are specifically prohibited in Q (Matt 10:10), he prohibits them from taking what would generally have been viewed as necessary travel provisions. No "bread" (ἄρτον) or provisions for eating. No "money" (χαλκόν) in their belt, a common place for carrying money. No "beggar's bag" (πήραν) as a means for carrying supplies received along the way. And not even a second coat for the journey, a change of clothing.

This rigorous list certainly deprives the missioner of any sense of self-sufficiency. Theissen (*ZTK* 70 [1973] 259) and Hoffmann (*Studien,* 246–47) take these demands to be even more stringent than the style exhibited by the stereotypes of frugality, the Cynic-Stoic preachers who demanded a "radical freedom from all possessions" (Hengel, *Leader,* 28). This list even prohibits "bread" and a "beggar's bag," two provisions allowed for the Cynic. Hengel (*Leader,* 28) sees here an intentional parody of the frugality demanded by the Cynic itinerant preachers (cf. 1 Thess 2:1–12). Such a reading may reflect conditions in the early Church mission that found itself "competing" with other movements.

In the setting of Jesus' ministry, these rigorous demands made for traveling light (Lohmeyer, 114) and left the missioners dependent on God's provisions for them (Grundmann, 169) through the beneficiaries of their ministry (6:10). The allowance here of a staff and sandals in contrast to Q represents a development in the tradition stemming perhaps from a different geographical setting that made a staff for self-defense and sandals for the journey necessary or from a difference in duration of the journey (Best, *Jesus,* 190).

10 Moving to direct address, Jesus next instructs the Twelve regarding their stay in a given place. First, they are to stay in the same home rather than to move about. Perhaps this was to prevent the missioners from seeking a better place in keeping with the stringency of the earlier instructions (Pesch, 1:329). Haenchen (232) thought it helped avoid any jealousy that might arise over the privilege of having such guests in one's house. In any case, the instruction implies an extended visit. We find different instructions in *Did.* 11:4 where an an extended stay is a sign of a "false prophet." The difference, however, corresponds to the different mission settings. Whereas the missioners in Mark's setting were establishing a witness in a community, the *Didache* described established churches visited by itinerant ministers.

11 The instructions then conclude with directions on how the missioners should respond to a place that rejects them. This note takes on special pertinence when set against Jesus' rejection in 6:1–6 by his own hometown. Yet the precise meaning of these directions is not clear. First, the missioners were to "shake the dust from the bottoms of their feet." Clearly this is a symbolical gesture, but what did it actually symbolize? The Jews customarily shook dust from their feet when returning from gentile territory (Str-B, 1:511). Does this mean that the place was declared "pagan" (Grundmann, 169)? Or was it a gesture of judgment symbolizing the termination of any further contact and communication with the place and denying any further opportunity to hear the message of salvation or experience the ministry of healing and deliverance (cf. 6:5; Pesch, 1:329; Gnilka, 1:240)? Or did this gesture show that the agents had done their job and were "washing their hands" of any further responsibility (cf. Acts 18:6, Cranfield, 201; Grundmann, 169)? The action contains an element of each suggestion, but it is no longer possible to say which was primary.

"For a witness against them" (εἰς μαρτύριον αὐτοῖς) could mean: (a) a witness to God's grace (Grundmann, 169), (b) a warning calling for repentance (Lane, 209), or (c) evidence against them in the final judgment (Pesch, 1:329; Gnilka, 1:240). But only the third comes into play, since the locale has rejected them and their message. The missioners' departure and parting gesture testify to their rejection and against those who have spurned their only hope for acquittal at the last judgment. The consistent use of μαρτύριον with the dative of disadvantage in the NT supports this rendering here (see *Comment* on 1:44).

12 The pericope concludes with a brief statement of their activities. They "preached that people should repent" (ἐκήρυξαν ἵνα μετανοῶσιν). "Preaching" was one of the two tasks the Twelve were sent to do at their calling (3:14). Their preaching of repentance places them in line with the Baptist's (1:4) and Jesus' (1:15) repentance preaching (cf. 13:10). In view of the Baptist's eschatological role (1:4–8; 9:11–13) and Jesus' preaching of the coming Kingdom (1:14–15) in Mark, one can hardly deny the eschatological thrust of this preaching (cf. Hoffmann, *Studien,* 239). This is all the more true, since the Twelve represented an extension of Jesus' ministry (Stock, *Boten,* 94). For Mark's context, this preaching appears to have had Jesus as its focus (see *Comment* on 6:14).

13 This thrust is particularly evident in the second mention within this pericope of the work of exorcism, "They cast out many demons" (cf. 6:7). Exorcism was the second task given the Twelve at their calling (3:14). The statement concludes with mention of their anointing the sick "with oil" and healing them. "Oil" has a therapeutic quality in Isa 1:6, but this is the only reference to oil in a healing context in the Gospels. It most likely has its roots in the early Christian use of oil as a symbol of God's healing (cf. James 5:14–15) rather than a healing potion (Gnilka, 1:240).

Explanation

Until now, the role of the Twelve has been to "be with Jesus" (3:14), an exclusive relationship as seen by Jesus' refusal of the Gerasene's request after his deliverance (5:18–19). This calling and companionship had set the Twelve apart as a special community. They had experienced Jesus' ministry of teaching that included healing and exorcisms. Here for the first time they actively share in Jesus' ministry.

Their calling had presumed a sharing in the mission. The first disciples were called to be "fishers of men" (1:17) and the Twelve were called to be "sent" to "preach" and to have authority over "the demons" (3:14–15). In this narrative the Twelve receive a commission to preach repentance and to cast out demons as well as to heal the sick (6:12–13) and to teach (6:30), a commission that covers the spectrum of Jesus' ministry and corresponds to their "being sent" as Jesus' authorized representatives. To this extent, by participating in and carrying out Jesus' ministry in a special way, the Twelve play a special role among the "disciples" in Mark.

The instructions demand the disciples to travel light, unencumbered by provisions for their journey. Eschewing even the characteristic "beggar's bag" and bread of the itinerant Cynic preachers, they were to receive their provisions solely from those who heard and received them. At the same time, they were instructed to move on when rejected by a place whose people refused to listen to them, an ominous note that corresponds to Jesus' own experience of rejection.

This participation by the Twelve in Jesus' ministry and its apparent success contributes greatly to the irony in Mark's portrait of the Twelve in this segment of the Gospel (6:7–8:26). On the one hand, it opens with this special mission whose success reported in 6:30 apparently reached to Herod's court (6:14) and led to a relentless response by the crowds (6:31–33). On the other hand, the very Twelve who experienced a special calling and relationship with Jesus and now participate fully in this ministry are seen to lack understanding (6:52; 7:18; 8:14–21) and even reflect a "hardened heart" (6:52; 8:17–18). This growing irony between the Twelve's special privilege and lack of understanding has its seed in the previous section (e.g., 4:11; cf. 4:13; 4:33–34; cf. 4:41).

B. The Death of John the Baptist (Mark 6:14–29)

Bibliography

Black, D. A. "The Text of Mark 6.20." *NTS* 34 (1988) 141–45. **Dormeyer, D.** *Die Passion Jesu als Verhaltensmodell: Literarische und theologische Analyse der Traditions-und Redaktionsgeschichte der Markuspassion.* NTA 11. Münster: Aschendorff, 1974. **Gnilka. J.** "Das Martyrium Johannes des Täufers (Mk 6,17–29)." In *Orientierung an Jesus*, FS J. Schmid, ed. P. Hoffmann. Freiburg: Herder, 1973. 78–29. **Hoehner, H. W.** *Herod Antipas.* SNTSMS 17. Cambridge: Cambridge UP, 1972. **Pesch, R.** "Zur Entstehung des Glaubens der Auferstehung Jesu." *TQ* 153 (1973) 201–28. **Schenk, W.** "Gegenschaft und Tod des Täufers: Erwägungen zur Christologie und ihre Konsequenzen." *NTS* 29 (1983) 453–83. **Wink, W.** *John the Baptist in the Gospel Tradition.* SNTSMS 7. Cambridge: Cambridge UP, 1968. **Wolff, C.** "Zur Bedeutung Johannes des Täufers im Markusevangeliums." *TLZ* 102 (1977) 857–65.

Translation

[14] *King Herod heard, for* Jesus'[a] *fame*[b] *had become known, that they*[c] *were saying, "John the Baptizer has risen from the dead. Therefore, these powers are at work in him."* [15] *But others were saying, "He was Elijah." Still others were saying, "He is a prophet like one of the prophets."* [16] *When Herod heard this, he said, "John*[d] *whom I beheaded, he is raised from the dead."*[a]

[17]*For Herod himself had sent* [e] *and had John taken into custody and bound in prison on account of Herodias, the wife of Philip his brother, because he had married her.* [18]*For John had said to Herod, "It is illegal for you to have the wife of your brother."* [19]*Herodias had it in for him and wanted to kill him, but was not able to do so.* [20]*For Herod feared John, knowing him to be a just and holy man. And he protected him. When he heard him, he did* [f] *many things and heard him gladly.*

[21]*On an appropriate day* [g] *when Herod held a banquet on his birthday* [h] *for his political magistrates, military commanders and the prominent men of Galilee,* [22]*and when his* [i] *daughter, Herodias, entered and danced, she pleased Herod and his dinner companions. The king said to the young girl, "Ask me whatever you wish and I shall give it to you."* [23]*And he repeatedly* [j] *swore to her, "Whatever you request of me I shall give you up to one half of my kingdom."* [24]*After leaving, she asked her mother, "What shall I request?" She said, "The head of John the Baptizer."*

[25]*Immediately entering in a hurry to the king, she made her request, saying, "I want you to give me at once the head of John the Baptist on a platter."* [26]*And the king became* [e] *very sad. Yet he did not want to refuse her because of his oath and his dinner companions.*

[27]*Immediately the king sent* [e] *the executioner* [k] *and ordered him to bring John's* [a] *head. Departing, the executioner* [a] *beheaded John* [a] *in prison* [28]*and brought his head on a platter and gave it to the girl. The girl gave it to her mother.* [29]*And when John's* [a] *disciples heard, they came and took his corpse and placed it in a tomb.*

Notes

[a] Romanized words added from context.

[b] τὸ ὄνομα αὐτοῦ means more than "his name" in this context. Since the name often means the person, one might say, "*He* had become known."

[c] Read ἔλεγον with B (D) W *pc* a b ff² vgmss samss rather than ἔλεγεν with ℵ A C L Θ *f*¹.¹³ despite MSS evidence because the latter is attracted to ἤκουσεν.

[d] This is a *casus pendens* attracted to the relative pronoun and resumed by the demonstrative οὗτος (Cranfield, 207).

[e] Circumstantial use of participle.

[f] Read ἐποίει with A C D *f*¹.¹³ Majority text lat sy, since the adverbial use of πολλά always follows the verb (Black, *NTS* 34 [1988] 143). Cf. ἠπόρει as read by Nestle²⁶ with ℵ B L (W) Θ copsa bo (Metzger, *Textual Commentary*, 89). Others have taken ἐποίει as a possible Semitism, "did many things" = "heard him many times" (e.g., Klostermann, 59), though without supporting evidence.

[g] Genitive absolute (γενομένης ἡμέρας εὐκαίρου) used temporally and explained by the following clause.

[h] In Attic Greek, γενέθλια meant birthday and γενέσια the celebration of the birthday of the dead. γενέσια comes to mean both (BGD, *s.v.*).

[i] Read αὐτοῦ ℵ B D L Δ 565 *pc* on the strength of the MSS evidence (Metzger, *Textual Commentary*, 90) rather than αὐτῆς τῆς with A C Θ *f*¹³ and Majority text as a later correction in line with Matt 14:6.

[j] Read adverbial πολλά with 𝔓⁴⁵ D Θ 565 700 it (see *Comment* on 5:43). It is easier to explain its omission than its addition; cf. ℵ A B C² *f*¹³ Majority text lat samss bo.

[k] σπεκουλάτορα is a Latin loanword used in Greek, Hebrew and Aramaic. Originally this official belonged to the emperor's staff as a scout or spy, but later the term came to mean executioner as a loanword.

Form/Structure/Setting

This section appears to contain two parts, often treated separately. First, we have a "report" (Pesch, 1:333) of Herod's and the public's opinion of

Jesus (6:14–16). Then we have the story of the Baptist's death (6:17–29), whose form has been much debated. Yet, as will be seen, in Mark's narrative, these two parts are combined into one account with the latter clarifying the mention of Herod's killing of the Baptist in the former.

Form-critically, 6:14–16 could stand alone as an apophthegm concluding with Herod's dramatic statement, "John whom I beheaded is alive!" But such a story begs any credible setting in history. To assign it to John's disciples under the assumption that Herod's judgment would then represent the antago-nist's own recognition of divine vindication for the martyr by bringing him back to life resorts to fanciful assumptions (cf. Pesch, 1:333–34). Could John's loyal disciples have ever seen Jesus as the Baptist *redivivus* or even as his alter ego? Without any evidence that this unit existed independently, we must read it as part of 6:17–29. Its thrust is Herod's opinion of Jesus (6:14a, 16). And since he thought Jesus to be John whom he had beheaded, this unit provides the setting for that story.

The story of John's death creates another form-critical dilemma because it does not fit any particular form. Bultmann (301–302) and Haenchen (241–42) maintained that it was a legend about the Baptist around whom the story revolved. Gnilka, however, following Dormeyer's (*Passion*, 43–47) division of martyr stories into Jewish martyrdom accounts and hellenistic acts of the martyrs assigns this story's underlying form to the former (245–46; Gnilka, *Orientierung*, 85–68).

For Dormeyer (*Passion*, 47) the distinguishing features of these categories lay in the handling of the martyr. The hellenistic acts of the martyrs concen-trated on the trial where the martyr gave a good account of himself. The Jewish stories of martyrdom (e.g., Azariah—2 Chron 24:20–22; Eleazar—2 Macc 6:18–31; the Maccabean brothers—2 Macc 7; Akiba—*b. Ber.* 61b) concen-trated on the martyr's death at the hand of an evil adversary. Gnilka (1:246) adds that the martyr not only refuses to transgress the law but views oneself as the guardian of the law.

Mark's account obviously goes beyond any such Jewish stories of martyrdom. Therefore, Gnilka posits three stages in its development (1:245–46; *Orientie-rung*, 85–87). First, the account of the martyrdom included Herod's arrest and execution of the Baptist because of John's legal opposition to Herod's marriage. Then embellished with a banquet scene employing numerous OT and hellenistic motifs the account became a popular tale. Finally, Mark adapted it to 6:14–16 by reworking the opening section with his own transition to the story (6:17–18). The later embellishment explains why Herod, the wicked adversary, now plays such a prominent role. In any event, the form-critical question has more to do with the origin and history of the account than with its interpretation.

Much has been made about the differences between Mark's and Josephus' accounts (*Ant.* 18.5.2–4). The basis for the Baptist's arrest (political vs. per-sonal), his place of imprisonment (Machaerus vs. Tiberias), the daughter's name (Herodias vs. Salome), the identity of Herodias' former husband (Herod vs. Philip) and the incongruity of a princess dancing at such a bawdy occasion have all led to assigning Mark's details more to folklore than to how it actually happened. A closer look (see *Comment*), however, reduces the relief in most of these contrasts.

As to source, with hardly an exception (cf. Schenk, *NTS* 29 [1983] 464) the commentators treat 6:14–16 as a composite unit at the heart of which lies a tradition containing various views of Jesus' ministry (6:14b–15). We find the same views again in 8:28, though in an abbreviated and less balanced form. This has led Pesch (1:332) to view the two passages as variants of the same tradition. Others have taken 6:14b–15 to represent more closely the tradition with Mark abbreviating it again in 8.28 (Ernst, 170, Gnilka, 244–45; cf. Bultmann, 302; Schweizer, 132; see *Comment* on 8:28). Unlikely to have circulated as an isolated unit, 6:14b–15 most probably belonged originally to a miracle story or stories offering an acclamation (Gnilka, 1:245; cf.δυνάμεις).

Who formed the present story of 6:14–16? Although some have assigned it to a pre-Markan redactor (Ernst, 185; Pesch, 1:332), unless it was redacted solely with a view to introducing the following story, the lack of any historical setting for such a unit makes this alternative most unlikely. John's disciples, perhaps interested in Herod's opinion, are not likely to have thought of Jesus as being the Baptist *redivivus* (cf. Ernst, 179). If we take 6:14–16 to have been redacted to form a unit with 6:17–29, we have a story about Herod's view of Jesus with an extended description of his killing the Baptist. What purposes might this composite of 6:14–29 have served in the early Church? From the standpoint of a "historical" setting, the composite unit best fits Mark's purposes for his portrait of Jesus.

Therefore, the evangelist combined two traditions, one containing views of Jesus (6:14a–15) including his being John the Baptist *redivivus* and another tradition about the death of John (6:17–29), by having Herod, the Baptist's killer in 6:17–29, share the view about the Baptist *redivivus* in 6:14a, 16. He connects the two tightly together with the γάρ-sentences of 6:17–18 (Taylor, 308; Schweizer, 132; Gnilka, 1:244; Wolff, *TLZ* 102 [1977] 859).

In 6:17–29 Mark has taken over a traditional story (cf. Schenk, *NTS* 29 [1983] 464–70; Schmithals, 1:316). Although some have assigned the origin of this story to a circle of the Baptist's disciples (Bultmann, 301; Lane, 215; Pesch, 1:343), one can only speculate about its original setting. The story has no Christian features, but Mark's familiarity with it suggests a broader circulation than the Baptist's disciples. His own redactional impact appears at the outset where he reworks the setting of 6:17–18 and combines it with 6:14–16. Otherwise, the adverbial πολλά in 6:23, the comment, ἡδέως αὐτοῦ ἤκουεν (6:20, cf 12:37), and his description of John as the "Baptizer" (τοῦ βαπτίζοντος) in 6:24 (cf. 6:14, 25) may reflect an occasional thumbprint.

Structurally, 6:14–16 begins with Herod's hearing the various views about Jesus (6:14–15). He states his own opinion in 6:16, agreeing with those who believed Jesus to be the Baptizer who had come back from the dead. Furthermore, he declares his role in John's death (6:16), and this becomes the setting for retelling how it had happened. Since John's death occurred at an earlier time in Mark's story line than the events of 6:16–17, it is told in the pluperfect tense. Furthermore, each of the γάρ-explanations in 6:17–18, 20 antedates the preceding. The story begins with a statement of its conclusion.

The story has two parts (Gnilka, *Orientierung*, 84–86). First, we have a setting (6:17–20) describing John's imprisonment (6:17a), the grounds for that imprisonment (6:17b–18), and Herod's attitude in contrast to Herodias' toward John (6:19–20). Then comes the nub of the story, John's execution

(6:21–29). A banquet and a dance provide the occasion (6:21–22a). An oath (6:22b–25) provides the basis. And a command and its fulfillment (6:26–29) provide the denouement. A solemn burial scene completes the story (6:29). Meanwhile, we have come full circle to 6:14–16 and the question of John's coming back from the dead.

Regarding the setting in Mark's Gospel, several find the evangelist beginning here a new section that places Jesus beyond Galilee (Taylor, 307; Cranfield, 204; Lane, 210). But this seems most odd, since it clearly interrupts the mission of the Twelve in 6:7–13, 30. Thus the new section begins more logically with 6:7–13.

As an interlude or a parenthesis in Mark's narrative, 6:14–29 does provide an extended period during which the Twelve can carry out their mission. But is the connection only parenthetical? If, as has been suggested, Mark has redactionally framed the public opinion of Jesus (6:14b–15) with Herod's hearing this in 6:14a, 16, does he imply with his parenthetic γάρ-explanation (6:14a) that Herod had heard about Jesus, whose "name had become known," as a result of the mission of the Twelve (Lane, 211; Reploh, *Lehrer*, 55–56; Schmahl, *Zwölf*, 81)?

The objection that Herod had heard what others were saying about "Jesus" rather than the Twelve (Best, *Jesus*, 192) overlooks the nature of the Twelve's commission. As "apostles" (6:30) "sent" (6:7) by Jesus, they went as his authorized representatives. They represented him and ministered in his name (cf. 9:38–40). Consequently, in Mark's context Jesus' ministry (4:1–5:43) expanded and extended by the mission of the Twelve (6:7–13, 30) provided the logical background for the spread of Jesus' fame that reached all the way to Herod.

Apart from the introductory material about the Baptist (1:4–8), this is Mark's only story without any reference to Jesus. Furthermore, the disciples have continually been with Jesus since their call. Now sent out on their own, Jesus moves off the stage.

But Jesus does not move entirely out of the action. Viewed within the framework of Mark's Gospel, 6:14–29 provides a key scene. Herod identifies Jesus with John. This identification has already been subtly made by Mark. The Baptist came as the forerunner of Jesus in his preaching (1:4–8) and in his passion (1:14a), since Jesus begins his ministry "after John had been handed over." Therefore, the cruel fate of the Baptist becomes a harbinger of Jesus' ultimate rejection.

Many commentators have noted the parallels between this story and Jesus' passion: arrest—6:17, cf. 14:46; 15:1; death plot—6:19, cf. 14:1b; fear—6:20, cf. 11:18, 32; 12:12; 14:2; innocent man executed under pressure—6:26c, cf. 15:10, 14–15; burial—6:29, cf. 15:45–46 (Wolff, *TLZ* 102 [1977] 859; Gnilka, *Orientierung*, 80–81; Ernst, 186). The parallel is drawn by Jesus himself in 9:11–13 between the Baptist, as Elijah, and the Son of man, and this cruel story anticipates the cryptic statement, "They did to him what they wished" (9:13). Therefore, this story of the "forerunner" set in the context of Herod's and the public's views about Jesus (6:14–16) points to Jesus' first passion announcement in 8:31 which comes as part of the answer to who Jesus is in 8:27, the very question behind the "answers" of 6:14–16 as well.

By having Herod identify Jesus with John and by relating the latter's death during this interlude of the mission of the Twelve, Mark ironically allows Herod to make the connection necessary for ultimately understanding Jesus. The disciples themselves, despite their presence with Jesus and their mission for him, struggle in vain to make this connection in the next major section of Mark's Gospel, 8:27–10:52.

Therefore, 6:14–29 is parenthetical only in terms of the sending and return of the Twelve. Thematically, Mark has selected and introduced a story closely interwoven with the flow of Jesus' story.

Comment

14 "King Herod" refers to Herod Antipas, born in 20 BC to Herod the Great and his Samaritan wife, Malthace. He became tetrarch of Galilee and Perea, the area of Jesus' ministry in Mark, in 4 BC at the age of sixteen and ruled until AD 39 when he was banished to Gaul. According to Josephus, his banishment grew out of Herodias' ambitious desire that he officially seek the title of "king" from the Roman Caesar Caligula. His opponents took the occasion to reveal his stockpiling of weapons for which he was banished (*Ant.* 18.7.2). "King" Herod, therefore, represents a popular designation rather than an official title.

What Herod had "heard" (ἤκουσεν) were the different opinions expressed publicly about Jesus (6:14b–15). But an awkward γάρ-explanation clause interrupts the flow to explain how Herod had heard this. Jesus' "fame," literally his "name" (ὄνομα, see *Note* b), had spread even to "King Herod." At the same time, this explanation in the larger setting of the mission of the Twelve (6:7–13, 30) may indicate the popular stir caused by Jesus' ministry but particularly by the mission of the Twelve sent as representatives in his name (cf. 6:30–33). This would make 6:14–29 more than a literary parenthesis to create a time span for the mission between 6:7–13 and 6:30. The mission leads to this story about Herod's own response and the foreboding story of the Baptist's fate which prefigures Jesus' ultimate course (cf. 9:11–13).

The public opinions follow in descending order. John the Baptist raised from the dead associates Jesus with the most recent prophetic image in the mind of the populace. Grundmann (170) has noted the obvious parallels: (a) both were itinerant preachers, (b) both worked with the people at large without close association with any particular group or sect, (c) both preached repentance in view of the coming Kingdom. Certainly, this association and the prominence of the Baptist at the head of the list speaks of the popular impact of his ministry in the area. But the point of comparison in the text is their "mighty works."

"These powers are at work in him" (ἐνεργοῦσιν οἱ δυνάμεις ἐν αὐτῷ) obviously refers to the "mighty works" done by Jesus (cf. 6:2; 4:35–5:43) and quite likely by the Twelve as his agents (6:12–13, 30) that contributed to his "fame." But the reference is made to "the powers" themselves in a more hellenistic sense as miracle-working powers "at work" (ἐνεργοῦσιν taken intransitively; cf. Lohmeyer, 115) in the miracle worker (cf. 5:30; Kertelge, *Wunder*, 121; Pesch, 1:332). But does this allusion to Jesus' work indicate that the supernatural powers accompany one raised from the dead (Grundmann, 170) or are the powers at work in Jesus an indication that the Baptist too accomplished "mighty works" (Pesch, 1:334; Gnilka, 1:247; Ernst, 170)? The latter is more likely, since we have no other evidence associating supernatural powers accompanying one raised from the dead (Haenchen, 235), and the comparison of the Baptist with Elijah and his role as a prophet might indicate aspects of his ministry missing from our sparse information about him (cf. John 10:41).

15 "He is Elijah" links Jesus with the popular expectation based on Mal 3:1; 4:5–6 that Elijah would return to announce the day of the Lord. Elijah also played the role of a patron saint in Judaism as one who helped and protected the needy (Grundmann, 170; Haenchen, 236). Jesus' preaching (1:14–15) called urgently for repentance in view of the reign of God, and his healings and exorcisms brought wholeness and deliverance to the sick and oppressed. "One of the prophets" most likely refers to one of the order of the OT prophets indicating the stature accorded the ministry of Jesus. Luke 9:8 maintains the theme of returning to life on earth (the Baptist, Elijah) by adding, "one of the ancients raised from the dead."

These examples of public opinion appear again in 8:28 in answer to Jesus' question of the Twelve at Caesarea Philippi. They consistently point to the prophetic character of his ministry. Interestingly, none suggests him to be the Messiah. But each moves considerably beyond the answer given to the question by his "hometown" (6:2–3). Each opinion views him to be a man of God. That was enough to get him killed, as the Baptist's story proved. Yet the Baptist's death is only a preview of Jesus' violent death (9:11–13). The latter's death, according to Mark's story, comes for a different reason than simply sharing the fate of the prophets (cf. 10:45).

16 "When Herod heard" (ἀκούσας δὲ ὁ Ἡρῴδης) resumes the starting point of 6:14 and leads to Herod's conclusion, namely, that Jesus was John the Baptist whom he had beheaded. This identification closely links Jesus with the Baptist for the reader who has already met the Baptist as the "forerunner" of Jesus' message and fate in 1:4–15 at the "beginning of the Gospel concerning Jesus Messiah, Son of God" (1:1–3). Jesus himself will also make the connection in 9:11–13 between Elijah (the Baptist) and the Son of man. Therefore, the story that follows underscores the dark element in Jesus' ministry, his coming death, latent in the rejections of 3:1–6, 20–29; 6:1–6. But even the fate of the prophet per se fails to explain Jesus' mission. He was more than a prophet in his death as well as in his life. This point becomes the focus of the disciples' struggle to comprehend Jesus' teaching from 8:27–10:52.

Herod's opinion sets the stage for the telling of the story of the Baptist's death (6:17–29) with themes that are repeated in Jesus' own passion story.

17 Mark introduces the story of the Baptist's death with a γάρ-explanatory that makes this story subordinate to Herod's conclusion, "John, whom I beheaded, he is raised from the dead." We now learn about the "beheading" of John.

"Taken into custody and bound" (ἐκράτησεν, ἔδησεν) are common terms used for arrests. But the prefiguring of Jesus' own course by the Baptist gives added force to these words used in Jesus' own arrest (14:1, 44, 46, 49; 15:1). According to Josephus (*Ant.* 18.5.2), Herod had John imprisoned and eventually beheaded at Machaerus, a fortress east of the Dead Sea.

"On account of Herodias" (διὰ Ἡρῳδιάδα) gives the grounds for the Baptist's arrest and introduces the force behind his death in this story. Josephus (*Ant.* 18.5.2) attributes Herod's actions to fear of the Baptist's popular influence among the people. Though different, these two tendentious grounds need not be totally incompatible. Josephus' concern lay naturally along political lines; this story develops the personal intrigue within the court.

"Herodias, the wife of Philip his brother" identifies Herod's wife. She was also his niece, the daughter of his brother Aristobulus. But who is "Philip his brother"? Many have assumed this refers erroneously to Philip the Tetrarch, half-brother to Herod and son of Herod the Great's fifth marriage (Cleopatra of Jerusalem), who had actually married Salome, Herodias' daughter (Josephus, *Ant.* 18.5.4). According to Josephus (*Ant.* 18.5.4), Herodias originally had married another Herod, a son of Herod the Great's third marriage (Mariamne II). Such confusion might be expected when dealing with Herod the Great's family that included eight wives and many sons with the name "Herod." Yet it is more likely that "Philip" was a second name for another Herod and does not mean Philip the Tetrarch (Haenchen, 237; Hoehner, *Antipas*, 132–136).

18 The evangelist uses another γάρ-sentence to explain the rather vague "because he (Herod) had married her." It was the marriage itself and the Baptist's statements about it that had aggravated Herodias. "John had said to Herod" describes the Baptist in a court setting not unfamiliar to the prophets (e.g., Jer 38:14–26; Sir 48:22; cf. Mark 13:9; Acts 25:23–24, Gnilka, *Orientierung*, 87).

The Baptist charged Herod with an illegal marriage based on the law of forbidden marriages that specifically excluded marrying one's brother's wife (Lev 18:16; 20:21) except for the occasion of a levirate marriage to raise children to an older brother. Thus the story depicts the martyr as an advocate of the law before the authorities (cf. 2 Macc 6:18–31; *4 Macc* 5:1–6:3; Gnilka, *Orientierung*, 87).

Josephus also indirectly connects Herod's marriage to Herodias and the death of the Baptist. In order to make room for Herodias, Herod had sent his first wife, the daughter of Aretas IV, king of neighboring Nabatea, home. Aretas, taking this act as a personal slight, made war with Herod, an action, according to Josephus (*Ant.* 18.5.2), that the people took to be God's punishment for his killing of the Baptist. Consequently, Josephus' and Mark's grounds for the Baptist's death might reflect two sides of the same coin. Had John publicly attacked Herod's marriage as contrary to the law, Herod, who already had problems with his neighbor, might have seen the Baptist's influence within his own boundaries as seditious and dangerous (Hoehner, *Antipas*, 142–45).

19 For Mark's story, however, the martyr's death comes ultimately from the intrigue of a scheming woman. Herodias' desire to kill the Baptist like the designs of Jezebel on Elijah (1 Kgs 19:2) introduces the first of the story's several OT images. The typology falls short, not least in the fact that Herodias succeeds where Jezebel fails in getting her respective desires, but the early Church connection between the Baptist and Elijah (1:2–3; 9:11–13) makes this parallel inevitable. Her grudge against the Baptist and desires for his death were initially thwarted (καὶ οὐκ ἠδύνατο).

20 Ironically, the Baptist's antagonist had become his protector (συνετήρει αὐτόν). Mark with his third γάρ-statement explains why Herodias could not carry out her wishes. "Herod feared John, knowing him to be a just and holy man." This statement begins the description of Herod's dilemma before an innocent man on whom he will have to pass sentence, a scene replayed by Pilate before Jesus in 14:6–15. The Baptist's innocence is stated explicitly in Herod's respect for him as "just" (δίκαιον) and "holy" (ἅγιον) and implicitly in Herod's response to their conversations. The Baptist's words had gotten him arrested. Yet Herod liked to hear him (ἡδέως αὐτοῦ ἤκουεν) and even "did many things" that John told him (πολλὰ ἐποίει).

21 The scene shifts from John in prison to a banquet hall. Herod's birthday (see *Note* h) provides the occasion for a great feast and eventually for Herodias to have her way. To celebrate with him Herod had invited important guests from Galilee—"political magistrates" (μεγιστᾶσιν), "Roman military commanders" (χιλιάρχοις) and "prominent men" (πρώτοις). The logistics of arranging for such a group in a festive setting has led most to assume the location, though unstated, to have been Tiberias where Herod had established the residency for his court. Josephus informs us that pious Jews avoided this city because it had been built on a cemetery (*Ant.* 18.2.3). We have no mention in the Gospel tradition of Jesus ministering in this city south of Capernaum. In the only reference to the city in the Gospels, John 6:23 does note that the Feeding of the 5000 (Mark's next pericope—6:30–44!) takes place in the vicinity of Tiberias. Since Mark gives no precise location for the Feeding, we have no solid basis for assuming he associated either of the adjoining pericopes with Tiberias.

22 A series of three genitive absolutes sets the scene (γενομένης ἡμέρας . . . εἰσελθούσης τῆς θυγατρός . . . ὀρχησαμένης). When the appropriate day and moment arrived, "Herod's" daughter (αὐτοῦ, see *Note* i) entered to dance for the crowd. Two issues emerge. First, the question arises about whose daughter is involved. If we take the best attested reading (see *Note* i), she is "his" or Herod's daughter. Yet the story clearly indicates that she is Herodias' daughter and working for her "mother" (cf. 6:24, 28; Matt 14:6). "His" daughter would then make her a part of his extended family, "his" step-daughter. Second, by taking αὐτοῦ as the reading, the daughter is named "Herodias." Yet Josephus tells us that Herodias' daughter from her first marriage was Salome the wife of Philip the Tetrarch (*Ant.* 18.5.4). This would mean that the daughter's name had become confused with the mother's.

More importantly, many have found the idea of a king's daughter dancing the dance of prostitutes in such a bawdy setting too preposterous to believe. But assuming that this connoted to the ancient hearer such a ribald and incredulous event, it could indicate the degree of disrepute Herod's rule and family life had among the people (Gnilka, *Orientierung*, 89).

23 Herod found the dance so pleasing that he in a grandiose gesture offered her anything she might request. To reinforce his promise, he took an oath similar to Ahasuerus' promise to Esther (Esth 5:3; 7:2) of "up to half of my kingdom." That Herod was a vassal of Rome only makes this oath the more brash. But it sets the trap in which he himself is ensnared.

The heart of the narrative reflects much movement—entering, exiting and reentering. The spotlight shifts from Herod and his guests to the daughter, from the daughter to her mother and back to Herod (6:20–26). And the pace quickens with each verse.

24 Without a moment's hesitation, when the girl asks her mother's advice, she receives the one request—"the head of John the Baptizer!" Herodias has her chance to carry out her wicked designs on John. Mark leaves his thumbprint, "the Baptizer" (6:14) rather than the more usual "Baptist" (6:25; see *Comment* on 1:4), on the tradition.

25 With words almost of urgency (εὐθύς, μετὰ σπουδῆς, ἐξαυτῆς) the young girl relays her request to Herod with the added note, "on a platter" (ἐπὶ πίνακι). It was not sufficient merely to take John's life; she literally wanted to have his head given to her. We have a similar example in *Midr. Esth.* 1:19, 21 where Vashti's head is brought to the king on a platter.

26–27 Herod has become entrapped in his own device. Despite his great sadness and feelings to the contrary, he keeps his oath and faith with his fellow diners by granting her request. Torn between the life of an innocent man and his word and prestige, Herod chooses the latter. He orders the "executioner" (σπεκουλάτορα) to bring the head. Pilate makes a similar decision under the pressures of the moment and the crowd in 15:14–15.

28 The drama ends with the order being carried out and the head given to the girl on a platter. She in turn gives the head to her mother. We have come full circle. Herodias, who at the beginning of the story was the cause for John's imprisonment, now ends the story with her prize. Evil appears to have won the day. "They did to him whatever they pleased" and will do the same to the Son of man (9:12–13).

The story leaves us with the impression that all transpired within one evening. If, however, the banquet was at Tiberias as often assumed, then the Baptist's death had to have taken place there as well. The journey from Tiberias to Machaerus, the place of his execution according to Josephus (*Ant.* 18.5.2), was far too long to be made overnight. One can resolve the dilemma by moving the banquet to Machaerius and explain the presence of the dignitaries in light of the festive occasion (Lane, 216; Hoehner, *Antipas*, 146–48) or attribute the implied shift in setting to the later embellishment of the original story with the banquet scene (Gnilka, *Orientierung*, 87).

29 The curtain falls as John's disciples take the beheaded "corpse and place it in a tomb." In a similar manner, Joseph of Arimathea will get Jesus' corpse from Pilate and place it in a tomb (15:46). The role of the "forerunner" has ended.

Explanation

The story takes on significance for Mark's Gospel through its location and the relation of John the "forerunner" to Jesus. By intercalating 6:14–29 between the sending of the Twelve (6:7–13) and the report of their return (6:30), the evangelist provides more than a dramatic interlude for their mission. The setting suggests that the story of the Baptist's death was triggered by Herod's reaction to the positive effect of the Twelve's mission. This had resulted in Herod's hearing about Jesus whose ministry reminded him of the Baptist (6:14). Immediately following this story, Mark relates the return of the Twelve and the relentless press of the crowds (6:30–32). Thus the disciples' mission, corresponding to Jesus' own ministry (cf. 3:1–6, 20–35), raises the specter of rejection in the moment of success.

One cannot miss the Baptist's role as "forerunner" for Jesus in this story. In 6:16 Herod explicitly identifies Jesus with John. He joins the crowds who believe Jesus to be a prophet—either the Baptist (a "just and holy man"— 6:20), Elijah, or in the line of the prophets (6:14b–15). The reader, however, knows that Jesus is not John but one greater than John whose way the Baptist prepared by his preaching and his death (cf. 1:4–8, 14a; 9:13). The description of his death anticipates in language and motifs Jesus' own coming death.

Consequently, 6:14–29 does not come as a surd in the middle of Mark's narrative. It plays an integral role in the story line by pointing again (cf. 3:1–6; 20–35; 6:1–6a) to Jesus' rejection within a story (6:7–13, 30) that speaks positively of his ministry as carried out by the disciples. The motif of Jesus' rejection becomes more prominent in the subsequent segment of Mark's narrative (8:27–10:52) in which the disciples themselves struggle to comprehend Jesus' own teaching about his coming rejection and death. In this section (6:7–8:26), however, the disciples exhibit a lack of understanding about who Jesus is even in his "successful" ministry (6:52; 7:18; 8:17–21), a ministry which they directly share (6:7–13, 30–44; 8:1–10).

C. The Feeding of the Five Thousand   (6:30–44)

Bibliography

Achtemeier, P. "Toward the Isolation of Pre-Markan Miracle Catenae." *JBL* 89 (1970) 265–91. ———. "The Origin and Function of the Pre-Markan Miracle Catenae." *JBL* 91 (1972) 198–221. **Best, E.** *Following Jesus.* 1981. **Boobyer, G. H.** "The Eucharistic Interpretation of the Miracles of the Loaves in St. Mark's Gospel." *JTS* 3 (1952) 161–71. ———. "The Miracles of the Loaves and the Gentiles in St. Mark's Gospel." *SJT* 6 (1953) 77–87. **Clavier, H.** "La multiplication des pains dans le ministère de Jésus." *SE* 1 (1959) 441–57. **Derrett, J. D. M.** "Leek-Beds and Methodology (πρασιαί πρασιαί [Mk 6,40])." In *Studies in the New Testament.* Leiden: Brill, 1978. 1–3. = *BZ* 19 (1975) 101–03. **Donfried, K. P.** "The Feeding Narratives and the Marcan Community." In *Kirche,* FS G. Bornkamm, ed. D. Lührmann and G. Strecker. Tübingen: Mohr, 1980. 95–103. **Egger, W.** *Frohbotschaft und Lehre.* 1976. **Farrer, A.** "Loaves and Thousands." *JTS* 4 (1953) 1–14. **Fowler, R.** *Loaves and Fishes: The Function of the Feeding Stories in the Gospel of Mark.* SBLDS 54. Chico, CA: Scholars, 1978. **Friedrich, G.** "Die beiden Erzählungen von der Speisung in Mark 6, 31–44, 8, 1–9." *TZ* 20 (1964) 10–22. **Heising, A.** "Exegese und Theologie der Alt- und Neutestamentlichen Speisewunder." *ZTK* 86 (1964) 80–96. **Iersel, B. W. van.** "Die wunderbare Speisung und das Abendmahl in der synoptischen Tradition (Mk VI. 35–44 par VIII. 1–20 par)." *NovT* 7 (1964) 167–94. **Jenkins, L. H.** "A Marcan Doublet." In *Studies in History and Religion,* FS H. W. Robinson, ed. E. A. Payne. London: Lutterworth, 1942. 87–111. **Keck,**

L. E. "Mark 3:7–12 and Mark's Christology." *JBL* 84 (1965) 341–58. **Kertelge, K.** *Die Wunder Jesu im Markusevangelium.* 1970. **Koch, D.-A.** *Die Bedeutung der Wundererzählungen für die Christologie des Markusevangeliums.* 1975. **Kuhn, H.-W.** *Ältere Sammlungen im Markusevangelium.* 1971. **Lang, F. G.** "'Über Sidon mitten ins Gebiet der Dekapolis': Geographie und Theologie in Markus 7,31." *ZDPV* 94 [1978] 145–60. **Loos, H. van der.** *The Miracles of Jesus.* NTS 8. Leiden: Brill, 1965. **Masuda, S.** "The Good News of the Miracle of the Bread. The Tradition and Its Markan Redaction." *NTS* 28 (1982) 191–219. **Montefiore, H.** "Revolt in the Desert? (Mark vi. 30ff.)." *NTS* 8 (1961–62) 135–41. **Neirynck, F.** *Duality in Mark.* 1973. **Neugebauer, F.** "Die wunderbare Speisung (Mk 6,30–44 parr.) und Jesu Identität." *KD* 32 (1986) 254–77. **Patsch, H.** "Abendmahlterminologie ausserhalb der Einsetzungsberichte: Erwägungen zur Traditionsgeschichte der Abendmahlsworte." *ZNW* 62 (1971) 210–31. **Reploh, K.-G.** *Markus—Lehrer der Gemeinde.* 1969. **Roloff, J.** *Apostolat-Verkündigung—Kirche.* Gütersloh: Mohn, 1965. ———. *Das Kerygma der irdische Jesus.* 1970. **Schenke, L.** *Die Wundererzälungen des Markusevangeliums.* 1974. ———. *Die wunderbare Brotvermehrung: Die neutestamentlichen Erzählungen und ihre Bedeutung.* Würzburg: Echter, 1983. **Snoy, T.** "La rédaction marcienne de la marche sur les eaux (Mc., VI:45–52)." *ETL* 44 (1968) 205–41, 433–81. **Theissen, G.** *The Miracle Stories of the Early Christian Tradition.* 1983. **Thiering, B. E.** "'Breaking of Bread' and 'Harvest' in Mark's Gospel." *NovT* 12 (1970) 1–12. **Ziener, G.** "Die Brotwunder im Markusevangelium." *BZ* 4 (1960) 282–85.

Translation

[30] *And the apostles gathered around Jesus and reported to him all that they did and taught.* [31] *And he said to them, "Come away by yourselves to an uninhabited place to rest for a while." For many were coming and going, and they did not even have an opportunity to eat.*

[32] *And they went in a boat to an uninhabited place alone.* [33] *And many saw them going, recognized them, and ran there on foot from all the cities and arrived ahead of them.*

[34] *When he got out of the* boat,[a] *he saw a large crowd and had compassion on them, for they were as sheep without a shepherd. And he began to teach them many things.*[b]

[35] *When the hour was now quite late, Jesus'*[a] *disciples came to him and said, "This is an uninhabited place and the hour is now late.* [36] *Send them away in order that going into the surrounding hamlets and villages they might buy for themselves something to eat."* [37] *But he answered and said to them, "You give them something to eat!" And they said to him, "Should we go and purchase two hundred denarii worth of bread and give them to eat?"* [38] *But he said to them, "How many loaves do you have? Go and see." When they knew, they said, "Five loaves and two fish."*

[39] *And he ordered them all to recline in companies*[c] *on the green grass.* [40] *And they reclined by groups*[d] *of fifty and a hundred.* [41] *And taking the five loaves and the two fish and looking to heaven, he blessed, and broke the loaves and gave them to his*[e] *disciples that they might serve them. And he divided the fish for all.* [42] *And all ate and were filled.*

[43] *And they picked up twelve baskets full of broken pieces and fish.* [44] *And those eating the loaves*[f] *were about five thousand men.*

Notes

[a] Romanized words supplied from context.
[b] Cf. 4:2 and 7:13. Perhaps an adverbial use of πολλά "at length."

c Συμπόσιον means a festive company often used of drinking together or a banquet setting, and is used distributively here.

d πρασιαί πρασιαί literally designates a garden of herbs or leeks, and comes to mean a small area, "garden plot" (BGD, ad loc.). It is used distributively here, "group by group" in orderly arrangement (cf. Derrett, *Studies*, 1–3).

e Read αὐτοῦ with P45 A D W Θ f1.13 Majority text lat sy samss in contrast to ℵ B L Δ 33 892 1241 pc bo. The text is fairly evenly divided. Mark generally uses αὐτοῦ rather than τοῦ with "disciples" (cf. 6:1, 35, 45; Metzger, *Textual Commentary*, 91).

f Read τοὺς ἄρτους with A B L Majority text f syp.h bo. Witnesses against (P45 hea D W Θ f1.13 28 565 700 lat sa) include Western readings that generally have a longer text. The elimination may be an attempt to align the text with bread *and* fish, though reading it is consistent with the emphasis on the "bread" in the account (Metzger, *Textual Commentary*, 92)

Form / Structure / Setting

Form-critically, 6:30–44 consists of a summary report and a miracle story with an extended introduction. In Mark these are so combined with the one leading so logically into the other that we have taken the complex as one pericope. Most commentators have divided this material into two parts. Where, however, is the line of demarcation? It has been variously drawn between 6:31/32 (e.g., Schweizer, 135–36; Pesch, 1:345), 6:32/33 (e.g., Kertelge, *Wunder*, 130), 6:33/34 (e.g., Schmidt, 186–90; Bultmann, 231; Schenke, *Wundererzählungen*, 217–21), and 6:34/35 (e.g., Taylor, 318; Egger, *Frohbotschaft*, 121–31).

In a detailed analysis, Egger (*Frohbotschaft*, 121–22) has taken 6:30–34 to be a summary report providing a transition to the feeding miracle in 6:35–44. But this designation places too much structural weight on Jesus' teaching (6:34) as the concluding element in tandem with the disciples' report of their teaching in 6:30 rather than recognizing the former as an integral part of 6:35–44. This division also fails materially to correspond to the change in subjects from the disciples in 6:30 to Jesus in 6:34 and to account for the primary action at the heart of 6:32–34, i.e., the futile attempt to evade the crowds.

Indeed, only 6:30 represents a summary report (cf. 6:7b). It clearly connects the report by the disciples to the mission of 6:7–13. Jesus' suggestion (6:31) that they get alone to find some rest arises from this report and provides the transition to the scene in 6:32 which begins the extended introduction of the feeding miracle.

The miracle story itself falls under the specific category of a gift miracle marked by: (a) the spontaneity of the miraculous action, (b) the unobtrusiveness of the miracle itself and (c) a clear demonstration (Theissen, *Miracle Stories*, 103). This particular story is reminiscent of several OT passages such as the miraculous feeding of the people in the wilderness (Exod 16; Pss 78:18–30; 105:40) and the feeding miracles of Elijah and Elisha (1 Kgs 17:8–16; 2 Kgs 4:1–7, 42–44).

Mark has a second feeding in 8:1–10 with numerous similarities: Jesus' compassion, an uninhabited place, conversation revealing the disciples' confusion, assessment of provisions, prayer of thanks, distribution of food by the disciples, collection of leftovers, and number of people fed (Gnilka, 1:255). At the same time, the differences in setting, occasion, amount of food, number of baskets and people present raise a question about a previous relationship of these stories in the tradition (see 8:1–9).

As to source, most interpreters regard 6:30–31 as stemming from Mark's redaction. Motifs (the combination of doing and teaching, moments of privacy), vocabulary (συνάγειν, κατ' ἰδίαν, ὅσος) and style (γάρ-explanatory) support this conclusion. The unusual presence of ἀπόστολοι and the invitation to rest in an "uninhabited place" (cf. 1:35), however, may suggest that Mark has re-worked traditional material to form this summary (Best, *Jesus,* 192–93; Cranfield, 213; Ernst, 187; Roloff, *Apostolat,* 142). His account of the sending in its present form (6:7–13), though based on a historical event and using traditional material for the instructions (6:8–11), comes more from the evangelist's pen than from a specific traditional unit. The same would most likely obtain for this summary report (cf. Luke 9:10; 10:17). By adding the suggestion that the returning disciples seek solitude and rest in order to eat (6:31), the evangelist combines their return from the mission (6:30) with the miracle of the Feeding.

Some have traced this story and those that follow to a "doublet" in the pre-Markan tradition between 6:30(31)–7:37 and 8:1–26 based on the similarity of themes and sequence (Klostermann, 74–75; Jenkins, *Studies,* 87–111). Taylor's (628–32) examination of this material, however, has shown this similarity extending to certain events (e.g., 6:34–44; 8:1–10) to be more apparent than real when applied to the entire complex. The actual arrangement of the pericope stems for the most part from the evangelist's use of his tradition.

Mark most likely found the miracle story with its extended introduction in the larger collection of miracle stories behind 4:35–5:43 (Keck, *JBL* 84 [1965] 341–58; Kuhn, *Sammlungen,* 203–10, 217–18; Pesch, 1:277–81). Not only does the unusual command that the young girl be fed that concludes 5:43 lead thematically to the feeding in 6:35–44 (cf. 5:43b and 6:37a), but the Elijah/Elisha motif behind Jesus' raising of Jairus' daughter also stands behind Jesus' surprising provision for the crowd here. The latter motif may have given rise to Mark's own use of the Baptist and Elijah that led into the previous story of the Baptist's death (6:14–29).

In a recent study, Fowler (*Loaves, 68–90*) rejects the thesis of a pre-Markan miracle collection and, after examining 6:30–44 on the basis of vocabulary, style, and themes, has concluded: "The story is Markan from beginning to end" (68), a Markan "doublet" constructed from the traditional story of 8:1–10. His conclusion runs contrary to the evidence that has led most commentators to take 8:1–10 to be later not earlier than the story in 6:34–44 (see pp. 402, 406). Furthermore, Fowler's Markan "characteristics" in the Feeding itself (6:35–44; cf. 6:30–34) have not been understood as so distinctive as to lead others to ascribe this story to the evangelist (cf. Masuda, *NTS* 28 [1982] 191–219).

The extended introduction (6:32–34) to the Feeding story betrays traits of the pre-Markan collector of the miracle stories and represents a pre-Markan redactor's effort to link the Feeding with the previous miracle story (5:21–43; cf. Lührmann, 119). The original introduction to the miracle story lies behind 6:34 with the note of Jesus' looking on a large crowd with compassion (cf. 8:2). Thus using the now familiar theme of Jesus crossing with his disciples "in a boat" (4:36; 5:2, 18, 21; 6:45) "to the other side" (4:35–36; 5:1–2, 18, 21) to evade the crowds (4:35–36; cf. 3:9 and 5:17), the collector introduces the crowds drawn from "all the cities," a hyperbole similar to the broad generalizations in the summaries of 3:7 and 6:53–56.

Mark's own contribution appears limited to the adapting of 6:31–32 and the additional note in 6:34, "He began to teach them." The typically Markan use of ἄρχεσθαι with the infinitive and the emphasis on Jesus' teaching point to Mark's hand. Again we have Jesus' teaching as a superscript for a miracle (cf. 1:21–27; 6:2) indicating the didactic force of Jesus' miracles for Mark (cf. 6:52).

The miracle story consists of three parts. First, we have a setting in the form of a conversation between Jesus and his disciples (6:35–38). Then comes the actual miracle itself, the feeding of a great crowd with few provisions (6:39–42). The story concludes with a demonstration of the miracle in that five thousand ate to their fill with food left over (6:43–44).

Lohmeyer (121–22) and Pesch (1:345, 349–50) take this unit to begin the next major section in Mark (6:30–8:26) developed around the idea of eating (ἐσθίειν). This, however, breaks the important connection seen between 6:7–13 and 6:30. The report of the Twelve resumes and concludes the mission of 6:7–13. By intercalating the Baptist's death (6:14–29) into the summaries in 6:12–13, 30, the evangelist has created an extended time span which the activities reported in 6:30 have filled. These activities have created such great response that Herod Antipas has heard about Jesus and the crowds have pursued him unrelentingly (6:14, 31–34).

In the context of Mark's Gospel, this miracle story begins a series in which the disciples' lack of understanding, a note introduced earlier (cf. 4:13, 41), becomes more pronounced. It stands in ironic tension with their preceding mission as commissioned agents of Jesus' ministry (6:7–13, 30) to heal, exorcise and preach repentance, as the crowds suggest, with great success. The opening dialogue between the disciples and Jesus (6:35–38) reveals their confusion. But the evangelist highlights their failure to understand the significance of the miracle itself in his comment at the end of the next story in 6:52.

Comment

30 "The apostles" (ἀπόστολοι) occurs only here and in a disputed reading in 3:14. Contextually, it picks up the ἀποστέλλειν of 6:7 and designates those sent as the "sent ones" or "missionaries." It points primarily to their role rather than their status, so there is no reason to take the term as a title, "the Apostles" (Reploh, *Lehrer*, 55). Yet in the broader context of the early Church, by Mark's day ἀπόστολος had definitely become a technical term for the Apostles. Consequently, it would be almost impossible for Mark's readers to read "apostles" without the larger context coloring its meaning here (Best, *Jesus*, 192–93; Roloff, *Apostolat*, 142).

Taken functionally, "apostle" carries more significance than either the term "sent one" or "missionary" expresses today. With its background in formative Judaism's use of a שׁלִיחַ, šālîaḥ (H. K. Rengstorf, *TDNT* 1 [1964] 414–30), ἀπόστολος denotes an official, an authorized representative or agent either of a person or a group (e.g., a synagogue). This agent operates in the name of the one having given the authorization. Therefore, the term "apostles" and their action of reporting to Jesus demonstrate the Twelve's dependent relationship to Jesus. Their mission was an extension of his mission.

"All they did and taught" (πάντα ὅσα ἐποίησαν καὶ ἐδίδαξαν) summarizes their mission endeavors. What they "did" (ἐποίησαν) obviously included the exorcisms and healings mentioned in 6:13 and perhaps even the preaching of 6:12. Typical of Mark, however, the Twelve also report their ministry of "teaching" in keeping with the evangelist's accent on Jesus' ministry of "teaching" (see *Comment* on 1:21; 3:6b; 6:6b). Here again we see the essential relationship between the mission of the Twelve and Jesus' mission.

31 "An uninhabited place" (ἔρημος τόπος) occurs in 1:35, 45 where Jesus attempts to move out of the towns and villages away from the people (see *Comment* on 1:35). The phrase may have been drawn from the following story (6:35) where it provided the setting for Jesus' feeding of the multitude. Here it signifies a place of privacy away from the town or village. But 6:35 shows, as in 1:45, that an uninhabited place does not guarantee privacy.

"To rest for a while" (ἀναπαύσασθε ὀλίγον) implies the necessity of the disciples finding some time to recuperate after their mission. Unlike the references to Jesus' desire to be alone for prayer (cf. 1:35; 6:45–46), this is a call for the disciples to rest and it stands out in Mark's Gospel. It may well reflect the same attitude as the following reference to Jesus' compassionate response to the "sheep without a shepherd" (6:34) and expresses his concern for his disciples who had been so preoccupied with the comings and goings of the people that they could not even find time to eat.

We find a similar situation in 3:20–21, 31–35 where Jesus' ministry attracted such a crowd in a home that he could not eat. Here the crowds disturb the eating pattern of the disciples which implies a direct connection between the press of the crowds and the mission of the Twelve.

32 In 6:30–31 the "apostles" had occupied center stage with their report to Jesus and his exhortation for them to seek some rest away from the crowds. They remain in the scene, but Jesus emerges as the primary subject of what follows. This significant shift (overlooked by Fowler, *Loaves,* 69–70) may indicate traces of a pre-Markan introduction of the Feeding miracle added by the redactor of the miracle stories to connect the Feeding with the other miracle stories in 4:35–5:43. One could easily omit 6:30–31 as well as 6:1–29 and continue the series of narratives from 5:43. By combining 6:32–44 with 6:30–31 through his "progressive doublestep expression" (Neirynck, *Duality,* 208–09), Mark subtly changes the nuance of this transitional material (6:32–33) from simply setting the scene for Jesus' feeding of the multitude who had preceded him to an "uninhabited place" (6:32, 35) to a description of the futile attempt by Jesus and the "apostles" to find an "uninhabited place" (6:31–32) "alone" (κατ᾽ ἰδίαν, 6:31–32).

The departure "by boat" corresponds to Jesus and his disciples' movement by boat throughout this collection of miracle stories (4:36; 5:2, 18, 21; see 6:45). The destination, "an uninhabited place" (εἰς ἔρημον τόπον), was the setting for the feeding (6:35) in the pre-Markan tradition. In the context of 6:31, the "uninhabited place" was meant to be a place of rest away from the crowds. Despite the common association of the "wilderness" (ἔρημος, see *Comment* on 1:4, 13) with an "uninhabited place" (ἔρημος τόπος, see *Comment* on

1:35), neither the underlying tradition nor the evangelist implies an identity or even a typology between the two. The locale remains unidentified in Mark. Luke 9:10 places it near Bethsaida; John 6:23 near Tiberias.

33 "Many saw them going . . . ran there on foot from all the cities" expresses the futility of the disciples' quest for solitude. At the same time, it leads into the feeding of the "multitude" in 6:35–44. "Arrived ahead of them" (προῆλθον) completes the setting by having the crowds on hand for Jesus' show of compassion (6:34; cf 8:2) when he disembarks.

In creating this transitional scene, the collector of the pre-Markan miracle stories may well show more familiarity with the geography of the area than is generally assumed (cf. Snoy, *ETL* 44 [1968] 205–41; Fowler, *Loaves,* 65–66). If one thinks of Jesus crossing the sea from east to west by boat (see *Comment* on 5:1; 6:45), it does indeed stretch one's imagination to think that a crowd could outrun him by foot. But if one thinks more in terms of the many coves along the western shores of the sea between Tiberias and Bethsaida, such a feat by an enthusiastic crowd is not so stupendous (Pesch, 1:349), and it hardly requires a "premeditated" rendezvous (cf. Montefiore, *NTS* 8 [1961–62] 136).

34 This verse most likely contains remnants of an earlier tradition of the Feeding miracle. In the context of 6:32, "departing" (ἐξελθών) refers to Jesus' "coming out" of the boat, and the "great crowd" (πολὺν ὄχλον; cf. πολλοί, 6:33) refers to the gathered multitude "from all the cities" who had run ahead of them. Jesus reacts with "compassion" when he sees the crowds rather than with agitation at not being able to get away from the public (cf. 6:30–31). But his "compassion" here does not grow out of the urgency of this situation (cf. 8:2), but out of his concern for them as "sheep without a shepherd."

"Sheep without a shepherd" reflects an OT image used of Israel (Num 27:17; 1 Kgs 22:17; Ezek 34:5) and introduces one of several OT motifs that appear in the following story. It places the miracle under the motif of Jesus as the good shepherd, the promised eschatological shepherd, who feeds the sheep (cf. Ezek 34:23: "I will set up over them one shepherd, my servant David, and he shall feed them: he shall feed them and be their shepherd"). This perspective may well hold the Christological key to this miracle story in which Jesus provides food and table fellowship for the multitude (Roloff, *Kerygma,* 243; Friedrich, *TZ* 20 [1964] 15–20; Ziener, *BZ* 4 [1960] 283–84).

"And he began to teach them" (ἤρξατο διδάσκειν αὐτούς) most likely is Mark's redactional note to accent again Jesus' role as teacher, particularly within the context of his healing and exorcism ministry (cf. 1:21–27; 6:2–3), and points to Mark's perception of the didactic role of Jesus' total ministry (see *Comment* on 6:52). To say that Mark changes the thrust of Jesus' compassionate response from feeding to teaching (Egger, *Frohbotschaft,* 130–31; Gnilka, 1:259) draws too great a contrast between the evangelist's emphasis on Jesus' "teaching" and his "mighty works" (see *Comment* on 6:2). One could assume that the crowds had come to see and hear Jesus and that he had fulfilled their wishes.

35–36 "The hour was now quite late" (ἤδη ὥρας πολλῆς γενομένης) most likely refers to late afternoon near sunset, the normal dinner hour (Grundmann, 181; Gnilka, 1:259). The time of day and the location, "an uninhabited place" (ἔρημος ὁ τόπος), has led the disciples to ask Jesus to dismiss the crowd to go into the "surrounding hamlets and towns" (εἰς τοὺς κύκλῳ ἀγροὺς καὶ κώμας) to buy something to eat. In contrast to the Feeding in 8:1–2, where Jesus takes the initiative and calls the disciples, here the disciples come to Jesus with their request on behalf of the people. But there is little hint of urgency or need of a miracle, since ample provisions can be found nearby.

37 Jesus' response, however, confuses the disciples. "You (ὑμεῖς) give them something to eat!" Their response, more a rhetorical question than one expecting an answer, expresses the impossibility of Jesus' command given their resources. A denarius equaled a day's wages. Two hundred denarii, assuming that would suffice (see Neugebauer, *KD* 32 [1986] 258; Schmid, 127), certainly represented more than their resources could cover.

38 Without answering their question, Jesus next asks them to determine what food was present. They report five loaves and two fish. This information concludes the opening scene, and the action moves to Jesus providing miraculously for those present.

39–40 He orders the crowd to "be seated," to take their normal positions for a meal ("to recline"—ἀνακλῖναι), in "companies" (συμπόσια), a word connoting a special kind of bond. It is used of a "drinking party, a banquet" (BGD, ad loc.). The symbolism of fellowship around the table reflecting a new kind of communion or community runs through Jesus' ministry. Here the arrangement in groups according to fifties and hundreds doubtless has more than a utilitarian function. In Exod 18:25 (Num 31:14) Moses arranged the Israelites in groups of 1000, 500, 100, and 10 under their respective leaders. The Qumran literature takes such groupings as an eschatological model for their own sectarian life (1QS 2:21–22; CD 13:1; 1QM 4:1–5:17; 1QSa 1:14–15, 28–29) and specifically for the messianic banquet (1QSa 2:11–22). Thus, the arrangement points back to the time of God's miraculous provision for the needs of the people in the wilderness and hints at the eschatological moment in the gathering of God's people into communities at the end time (Gnilka, 1:261).

The "sheep without a shepherd" (6:34; cf. Exod 34:5) have received a "shepherd." It may be going too far to take the "green grass" (τῷ χλωρῷ χόρτῳ; cf. John 6:10) as an allusion to the messianic age when the "desert will blossom" (Friedrich, *TZ* 20 [1964] 18–20) or as a vivid recollection of an eyewitness account (Schmidt, 191). In the context of Jesus' compassion for the "sheep" it may well reflect the shepherd's role in Ps 23 of leading the sheep "in green pastures" (van Iersel, *NovT* 7 [1964] 188; Heising, *ZTK* 86 [1964] 91). Thus Jesus is the eschatological shepherd (Ezek 34:23; Jer 23:4; *Pss. Sol.* 17:40) who gathers God's people into community and provides for their needs (Pesch, 1:350).

41 The miracle follows unobtrusively. In keeping with the role of the father in the Jewish household, Jesus took the bread at hand and proceeded as with a normal meal. Only one difference stands out. After taking (λαβών) the bread (literally "the five breads" [τοὺς πέντε ἄρτους], commonly rendered "the loaves") and the two fish, he "looked to heaven" (ἀναβλέψας εἰς τὸν οὐρανόν) and offered the blessing (εὐλόγησεν; cf. 8:6). Some commentators have found the gesture of prayer contrary to the normal Jewish gesture of looking down when praying (Str-B, 2:246). And since in 7:34 and in John 11:41 we find a similar gesture of prayer just prior to a miracle, they have assumed that Jesus looked to God for the power to do this mighty work while saying the blessing (Cranfield, 219; Pesch, 1:352–53). This conclusion, however, overlooks other references to a similar gesture in prayer in the NT period (e.g., Luke 18:13; Josephus, *Ant.* 11.56), a gesture frequently found in the OT (Lohmeyer, 127, n. 7; Neugebauer, *KD* 32 [1986] 260; cf. Ps 121:1). Such a gesture comes appropriately at this point, since in Jewish practice God rather than the food (cf. 8:7) is the object of the blessing (cf. ancient blessing for bread quoted by Taylor, 324: "Blessed art Thou, O Lord our God, King of the world, who bringest forth bread from the earth").

Jesus then broke (κατέκλασεν; cf. 8:6) the finger-thick, plate-shaped "loaves" (τοὺς ἄρτους) and gave (ἐδίδου) them to the disciples to distribute. This follows the normal pattern of the meal in which the father or the host blesses God for the bread, then breaks it and passes it to the others as a sign of the beginning of the meal (Str-B, 4:611–39).

Then he divided the fish for all (καὶ τοὺς δύο ἰχθύας ἐμέρισεν πᾶσιν). The difference in language pertains to the foods involved rather than a secondary addition (Roloff, *Kerygma*, 244; cf. van Iersel, *NovT* 7 [1964] 174–75). The "breaking" of the bread is a formulaic expression signifying the beginning of the meal as well as the rite of eating in the Jewish household. It only secondarily has to do with "dividing" the bread for distribution. Since one does not formally give a blessing over the main course or "break fish" as one "breaks bread," it is not surprising that Jesus simply "divides" (ἐμέρισεν) the fish for all to eat.

Yet there does appear to be an emphasis on the "bread" in the story (cf. Matt 14:19–21). The statement about the fish appears less developed. This is particularly true of the leftovers in 6:43 where "and from the fish" sounds like an afterthought. And if "the loaves" (τοὺς ἄρτους) is to be read in 6:44 (see *Note* e), the story clearly concluded without further mention of the fish.

Consequently, some have seen eucharistic overtones behind these words (e.g., Lohmeyer, 127, n. 5; Taylor, 324; Clavier, *SE* 1 [1959] 441; Ziener, *BZ* 4 [1960] 282–85; esp. van Iersel, *NovT* 7 [1964] 167–94; Ernst, 192), and Achtemeier has located the miracle catenae in a "eucharistic liturgy" based on the two Feeding miracles (*JBL* 91 [1972] 208–09). Yet significant differences make a eucharistic interpretation at best remote (Boobyer, *JTS* 3 [1952], 161–71; Patsch, *ZNW* 62 [1971] 219–228; Roloff, *Kerygma*, 241–46; Pesch, 1:352; Gnilka, 1:261).

First, the absence of wine and the presence of fish speak against its ever having been taken as a eucharistic meal (cf. Matt 14:19). Second, and most importantly, the words "took" (λαβών), "blessed" (εὐλόγησεν), "broke" (κατέκλασεν) and "gave" (ἐδίδου) that appear reminiscent of the Lord's Supper (14:22) are not themselves evidence of a eucharistic meal (cf. Acts 27:35) and cannot mask the absence of "This is my body/blood" which makes the Lord's Supper unique. Third, the gathering of the leftovers plays a significant role in the miracle story but has no place in the Lord's Supper. Therefore, we have the normal procedures for an average meal in a Jewish household (Roloff, *Kerygma*, 244).

While hardly constructed or modified to reflect a eucharistic meal, the prominence given the bread throughout and the inescapable similarity in the language to that of the beginning of the Lord's Supper (which in itself uses the language and custom of the Jewish meal) may reflect influence from the Lord's Supper liturgy on the wording of 6:41 and explain why the fish are relegated a lesser role, especially in the parallel accounts in Matthew and Luke (van Iersel, *NovT* 7 [1964] 171, 174–75). This indirect influence becomes even more evident when the second Feeding comes into consideration (Patsch, *ZNW* 62 [1971] 227–28; see 8:1–10).

The miraculous feeding takes place as though it were nothing out of the ordinary. The crowd appears oblivious to the event and the disciples carry out their task without comment. Yet the disciples' awareness and lack of understanding do come into play again in 6:52 for Mark. Consequently, one of the most spectacular of Jesus' miracles takes place essentially unnoticed.

42 "And all ate and were filled" provides the confirmation of the miracle. The need of the moment, food for an evening meal, had been met. "All" (πάντες) had eaten to their satisfaction (ἐχορτάσθησαν).

43 The demonstration takes place in the gathering of "twelve baskets" of leftovers. "Basket" (κόφινος) refers to an apparently distinctively Jewish basket noted by Juvenal (3.14; 6.542) as characteristic of a poorer class of Jews in Rome (BGD, *s.v.*).

"And fish" (καὶ ἀπὸ τῶγ ἰχθύων) appears almost as an afterthought. "Pieces" (κλάσματα) could have included both bread and fish, though only the bread was "broken" (κατέκλασεν; cf. 6:41). But "the loaves" of 6:44—either originally or later—indicates the prominence of the "bread" motif. So "and fish" picks up the fish of 6:41 and balances the story that tends to accent the bread and de-emphasize the fish (cf. Matt 14:15–21; Luke 9:12–17).

"Twelve" has often been taken symbolically in contrast to the "seven" in 8:1–9 for either the Twelve Apostles in contrast to the Seven "Deacons" of the "Hellenists" of Acts 6:1–6 (e.g., Thiering, *NovT* 12 [1970] 4; Lang, *ZDPV*, 94 [1978] 158–59) or the twelve tribes of Israel in contrast to the seven or seventy nations (Gentiles) of the world (e.g., Farrer, *JTS* 4 [1953] 4–5; Thiering, *NovT* 12 [1970] 3; Pesch, 1:355, 404; van Iersel, *NovT* 7 [1964] 181). In either case, this Feeding would then pertain to Jesus' ministry to the "Jews" and the subsequent Feeding to the "Gentiles."

Nothing in this account when taken by itself would lead necessarily to such a subtle reading beyond the obvious correlation between the number twelve and the same number of tribes and apostles. One could just as easily argue that the number devoid of any symbolism simply meant that each of the twelve disciples who had played such a prominent role in this story had received a basket of leftovers. But the possibility that more lies behind the numbers "twelve" and "seven" does arise when the two accounts are taken together in the larger context of Mark's narrative.

Mark's selection and arrangement of the two Feedings with the first in the Jewish setting of Galilee and the second in the gentile territory of the Decapolis (see *Comment* on 8:1; 7:31) may imply a subtle allusion behind "twelve" to the tribes of Israel. Certainly, the lack of correlation between the baskets (seven) and the number of disciples in 8:1–9 argues against connecting literally or symbolically the twelve baskets here with the twelve disciples or twelve apostles.

The abundance of food adds to the eschatological significance of the Feeding as God's gracious, abundant provision characteristic of the age of salvation. At the same time, this note recalls a similar story in 2 Kgs 4:44–45. Elisha feeds a hundred men with twenty loaves of barley bread with food left over. The story has several parallels including a servant at the outset who is puzzled by the prophet's command to feed the people with so little bread. If, as has been true for Elijah in previous stories (5:21–43; 6:14–16), a parallel is to be drawn with Elisha, this story shows by its magnitude that a "greater than Elisha" is here.

44 "Five thousand men" (πεντακισχίλιοι ἄνδρες) most likely specifies "men" rather than "persons" (cf. 8:9). Matt 14:21 renders this "without women and children." Not only does the lexical force of ἄνδρες (BGD, ad loc.) support this, but the grouping of the people in companies (6:40) reminiscent of Moses' grouping of the men of Israel in the wilderness and the grouping of the males at Qumran in their eschatological community provide a conceptual parallel (Friedrich, *TZ* 20 [1964] 18–19). As such, the statement does not intend to emphasize the magnitude of the miracle through deliberate understatement (so Matt 15:38; cf. Mark 8:9).

Much has been made of the numbers in this story. Some associations are inevitable; some too subtle (e.g., Farrer, *JTS* 4 (1953) 1–14; Thiering, *NovT* 12 [1970] 2–5). In contrast to 8:1–9 Jesus feeds a greater number (5000 "men" vs. 4000 total) with less (five loaves vs. seven loaves) and has more left over (twelve baskets vs. seven). The "twelve baskets," however, in a setting of the gathering of the people into groupings and the work of the Twelve might well point to the eschatological people of God symbolized by the sheep gathered and fed by God's promised "shepherd." Jesus comes as the promised one to inaugurate God's new day of blessing.

Explanation

Mark most likely found this story as the sequel to the raising of Jairus' daughter (5:21–43) in a miracle collection. Connected by a feeding motif (5:43), the two stories draw special parallels between Jesus' ministry and that of Elijah/Elisha (1 Kgs 17:10–16, 17–24; 2 Kgs 4:32–37, 42–44) who raised the dead and miraculously fed the hungry (in the same context!).

But Jesus was greater than Elijah or Elisha. Not only do the stories attest this by the contrast in manner (5:21–43) and scope (6:35–44) but also by showing Jesus to be the promised shepherd who feeds his sheep (6:34). The original introduction (6:34) described the masses in language reminiscent of an OT image for the People of God, "sheep without a shepherd" (Num 27:17; 1 Kgs 22:17; Ezek 34:5). By providing food for them, Jesus shows himself to be God's promised "servant David . . . (who) shall feed them and be their shepherd" (Ezek 34:23).

Mark does little to alter these traditional motifs. In fact, he underscores the surface connection between Jesus and Elijah by introducing the story of the Baptist's death with the question of whether Jesus was "Elijah" as well as the Baptist *redivivus* (6:14–16). And he uses the crowds as the backdrop for the disciples' report from their mission (6:31). Consequently, the reader, informed at the outset that Jesus is the "Messiah, Son of God" (1:1), an identity reinforced by Isaiah's promise (1:3), God's own voice (1:11) and even the demons' perception (1:24; 5:7), recognizes these connections and understands that Jesus is greater than Elijah.

But his handling of this pericope does introduce an additional motif. Instead of leaving the Feeding story as the sequel to the raising of Jairus' daughter, the evangelist has placed it in another segment of his narrative that opens with the mission of the Twelve (6:7–8:26). Basic to this segment is the disciples' failure to understand Jesus and his ministry despite their special relationship with him and their having participated so "successfully" in his work (6:7–13, 30–31). And Mark uses the story here to accent this theme.

The disciples share in Jesus' ministry by taking the initiative (6:35), directly participating in obtaining the food (6:37–38), and distributing it (6:41). Yet Mark, doing little to highlight their misunderstanding of Jesus' initial command to feed the crowd (6:37), makes clear by their reaction to Jesus in the following story (6:45–51) and by his concluding, redactional comment in 6:52 that they did not understand what the miracle was saying about who Jesus really was. He returns again to this motif with even greater development in 8:14–21 after the second Feeding story.

D. Jesus Walks on the Sea (6:45–52)

Bibliography

Achtemeier, P. "Toward the Isolation of Pre-Markan Miracle Catenae." *JBL* 89 (1970) 265–91. ———. "Person and Deed: Jesus and the Storm-Tossed Sea." *Int* 16 (1962) 169–76. **Betz, O.** "The Concept of the So-called 'Divine Man' in Mark's Christology." In *Studies in New Testament and Early Christian Literature*, FS A. P. Wikgren, ed. D. E. Aune. NTS 33. Leiden: Brill, 1972. 229–40. **Bonnard, P.** "La méthode historico-critique appliquée à Marc 6,30 à 7,30." *FoiVie* 77 (1978) 6–18. **Derrett, J. D. M.** "Why and How Jesus Walked on the Sea." *NovT* 23 (1981) 330–48. **Hegermann, H.** "Bethsaida und Gennesar: Eine traditions- und redaktionsgeschichtliche Studie zu Mk 4–8." In *Judentum, Urchristentum, Kirche*, FS J. Jeremias, ed. W. Eltester. BZNW 26. Berlin: Töpelmann, 1960. 130–40. **Heil, J. P.** *Jesus Walking on the Sea: Meaning and Gospel Functions of Matt 14:22–33, Mark 6:45–52 and John 6:15b–21.* AnBib 87. Rome: Pontifical Biblical Institute, 1981. **Jeremias, J.** *New Testament Theology.* 1971. **Kertelge, K.** *Die Wunder Jesu in Markusevangelium.* 1970. **Koch, D. A.** *Die Bedeutung der Wundererzählungen für die Christologie des Markusevangeliums.* 1975. **Kremer, J.** "Jesu Wandel auf dem See nach Mk 6,45–52." *BibLeb* 10 (1969) 221–32. **Quesnell, Q.** *The Mind of Mark: Interpretation and Method through the Exegesis of Mark 6,52.* AnBib 38. Rome: Pontifical Biblical Institute, 1969. **Ritt, H.** "Der 'Seewandel Jesu' (Mk 6, 45–52 par): Literarische und theologische Aspekte." *BZ* 23 (1979) 71–84. **Schenke, L.** *Die Wundererzählungen im Markusevangelium.* 1974. **Snoy, T.** "Marc 6,48." In *L'évangile selon Marc: Tradition et Redaction*, ed. M. Sabbe. BETL 34. Gembloux: Duculot, 1974.

347–63. ———. "La rédaction marcienne de la marche sur les eaux (Mk 6,45–52)."
ETL 44 (1972) 205–41, 433–81. **Theissen, G.** *The Miracle Stories of the Early Christian
Tradition.* 1983.

Translation

⁴⁵*And* Jesus[a] *immediately urged his disciples to embark into the boat and to go
ahead to the other side*[b] *toward Bethsaida, while he dismissed the crowd.* ⁴⁶*After
he had taken leave of them, he went to the mountain to pray.*

⁴⁷*When evening had come, the boat was out on the sea, and he was alone on
land.* ⁴⁸*And around the fourth watch of the night he saw the* disciples[a] *distressed
while rowing, for the wind was against them, and he went to them walking on the
sea and wanted to pass them by.* ⁴⁹*When they saw him walking on the sea, they
thought he was a ghost. And they screamed.* ⁵⁰*For all saw him and were terrified.
But he immediately spoke with them and said to them, "Take courage! It is I. Do
not be afraid any more!"* ⁵¹*And he entered the boat with them, and the wind
abated. And they were absolutely amazed.* ⁵²*For they did not understand about the
loaves. Rather their hearts were hardened.*

Notes

[a] Romanized words added from context.

[b] εἰς τὸ πέραν is omitted by 𝔭⁴⁵vid W *f*¹, possibly in an attempt to smooth out the geographical
details.

Form / Structure / Setting

Form-critically this miracle story apparently combines the characteristics
of a true epiphany and rescue story. Although "any miracle can be regarded
as an epiphany" (Theissen, *Miracle Stories,* 94), in an epiphany more narrowly
conceived the divinity of the person becomes apparent in the person and
not merely in the effects of the person's actions or attendant phenomena.
Theissen lists extraordinary visual and auditory phenomena, terrified reaction
of human beings, a word of revelation and a miraculous disappearance as
traits of an epiphany story (*Miracle Stories,* 95). By contrast, a rescue story
opens with a setting and description of an emergency, the miracle of rescue,
and a confirmation followed by a response of admiration (Theissen, *Miracle
Stories,* 99–103). The miracle is the focal point.

Most have taken this formally complex story as the final stage in a development from a rescue story to an epiphany story (Dibelius, 100), or from an
epiphany story to a rescue story (Gnilka, 1:267), or a combination of an
epiphany and a rescue story (Lohmeyer, 77). Theissen denies any convergence
of forms or stories by referring to this as a "soteriological epiphany," an
epiphany story that brings rescue (*Miracle Stories,* 101). But a closer look at
the story itself indicates that an earlier epiphany story has taken on aspects
of a rescue story, perhaps under the influence of 4:35–41 (Koch, *Wundererzählungen,* 105–6).

As to source, the only question arises over whether Mark found this story
as an isolated traditional unit (Snoy, *ETL* 44 [1972] 205–41), a part of another

cycle of miracle stories (Achtemeier, *JBL* 89 [1970] 282–84) or already combined with 6:32–44. The awkward dismissal of the crowds (6:45–46) together with the difficulties in the chronological sequence between the events in 6:30–44 and 6:45–52 (Haenchen, 252, n. 2) does suggest a combination of two originally independent stories, but the combination of a Feeding and a Crossing in 8:1–10 and John 6:1–21 argues for Mark having found these two combined in his tradition. When and why is even more speculative. Should John 6:1–21 be independent of Mark 6:34–52 (R. Brown, *The Gospel According to John, I–XII*, AB 29 [Garden City, NY: Doubleday, 1966] 236–50, 252–54), then this combination would have taken place early in the developing tradition. If, however, John 6:1–21 is related in any way to Mark or the tradition underlying 6:45–52, the combination may well have been made by the redactor of the miracle collection in view of the thematic relationship between 6:45–51, the last miracle in the cycle, and 4:35–41, the first miracle in the cycle.

Mark's own redaction is limited primarily to the explanatory sentence in 6:52 (Taylor, 330–31; Lohmeyer, 134; Kertelge, *Wunder*, 145–46; Koch, *Wundererzählungen*, 107; Pesch, 1:359).

The narrative flow takes some awkward turns in the story. It opens with Jesus ordering his disciples to cross to the other side while he dismisses the crowds (6:45). Then Jesus takes leave of what now has to be the crowds (6:46), though the disciples would fit more naturally. Toward the end of the story we seem to have two conclusions. First, Jesus appears to the terrified disciples, assures and calms them by identifying himself, and joins them in the boat (6:50–51a). Second, when he joins them in the boat, the winds cease and the disciples again react with great amazement (6:51b), which Mark explains to be the result of their failure to understand the previous feeding miracle (6:52). As will be seen in the *Comment*, the awkward elements in the narrative flow again supply important clues regarding a new direction for the story.

If Mark found this story in a collection of miracle stories, a summary report (6:53–56) follows to round off the collection just as it began (cf. 4:7–12). Thus this miracle comes as the final, climactic story in the series and stands juxtaposed to the first miracle in the series (4:35–41). Both take place at night on the storm-tossed sea. And as an epiphany story, it answers ("It is I," ἐγώ εἰμι) the question raised ("Who is this . . . ?") by the earlier rescue story.

For Mark's narrative, however, this story graphically illustrates the disciples' lack of understanding about Jesus. The evangelist enlarges on their question of 4:41 by using their amazement in 6:51 to point out their failure to grasp the meaning of the Feeding miracle (6:52). Therefore, even an epiphany, a self-revelation of Jesus, fails to answer their "Who is this?" question. Mark continues to expand this theme of the disciples' lack of understanding in this section, especially in the sequel (8:14–21) to the second feeding miracle.

Comment

45 "Immediately urged" (εὐθὺς ἠνάγκασεν) closely ties this story with the previous one and expresses a sense of urgency. But no grounds are given for this urgency. We have no hint of the crowd reacting to the Feeding miracle as in John 6:15. Thus to suggest the need to remove the disciples from the scene before they revealed the miraculous nature of the feeding to an overly enthusiastic crowd (Cranfield, 225) may be reading Mark too much in light of John.

"To the other side" (εἰς τὸ πέραν) has generally been taken to mean "the other side of the sea." If "Bethsaida" is the destination, this would mean that Jesus and the disciples had crossed to an "uninhabited place" (6:32–34) somewhere on the east side (6:35) where the feeding took place. This location, however, creates a major geographical problem for the present introduction of the Feeding miracle in which the crowd gathered by foot in advance of Jesus' arrival by water (see *Comment* on 6:32–33). Furthermore, we learn in 6:53 that the disciples actually land at Gennesaret, a location between Tiberias and Capernaum, southwest of Bethsaida.

These geographical details have caused some to conclude that 6:45–52 was originally a separate story which Mark, confused about the geography, first combined with 6:34–44 (e.g., Snoy, *ETL* 44 [1968] 234–36; Achtemeier, *JBL* 89 [1970] 282–84). Accordingly, the landing at Gennesaret (6:53) originally followed the Feeding (6:44) until Mark inserted the story of 6:47–51 with his introduction (6:45–46) and conclusion (6:52).

As we shall see, there are grounds for viewing this story to have been originally separate from the previous Feeding at one point in the tradition, but the geographical details do not necessarily support Markan redaction nor are they as contradictory as they may appear. If, as has been suggested in 6:30–44, a pre-Markan collector of miracle stories has extended an earlier introduction for the Feeding miracle by having Jesus and his disciples reach the area by boat while the crowd precedes them by land (6:32–33) and if the collector combined this story involving a boat trip at night with the story of the Feeding by again using his familiar "boat" and "crossing" motif, the geographical details would come from the pre-Markan redactor of the collection and offer no clues about Mark's own redaction.

Even the pre-Markan redactor of the miracle collection may not have been as reckless with the geographical details as has been assumed. If "the other side" (εἰς τὸ πέραν) does not necessarily refer to the "east side" of the sea (see *Comment* on 5:21), the geographical details can fit logically together. After "crossing" from the east side (Gerasa, 5:1–20) to some point on the west side (5:21), Jesus could have left the synagogue ruler's house to "cross" merely one of the many coves or small inlets of the sea on the west side (6:32) where he met a large crowd who had preceded him on foot (6:33–34). After feeding this crowd, he then sent his disciples "across" another stretch of the sea "in the direction of (πρός) Bethsaida" rather than "to Bethsaida" as their destination (Pesch, 1:359). Instead they land at "Gennesaret" (6:53) where they again encounter a crowd (6:54–55). Thus, the collector of the miracle stories consistently ties the units together by moving Jesus and the disciples from one location near the sea to another by boat.

"While he dismissed the crowd" (ἕως αὐτὸς ἀπολύει τὸν ὄχλον) has little to do with the present story but does add a connection to the previous Feeding. Was it necessary, however, to urge the disciples into a boat and onto the sea before dismissing the crowd? This rather strained opening suggests a bridge constructed by the pre-Markan redactor between two originally separate stories. The urgent compelling of the disciples to embark and set out in the direction of Bethsaida provides the necessary sea setting for this story (6:47–51). The dismissal of the crowds simply provides a connecting link with the preceding story.

46 "When he had taken leave of them" (ἀποταξάμενος αὐτοῖς) has to refer now to the "crowd" of 6:45. Yet the story involved Jesus and the disciples. Therefore, we may have here a remnant of the story's original introduction that spoke of Jesus' taking leave of his disciples to stay behind for a time of prayer.

"The mountain" (τὸ ὄρος) may relate to the epiphanic thrust of the story. God appeared to Israel from the mountain (Deut 33:2; Hab 3:3), and Jesus "appears" to the disciples after being on the mountain with God in prayer (Pesch, 1:360; Gnilka, 1:268). Here and in 1:35 Jesus takes time out from his public ministry to pray alone (cf. 14:32).

47 This verse clearly provides the setting for what follows. The boat with the disciples is out on the sea; Jesus is alone on land. But it also contains a temporal element in tension with the previous story.

"When evening had come" (ὀψίας γενομένης) generally refers to late afternoon or early evening and corresponds to a similar expression in the setting of the Feeding—"the hour was now quite late" (ἤδη ὥρας πολλῆς, 6:35). This correspondence hardly allows sufficient time to feed five thousand people, collect the leftovers, and dismiss the crowd. This tension suggests that the two stories, each with temporal settings essential to their respective narratives, were originally unrelated. The lateness of the hour offered the setting for a feeding; the coming night provides the appropriate setting for an epiphany.

We found a similar tension at the outset of the miracle collection between the stilling of the storm at night and the subsequent arrival at Gerasa apparently in broad daylight (cf. 4:35–41 and 5:1–20). It is a temporal tension within the collection that reflects the combination of fixed traditional materials whose various time frames were inherent to the stories. The redactor could combine the traditional units rather artificially with a travel motif (e.g., "boat," "crossing") but could not alter the temporal settings without doing violence to the crucial settings of the stories.

48 "Around the fourth watch of the night" (περὶ τετάρτην φυλακὴν τῆς νυκτός) reckons according to Roman time (Jews had three watches in a night) between three and six in the morning. In 1:35 Jesus had arisen "very early" to pray (cf. Ps 129:6 LXX). Similarly, God destroyed the Egyptians in the sea during the "morning watch" (Exod 14:24). This would mean that the disciples, who had left in late afternoon or evening, had struggled most of the night and made little headway.

"Distressed while rowing" (βασανιζομένους ἐν τῷ ἐλαύνειν) graphically describes their struggle and begs for an explanation. γάρ provides one at some point in the development of the tradition. They had encountered a contrary wind. Though typical of Mark's style, this γάρ-explanation is more than a parenthetic comment. The wind plays a further role in the story (6:51; see

John 6:18) and may have been added by the collector of the miracle stories under the influence of 4:35–41. The introduction of the contrary wind changes the thrust of the story from a pure epiphany story to a rescue story (6:51).

The note that Jesus "saw" (ἰδών) them may connote his miraculous "telescopic" vision to be able to see so far away in the dark hours of the fourth watch (cf. Philostratus, *Vit. Apol.* 5.30; 8.26, so Gnilka, 1:268). Others have noted the vantage point of the mountain (e.g., Taylor, 328–29). But limited visibility is assumed by the story, since the disciples mistook Jesus for a ghost when they saw him.

"He went to them walking on the sea" suggests his desire to aid them in their struggle. But the next statement throws the whole verse into confusion by asserting that he wanted "to pass them by" (παρελθεῖν αὐτούς). If the accent falls on the disciples and their struggle with the boat, this action is uncharacteristically calloused of Jesus and has led to several explanations (Sabbe, *Marc*, 347–61).

Some have taken "wanted" (ἤθελεν) as an auxiliary verb with future force (cf. μέλλειν) meaning "about to" (e.g., Cranfield, 226), a reading without NT parallel (BGD, *s.v.*). Others take it to express the disciples' mistaken impression of what Jesus was about to do (Taylor, 329), which illogically shifts the point of view from Jesus as the subject to the disciples. Another explanation takes the καί as epexegetic, "For he intended to pass their way" (van der Loos, *Miracles*, 652–53), rather than conjunctive. Still others take the statement at face value and explain it either in terms of Jesus' desire to test the disciples' faith (Schweizer, 142) or to remain incognito, alone (6:46–47), away from his disciples, in keeping with Mark's redactional notes in 3:13; 7:24 and 9:30 (Snoy, *Marc*, 361–63).

Yet this statement holds the key to the original thrust of the story. Jesus, not the disciples, stands at the center of the story. He had sent the disciples on their way. He had remained behind alone to pray on the mountain. He saw the disciples in distress, and he, walking on the sea, went to them (πρὸς αὐτοὺς περιπατῶν), an act that makes little sense if he desired to remain "alone." Nor does the desire to "walk on by" fit either the situation or Jesus' usual way of dealing with those in need.

Thus to "pass by them" (παρελθεῖν αὐτούς) most probably has its significance in the similar language used in an epiphany of God to Moses (Exod 33:19–23; 34:6) and Elijah (1 Kgs 19:11) as the One who "passed by them" in a moment of self-revelation (Lohmeyer, 133–34; Kremer, *BibLeb* 10 [1969] 226–28; Pesch, 1:361). Therefore, instead of a story about Jesus' rescue of his disciples who are distressed but not in danger (cf. 4:35–41), this is an epiphany story about Jesus' self-revelation to his own followers.

Much has been made of Jesus' "walking on the sea" (περιπατῶν ἐπὶ τῆς θαλάσσης). Some have attempted to avoid the difficulties involved by having Jesus walk on submerged stones or "mud flats" exposed by the wind (e.g., Derrett, *NovT* 23 [1981] 342–47) or rendering ἐπί as "by" (cf. John 21:1; Acts 5:23) rather than "on" the sea (e.g., Jeremias, *Theology*, 87). Not only do such explanations miss the epiphanic character of the story, but "on land" (ἐπὶ τῆς γῆς) of the preceding verse confirms the rendering "on the sea" (Taylor, 329). It may not be mere coincidence that both Moses and Elijah, who experienced an epiphany of God "passing by," also miraculously crossed a water barrier. Each, however, did so by parting the waters (Exod 14:21–22; 2 Kgs 2:8) and crossing on dry land. Though parallels to walking on water have been noted in hellenistic literature (van der Loos, *Miracles*, 655–57; Lucian, *Philopseudes*, 13; Porphyrius, *Vit. Pyth.* 29; Dio Chrysostom, *Or.* 3:30–31), the background here is clearly OT. Job 9:8, 11 LXX offers the closest verbal parallel.

49 The disciples respond out of fear rather than faith (Ernst, 196). Yet their reaction corresponds to that of an epiphany. First, they cannot believe their eyes and mistake Jesus for a "ghost" (φάντασμα). Then they scream (ἀνέκραξαν) in fear.

50 "For all saw him and were terrified" includes the whole group both as witnesses and as respondents. Jesus speaks to them first to assure them, "Take courage" (θαρσεῖτε), and then to comfort them, "Do not be afraid any more" (μὴ φοβεῖσθε). But not before giving them the reason by identifying himself, "It is I" (ἐγώ εἰμι), in between.

In the earlier pre-Markan setting, "It is I" (ἐγώ εἰμι) expressed more than an identification formula (cf. Taylor, 330). At the level of the reader/hearer Jesus' coming to the disciples from prayer on the mountain and his miraculous walking on the sea to "pass by" makes ἐγώ εἰμι an echo of the OT revelation formula of God (Exod 3:14; Isa 41:4; 43:10–11) and sets this story off from the post-Easter appearance stories (cf. Luke 24:37; Gnilka, 1:270).

The reader/hearer perceives what the disciples could have heard, and may have heard at the level of the pre-Markan tradition, a statement of self-revelation, a divine revelation to the disciples through Jesus who comes to them walking on the sea (Pesch, 1:362). Consequently, as the concluding story of the miracle collection, it provides the answer to the "Who is this?" question posed by the disciples after Jesus stills the storm in the opening story of the collection (4:41).

At the level of the story as told now by the evangelist, Jesus assures his disciples by identifying himself, "It is I." The following events do not diminish the epiphanic character of this statement, but Mark's explanation (6:52) of the disciples' response to the ensuing "rescue" (6:51) shows that the disciples did not recognize this epiphanic self-disclosure. Recognizing "it is I" to be simply Jesus' identification of himself, the frightened disciples are then "amazed" by what happens when he joins them in the boat because they did not "understand the loaves" (6:51).

51 "He entered the boat with them" (ἀνέβη πρὸς αὐτοὺς εἰς τὸ πλοῖον) may well have concluded the epiphany story at its earliest stage. The moment of revelation completed, Jesus joins his disciples in the boat. Formally, epiphany stories conclude with the sudden disappearance of the person or means of disclosure and they have no concluding response or further demonstration. But the current story continues by noting that the contrary wind of 6:48 suddenly abates (so 4:39) when Jesus enters the boat. This evokes a second response that is even more intense than the reaction to Jesus' appearance.

"They were absolutely amazed" (λίαν ἐκ περισσοῦ ἐν ἑαυτοῖς ἐξίσταντο). This conclusion, which may have been added at the time of the collection of these related stories, changes the thrust of the story from being primarily a self-disclosure by Jesus to a story about two miracles: Jesus' walking on the sea and his stilling the wind. Both leave the disciples absolutely astounded.

This second reference to the disciples' amazement, however, need not have been negative (cf. 2:12; 5:42). The calming of the wind simply completes the story by eliminating the obstacle that hindered them from reaching their destination. If Jesus is indeed the one in whom God reveals himself to the disciples, it follows that he can and will remove any hindrance in their way (cf. 4:35–41). When it happens, they are all the more awed (cf. Matt 14:33, "Truly, you are the Son of God!").

52 Mark, however, removes all ambiguity about the disciples' response by adding another of his characteristic γάρ-explanatory sentences that closely links this story with the Feeding of the crowd. Since these explanatory clauses always refer directly to what immediately precedes, the evangelist explains the disciples' astonishment at the miraculous quieting of the wind by pointing to their lack of understanding of the "loaves" (ἄρτοις). Since, however, their reaction followed Jesus' words of encouragement and particularly his identifying ἐγώ εἰμι in 6:49–50, it also indicates that the disciples heard ἐγώ εἰμι as an identifying "it is I" rather than as a divine disclosure in this epiphanic setting as well. Therefore, the disciples' failure to "understand the loaves" pertains not only to their astonishment at the miraculous abating of the wind but it also reveals their failure to comprehend the main event in this story. For Mark the disciples' amazement betrays their lack of understanding about who Jesus really is and recalls their earlier question that concludes the opening miracle in this series (4:41), "Who is this that the wind and sea obey?"

With a γάρ-explanation, the evangelist informs the reader that the disciples had missed something implicit in the previous Feeding miracle and this resulted in their amazement at Jesus' actions here. The ἄρτοις obviously refers to the story of the Feeding (so τοὺς ἄρτους—6:37, 38, 41, [44]; cf. 8:17–21) rather than being a theological symbol in itself (cf. Quesnell, *Mark,* 190–208). But what had they failed to understand? One is tempted to return to the clue given the reader at the outset of that story when Jesus looked with compassion at the crowd described as "sheep without a shepherd" (6:34). His subsequent action on their behalf could suggest that he was the promised, eschatological Shepherd (see *Comment* on 6:34).

But the evangelist moved away somewhat from emphasizing Jesus' response to the crowd's physical needs by adding that Jesus' compassion resulted in his "teaching them." This accent becomes Mark's superscript for the Feeding miracle (see *Comment* on 6:34). But we learn now that the disciples themselves had failed to comprehend what Jesus' "teaching" through word and deed had taught about himself, even though they had actually participated in the miracle itself by distributing the food and gathering the leftovers. Their astonishment reflects much more than their surprise at his ability to perform miracles. It reflects a deeper question about who this one really is who performs the miracles. By implication, had they understood the point of Jesus' "teaching" by word and deed, they would have grasped the significance of his self-disclosure in 6:50 and understood the quieting of the wind. But their "heart was hardened" (ἦν αὐτῶν ἡ καρδία πεπωρωμένη), a description given Jesus' opponents in 3:15 and repeated again with reference to the disciples in 8:17.

This explanation accents the disciples' failure to understand, a motif which first appeared in 4:13 (see *Comment* on 4:13) and comes to a head in 8:17–21 (see *Comment* on 8:17–21). At the same time, the disciples are depicted as "insiders" in 6:7–13, 30, who actively participate in Jesus' ministry, and they play a key role in the very incident they fail to understand (6:32–44). This tension in the portrait corresponds with 4:11, 13 where as "insiders" to whom the "mystery of the Kingdom" has been given (4:11, 34) they fail to understand the "parable" (4:13, see *Comment* on 4:13; cf. 7:18).

Explanation

An earlier form of the story, most likely separate from the Feeding of 6:35–44, depicted Jesus' coming to his disciples as an epiphany. Using language drawn from the experience of Moses and Elijah of God's self-revelation as a "passing by," the story underscores the epiphany by having Jesus identify himself with the pregnant, "It is I" or "I am." The "I am" formula in this epiphanic setting with Jesus coming from the mountain during the early morning hour of prayer to his own corresponds with the disciples' exclamation of Matt 14:33: "Truly, you are the Son of God." The formula answers the question of who Jesus is.

Later the story came to be associated with the Feeding miracle (6:45b; see John 6:1–21) and was used by the collector of the miracle cycle underlying Mark 4–6 to form an inclusio with the first miracle of the cycle, the stilling of the storm in 4:35–41. Both stories involve the disciples in a boat struggling against the elements. Whereas the first story concluded with the question posed by the disciples: "Who is this that the wind and the sea obey him?" (4:41), this story answered that question with the epiphanic appearance of Jesus and his "I am." In keeping with a recognition of the epiphany, their initial response was fear (6:49–50). Jesus' joining them in the boat and the immediate abating of the wind completes the story in a manner appropriate to Jesus' self-revelation and his manner of helping those in need. Their subsequent amazement at the miraculous calming of the wind (6:51), in contrast to the epiphanic response of amazement, formally corresponds to the wonder generated by a miracle (see 2:12; 5:42).

Mark, however, interprets the disciples' amazement negatively. By adding an explanation to the story (6:52), he changes the story's thrust from an epiphany that answers the earlier question of who Jesus is to a story that underscores the disciples' lack of understanding. In fact, he makes this change in thrust by basing it on their failure to understand the previous miracle of the loaves.

In so doing, Mark continues to develop his ironic portrait of the Twelve as "insiders" specially called to be with him (1:16–20; 3:13–19), privileged to have Jesus' personal instruction (3:31–35; 4:11, 13–20, 34), and commissioned to share directly in his ministry (6:7–13, 30, 35–44), yet like the "outsiders" they find Jesus' teaching in both word and deed to be more a "riddle" (4:13, 41; 6:37). He even accuses them here of "hardness of heart," a characteristic of Jesus' actual opponents in 3:5. This ironic portrait dominates the section (6:45–52; 7:18–23) that opens with their commission to share successfully in Jesus' ministry (6:7–13, 30) and concludes with a specific statement about their lack of understanding (8:14–21).

E. Healings in Gennesaret (6:53–56)

Bibliography

Achtemeier, P. "The Origin and Function of the Pre-Markan Miracle Catenae." *JBL* 91 (1972) 198–221. ———. "Toward the Isolation of Pre-Markan Miracle Catenae." *JBL* 89 (1970) 265–91. **Dalman, G.** *Sacred Sites and Ways: Studies in the Topography of the Gospels.* Tr. P. Levertoff. New York: Macmillan, 1935. **Egger, W.** *Frohbotschaft und Lehre.* 1974. **Hedrick, C. W.** "The Role of 'Summary Statements' in the Composition of the Gospel of Mark: A Dialogue with Karl Schmidt and Norman Perrin." *NovT* 26 (1984) 289–311. **Hegermann, H.** "Bethsaida und Gennesar: Eine traditions- und redaktionsgeschichtliche Studie zu Mk 4–8." In *Judentum, Urchristentum, Kirche,* FS J. Jeremias, ed. W. Eltester. BZNW 26. Berlin: Töpelmann, 1960. 130–40. **Kertelge, K.** *Die Wunder Jesu im Markusevangelium.* 1970. **Koch, D.-A.** *Die Bedeutung der Wundererzählungen für die Christologie des Markusevangeliums.* 1975. **Kuhn, H.-W.** *Ältere Sammlungen im Markusevangelium.* 1971. **Maloney, E. C.** *Semitic Interference in Marcan Syntax.* SBLDS 51. Chico, CA: Scholars Press, 1981. **Snoy, T.** "La rédaction marcienne de la marche sur les eaux (Mc 6,45–52)." *ETL* 44 (1968) 205–41, 433–81.

Translation

[53] *Crossing to land they came to Gennesaret* [a] *and entered the harbor.* [54] *And when they had come out of the boat, the* people,[b] *immediately recognizing* Jesus,[b] [55] *ran through that whole region and began to bring the ill on their* [c] *mats* [d] *to where they heard he was.* [56] *And wherever he entered villages, cities or farms, they would place the sick in the market places* [e] *and appealed to him that they might touch the tassel of his robe. As many as touched him were made well.*

Notes

[a] Γεννησαρ in D it vg[mss] sy[s.p].
[b] Romanized words added. The main verb (περιέδραμον) is impersonal.
[c] Perhaps a "deictic article" (Maloney, *Interference,* 105–6) referring to objects at hand in the mind of the reader (τοῖς κραβάττοις).
[d] See 2:4, *Note* e.
[e] Technically only cities and larger villages had "market places" (ἀγοραῖς). Thus the term is corrected to "wide streets" (πλατείαις) in D 565 700.

Form / Structure / Setting

Form-critically, this pericope represents a classic summary report. But one must remember that summary reports in Mark do not simply offer a summary of what has preceded or what will follow. Each summary generalizes traits of individual stories. They make their own broad statement about Jesus' ministry.

As to source, the views run the gamut from essentially a pre-Markan tradition (Schmidt, 195; Egger, *Frohbotschaft*, 134; Ernst, 198; Schmithals, 1:339) to a complete Markan construction (Bultmann, 341; Gnilka, 1:271–72; Kertelge, *Wunder*, 35, n. 32; *Wundererzählungen*, 169; Achtemeier, *JBL* 89 [1970] 284) with some who attribute the composition to Mark "on the basis of tradition" (Lohmeyer, 136; Taylor, 331; Cranfield, 229).

Gnilka (1:272, n. 2), for example, assigns this to Mark's redaction because of style (genitive absolute; ἄρχεσθαι with infinitive—6:54–55) and vocabulary (εὐθύς, κράβαττος, κώμη, ὅσος, οἱ κακῶς ἔχοντες). But granting the "Markan" character of such style and lexical elements does not necessarily mean a Markan composition. In fact, this unit has many connections with previous parts of the pre-Markan miracle collection.

Mark's only other and equally awkward use of διαπερᾶν for a sea crossing occurs in 5:21 (see *Comment* on 5:21). Similarly, with the exception of the traditional story of John the Baptist's death (6:17–29), the genitive absolute construction has only occurred to this point in the Gospel in the "seams" of the miracle collection, and the same genitive absolute (ἐξελθόντων αὐτῶν ἐκ τοῦ πλοίου) appears in the seam of 5:2 (see *Comment* on 5:21). The motif of the public recognition and pursuit of Jesus occurs in the seam of 6:33. "Region" (χώραν) appears in 5:1 and 10 (see *Comment* on 5:1), and the listing of "towns, cities and farms" is atypical of Mark, though "city" and "farms" appear together in the Gerasene story (5:14). Finally, the theme of healing by touch has its locus in the healing of the woman with a hemorrhage (5:25–29) after being introduced in the summary report of 3:7–12 (3:10).

These points of connection with elements of a possible miracle collection strongly suggest that this summary report came from the redactor of that collection. To the extent that these connections are more distinctive of certain related stories than of the rest of Mark's Gospel they point to a pre-Markan tradition. Add to this evidence the uncharacteristic depiction of Jesus as totally passive, without one reference to his teaching or exorcising and you have a unit not unlike the tradition underlying 3:7–12 which forms the opening bracket or introduction to a series of miracle stories for which this summary forms the concluding bracket that accents the popularity of Jesus' healing ministry.

As to structure, the summary report opens with a statement of Jesus' arrival in Gennesaret (6:53). From that point on he is the focal point of the narrative but not the subject. Two statements highlight his healing ministry by describing the actions of the friends of those who are ill who carry the sick to Jesus (6:54–55) or make certain that they are placed where they might be healed by touching his clothing (6:56). The narrator then concludes the summary with a statement of the results: "As many as touched him were healed." The pervasive use of the imperfect tense provides the sense of an extended period covered by the report.

As to setting, assuming this summary concluded a series of miracle stories which Mark has incorporated into his Gospel (3:7–12; 4:35–5:43; 6:32–52; 6:53–56), it offered an appropriate finale for materials depicting Jesus' power through his miracles. The collection included more than simply "healing miracles" (cf. 4:35–41; 6:32–52), but the introductory summary (3:7–12) and this concluding summary (6:53–56) depict the peoples' helplessness primarily in terms of their physical illnesses.

Mark has chosen to use these summaries differently from their role in the miracle collection. First, he uses the opening summary in 3:7–12 to bring to a head a section of healings (1:21–3:12) that began with (1:21–28) and included exorcisms (1:34). Consequently, he appropriately added Jesus' response to "unclean spirits" as the concluding note of that summary (3:11–12). The summary of 6:53–56, however, does not play the same role as a structural marker in his Gospel (cf. 6:6b as the concluding summary for a section accenting Jesus' teaching in 3:20–6:6a). Rather the evangelist, following his tradition, employs this summary as another miracle story without any reference to the previous themes of either exorcisms (3:11–12) or teaching (6:6b).

Comment

53 "Gennesaret" (Γεννησαρέτ) found only here (par Matt 14:34) and in Luke 5:1 is "foreign to Aramaic-speaking people" (Dalman, *Sites*, 121). Most likely a derivative of the more common "Gennesar" (Γεννησαρ, so 1 Macc 11:67; Josephus, *Ant.* 5.7; 18.2.1; *War* 3.10.7), it identifies the fertile, densely populated, three-by-one-mile plain along the western shore of the Sea of Galilee between Tiberius and Capernaum. Lagrange (177), with few followers, suggests a village whose name comes from the plain by adding a feminine suffix to Gennesar.

This apparent landing at Gennesaret creates another geographical tension in Mark's story. In 6:45 Jesus sent his disciples ahead by boat in the direction of Bethsaida on the north shore. But they land far short at Gennesaret. Why?

For some interpreters, the answer lies in rearranging the text. For example, some take this note (6:53) to have originally concluded the feeding miracle (Grundmann, 187) and the sending of the disciples to Bethsaida (6:45–51) to have preceded the story of 8:22–26 that notes their arrival (Snoy, *ETL* 44 [1968] 234–36; Achtemeier, *JBL* 89 [1970] 281–84). Schmithals (1:339), on the other hand, locates 6:53 originally between 5:20 and 5:22 and Marxsen (*Mark*, 69, n. 52) assigns it to 7:1–23. In any case, the confusion supposedly results from the evangelist's ignorance of his geography.

Other interpreters accept the tension as stemming from the combination of two originally independent traditions (6:45–51; 6:53–56) but take it as attesting to the relative insignificance of the geography in relation to the significance of the miracles (Egger, *Frohbotschaft*, 137–38; Ernst, 198). In other words, the focus on Jesus' miraculous activity overshadowed any logical geographical concerns of either Mark or his tradition in bringing the two originally independent traditions together.

And others explain the tension away. For example, some attribute the change in destination to the strong wind encountered by the disciples in the previous story (Taylor, 332; Lane, 240), an answer that seems somewhat at odds with the calming of the wind when Jesus embarked into the boat (6:51). Some argue that they actually reached Bethsaida in 6:45–52, a place of rest and repose in Mark. This notice of arrival at Gennesaret, a place of Jesus' ministry among the crowds in Mark, refers to yet another trip by boat, perhaps from Bethsaida (Hegermann, *Judentum*, 133–34). Pesch simply concludes that they turned to shore at Gennesaret as planned after the wind died down, since 6:45 only states that they were headed "toward Bethsaida" without necessarily implying they were actually sailing "*to* Bethsaida" (Pesch, 1:359; see *Comment* on 5:45).

Assuming, as we have argued, that this summary report comes from the pre-Markan redactor of a miracle cycle, the unnecessary presence of a specific geographical location, "Gennesaret," suggests the use of a tradition. Since 6:53 could hardly have stood alone in the tradition, its original place might well have been at the conclusion of the feeding in 6:44 (cf. John 6:23, "Tiberias near to the place where they ate the bread . . ."). The "crossing on land" (διαπεράσαντες ἐπὶ τὴν γῆν) to Gennesaret, a more natural use of διαπερᾶν (see *Comment* on 5:21), does not imply by boat. But when the story of the Walking on the Sea (6:45–52) was combined with the Feeding of 6:32–44, the reference to Bethsaida (6:45) replaced this geographical note which then became the locale (6:53) for the narrator's concluding summary of 6:54–56. And since, as Pesch has noted (1:359), the disciples were sailing *toward* (πρός) Bethsaida rather than *to* (εἰς) Bethsaida (6:45), the redactor could insert 6:45–51 between 6:44, 53 and have them now land by boat (προσωρμίσθησαν) after "crossing" (see *Comment* on 5:21) to Gennesaret without convoluting the geography.

54 This verse contains motifs expressed almost verbatim in two earlier seams of 5:2 (disembarking from the boat) and 6:33 (the crowd's recognition of Jesus).

56 This verse specifies the general thought of 6:55. Jesus stands at the center of the activity, but all the activity is going on around him. He does not even speak. Yet the broader context of Mark 6 and 7 hardly suggests that he had resigned himself to the public's inability to receive or their lack of preparation for receiving the word (cf. Lane, 241; similarly Taylor, 333; Schweizer, 153).

The accent falls on Jesus' healing ministry which takes place by the sick touching a part of his clothing. The curtailing of Jesus' activity underscores his power to heal through the action of the sick in touch with him rather than his *passivity* (Koch, *Wundererzählungen*, 171).

Taken out of context, one might read this as nothing less than magic (Kertelge, *Wunder*, 36; Grundmann, 187). But read in the context of 3:10, where the sick sought to touch Jesus, 3:27–28, where the woman sought to touch his clothes, the desire here to touch only the extremity of his clothing represents an intensification or progression not so much in Jesus' power to heal as the faith of those seeking his help. One has to read this summary of the miracle collection in view of the woman's healing and its explication based on her faith (5:25–34) that lies at the core of that miracle cycle. And one must read this also in view of Jesus' limited healing ministry at Nazareth (6:5–6) because of lack of faith. All three accounts point the reader to the posture of the people involved more than to Jesus' "power" (see *Comment* on 5:30).

"Tassel" (κρασπέδου) could refer to the "hem" of a garment (BGD, *s.v.*). But it most likely refers to one of four "tassels" (צִיצִת, *ṣîṣit*) worn by Jewish men on their robes in keeping with the Mosaic prescription of Num 15:38–39 LXX; cf. Deut 22:12. These tassels consisted of four blue and white threads to remind the wearer to do the commandments of the Lord (Matt 23:5).

The efficacious power of Jesus displayed throughout this miracle collection (3:7, 9–10; 4:35–5:43; 6:32–51) is seen in the concluding statement: "As many as touched him were made well" (ἐσώζοντο, see *Comment* on 5:34).

Explanation

This summary report coming most likely from the redactor of a miracle collection underlying Mark 4:35–6:53 (4:35–5:43; 6:32–56) formed an inclusio with an opening summary account now found behind Mark 3:7–12 (3:7, 9–10). Both summaries accent the press of the crowds to bring their sick to Jesus for healing. Both accounts accent Jesus' healing through the touch of those seeking his healing (3:10; 6:56).

The focus on the initiative of the sick to touch Jesus, however, has its own distinctive thrust as seen by the story of the woman with a hemorrhage that lies at the heart of this cycle (5:25–34). In the dialogue with the woman, Jesus makes clear that her faith that led to her actions was really behind her healing ("Your faith has made you well," 5:34), a faith that was crucial in Jesus' response to Jairus' request for help in the ultimate healing miracle of raising someone from the dead (5:36). Furthermore, the other miracles in the cycle point to Jesus' person rather than to his power per se. The first (4:35–41) and last miracle (6:45–51) involve the disciples' question ("Who is this?" 4:41) and the answer ("I am," 6:50) about Jesus' identity. The Gerasene demoniac (5:1–20) recognizes Jesus both through his submissive actions and by his word ("Son of the Most High God," 5:7). And the feeding (6:32–44) portrays Jesus as the promised Shepherd who feeds God's people (6:34).

Mark recognizes this point of the miracle collection. By utilizing a major part of the miracle cycle in a section that emphasizes Jesus' teaching (3:20–4:34), by adding the motif of Jesus' teaching in 6:34b and by introducing both Jesus' "mighty works" and his "teaching" in the scene in Nazareth (6:1–6a), the evangelist shows that Jesus' deeds make a statement about who he really is (cf. 1:21–28). Jesus' words and work proclaim the "good news of God," the coming of God's sovereign rule in his ministry (1:14–15). And Mark, by introducing the Nazareth story into the miracle cycle (6:1–6a), also recognizes the essential role that faith played in Jesus' response to the needy, a motif which he found in his tradition (e.g., 5:34, 36).

Nevertheless, by using this summary account as another miracle story pointing to the believing response of the sick and needy, the evangelist sets their response in stark contrast to the disciples whom he has just depicted as failing to comprehend Jesus and his ministry (6:52). The evangelist in no way implies that the faith of those seeking Jesus' healing is inadequate, limited to their fascination with the miraculous. But he does hold especially accountable for their density of mind those whom Jesus had selected to accompany him and to share in his ministry. This theme appears again in 7:17–18 and comes to a climax in 8:14–21.

F. On Tradition and Defilement (7:1–13)

Bibliography

Banks, R. *Jesus and the Law in the Synoptic Tradition.* SNTSMS 28. Cambridge: University Press, 1975. **Berger, K.** *Die Gesetzesauslegung Jesu,* I. WMANT 40. Neukirchen-Vluyn: Neukirchener Verlag, 1972. **Booth, R. P.** *Jesus and the Laws of Purity: Tradition History and Legal History in Mark 7.* JSNTSup 13. Sheffield: University of Sheffield Press, 1986. **Carlston, C. E.** "The Things That Defile (Mark vii. 14) and the Law in Matthew and Mark." *NTS* 15 (1968–69) 57–69. **Derrett, D. J. M.** "KOPBAN, O EΣTIN ΔΩPON." *NTS* 16 (1969–70) 364–68. **Falk, Z. W.** "On Talmudic Vows." *HTR* 59 (1966) 309–12. **Fitzmyer, J.** "The Aramaic Qorban Inscription from Jebel Hallet Et-turi and Mk 7:11/Mt 15:5." *JBL* 78 (1959) 60–65 = *Essays in the Semitic Background of the New Testament.* London: Geoffrey Chapman, 1971. 93–100. **Hengel, M.** "Mk 7,3 πυγμῇ: Die Geschichte einer exegetischen Aporie und der Versuch ihrer Lösung." *ZNW* 60 (1969) 182–98. ———. "Die Ursprünge der christlichen Mission." *NTS* 18 (1971) 15–28. **Hübner, H.** *Das Gesetz in der synoptischen Tradition.* Witten: Luther, 1973. ———. "Mark vii. 1–23 und das 'jüdisch-hellenistische' Gesetzes Verständnis." *NTS* 22 (1976) 319–45. **Kümmel, W. G.** "Äussere und innere Reinheit bei Jesus." In *Das Wort und die Wörter,* FS G. Friedrich, ed. H. Balz and S. Schulz. Stuttgart: Kohlhammer, 1973. 35–46. = *Heilsgeschehen und Geschichte,* II. MTS 16. Marburg: N. G. Elwert, 1978. 117–29. ———. "Jesus und der jüdische Traditionsgedanke." *ZNW* 33 (1934) 105–30. = *Heilsgeschehen und Geschichte,* I, ed. E. Grässer, O. Merk, A. Fritz. MTS 3. Marburg: N. G. Elwert, 1965. **Lambrecht, J.** "Jesus and the Law: An Investigation of Mk 7, 1–23." *ETL* 53 (1977) 24–82. **Lührmann, D.** "Die Pharisäer und die Schriftgelehrten im Markusevangelium." *ZNW* 78 (1987) 169–85. ———. ". . . Womit er alle Speisen für rein erklärten (Mk 7,19)." *WD* 16 (1981) 71–92. **McEleney, N. J.** "Authenticating Criteria and Mark 7, 1–23." *CBQ* 34 (1972) 431–60. **McHardy, W. D.** "Mark 7, 3—A Reference to the Old Testament?" *ExpTim* 87 (1976) 119. **Marxsen, W.** "Redaktionsgeschichtliche Erklärung der sogenannten Parabeltheorie des Markus." In *Der Exeget als Theologe: Vorträge zum Neuen Testament.* Gütersloh: Mohn, 1968. 13–28. **Merkel, H.** "Mk 7,14—das Jesuswort über die innere Verunreinigung." *ZRGG* 20 (1968) 340–63. **Neusner, J.** "'First Cleanse the Inside.'" *NTS* 22 (1975–76) 486–95. ———. "The Idea of Purity in Ancient Judaism." *JAAR* 43 (1975) 15–26. **Paschen, W.** *Rein und Unrein: Untersuchung zur biblische Wortgeschichte.* SANT 24. München: Kösel, 1970. **Quesnell, Q.** *The Mind of Mark: Interpretation and Method through the Exegesis of Mark 6, 52.* AnBib 38. Rome: Pontifical Biblical Institute, 1969. **Reynolds, S. M.** "Πυγμῇ (Mark 7, 3) as 'Cupped Hand.'" *JBL* 85 (1966) 87–88. ———. "A Note on Dr. Hengel's Interpretation of Πυγμῇ in Mark 7, 3." *ZNW* 62 (1971) 295–96. **Ross, J. M.** "With the Fist." *ExpTim* 87 (1976) 374–75. **Suhl, A.** *Die Funktion der alttestamentlichen Zitaten und Anspielungen im Markusevangelium.* Gütersloh: Mohn, 1965. **Weis, P. R.** "A Note on ΠΥΓΜΗΙ." *NTS* 3 (1956–57) 233–36. **Zeitlin, S.** "Korban." *JQR* (1962) 160–63. ———. "Korban: A Gift." *JQR* 59 (1968) 133–35.

Translation

[1] *The Pharisees and some of the scribes who had come from Jerusalem gathered around Jesus.*[a] [2] *And when they saw that some of his disciples were eating the loaves with defiled hands,*[b] *that is, with unwashed hands*[c]—[3] *for the Pharisees and many of the Jews, keeping the tradition of the elders, do not eat if they do not*

wash their hands with cupped hands.[d] [4] *They do not eat* anything[a] *from the market-place if it is not thoroughly washed.*[e] *And there are many other* customs[a] *which they have received as tradition*[f] *to keep, like the thorough washings of cups, pitchers, copper pots*[g]— [5]*and*[h] *the Pharisees and scribes asked him, "Why do your disciples not walk according to the tradition of the elders but eat with defiled hands?"*

[6]*And he said to them, "Isaiah did a good job of prophesying concerning you hypocrites, as it is written, 'This people honors me with their lips, but their heart is far from me.* [7]*They worship me in vain, teaching as teachings human commandments.'* [8]*Neglecting the commandment of God you keep the tradition of men."*

[9]*And he said to them, "You do a good job of nullifying the commandment of God in order that you might establish*[i] *your tradition.* [10]*For Moses said, 'Honor your father and mother,' and 'Let the one who speaks evil of one's father or mother be put to death.'* [11]*But you say, 'If anyone should say to one's father or mother, "Whatever you might be benefited from me is Corban"' (which means "gift"),* [12]*you no longer allow that person to do anything for his or her father or mother,* [13]*thus annulling the word of God with your tradition which you have passed on. And you do many similar things."*

Notes

[a]Romanized words added.

[b]Lohmeyer (139, n. 1) notes that either ἰδόντες τινὰς . . . ἐσθίοντας (so A D W Θ 02744 *f*[1.13]; so 1:10; 6:48, 49) or ἰδόντες ὅτι ἐσθίουσίν τινες (cf. 2:16; 9:25) would have been more appropriate. Taylor (334) and Cranfield (231) take the τινὰς to be a hyperbaton (the "displacement of the subject or object of a subordinate clause so that it becomes the subject or object of another clause," Cranfield, 231).

[c]This sentence breaks off (an anacoluthon) and awkwardly resumes in 7:5. Several mss seek to smooth out the awkward hyperbaton by omitting ὅτι and substituting ἐσθίοντας for ἐσθίουσιν (A D W Θ *f*[1.13] Majority text). Read the text with ℵ B L Δ 892 1241 1424 *pc*.

[d]The difficult πυγμῇ is rendered as πυκνά ("often") in ℵ W f vg syp.h bo, omitted by Δ sys sa and read by A B (D) L Θ 0131 0274 *f*[1.13] Majority text it.

[e]Read βαπτίσωνται A D W Θ*f*[1.13] Majority text latt meaning "to immerse" rather than ῥαντίσωνται meaning "to sprinkle" (ℵ B *pc* sa).

[f]"Received as tradition" renders the technical use of παρέλαβον.

[g]A D W Θ *f*[1.13] Majority text latt syp.h samss Nestle[26] (brackets) read καὶ κλινῶν but strong witnesses omit it (ℵ B L Δ *pc* bo). The emphasis on eating utensils makes this reading a likely gloss by one who understood the passage in light of Lev 15 rather than as the "tradition of the elders."

[h]The sentence begins with καί, as though it had not begun in 7:1–2.

[i]Read στήσητε with D W Θ *f* 28 565 it sys.p as counter to ἀθετεῖτε. Cf. τηρήσητε with ℵ A L *f*[13] Majority text vg syh (τηρῆτε in B).

Form/Structure/Setting

Form-critically this pericope has undergone numerous analyses with vastly diverging results. The diversity of opinion relates both to the text as it stands as well as to possible traditional units from earlier settings. For example, Cranfield (231) and Lambrecht (*ETL* 53 [1977] 25, 57) take Mark's story like Matt 15:1–20 to be conceived as a unit (Cranfield, a unit of tradition; Lambrecht, a Markan redactional product), though neither offers a formal classification of the complex unit. By contrast, Taylor (334, 339, 342) finds here three related units with 7:1–8 the "pronouncement story" to which Mark has appended the related "isolated sayings" of 7:9–13 and 7:14–23.

Yet an analysis of the material from the perspective of its history of tradition appears to support the formal division of 7:1–23 into two separate forms, a controversy narrative and a teaching narrative (e.g., Kümmel, *Heilsgeschehen,* 2:29; idem, *Wort,* 37; Pesch, 1:367–77; Gnilka, 1:277–78; Ernst, 200). The controversy narrative (7:1–13) consists of a setting (7:1–2) with parenthetical explanation (7:3–4), the accusation (7:5), and Jesus' response regarding the question of the tradition of the elders based on Isa 29:13 and illustrated by the Corban example (7:6–8, 9–13). The teaching narrative (7:14–23) first addresses the crowd with a parabolic saying set in antithetical parallelism (7:14–15) which becomes the basis for private instruction for the disciples that explicates both halves of the parallelism (7:18–19, 20–23).

The issue becomes acute when one asks whether Mark (or his tradition) understood these two forms to be treated as separate episodes pertaining to different topics (i.e., tradition of the elders and clean and unclean food) or one episode about defilement. The key lies in the much more complex issue of the development of the multilayered tradition underlying the text as it now stands as well as in its present setting in Mark's Gospel.

The parenthetical comments in 7:2, 3–4, 19c point to more than one level in the development of this material. But attempting to define the discrete traditional units, their original *Sitz im Leben* and the tradition history in which they were brought together has produced many hypotheses. The discussion has generally divided over whether 7:6–13 in part or as a whole (e.g., Bultmann, 61; Taylor, 334; Kümmel, *Heilsgeschehen,* 2:29; Hübner, *Gesetz,* 143–44; Gnilka, 1:227; Pesch, 1:367) or 7:15 (e.g., Grundmann, 188–89; Schweizer, 146; Berger, *Gesetzesauslegung,* 461–62; Lambrecht, *ETL* 53 [1977] 66–69; Lührmann, *WD* 16 [1981] 81; Booth, *Purity,* 67) originally answered the opponents' charge. Behind this discussion lies the fundamental question of whether the original charge pertained to "unwashed hands" or to the "tradition of the elders."

An examination of the constituent elements suggests a development of several stages in the tradition that reflects the changing concerns of the early community (Berger, *Gesetzesauslegung,* 461–65; Lührmann, *WD* 16 [1981] 81–91; Booth, *Purity,* 55–114; cf. Lambrecht, *ETL* 53 [1977] 66–67, see 28–39 for a good survey of viewpoints). The original core, whose roots may well extend into Jesus' ministry, lies behind 7:1–2, 5b, 15 containing the situation (Jesus, the "Pharisees" and the disciples), charge (eating with "defiled hands"), and response (in the antithetical form of a wisdom saying).

This core provided the basis for addressing a related question in the primitive Church about the validity of the "tradition of the elders" by the identification of the ritual cleansing of one's hands with the "tradition of the elders" (7:5a). The addition of Jesus' response based on Isa 29:13 (7:6–8) and the Corban example (7:9–13) addressed this broader issue of the Jewish Christian community. Jesus' original response (7:15), which became separated from 7:5 by the intervening 7:6–13, still addressed the specific issue of eating with "defiled hands" (7:5b). But removed from the immediate context of 7:5b, the parabolic saying in 7:15 attracted the commentary found in 7:17–19, 20–22 (23) which refocused the thrust of 7:15 more toward the question of food that had been eaten with defiled hands.

The subsequent parenthetical explanations of the issues in 7:2, 3–4 reflect a development aimed at a "gentile" Christian audience for whom the Jewish practices and "traditions" were unknown. The parenthetical comment in 7:19c that draws the logical implications of 7:15 interpreted by 7:18b–19 now addresses the issue of "clean and unclean" food (e.g., Lev 11–19). These comments clearly assume a setting in the Church where more than ritual defilement or the "tradition of the elders" was at stake.

The final stage in the formal development (if not already precipitated by the modifications in the previous stage) came when 7:15 was set off from 7:1–13 by the change of scene in 7:14 and 7:17–18a. This most likely stemmed from the evangelist's redaction (see *Comment* on 7:14, 17). Form-critically, this last stage produced two separate forms addressing related but different issues (controversy narrative—7:1–13; and teaching narrative—7:14–23).

As to source, despite those who would take 7:1–23 to be a collage of traditions brought together by Mark (e.g., Lambrecht, *ETL* 53 [1977] 24–73; Quesnell, *Mind*, 90–91), the development traced above suggests that Mark found the mix of traditions—some rooted in Jesus' ministry (e.g., 7:[6–7] 9–13, 15), others in the Church's elaboration (e.g., 7:18b–19, 20–22 [23])—already combined. Less certain is the extent to which Mark found the parenthetical elements in the tradition or added them for his audience (see *Comment* on 5:2, 3–4, 19) and whether Mark found the shift in scenes in 7:14, 17 in the tradition or added it (see *Comment* on 7:14, 17).

As to structure, the disciples' behavior noted in 7:2 now gives occasion for Jesus' opponents to question why the disciples do not "walk according to the tradition of the elders" (7:1–2, 5). He responds by first arguing *ad hominem* from Isa 29:13 about the opponents' "hypocrisy" (7:6–8) and then illustrating the point by using the example of Corban (7:9–13). The specific occasion, "defiled hands" (κοιναῖς χερσίν), has been absorbed by the larger question of "tradition." The parenthetical comments of 7:2, 3–5 interrupt the narrative flow to inform the reader about Jewish practices and underscore the focus on the "tradition of the elders" (7:3—κρατοῦντες τὴν παράδοσιν τῶν πρεσβυτέρων; 7:4—ἄλλα πολλά ἐστιν ἃ παρέλαβον κρατεῖν).

The setting in Mark's narrative for these two pericopes dealing with defilement, just prior to Jesus' excursion into gentile territory where he has dealings with both the "Greek, Syrophoenician" woman (7:24–30) and the deaf mute in the Decapolis (7:31–37), raises the issue of social boundaries. By confronting the purity laws that set "the Jews" apart (illustrated by 7:2–4 and 7:19b) as focusing on externals rather than what is from within, Jesus can move freely into the gentile area and among Gentiles. As Gnilka (1:279) puts it, a spiritual break precedes a geographical break in Jesus' ministry with Israel. For Mark, therefore, the original issue of purity seen in 7:1–5, almost eclipsed by the later focus on the "tradition of the elders," becomes central again to show Jesus' response to it.

At the same time, by referring to some of the disciples' eating "the loaves" (pl. τοὺς ἄρτους), Mark may be deliberately connecting this scene with "the loaves" (τοὺς ἄρτους) in 6:41, 44 and the reference to "the loaves" (τοὺς ἄρτους) in 8:14–21. The connection between the disciples' lack of understanding of "the loaves" (τοὺς ἄρτους) in 6:51 and 8:14–21 corresponds as well to their lack of understanding in 7:15 (cf. Quesnell, *Mind*, 228–29).

Comment

1 The setting is a typical scene without any temporal or geographical details. The participle ἐλθόντες can modify either "the Pharisees and some scribes" or simply "some scribes." Since Mark uses a similar phrase to refer to the scribes in 3:22 (see *Comment* on 3:22), it likely qualifies the latter here. By qualifying them in this manner, the evangelist apparently sets the scene in Galilee (cf. 6:56).

2 See *Notes* b, c, for the awkward construction of this verse.

"The loaves," lit. "the breads" (τοὺς ἄρτους), instead of the normal singular ἄρτον without the article meaning "to eat food" (Lohmeyer, 139, n. 1), may well allude to "the loaves" of 6:41, 44 (cf. τοὺς ἄρτους, the "leftovers" of 6:43?). If so, it ties this scene to that of "the loaves" which the disciples did not understand in 6:52 (cf. 7:17–18a) and will not understand after the feeding in 8:1–9 (see 8:14–21).

"With defiled hands" (κοιναῖς χερσίν) uses "common" (κοιναῖς) in the biblical sense of "ritually unclean" (cf. Acts 10:14, 28; 11:8; Rev 21:27; see Paschen, *Rein*, 165–68). A parenthetical comment "with unwashed hands" (τοῦτ᾽ ἔστιν ἀνίπτοις; cf. Lev 15:11 LXX) clarifies the meaning for the reader. It assumes the reader is either unfamiliar with the technical κοιναῖς χερσίν or the Jewish custom of "hand washing." If this explanation comes from the same redactor as the explanatory parenthesis in 7:3–4, it refers to the latter (cf. 7:3a, 4). Although this comment is frequently assigned to Mark (e.g., Lambrecht, *ETL* 53 [1977] 40), the evangelist's consistent use of ὅ ἐστιν elsewhere (cf. 3:17; 7:11, 34; 12:42; 15:16, 42) rather than τοῦτ᾽ ἔστιν suggests the explanation was pre-Markan, though Mark may well have changed the more idiomatic ἄρτον ἐσθίειν to the contextually related τοὺς ἄρτους.

3 Many interpreters have also assigned this parenthetical comment to Markan redaction (e.g., Taylor, 335; Kümmel, *Heilsgeschehen*, 2:29; Schweizer, 145, 147; Lambrecht, *ETL* 53 [1977] 41, 48; Quesnell, *Mind*, 90; Gnilka, 1:227; Booth, *Purity*, 35–36). But the lexical (cf. the only occurrence of "the Jews" as a collective designation) and stylistic evidence (cf. the ellipses) counter this conclusion. Materially, the explanation hardly underscores satirically the "absurdity" of Jewish legalism (Schweizer, 147) but rather ascribes the question of "unwashed hands" to the "tradition of the elders" (7:3) and supports it with similar examples (7:4). In other words, the parenthesis comes from the need to explain to the reader how "defiled hands" led to the discussion of the "tradition of the elders" for those unfamiliar with that "tradition." Since Mark's use of this pericope in the context of his Gospel (cf. 7:24–37) relates more to the question of "defiled hands" (7:2, 5b) than the issue of the "tradition of the elders," he had little reason to underscore the latter. Therefore, the parenthesis and the explanation of "defiled hands" in 7:2 more likely stem from an earlier redactor attempting to explain the disciples' behavior in light of the "tradition" that Jesus rejects in 7:6–13.

"All the Jews" (πάντες οἱ Ἰουδαῖοι) has come under criticism as being historically inaccurate (e.g., Grundmann, 193; Gnilka, 1:281). Technically, only "the Pharisees," who sought to create "in everyday life the conditions of purity required in the Temple" (Neusner, *NTS* 22 [1975–76] 494, n. 2; idem, *JAAR* 43 [1975] 25), and the Essenes, who appear to have rigorously applied the purity provisions of the priests (Exod 30:17–21; 40:12) to the laity, were so concerned about purity. Thus some have avoided the problem by assuming without documentation that it reflects the practice of (western) Diaspora Judaism (Klostermann, 67; Lohmeyer, 139; Rawlinson, 94). But the reference to "the Pharisees" alongside of "all Jews" certainly cautions one from reading "all the Jews" as though meant inclusively.

"All the Jews" reflects the accepted practice of generalizing about a group. Mark uses πᾶς this way in 1:5, 32, 33; 6:33; 11:11—and the second century B.C. *Ep. Arist.* 305 provides a perfect parallel to this passage: "And as the custom of *all the Jews,* they washed their hands and prayed to God." The phrase, "the Jews," does indicate that the writer and implied reader/hearer viewed "the Jews" as different and strongly suggests a gentile setting for this generalization.

"Wash their hands" belongs to the ritual cleansings covered by the sixth division of the Mishnah (*Tohorot*) with twelve tractates, the eleventh of which is on "hands" (*Yadaim*). As with much of the Mishnah and traditional law, the question arises about how far back in history these traditional laws may go. That this concern extended back to Jesus' ministry seems amply attested by passages in *Ep. Arist.* 305; Jdt 12:7 and *Sib. Or.* 591–93 (see Neusner, *NTS* 22 [1975–76] 494, n. 2). Booth (*Purity,* 155–87) concludes, after an extensive look at the Jewish law and its development, that traditional law as such did not demand washing before eating. But strong evidence indicates that these rules for hand washing did apply among certain of the "Pharisees," the *haberim* who voluntarily undertook obligations especially regarding tithes and purity not required by general law (*Purity,* 189–203).

"With cupped hands" (πυγμῇ) presents one of the lexical anomalies of the NT (see *Note* d for *v.l.*). Wellhausen (57) years ago stated an opinion that still prevails today: "No one knows what πυγμῇ means!" Hengel (*ZNW* 60 [1969] 182–98) in the most extensive discussion of the problem traces the numerous attempts at rendering this word (183–85). He notes four: (a) a unit of measure (e.g., "cubit") meaning here "to the elbow"; (b) "with the fist," i.e., rubbing the fist into the other hand (e.g., BGD, *s.v.;* Schweizer, 148; Taylor, 335); (c) "to the wrist" (e.g., Black, *Approach,* 9); (d) "with a handful of water" (e.g., Schniewind, 104). One could add the renderings based on an awkward rendering of an Aramaic expression (see Weis, *NTS* 3 [1956–57] 233–36) and Reynolds' "with cupped hands" (*JBL* 85 [1966] 87–88; *idem, ZNW* 62 [1971] 295–96). The RSV epitomizes the dilemma by not even attempting to translate this word.

Hengel (*ZNW* 60 [1969] 192–95) makes a strong case for πυγμῇ being a "Latinism" by arguing first that since this term is part of an explanation of an unfamiliar practice it must have been intelligible to the reader. Thus it cannot have been a mistranslation of an Aramaic expression or a reference to a special, obscure rabbinic practice (e.g., Reynolds' "cupped hand") whose knowledge could be assumed of the reader for whom this "Jewish" practice was being explained. Second, he notes that the Latin versions use *pugillo,* the diminutive of *pugnus* used here and elsewhere in the Scriptures as a unit of measure or a "fistful." And noting that *pugillo* and *pugnus* are interchangeable in Latin, Hengel takes this to show that πυγμῇ is a Latinism enhanced by the common root between πυγμῇ and *pugnus*. He then counters the lack of literary parallels for this usage as being the result of the nonliterary character of this text and perhaps a limited geographical usage of this term.

Reynolds, however, in a brief rejoinder takes issue with Hengel's ingenious explanation at three points (*ZNW* 62 [1971] 295). First, he notes that *m. Yad.* 1:2 expressly forbids pouring water from "cupped hands" (a note that may well assume its disputed practice, so Hengel, *ZNW* 60 [1969] 195). Second, he argues that the word for hand always appears in the dual form and calls for a plural rather than a singular rendering (e.g., πυγμαῖς). Further, the amount of water prescribed for washing hands can only be held in a "cup formed by two hands." And finally, borrowing from another language ("Latinism") seems hardly appropriate when the language has a precise equivalent for "handful" (cf. δράξ and even a diminutive, δράγμα).

Of the options, either "with cupped hands" in the sense of pouring water over hands that are held out with fingers "cupped" instead of in a tight fist (so Reynolds) or "with cupped hands" as a measure of water ("fistful") seems the most likely. Enough questions surround each to prevent one from knowing precisely what presumably was clear to the reader.

"Tradition of the elders" (παράδοσιν τῶν πρεσβυτέρων; cf. Gal 1:14) refers to the oral tradition that the Pharisees in particular held to be as binding as the written Law. R. Akiba referred to "the tradition [as] a fence around the Law" (*m. 'Abot* 3:14). Codified into the Mishnah toward the end of the second century A.D., one tractate of this "tradition," *m. Yadim*, specifically deals with the washing of hands. For example, *m. Yad.* 1–2 describes the water, amount (ca. 1½ eggshells) and means necessary to wash one's hands ritually. However, it is unclear how much of this "tradition" goes back to Jesus' day. The issue itself of the "washing of hands," however, existed beyond doubt (see Hübner, *Gesetz*, 163–64; Neusner, *NTS* 22 [1975–76] 494–95; Booth, *Purity*, 189–203).

4 The meaning of "from the marketplace" (ἀπ' ἀγορᾶς) also remains unclear because of an ellipsis in the sentence. Some have rendered it as a modifier of the personal subject of the following verb—"*When they come* from the marketplace" (e.g., Cranfield, 234; Gnilka, 1:181–82). Others relate it to impersonal things (e.g., food, drink, utensils) brought from the marketplace, the object of the following verb—"*Anything* from the marketplace" (e.g., Taylor, 336; Pesch, 1:371).

Against understanding it to be a reference to persons, which is the natural reading with plural middle βαπτίσωνται (cf. 2 Kgs 5:14; cf. *Note* e) is the lack of evidence in Jewish sources for such practice (cf. Judith's bathing in Jdt 12:7). When taken with 7:3 this statement does move logically from the washing of hands before eating to the washing of one's entire body, assuming defilement from contacts in the marketplace. Nevertheless, the following clause uses the cognate noun (βαπτισμούς) in reference to objects. Therefore, it could imply cooking utensils in general or food in particular brought from the marketplace, a general statement specified by what follows.

"Many other things received as tradition" (see *Note* f) generalizes from the "tradition" about washing but does not move beyond the "tradition" regarding the relationship between "eating" and defilement. The following examples still have to do broadly with defilement and eating. This general statement makes a further connection between the disciples' conduct and the issue of "tradition" pointing to the charge in 7:5a and Jesus' response in 7:6–13.

"Cups, pitchers, and copper pots" are utensils used in preparing and serving food. "Pitchers" (ξεστῶν) is another Latinism. A *sextarius* is a Roman unit of dry measure of about a pint or half liter. Like our "bushel" it comes to mean as here a container, a "pitcher" or a "jug." We have a materially related saying in Q (Matt 23:25–26 // Luke 11:32–41) where Jesus charges the Pharisees with concentrating on cleaning the "outside of the cup. . . ." But the reference hardly seems sufficient to suggest a direct connection between that saying and this explanation (cf. Lambrecht, *ETL* 53 [1977] 45–47).

5 This verse resumes the scene of 7:2 almost as though it had been forgotten. The disjuncture may stem in part from the shift from an earlier question pertaining solely to the disciples' eating with κοιναῖς χερσίν (cf. 7:2a, 5b) to the question about their failure to follow the "tradition of the elders" and sets the stage for Jesus' response in 7:6–13.

"Not walk according to the tradition of the elders" becomes the primary question of 7:1–13 (cf. 7:2!). The verb "walk" (περιπατοῦσιν) occurs only here in the Synoptics with the more technical meaning of *halacha*, "to live by." This question takes the initial concern of "defiled hands"—an episode that could easily have taken place in Jesus' ministry in view of the disciples' conduct displayed elsewhere (e.g., 2:23–28)—and turns it into the larger question about the role of the "tradition of the elders." This adjustment most likely took place in the formative stages of the primitive Church where some of the inner Jewish struggles between the Pharisees and other Jews about the validity of the "tradition" were carried over.

"With defiled hands" (κοιναῖς χερσίν), a remnant of the initial question, is not dropped but now specifies the charge that the disciples do not hold to the "tradition of the elders." Jesus' answer to this initial charge was most likely the saying now found in 7:15. When the issue of the "tradition" became paramount, the response in 7:6–13 intervened (see *Comment* on 7:15).

6 Jesus responds to the "tradition" question of 7:5 *ad hominem* by first citing Isa 29:13 as a statement appropriate (καλῶς) to his opponents. The question of whether he could have ever used this argument hinges for many on whether it is based on the LXX or not.

Without question the present form of 7:6–7 corresponds much more closely to the LXX than to the MT. Whereas the MT concludes by charging the people with lip service stemming from a "commandment of men learned by rote" (RSV; cf. מצות אנשים מלמדה, *miṣwat ʾănāšîm mĕlummādāh*), the LXX has "teaching commandments of men and teachings" (διδάσκοντες ἐντάλματα ἀνθρώπων καὶ διδασκαλίας). Mark's text has sharpened the last phrase to "teaching teachings and commandments of men" (διδάσκοντες διδασκαλίας ἐντάλματα ἀνθρώπων). Col 2:22 has a similar reference, "according to the commandments and teachings of men" (κατὰ τὰ ἐντάλματα καὶ διδασκαλίας τῶν ἀνθρώπων).

Jesus calls the opponents "hypocrites" (ὑποκριτῶν), a word in classical Greek that means "to play a part," an "actor." It does not carry the moral overtone of fraud that our English word does today. Rather it refers to the discrepancy in the behavior of one who unconsciously has alienated oneself from God, an "ungodly" person (cf. חנף, *ḥānēp*), by one's actions (U. Wilkens, *TDNT* 8

[1972] 564). Isa 29:13 illustrates the point and becomes the basis for Jesus' charge against the opponents.

According to Isa 29:13 the people "draw near with their mouth and honor me with their lips, while their hearts are far from me" (RSV). Mark 7:6 abbreviates this along with the LXX and simply contrasts honoring "me with their lips, but their heart is far from me." The change is hardly significant for the argument so far. In both the MT and the LXX the discrepancy in behavior lies in the difference between lip service and where one's heart really is.

7 The second part of the citation in the MT explains that their "reverence" of God comes from the commandments of men which they have learned. In other words, it does not come from the heart. By contrast, the LXX declares that their "honor" or "worship" (σέβονται) is "in vain" (μάτην) since they are "teaching the commandments of men and teachings" (διδάσκοντες ἐντάλματα ἀνθρώπων καὶ διδασκαλίας). Mark differs from both by sharpening the charge "teaching as teachings the commandments of men" (διδάσκοντες διδασκαλίας ἐντάλματα ἀνθρώπων).

Does this difference in rendering mean that Jesus' response of 7:6–7 has to be based on the LXX and thus from a "hellenistic" Jewish Christian community (e.g., Nineham, 194–95; Kümmel, *Heilsgeschehen*, 2:29; Gnilka, 1:227; Lührmann, *WD* 16 [1981] 80–81) or from Mark himself (e.g., Suhl, *Zitate*, 81; Berger, *Gesetzesauslegung*, 485–86; Lambrecht, *ETL* 53 [1977] 51–55)? The answer lies in the application of this passage in 7:8.

8 "Neglecting the commandment of God" (ἀφέντες τὴν ἐντολήν) charges the opponents with negligence in reference to God's commandment. But what commandment? Pesch (1:373), placing this saying in the broader context of Jesus' ministry, reads "the commandment of God" to mean the great commandment of Deut 6:4–5 to love the Lord God with all one's heart, soul, and might. Since their "heart" was not in their "honor," they had neglected God's commandment. In the context of 7:9–13, the "commandment of God" points to God's Law as the written law in contrast to "tradition" which consists of "human" commandments. In either case God's commandment is being neglected.

"Keep the tradition of men" (κρατεῖτε τὴν παράδοσιν τῶν ἀνθρώπων). The "tradition of the elders" (7:3, 5) is now identified as "human tradition" and equated with the charge of Isa 29:13 that the people were following the "commandment(s) of men" (so מצות אנשים [miṣwat ᵓānāšîm] and ἐντάλματα). Therefore, their "hypocrisy," the discrepancy in their behavior, was their failure to observe God's commandment by following instead human commandment(s)/tradition. Since this is ultimately the point of both the MT and the LXX, the argument does not necessitate the use of the LXX. Even the sharpening of the LXX in 7:7 ("teaching as teaching") does not alter the situation, since Jesus' charge of hypocrisy (7:6) is directed at "false teaching" only to the extent that it leads to the discrepancy of neglecting the "commandment of God" (cf. Banks, *Law*, 134). The opponents are not "hypocrites" here because they "teach falsely" but because their "false teaching" ("human commandments") causes them to neglect God's commandment.

The similarity of citation between 7:7 and Col 2:22 need not lead to deducing any "Pauline" influence on Mark or to their having a text in common different from either the MT or the LXX (so Taylor, 337; Mann, 313). The similarity of form and usage does, however, suggest that Isa 29:13 was used to address similar questions pertaining to different "regulations" in the early Church (cf. *Pap. Eger.* 2). The LXX may have influenced the present wording, which should come as no surprise in light of the extensive use of the LXX by the early Church. But this verbal correspondence does not provide sufficient grounds for denying that the Hebrew text of Isa 29 was first applied to an issue similar to one depicted in 7:1–13 by Jesus during his ministry.

9 In 7:9–13 Jesus offers a second, more direct response to the question about "tradition" by using the Corban practice to illustrate the point made in 7:8. Kümmel (*Heilsgeschehen,* 2:29) and Hübner (*Gesetz,* 144–46) take this to be Jesus' "original" response to the Pharisees' charge in 7:5 with 7:6–8 added later. Others attribute its present location to Mark's redactional employment of a different tradition to illustrate the response in 7:6–8 (Taylor, 339; Grundmann, 189; Schweizer, 145; Carlston, *NTS* 15 [1968–69] 91; Gnilka, 1:277). The oft cited "Markan" καὶ ἔλεγεν αὐτοῖς (e.g., Lambrecht, *ETL* 53 [1977], 42) cannot be rigidly held as the decisive factor (cf. *Comment* on 4:11). Rather the play on words between καλῶς in 7:6 ("Isaiah did a good job . . .") and here ("You do a good job . . .") suggests an earlier combination of 7:6–8 and 7:9–13. Furthermore, the shift from "tradition of men" to "your tradition" (cf. 7:8) suggests that 7:9–13 is a subsequent specification of 7:6–8. The broadening of the issue from "defiled hands" to "tradition of the elders" noted above suggests that the response of 7:9–13 came into this pericope as the answer to the broader issue of "tradition" (see *Comment* on 7:15). Clearly adapted now to 7:1–8, 7:10–12 may well have had its roots in Jesus' ministry.

The charge in 7:9 sharpens the point of 7:8. Whereas the opponents "neglect (ἀφέντες) the commandment of God" in 7:8, they actually "nullify (ἀθετεῖτε) the commandment of God" here. And "the tradition of men" becomes "your (ὑμῶν) tradition" which they "establish" (στήσητε; cf. *Note* i). The direct address assigns the responsibility to Jesus' opponents.

10 For evidence of God's commandment, Jesus first cites Moses and the fifth commandment almost verbatim with Exod 20:12a LXX (Deut 5:16a): "Honor your father and your mother." In addition, he cites Exod 21:16 LXX (Lev 20:9): "Let the one who speaks evil (κακολογῶν) of his father or mother be put to death." The Hebrew text (21:17, מְקַלֵּל, *měqallēl*) specifies, "The one who *curses* . . . ," a meaning foreign to κακολογεῖν (BGD, *s.v.*). In either case, this reference applies here to the Corban statement.

11 "But you say" (ὑμεῖς δὲ λέγετε) stands in stark contrast to "For Moses said" (cf. 7:10, Μωϋσῆς γὰρ εἶπεν) to show how the "tradition" counters the "commandment."

"Corban" (κορβᾶν) renders קָרְבָּן, *qārbān.* Zeitlin (*JQR* 53 [1962] 160) traces the meaning of this formula from a designation of an "offering" in the Pentateuch to a "vow or oath" and later to a "prayer." Though only used as an "offering" in the Hebrew Scriptures, contemporary evidence in the first century supports its use as a "vow." In addition to such usage in Philo (*Spec. Leg.* 2:16–17) and Josephus (*Ant.* 4.72–73; *Apion* 1.167), Fitzmyer cites a "perfect contemporary parallel" found on an ossuary lid from a Jewish tomb located southeast of Jerusalem and dating from the beginning of the Christian era (*Essays,* 100).

We find an interesting parallel to 7:10–11 in *m. Ned.* 5:6: "It once happened that a man at Beth Horon, whose father was forbidden by *vow to have any benefit from him,* was giving his son in marriage, and he said to his fellow, 'The courtyard and the banquet are given to thee as a gift, but they are thine only that my father may come and eat with us at the banquet.' His fellow said, 'If they are mine, they are dedicated to Heaven.' The other answered, 'I did not give thee what is mine that thou shouldest dedicate it to Heaven.' His fellow said, 'Thou didst give me what is thine only that thou and thy father might eat and drink and be reconciled one with the other, and that the sin should rest on his head!'" (Danby, *Mishnah,* 271, italics mine).

Despite the parallels, how the Corban formula functioned in Jesus' day is less certain. On the one side, several interpret the formula against its Scriptural background as being a dedicatory formula in the form of a vow that dedicates the object in question to God or the Temple. By relegating something to the realm of the sacred one withdraws it from secular use (Str-B, 1:711; K. H. Rengstorf, *TDNT* 3 [1965] 862). On the other side, it becomes quite evident in the Mishnah that the formula also functions more like a ban than a dedicatory formula (cf. Taylor, 342; Falk, *HTR* 59 [1966] 309–12). Fitzmyer (*Essays,* 97) notes that it comes to mean no longer "an offering to God" but "acquires the form of an asseveration and even an imprecatory interjection" as seen in *m. Ned.* 8:7. In this setting, one did not declare the object an offering to God or the Temple but simply vowed that it would not be used by anyone else for their benefit "as if it were an offering" (Falk, *HTR* 59 [1966] 310; Hübner, *Gesetz,* 148).

It is no longer possible to know when the shift in usage took place. The effect remains the same. Consequently, it makes little difference whether we render Mark's formula, "Whatever you might be benefited from me is *an offering to God!*" or "*Corban* is whatever you might be benefited from me!" meaning, "You shall have no benefit from what is mine!" Either way the parents in question are denied the benefit. The context gives little hint whether the "benefit" was withdrawn from all "secular" use and makes moot the suggestion that the actual "gift" could have been transacted later or at death (e.g., Grundmann, 193).

"Which means *gift*" (ὅ ἐστιν δῶρον) is typical of Mark's rendering of "foreign" words (see *Comment* on 7:2) and most likely is redactional. Josephus uses the same terminology (*Ant.* 4.73: δῶρον δὲ τοῦτο σημαίνει κατὰ ῾Ελλήνων). We cannot, however, gain any precise information from the use of δῶρον, since this term renders קָרְבָּן, *qārbān,* in Leviticus and Numbers.

12 "You no longer allow . . ." implies that the opponents held the Corban formula as absolutely binding, an implication evident in the example from *m. Ned.* 5:6 cited above. This view has been disputed, however, in light of *m. Ned.* 9:1: "R. Eliezer says: 'They may open for men the way (to repentance) by reason of the honour due to father and mother.' But the Sages forbid it. R. Zadok said: 'Rather than open the way for a man by reason of the honour due to father and mother, they should open the way for him by reason of the honour due to God; but if so, there could be no vows.' But the Sages agree with R. Eliezer that in a matter between a man and his father and mother, the way may be opened to him by reason of the honour due to his father and mother" (Danby, *Mishnah,* 275). Falk (*HTR* 59 [1966] 311), for example, concludes, "While Jesus considered the vow to be illegal and void, the Rabbis held it to be merely voidable." But the very point of the discussion in *m. Ned.* 9:1 and the example cited in *m. Ned.* 5:6 indicate that some besides Jesus also understood the vow to be binding.

13 "Thus annulling the word of God with your tradition." From "neglecting" (7:8) to "nullifying" (7:9) to "annulling" (ἀκυροῦντες), the charge that "tradition," "your tradition" (παραδόσει ὑμῶν), contravenes God's commandment, God's word (τὸν λόγον τοῦ Θεοῦ) is now complete. Jesus does not place "commandment" against "commandment" by setting the commandment to fulfill one's vows (Num 30:3) over against the commandment to honor one's father and mother (Exod 20:12), as though honor to God supersedes honor to one's parents (e.g., Kümmel, *Heilsgeschehen*, 2:30; Nineham, 195–96; cf. Hübner, *Gesetz*, 153), but he places human tradition against God's word.

"Which you passed on" (ἦ παρεδώκατε) further implicates the opponents by making them more than passive receivers and followers of "tradition." It is "your tradition" that you actively hand down.

"And you do many similar things" moves from the specific Corban illustration to include many related uses of "tradition" to set aside God's commandment. This generalizing comment may reflect an editorial comment of Mark (e.g., Lambrecht, *ETL* 53 [1977] 41; Quesnell, *Mind*, 90–91). Since, however, his concern lies more with the issue of defilement than with "tradition," this probably entered the tradition at the same time as the parenthetical explanation of 7:3–4. It fits with the generalizing comment of 7:4b.

In 7:1–13 Jesus now answers the charge that his disciples fail to "walk according to the tradition of the elders" in eating with "defiled hands" by responding that the "tradition of the elders" was not of God (7:6–9) but actually represented "human commandments" that contravened "the commandment of God" (7:8–9, 13). This is clearly seen in the Corban practice that set aside one's obedience to the fifth commandment (7:10–11).

Explanation

This pericope comes as the end product of a rather complex development in the tradition. Originally found by Mark as part of the larger unit of tradition behind 7:1–23, it now stands alongside 7:14–23 as a unit in itself.

The earliest core of this tradition centered around a dispute between Jesus and his opponents over his disciples' eating with "defiled hands" (7:1–2, 5b). Jesus addressed the charge with a response now found in 7:15 that engaged the opponents' concerns at a different level. Instead of the issue of "defiled hands," he raised the issue of what really defiles a person. By moving from the concern with externals to focus on what comes from one's person as the cause for defilement, Jesus challenged his opponents with a more radical understanding of "purity" rooted in one's person. Without disdaining the Law, he called for conduct congruent with God's will, not necessarily defined by the rules and regulations of the Law but indicative of one's relationship with God.

This story about "defiled hands," when viewed as an example of the Pharisees' "tradition of the elders," provided the early Church an occasion to broaden the question (7:5a) and incorporate other traditional material pertaining to the issue of "tradition" (7:6–13). At this second stage in the development of the narrative, Jesus charges the Pharisees (7:6–8) with an external show of allegiance to God's demand (lip service) while ignoring the personal rupture in their relationship with God ("their hearts are far from me"), a motif that consistently characterizes Jesus' response to them throughout the Gospel tradition. Then he charges them in particular with pursuing their "tradition," "human commandments" as prophesied by Isaiah, and contravening God's Law (7:9–13). He cites the use of Corban to void the fifth commandment regarding the honor of one's parents. Without doubt this account provided the early Jewish Christian community a basis for rejecting any attempt by some to import "tradition" as binding for the primitive Church.

At a subsequent stage and in a different setting this story loses some of its force because of the audience's apparent ignorance of the issues involved. To explain these issues, several parenthetical comments were added (7:2b, 3–4, 8b). "All the Jews" (7:3) indicates this to have been a gentile context for which neither "defiled hands" nor the "tradition of the elders" made much sense and in which, certainly, neither was a problem. The addition of the "explanation" of 7:15 in 7:18b–19, 20–22 shows that the question of "foods," however, continued to be an issue (cf. Rom 14:1–12, 14; 1 Cor 8) to which the developed narrative of 7:1–23 provided direction based on Jesus' ministry.

By changing the setting in 7:14–23, the evangelist creates two scenes with the first accenting the issue of "tradition" (7:6–13). Yet the "tradition of the elders" hardly seems appropriate as an issue paramount for Mark or his community. Unlike Matthew, Mark does not make a special effort to set Jesus and his demands over against the Pharisees. He does depict them as Jesus' deadly adversaries, especially in conjunction with the "scribes." But this has more to do with the causes leading to Jesus' death than with a challenge to their teaching regarding the Law per se.

Consequently, the focus of 7:1–13 for Mark falls more on the initial issue of defilement. The disciples' behavior raises the question of the social boundaries by failing to do what was acceptable to the "Pharisees and scribes from Jerusalem." Jesus counters by dismissing these boundaries as "human" and calls for a different basis rooted in one's personal relationship with God. This reading coincides with Jesus' initial thrust in the conflict behind 7:1–23 and sets the stage in Mark's story for his work among the "Gentiles" in the episodes of 7:24–37; 8:1–9, 22–26. It also explains how Jesus could touch a leper in 1:41, a corpse in 5:41, be touched by a defiling woman in 5:27–28, eat with "sinners" in 5:17 and minister to one in swine country (5:1–20) without fear of "defilement." Jesus himself had broken down the religiously defined social boundaries based on ritual defilement.

G. On Defilement (7:14–23)

Bibliography

Allison, D. C. "The Eye Is the Lamp of the Body (Matthew 6.22–23 = Luke 11.34–36)." *NTS* 33 (1987) 61–83. **Banks, R.** *Jesus and the Law in the Synoptic Tradition.* SNTSMS

28. Cambridge: University Press, 1975. **Berger, K.** *Die Gesetzesauslegung Jesu*, I, WMANT 40. Neukirchen-Vluyn: Neukirchener Verlag, 1972. **Best, E.** *Following Jesus: Discipleship in the Gospel of Mark.* JSNTSup 4, Sheffield: University of Sheffield, 1981. **Black, M.** *An Aramaic Approach to the Gospels and Acts.* 1967. **Booth, R. P.** *Jesus and the Laws of Purity: Tradition History and Legal History in Mark 7.* JSNTSup 13. Sheffield: University of Sheffield Press, 1986. **Carlston, C. E.** "The Things That Defile (Mark vii. 14) and the Law in Matthew and Mark." *NTS* 15 (1968–69) 57–69. **Hengel, M.** "Die Ursprünge der christlichen Mission." *NTS* 18 (1971) 15–28. **Hübner, H.** *Das Gesetz in der synoptischen Tradition.* Witten: Luther, 1973. ———. "Mark vii. 1–23 und das 'jüdisch-hellenistische' Gesetzes Verständnis." *NTS* 22 (1976) 319–45. **Jeremias, J.** *New Testament Theology.* 1971. **Kümmel, W. G.** "Äussere und innere Reinheit bei Jesus." In *Das Wort und die Wörter*, FS G. Friedrich, ed. H. Balz and S. Schulz. Stuttgart: Kohlhammer, 1973. 35–46. = *Heilsgeschehen und Geschichte*, II. MTS 16. Marburg: Elwert, 1978. 117–29. **Lambrecht, J.** "Jesus and the Law: An Investigation of Mk 7, 1–23." *ETL* 53 (1977) 24–82. **Lemcio, E. E.** "External Evidence for the Structure and Function of Mark iv. 1–20, vii. 14–23 and viii. 14–21." *JTS* 29 (1978) 323–38. **Lührmann, D.** ". . . Womit er alle Speisen für rein erklärten (Mk 7, 19)." *WD* 16 (1981) 71–92. **McEleney, N. J.** "Authenticating Criteria and Mark 7, 1–23." *CBQ* 34 (1972) 431–60. **Marxsen, W.** "Redaktionsgeschichtliche Erklärung der sogenannten Parabeltheorie des Markus." In *Der Exeget als Theologe: Vorträge zum Neuen Testament.* Gütersloh: Mohn, 1968. 13–28. **Merkel, H.** "Mk 7,14—das Jesuswort über die innere Verunreinigung." *ZRGG* 20 (1968) 340–63. **Neusner, J.** "'First Cleanse the Inside.'" *NTS* 22 (1975–75) 486–95. **Paschen, W.** *Rein und Unrein: Untersuchung zur biblische Wortgeschichte.* SANT 24. München: Kösel, 1970. **Quesnell, Q.** *The Mind of Mark: Interpretation and Method through the Exegesis of Mark 6, 52.* AnBib 38. Rome: Pontifical Biblical Institute, 1969.

Translation

[14] *Summoning again the crowd he said to them, "Listen to me, all of you, and understand.* [15] *There is nothing which enters a person from outside that is able to defile. But the things which come out of a person are the things that defile."*[a]

[17] *And when he had entered a house away from the crowd, his disciples asked him about the parable.* [18] *And he said to them, "Are you also as lacking in understanding? Do you not know that nothing entering into a person from outside can defile* [19] *because it does not enter into one's heart but into the stomach and comes out into the latrine?"*[b] *(Thus he cleansed*[c] *all foods).*

[20] *And he said, "What comes out of a person, that defiles.* [21] *For from inside, from people's hearts, evil devisings come out: immoralities, thefts, murders,* [22] *adulteries, greedy actions, evil deeds, deceit, sensuality, selfishness, blasphemy, arrogance, lack of moral sense.* [23] *All these evil things come out from inside and defile a person."*

Notes

[a] Omit 7:16 with ℵ B L Δ* 0274 28 sa[mss] bo[pt] against A D W Θ *f*[1.13] Majority text latt sy which may have added it from a similar setting in 4:9, 23 (Metzger, 94).

[b] Place the question mark here rather than after βρώματα which offers a parenthetical comment (see *Comment* on 7:19).

[c] καθαρίζων agrees with the subject of ἔλεγεν (see *Comment* on 7:19).

Form/Structure/Setting

.As Mark's text now stands, 7:14–23 offers a teaching narrative. Beginning with a parabolic saying addressed to the crowd (7:14–15), the narrative proceeds with a two-part explanation to the disciples (7:17–19, 20–23). This form, however, most likely came about with Mark's own redactional setting for this material (see *Comment* on 7:14). For a discussion of the form of the tradition(s) underlying 7:1–23, see pp. 360–62.

As to source, most see a development in the pre-Markan tradition. Generally, 7:15, the heart of this unit, is viewed to have circulated originally as an independent logion (Bultmann, 74; Kümmel, *Wort*, 37; Hübner, *Gesetz*, 159, 164; Schweizer, 146; Berger, *Gesetzesauslegung*, 463; Lambrecht, *ETL* 53 [1977] 69; Gnilka, 1:271–78; Pesch, 1:378) with roots in Jesus' ministry (see Kümmel, *Wort*, 35–46; cf. Berger, *Gesetzesauslegung*, 465–69). Yet such an open saying had to have had a specific referent in Jesus' ministry similar to the one in this context. Did the saying spawn the setting of 7:1–2, 5 (e.g., Berger, *Gesetzesauslegung*, 463–64; Lambrecht, *ETL* 53 [1977] 69) or 7:14–23 (e.g., Taylor, 343; Kümmel, *Wort*, 37; Pesch, 1:378) in the early Church debates or might 7:1–2, 5 represent the setting from Jesus' ministry (see Lührmann, *WD* 16 [1981] 88–89; Booth, *Purity*, 96–114)? While one can argue that the present setting is "secondary," the temporally and locally generic character of 7:1–2, 5 prevents one from arguing either for or against its primacy in Jesus' ministry.

Mark's redactional work emerges at the outset. He has most likely created the shift in scene to address the crowds from whom Jesus withdraws to "a house" where privately he responds to the disciples' further question (see *Comment* on 7:14, 17–18). Though some have assigned part (e.g., 7:17–19—Carlston, *NTS* 15 [1968–69] 91; 7:23—Gnilka, 1:278) or all (e.g., Kümmel, *Wort*, 37; Schmithals, 1:341) of 7:17–23 to Markan redaction, most take 7:18b–23 to be a commentary on 7:15 developed in the pre-Markan tradition (e.g., Taylor, 343; Lambrecht, *ETL* 53 [1977] 66; Pesch, 1:378; Lührmann, *WD* 16 [1981] 85–88).

Structurally, Daube (*Rabbinic Judaism*, 141–50) has found a rabbinic pattern behind this section. It consists of: (a) an opponent's question, (b) a public but opaque response, (c) a disciple's request for clarification and (d) an explanation given in a smaller, private setting. The first element would have to be implicit (cf. 7:5), if present at all. Lemcio (*JTS* 29 [1978] 324–31) has traced a "traditional" pattern of (a) "ambiguity" (7:15), (b) "incomprehension" (7:17), (c) "surprise/critical rejoinder" (7:18a), and (d) explanation (7:18b–23) behind this pericope, 4:1–20 and 8:14–21 (see pp. 202, 419). While it accurately describes the narrative flow from 7:15–23 (cf. 7:14, an integral part in Mark's structure), the presence of (b) "incomprehension," and (c) "surprise/critical rejoinder" might well have coincidentally resulted from Mark's redactional setting (see *Comment* on 7:17–18a).

7:14–23 falls neatly into two parts based on audience. After summoning the crowd to attentive listening in 7:14 and giving the parabolic saying about what defiles in 7:15, the scene shifts to a house where Jesus explains the "parable" to his disciples (7:17–23). The explanation itself follows the parallelism of the saying. The rather crass exposition in 7:18b–19 explains why what enters one cannot defile, and 7:20–22 explains why what comes out defiles and illustrates this with a catalogue of vices. The narrative then concludes with a summary comment on this last point (7:23). A parenthetical comment in 7:19c specifically calls the reader's attention to the implication of 7:15 for all foods.

Since 7:14–23 belonged originally with 7:1–13, it inevitably relates thematically. "Defilement" (κοινοῦν) links the two (7:2, 5, 15, 18, 20, 23). By separating the material into two narratives, the evangelist highlights this central issue in 7:14–23. At the same time, by leaving 7:14–23 in the immediate context of 7:1–13, he also reemphasizes this issue underlying 7:2, 5b which had been somewhat eclipsed by the later focus on the "tradition of the elders" in 7:5a, 6–13. Though Jesus does not actually eat with the "Greek" woman of Syrophoenicia in 7:24–30, the allusion to "bread" in that pericope and Jesus' contact with and help for her and the deaf mute in 7:31–37 directly relates to the theme of clean and unclean. Therefore, it can hardly be fortuitous that Mark locates 7:1–23 in this setting in his Gospel.

At the same time, this narrative accents the lack of the disciples' understanding, a theme that began in Jesus' first extended teaching (4:10–13, 33–34), became pronounced in 6:52 and becomes a subject in itself in 8:14–21.

Comment

14 Numerous signals indicate Markan redaction in 7:14a (see Lambrecht, *ETL* 53 [1977] 57; cf. Marxsen, *Exeget*, 16–20). First, Mark frequently uses the participle προσκαλεσάμενος to set the stage for a statement or pericope (see *Comment* on 6:7). Second, the evangelist turns to "the crowd" (τὸν ὄχλον) "again" (πάλιν) (see *Comment* on 2:1). Thirdly, the framework of Jesus' publicly addressing the crowd (7:14–15) and then privately explaining the implications to the disciples because of their lack of understanding (7:17–18a) corresponds both to his embellishment of 4:1–20 (cf. 4:13) and the arrangement of 10:2–12. But by developing the scene in 7:14a, the evangelist breaks an awkwardly complex composite of traditions into two scenes with the first (7:1–13) providing the backdrop for the second (7:14–23).

"Summoning again the crowd" may be reminiscent of 4:1–2, the setting for Jesus' last extensive teaching "in parables" (Carlston, *NTS* 15 [1968–69] 92), or it could pick up "the crowd" motif "again" from 6:45 where Jesus dismissed "the crowd."

"Listen to me, all of you, and understand" (ακούσατέ μου πάντες καὶ σύνετε) recalls the exhortations to "hear" (ἀκούετε) enclosing the parable of 4:3–9 (see *Comment* on 4:3, 9). The combination of "hear and understand" is unique to 7:14 (// Matt 15:10) but the addition of "to understand" merely reinforces the intent of the call to "hear" (cf. 4:12 [Isa 6:9–10]). Ironically, it underscores the lack of "understanding" on the part of the "hearers"—both "the crowd" and especially "the disciples" as noted in 7:18. Since the disciples' lack of understanding is a developed Markan theme for this section of the Gospel (e.g., 6:52; 7:18; 8:14–21), this exhortation stems most likely from the evangelist.

15 This saying provides the "parable" around which 7:14–23 now centers. *Gos. Thom.* 14 shows that this saying existed in the tradition as an isolated saying, but it could also have served as the original response to the issue of "defiled hands" raised by the setting in 7:1–2, 5b (see Lührmann, *WD* 16

[1981] 88–89). When the story was expanded to address the question of "tradition" (7:5a, 6–13), this response still addressed the issue of defilement as the concluding statement. When, however, the explanations of 7:18b–19, 20–22 were added, the focus changed again from the narrow issue of eating with "defiled hands" to the broader question of what actually defiled a person (Lührmann, *WD* 16 [1981] 77–88). Once Mark changed the setting in 7:14, this became the primary thrust of the saying. It took on a life of its own related to but distinct from the questions in 7:5.

Constructed in the form of an antithetical parallelism, 7:15 is a typical wisdom saying. The specification of "mouth" (στόμα, στόματος) in both members of the parallelism in Matt 15:11 represents a secondary application of the more general statement (cf. Lohmeyer, 141–42). Kümmel (*Wort*, 37–38) argues for the integrity of the present saying against any who would soften or abbreviate it (cf. Taylor, 343; Merkel, *ZRGG* 20 [1968] 352–54).

"Nothing . . . outside" (οὐδέν . . . ἔξωθεν) presently lacks a clear referent. The *Comment* on 7:18b–19 applies it to what enters the mouth as food and the parenthetical comment in 7:19b makes this reference explicit (τὰ βρώματα). But was food the original referent? If so, many have asked how one then accounts for the extended debate in the early Church over clean and unclean food (e.g., Acts 10:14–15; 15:28–29; Rom 14:14; Gal 2:11–14; Col 2:20–22) when the tradition offered such a clear word from Jesus (e.g., Taylor, 343; Nineham, 191; Carlston, *NTS* 15 [1968–69] 95; Banks, *Jesus*, 141).

The referent in the pre-Markan tradition behind 7:1–13 appears to have been the issue of eating with "defiled hands" to which this saying provided Jesus' response (cf. κοιναῖς χερσίν, 7:2, 5b and κοινῶσαι, κοινοῦντα, 7:15). The underlying assumption countered by the declaration that "nothing . . . from outside" could "defile" a person was that "defiled hands" could through contact "defile" one's food and eating "defiled food" would "defile" the person. Hübner notes OT and Rabbinic evidence for this assumption (*Gesetz*, 160–64; Booth, *Purity*, 194–203). Therefore, 7:1–2, 5b, our earliest traditional context, applied 7:15 ultimately to food, though to food eaten with "defiled hands" and not directly to the question of unclean foods or the food laws of Lev 11 per se. Such a referent could well have had its place in Jesus' ministry. The parenthetical comment in 7:19b does, however, take the next logical step by applying it to "all foods" and not merely to those supposedly defiled by the eating with defiled hands.

"The things coming out of a person . . ." (τὰ ἐκ τοῦ ἀνθρώπου ἐκπορευόμενα) can refer more generally to all that comes from within a person including thoughts, actions, and words. Rather than remove the issue of defilement, this saying actually broadens and refocuses it in a manner not unlike Jesus' demands in the Antitheses of Matt 5:21–22, 27–28, 33–37 and the divorce pericope in Mark 10:2–12. By implication the opponents' concern over minutiae had distorted the bigger picture. One's purity or acceptability before God involved one's entire person, one's "heart," as seen reflected in one's thoughts and conduct (see Neusner, *NTS* 22 [1975–76] 494, n. 2).

By responding in this manner to the question about eating with "defiled hands" in particular and "defilement" in general, 7:15 in the broader context of Jesus' ministry corresponds to the Gospels' portrait of him in "defiling" settings. As Kümmel (*Wort,* 41) has noted, Jesus did not shy away from eating in homes where it was doubtful that the food served was ritually clean and with people where it could not be foreseen that he would not defile himself in other ways (e.g., 2:16). And Mark has three miracles in which Jesus finds himself in a defiling situation. He touched the leper in 1:41 and the corpse of Jairus' daughter in 5:41 and was touched by the hemorrhaging woman in 5:27–29.

Consequently, one need not posit (a) a "much less specific form" (Carlston, *NTS* 15 [1968–69] 95; Jeremias, *Theology,* 210; cf. Merkel, *ZRGG* 20 [1968] 351); (b) a failure in understanding by the primitive Church (Haenchen, 266; Mann, 315); or (c) a paradoxical hyperbole (Quesnell, *Mind,* 98) to account for the absence of the saying's direct impact on the early Christian struggle with the food laws. If the saying existed originally as an isolated saying devoid of specific context, the question does become more acute since its applicability to the controversy over foods is self-evident. But if the saying's "original" context in Jesus' ministry lies behind the narrative as we now have it, one can see how it only later became an authoritative word regarding foods per se.

As the response to the original query about the disciples' eating with "defiled hands," this saying fits the manner of Jesus' response in similar situations. Jesus frequently refuses "to debate within the terms of his opponents. Rather has he tended to answer in such a way as to lift the discussion to a higher level" (Banks, *Jesus,* 140). Here he addresses the question of "defiled hands" by addressing the larger issue of defilement itself. To this extent, he speaks as elsewhere more "prophetically" than "programmatically" regarding the law and its demand (Lührmann, *WD* 16 [1981] 84). He does not "programmatically" abrogate or even reinterpret the law. He "prophetically" summons the hearer to do God's will from the whole person. Instead of attacking the ritual or ceremonial law of purity, Jesus calls for a total purity, the sanctification of the whole person, as anticipated for the age of salvation (Pesch, 1:379). Thus his call corresponds to his proclamation of the "gospel of God," the coming of the Kingdom in his ministry (see *Comment* on 1:14–15).

The early Church, however, seeking to implement this for their needs returned to the narrower question about "defiled hands" (7:1–2, 5b) and turned the issue into a debate about the validity of the "tradition of the elders" by expanding the question in 7:5a and adding relevant tradition in 7:6–13. In doing so, it becomes obvious that that community in no way understood Jesus' "original" response in 7:15 to be in reference to the Levitical food laws. In fact, it was precisely the Pharisees' use of "tradition" to contravene the Mosaic law that made them "hypocrites." So one could evidently still take seriously 7:15, buttressed by the argument in 7:6–13, in the narrow terms of "defiled hands" and follow the Levitical food laws. This seems to have been how 7:15 was preserved in its present form in the primitive Church. Thus one need not assign its preservation from the outset to a less rigorously law-observant group in Jerusalem like the "Hellenists" of Acts (e.g., Hübner, *Gesetz,* 175; *NTS* 22 [1976] 340–45).

16 Though some have chosen to read this verse as appropriate to the "parable" setting (e.g., Taylor, 344; Schmithals, 1:343; Berger, *Gesetzesausle-*

gung, 479), most take it to be a later, copyist addition drawn from the similar literary context of 4:9, 23 (See *Note* a).

17 This verse opens with a temporal clause, "When he had entered a house away from the crowd" (ὅτε εἰσῆλθεν εἰς οἶκον ἀπὸ τοῦ ὄχλου), that changes the scene. As in 4:13, 33–34, the disciples receive special instruction about the "parables" in distinction from "the crowd." Though some have assigned this to pre-Markan tradition (e.g., Marxsen, *Exeget,* 16–20; Pesch, 1:380; Gnilka, 1:278), the compelling evidence supporting Mark's redactional work behind the setting in 7:14 strongly suggests that he introduces this contrasting scene shift here (so Taylor, 344; Grundmann, 195; Lambrecht, *ETL* 53 [1977] 61–62). The motif itself of contrasting Jesus' public and private teaching came to Mark in the tradition behind 4:1–20 (see *Comment* on 4:10, 13), but he employs it here, in 9:28, 33, and 10:10 by setting Jesus and the disciples "in a house" (see Best, *Jesus,* 226–27). The last time Jesus and the disciples retired to a "house" (οἶκον) apart from Jairus' (5:38) was in 3:20 (see *Comment* on 3:20).

"His disciples asked him about the parable" (ἐπηρώτων αὐτὸν οἱ μαθηταὶ αὐτοῦ τὴν παραβολήν). Mark again leaves his thumbprint with his characteristic verb of asking (ἐπηρώτων, see *Comment* on 4:10). He also identifies the saying in 7:15 as a "parable" (see *Comment* on 4:11) which he had exhorted "the crowd" to "hear and understand" (7:14).

18 Mark's redactional thematic and stylistic traits introduce Jesus' response to the disciples' question. The evangelist opens with his typical "and he said" (καὶ λέγει αὐτοῖς, see *Comment* on 4:11) to introduce Jesus' own question about the disciples' lack of understanding. And their lack of understanding becomes a major issue in 8:14–21 (see *Comment* on 4:13; 6:52).

"Are you also as lacking in understanding?" (οὕτως καὶ ὑμεῖς ἀσύνετοί ἐστε;). We learn two things from this question. First, "the crowd" to whom the "parable" was addressed (7:14) failed to grasp it. And second, "the disciples" in not grasping it are no different from "the crowd" in that respect. We have the same situation as in 4:13 compared to 4:11–12 (see *Comment* on 4:13). The difference, however, lies in their receiving, despite Jesus' rebuke, a further explanation. Therefore, Mark uses the disciples' question in private as the occasion for Jesus' explanation of 7:15.

"Do you not know . . . ?" (οὐ νοεῖτε;) sets the explanation in the form of a question. A similar combination of "understand" (συνίετε) and "know" (νοεῖτε) appears in Jesus' accusing query of 8:17 (cf. *Comment* on 4:13). At the same time, this second question poses a "rationalistic" or self-evident explanation to the first part of the parallel constructed saying in 7:15a: "Nothing entering into a person from outside can defile."

19 "Because it does not enter into one's heart but into the stomach. . . ." The reason given points directly to what enters through the mouth. This explanation corresponds neither in thrust nor in style to Mark's redaction (cf. Kümmel, *Wort,* 37; Schmithals, 1:341). Most agree that the evangelist found it combined with 7:15 in his tradition. This means that the original thrust of 7:15 had changed. From responding to the initial question about "defiled hands" (7:1–2, 5b) in terms of the larger issue of what defiles in general, the accent shifts from defilement in the second half of the saying

(7:15b) to the more narrow issue of "food" that enters one's mouth (so Matt 15:11). This change in emphasis came at some point after the issue of "tradition" (7:5b, 6–13) had been added but prior to Mark's use of the material.

"Into one's heart but into the stomach. . . ." (εἰς τὴν καρδίαν ἀλλ᾽ εἰς τὴν κοιλίαν) does draw on Jesus' response to the "tradition" question from Isa 29:13 (7:5a, 6–7) by noting that what enters "from outside" has no direct effect on one's "heart" (καρδίαν), the ultimate basis for one's relationship with God. Rather what enters "from outside" enters "the stomach" (εἰς τὴν κοιλίαν) and "comes out into the latrine" (εἰς τὸν ἀφεδρῶνα ἐκπορεύεται). Therefore, this explanation still takes 7:15 as the answer to the initial charge concerning the disciples' eating with "defiled hands" and in the process risking "defiling" their food. Since, however, on the basis of this argument "defiled" food does not "defile" the person, the disciples are exonerated for their behavior. The explanation subtly moves from "how" one eats to "what" one eats (Lührmann, WD 16 [1981] 86). It is only a short step then to the parenthetical comment that follows about "all foods."

"(Thus he cleansed all foods)" (καθαρίζων πάντα τὰ βρώματα). This comment raises two issues: to what does it refer and from whom does it come? Grammatically, this participial construction hangs awkwardly without obvious syntactical connection. Several, as exemplified by Black (Approach, 217–18), have sought to link it more directly to what immediately precedes as done by the Sinaitic Syriac. By taking "foods" (βρώματα) as singular and the participle as a passive, the sentence reads, ". . . for it enters not his heart but his belly, *all the food being cast out and purged away*" (Black, Approach, 217). Others view this as a possible anacoluthon drawing an obvious, if sarcastic, conclusion that the digestive process "cleanses all foods" (cf. Klostermann, 71; Grundmann, 195; Gnilka, 1:285). Most, however, take καθαρίζων to agree syntactically with the subject of λέγει in 7:18, i.e., Jesus (Lohmeyer, 142; Schweizer, 150; Berger, Gesetzesauslegung, 481; Lambrecht, ETL 53 [1977] 63; Pesch, 1:381; Lührmann, WD 16 [1981] 85).

The awkward construction has led some to suggest that its presence might reflect a later incorporation into the text of a scribal gloss (Lohmeyer, 142; Haenchen, 264, n. 3; Nineham, 196; Schweizer, 150). But more attribute it to the evangelist (Taylor, 345; Cranfield, 241; Klostermann, 71; Lambrecht, ETL 53 [1977] 41; Gnilka, 1:278; Quesnell, Mind, 90–91). A few guardedly handle it as part of the pre-Markan narrative (Carlston, NTS 15 [1968–69] 91; Pesch, 1:378; cf. Lührmann, WD 16 [1981] 85 ["narrator"]).

We have seen above that this comment grows logically out of the explanation in 7:18b–19. Thus it belongs syntactically with the subject of λέγει and states directly that Jesus not only declared food eaten with "defiled hands" to be clean but "all foods." This comment clearly pertains to the Levitical food laws and stems from a setting in the early Church that no longer observed them. But did Mark add it?

While this viewpoint may well have been shared by Mark's community, the issue as such does not emerge elsewhere in Mark's work. As we have seen, Mark's interest in 7:1–23 appears to focus more on what defiles than on the narrower concern about food laws. Furthermore, this awkward participial construction not only uses a *hapax legomenon* for "foods" but it fails to follow the normal pattern of the evangelist's parenthetical comments, generally a statement introduced by a conjunction. Therefore, it may well have been introduced into the story along with the other comments in 7:2b, 3–4 that clarify the behavior of the disciples, the Pharisees, and the logical implications of Jesus' explanation in 7:13, 18b–19.

20 This verse introduces the explanation of the second half of 7:15b, which it cites almost verbatim.

21–22 The explanation consists of a catalogue of vices which come "from within" and defile a person. The list includes thirteen vices summarized by the first, "evil thoughts" (οἱ διαλογισμοὶ οἱ κακοί). The following twelve fall into two groups of six each with the first group in the plural and second in the singular.

"Evil thoughts" renders οἱ διαλογισμοὶ οἱ κακοί too blandly for this context. Since these "thoughts" come from one's "heart" or person and give rise to the evil behaviors and attitudes that follow, "evil devisings" comes closer to capturing its thrust (Taylor, 345). This list of vices, unique to the Synoptics, has numerous parallels elsewhere in the NT (e.g., Rom 1:29–31; 1 Cor 5:10–11; 2 Cor 2:20–21; Gal 5:19–21; Col 3:5–8; 1 Tim 1:9–12; 2 Tim 3:2–5) and in hellenistic Jewish writings (see Berger, *Gesetzesauslegung*, 390–92). But the only real common denominator between the lists is that most begin with the vices of immorality (cf. Taylor, 347).

"Selfishness" renders the ethically loaded "evil eye" (ὀφθαλμὸς πονηρός). This phrase occurs in Jewish writings (e.g., Deut 15:9 LXX; Sir 14:10; 31:13) where "eye" signifies "intent" and "evil" or "bad eye" is generally the "antithesis of generosity: selfishness, covetousness, an evil and envious disposition, hatred of others" (Allison, *NTS* 33 [1987] 77; cf. Matt 20:15 RSV).

"Lack of moral sense" renders ἀφροσύνη, a word that occurs in the LXX for one lacking ethical or religious perception (Cranfield, 242).

23 This verse simply summarizes the thrust of the catalogue as an explanation of how one is "defiled" by the "vices" (πάντα ταῦτα τὰ πονηρά) that come "from within." As a summary statement, it places the weight again on the second half of 7:15, which specifies what really "defiles" a person. At the same time, it raises for the final time the key term "defilement" sounded in the opening scene of 7:1–2. It is impossible to say with certainty whether Mark composed this conclusion to accent the broader issue of what does and does not defile (e.g., Hübner, *Gesetz*, 7:15–22; Lambrecht, *ETL* 53 [1977] 65) or whether it formed a concluding inclusio with 7:2 in the expanded pre-Markan tradition. In either case, this story ends on the broader note of "all these evil things coming from within a person" rather than the narrower question of foods.

Explanation

This narrative discourse now has a different audience and slightly different focus from the controversy narrative in 7:1–13. This change in audience and ensuing separation of 7:15–22 (23) from 7:1–13 resulted from Mark's own arrangement of this material to address "the crowd" (7:14) and instruct the "disciples" (7:17–18b).

As an earlier part of the tradition behind 7:1–23, 7:15–22 (23) developed the two aspects of Jesus' antithetically formulated response in 7:15 to what may well have been the original question about eating with "defiled hands" (7:2, 5b). Even after the issue of "tradition" became paramount (7:5a, 6–13), Jesus' saying in 7:15 continued to answer specifically the question about eating with "defiled hands" by changing the level of debate to the fundamental question about what really defiles a person. This response, however, was eclipsed by the focus on "tradition" at the stage when that issue's importance led to its being incorporated into the narrative.

The addition of the commentary in 7:18b–19, 20–22 (23) to 7:15 accented again the question of eating with "defiled hands" and its consequence. In a community for whom the "tradition of the elders" provoked little concern, Jesus' rejection of the tradition of the elders' "human" rather than "divine" commandments" (7:6–13), tended to be at best academic. That food defiled by one eating with "defiled hands" did not defile a person (7:15) took on added significance. The accent fell equally on both halves of the antithetical parallelism, and especially emphasizing that defilement comes not from what enters but from what comes out of a person.

This conclusion finds rather crude, logical support in the way food passes through the stomach and is eventually eliminated as waste without any "contact" between it and one's "heart" (7:18b–19). Since the "heart" is the determinant factor in one's standing before God, it follows that "defiled" food cannot defile one's "heart" or "person." By contrast, all sorts of evil thoughts, attitudes and conduct emerge from within one's "heart" or person (7:20–22) and these make one "defiled" or unworthy of a direct relationship with God. Thus eating with "defiled hands" has no consequence.

Such an understanding of 7:15 leads logically to the next step reflected in the parenthetical comment in 7:19c. Jesus' saying in 7:15 explained with reference to what one eats by 7:18b–19 means that no foods, even those forbidden by the Levitical law (Lev 11–15), could defile one before God. In essence, Jesus "makes all foods clean." Thus what was latent in Jesus' response of 7:15 to the question about eating with "defiled hands" becomes explicit in the early Church's struggle with the purity laws pertaining to what should and should not be eaten.

Mark's concern is twofold. First, he is concerned to show that Jesus had removed the social boundaries that had separated people on the basis of "defilement." We noted this in his location of the two narratives just prior to Jesus' ministry to Gentiles in 7:24–37. His making of 7:15–22 (23) into a separate narrative by his change in setting (7:14) underscores its focus on what it is that defiles a person. We have no evidence that any of the issues ("defiled hands," "tradition of the elders," or even "foods") per se concerned Mark or his community. But both 7:1–13 and 7:14–23 explain how Jesus could move beyond the "purity" boundaries of Judaism and even the primitive Christian community. At the same time, it may point to the rather open character of Mark's community and the extent of their own mission.

Mark's second concern lies in his depiction of the disciples. This narrative resulted from the evangelist's arrangement of the setting first with "the crowd" (7:14) and then privately with "his disciples" (7:17). Furthermore, defining

Jesus' saying as a "parable," Mark portrays the disciples like "the crowd" as lacking understanding of Jesus' point. We found the same portrait in 4:13. The motif of the disciples' lack of understanding builds to a crescendo in 8:14–21. It certainly is one of the outstanding features of this section (6:7–8:26) of the Gospel (6:9; 6:52; 7:18a; 8:14–21). But despite their similarity to "the crowd" in failing to grasp Jesus' meaning and Jesus' disparaging remarks to them, they also differ from "the crowd" in that Jesus gives them special instruction indicative of their relationship to him (cf. 4:11, 13–20, 34).

Once again we have an ironic twist in Mark's portrait of the disciples. Using the motif of their lack of understanding which he found rooted in his tradition (e.g., 4:[10], [13]–20; 4:41; 6:37), he combines this with the disciples' privileged place by having them privately instructed by Jesus. In this way, they act as a foil by which Mark instructs and encourages his own community in the struggle and privilege of discipleship.

H. The Syrophoenician Woman (7:24–30)

Bibliography

Burkill, T. A. "Historical Development of the Story of the Syro-phoenician Woman." *NovT* 9 (1967) 161–77. ———— "The Syrophoenician Woman, the Congruence of Mk 7, 24–31." *ZNW* 57 (1966) 22–37. **Dalman, G.** *Sacred Sites and Ways.* Tr. P. Levertoff. New York: Macmillan, 1935. **Dermience, A.** "Tradition et rédaction dans la pericope de la Syrophonicienne: Marc 7, 24–30." *RTL* 8 (1977) 15–29. **Derrett, J. D. M.** "Law in the New Testament: The Syro-Phoenician Woman and the Centurion of Capernaum." *NovT* 15 (1973) 161–86. **Haenchen, E.** "Die Komposition von Mk 7:27–9:1 und Par." *NovT* 6 (1963) 81–109. **Iersel, B. W. van.** "Die wunderbare Speisung und das Abendmahl in der synoptischen Tradition." *NovT* 7 (1964) 167–94. **Jeremias, J.** *Jesus' Promise to the Nations.* SBT 14. London: SCM, 1958. **Kelber, W.** *The Kingdom in Mark: A New Place and a New Time.* Philadelphia: Fortress, 1974. **Kertelge, K.** *Die Wunder Jesu.* 1970. **Klauck, H. J.** *Allegorie und Allegorese in synoptischen Gleichnistexten.* NA 13. Münster: Aschendorff, 1978. **Koch, D.-A.** *Die Bedeutung der Wundererzählungen für die Christologie des Markusevangeliums.* 1975. **Manson, T. W.** *The Sayings of Jesus.* Repr. 1957. **Petersen, N. R.** "The Composition of Mark 4:1–8:26." *HTR* 73 (1980) 185–217. **Quesnell, Q.** *The Mind of Mark: Interpretation and Method through the Exegesis of Mark 6:52.* AnBib 38. Rome: Pontifical Biblical Institute, 1969. **Roloff, J.** *Das Kerygma und der irdische Jesus.* 1970. **Schenke, L.** *Die Wundererzählungen des Markusevangeliums.* 1974. **Standaert, B. H. M. G. M.** *L'évangile selon Marc: Composition et genre littéraire.* Zevenkerken-Brugge, 1984. **Storch, W.** "Zur Perikope von der Syrophönizierin. Mk 7,28 und Ri 1,7." *BZ* 14 (1970) 256–57. **Theissen, G.** *The Miracle Stories of the Early Christian Tradition.* 1983.

Translation

[24]*Arising, Jesus[a] went from there to the territory of Tyre.[b] After he had entered a house, he wanted no one to know about it,[a] but he was not able[c] to escape notice.* [25]*Rather, immediately after hearing about him, a woman whose[d] daughter had an unclean spirit came and fell at his feet.*

^{26} *The woman was a Greek, a Syrophoenician* ^{e} *by birth. And she kept asking* ^{f} *him to cast out the demon from her daughter.* ^{27} *And he said to her, "Let the children first be filled. For it is not right to take the children's bread and throw it to the dogs."* ^{28} *But she answered and said to him, "* ^{g} *Lord, even the dogs under the table eat from the crumbs of the children."*

^{29} *Jesus said to her, "Because of this word, go, the demon has departed from your daughter."* ^{30} *After she went to her house, she found the child lying on the bed and the demon having departed.*

Notes

^{a} Romanized words added from context.

^{b} Several witnesses read καὶ Σιδῶνος (ℵ A B $f^{1.13}$ Majority text *pc* lat sy$^{p.h}$ co), an assimilation to Matt 15:21 and Mark 7:31 (Metzger, *Textual Commentary*, 95). The two cities are commonly associated, and the reference to Sidon is unlikely to have been dropped. Text in D L W Δ Θ 565 *pc* it sy^s Or.

^{c} ἠδυνήθη is read by ℵ B and is an Ionic aorist of δυνέσθαι occurring frequently in the LXX and papyri but only here and in Matt 17:16 (B) in the NT (Taylor, 349). It is attested by A D L W Θ $f^{1.13}$ 892 1006 1342 1506 Majority text.

^{d} Awkward use of the resumptive pronoun following a relative pronoun (ἧς . . . αὐτῆς); see Taylor, 60.

^{e} B E F G H W $f^{1.13}$ 700 1006 1342 1506 2542 *pm* read Συρα Φοινικισσα; D it, simply Φοίνισσα. The reading ἡ δὲ γυνὴ ἦν χήρα Φοινίκισσα behind sy$^{sin.cur}$ followed by Lohmeyer (146), Grundmann (198) and Burkill (*ZNW* 57 [1966] 23) draws heavily on 1 Kgs 17–24 without Greek MS support.

^{f} "Kept asking" literally renders the imperfect ἠρώτα.

^{g} ναί read by ℵ A B D H L Δ f^1 33 579 892 1006 1342 1506 Majority text lat it sy$^{p.h}$ aligns Mark (only occurrence) with Matt 15:27 (8x Matt, 4x Luke). Text in D P^{45} W Θ f^{13} 565 700 it sy^s.

Form / Structure / Setting

Form-critically, the range of forms suggested for this narrative extend from apophthegm or pronouncement story (e.g., Taylor, 347) as a teaching narrative (e.g., Gnilka, 1:291) to a miracle story (e.g., Nineham, 198) with Koch calling it an apophthegmatic miracle story (*Wundererzählungen*, 85–86). Yet even Taylor qualifies his choice as being uncharacteristic of the form, and many interpreters have noted that the key ingredient of the healing miracle, the healing act, is missing. This has led to the positing of either an underlying apophthegm with the miracle features added later (e.g., Lohmeyer, 145) or a miracle story with the dialogue added subsequently (e.g., Kertelge, *Wunder*, 121). Burkill has even suggested that Jesus' aphoristic saying in 7:27b existed originally as an isolated saying which developed in four stages to what we find now in Mark and Matthew (*NovT* 9 [1967] 175–77).

Pesch (1:385–86; Klauck, *Allegorie*, 275) taking a lead from Theissen's analysis of miracle stories (see *Miracle Stories*, 113) notes that an overly developed exposition at the expense of other features, such as the act of healing itself, is a feature of "distance healing." Finding a formal parallel between this story and the Healing of the Centurion's Servant (Matt 8:5–10 par Luke 7:1–10; cf. John 4:46–54), Pesch then uses "distance healing narrative" as the formal designation (so Grundmann, 197; Klauck, *Allegorie*, 275).

The only examples of "distance healing narratives" in our Gospels involve Jesus healing Gentiles. While this may be coincidental, it could be that the situation of Jesus and a Gentile had something to do with the greater emphasis on the dialogue and the healing taking place from a "distance" for "purity" reasons rather than the form shaping the story. If so, the content shapes the form rather than the form shaping the content. This would also explain why this story fails to "fit" any "normal" formal pattern (see Schmithals, 1:356). Certainly, the interdependence of miracle and dialogue in this pericope precludes the attempts to trace its development from one form to another (so Schweizer, 151; Koch, *Wundererzählungen,* 86).

As to source, most assign the story with a few redactional additions to Mark's tradition. Matt 15:21–28 has a parallel with significant differences leading some to conclude that both were selectively drawing from a common source (e.g., Cranfield, 247). Most, however, view Matthew's story to be the evangelist's redactional product that included combining Mark with other traditional material drawn from Q and M (e.g., Taylor, 347; Manson, *Sayings,* 200–01; Burkill, *ZNW* 57 [1966] 25–28).

Almost without exception (cf. Taylor, 349; Cranfield, 246; Grundmann, 197), 7:24a (e.g., Pesch, 1:385; Ernst, 210) or 7:24–25a has been attributed to Mark's redaction (e.g., Klostermann, 71; Burkill, *ZNW* 57 [1966] 34; Kertelge, *Wunder,* 151; Koch, *Wundererzählungen,* 89; Schweizer, 151; Gnilka, 1:290). And many interpreters assign πρῶτον or the entire phrase of 7:27a to Mark's redaction as well (e.g., Schweizer, 151; Kertelge, *Wunder,* 153; Grundmann, 197; Klauck, *Allegorie,* 273; Gnilka, 1:290). If sustained, both redactional elements color how Mark utilized this traditional unit (see *Comment* on 7:24, 27).

The setting of this pericope in Mark's immediate context appropriately follows the two narratives on defilement (7:1–13, 14–23). Jesus now enters the gentile territory of Tyre north of Galilee and has contact with a specifically designated gentile woman whose daughter has an "unclean" spirit. Jesus' behavior illustrates his removal in 7:1–23 of the social boundaries of traditional Judaism based on ritual defilement (Kelber, *Kingdom,* 59). One can hardly miss the ramifications of this story for a community consisting at least in part of Gentiles (cf. "all the Jews," 7:3) and engaged in mission to Gentiles. At the same time, the story's content addresses the particular issue of Jesus' mission with reference to both Jews and Gentiles.

But this story also comes as a part of a larger piece in Mark's Gospel. The catchword "bread" (ἄρτος) connects at least verbally the two Feedings (6:30–44; 8:1–9), their following episodes of Walking on the Sea (6:45–52) and the discussion of "bread" (8:14–21) as well as the discussion of the disciples' behavior in 7:1–23. Furthermore, "eating their fill" in 7:27a has a counterpart in the two Feedings (6:42; 8:4, 8). Are these links merely mechanical devices for combining disparate traditions or do they reflect a special purpose behind Mark's combination? Furthermore, does this gentile woman who stands in contrast to the "children of God" also stand in contrast to the disciples as portrayed in this section? One can better answer these questions regarding the larger setting in Mark after an analysis of the story.

Comment

24 "From there" (ἐκεῖθεν) begins this section. Though Gennesaret (6:53) is often taken as the point of reference, Mark's consistent use of ἐκεῖθεν in contexts where the one leaves a "house" (6:1 [5:38–43]; 6:10–11; 9:30 [9:28–29]; 10:1 [9:33–50]) makes the "house" in 7:17 the place of departure. This idiosyncratic usage indicates both Mark's redactional hand and a desire to provide at least some continuity to the narrative flow of his text. Furthermore, the close lexical similarity between this opening statement and 10:1 also suggests Mark's redactional hand behind this "seam."

"The territory of Tyre" (τὰ ὅρια Τύρου) refers generally to the area under the jurisdiction of the coastal city of Tyre bordering on the north of Galilee running from the Mediterranean to Lake Simhu (Dalman, *Sites*, 197). This vague setting, if not traditional (e.g., Schenke, *Wundererzählungen*, 254), was perhaps drawn from the reference to the woman in 7:26 and serves to take Jesus from Galilee, the center of his activities to this point in Mark's narrative. Tyre, often linked with Sidon in Scripture (Isa 23:1–12; Jer 47:4; Joel 3:4–8; Zech 9:2; cf. 7:31), was a gentile area, whose inhabitants Josephus describes as "notoriously our bitterest enemies" (*Apion*, 1.13).

"After he had entered a house" (εἰσελθὼν εἰς οἰκίαν) gives Jesus' location but without mentioning a city, town or even how far he had gone into the area. Jesus as the subject of the sentences appears to be travelling alone. But one cannot press this too far in Mark's narrative. We find the same construction in 2:1, 15; 3:20; 7:17; 9:28 only to learn in the broader context that Jesus was not alone. We have no reason to assume here that he had left his disciples behind.

On this occasion, however, the entrance into a house does not set the stage for Jesus to instruct the disciples directly. Could it be implied that as elsewhere the introduction of the setting in a house by Mark signalled what follows to be instruction for the "disciples," i.e., Mark's readers? This would give strong indication that the "disciples" represented to an extent at least Mark's own audience.

"He wanted no one to know about it" (οὐδένα ἤθελεν γνῶναι) removes any doubt about Jesus' foray into this territory. He simply sought privacy away from the public. This excludes any desire by Jesus to engage in mission activity in this area and helps set the stage for the following dialogue that results in his working here nonetheless. Whatever role Mark or his tradition had in developing this setting, it did not violate the synoptic tradition as we know it which limits Jesus' ministry primarily to the areas of Galilee and Judea. Regardless of how much such a "mission" to the Gentiles might have supported the Church's gentile mission, this story along with that of the Centurion stays within the limits of the exception rather than the rule for Jesus' ministry.

"But he was unable to escape notice" (οὐκ ἠδυνήθη λαθεῖν). Even in gentile territory, Jesus could not escape public notice. The reference in 3:8 to people coming from Tyre and Sidon to hear and be healed by Jesus has already informed the reader that Jesus' fame had spread throughout the area. To attribute this move to Mark's "messianic secret" by which Jesus seeks to remain incognito (Wrede, *Secret*, 36–38) fails to note that here as in 1:45 and 6:31 Jesus sought privacy away from the crowds precisely because his "identity" was known and it always led to mission (e.g., 1:44–45; 2:1–2; 3:20; 6:31). Consequently, his identity and his mission are inseparable in Mark.

25 "Unclean spirit" (πνεῦμα ἀκάθαρτον), described from a Jewish perspective (see *Comment,* on 1:23), may reinforce the "unclean" setting for Jesus in 7:24–25 and offers a link with the discussion of defilement in 7:1–23. Mark may possibly have chosen to use this designation here (e.g., Klauck, *Allegorie,* 273). This designation changes to δαιμόνιον in 7:26, 29, 30 in keeping with Mark's style of using δαιμόνιον with βαλλεῖν (see *Comment,* on 1:23).

"Fell at his feet" (προσεπεσεν πρὸς τοὺς πόδας αὐτοῦ) occurs one other time in Mark with reference to Jairus, who requests help for a daughter (5:22). The contrast in types between a gentile woman and a president of the synagogue could not be more exaggerated. This gesture of supplication places one at the mercy of the other (cf. 1:40; 5:23).

26 "The woman was a Greek" (ἡ γυνὴ ἦν Ἑλληνίς) identifies her as a Gentile. While "Greek" may at times imply cultural standing of one "hellenized" or Greek speaking and educated and thus of the upper class (Gnilka, 1:292; Klostermann, 71), to refer to the "Greeks" in the early Christian mission meant primarily to contrast religiously the Jews and "the Greeks" with the latter synonymous with "non-Jews" or "pagans" (e.g., Rom 1:16; 2:9, 10; 3:9; 10:12; 1 Cor 1:24; 10:32; Gal 3:28; Col 3:11). The designation underscores the "gentile" setting of this territory. It also sharpens the issue in the ensuing dialogue about Jews and Gentiles in 7:27–28.

"A Syrophoenician by birth" (Συροφοινίκισσα τῷ γένει) identifies more narrowly her "citizenship" in contrast to a "Libophoenician" (Λιβυφοῖνιξ) or "Carthaginian" from northern Africa. In church tradition she becomes known as Justa and her daughter as Bernice (Pseudo-Clem. *Hom.* 2:19; 3:73). Despite the claims of some (cf. Grundmann, 198; Kertelge, *Wunder,* 152; Derrett, *NovT* 15 [1973] 162–74), the points of contact between this story and that of Elijah and the widow of Zarephath (1 Kgs 17:7–24) are too limited to be sustained. Standaert (*Marc,* 475–76), noting that this term, rare in Greek and Latin literature, occurs only twice in Latin sources (Lucilius, *Lives* 15, frag, 496-97; Juvenal, *Satires* 8.158-62) to refer to one who moves in the infamous part of Rome and to one of poor reputation, a prostitute, has suggested this nuance may also have set the woman off as morally unclean as well. "By birth"(τῷ γένει), however, puts the stress on her "gentile" origins rather than her moral character.

"To cast out the demon" (τὸ δαιμόνιον ἐκβάλῃ) shows that the woman had heard not only of Jesus' presence in the area but also that he had the power to exorcise demons. This implied that Jesus' fame had clearly spread to the populace of Tyre (cf. 3:8). By seeking him out and asking for his help, she entrusted herself to him and acknowledged without question his power to accomplish the task.

27 "Let the children first be filled" (ἄφες πρῶτον χορτασθῆναι τὰ τέκνα). Several have taken this part of Jesus' response as a secondary softening of his answer that now actually preempts the force of the woman's rejoinder in 7:28. Many have assigned it to Mark (e.g., Kertelge, *Wunder,* 153; Schweizer, 151; Gnilka, 1:290, 292; Klauck, *Allegorie,* 279) or a pre-Markan redactor (e.g., Roloff, *Kerygma,* 160, n. 200; Koch, *Wundererzählungen,* 88; cf. Schenke, *Wundererzählungen,* 256–57).

The crux of this statement lies more with "be filled" (χορτασθῆναι) than with "first" ($\pi\rho\tilde{\omega}\tau o\nu$), although the latter generally gets most of the attention. The only other occurrences of this verb in Mark come in the two Feeding stories (see 6:42 and 8:8). This has led to the suggestion that Mark added the clause here to interpret the first Feeding as the "children's" or for the Jews and the second Feeding as the "dog's" or for the Gentiles (see *Comment*, on 8:3) in support of the legitimate place of both Jewish and gentile Christians at the Lord's Table (e.g., Burkill, *ZNW* 57 [1966] 29–30; van Iersel, *NovT* 7 [1964] 188–89; Klauck, *Allegorie*, 273, 279; Quesnell, *Mind*, 224–28). But this allusion is not only too subtle for Mark's style but it fails to stand up under scrutiny.

Without question "bread" ($\check{\alpha}\rho\tau o\varsigma$) and "filled" ($\chi o\rho\tau\acute{\alpha}\zeta\epsilon\iota\nu$) also occur in the two Feedings. But need that be any more than coincidence in view of the common setting they share, namely, eating in which "bread" ($\check{\alpha}\rho\tau o\varsigma$) and "eating to one's fill" ($\chi o\rho\tau\acute{\alpha}\zeta\epsilon\iota\nu$) have their own logical place (cf. Matt 5:6; Luke 6:21)? Furthermore, such a reading takes Jesus' response about "being filled" either more literally (a reference to the Feedings) than the immediate context in this pericope necessitates or more figuratively (in reference to the Feedings) than the Feeding stories themselves allow. This pericope can and must determine first the referents of "the children," the "dogs," the "bread" and then "being filled."

What then is the meaning of the children's "being filled?" No one questions in view of the general biblical use and the immediate context that the "children" refers to the "Jews." "Being filled" then has to refer to Israel's place in salvation history and her claim to God's blessing. Therefore, Jesus' opening remark stakes Israel's claim to God's blessing as paramount. But was it exclusive?

"First" ($\pi\rho\tilde{\omega}\tau o\nu$) implies that Israel's claim was not exclusive. That Israel's "being filled" connoted a sequence of God's salvation "to the Jew first and then to the Greek" certainly represented the principle of Paul's mission (Rom 1:16) as well as the schematic of the mission in Acts. But could it have had its roots here in Jesus' ministry (cf. Jeremias, *Promise*, 29–30)? The answer hinges on the internal logic of Jesus' response and the woman's rejoinder.

"For it is not right to take the children's bread and throw it to the dogs." Much has been made of the apparently harsh words used by Jesus (see Burkill, *NovT* 9 [1967] 170–73). Ample OT (Deut 23:19; 1 Sam 17:43; 24:14; 2 Sam 9:8; 16:9; 2 Kgs 8:13; Prov 26:11; Sir 13:18; O. Michel, *TDNT* 3 [1965] 1101–02) and rabbinic (Str-B, 1:724–26) evidence supports the pejorative use of "dogs." But did Jesus use the term primarily pejoratively here?

The appeal to the diminutive $\tau o\tilde{\iota}\varsigma$ $\kappa\upsilon\nu\alpha\rho\acute{\iota}o\iota\varsigma$ as an ameliorating "pet dogs" or even "household dogs" supported by their presence "under the table" (e.g., Lohmeyer, 147; Grundmann, 198; Lane, 262; Schweizer, 152) begs the question. Apart from the fact that the passage has several diminutives without significant force (e.g., $\theta\upsilon\gamma\acute{\alpha}\tau\rho\iota o\nu$, $\kappa\upsilon\nu\acute{\alpha}\rho\iota o\nu$, $\psi\iota\chi\acute{\iota}o\nu$, $\pi\alpha\iota\delta\acute{\iota}o\nu$), Jesus' reply makes use of a household scene to contrast between the "children" and the "dogs" with the former referring to the Jews and the latter to the Gentiles, a contrast in kind rather than degree.

Jesus flatly refuses the woman's (a "dog" or a Gentile) request for his redemptive help ("the bread" [$\tau\grave{o}\nu$ $\check{\alpha}\rho\tau o\nu$]) that belongs exclusively to "the children" (the Jews). Even should we read this reply as an explanation of the first response (cf. "for" [γάρ]), the temporal qualification in 7:27a merely softens Jesus' reply by leaving open the possibility for the "dogs," the Gentiles, to receive help but only after the "children," the Jews, have "been filled." Since that time was not completed in terms of the immediate situation, the temporal clause offered neither comfort nor hope for the woman whose time as a Gentile by her own admission (7:28) had not come. In short, Jesus rejected her request because of who she was, a Gentile.

28 The woman's rejoinder, however, makes clear that she took Jesus' answer to refer to Israel's privilege exclusively rather than temporarily, which supports the suggestion that πρῶτον is a later, temporal qualification. She recognized the "divinely ordained division between God's people and the Gentiles" (Jeremias, *Promise*, 30).

"Even the dogs" (καὶ τὰ κυνάρια) accepts the contrast in kind and that the "bread" was for the "children" not for the "dogs." The woman, however, takes the figurative scene and extends its application by noting that "*even the dogs under the table*" do have a claim, though it be only for the "crumbs" (ψιχίων). Hardly an allusion to the "superabundance" of the Messianic age comparable to the leftovers of the two Feedings (Burkill, *ZNW* 57 [1966] 29–30), the "crumbs" (τῶν ψιχίων) play a different role in this story. The statement recognizes the "children's" prerogative and the subordinate order of the "dogs'" claim. Yet the fact that the "dogs" eat the "childrens' crumbs" (ἀπὸ τῶν ψιχίων τῶν παιδίων) *during* the meal belies any trace of temporal order in her claim. Therefore, the woman's response did not use the loophole implied by "Let the children *first* be filled."

The logic of the dialogue, therefore, suggests that the temporal sequence in Israel's privilege implied by 7:27a does not reflect a secondary addition to soften Jesus' reply (Jeremias, *Promise*, 29, n. 2). But might not the entire clause or just the key term πρῶτον have been added to echo the early Christian mission struggles with the prerogatives of the Jews and the mission to the Gentiles? Mark appears to be beyond these debates. In fact, the very point of the setting of 7:1–23 makes the distinction between Jew and Greek irrelevant. But what about a pre-Markan setting?

Was there ever a wing in the primitive Christian Church so exclusively Jewish as to deny a mission at least at some point to the Gentiles? One would have to posit such a front if 7:27a were to reflect conflicting mission objectives. But Roloff correctly notes the absence of any trace of a Jewish Christianity that so absolutely rejected the possibility of a gentile mission (Roloff, *Kerygma*, 161, n. 201; cf. Jeremias, *Promise*, 71). This saying then like Matt 15:24 could accurately reflect Jesus' own ministry as one sent to the "house of Israel" to declare God's day of salvation to his people. This gentile, Syrophoenician woman did not qualify on that basis.

Jesus' ministry did not exclude Gentiles entirely as the synoptic tradition indicates, but the Gentiles participated by receiving the "children's crumbs" through an act of faith in Jesus as the one sent to Israel. For Mark, however, this very participation became possible because of the ultimate thrust of Jesus' redemptive ministry that removed the social/ritual boundaries between Jew and Greek, clean and unclean (e.g., 1:40–45; 5:1–20, 21–43; 7:1–23, 24–30). To that extent, the temporal "first" was a matter of the past.

"Lord" (κύριε) connotes more than a polite "sir" by a Gentile (e.g., Taylor, 351; Schweizer, 152). As the context indicates, the woman acknowledged in the address typical of gentile Christianity that Jesus was "Lord" (Gnilka, 1:293; Ernst, 213). This "title" of "Lord" that consistently comes on the lips of "believers" in Matthew occurs only this one time with confession overtones in Mark and sets the stage for Jesus' concluding remark and his offer of help to the woman.

29 "Because of this word" (διὰ τοῦτον τὸν λόγον) draws attention to the woman's response. Matt 15:28 captures its thrust by referring to her response as "great faith" (μεγάλη ἡ πίστις). Mark, whose stories have made so much of faith or its absence (cf. 2:1–12; 5:21–43; 6:1–6a), lets the story stand as evidence. It portrays her as coming to Jesus in need and recognizing him to be one who could exorcise the demon from her daughter (7:26). Acknowledging Jesus through her gesture of prostration, she addressed him as "Lord." When refused because of who she was, a Gentile asking for the blessing that rightfully belonged to the Jews, she accepted Israel's prerogative but laid claim to God's benefit that came through the Jews, the crumbs from the childrens' table. In short, she had yielded to one in whom the God of Israel was at work. This was her "great faith" (Roloff, *Kerygma*, 160).

"The demon has departed from your daughter" (ἐξελήλυθεν ἐκ τῆς θυγατρός σου τὸ δαιμόνιον) declares what has happened without any direct act or word of healing being given by Jesus. Yet this word implies that he had answered her request rather than having a telepathic awareness of a sudden recovery (e.g., Taylor, 351; Mann, 319).

30 "She found her daughter . . . the demon having departed" confirms the miracle.

Explanation

Mark takes a story about a gentile woman, a Syrophoenician, who comes to Jesus requesting his help and places it in the context of a broader discussion of defilement (7:1–23) to illustrate the force of Jesus' ministry in removing all barriers between Jews and Gentiles. He underscores this by placing Jesus in the "territory of Tyre," an area synonymous with non-Jews.

Yet Mark does not depict Jesus as desiring to engage in a gentile mission either by his movement from Galilee into gentile territory or by his response to the woman seeking his help. To the contrary, Mark makes clear that Jesus withdrew to this area to avoid the public. His retiring to a house may reinforce this desire, but as elsewhere it offers a setting for instruction.

The instruction, however, comes much more indirectly. No mention is made of the disciples, the ones Jesus generally instructs in a house setting. What follows is a story rather than an address. But the house setting suggests the story to be instructive, at least for Mark's audience regarding Jesus' ministry.

Though Jesus has just removed the issue of defilement in 7:1–23, he maintains the distinction between the "Jews and the Greeks" by drawing attention to Israel's prerogative. As the "children," they have a claim on the "bread," God's blessing through Jesus. In other words, this story, despite its setting and characters, does not imply that Jesus removed the divinely set prerogative of Israel for his mission.

The woman's response accepts this prerogative but notes that the "dogs" also have a claim. This claim means that the Gentiles can also receive God's blessing but do so by recognizing Jesus to be God's blessing for Israel. Recognizing her "faith," Jesus provides her daughter the same deliverance he has offered to Israel. This deliverance has been typified by Mark in Jesus' power to exorcise the demonic (cf. 1:21–28). In other words, the Kingdom of God at work in Jesus' ministry extends to the Gentiles.

Mark makes little of the temporal sequence implied by the statement that "the children first be filled." By letting it stand, this reference (7:27a) does not deny Israel's place in salvation history. Set in the immediate context of Jesus' ministry which removes the social and ritual boundaries between Jew and Greek (7:1–23) it does imply that Israel's "first" is now a point of history rather than a current principle behind the Church's mission strategy.

The woman's reply to Jesus demonstrates that the response of one's heart ultimately qualifies one's relationship to God (cf. 7:15–23). This message becomes clear when the woman's posture toward Jesus negates her being a Syrophoenician, a Greek, from the territory of Tyre, one of the "dogs" who have no claim on the "childrens' bread." At the same time, one cannot avoid the contrast the woman offers not only to the "Jews" who reject Jesus in the previous narratives (cf. 7:1–13) but also to the disciples whose misunderstanding Mark has accented in the surrounding stories (see 6:52; 7:18; and 8:14–21).

Therefore, this story about Jesus' ministry that crosses the social boundaries of the day remains both consistent to what the tradition indicates about Jesus' primary concern for Israel and makes clear how that ministry provided the impetus for the early Church to transcend these boundaries based on one's response to Jesus.

I. The Healing of the Deaf-Mute (7:31–37)

Bibliography

Baird, T. "Translating *orthos* at Mark 7:35." *ExpTim* 92 (1981) 337–38. **Black, M.** "ΕΦΦΑΘΑ (Mk 7,34), [ΤΑ] ΠΑΣΧΑ (Mt 26,18), [ΤΑ] ΣΑΒΒΑΤΑ (*passim*), [ΤΑ] ΔΙΔΡΑΧΜΑ (Mt 17,24 bis)." In *Mélanges Bibliques*, FS B. Rigaux, ed. A. Descamps. Gembloux: Duculot, 1970. 37–62. **Bonner, C.** "Traces of Thaumaturgic in Miracles." *HTR* 20 (1927) 171–81. **Burkill, T. A.** "The Syrophoenician Woman, the Congruence of Mk 7,24–31." *ZNW* 57 (1966) 23–37. **Dalman, G.** *Sacred Sites and Ways: Studies in the Topography of the Gospels.* Tr. P. Levertoff. New York: Macmillan, 1935. **Emerton, J.** "ΜΑΡΑΝΑΘΑ and ΕΦΦΑΘΑ." *JTS* 18 (1967) 427–31. **Kertelge, K.** *Die Wunder Jesu in Markusevangelium.* 1970. **Koch, D.-A.** *Die Bedeutung der Wundererzählungen für die Christologie des Markusevangeliums.* 1975. **Lang, F. G.** "'Über Sidon mitten ins Gebiet der Dekapolis': Geographie und Theologie in Markus 7,31." *ZDPV* 94 (1978) 145–60. **Luz, U.** "Das Geheimnismotiv und die markinische Christologie." *ZNW* 56 (1965) 9–30 = "The Secrecy Motif and Marcan Christology." In *The Messianic Secret*, ed. C. Tuckett. London/Philadelphia: SPCK/Fortress, 1983. 75–96. **Marxsen, W.** *Mark the*

Evangelist. 1969. **Morag, S.** "Ἐφφαθά (Mark vii. 34): Certainly Hebrew, Not Aramaic?" *JSS* 17 (1972) 198–202. **Parker, S. T.** "The Decapolis Reviewed." *JBL* 94 (1975) 437–41. **Rabinowitz, I.** "'Be Opened' = Ἐφφαθά (Mark 7,34): Did Jesus Speak Hebrew?" *ZNW* 53 (1962) 229–238. ———. "ΕΦΦΑΘΑ (Mark VII. 34): Certainly Hebrew, Not Aramaic." *JSS* 16 (1971) 151–56. **Robinson, J. M.** *The Problem of History in Mark.* SBT 21. London: SCM, 1957. **Schenke, L.** *Die Wundererzählungen des Markusevangeliums.* 1974. **Theissen, G.** *The Miracle Stories of the Early Christian Tradition.* 1983.

Translation

[31] *Departing again from the territory of Tyre,* Jesus[a] *went through Sidon*[b] *into the middle of the territory of the Decapolis to the Sea of Galilee.* [32] *And they brought to him a deaf man who could hardly speak and appealed to him to lay his hand on him.* [33] *Taking* the man[a] *away from the crowd privately,* Jesus[a] *put his fingers into* the man's[a] *ears and spitting he touched* the man's[a] *tongue.* [34] *Looking to heaven he sighed and said to him, "Ephphatha," which means "be opened."* [35] *Immediately his ears were opened and his tongue's fetter was loosed and he began speaking properly.* [36] *And Jesus commanded them to tell no one. But the more he commanded them, the more they proclaimed it.* [37] *They were absolutely overwhelmed saying, "He has done all things well. He makes the deaf to hear and the mute to speak!"*

Notes

[a] Romanized words added from context.

[b] Several witnesses read καὶ Σιδῶνος ἦλθεν to smooth the apparent awkwardness of the itinerary (p45 A W f1.13 1006 1506 Majority text syr samss). The text is supported by ℵ B D L Δ Θ 33 565 700 892 1342 2427 lat samss bo.

Form / Structure / Setting

Form-critically, this story represents a classic healing narrative. Kertelge (*Wunder,* 158) refers to it as a "hellenistic" miracle story because of the numerous thaumaturgic elements such as touching the affected organs, spitting, looking to heaven, inhaling deeply, and a ῥῆσις βαρβαρική that play an important role in those stories. Generally, the healing narratives in the Gospels place much more emphasis on Jesus' word. Even here the actual healing takes place when Jesus commands, "Be opened!"

As to source, most assign 7:32–35, 37a to Mark's tradition. Dibelius (73) raised questions about the general acclamation in 7:37 following a particular episode and attributed it to a separate group of stories (so Taylor, 352; Nineham, 202). The stylistic and structural similarity between this healing and the healing of the blind man in 8:22–26 has led several to view these stories as having been paired originally in the tradition so that 7:37 would have served as the acclamation for both miracles (e.g., Cranfield, 253; Gnilka, 1:296; Ernst, 215).

Apart from Schmithals (1:357–58), the itinerary of 7:31 leading into this story has been assigned in part or as a whole to Mark's redaction. A few assign the mention of the Decapolis to the traditional story (e.g., Schmidt,

200–01; Marxsen, *Mark,* 70; Pesch, 1:393; Schenke, *Wundererzählungen,* 269). But most assign it (cf. 5:20) and the "Sea of Galilee" (cf. 1:16) to Mark along with the reference to Tyre drawn from the previous story and combined with Sidon, its close neighbor (cf. 3:8; see *Comment* on 7:24). In addition, most assign 7:36 to Mark based on his "secret" motif and/or its disruption of the narrative flow (Klostermann, 74; Lohmeyer, 151; Grundmann, 201; Haenchen, 270–77; Luz, *ZNW* 50 [1905] 10, Kertelge, *Wunder,* 157, Schweizer, 154; Gnilka, 1:296; Schmithals, 1:357; Schenke, *Wundererzählungen,* 271; cf. Theissen, *Miracle Stories,* 68–69; Pesch, 1:398; Ernst, 214–15).

As to structure, Grundmann (200–01) has divided 7:32–37 into six strophes of three lines each. Lohmeyer (149) omitting 7:36 notes that the narrative consists of five sentences, each having three predicates that form short, uniform clauses. And Kertelge (*Wunder,* 157) has alluded to the "poetic" form of the story based on its rhythmic construction. Apart from the secrecy command in 7:36 which stands in tension with the withdrawal from the crowds in 7:33 and the notice of amazement in 7:37a, the narrative moves smoothly along the lines of a healing story. The companions and crowd form the subject of 7:32 and 7:37, surrounding the healing event of 7:33–35.

The setting of this story following Jesus' encounter with the Syrophoenician woman and introduced by the itinerary of 7:31 continues the motif of Jesus' work among the Gentiles or at least in gentile territory. With no change of venue given at the outset of 8:1, this pericope also suggests that the ensuing Feeding takes place in the same area. The locale, which Mark was at least in part responsible for creating, speaks for itself as in 5:1–20. Yet the evangelist reflects no particular interest in accenting this point by defining the crowd or the deaf-mute as particularly gentile or "Greek" (cf. 7:26).

This story also plays a role in Mark's larger context. We have noted several occasions where he has underscored the disciples' lack of understanding in the previous stories (e.g., 6:52; 7:18). This motif comes to a head in a conversation after the next Feeding when Jesus accuses them of having "eyes" that do not see and "ears" that do not hear (8:14–21). The healing of the blind man at Bethsaida (8:22–26)—the second member along with this story of a probable traditional pair of miracles—follows this critique. At the same time, the crowd's acclamation in 7:37 in reference to the fulfillment of Isa 35:5–6 corresponds to Peter's subsequent confession at Caesarea Philippi in 8:27–30. Thus Jesus' role in healing the deaf-mute in the Decapolis and the blind man at Bethsaida has a deeper significance for his relation with the disciples and their seeing and hearing what he was revealing to them about God.

Comment

31 This verse in the eyes of many describes what is at best an improbable if not nonsensical route. Abandoning any attempt at making sense of it, several like Cranfield (250) have concluded "that this verse reflects a certain vagueness on Mark's part about the geography of northern Palestine." Taken literally and in sequence, the route is comparable to going from New York City to the Chesapeake Bay through Boston (254). The matter becomes the more difficult if the statement simply seeks to move Jesus from "New York" to the "Bay." And add to this itinerary the further problem of the apparent dislocation of the Chesapeake Bay to the middle of Maryland and you have the basis for the despair.

"From the territory of Tyre" refers back (cf. πάλιν) to 7:24 (see *Comment* on 7:4).

"Through Sidon" (διὰ Σιδῶνος) denotes a city twenty miles north of the other major coastal city of Tyre located in the area north of Galilee. The territory of Sidon extended from the Mediterranean on the west to the area of Damascus on the east. "Through Sidon" most likely refers to the city but may refer to the territory and could have been added in view of its common association with Tyre (see *Comment* on 7:24). In any case, Jesus travels north from the location in the previous story.

"To the Sea of Galilee" (εἰς τὴν θάλασσαν τῆς Γαλιλαίας) appears to be the final destination. This is the second occurrence in Mark of the full designation "Sea of Galilee" (see *Comment* on 1:16) and may serve here to distinguish this "sea" from the Mediterranean Sea on which both Tyre and Sidon lie.

"The middle of the territory of the Decapolis" (ἀνὰ μέσον τῶν ὁρίων Δεκαπόλεως, see *Comment* on 5:20) presents two options. First, as a qualifier of "Sea of Galilee" it would mean "to the Sea of Galilee in the middle of the territory of the Decapolis." This reading conflicts with the geographical data, since the sea borders only a part of the Decapolis and certainly is not in the middle of it. The rendering "*within* the territory" (e.g., Cranfield, 250; Lane, 265) eases this tension somewhat but lacks lexical support (Lang, *ZDPV* 94 [1978] 153, n. 47). Second, as a location itself, the phrase would mean "through the middle of the territory of the Decapolis." This alternative has Jesus coming through "the middle of the Decapolis" from the north to the Sea of Galilee (e.g., Lang, *ZDPV*, 94 [1978] 152–54) in keeping with the use of ἀνὰ μέσον. Its location following rather than preceding the ultimate destination point, the Sea of Galilee, makes this construction awkward at best, but corresponds to Mark's style of placing last in a list the immediate locale for what follows (cf. 10:1 and 11:1). This construction may also suggest Mark's having found the location at the opening of the miracle story in 7:32–37 (e.g., Schmidt, 201; Marxsen, 70; Pesch, 1:393; Schenke, *Wundererzählungen,* 269).

Numerous attempts have been made at tracing a journey behind these data. Wellhausen's conjecture (58, followed by Klostermann, 73; Taylor, 353; Mann, 322) that διὰ Σιδῶνος mistranslates an underlying בציד׳ן meaning Bethsaida so that Jesus returned from the territory of Tyre through Bethsaida to the east bank of the Sea of Galilee greatly simplifies the problem. But it lacks textual support and also assumes an underlying Aramaic tradition that either Mark or a pre-Markan redactor mistranslated, a view that is hardly consistent with the hellenistic tone of this story.

Two other suggestions have emerged as possibilities. Dalman (*Sites,* 200–01; so Cranfield, 250; Lane 265; Schmithals, 1:357–58) proposed a route from Tyre via Sidon across to Caesarea Philippi and down through Philip's territory to the sea at Hippos. But this route hardly runs through "the middle of the Decapolis." A second alternative explored more recently in detail by Lang (*ZDPV* 94 [1978] 146, 152–54; so Grundmann, 201) and proposed initially by H. J. Holtzmann (*Die Synoptiker,* HC I/1, 3d ed. [Tübingen: Mohr,

1901], 144–45) runs from the territory of Tyre north to Sidon then across Lebanon to the territory of Damascus which bordered the eastern territory of Sidon and then southeast through perhaps the Decapolis cities of Dium, Abila, Gadara and eventually through Hippos to the sea. This extended route is geographically possible and takes all the places in 7:31 into account, including "the middle of the Decapolis."

Either alternative implies that Jesus took a longer than necessary journey to reach the Sea of Galilee in the area of the Decapolis. Ultimately, therefore, the question comes down to whether Mark's redaction accidentally produced a confused "itinerary" by virtue of his combining traditional materials (e.g., Marxsen, *Mark,* 70; Schweizer, 154; Haenchen, 276; Pesch, 1:373) that may or may not reflect on his geographical knowledge or whether Mark has deliberately though awkwardly constructed an itinerary *de novo* or from the tradition behind 7:24–30 and 7:32–37.

In the first case, Mark has simply made a mess of getting Jesus from the "territory of Tyre" to the "Sea of Galilee in the middle of the territory of the Decapolis." In the second case, Mark has given us more than a transitional verse in 7:31. He has given us a journey that comes to a stop with the healing in 7:32–37 and the Feeding in 8:1–9.

Lang (*ZDPV* 94 [1978] 145–60) argues convincingly that Mark intended the latter by having Jesus travel through the gentile lands north and east of Galilee. Schweizer (154) concludes that this itinerary was Mark's attempt to name the foreign lands around Galilee and show that the message was available to the gentile world. One must, however, guard against viewing this itinerary more technically as a mission to the Gentiles by Jesus for Mark. Mark makes it clear at the outset that Jesus did not want to work publicly in the territory of Tyre (cf. 7:24). The story itself distinguishes between the claim of the Jews and the Gentiles on Jesus' ministry. And Mark does not depict Jesus pausing along this route to teach or heal anywhere else prior to this story at the end of the journey.

Consequently, the evangelist may well have found this miracle story located "in the middle of the Decapolis" in the tradition behind 7:32–37 (cf. 5:1–20). And since the Feeding in 8:1–10 concludes with a sea crossing, Mark had to take Jesus through the "middle of the Decapolis" to the Sea of Galilee where he boarded the boat immediately after feeding the four thousand. If this was meant to be more than a transition between 7:24–30 and 31–37 but not a mission to the Gentiles during Jesus' ministry, why then have Jesus make this extensive trip? The answer lies in Mark's setting 7:24–8:10 in the immediate context of the defilement question behind 7:1–23. Constrained by his loyalty to the tradition of Jesus' ministry, Mark could not develop a full-fledged mission to the Gentiles when the tradition did not support it. So the evangelist made use of isolated traditions (e.g., 7:24–30; 7:32–37; cf. 5:1–20) about Jesus ministering in gentile lands to show how Jesus' teaching on defilement (7:1–23) was borne out by his own travel into areas to the north (Tyre and Sidon) and east (the Decapolis) of Galilee beyond the social and political boundaries of Judaism. It was Mark's way of showing that the mission extending far beyond these boundaries by his day had its legitimacy in Jesus' own ministry of word and deed.

32 "They brought" (φέρουσιν). The story proper begins here with no identification of who or where. Even if "in the middle of the Decapolis" were originally the setting, it fails to give a specific location. Pesch (1:394) attributes this lack of specificity to the character of oral tradition for which the story's use filled in the blanks. Obviously, Jesus was one subject. But was the man a Jew or a Gentile? And who were those who "brought" him to Jesus?

In Mark's narrative the setting of 7:1–23 and 24–37 and particularly the itinerary of 7:31 leads the reader to view the man as a Gentile. Those bringing him to Jesus obviously have an expectation which implies knowledge of at least Jesus' reputation to heal. Read in the larger context of Mark's narrative, their coming may have resulted from the "preaching" of the Gerasene demoniac in the Decapolis (cf. 5:1–20) about all that Jesus had done for him (Schmithals, 1:358).

"A deaf man who could hardly speak" (κωφόν καὶ μογιλάλον). κωφός used more specifically here as "deaf" has the general meaning of "blunt" or "dull" (BGD, s.v.). "Could hardly speak" renders the extremely rare μογιλάλος. An NT *hapax legomenon,* it appears once in the LXX, in Isa 35:6. Since the Isaiah passage appears again behind the acclamation of 7:37, it clearly influenced the choice of wording here. Whether the man was actually mute (cf. ἄλαλος, 7:37) or had a severe speech impediment—perhaps as a byproduct of his deafness—(cf. ἐλάλει ὀρθῶς, 7:35) is immaterial. Since 7:35 gives the results of Jesus' healing based on the condition described in 7:32, the latter is more likely. Mark 7:37 interprets Jesus' healing more generally in view of Isa 35:5–6. In either case, the man's hearing and his speaking ability needed healing.

"Lay a hand on him" (see *Comment* on 5:23).

33 "Taking him away from the crowd privately" has been variously explained as: (a) Mark's penchant for getting Jesus alone away from the crowds (Schenke, *Wundererzählungen,* 270–71); (b) a part of Mark's Messianic Secret (e.g., Nineham, 203; Gnilka, 1:297); (c) the desire to avoid the curiosity seekers in the crowd (e.g., Grundmann, 201; Ernst, 216); or (d) a means of preserving the secret process of the healing (Klostermann, 73; Pesch, 1:394; Gnilka, 1:297; see Theissen, *Miracle Stories,* 68–69). Though Mark may have enhanced the motif of privacy (cf. κατ᾿ ἰδίαν, see *Comment* on 4:34), this is one of only two times that Jesus takes someone aside for healing. The other is the structurally and stylistically similar miracle of 8:22–26 (23). Furthermore, the secrecy motif corresponds with the presence of several other actions which may well suggest the pre-Markan shaping of this story in a "hellenistic" context (Kertelge, *Wunder,* 158–59; Pesch, 1:395–96), a context appropriate for Jesus' healing of a Gentile in gentile territory. "Put his fingers into the man's ears and spitting touched his tongue" are two such gestures obviously related to the man's condition. More appears to be implied than that Jesus merely touched the man's impaired organs to establish contact and offer the hope of or even to summon healing through touch because words would have been inadequate (cf. Grundmann, 202; Schweizer, 154; Ernst, 216). The summaries of 6:56 and 3:10 as well as the healing of the woman in 5:25–34 have highlighted touch as a means of healing (see *Comment* on 5:30), and Jesus' spitting connotes more than a gesture of communication. Thus each gesture represents an integral part of the healing miracle.

The text does not say why Jesus spit or what he did with the spittle. We do know, however, that spittle supposedly had a therapeutic function in both the Greco-Roman (e.g., Pliny, *Nat. Hist.* 28.4.7; Tacitus, *Hist.* 6.18; Suetonius, *Vesp.* 7) and the Jewish world (Str-B, 2:15–17). In 8:22–26 and in John 9:1–7 Jesus mixes spittle with some earth and uses it to heal blindness. In Gal 4:14 spitting has an apotropaic function against evil spirits and disease (H. Schlier, *TDNT* 2 [1964] 448).

34 "Looking to heaven" (ἀναβλέψας εἰς τὸν οὐρανόν) combined with the "sighing" (ἐστέναξεν) introduces two other gestures. The identical phrase, "looking to heaven," appears in 6:41 at the outset of the miracle of the Feeding. Yet some interpreters have distinguished between the two statements by taking the first to be a gesture of prayer and the second a thaumaturgic gesture of receiving superhuman power (e.g., Pesch, 1:396; Gnilka, 1:297). Context certainly qualifies a phrase's meaning and the blessing that follows in 6:41 supports taking the gesture there as a moment of prayer as in John 11:41. The absence, however, of any reference to prayer in this context need not exclude its being implied nor does the one alternative exclude the other. Jesus needed power to feed the multitude and to raise Lazarus just as he needed power to heal this deaf-mute. In all three cases, his looking to heaven points to his relation with God from whom he receives the power to feed the hungry, heal the sick and raise the dead.

"He sighed" (ἐστέναξεν). This action has also been taken as a therapeutic gesture with parallels in ancient magical healings (e.g., Dibelius, 85–86). Some have interpreted it as an expression of "pneumatic excitement" typical of ancient miracle stories (Bonner, *HTR* 20 [1927] 171–81; Dibelius, 85–86). But this gesture too is associated with prayer. It can represent a sign of deep distress that leads to prayer (Exod 2:24; 6:5; Tob 3:1; cf. Rom 8:22–27). Theissen (*Miracle Stories,* 65; similarly J. Schneider, *TDNT* 7 [1971] 600, 603) labels it a "prayer-like gesture" in healing stories and points to parallels in the OT (e.g., 1 Kgs 17:21) and Judaism (*b. Ber.* 9:1). And when the disciples are unable to exorcise the mute demon in 9:14–18, Jesus explains to them that such healing comes only by prayer (9:29). Thus like the previous gestures, this gesture with apparent thaumaturgic parallels in pagan miracle stories takes its own special twist here.

Jesus touches the affected organs, spits, and looks to heaven with a deep sigh, any one of which could have been the means of healing. But the actual healing takes place through Jesus' authoritative word. The presence and accumulation of the therapeutic gestures form part of the process. Their presence in one event set in the Decapolis may point to the "hellenistic" setting of this story. Consequently, these details may reflect the story's original *Sitz im Leben* in "hellenistic" Jewish Christianity (Grundmann, 200; Pesch, 1:399; Gnilka, 1:296; Ernst, 215) or, more likely, the astuteness of the early Christian mission's "contextualization" of the miracle stories by adapting a story with Aramaic background to a hellenistic social setting.

"Εφφαθα" was often assumed to be an Aramaic ʾithpeʿel(paʿal) (with the ת assimilated [אפתח for אתפתח]) until Rabinowitz disputed this for lack of literary evidence and argued for a Hebrew niphʿal הפתח of פתח (Rabinowitz, *ZNW* 53 [1962] 236–37; *JSS* 16 [1971] 151–56; similarly, Lohmeyer, 150). Black ("ΕΦΦΑΘΑ," 57–60) and Emerton (*JTS* 17 [1967] 427–31) argued for the Aramaic based on a difference in vocalization and writing of the form in question. But Morag (*JSS* 17 [1972] 198–202) appears to have solved the mystery by finding the missing evidence in an analysis of Samaritan liturgical poetry supporting a "historical spelling" in Aramaic for the assimilated pronunciation of the actual verb in question and several parallels. He concluded that taking the verb "as Aramaic is as valid as . . . considering it to be Hebrew" (*JSS* 17 [1972] 202).

Like the other gestures in the story, Jesus' word of healing has been taken as a thaumaturgic device common to ancient miracles, the ῥῆσις βαρβαρική or magical formula in a foreign language (e.g., Bultmann, 213; Kertelge, *Wunder*, 159; Theissen, *Miracle Stories*, 64; Pesch, 1:396). There is no question for a Greek-speaking audience that the Aramaic command would be unintelligible. In keeping with the stylized thaumaturgical elements of the story, it could have served as a ῥῆσις βαρβαρική. But the healing takes place here as in so many of the Gospel healings through Jesus' command. Assuming that this story circulated originally among some at least who were bilingual (where else would the appropriate Aramaic word come from?), we see that the "foreign" character of this command loses its mystery. Certainly, it did for Mark who translated it for his readers (cf. *Comment* on 7:2).

35 The healing follows "immediately" (εὐθέως) in the description of the man's use of his faculties. "His ears," literally, his "hearing" (ἀκοαί; cf. τὰ ὦτα, 7:33) were "opened" (ἠνοίγησαν) and "he began speaking properly" (ἐλάλει ὀρθῶς). The latter followed the loosing of his "tongue's fetter" (ἐλύθη ὁ δεσμὸς τῆς γλώσσης). Some interpreters following the evidence cited by Deissmann (*Light from the Ancient East*, [London: Hodder and Stoughton, 1927], 307–10) equating "binding" with the demonic have found an allusion here to the demonic (e.g., Grundmann, 202; Pesch, 1:397). Whereas the phrase may have its origin in the popular concept of the demonic cause of one to be "tongue tied," reading it more than figuratively here seems to read too much into an account which offers no other hint of the demonic or even the hostility that accompanies such encounters (Robinson, *History*, 40; cf. 9:25–27).

36 Jesus "commanded them" (διεστείλατο αὐτοῖς) turns the attention abruptly back to the "crowd" (7:33) or to those who had brought the man to Jesus (7:32). It is a secrecy command similar to 1:44 and 5:43. And as in 1:44–45 (cf. 5:43) the command is disregarded. But the situation is intensified here. The people disregard the command in proportion to Jesus' insistence on it. The more "he was commanding them" (ὅσον δὲ αὐτοῖς διεστέλλετο), "even more they were preaching" (αὐτοὶ μᾶλλον περισσότερον ἐκήρυσσον). The imperfect tenses underscore the activity and the disjunctive δέ the contrast.

Most commentators take this verse to come from Mark's redaction in keeping with his "secrecy" motif. Koch (*Wundererzählungen*, 72–73) notes that 7:36 interrupts the story's narrative flow, counters the tendency seen in the acclamation of 7:37 to praise the wonder-worker by emphasizing the miraculous deeds and awkwardly has the subjects "preaching" before they are "overwhelmed" (7:36b cf. 7:37a). All three difficulties are removed, if 7:36 was added later by Mark.

Pesch (1:398) by contrast argues for its presence in the pre-Markan tradition as part of the command to secrecy integral to ancient miracle stories and found here in the withdrawal from the crowd in 7:33a and the ῥῆσις βαρβαρική in 7:34 (Theissen, *Miracle Stories,* 68–69). But a tension exists between the withdrawal motif and the Aramaic word of healing on the one hand and this command on the other. Why this injunction and to whom, if the withdrawal and the ῥῆσις βαρβαρική were indeed intended to protect the secret means of the healing? Why would Mark have added it this one time (assuming the previous commands to have been traditional, see *Comment* on 1:44; 5:43)?

The answer may indeed lie in Mark's redactional work. The evangelist clearly did not take the Aramaic command as a ῥῆσις βαρβαρική here or in 5:43. His Greek translation in both cases makes that obvious. Nor did he take the secrecy injunction in 1:44 as inviolate (see *Comment* on 1:45). Furthermore, that he did not take the withdrawal in 7:33a as a secrecy motif is seen in the "preaching" by more than one person in 7:36b–37 (cf. plural "them," αὐτοί). If, however, the secrecy motif had become part of the tradition for the stylistic reasons noted above (7:33–34), the secrecy command would have been directed originally at the man himself (cf. 1:44a). He was not to divulge the "secret" of how Jesus had healed him in private.

Mark, however, finding this story with the public acclamation of 7:37 took the acclamation to refer to Jesus' healing ministry in general (7:36b) and modified the secrecy command of the tradition (7:36a) along the same lines he used in 1:44–45. By changing the singular to the plural in 7:36a and adding the ignoring of the injunction intensified by his characteristic words ὅσον and κηρύσσειν (7:36b), the evangelist changed the injunction of the tradition from referring to the secret means used in a private healing to refer now to Jesus' own role in the healing.

Jesus' role once known always draws a crowd in Mark. And the nature of the healing ministry defies concealment. So the evangelist adapts the secrecy command to accent the futility of any attempt by Jesus to keep a low profile. At the same time, the violation of the injunction, as in 1:44–45, serves as a literary device to set the stage for the "crowds" that follow (cf. 8:1–9). In Mark's narrative the stage for this healing in "the middle of the Decapolis" may itself have been set by the "preaching" of the Gerasene demoniac "in the Decapolis" (5:20). This healing then becomes the basis for the further "preaching" in 7:36b–37 (see *Comment* on 5:20) that leads to the crowds in 8:1–9. In 5:43 and 8:26, however, where the injunction is apparently observed, no mention of a "crowd" follows.

37 "Absolutely overwhelmed" (ὑπερπερισσῶς ἐξεπλήσσοντο) describes the crowd's response to the healing. With Mark, having modified the secrecy command of 7:36 by addressing it now to the public and adding their contrary behavior, this delayed reaction comes as a surprise. Originally, the statement expressed the crowd's reaction when learning of the man's healing. Mark has let it stand and used the formal acclamation as the content of the "preaching" (ἐκήρυσσον) in 7:36b.

"He has done all things well" (καλῶς πάντα πεποίηκεν) echoes the words of Gen 1:31 regarding God's work at creation. This declaration at least ascribes to Jesus the work of God and may reflect the hope of the restoration of fallen creation, Israel's hope for the age of salvation as promised by the prophets (Gnilka, 1:298; Ernst, 217). Instead of a divine miracle worker, Jesus' healing represents God's work of doing "all things well."

The motif of the messianic age rings loudly through the second part of the acclamation based on the promise of Isa 35:5–6: "He makes the deaf to hear and the mute to speak" (cf. Matt 11:1–7; Luke 7:18–23). As part of Isaiah's promise of the age of salvation, this acclamation by the "Gentiles" shows that their "ears" and their "tongues" can hear and declare the "good news" of the day of salvation. As in 1:14–15, Jesus' work signals the coming of the "Kingdom of God," the "good news of God" (see *Comment* on 1:14, 15).

Explanation

Most likely one of two stories transmitted together as a pair (7:31–37; 8:22–26) with a common acclamation (7:37), this story with its grouping of several thaumaturgical traits despite healing through an efficacious word may well illustrate "contextualization" in the early Church. Set in the "middle of the Decapolis," gentile territory, the story with its Aramaic background reflects a hellenistic coloring of the details appropriate to a gentile mission setting. It depicts Jesus as being familiar with common hellenistic thaumaturgical practices. But the response shows him to be more than simply another miracle worker.

The story tells us little about the man or his friends. We only know they came to Jesus for healing. When Jesus heals the man, "they" bear witness to who he is. Praising Jesus as the one who does "all things well," a phrase reminiscent of Gen 1:31 that describes God's work in creation, they associate this act of making one whole with God's own work at creation. At the same time, "they" echo the words of Isa 35:5–6 that promised healing to the deaf and mute as part of the new day of God's salvation. In this way, the story dramatizes the summary message of Jesus in 1:14–15 about the "gospel of God." The "appointed time has come to pass." God's promised sovereign rule has come into history. And it was known in gentile territory.

Mark's own contribution involves both the location of this story and his shifting of the silence command. Linked by an extended itinerary (7:31) with the story of the Syrophoenician Woman (7:24–30) as a second episode outside of Galilee, this story shows Jesus continuing to minister in gentile areas. It also provides the locale for the Feeding story that follows (8:1–9). Therefore, instead of simply being an incursion into gentile territory as in 5:1–20, this story provides part of the framework for an extended period of ministry beyond Galilee before Jesus returns briefly to Gennesaret in 8:10–13.

By addressing the silence command to the public (7:36) instead of to the man in a private setting as originally (7:36), the thrust of the command shifts from its usual role pertaining to the *means* of healing to the *work* of the healer. Furthermore, the disregard for the injunction proportionate with the command demonstrates for Mark the ultimate futility of concealing the nature of Jesus' ministry (cf. 1:45; 4:21–22). And as usual, "preaching," which may in Mark's story have led to this episode (cf. 5:20), draws a crowd (cf. 1:44–45) and sets the stage for the Feeding in 8:1–9.

Mark does little to alter the story's formal acclamation of 7:37. But read in conjunction with what has come before in the Gospel, this "preaching" has as its content the redemptive historical significance of Jesus' ministry. He is the one who is inaugurating the age of salvation implicit in his teaching (cf. 4:1–34) and explicit in his deeds for those who have the ears to hear and the eyes to see (4:11–12). This message was not only proclaimed by Jesus (1:14–15), but it was the "word" proclaimed by the leper in 1:45 and the message about what God/Jesus had done for the Gerasene demoniac in 5:1–20. "Preached" in violation of the injunction in 7:36a, this message had nothing to do with a wonder worker, who sought to keep his magic a secret. Rather it spoke of Jesus as the one who fulfills God's promise of salvation (cf. Matt 11:3–5). The Gentiles, however, are the first to spell this out (cf. 15:39), while the disciples are depicted in this section as confused, misunderstanding, "deaf," "blind," and "hardhearted" (6:45–52; 7:17–18; 8:14–21).

If, however, as is likely, Mark separated this story from its traditional mate in 8:22–26, his location of the two stories prepares for a strong comment contextually about the disciples. This subsection of Mark's Gospel (6:7–8:26), after opening with the disciples commissioned to share in Jesus' ministry, depicts them as struggling in their understanding of Jesus and what he is really about (6:34–44, 45–52; 7:14–23; 8:1–9; and esp. 8:14–21). Meanwhile, the people in gentile territory, in the "middle of the Decapolis," proclaim Jesus to be the one in whom God is at work ("does all things well") effecting the promised day of salvation according to Isa 35 when the deaf hear, the mute speak and the blind see (cf. 1:1–2a; 1:14–15!). Perhaps, in view of this contrast between the response in gentile territory (cf. 7:24–30, 31–37) and that of the disciples in this section, it does not come as coincidence that a gentile centurion declares the ultimate confession of Jesus' dignity in 15:39, a confession that contrasts with Peter's myopic confession in 8:29.

Lest one conclude, however, that Mark intended by this contrast to indict the disciples and their response as a form of rejection, he uses the second of the two traditional stories (8:22–26), strategically placed after the warning about the "leaven" and the painful, exposing questions by Jesus directed at the disciples' lack of understanding (8:14–21), to show that they had received the first touch. Unlike the "outsiders" and the opponents of Jesus, the disciples were suffering not from blindness but myopia. They needed a second touch. The total healing of the Blind Man of Bethsaida promised that hope for the disciples too.

J. The Feeding of the Four Thousand (8:1–9)

Bibliography

Boobyer, G. H. "The Miracles of the Loaves and the Gentiles in St. Mark's Gospel." *SJT* 6 (1953) 77–87. ——— "The Eucharistic Interpretation of the Miracles of the Loaves in St. Mark's Gospel." *JTS* 3 (1952) 161–71. **Clavier, H.** "La multiplication des pains dans le ministère de Jésus." *SE* 1 (1959) 441–57. **Danker, F. W.** "Mark 8,7." *JBL* 82 (1963) 215. **Donfried, K. P.** "The Feeding Narratives and the Marcan Community." In *Kirche*, FS G. Bornkamm, ed. D. Lührmann and G. Strecker. Tübingen:

Mohr, 1980. 95–103. **Farrer, A.** "Loaves and Thousands." *JTS* 4 (1953) 1–14. **Fowler, R. M.** *Loaves and Fishes: The Function of the Feeding Stories in the Gospel of Mark.* SBLDS 54. Chico, CA: Scholars Press, 1978. **Friedrich, G.** "Die beiden Erzählungen von der Speisung in Mark 6,31–44, 8,1–9." *TZ* 20 (1964) 10–22. **Hegermann, H.** "Bethsaida und Gennesar: Eine traditions- und redaktionsgeschichtliche Studie zu Mk 4–8." In *Judentum, Urchristentum, Kirche,* FS J. Jeremias, ed. W. Eltester. BZNW 26. Berlin: Töpelmann, 1960. 130–40. **Heising, A.** "Exegese und Theologie der Alt- und Neutestamentlichen Speisewunder." *ZTK* 86 (1964) 80–96. **Iersel, B. W. van.** "Die wunderbare Speisung und das Abendmahl in der synoptischen Tradition (Mk VI. 35–44 par VIII. 1–20 par)." *NovT* 7 (1964) 167–94. **Jenkins, L. H.** "A Marcan Doublet." In *Studies in History and Religion,* FS H. W. Robinson, ed. E. A. Payne. London: Lutterworth, 1942. 87–111. **Kelber, W.** *The Kingdom in Mark.* 1974. **Kertelge, K.** *Die Wunder Jesu im Markusevangelium.* 1970. **Koch, D.-A.** *Die Bedeutung der Wundererzählungen für die Christologie des Markusevangeliums.* 1975. **Kuhn, H.-W.** *Ältere Sammlungen im Markusevangelium.* 1971. **Lang, F. G.** "'Über Sidon mitten ins Gebiet der Dekapolis': Geographie und Theologie in Markus 7,31." *ZDPV* 94 (1978) 145–60. **Masuda, S.** "The Good News of the Miracle of the Bread: The Tradition and Its Markan Redaction." *NTS* 28 (1982) 191–219. **Neugebauer, F.** "Die wunderbare Speisung (Mk 6,30–44 parr.) und Jesu Identität." *KD* 32 (1986) 254–77. **Patsch, H.** "Abendmahlsterminologie ausserhalb der Einsetzungsberichte." *ZNW* 62 (1971) 210–31. **Roloff, J.** *Das Kerygma und der irdische Jesus.* 1970. **Schenke, L.** *Die Wundererzählungen des Markusevangeliums.* 1974. ——— *Die wunderbare Brotvermehrung: Die neutestamentlichen Erzählungen und ihre Bedeutung.* Würzburg: Echter, 1983. **Theissen, G.** *The Miracle Stories of the Early Christian Tradition.* 1983. **Thiering, B. E.** "'Breaking of Bread' and 'Harvest' in Mark's Gospel." *NovT* 12 (1970) 1–12. **Wendling, E.** *Die Entstehung des Marcus Evangeliums.* Tübingen: Mohr, 1908. **Ziener, G.** "Die Brotwunder im Markusevangelium." *BZ* 4 (1960) 282–85.

Translation

¹*In those days there was again* [a] *a great crowd that did not have anything to eat. Summoning the disciples, Jesus* [b] *said to them,* ²*"I have compassion on the crowd because they have stayed with me three days* [c] *and have not had anything to eat.* ³*If I send them home without food, they will collapse in the way. Some of them come from a long distance."* ⁴*His disciples asked him, "From what source can anyone fill these people with bread here in the wilderness?"* ⁵*He asked them, "How many loaves do you have?" They said, "Seven."*

⁶*He commanded the crowd to recline on the ground. Taking the seven loaves and giving thanks, he broke them and gave them to his disciples to serve, and they served them to the crowd.* ⁷*They also had a few small fish. Blessing these,* [d] *Jesus* [b] *told them to serve these also.* ⁸*They ate and were filled. And there were seven large baskets of leftover pieces.* ⁹*About four thousand were present, and he sent them away.*

Notes

[a]Some MSS read παμπολλοῦ for πάλιν πολλοῦ (א 1006 1506 Majority text sy[h] sa[mss] bo[mss]), a word not found in the Bible.

[b]Romanized words added from context.

[c]ἡμέραι τρεῖς is a *nominativus pendens* or a "parenthetic nominative" (Taylor, 358).

[d]A few MSS omit αὐτά in keeping with the Jewish practice of thanking/blessing God rather than the food (E G H 33 579 700 1006 1506 *pm*).

Form / Structure / Setting

Form-critically, this pericope falls into the same category of gift miracles as the previous Feeding (see 6:30–44). Consequently, we find greater development of the opening dialogue, little description of the actual miracle, and no response by those involved. In contrast to the Feeding of the Five Thousand (see *Comment* on 6:34), this setting represents one of dire need (8:1–2), a typical trait of miracle stories (Friedrich, *TZ* 20 [1964] 13–14; Roloff, *Kerygma*, 243).

As to source, some interpreters have assigned this story to Mark's redaction (e.g., Wendling, *Entstehung*, 68–75; Dibelius, 78, n. 1; Schmithals, 1:363); others argue for the "historical integrity" of the account (e.g., Lane, 272), and Fowler argues that this Feeding represents the earlier tradition from which Mark developed 6:30–44 (*Loaves*, 43–90). But the vast majority of commentators have viewed this story as a "doublet" of 6:34–44, a variant tradition of the same story (cf. Donfried, *Kirche*, 95–103).

Nineham notes the similarities that point to a common story: (a) a deserted setting (6:35; 8:4), (b) the same question about available food (6:38; 8:35), (c) a command to recline (6:39; 8:6), (d) essentially the same words and sequence used for serving loaves (6:41; 8:6), (e) the same result (6:42; 8:8), (f) gathering of leftovers (6:43; 8:9), (g) a dismissal and boat journey (6:45; 8:10). In addition, many interpreters have pointed out the disciples' surprising lack of understanding in 8:4 should they have previously fed an even larger crowd.

At the same time, this story, most likely the later of the two variants, differs significantly from the first. The setting differs (cf. 6:32–34), and apart from the obvious difference in the numbers of loaves, fish, baskets and crowd, thematic differences also appear. For example, the disciples play a more passive, supporting role with Jesus taking the initiative (8:1–5). OT motifs, the seating by groups (cf. 6:40) and Jesus' look to heaven (8:6 cf. 6:41) are missing, and we have a separate fish course in 8:7. Significant differences in wording also occur (e.g., ἔρημος ὁ τόπος, 6:35 cf. ἐρημίας, 8:4; ἐπὶ τῷ χλωρῷ χόρτῳ, 6:39; cf. ἐπὶ τῆς γῆς, 8:6; εὐλόγησεν, 6:41; cf. εὐχαριστήσας, 8:6 and κόφινος, 6:43; cf. σπυρίδα, 8:8). Add to this combination of similarities and dissimilarities the proximity of the Johannine account to 8:1–10 and you have strong evidence supporting Mark's use of an independent traditional variant of the Feeding tradition.

But where does this variant come from? Many assign it to a hellenistic-Jewish Christian community based on the use of the eucharistic formula in 8:6 which appears in Luke 22:19 and 1 Cor 11:24. But the interchangeable character of εὐλογεῖν and εὐχαριστεῖν (see *Comment* on 8:6) seriously weakens the argument. The fish course (8:7) also seems to reflect a more gentile or hellenistic setting because of its insensitivity to the Jewish custom of the blessing which is given over the bread and always blesses God rather than the food (εὐλογήσας αὐτά). Yet one could avoid this confusion by assigning 8:7 to a later development in the tradition (e.g., van Iersel, *NovT* 7 [1964] 185). Therefore, much depends on whether Mark found this tradition in a collection of materials reflecting a more "hellenistic"-Jewish Christian community and on whether the change in numbers, particularly the use of "seven," has significance. Assuming a subsequent development behind 8:7, we see that nothing else in the story (8:1–6, 8–10) offers convincing evidence for determining its original *Sitz im Leben*.

Redactionally, the *hapax legomena* (e.g., προσμένειν, ἐκλύειν, περίσσευμα, ἐρημία, σπύρις), the forms unique to Mark (e.g., εἶχον, ἤκησιν, δυνήσεται) and the difference between εὐχαριστήσας in 8:6 and εὐλογήσας in 14:22 counter the claim for this being a Markan redactional doublet. Most assign Mark's thumbprint to the opening (8:1) and ending (8:9b) of the account (see *Comment* on 8:1, 9).

Structurally, the story follows the usual form of a miracle story. The narrator sets the stage in 8:1 which Jesus repeats in direct discourse to the disciples in 8:2–3. The disciples counter by emphasizing the impossibility of meeting the need in view of the location (8:4). Jesus poses then a counter question in 8:5. The narrator takes over again in 8:6 to finish the story. The miracle occurs unobtrusively with Jesus giving bread and fish to the disciples to serve (8:6–7). In 8:8 we find the demonstration and confirmation in the crowd's eating to their fill and the gathering of seven baskets of leftovers. The story ends in a dismissal without any response (8:9).

The setting of the story in Mark is critical for its significance. Nothing in the story itself provides an adequate basis for taking it as anything more than simply a second Feeding miracle, another miracle story. But its setting in the pre-Markan tradition and certainly in Mark's context may supply the clue for why the evangelist used this story at this point in his narrative.

Several have assigned the story to a larger "doublet" in 6:35–7:37 and 8:1–26 (e.g., Jenkins, *Studies*, 87–111; Klostermann, 74–75; Haenchen, 283–84; see Quesnell, *Mind*, 28–38, and Kuhn, *Sammlungen*, 29–32, for survey of options) but this hypothesis has not held up (e.g., Taylor, 628–32; Gnilka, 1:315). Mark 8:11–13 hardly represents a doublet of 7:1–23 nor can 8:22–26 be a doublet of 7:31–37.

Mark, however, may well have found this miracle story in combination with 7:24–30; 7:31–37 and 8:22–26 (Roloff, *Kerygma*, 243, n. 15; van Iersel, *NovT* 7 [1964] 185). We have noted the "hellenistic" thaumaturgic traits of 7:31–37 whose closest parallel among the miracle stories of Mark comes in 8:22–26, which has been paired with it (see 8:22–26). The Syrophoenician story has obvious "hellenistic" overtones (see 7:24–30). Such a grouping in the tradition would account for the "hellenistic" blessing in 8:7 and perhaps color the more neutral elements such as "from a long distance" (see *Comment* on 8:3) and "giving thanks" (see *Comment* on 8:6). Such a collection of traditional materials would also explain why Mark took it as a second miracle of Feeding and used it in his present location.

We are on much firmer ground when we turn to Mark's own setting for the story. Despite those who would argue that he has placed this Feeding in Galilee by having Jesus reach the Sea of Galilee in 7:31 (e.g., Marxsen, 69–70; Koch, *Wundererzählungen*, 90), we found that the healing of the deaf-mute took place in the area of the Decapolis after the evangelist sketched an extended journey for Jesus from Tyre through Sidon to the Decapolis (see *Comment* on 7:31). He does not change the venue for this miracle but links it with what has happened "in those days" (8:1). After the miracle,

Jesus embarks with his disciples and departs for Dalmanutha, a place unknown to us but assumed to be on the western shore (see *Comment* on 8:10). This too would suggest the Feeding took place for Mark on the east side of the Sea of Galilee. Therefore, Mark's narrative framework places this story in gentile territory (Kertelge, *Wunder*, 143; Grundmann, 204; Pesch, 1:400; Lang, *ZDPV*, 94 [1978] 158; Ernst, 218).

Does Mark's location of this story imply, as has been suggested since the early Church, a Feeding for Gentiles in contrast to the previous Feeding which was for Jews (e.g., more recently, Grundmann, 204; van Iersel, *NovT* 7 [1964] 183–86; Pesch, 1:403–5; Kelber, *Kingdom*, 59–62)? Support has been found in the reference to the "children" and the "dogs" in 7:27, but 7:27 clearly states that the time for the Gentiles has not yet arrived in Jesus' ministry between the two Feedings (see *Comment* on 7:27). Furthermore, if such had been intended by Mark, he certainly chose to express it in an uncharacteristically "roundabout way" (Nineham, 208).

Nevertheless, Mark's geographical and literary setting does imply that this Feeding involved Gentiles (Kelber, *Kingdom*, 59–61). Following as it does the discussions of 7:1–23 with both the Pharisees and the disciples about purity laws regarding eating that had formed part of the social boundaries between Jews and Gentiles, this Feeding set in gentile territory would certainly have included Gentiles (see *Comment* on 8:3). They, like the Syrophoenician woman and the deaf-mute, receive the benefit of Jesus' redemptive ministry in their territory.

At the same time, this Feeding is followed by another query from the Pharisees (8:11–13), a request that leads to a dialogue between Jesus and his disciples (8:14–21) that exposes anew their blindness. They stumble again over the "loaves" (cf. 6:52) in what amounts to Jesus' most harsh critique of their lack of understanding. Schweizer (156) hardly exaggerates when he takes these two Feedings in Mark to "show how absolutely and unimaginably blind man is to the activity of God."

Comment

1 This verse contains several characteristically Markan words or phrases such as the resumptive use of πάλιν, a "great crowd" (πολλοῦ ὄχλου, see *Comment* on 4:1), and προσκαλεῖσθαι at the beginning of a pericope (see *Comment* on 6:7).

"In those days" (ἐν . . . ταῖς ἡμέραις) does not occur as frequently (1:9; cf. 13:24), but it could also be Markan. It connects this story temporally with the previous event or events during Jesus' journey outside Galilee (7:24–37). Consequently, 7:31 would most likely provide a general location somewhere in the territory of the Decapolis (cf. Lohmeyer, 152; Marxsen, 69–70; Koch, *Wundererzählungen*, 90).

"There was again a great crowd" (πάλιν πολλοῦ ὄχλου ὄντος) renders one of the two genitive absolutes, and the resumptive "again" (πάλιν) points back to the first Feeding of a "great crowd" (πολὺν ὄχλον) in 6:34. But in this story Jesus takes the initiative by summoning the disciples (προσκαλεσάμενος τοὺς μαθητάς). Though not mentioned since 7:17, the narrative implies their presence with Jesus during the intervening events.

2 The setting and need become clear through the ensuing dialogue between Jesus and his disciples. "I have compassion for the crowd" (σπλαγχνίζομαι ἐπὶ τόν ὄχλον) is reminiscent of, but contrasts with, the scene in 6:34. There Jesus' compassion arose from the crowd's "spiritual need" as "sheep without a shepherd"; here he senses their "physical need" for sustenance (Haenchen, 278). The crowd has "stayed" (προσμένουσιν) with Jesus "three days" (ἡμέραι τρεῖς) and "have nothing to eat" (οὐκ ἔχουσιν τί φάγωσιν).

This setting gives only the barest details with no further information about what they had been doing or why they had been together. The reader can assume from Mark's narrative context that the crowd had gathered in part because of what they had heard about Jesus, perhaps even from the preaching of those with the deaf-mute in 7:35–36. The frequent association of Jesus' healing and teaching with the gathering of large crowds to this point in Mark's story (e.g., 1:31–32, 45; 2:2; 3:7–8, 20; 4:1–2; 6:32–44) leads the reader to assume the same for this occasion.

3 The need rapidly becomes an emergency, when Jesus tells his disciples that the crowds will "collapse" (ἐκλυθήσονται) from lack of food (νήστεις), if he were to send them home. "Some of them had come from a long distance" (τινες αὐτῶν ἀπό μακρόθεν ἥκασιν). In the immediate context of Jesus' own extensive travel in 7:31, this statement could simply indicate that some had accompanied him from earlier locales in the itinerary. At least some had come a long distance to be with him which reinforces their desperate situation.

This phrase could also allude to Gentiles as constituents of the crowd. Danker (*JBL* 83 [1963] 215) has noted that "come from afar" (μακρόθεν ἥκασιν) connotes "Gentiles" in Josh 9:6 LXX and Isa 60:4 LXX. Van Iersel (*NovT* 7 [1964] 184–85), though disputing the Isaiah reference (applies to Jews from the dispersion; cf. Isa 5:26; 43:6; 49:12; 60:4, 9; Jer 30:10), concurs with Danker's thesis and points to the rabbinic use of "far" (רחוקים, rĕḥôqîm, Str-B, 3:585–86) to refer to Gentiles and the early Church's use of μακράν (e.g., Acts 2:39; 22:21; Eph 2:11–12) to distinguish the Gentiles from the Jews. This reading becomes even more plausible when the story is taken in the Markan context of Jesus' travel in gentile territory. "Some" (τινες) would then imply that "some" of the crowd at least were Gentiles (Grundmann, 205; Pesch, 1:402–3; cf. Schweizer, 156).

4 The disciples' query underscores the dire situation by noting the impossibility of "anyone" (τις) feeding such a crowd "in the wilderness" (ἐπ᾿ ἐρημίας, see *Comment* on 1:4; 1:35; cf. ἔρημος ὁ τόπος in 6:31, 35). Skepticism occurs as a regular feature in miracle stories (Theissen, *Miracle Stories*, 56), but it takes on special significance here in Mark's story. Not only does it enhance the drama, but it also indicates the disciples' lack of understanding about Jesus. Each appearance of the disciples since 6:32 has made this point. According to Mark's story line, they are the more culpable for having already experienced Jesus' response to a similar situation in the first Feeding where the issue was not *where* one could get the food but *how* they could afford it. Mark explicitly returns to their obtuseness in a subsequent dialogue (8:14–21). Furthermore, read in the context of 7:24–37, their perplexity contrasts markedly with both the "faith" of the Syrophoenician woman (7:24–30) and the companions of the deaf-mute (7:31–37).

5 Jesus inquires and learns that they have "seven loaves." Much has been made of the number "seven" in contrast with the "five" of 6:34–44. Pesch (1:403; similarly, Ernst, 219–20) compares the seven Noachic commandments (cf. Gen 9:4–6: [1] administration of justice, [2] prohibition of idolatry, [3] blasphemy, [4] immorality, [5] murder, [6] stealing, and [7] eating a part of a live animal) as a form of natural law for humankind compared with the five books of the Torah, the Mosaic Law given to the Jews. Gnilka rejects the earlier association of the "seven" with Acts 6:3 and applies the more common biblical meaning of fullness or completion as an expression of the completion of the blessing (1:303). Farrer (*JTS* 4 [1953] 4–5) combines the "seven" with the "five" of the previous Feeding to equal twelve in keeping with the twelve loaves of shewbread (Lev 24:5–8) to represent the "(twelve) children of Israel."

Unfortunately, nothing within the story itself supplies a solid clue. The gathering of "seven" baskets of leftovers most likely corresponds in some way with the "seven loaves." But to what do the "seven" baskets refer (see *Comment* on 8:8)? Did the "seven loaves" influence the number of baskets or vice versa? The lack of correspondence between the "twelve" disciples who serve both "five loaves" and "seven loaves" respectively rules against any connection of the number of loaves with the ones serving and thus rules out any allusion to the "seven deacons" of Acts 6.

Perhaps the number came about during the development of the tradition which here accents the "loaves" by omitting any reference to the fish until after the serving of the bread (8:7). Should this reflect a eucharistic influence, the "two fish" of 6:38 combined with the "five loaves" would give the "seven loaves" for this meal and the number would have no special significance in itself.

6 Jesus orders the crowd to recline (ἀναπεσεῖν) without mention of specific groupings (cf. 6:39) "on the ground" (ἐπὶ τῆς γῆς) in contrast to the "green grass" (cf. 6:39). The OT allusions of the first Feeding are missing.

"Taking the seven loaves" (λαβὼν τοὺς ἑπτὰ ἄρτους) corresponds to the role of the Jewish father at the meal who takes bread, breaks and passes it to others after saying the blessing. No mention has been made of any fish up to this point (cf. 6:41).

"Giving thanks" (εὐχαριστήσας) differs from the first Feeding in two ways. First, nothing is said about Jesus "looking to heaven" (cf. 6:41). Second, and more importantly, the wording changes from "blessing" (εὐλογήσας) in 6:41 and 14:22 to "giving thanks" (εὐχαριστήσας). This difference has generally been attributed to the influence of a eucharistic tradition found in Luke 22:19 and 1 Cor 11:24 on the pre-Markan tradition (e.g., van Iersel, *NovT* 7 [1964] 178; Kertelge, *Wunder*, 140; Patsch, *ZNW* 62 [1971] 227; Pesch, 1:404; Ernst, 220). The change in wording itself, however, need not point in that direction, since the two verbs appear to be used interchangeably (Patsch, *ZNW* 62 [1971] 218–19; Gnilka, 1:303). Mark illustrates this in our immediate context where a "blessing" is given for the fish in 8:7. In 14:22 Jesus gives a "blessing" for the bread followed by "thanks" for the cup in 14:23. Paul uses "thanks" (εὐχαριστεῖν) for the Lord's Supper in 1 Cor 11:24 but also for a normal meal in Rom 14:6 and 1 Cor 10:30 (cf. 1 Tim 4:3–4; Acts 27:35).

Taken in the context of this story as a whole, however, the change in expressions may indeed reflect a eucharistic influence on the tradition. We have already noted in contrast to the first Feeding the absence of any reference to fish, which plays no part in the Lord's Supper. This tendency to deemphasize the fish appears in the Matthean and Lukan parallels to the Feeding of the Five Thousand (van Iersel, *NovT* 7 [1964] 171–73). Furthermore, the fish do come into play but as a separate course in 8:7, which suggests that they had been pushed to the background here as well. Therefore, the description of Jesus' handling of the loaves may well reflect the use of terminology familiar to the early Church from the Lord's Supper, and the presence of "giving thanks" (εὐχαριστεῖν) in the Lukan and Pauline tradition may suggest that a similar "hellenistic" setting left its mark on the tradition here (Patsch, *ZNW* 62 [1971] 219–28).

However, the presence of the fish and the absence of the cup and words interpreting the bread preclude any attempt to take this Feeding as a eucharistic meal. And since Jesus' actions with the bread corresponded with the typical role of the Jewish father at a meal, we need to proceed cautiously even in assigning a eucharistic interpretation to the Feeding or the Feeding to a "eucharistic catechism" (Roloff, *Kerygma,* 241–45; Gnilka, 1:303; cf. van Iersel, *NovT* 7 [1964] 178–79; Pesch, 1:403–4). At most we have here a liturgical tradition exerting indirect influence on the development of a separate meal tradition (Patsch, *ZNW* 62 [1971] 210–31).

"Broke" (ἔκλασεν; cf. κατέκλασεν, 6:41) corresponds more directly with the verb used in the Lord's Supper of 14:22; Luke 22:19; and 1 Cor 11:24. But we find the same verb used in reference to Paul's "breaking" bread in Acts 27:35. The term belonged to the customary manner for beginning a meal.

"Gave it to his disciples to serve" (ἐδίδου τοῖς μαθηταῖς αὐτοῦ ἵνα παρατιθῶσιν) incorporates the disciples in the miracle despite their lack of understanding (see *Comment* on 6:41).

7 "They had a few little fish" (ἰχθύδια ὀλίγα) introduces the fish into the story for the first time. Because of our knowledge of the previous Feeding, this remark comes almost as an afterthought leading several to consider it a secondary addition (e.g., van Iersel, *NovT* 7 [1964] 176–77; Patsch, *ZNW* 62 [1971] 222–23; Fowler, *Loaves,* 53–54). Yet were this our only account of the Feeding, it would not seem so abrupt. The "bread" was always the first course followed by the "main" course. The diminutive "little fish" (ἰχθύδια) and the vague number, "a few" (ὀλίγα), correspond to the setting that accents the bread and the need. We noted above that the pushing of the fish more into the background may have led to the combination of "five" loaves and "two" fish of a variant tradition into "seven" loaves. The fish becomes "little fish" and the specific number becomes "a few."

"Blessed them" (εὐλογήσας αὐτά) raises a special issue. First, the blessing normally accompanies the breaking of the bread and not the main course. This blessing sets the fish off as distinct from the bread (see *Comment* on 6:41) and gives it greater prominence than normal for a Jewish setting. Second, the Jewish blessing or thanks was directed to God, the primary object, rather than for the elements of the meal. One blesses God not the fish. Consequently, many interpreters have attributed the verse to a later hellenistic redaction unfamiliar with the Jewish customs regarding the blessing, perhaps mistaking it for a miracle formula (e.g., Grundmann, 205; Gnilka, 1:303; van Iersel, *NovT* 7 [1964] 185). Yet, though one might imagine an early Christian community unaware of the special nuances of the Jewish blessings at the meal, it is hard to imagine any Christian community that would mistake a blessing with a miracle-working formula.

Despite the tendency to align the details with the Lord's Supper, it remains most unlikely that the story which doubtless included fish originally (cf. 6:34–44) should have been so stylized along the lines of the Lord's Supper that the fish were totally eliminated only to be reintroduced awkwardly by a "hellenistic" redactor at a later time (so, e.g., van Iersel, *NovT* 7 [1964] 185; Patsch, *ZNW* 62 [1971] 222–23). Rather the isolation of the fish with its own blessing most likely reflects the influence of the Lord's Supper liturgy on the story that eventually led to describing Jesus' handling of the fish separately but parallel to the loaves by a community unfamiliar with the Jewish blessing formulas.

8 "They ate and were filled" (ἔφαγον καὶ ἐχορτάσθησαν, see *Comment* on 6:42 and 7:27) consummates the miracle. The need has been met.

"Seven large baskets of leftover pieces" gives the first of two demonstrations of the miracle, the second being the number of people fed in 8:9. The "large baskets" (σπυρίδας; cf. κοφίνων in 6:43; 8:19) renders the same word used for the "basket" in which Paul was let down from a wall (Acts 9:25).

"Seven" baskets obviously contrasts with the "twelve" baskets of 6:43 leading many interpreters to see a further reference to a "hellenistic" setting, particularly in view of the "Hellenists'" seven "deacons" of Acts 6:1–6 (e.g., Klostermann, 75; Grundmann, 284; Thiering, *NovT* 12 [1970] 4; Lang, *ZDPV*, 94 [1978] 158–59; cf. van Iersel, *NovT* 7 [1964] 185–86; Masuda, *NTS* 28 [1982] 205). Pesch (1:404) finds an allusion to the "seven" or "seventy" nations without explaining either the connection between "seven" and "seventy" or why "seventy" baskets were not left over should the number have been a reference to the nations of the world.

As usual with numerology, the variables in this case create so much uncertainty that any "interpretation" must remain highly speculative. We do have a second Feeding which differs in details from the first. The first Feeding took place in Galilee in part as a response to the crowds generated by the disciples' mission and Jesus' ministry in Mark's story. The second Feeding takes place outside Galilee after Jesus moves throughout the area north and east of Galilee where he heals two people (7:24–37) after a discussion about the socio-religious boundaries of purity regarding foods (7:1–23). Set in gentile territory, one must assume Gentile participation in this meal, possibly a result in part of the preaching of the preceding narrative (7:35–36). "Twelve" and "seven" come naturally to mind from the Acts' account of the leadership struggle in the primitive Church, the one group led by the Twelve Apostles and the other by the Seven around Stephen. Unfortunately, our knowledge of the latter figure comes solely from Acts 6 whose knowledge by or influence on Mark 8:8 can only be arbitrarily posited. Even should one grant the allusion to the "Seven" or the "Hellenists" of Acts 6, one cannot forget that they hardly represented the "Gentiles" and only in an extended manner the mission to the Gentiles. Furthermore, the "Twelve" disciples play an important supporting role in this Feeding too.

Perhaps the answer is much less exotic. Rather than influencing the number of loaves in 8:5, perhaps the number of loaves influenced the number of baskets. Each loaf produced not only enough to fill the desperately hungry crowd but enough was left over for the remnants of each loaf to fill a large basket. The leftovers again pointed to God's abundant supply characteristic of the day of salvation proclaimed in 7:36 (see *Comment* on 6:43). That the number is less than the twelve baskets in 6:43 is no more anomalous than the lesser number of those fed. And the very existence of "seven" here may well indicate the lack of any symbolical significance behind the number "twelve." At least the significance was lost in this variant.

9 "Four thousand" has also prompted much debate. Farrer (*JTS* 4 [1953] 4–5) seeks a hidden meaning by viewing both Feedings together with five loaves for five thousand and seven loaves for potentially seven thousand. Taken together the two totals would equal the completed number of twelve thousand, an allusion to the twelve-tribed Israel. Accordingly, the story implies a future Feeding of Three Thousand (similarly Thiering, *NovT* 12 [1970] 4), since only four thousand were fed. Such a speculative reading assumes without support an anticipated third Feeding and either the prior existence of these two variants together in a tradition or an overly subtle Markan redaction of 8:1–9 according to this scheme.

Other interpreters find in "four thousand" a hint of the "four corners" of the universe, the four points of a compass, another allusion to the Gentiles or the nations of the world (e.g., Pesch, 1:404; Thiering, *NovT* 12 [1970] 4). This too may be overinterpreting the story. If the five thousand had little obvious significance in the first Feeding, "four thousand" could hardly be more significant even for Mark who obviously took these stories as two separate accounts whose significance lies in the event rather than the numbers (see *Comment* on 6:52 and 8:19–20).

"And he sent them away" (καὶ ἀπέλυσεν αὐτούς) represents the formal dismissal (cf. 6:45). Although several assign it to Mark's redaction (e.g., Schenke, *Wundererzählungen*, 282; Gnilka, 1:301; Pesch, 1:400), it does have a formal function in a story that ends as did the first feeding without a formal response. Here it belongs in part to the demonstration, since Jesus had not dared "send them away" earlier lest they collapse because of hunger (8:3). Not only had they eaten to their fill, they were able now to depart without risk. Their need had been amply met.

Explanation

This Feeding miracle was most likely transmitted in the tradition along with other stories like 7:24–30, 32–37; 8:22–26 that reflect more of a gentile, "hellenistic" orientation. To that extent, it represents a later variant of the Feeding narrative behind 6:34–44. The difference in orientation would explain the change in wording between "blessing" and "giving thanks," with the latter corresponding to the eucharistic formula of Luke 22:19 and 1 Cor 11:24, and a separate "blessing" of the fish. The different orientation, however, offers little clue about the change in details from five loaves and two fish to seven loaves and a few fish or from five thousand to four thousand. At best, the combination of five loaves and two fish might have led to the "seven" loaves in a setting accenting more the breaking of bread under indirect influence of the Lord's Supper. And the "seven" loaves in turn may have influenced the "seven" large baskets of leftovers, a basketful per loaf.

The transmission of the Feeding along with traditions of similar thrust would also help explain Mark's own use of the story at this juncture in his Gospel. It appropriately comes during Jesus' time outside Galilee where he has ministered to a Gentile, a "Greek" (7:24–30), and has healed the deaf-mute in a story uncharacteristically filled with thaumaturgical actions in the Decapolis (7:31–37). The story is then followed by another healing miracle with similar thaumaturgical traits in Bethsaida (8:22–26) with the Pharisees' request for a sign (8:10–13) and the warning about the leaven of the Pharisees and Herod's intervening (8:14–21).

Jesus responds in the Feeding to the physical needs of the people. Missing are the OT motifs of "sheep/shepherd," "green grass," and "companies" of people found in the Feeding of the Five Thousand. The disciples play much more of a supporting role in the cast here, though their question about an adequate source of food betrays their failure to recognize Jesus' ability to provide for this need, a failure that seems all the more culpable after their having already fed a larger multitude with fewer supplies.

For Mark the Feeding has two foci. Clearly, the Feeding of the Four Thousand points to Jesus' miraculous, abundant provision for the physical needs of the multitude. This motif is inherent in the story about feeding four thousand desperately hungry people with seven loaves, a few little fish and still gathering seven large baskets full of leftovers. But set as it now is in a section of material where Jesus is outside Galilee involved with Gentiles and after the dispute with the Pharisees about purity laws and social boundaries set by food regulations that separated Jews and Gentiles (7:1–23), this Feeding—if not explicitly including Gentiles ("from afar," 8:3)—implicitly includes them by location and demonstrates the removal of such social boundaries by Jesus' ministry. While not intended to provide an exclusively gentile Feeding set in contrast to an earlier exclusively Jewish Feeding, the literary and geographical setting of this Feeding bears witness to the breaking down of the boundaries between Jews and Gentiles rooted in Jesus' ministry.

Mark's second thrust in using this story comes from what follows. On the one hand, after the return to Galilee, the Pharisees' request for a divine sign (8:10–13) shows the blindness to what God is doing in Jesus and signals again the rejection and opposition to Jesus' ministry among his own people in contrast to the "Gentiles" outside Galilee. On the other hand, this Feeding along with the first provides a foil against which the disciples' own lack of perception and understanding stands out and leads to the warning and challenge lest they too succumb to the "leaven of the Pharisees" (8:14–21; cf. 6:52). The Feeding with all its implications bears witness to who Jesus is but also by what follows to the fact that one can only see and hear this with the eyes and ears of faith.

K. The Demand for a Sign   (8:10–13)

Buchanan, G. W. "Some Vow and Oath Formulas in the New Testament." *HTR* 58 (1965) 319–24. **Edwards, R. A.** *The Sign of Jonah in the Theology of the Evangelists and Q.* SBT 2nd Series 18. London: SCM, 1971. **Fowler, R. M.** *Loaves and Fishes.* SBLDS 54. Chico, CA: Scholars, 1981. **Koch, D.-A.** *Die Bedeutung der Wundererzählungen für die Christologie des Markusevangeliums.* 1975. **Laufen, R.** *Die Doppelüberlieferungen der Logienquelle und des Markusevangeliums.* BBB 54. Bonn: Peter Hanstein, 1980. **Linton, O.** "The Demand for a Sign from Heaven (Mk 8, 11–12 and Parallels)." *ST* 19 (1965) 112–29. **Lührmann, D.** *Die Redaktion der Logienquelle.* Neukirchen-Vluyn: Neukirchener Verlag, 1969. **Robbins, V. K.** "*Dunameis* and *Semeia* in Mark." *BR* 18 (1973) 5–20. **Schenk, W.** "Der Einfluss der Logienquelle auf das Markusevangelium." *ZNW* 70 (1979) 141–65. **Schenke, L.** *Die Wundererzählungen des Markusevangeliums.* Stuttgart: Katholisches Bibelwerk, 1974. **Schmitt, G.** "Das Zeichen des Jona." *ZNW* 68 (1978) 123–29. **Schulz, S.** *Q: Die Spruchquelle der Evangelisten.* Zürich: Theologischer Verlag, 1972. **Vögtle, A.** "Der Spruch vom Jonazeichen." In *Das Evangelium und die Evangelien: Beiträge zur Evangelienforschung.* Düsseldorf: Patmos, 1971. 103–36. = *Synoptische Studien.* FS A. Wikenhauser, ed. J. Schmid and A. Vögtle. Munich: Zink, 1953. 230–77.

Translation

[10] *And immediately embarking into the boat with his disciples, he went to the district of Dalmanutha.*[a] [11] *The Pharisees came and began to dispute with him, seeking from him a sign from heaven in order to test him.* [12] *Sighing deeply in his spirit, he said, "Why does this generation seek a sign? Truly I say to you, 'May I be accursed,*[b] *should a sign be given to this generation.'"* [13] *Leaving them and embarking again,*[c] *he went to the other side.*

Notes

[a] Numerous variants reflect the questions surrounding this locale: (a) Δαλμουναι W; (b) Μαγδαλα Θ *f*[1.13] 205 565 2542 *pc*; (c) Μαγαδα D sy[s]. Δαλμανουθα ℵ A (B) C L 0274 33 1006 1342 1506 2427 Majority text vg sa[ms] bo.

[b] Ellipsis of an oath formula found in the OT (e.g., 1 Kgs 3:14; Ps 94:11 LXX). εἰ renders ΠΝ, ᵓ*im* (Taylor, 362; Klostermann, 76; Buchanan, *HTR* 58 [1965] 324–26).

[c] Text reads πάλιν ἐμβὰς (ℵ B C L Δ), with variants ἐμβὰς πάλιν εἰς (τὸ) πλοῖον (A *f*¹ 0131 Majority text sy[s.h]) and ἐμβὰς πάλιν (𝔓⁴⁵ D W Θ *f*¹³ 28 33 565 *pc* it vg[cl] bo[pt]).

Form / Structure / Setting

Form-critically, the pericope belongs to the broad category of apothegms with a Jesus logion at the center. Read in Mark's larger context, it doubtless functions as a controversy narrative with the Pharisees playing an adversarial role attempting to test Jesus (8:11). Less certain is whether this form stems from an earlier tradition or results from Mark's redaction.

As to source, the Jesus logion has a parallel in Matt 16:1–4 and Matt 12:38–39 // Luke 11:29 (Q) with a major difference. Whereas Jesus flatly refuses the request in Mark, he offers the sign of Jonah as the one exception in the parallels. This difference has led several interpreters to take 8:12 in particular and 8:10–13 in general to be a Markan redactional reworking of Q or a tradition parallel to Q. They have generally based their viewpoint on the assumption that one can more easily explain Mark's elimination of the Jonah sign than its later addition (e.g., Bultmann, 118, n.1; Taylor, 361; Vögtle, *Evangelium*, 134; Schenke, *Wundererzählungen*, 287–88; Schulz, *Spruchquelle*, 254, n. 527; Schenk, *ZNW* 70 [1979] 153–56; Schmithals, 1:367; similarly, Mann, 331). Others acknowledging the force of that argument but finding little betraying Markan redaction in 8:12, have assigned the redaction to a pre-Markan stage in which Mark found the tradition "polished and abbreviated from Q" (e.g., Schweizer, 158; Gnilka, 1:305; Lührmann, 135–36).

The evidence supporting pre-Markan tradition clearly outweighs the argument for Markan redaction. First, the specific geographical reference to Dalmanutha, despite its uncertainty, runs contrary to Mark's vague handling of locales. Second, the language, style, and structure of 8:11–12 when taken together strongly suggest a Semitic, non-Markan source (e.g., periphrasis for "God" with "heaven" and the *divinum passivum* δοθήσεται; the asyndeton construction; πνεύματι = בָרוּחַ, *bĕruaḥ*; the rhetorical question; "this generation" = הַדֹר הַזֶּה, *hador hazzeh*, with post-positive αὕτη; ἀμήν-formula; אִם כִּי, *kī 'im* = εἰ in an oath formula; use of σημεῖον = אוֹת, *'ōt*, so Pesch, 1:409; Vögtle, *Evangelium*, 109–10). Any one of these alone might not be significant but each gains weight in combination with the others in one brief section.

This leaves unresolved the apparent tension between the Q and Markan sayings about "signs." One might resolve the tension by taking them as two independent traditions. Or one might posit a development of a single saying whose roots extend to Jesus' ministry. Which stands closer to the original saying? The numerous Semitisms in Mark indicate the earlier wording, but this does not explain the absence of the Jonah exception. Was then an earlier saying modified by the addition of the sign of Jonah (e.g., Lührmann, *Logienquelle*, 34–43; Edwards, *Sign*, 83–87) or was it kerygmatically sharpened by removing the one exception, the sign of Jonah (Vögtle, *Evangelium*, 134; Taylor, 361; Schweizer, 158; Gnilka, 1:305)? The clue most likely lies in the linking of the request for a sign (Luke 11:29 // Matt 12:39) with the double saying of judgment (Luke 11:31–32 // Matt 12:41–42) now facilitated by the Son of man saying in Luke 11:30; cf. Matt 12:40 (see Lührmann, *Logienquelle*, 38–42; Edwards, *Sign*, 83–84).

Mark's redaction involves primarily the framework of this apophthegm. Although some have argued that the sequence of a boat crossing and the demand for a sign belong to the tradition of the Feeding as seen in a similar sequence in John 6:1–30 (e.g., Grundmann, 206; Haenchen, 287), the similarity is more apparent than real and comes from Mark's redactional arrangement. It may reflect the evangelist's desire to coordinate the events after the Feeding here with the order of events after the previous Feeding. There the evangelist found the Feeding and crossing combined in the tradition (see pp. 347–49). But in 7:1–13, he introduced the conflict scene with the "scribes from Jerusalem and the Pharisees," after which Jesus leaves the area (7:24). Here the evangelist provides a crossing (8:10) to "Dalmanutha" where Jesus again encounters the "Pharisees."

The vocabulary used to describe Jesus' journey to and from Dalmanutha could easily have been drawn by the evangelist from the previous references to similar boat journeys (e.g., ἐμβαίγογτος αὐτοῦ εἰς τὸ πλοῖον—5:18; cf. 4:1; εἰς τὸ πέραν—4:35; 5:1; 6:45). That the disciples explicitly accompany him fits not only their role in the Feeding but sets the stage for the critical dialogue of 8:14–21. Among those who consider Mark to be working with a given tradition, we find less agreement about the extent to which he has intervened in redacting the setting of 8:11. Some have put the "Pharisees" and "to test him" on Mark's account too (e.g., Kertelge, *Wunder*, 23; *Wundererzählungen*, 155; Gnilka, 1:305; cf. Pesch, 1:405; Lührmann, 136).

Structurally, Jesus moves by boat from the scene of the Feeding to another destination where he is met by the Pharisees who demand an authenticating sign (8:10–11). This sets the stage for Jesus' response in direct address, a double saying in the form of a rhetorical question and an oath formula introduced by an ἀμήν-formula (8:12). The episode concludes with Jesus leaving the Pharisees and departing again by boat for "the other side" (8:13).

The setting following the Feeding corresponds to the crossing after the previous Feeding (6:30–52) in Mark's larger context. And though a summary statement about Jesus' ministry corresponding to that of 6:53–56 is missing here, the encounter with the "Pharisees" in 8:11–12 is reminiscent of the encounter with the "scribes" and "Pharisees" in 7:1–13, a dialogue that led up to Jesus' departure in 7:24 for the territory of Tyre. In a similar way, Jesus departs from Dalmanutha for "the other side" in 8:13, a crossing that provides the setting for a dialogue between him and the disciples (8:14–21, cf. 7:14–23). Therefore, Mark appears to have shaped and set this pericope in line with similar events and the order of 6:30–7:23.

Mark's immediate setting contrasts the Pharisees' response to Jesus' ministry with that of the Syrophoenician, the deaf-mute along with those "preaching" the fulfillment of Isaiah in 7:36–37, and implicitly the four thousand including Gentiles in a gentile setting. At the same time, this story sets the stage for the crucial dialogue about the disciples' own lack of understanding in 8:14–21. They appear more like the Pharisees than the Gentiles, a situation that lends gravity to the warning about the "leaven of the Pharisees and the Herodians" (8:15).

Comment

10 "Immediately embarking into the boat with his disciples" (εὐθὺς ἐμβὰς εἰς τὸ πλοῖον μετὰ τῶν μαθητῶν αὐτοῦ) after the Feeding of the Four Thousand reminds the reader of the same sequence after the Feeding of the Five Thousand. Instead, however, of a dramatic story about a crossing in adverse conditions (cf. 4:35–41; 6:45–52; John 6:12–21), this statement simply moves Jesus from one location to another by using the mode familiar to the reader (cf. 4:35–6:56). Jesus accompanies the disciples from the point of departure (cf. 6:45; John 6:16–21).

"The district of Dalmanutha" (τὰ μέρη Δαλμανουθά), unfortunately, provides little information, since the place name is unknown to us otherwise. It may stem from an early corruption of the text. Matt 15:39 reads Magadan or Magedan perhaps from Magdala, the most important town on the west shore prior to the founding of Tiberias (see *Note* a). Since Mark does not create specific place names elsewhere in his redaction and since one is more likely to use a well-known rather than a rare place name when creating a scene, this geographical reference most likely belongs to a pre-Markan tradition (Schmid, 210; Kertelge, *Wunder,* 140; Pesch, 1:405–6; Gnilka, 1:305; Ernst, 222; cf. Fowler, *Loaves,* 51–53; Schenke, *Wundererzählungen,* 282; Schmithals, 1:367). Most assume it refers to a location on the west side of the sea.

11 "The Pharisees" (οἱ Φαρισαῖοι, 2:24; 3:6; 7:1, 5) along with the "scribes" (2:6; 3:22; 7:1, 5) and the "scribes of the Pharisees" (2:16) have consistently appeared in an adversarial role to this point in Mark's narrative. Furthermore, their appearances have exclusively involved either issues surrounding the Law or the questions of Jesus' authority. Issues surrounding the Law have had to do specifically with purity issues and sabbath practices like eating with sinners, "reaping" on the sabbath, healing on the sabbath, and eating with defiled hands. They have questioned the authority by which Jesus ministers, forgives sins, and casts out demons. Here we have to do with the authority, the need for Jesus to authenticate himself. But the question is set against the backdrop of the discussions regarding purity laws in 7:1–23 and Jesus' ministry to Gentiles in gentile territory 7:24–8:9 that raise again the broader purity issue of the Law. The "Pharisees" apropos their concern for purity pose the question (cf. Matt 16:1; 12:38–39 // Luke 11:29–30). For Mark, it is a controversy narrative.

"Came" (ἐξέρχεσθαι), literally, "to come out" but 1:38 and 3:21 demonstrate a more general sense of "to come."

"Disputed with him" (συζητεῖν) appears in four other contexts in Mark, each involving a difference of opinion (1:27; 9:1; 9:14, 16; 12:28). It indicates confusion and not necessarily opposition. The nature of the dispute here becomes clear in their request for a sign.

"Sign" (σημεῖον) consistently differs in Mark from "wonders" or "miracles" (δυνάμεις). Nowhere in the Synoptics does "sign" refer to a "miracle" or is a miraculous event called a "sign." Coming as this story does at the height of Jesus' miracle working in Mark (cf. 4:35–5:43; 6:30–8:9) and in view of the repeated summary statements reflecting Jesus' reputation as a miracle worker (1:32–34, 45; 3:7–12; 6:53–56) extending even to gentile territory (7:25, 32), the reader can hardly doubt that the Pharisees knew about Jesus' miracles. Indeed, his deeds as well as his words had raised their question.

They sought a "sign" in the OT Jewish sense, a confirmation or authentication of Jesus' ministry (e.g., 1 Sam 2:30–33; 10:1–8; Deut 13:1–2; Isa 7:10–14; Linton, *ST* 19 [1965] 112–29; K. H. Rengstorf, *TDNT* 7 [1971] 234–36). Since they wanted "outward compelling proof of divine authority" (Cranfield, 257) rather than a display of power, σημεῖον (cf. אוֹת, *'ōt*) instead of δύναμις became the appropriate term. The latter left too many questions (cf. 1:27; 3:22).

"A sign from heaven" (σημεῖον ἀπὸ τοῦ οὐρανοῦ) can be understood in two ways. The first occurs in an apocalyptic setting and refers to signs in the heavens of cosmic proportions commonly associated with the end of time, a period of catastrophe and judgment (e.g., 13:24–25; cf. 4 Ezra 5:4; 7:39; so Lohmeyer, 155; Grundmann, 207; Schweizer, 159). Accordingly, the Pharisees wanted Jesus to produce a convincing "apocalyptic" sign authenticating the eschatological character of his ministry. The second takes "from heaven" to be simply a periphrasis for "from God" (e.g., K. H. Rengstorf, *TDNT* 7 [1971] 235–36; Pesch, 1:407; Gnilka, 1:307). Accordingly, they were asking that God personally step in and confirm Jesus' credibility.

Of the two alternatives, the latter fits this context better. First, their request corresponded to the OT Jewish concern to authenticate a prophet's implicit or explicit claim (e.g., Deut 13:2–6; 18:18–22; 2 Kgs 20:1–11; Isa 7:10–14; cf. 1 Cor 1:22), a concern that became applicable to the eschatological prophet or messiah as well (Str-B, 1:640–41; 721–22; Mark 13:22). Second, Mark's narrative has portrayed Jesus from the outset as the one coming to announce the Kingdom (1:14–15; 4:1–34) whose presence and work fulfills the promise of Scripture, especially Isaiah (cf. 1:1–15; 7:36). But this ministry has succeeded in only confounding the religious representatives, the "scribes and Pharisees." Third, the use of the divine passive ($\delta o\theta\acute{\eta}\sigma\epsilon\tau\alpha\iota$) in 8:12 indicates that they had wanted God to grant them such an authenticating sign. Therefore, "from heaven" as a periphrasis for "God" belongs with the *divinum passivum* of 8:12 in a pre-Markan tradition reflecting Jewish sensitivity to the use of God's name (cf. Kertelge, *Wunder*, 24).

"In order to test him" ($\pi\epsilon\iota\rho\acute{\alpha}\zeta o\nu\tau\epsilon\varsigma$ $\alpha\dot{\upsilon}\tau\acute{o}\nu$). So far the Pharisees comply with normal Jewish concern about the word and work of one who claims to be ministering for God. One could hardly fault them for pursuing their concern with Jesus whose unorthodox "religious" impact was obvious to the reader. But the same expression occurs again in 10:2 and 12:15 and changes the mode from legitimate inquiry to harassment. Their question intends to compromise Jesus (cf. 1:13) either as one who cannot or will not provide the "sign." He loses in either case. Consistent with the portrait to this point in Mark's narrative, the statement betrays the Pharisees' orientation as adversaries.

12 "Sighing deeply in his spirit" ($\dot{\alpha}\nu\alpha\sigma\tau\epsilon\nu\acute{\alpha}\xi\alpha\varsigma$) renders an NT *hapax legomenon*, though the root ($\sigma\tau\epsilon\nu\acute{\alpha}\zeta\epsilon\iota\nu$) does occur in 7:34. For some the verb expresses a deep emotional reaction to pain parallel to the anger of 1:41 (cf. John 11:33). The unbelieving response of the Pharisees, the leading religious party of Israel, caused him deep pain in his spirit (Taylor, 362; Grundmann, 208; similarly, Lane, 277). For others the verb expresses more formally the "spiritual excitement" experienced by the prophet moved deeply in his person prior to an utterance or an action (cf. Ezek 21:11–12 LXX; Isa 21:2 LXX; John 13:21, Pesch, 1:408; similarly Ernst, 223). The latter alternative corresponds more with the context in which Jesus is asked like a prophet for an authenticating sign (8:11) and what follows also takes the form of a prophetic utterance, one of judgment.

"Why . . . seek a sign?" ($\tau\acute{\iota}$ . . . $\zeta\eta\tau\epsilon\tilde{\iota}$ $\sigma\eta\mu\epsilon\tilde{\iota}o\nu;$) begins Jesus' response with a rhetorical question that exposes the disposition of the questioners. Their request comes as incongruous, since they have rejected the "signs" that God has already given them through Jesus' ministry. Why then ask for a sign?

By addressing them as "this generation" ($\dot{\eta}$ $\gamma\epsilon\nu\epsilon\grave{\alpha}$ $\alpha\dot{\upsilon}\tau\eta$), Jesus uses a designation applied to the "generation" of Noah's day (Gen 7:1) and the stubborn, disobedient wilderness wanderers in Ps 95:10–11 (cf. Deut 32:5, 20). Here it is a pejorative term referring to those who turned their backs on God, "Sons in whom is no faithfulness" (Deut 32:20). The same designation occurs later in 8:38 and 9:19 with reference to Jesus' contemporary generation character-ized as "adulterous, sinful" (8:38) and "unbelieving" (9:19). For Mark, the Pharisees epitomize "this generation" who repeatedly refuse to respond to God's overture in Jesus and have the audacity to request a sign, a request that stems from their unbelief (cf. 6:5–6a).

"I assure you" (ἀμὴν λέγω ὑμῖν), a solemn introductory formula of prophetic character, sets the tone of the following pronouncement (see *Comment* on 3:28–29).

The pronouncement itself comes in the form of an elliptical oath formula. Literally, we have, "If a sign shall be given to this generation . . ." (εἰ δοθήσεται τῇ γενεᾷ ταύτῃ σημεῖον). The apodosis is missing. But many have found an underlying Hebraic idiom that renders the conditional literally, "If a sign shall be given to this generation, may I die!" or "may I be cursed!" (e.g., Taylor, 362; Klostermann, 76). Ps 94:11 LXX; Gen 14:23; Num 32:11: Deut 1:35; 1 Kgs 3:14 provide OT parallels for this single, NT occurrence of the oath formula. The thrust of such a formula is an emphatic denial of the request. Jesus absolutely refused to grant their request here and in a similar setting in 11:27–33.

Why does Jesus refuse to grant the "sign"? For some the answer lies in the "messianic secret" (e.g., Cranfield, 257; Kertelge, *Wunder*, 26; Schmithals, 1:367). But this answer misses the mark. The real issue here is unbelief, not concealment. Unbelief can never be alleviated (Gnilka, 1:307). On the one hand, to force the evidence upon one would make a faith response by its very nature impossible. On the other hand, the unbeliever despite the evidence will always find grounds for unbelief, especially if believing means abandoning the familiar, the source of security. For those who had the eyes of faith Jesus' ministry provided an ample "sign from heaven" of God's confirming work. For those blinded by unbelief no sign could adequately reveal the nature of Jesus' words and work. "This generation shall not be given a sign!"

13 "Leaving them" (ἀφείς) indicates that Jesus acts in keeping with his pronouncement of judgment. He chooses to depart from their presence rather than speak or work further "signs" among them or in their district.

"Embarking again" (πάλιν ἐμβάς) takes "again" with the second participle. Syntactically, one could translate it with the first in which case Jesus would be "leaving them *again*." He at least implicitly had left the "scribes and Phari-sees" on the previous occasion when he left Galilee for the territory of Tyre in 7:24 (cf. 7:1–23). That departure, however, was not as clear or as abrupt, since he had already withdrawn into a house before departing for Tyre (cf. 7:14). Furthermore, the variant readings support taking "again" with "embark-ing" (see *Note* c).

"He went to the other side" (ἀπῆλθεν εἰς τὸ πέραν) picks up the familiar but vague destination of previous crossings (e.g., 4:35; 5:1, 21; 6:45; see *Comment* on 5:21; 6:45). We learn in 8:22 that they came to Bethsaida.

How much significance can we place on this departure? The use of the boat and crossing motif in the earlier stories served the mechanical purpose of moving Jesus from one area to another around the Sea. Mark apparently selected this device to move Jesus from gentile territory back to Galilee and a confrontation with the religious representatives of Judaism whose unbelief had blinded them from seeing the "sign" of Jesus' ministry (8:10). With this departure (8:13), Jesus essentially concludes his public ministry in Galilee. The following episodes in Galilee pertain exclusively to his disciples (cf. 9:30–32, 33–50).

Does this change in venue signal a shift of Jesus' mission from the Jews to the Gentiles? Hardly. According to Mark's narrative, he has already travelled and worked in gentile territory (7:24–8:9) congruent with his teaching regarding the purity laws (7:1–23). But this departure quite likely does depict his general rejection by the Jews of Galilee, "this generation" epitomized by the Pharisees, and begins setting the stage for his ultimate rejection by the Jewish authorities in Judea. The conflict that has marked the relationship between Jesus and the Jewish religious representatives (e.g., 2:6, 16, 24; 3:6, 22; 7:1, 5) turns now to final rejection. The same pattern will emerge later in Judea where the conflict leads to rejection which ends in death whose shadow has followed Jesus from the beginning.

Consequently, the focus of Jesus' ministry turns next to the disciples instead of the public. He does heal a blind man in Bethsaida and exorcises the demon-possessed lad after the Transfiguration, but even these episodes speak directly to the needs of the disciples in 8:27–9:50. More immediately, this crossing sets the scene for the critical discussion about the "leaven of the Pharisees" and the disciples' own lack of understanding (8:14–21) typified by the blind man of Bethsaida (8:22–26).

Explanation

In this brief story, Mark moves Jesus with his disciples from the east shore of the Sea of Galilee by boat to "the district of Dalmanutha" and then to Bethsaida on "the other side" (8:10, 14). This journey implies a return to Galilee where the Pharisees meet them. The setting, therefore, contrasts with Jesus' ministry outside Galilee not only in location but also in response (cf. 7:24–30, 31–37; 8:1–9).

Coming where it does in the narrative, the reader assumes that the Pharisees know about Jesus and his ministry. Their request would make no sense otherwise. Consequently, Jesus' ministry of miracles, teaching, and questionable conduct, including the boundary-destroying claims of 7:1–23 and the work of 7:24–8:9 done at least implicitly as a man of God, led them to pose the relevant question about divine authentication. They asked for a "sign from heaven." But they did so to "test him."

Jesus' response exposes their design as well as their blindness by addressing them as "this generation." With an emphatic oath formula, he denies them any sign at all from God. By contrast to others who come to him in faith anticipating God's offer of help and healing, the Pharisees in their blindness had failed to see God's sign and to believe in Jesus or his ministry (cf. 3:1–6, 22–30). Signs are not a divine antidote for unbelief. And as though carrying out his judgment, Jesus left the Pharisees and sailed to "the other side." Their blindness was total and irremediable.

Mark has used the motif of rejection toward the end of the previous units in this section (1:16–8:26) of his Gospel (cf. 3:1–6; 6:1–6a). The motif serves as a constant reminder that Jesus' ministry knew rejection and opposition and as a pointer to his ultimate rejection in 11:1–16:8. But here it sets the stage additionally for a warning and challenge to the disciples which follows in 8:14–21. They themselves are in danger of the "leaven of the Pharisees" (8:15). Mark has highlighted the theme by underscoring the disciples' lack of understanding, a posture approximating that of the Pharisees more than that of the people even in gentile territory who recognize and commit themselves to Jesus. But he also uses this story to contrast the blindness of the Pharisees with that of the disciples. The one is total and permanent; the other is partial and temporary. Jesus abandons the one group; he concentrates on the other, especially in 8:27–10:52.

L. Warning against the Leaven of the Pharisees and Herod (8:14–21)

Bibliography

Beck, N. A. "Reclaiming a Biblical Text: The Mark 8:14–21 Discussion about the Bread in the Boat." *CBQ* 43 (1981) 49–56. **Boobyer, G. H.** "The Miracles of the Loaves and the Gentiles in St. Mark's Gospel." *SJT* 6 (1953) 77–87. **Countryman, W.** "How Many Baskets Full? Mark 8:14–21 and the Value of the Miracles in Mark." *CBQ* 47 (1985) 643–55. **Hawkin, D. J.** "The Incomprehension of the Disciples in the Marcan Redaction." *JBL* 91 (1972) 491–500. **Kertelge, K.** *Die Wunder Jesu im Markusevangelium.* 1970. **Lemcio, E. E.** "External Evidence for the Structure and Function of Mark iv. 1–20, vii. 14–23 and viii. 14–21." *JTS* 29 (1978) 323–38. **Manek, J.** "Mark viii. 14–21." *NovT* 7 (1964) 10–14. **Meagher, J.** *Clumsy Construction in Mark's Gospel: A Critique of Form- and Redaktionsgeschichte.* TST 3. Toronto: Edwin Mellen, 1979. **Neirynck, F.** *Duality in Mark.* 1972. **Quesnell, Q.** *The Mind of Mark: Interpretation and Method through the Exegesis of Mark 6,52.* AnBib 38. Rome: Pontifical Biblical Institute, 1969. **Reploh, K.-G.** *Markus—Lehrer der Gemeinde.* 1969. **Schenke, L.** *Die Wundererzählungen des Markusevangeliums.* 1974. **Sundwall, J.** *Die Zusammensetzung des Markusevangeliums.* Acta Academiae Aboensis—Humaniora IX, 2, Abo, 1934. **Wendling, E.** *Die Entstehung des Marcus-Evangeliums.* Tübingen: Mohr, 1908. **Ziener, G.** "Das Bildwort vom Sauerteig, Mk 8, 15." *TTZ* 67 (1958) 247–48.

Translation

[14] *The* disciples[a] *had forgotten*[b] *to take loaves of bread*[c] *except*[d] *for one with them in the boat.* [15] *And* Jesus[a] *began to admonish them, "Take care! Beware of the leaven of the Pharisees and the leaven of Herod!"*[e] [16] *And they continued discussing with one another the fact*[f] *that*[g] *they*[h] *had no loaves.* [17] *Jesus knowing this said to them, "Why are you discussing the fact that you have no loaves? Do you not yet know or understand? Do you have hardened hearts?* [18] *Having eyes do you not see? And having ears do you not hear? And do you not remember?* [19] *When*

I broke the five loaves for the five thousand, how many baskets full of broken pieces did you pick up?" They said to him, "Twelve." 20"When I broke[a] seven loaves for the four thousand, how many large basketfuls of pieces did you pick up?" And they said to him, "Seven." 21And he said to them, "Do you not yet understand?"

Notes

[a] Romanized words supplied from context.

[b] ἐπελάθοντο translated as pluperfect from context.

[c] Translates τοὺς ἄρτους to be consistent with 6:38, 52; and 8:5. English plural "breads" connotes something different from "loaves of bread."

[d] Several MSS smooth out the awkward καὶ εἰ μὴ ἕνα ἄρτον οὐκ εἶχον to ἕνα μόνον ἄρτον ἔχοντες (e.g., P45 [W] Θ f1.13 205 565 700 k sa).

[e] Some MSS align Ἡρῴδου with Ἡρῳδιάνων of 3:6 and 12:13 (P45 G W Θ f1.13 205 565 1506 2542 pc i k sa).

[f] Awkward construction smoothed by adding λέγοντες in A C L Θ f13 33 892 1006 1506 Majority text vg sy bo.

[g] This rendering takes ὅτι as introducing a noun clause. It could also be causal, since it is uncertain and moot whether this clause tells what they were discussing or why they were discussing it. The variant reading λέγοντες . . . ἔχομεν would change its thrust to *recitativum*.

[h] Some MSS have ἔχομεν for ἔχουσιν (א A C L Θ f13 33 892 1006 1506 Majority text vg syp.h bomss).

Form / Structure / Setting

This pericope exhibits numerous awkward elements that supposedly stem from Mark's clumsy combination of various traditions or simply his "opacity" in transmitting a story without himself understanding it (e.g., Meagher, *Construction*, 74–81). This awkwardness makes any attempt at classifying it form-critically, especially if the story represents a redactional amalgam, almost impossible. Most have grouped it with the teaching narratives (e.g., Beck, *CBQ* 43 [1981] 51–52; Gnilka, 1:310; Schenke, *Wundererzählungen*, 281; cf. Quesnell, *Mind*, 106).

A large consensus ascribes the story as we have it to Mark's redactional efforts. In fact, Schmithals (1:369–70) attributes the entire complex, including the reworking of a Q-saying on the "leaven" (Matt 13:33 // Luke 13:20–21), to Mark's redaction. Few interpreters would go that far, but some do consider Mark to have constructed the present narrative around a traditional saying about the "leaven of the Pharisees" (e.g., Schenke, *Wundererzählungen*, 291–92; Gnilka, 1:310).

Most commentators, however, posit an underlying story whose traditional fragments appear in at least 8:14, 16 (e.g., Grundmann, 228; Quesnell, *Mind*, 106; Schweizer, 160–61; Beck, *CBQ* 43 [1981] 55; Ernst, 225). Wendling (*Entstehung*, 75; similarly, Klostermann, 77) suggested it might have introduced another Feeding miracle, whereas Sundwall (*Zusammensetzung*, 52–53) argued it originally introduced the Feeding of 8:1–9. Perhaps the strongest argument for an underlying tradition lies in the awkward relationship between 8:14, 16 and 8:15, an insertion that has little to do with either verse. Would not 8:15 have been more integral to 8:14–21 if Mark had used it as the core text around which to construct the story? Furthermore, an underlying tradition might also account for the extreme awkwardness of 8:14b (καὶ εἰ μὴ . . . οὐκ εἶχον).

Besides the evangelist's redactional choice of locating this pericope at this particular juncture of his narrative and the probability of his introducing the warning about leaven (8:15) into the account, his redactional touch becomes much clearer in the second half. Here we find the climax of the repeated Markan theme about the disciples' lack of understanding (8:17b, 21; cf 4:13, 41; 6:37, 52; 7:18; 8:4). We also have the almost verbatim recall of the details of the two Feedings, not only as to the sequence and numbers but even the precise words for "baskets" (8:17c–23). This strongly indicates familiarity with the literary text of 6:35–44 and 8:1–9.

As to structure, the story falls into three or four parts. It opens with the setting describing the disciples' predicament of travelling without sufficient bread (8:14, 16). Then comes intrusively Jesus' warning about "leaven" (8:15). Next comes a dialogue between Jesus and his disciples set as a series of questions (8:17–21). The dialogue itself begins with a rhetorical question about their discussion (8:17a), turns into a series of rhetorical questions about their lack of understanding (8:17b) including two based on the prophetic indictment of Israel's blindness and deafness (8:18), and reviews the details of the two Feedings in a question and answer format (8:19–20) before posing once again the rhetorical question about their understanding (8:21). Without doubt 8:15, lacking any obvious structural role in the story, interrupts the narrative flow.

Lemcio (*JTS* 29 [1978] 325–31) argues for a common structure between this story and those of 7:14–23 and 4:1–20 with roots in OT and apocalyptic writings (see pp. 202, 373). He finds this pattern to consist of: (a) ambiguity (8:15), (b) incomprehension (8:16), (c) surprise/critical rejoinder (8:17–18), and (d) explanation (8:19–21). But just as that structure appears forced in 4:1–20 and 7:14–23, so it does here. Neither the "incomprehension" (8:16) nor the "explanation" (8:19–21) relates directly to the "ambiguity" (8:15).

Mark's setting does play a significant role for the reader in understanding this story in which many lines converge. In the immediate context, the story with its reference to the "leaven of the Pharisees" (8:15) follows immediately Jesus' encounter with the Pharisees who had asked for an authenticating sign (8:11–13). At the same time, the story connects with the two Feeding accounts, one of which has just taken place (8:1–9) and the other which is at the beginning of a series of stories that underscore the disciples' lack of understanding (6:30–44, 45–52; 7:14–23; 8:1–9). And the reader may recall that Mark's narrative sequence had been interrupted just prior to the first Feeding by the story of Herod's execution of John the Baptist, a story introduced by a reference to Herod's awareness of Jesus' "miracles" that had given rise to the question about Jesus' identity (6:14–16). Thus Herod's interest in Jesus' "miracles" and the Pharisees' demand for a "sign" enclose the two Feeding accounts. This story directly refers to both Herod and the Pharisees (8:15) as well as the two Feedings (8:19–20).

At the same time, the disciples themselves fail to grasp Jesus' intentions to feed miraculously the crowds in 6:37 and 8:5. Then after personally participating in feeding the five thousand, their astonished reaction to Jesus' epiphany during the night crossing shows they did not "understand about the loaves; rather their hearts were hardened," the very language used in the dialogue of this crossing (8:17, 21).

The disciples' failure to understand first surfaced with the question about "parables" in 4:10–12. Jesus informed them that they had been given the "mystery of the Kingdom" while those "outside" found the parables to be "riddles" according to the prophecy of Isa 6:9–10. Yet in the next verse (4:13) Jesus critically queried the disciples' failure to understand the parable in question (see *Comment* on 4:13). We find the same retort again in 7:18 when the disciples fail to grasp the "parable" of things clean and unclean (7:15). Here the reference to the prophets' indictment of Israel's failure to see and hear (7:18) sounds dangerously close to what Isa 6:9–10 had to say about "those outside" cited in 4:12 (see *Comment* on 4:12).

Finally, the story of the Feeding of the Four Thousand, the Pharisees' Demand for a Sign, and this episode in the boat fall significantly between two healing stories. The first has to do with a deaf-mute (7:31–37) and the second with a blind man (8:22–26). These stories along with the "not yet" of Jesus' question (8:17, 21) provide hope for the disciples' perception. Though the next major section of Mark's narrative begins with Peter's confession, Jesus concentrates his ministry on "curing" their deafness and blindness which continues to show itself in 8:27–10:52.

Perhaps more than coincidentally, Mark's narrative so far falls into three sections subsequent to the introduction of 1:1–15. The first unit begins with the calling of four disciples (1:16–20) then ends with the religious and political representatives of Judaism, the "Pharisees" and "Herodians," plotting his execution (3:1–6). The second begins with the call of the Twelve (3:13–19) and moves to its end with Jesus' rejection by home and hometown (6:1–6a). The third opens with the sending of the Twelve in mission (6:7–13) and winds down with both the rejection by the "Pharisees" (8:10–13) and this story (8:14–21) underscoring the disciples' own failure to perceive and understand (8:14–21). The previous units actually conclude with a summary account of Jesus' continued ministry in the face of rejection (3:7–12; 6:6b). No such summary follows this account. Instead we have the rather labored healing of the blind man (8:22–26) which may be symbolic of the disciples' own need for sight. The scope of Jesus' ministry narrows down considerably from this point in Mark's Gospel, and he concentrates most of his time and teaching on his disciples for whom the questions are posed but left unanswered.

Comment

14 "Forgotten to take loaves of bread" (ἐπελάθοντο λαβεῖν ἄρτους) sets the stage for the discussion in 8:16 that provokes Jesus' questions. One can hardly read this without thinking of the loaves in the previous Feedings (6:35–44; 8:1–9) or the reference to "loaves" in the discussion with the Syrophoenician woman in 7:27. At the same time, the lack of bread places the "disciples"— unnamed here but clearly understood from Mark's broader context—in the same situation of need experienced by the crowds in each of the Feedings.

"Except for one loaf" renders an awkward clause that forms an antithetical parallelism with the first. Literally it reads, "and they did not have except one loaf with them in the boat" (εἰ μὴ ἕνα ἄρτον οὐκ εἶχον, see *Note* d). This comment presents us with an enigma. On the one hand, it qualifies the absolute statement, "they had forgotten to take loaves of bread," by noting that they did have one loaf of bread with them. On the other hand, in 8:16 the disciples dispute among themselves because they did not have "loaves of bread" with them, as though nothing had been said to the contrary.

This enigma has been resolved in two ways. First, some have argued that the contradiction between no bread and one bread is more apparent than real because of the difficulty in rendering the Greek words into English. Since we do not use the plural "breads" as we do "rolls," for example, we cannot distinguish as the Greek does between "breads" (ἄρτους, 8:14a, 16, 17) and "bread" (ἄρτον, 8:14b), meaning that though they had not brought "breads," they did have a "bread." The thrust of the exception then would be that having "one bread," apart from an attempt to be precise, was hardly worth mentioning, and indeed was not mentioned in 8:16, 17 in view of the number needed for the group (see Boobyer, *JTS* 6 [1953] 84–85; Beck, *CBQ* 43 [1981] 53). But why mention the "one bread" at all? Many interpreters have found here a symbolic reference to Jesus as the "one bread" that was sufficient for their needs (e.g., Klostermann, 77; Grundmann, 208; Manek, *NovT* 7 [1964] 10–14; Quesnell, *Mind*, 231–32; Kertelge, *Wunder*, 172; Hawkin, *JBL* 91 [1972] 495–96; Pesch, 1:414; Gnilka, 1:312). By introducing this "exception" here, Mark prepares for the culpable failure of the disciples to comprehend the significance of having Jesus with them in the boat (cf. 4:35–41).

This significance has been variously interpreted as: (a) a eucharistic allusion to Jesus as the "one bread" (e.g., Quesnell, *Mind*, 242–43), (b) as the "one bread" sufficient for Jews and Gentiles (Boobyer, *JTS* 6 [1953] 170; Hawkin, *JBL* 91 [1972] 495), or (c) as the one capable of performing a miracle to meet their need (Schenke, *Wundererzählungen*, 310; Gnilka, 1:304). Certainly, John 6:48–51 takes the discussion in this general direction by identifying Jesus with "the bread of life." And nothing prevents Mark from working in such symbolism. But apart from its extreme subtlety (even John's symbolism specifically identifies Jesus as the "bread of life"), the shift to a symbolic use of "bread" does come quite unannounced to the reader, particularly since "bread(s)" is used literally throughout the account.

Perhaps a less sophisticated reason can explain the mention of "one bread." Had Mark created 8:14 from scratch, it seems most unlikely despite his purported stylistic "clumsiness" that he would have constructed it in this fashion (cf. the *v.l.* that seeks to make it smoother, *Note* d). Might not the "except one bread" represent a traditional splinter of the episode used by Mark in shaping this story? Accordingly, the tradition indicated that the disciples had only one loaf of bread. Mark, however, depicts a scene of dispute between Jesus and his disciples over the fact that they discuss their failure to "have loaves" (8:16–17; cf. 8:14a). Then Jesus reminds them of two previous occasions when they thought for all practical purposes that they "had no bread" (6:37; 8:4) but had more than enough with five loaves for five thousand and seven for four thousand with leftovers (8:19–20). Therefore, to draw the analogy the evangelist begins the story by declaring that the disciples "had forgotten to take loaves of bread" (sufficient for their needs) but deliberately leaves the qualification, "and they did not have except one loaf" (hardly worth mentioning). We have then in 8:14 the ingredients (need, limited resources) for another Feeding miracle (Wendling, *Entstehung*, 75; Boobyer, *JTS* 6 [1953] 84; Haenchen, 288; Schmithals, 1:369).

15 "Began to admonish" (διεστέλλετο) renders the imperfect of a verb used by Mark in the aorist tense elsewhere in silence commands (5:43; 7:36; 9:9). "Be careful!" (ὁρᾶτε) and "Beware" (βλέπετε ἀπό) is another example of duality in Mark. It underscores the intensity of the warning, especially combined with διαστέλλειν. The evangelist, who most likely constructed this introduction to the saying, clearly wanted to emphasize it.

"Leaven" (ζύμη) like "yeast" is naturally associated with bread. Its property of gradually pervading the dough serves as a positive (e.g., Matt 13:33 // Luke 13:31) though more often as a negative (e.g., 1 Cor 5:6; Gal 5:9) point of reference. The feast of unleavened bread and the requirement that a grain offering be without leaven (Lev 2:11) may have contributed to the negative connotation in Jewish circles that it has here, in Paul's use, and in the use by the Rabbis to symbolize the evil inclination within human beings (Str-B, 1:278–79; cf. H. Windisch, *TDNT* 2 [1964] 902–6).

This warning has at best a tangential relation to 8:14. The mention of bread and the shift to its common ingredient, "leaven," has some correlation. But the ensuing dialogue does not develop the warning. Instead 8:16–17a returns to the concern about the missing "loaves" of 8:14. Consequently, 8:15 stands as an intrusion within 8:14–21 when taken as a unit in itself. The appearance of the same warning in a different context in Luke 12:1 together with its intrusive character here points to the saying's traditional existence as an independent saying (cf. Schmithals, 369–70). Its awkward presence in 8:14–21 makes it an unlikely candidate for being the core of a Markan created narrative (cf. Schenke, *Wundererzählungen*, 291–94; Gnilka, 1:310).

Who then inserted it here? Several have discounted Mark's responsibility, since inserting sayings within traditional blocks is more characteristic of Matthew's than Mark's redactional style (e.g., Taylor, 366; Cranfield, 259; Lane, 280). That observation may well obtain for Mark's normal style of handling traditional units, but his "sandwich" technique of inserting tradition within tradition (see p. 169) does indicate some flexibility in handling tradition. More importantly, the warning, which remains undeveloped in 8:14–21 (cf. Matt 16:5–12), takes its significance from the broader Markan context. And this strongly suggests that Mark has not only located this pericope about "loaves of bread" in the larger context of Jesus' miraculous use of bread to feed multitudes (6:35–44; 8:1–9; cf. 8:19–20) but also has inserted this warning against the "leaven of the Pharisees and Herod" that refers back to the stories of Herod (6:14–29) and the Pharisees (8:10–13) that enclose these Feedings.

"The leaven of the Pharisees and the leaven of Herod" is unique to Mark. Whereas Luke 12:1 only refers to the "leaven of the Pharisees," Matt 16:6 refers to the "leaven of the Pharisees and the Sadducees." Since Mark and Matthew are most likely responsible for their differing second referents, one can posit the "leaven of the Pharisees" as the original referent. To survive, an independent logion must convey a certain intelligible meaning in itself. Yet its applicability to various contexts reflects an inherent ambiguity as well. Luke 12:1 identifies the "leaven" with "hypocrisy" (ὑπόκρισις); Matt 16:12 identifies it with "teaching" (διδαχή). Not unrelated, both have become stereotypical of the Pharisees in the Gospels. Mark, however, leaves the meaning of the "leaven" for the reader to identify.

The Markan clue may well lie in the combination of the Pharisees and Herod. Some have sought to distinguish the "leaven" of the former—"false and inconsistent piety"—from the latter—"godlessness of the man of the world" (so Cranfield, 261; similarly Lagrange, 208; Grundmann, 209). Most, however, have sought a common denominator between the "leaven" of the Pharisees and Herod. For some it represents the common but disparate nationalism that hoped for a unified nation under a revolutionary messiah (Pharisees) or consolidation of power (Herod Antipas). Accordingly, Jesus warned his disciples against a false messianic hope and/or a narrow nationalism (Lohmeyer, 157; Boobyer, *JTS* 6 [1953] 86; Pesch, 1:413; Ernst, 226). For others the "leaven" represents the intense hostility toward Jesus seen in the collusion in 3:6 of the religious and political representatives of the Jews (Haenchen, 288; Schmithals, 1:370–71).

None of the above suggestions takes seriously Mark's redactional insertion of this warning into the pericope. The connection between the interpretations of the warning with the thrust of this pericope becomes forced at best. Nor do the suggestions take seriously Mark's reference to the Pharisees and Herod at the end of a series of stories beginning and ending with miraculous feedings (6:30–8:9) enclosed by a story about Herod (6:14–29) and the Pharisees (8:10–13). Since Mark is responsible for this "coincidence," is it not likely that it sheds light on the "leaven of the Pharisees and the leaven of Herod?"

Without doubt the recounting of Herod's execution of the Baptist whom he saw to be a "just and holy man" (6:17–29) harbingers Jesus' own rejection and death. But this account begins with Herod's hearing about Jesus' fame arising from "the powers" (αἱ δυνάμεις) at work in him (see *Comment* on 6:14). Herod concluded that the Baptist had been raised from the dead (6:16). What follows in 6:17–29 is a flashback to the story of the Baptist's death. Compositionally, then, for Mark's readers Herod's response to Jesus' fame (6:14–16), not the story of the Baptist's death (6:17–29), fills the narrative time gap between the sending and the return of the Twelve (6:7–13, 30). This brief story shows that Herod had failed to grasp the import of Jesus' ministry precisely because of "the powers" (αἱ δυνάμεις) at work in him. Jesus' fame based on miracles (δυνάμεις) did not necessarily lead to faith (cf. 6:1–6a).

Similarly, the Pharisees had just encountered Jesus and demanded a "sign" (8:10–13). They too had failed to recognize Jesus' ministry but sought a confirming indication from God to validate his ministry (see *Comment* on 8:12; cf. 3:22–29). This despite, if not because of, the popular response to Jesus as teacher and healer. For Mark's readers the Pharisees' demand stands in sharp contrast to the many who do respond to him in faith seeking divine help. Jesus' miracles have not led them to faith in Jesus, the "sign" of God's redemptive work for those who have eyes to see.

In short, the "leaven of the Pharisees and the leaven of Herod" is unbelief, the failure to recognize Jesus as the one in whom God is uniquely and redemptively at work meeting the needs of those who entrust themselves to him (Reploh, *Markus,* 83; Quesnell, *Mind,* 254–55; Gnilka, 1:311). In Herod's case the "miracles" mislead; in the Pharisees' case they are inadequate. Here we find the connecting link between this warning and the rest of the story. Mark introduces the warning in a story that shows the disciples coming dangerously close to unbelief, to missing who Jesus really is and what he is about as seen by his ministry (cf. 4:41; 6:52; 8:17–21). "Leaven" is unbelief reflected in one's response to Jesus.

16 "They continued discussing" (διελογίζοντο) renders the imperfect as durative action implying that the disciples simply ignored Jesus' warning in their concern about not having bread (e.g., Taylor, 366; Grundmann, 208). Others translate it as an inceptive imperfect ("began to discuss") in keeping with the thesis that the disciples in a Johannine manner took literally what Jesus had meant figuratively (e.g., Lohmeyer, 158; Lane, 280; Pesch, 1:414). Matt 16:12 handles the story in this way. Such a reading does tie 8:15 more closely to 8:16, but it fits better with the *v.l.* (see *Note* f) and overlooks the deliberate setting of 8:14a. As Jesus' question shows, the disciples were in danger of misunderstanding Jesus rather than his reference to "leaven."

17 Jesus asks the disciples in the words the narrator has just used to describe the disciples' concern—"Why are you discussing the fact that you have no loaves?" For the third time, the reader learns that the disciples have no loaves of bread with them. Nothing further is said about the one loaf they did bring, since their failure to bring along the loaves made the one loaf meaningless.

Jesus, however, finds their discussion disturbing. It reflects a deeper problem than merely failure to bring along the necessary provisions. A series of rhetorical questions makes the point. After asking why they even bothered to discuss their lack of loaves, Jesus asks: "Do you not yet know or understand? Do you have hardened hearts?" These words, used by the narrator to describe the disciples after Jesus joined them in the boat following the first Feeding (συνῆκαν, πεπωρωμένη, 6:52), now come from Jesus in the form of a double question. He asked a similar double question in 7:18 (ἀσύνετοί ἐστε, οὐ νοεῖτε; cf. 4:13).

Clearly, the disciples' concern for the lack of loaves triggered Jesus' question about their comprehension (νοεῖτε, συνίετε) of someone or something much greater. This is seen by the query about their "hardened hearts" (πεπωρωμένην . . . καρδίαν). In 3:5 Jesus had been angered and deeply grieved by the "hard hearts" of those in a synagogue who had questioned his healing on the sabbath. The next verse (3:6) identifies his opponents who departed to take counsel with the "Herodians" about killing Jesus as the "Pharisees." For the reader, therefore, the disciples appear indeed in danger of the "leaven" of the Pharisees by sharing the same characteristic, "hardness of heart," assigned by the prophets to Israel who failed to grasp and respond to God's message (see *Comment* on 3:5).

18 Jesus' rhetorical questions continue by moving more directly to the prophetic accusation. In words similar to Isa 6:9–10 used in 4:12 to describe the blindness and deafness of "those outside," Jesus asks if they having eyes cannot see and having ears cannot hear (cf. Jer 5:21b; Ezek 7:2). Unlike the crowds and those seeking Jesus' help in the miracle stories of the Gospel, the disciples' response to Jesus in the time of their own need (4:35–41; 6:45–52; 8:14–21) parallels more closely the response of "the outsiders" for whom all things are in "riddles" (e.g., 4:13; 7:18), the response of Jesus' adversaries (3:5–6; 6:14–16; 8:15).

Mark does not take the ultimate step and make the equation. Jesus counters the disciples with rhetorical questions which implicitly include a challenge to a positive response rather than anger and deep grief (cf. 3:5). The series begins and concludes with the loaded "not yet" (οὔπω, 8:17, 21) holding out the real possibility that they, to whom the "mystery of the Kingdom" has been given, will know and understand. Their hearts are not hardened, they will see and hear. And perhaps not without significance, Mark chooses to use analogous prophetic texts to describe the disciples' blindness and deafness rather than Isa 6:9–10 which characterizes those who are clearly "outside" (see *Comment* on 4:12).

What do they "not yet" know, understand, see, or hear? The answer lies for Mark in the two ensuing questions referring to the two Feedings. No longer rhetorical in form, these questions demand an answer based on the disciples' remembering. But more than their "knowledge" of the facts is at stake. We are back to their need to "understand the loaves" (cf. 6:52).

19–20 In these two verses, Jesus asks specifically about the number of baskets left over after feeding the five and four thousand respectively. The wording of the questions agrees in detail with each Feeding, not only regarding the numbers ("five loaves for five thousand"; "seven loaves for four thousand") but even the words for the different baskets used in gathering the leftovers (κοφίνους, σπυρίδων). Since Mark most likely first combined the two Feeding stories, variants of a common tradition, in a sequential narrative, these questions as well as the rhetorical questions in 8:17 with their parallels in Mark's redactional work in 6:52 and 7:18 most likely stem from his own composition. In other words, Mark composed this dialogue to address the issue of the disciples' response to Jesus. Assuming his redactional insertion of the warning about the "leaven" in 8:15, we see that he shows how dangerously close the disciples had come at times in their unbelief to the "leaven of the Pharisees and Herod."

Recalling the Feedings, Jesus specifically asks how many baskets were left over after each of the two Feedings. The disciples correctly remember and respond accordingly, "Twelve," and, "Seven." These questions and their answers must address the underlying issue. One cannot ignore them. But what do they mean? By focusing on the numbers per se as symbolic, one might argue that Jesus wants the disciples to be open to the mission to both Jews and Gentiles against the narrow nationalism ("leaven") of the Pharisees and Herod (e.g., Boobyer, 84–86). But we have seen that little significance rides on the numbers in the respective Feedings (see *Comment* on 6:42; 8:8).

If we put Jesus' questions about the amount of leftovers together with the disciples' repeated concern over not having loaves of bread (8:14, 16, 17), which precipitated the series of questions culminating in the questions about the amount of leftovers (8:17b–20), it appears that Jesus has been uncovering their lack of faith in him. This lack of faith comes to the surface at the point of their own need (cf. 4:40; 6:52). Rather than trusting Jesus during the threatening storm (4:35–41), comprehending his epiphanic presence with them during another crossing (6:45–52), or recognizing his ability to provide food for the relatively small group from one loaf (8:14b) when he had abundantly fed thousands with even less, the disciples grumble about their not having brought enough loaves with them.

In constructing this third crossing in which the disciples' lack of faith is exposed, Mark does not expect the reader to think the disciples doubted Jesus' ability to perform miracles. They had been witnesses and party to more than enough examples to convince them of Jesus' ability. Rather like the Pharisees, Herod, the members of Jesus' home and hometown, and "those outside," they risked failing to grasp the significance of the miracles for who Jesus was as the one in whom God was at work for them, the one in whom they could place their total trust. So they responded with amazement when he came to their aid during the first crossing (4:35–41), amazement at his epiphanic presence during the second (6:52), and in their concern for having forgotten to bring loaves of bread with them forgot who was with them during this third crossing (8:14, 16, 17a).

21 Jesus repeats the question, "Do you not yet understand?" (οὔπω συνίετε). Again the rhetorical question and the "not yet," while reflecting a note of despair, does offer hope that the disciples will understand. Furthermore, this pericope is placed between the healing of a "deaf-mute" (7:31–37) and a blind man (8:22–26) which bespeaks Jesus' healing power for the "deaf" and "blind" disciples. And the next section of Mark's story (8:27–10:52) focusing on Jesus' instruction and the disciples' misunderstanding shows that even this "healing" takes place with a struggle.

Explanation

This pericope plays a much more significant role in Mark's narrative than is often assumed. First, it bears the most redactional marks of any pericope so far. Not only does the evangelist place this story strategically here, but he develops at best a fragment of tradition about the disciples' lack of sufficient bread (8:14b, 16a) by adding the warning against "leaven" (8:15) and a series of questions (8:16b–21) that point to the disciples' precarious response to Jesus. At the same time, he surrounds the story, which queries the disciples' "hearing" and "seeing," with episodes of Jesus healing the deaf and blind (7:31–37; 8:22–26). Second, this story develops the theme of the disciples' lack of understanding which has continually recurred in this section of his Gospel (e.g., 6:37, 52; 7:18; 8:4), a theme that emerged in the previous section (e.g., 4:10, 13; 4:40) and continues in the subsequent section (8:27–10:52).

Mark clearly depicts the disciples as having a special relationship with Jesus. Each of the sections from 1:16–8:26 begins with a special calling or commissioning of disciples to be with him and to participate in his ministry (e.g., 1:16–20; 3:13–19; 6:7–13). Yet despite their presence with Jesus and their sharing in his ministry, they appear to miss the significance of who Jesus is and what he is doing.

In the first Feeding, they described the impossible situation in economic terms, the prohibitive cost of procuring sufficient bread for the crowd (6:37).

Then after helping serve the people through Jesus' miraculous provisions they were astounded at his epiphanic disclosure to them on the sea, because they had not "understood the loaves, rather their hearts were hardened" (6:52). In the second Feeding, they described the impossible situation in logistic terms, the lack of supplies from which to procure sufficient food (8:4), and this after having already shared in Jesus' miraculous supply of a similar need. Here they themselves discuss their failure to bring sufficient bread (8:11, 16).

Jesus exposes their discussion for what it is, a lack of comprehension of who he was and the significance of his ministry, by warning the disciples about the "leaven of the Pharisees and the leaven of Herod" (8:15) and by posing a series of challenging questions to them (8:16b–21). The referent for the "leaven" lies in the evangelist's enclosure of the two Feeding stories (6:30–44; 8:1–9) with a story about Herod's mistaking Jesus for the Baptist because of his miracles (6:14–16) and the story of the Pharisees' request for a sign of divine authentication despite his miracles (8:10–13). The "leaven" was their unbelief, their failure to comprehend the uniqueness of Jesus and his ministry.

A series of rhetorical questions poses the issue sharply for the disciples (8:16b–18). The questions specifically address their lack of understanding and perception, even invoking prophetic language once addressed to unbelieving Israel (8:18). Then Jesus reminds the disciples through question and answer about the surplus from the two Feedings (8:19–20) thereby exposing their discussion about a lack of bread as indicative of their failure to understand and perceive that Jesus was there for just such times. But as the warning against the "leaven of the Pharisees and Herod" indicates, their lack of understanding went beyond an awareness of his ability to perform miracles. As privy and party to Jesus' numerous miracles including the two Feedings, the disciples least of all would have questioned his miracle-working power. But like the Pharisees and Herod they risked failing to comprehend what the miracles said about the person and work of Jesus. Thus the story ends once again with the rhetorical question, "Do you not yet understand?"

The story doubtless reflects in some ways the failure of the disciples to comprehend the scope of Jesus and his ministry before Easter. Though Mark did much to create this pericope, he did not create this motif. But the evangelist was doing more than recounting the disciples' response to Jesus during his earthly ministry. Both the redactional character of the story, especially the reference to the two Feedings which were aligned for the first time in Mark's Gospel, and the warning against the "leaven," with the alignment of its referent in the stories of Herod and the Pharisees surrounding the two Feedings, give us a clue that Mark wanted his readers, who alone had the relevant details based on his account, to hear for themselves the challenge addressed by Jesus to the disciples.

In this way, Mark appears to say that being an "insider," even a "disciple," did not guarantee that one "understood" or perceived the significance of Jesus and his ministry. One was in danger of being an "outsider" whose "heart was hardened, having eyes but not seeing, and ears but not hearing" (8:17b–18; cf. 3:5; 4:11–12). Yet the rhetorical form of the questions and the prefacing with "not yet" offers hope and a challenge to Mark's readers to respond in faith to Jesus. The healing of the blind man of Bethsaida in

the next story along with the healing of the deaf-mute in 7:31–37 orient that hope in Jesus' ministry itself.

M. The Blind Man of Bethsaida   (8:22–26)

Bibliography

Best, E. "Discipleship in Mark: Mark 8:22–10:52." *SJT* 23 (1970) 223–37 = *Disciples and Discipleship: Studies in the Gospel According to Mark.* Edinburgh: T. & T. Clark, 1986. 1–16. **Derrett, J. D. M.** "Trees Walking, Prophecy and Christology." *ST* 35 (1981) 33–54. **Hegermann, H.** "Bethsaida und Gennesar: Eine traditions- und redaktionsgeschichtliche Studie zu Mc 4–8." In *Judentum, Urchristentum, Kirche.* FS J. Jeremias, ed. W. Eltester. BZNW 26. Berlin: Töpelmann, 1960. 130–40. **Johnson, J. E.** "Mark VIII. 22–26: The Blind Man from Bethsaida." *NTS* 25 (1979) 370–84. **Koch, D.-A.** *Die Wundererzählungen Jesu im Markusevangelium.* 1970. **Kuby, A.** "Zur Konzeption des Markus-Evangeliums." *ZNW* 49 (1958) 52–64. **Lightfoot, R. H.** *History and Interpretation in the Gospels.* London: Hodder and Stoughton, 1935. **Luz, U.** "Das Geheimnismotiv und die markinische Christologie." *ZNW* 56 (1965) 9–30 = "The Secrecy Motif and the Marcan Christology." In *The Messianic Secret,* ed. C. Tuckett. London/Philadelphia: SPCK/Fortress, 1983. 75–96. **Miller, J. I.** "Was Tischendorf Really Wrong? Mark 8:26b Revisited." *NovT* 28 (1986) 97–103. **Roloff, J.** *Das Kerygma und der irdische Jesus.* 1970. **Ross, J. M.** "Another Look at Mark 8:26b" *NovT* 29 (1987) 97–99. **Snoy, T.** "La rédaction marcienne de la marche sur les eaux (Mc VI. 45–52)." *ETL* 44 (1968) 205–41, 433–81. **Wendling, E.** *Die Entstehung des Marcus Evangeliums.* Tübingen: Mohr, 1908.

Translation

[22] *And they came to Bethsaida. And they brought to Jesus[a] a blind man and appealed to him to touch him.* [23] *And taking the blind man's hand, he brought him out of the village. After spitting in his eyes and laying hands on him, Jesus[a] began asking him, "What do you see?"[b]* [24] *After regaining his sight, he said, "I see people walking but they are like trees."[c]* [25] *Then Jesus[a] again laid his hands on his eyes, and he saw clearly. He was restored and continued seeing all things distinctly.* [26] *And Jesus[a] sent him to his home saying, "Do not enter the village!"[d]*

Notes

[a] Romanized words added from context.

[b] εἰ used to introduce a direct question.

[c] The convoluted syntax defies literal translation (βλέπω τοὺς ἀνθρώπους ὅτι ὡς δένδρα ὁρῶ περιπατοῦντας). It is ameliorated by dropping ὁρῶ in C² D W Θ f¹.¹³ 205 565 1424 1542 al lat co.

[d] Several variants add an explicit secrecy command: (a) μηδενὶ εἴπῃς εἰς τὴν κώμην—D (e.g., Taylor, 373; Ross, *NovT* 29 [1987] 99); (b) μηδὲ εἰς τὴν κώμην εἰσέλθῃς μηδὲ εἴπῃς τινι ἐν τῇ κώμῃ— A C 33ᵛⁱᵈ 1006 1506 Majority text syᵖ·ʰ. These readings align the text with a similar prohibition in 1:44. Text (μηδὲ εἰς τὴν κώμην εἰσέλθῃς) is read by ℵ B L Δ* f¹ pc syˢ sa boᵖᵗ (Metzger, *Textual Commentary,* 99; cf. Miller, *NovT* 28 [1986] 97–103).

Form / Structure / Setting

Form-critically, this pericope represents a healing story. But like the healing of the deaf-mute in 7:31–37, it contains thaumaturgical elements that set it off from the other healing miracles of the Synoptics. Jesus removes the blind man from the initial scene, uses spittle and heals the man in stages by touching his eyes. Jesus' only words during the healing come in the form of a question about what the man sees. The story ends with a dismissal (8:26a) and an order not to return to the village (8:26b), which many interpreters take to be another form of a silence command (cf. 1:44; 5:43; 7:36). We have no acclamation or response (cf. 7:36b, 37).

A few interpreters have taken the structural similarity of 7:32–37 and 8:22–26 to indicate a doublet or variant (e.g., Wendling, *Entstehung,* 77; Bultmann, 213). For instance, we have in the two stories: (a) a man brought to Jesus for healing (7:32 = 8:22), (b) Jesus' removal of the man from the public (7:33 = 8:23), (c) the use of spittle and touch for healing (7:33 = 8:24, 26), (d) a silence command (7:37 = 8:26) about (e) something impossible to conceal.

The consensus, however, finds the differences too great to account for the stories in this manner (Taylor, 369; Cranfield, 263; Kertelge, *Wunder,* 161; Gnilka, 1:312–13; Pesch, 1:420; Ernst, 228). Yet the unusual similarities and the absence of both accounts in either Matthew or Luke do suggest that Mark found the two paired in the tradition. Such a close association could explain the assimilation of language and structure (Schweizer, 163; Ernst, 228). The similarities may also suggest their having been composed by the same author or community (e.g., Kertelge, *Wunder,* 163; Johnson, *NTS* 25 [1978–79] 374). Roloff (*Kerygma,* 127) assigns these stories without parallel or analogy in the synoptic tradition to a special group of popular narratives about Jesus' mighty works that was repressed because of their extensive hellenistic traits. One can only speculate on the basis of the limited data. But the combination of these two stories around the theme of Isa 35:5, which may have provided the choral response for the stories in reverse order in the tradition, does make sense (so Grundmann, 211; Schenke, *Wundererzählungen,* 308; Gnilka, 1:313; Ernst, 228).

Mark's redactional influence has generally been traced to the addition of the location at the outset (8:22a) and the silence command at the conclusion (8:26b). Only rarely has anyone assigned more to Mark's account (cf. Cranfield, 263; Mann, 336). If the evangelist indeed found 8:22–26 in combination with 7:32–37, the present location and order would also reflect his redactional handling of the tradition. The location of a healing of the blind appropriately follows the allusion to Jer 5:21 in 8:18 in a context that had underscored the Pharisees' demand for a "sign" (8:10–13) despite the "significance" of Jesus' ministry and the disciples' own failure to perceive and understand Jesus and his ministry (8:14–21).

Structurally, the narrator tells the story by setting the stage with the arrival presumably of Jesus and the disciples (cf. 8:14–21 and 27–30) and the approach of an unnamed group who ask Jesus to heal a blind man by touching him (8:22). Jesus removes the man from that scene, spits in his eyes and lays his hands on him (8:23a). Then a brief dialogue ensues with Jesus asking the man what he sees. His answer indicates that his healing was only partial (8:23b–24). So Jesus lays his hands on his eyes again with the result that the man's sight is fully restored (8:25). The story ends with the narrator informing the reader that Jesus dismissed the healed man to his house but forbad him from going into the village (8:26).

The central portion stands out, because it offers the only example in the healing stories of Jesus asking about the results of his work and the only account where the healing takes place in stages rather than immediately. Naturally, these features raise the question of whether they simply belong to the unusual details of the story or whether the evangelist intended them to have special, symbolical significance for his readers.

As to setting, the location of the story holds the key to its significance. But does it come as an epilogue looking back on what has happened (e.g., Klostermann, 77; Koch, *Wundererzählungen*, 71–72; cf. Roloff, *Kerygma*, 131) or as a prelude looking forward to what is to happen (e.g., Lightfoot, *History*, 90–91; Best, *Disciples*, 3; Grundmann, 211; Gnilka, 1:315; Ernst, 228)? Generally the preference has been the latter. But a prelude for what?

Lightfoot took it to refer to the following events in 8:27–30 because of a structural parallel between these two passages (e.g., 8:23b = 8:27b; 8:25 = 8:29a; 8:25b = 8:29b; 8:26 = 8:30; *History*, 90–91; similarly, Kuby, *ZNW* 49 [1958] 52–64, and Ernst, 228). Others focus on Jesus' gradual "healing" of the disciples through his teaching in 8:27–10:52, a section that concludes with Mark's second story about the healing of a blind man (e.g., Best, *Disciples*, 3; cf. Gnilka, 1:315). Still others find 8:22–26 to be the prelude for the ultimate healing which comes after the cross (e.g., Grundmann, 211; Kertelge, *Wunder*, 164).

In Mark's literary setting, this story belongs thematically with what has come before. In the preceding narrative (8:14–21), Jesus raised the issue of the disciples' blindness and deafness (8:18) as a rhetorical question with the repeated query about their "*not yet* understanding" (8:17, 21). Thus the story comes as evidence for hope that their "blindness" or lack of understanding can be remedied. The connection between the prophetic reference to blindness in 8:18 and the belabored healing of the blind man in 8:22–26 has to be more than coincidental (cf. Koch, *Wundererzählungen*, 71–72).

At the same time, the story itself precedes an entire section in which Jesus concentrates almost exclusively on the disciples (8:27–10:52) to prepare them for his coming death. But their final "healing" does not come by 10:52, nor does it come by 16:8. Their behavior throughout the passion narrative and on Easter Sunday (11:1–16:8) demonstrates that fact. Therefore, 8:22–26 can hardly serve as a prelude for either 8:27–10:52 or even 8:27–16:8 (Johnson, *NTS* 25 [1978–79] 375–83). It does, however, give a hint to what Mark's readers doubtless know, namely, that the disciples did gain their full sight but only after Easter. Only then did they fully comprehend who Jesus was and the significance of his ministry.

Why introduce the story at this point in the narrative? First, it belonged together with 7:24–30 and its "hellenized" twin 7:32–37 in a section that focused on Jesus' ministry in predominantly gentile territory. Second, it offered symbolically to the readers an explanation of the disciples' situation as depicted by the evangelist from 4:10–8:21 and prepared them for the disciples' obtuseness in 8:27–10:52.

The story also brings to a close the first half of Mark's narrative (1:16–8:26). This half consists of three sections (1:16–3:12; 3:13–6:6; 6:7–8:26). Each begins with an account focusing on the disciples (1:16–20; 3:13–19; 6:7–13). Each concludes with the motif of rejection (3:1–6; 6:1–6a; 8:10–21), but not before an additional note points to Jesus' redemptive ministry despite rejection (3:7–12; 6:6b; 8:22–26). In other words, Jesus' healing of the blind man, as did the previous summaries (3:7–12; 6:6b), shows that his ministry continues despite apparent setbacks. In this case, the story offers hope for the resistant, myopic disciples, while no such hope was offered at the end of the previous two sections to either the religious and political representatives in 3:1–6 (cf. 3:7–12) or to Jesus' hometown and household in 6:1–6 (cf. 6:6b).

Comment

22 "They came to Bethsaida" (ἔρχονται εἰς Βηθσαϊδάν). A large consensus assigns this introductory statement to Markan redaction. Pesch's lonely voice assigns it to pre-Markan tradition (1:417) on the grounds that the evangelist never employs specific locales in his transitions (cf. 1:21; 2:1; 3:1, 20; 5:1; 6:16; 7:24). But Mark appears to have arranged the itinerary from 7:24–8:21 that has Jesus moving from Gennesaret (6:53) to the territory of Tyre (7:24), then through Sidon across to and down through the middle of the Decapolis (7:31) to the Sea of Galilee which he crosses to Dalmanutha (8:10) from where he crosses back to Bethsaida (8:13–22). The journey covers the area bordering the northeast shore of Galilee, which was predominantly gentile. The materials involving a Syrophoenician woman, two miracle stories laced with an inordinate amount of hellenistic thaumaturgical traits (7:32–37; 8:22–26), and a second, "hellenized," Feeding located in the Decapolis aptly constitute all but two events (cf. 8:10–13; 8:14–21, both mostly redactional) of this "itinerary" since the discussion of the purity laws in 7:1–23 set aside that critical social boundary between Jew and Gentile (7:15–23).

Mark may well have taken "Bethsaida" from 6:45 when Jesus dismissed his disciples and the crowds after the first Feeding (6:45; cf. Snoy, *ETL* 44 [1968] 209, n. 6). Never reaching Bethsaida, they landed at Gennesaret (see *Comment* on 6:45, 53). By using it for the present destination, however, Mark does not intend it to be the final destination of the crossing in 6:45 or that 6:45–8:22 constituted one journey with an extended detour (cf. Kertelge, *Wunder*, 164; Johnson, *NTS* 25 [1978–79] 372). It merely gives the destination of the crossing in 8:10–21. Situated on the north and east shore of the Sea of Galilee, east of the Jordan River, "Bethsaida" lay outside the eastern border of Galilee and was under the aegis of Herod Philip. This locale offered a convenient and appropriate destination as a gentile setting for the second of two healings with "hellenistic" thaumaturgical traits (7:31–37; 8:22–26). Furthermore, it directs Jesus and the disciples toward Caesarea Philippi, the setting of the following story.

"Bethsaida" along with "Caesarea Philippi" was built by Philip the Tetrarch and named Julias after Caesar Augustus' daughter, Julia, (Josephus, *Ant.* 18.28; *War* 2.515). It became the capital of Gaulanitis. According to John 1:44 and 12:21, it was the home of Philip as well as Peter and Andrew (cf. *Comment* on 1:29). In the only other reference in the Synoptics, "Bethsaida" appears in conjunction with Chorazin in the woe formula of Matt 11:21 // Luke 10:13 according to which the two "cities" had failed to respond to the "mighty works" done among them.

"They brought to *Jesus* a blind man" (φέρουσιν αὐτῷ τυφλόν) begins like the story of the deaf-mute (cf. 7:32). The parallel extends to the end of the verse including much of the wording (e.g., φέρειν, παρακαλεῖν, ἵνα + subjunctive). The appeal differs slightly. Instead of requesting that Jesus specifically "lay his hand on him" (so 7:32; cf. 8:24, 25), they ask Jesus to "touch him" (αὐτοῦ ἅψηται; cf. *Comment* on 5:34). In either case, those bringing the one needing healing were simply asking Jesus to heal their friend.

23 "Taking the blind man's hand" provides a graphic detail of Jesus' assistance with a Markan *hapax legomenon* (ἐπιλαβόμενος; cf. ἀπολαβόμενος, 7:33; κρατεῖν τῆς χειρός, 5:41; 9:27).

"He brought him out of the village" (ἐξήνεγκεν αὐτὸν ἔξω τῆς κώμης). In 7:33 Jesus similarly removed the deaf-mute from the public eye, a thaumaturgic trait suggesting a desire to conceal the means of the healing (see *Comment* on 7:33). Taken accordingly, Jesus sought privacy in which to accomplish the miracle. But the apparent presence of people walking who looked like trees (8:24) inherent in the story makes it quite possible that more than a thaumaturgical concern for "privacy" or "secrecy" may lie behind this action. Indeed, separation from the "village" (ἔξω τῆς κώμης, 8:23) may be the actual point here (cf. ἀπὸ τοῦ ὄχλου, 7:33). See *Comment* on 8:26.

Many interpreters have found a tension in the designation of "Bethsaida" as a "village" (κώμη, 8:23, 26). Matt 11:20 calls it and Chorazin "cities" (πόλεις; cf. John 1:44; Josephus, *Ant.* 18.28). The textual variant, "Bethany" (Βηθανίαν, D *pc* it), a small town east of the Jordan (John 1:28), may represent an attempt to alleviate this tension. Generally, however, this tension is attributed to Mark's geographically uninformed insertion of "Bethsaida" into a traditional story referring to an unnamed "village" (e.g., Bultmann, 213; Lohmeyer, 158; Nineham, 219; Ernst, 229). Yet study has shown that despite its size and new name, "Bethsaida" did remain organizationally a "village" under Herod Philip (so A. H. M. Jones, *The Cities of the Eastern Roman Provinces,* 2nd ed. [Oxford: Clarendon Press, 1971] 282). Whether "village" represents Mark's attempt at precision in contrast to Matt 11:20; John 1:44; and Josephus, *Ant.* 18.28 is at best debatable.

"After spitting in his eyes" (πτύσας εἰς τὰ ὄμματα αὐτοῦ) implied more than simply a communication to the man that healing was coming (so Grundmann, 212; Gnilka, 1:314). Yet the repeated laying on of hands (8:25) suggests that the healing came primarily through that gesture. See *Comment* on 5:23, regarding laying on of hands; see *Comment* on 7:33, regarding the therapeutic use of spittle.

"What do you see?" (εἴ τι βλέπεις) poses the only such question in Jesus' miracles. He never asks the "patient" regarding the miracle or its success.

The ensuing answer allows Jesus and the reader to learn that the healing was only partial.

24 "After regaining his sight" (ἀναβλέψας). Most take the participle to be parallel with Jesus' "looking up" in 7:34 (e.g., ἀναβλέψας). But the verb functions very differently in the two contexts. Whereas it belongs to the thaumaturgic setting of 7:34 (see *Comment*), here it reflects a semi-technical meaning of "regaining sight" (e.g., 10:51–52 // Matt 20:34 // Luke 18:43; Matt 11:5 // Luke 7:22; John 9:11, 15, 18; Acts 9:12, 17, 18; 22:13; so Lagrange, 213; Johnson, *NTS* 25 [1978–79] 376–77). With this participle then we learn that Jesus had given the man his sight. Something had happened in Jesus' healing gestures.

"I see people walking as trees" (βλέπω τοὺς ἀνθρώπους ὅπ ὡς δένδρα ὁρῶ περιπατοῦντας) smoothes out an almost unintelligible statement (see *Note* c). Some interpreters have explained this awkwardness as a bad rendering of ⊤ by ὅτι rather than the pronoun οὕς (e.g., Taylor, 371; cf. Black, *Approach*, 53–54). The statement would then read, "I see people *whom* I see walking as trees." Black (*Approach*, 53–54), who finds even this rendering too awkward, takes the Greek to be a poor rendering of an idiomatic use of the emphatic hyperbaton in Aramaic. He suggests that it read, "I see men that like trees they are walking." Others, perhaps making virtue of a necessity, have explained the awkward syntax to be a dramatic depiction of the man's emotional state (e.g., Grundmann, 212; Ernst, 230). This view, however, seems unlikely, since the story accents to the point almost of redundancy in 8:25 the ultimate healing in contrast to this initial myopia.

25 "And *Jesus* again laid his hands on his eyes" (ἔιτα πάλιν ἐπέθηκεντὰς γεῖρας ἐπὶ τοὺς ὀφθαλμοὺς αὐτοῦ) gives the efficacious gesture. But unlike the other miracle stories, Jesus repeats his actions to complete the healing, a fact that has led to numerous explanations. Some take it as testimony to the magnitude of the miracle (e.g., Klostermann, 78; Ernst, 230). Yet healing a blind man hardly qualifies as the most difficult or greatest of Jesus' miracles. More often the healing in stages has been taken as symbolic of the disciples' experience of "two stage" healing. This explanation hardly suffices. Mark is only responsible for the location of the miracle story and not for the development of this particular motif. Therefore, we must assume the phased healing had significance for the story itself.

Perhaps the answer lies in Jesus' role as depicted by the story. The story as we have it resembles more a cure by a physician than a miraculous event (Roloff, *Kerygma*, 128). The protracted healing then is a narrative device (Gnilka, 1:314). Like a physician Jesus asks the man a leading question about his sight after ministering to him. Learning that the healing process was not complete, Jesus takes further therapeutic action. In a way, this story portrays Jesus more as the "great physician" (Roloff, *Kerygma*, 128; Pesch, 1:419) than the miracle worker.

There can be little doubt, however, that this story functioned symbolically in Mark's Gospel. He has most likely separated it from its traditional setting paired with the healing of the deaf-mute in 7:32–37, rearranged the order of the two stories and strategically located it here in his narrative after a pericope that accented the disciples' lack of perception, their having eyes without seeing and ears without hearing (8:14–21). But how does the story fit Mark's portrait of the disciples?

The disciples do not represent the deaf and blind in Mark's Gospel. That role is filled especially by the "scribes" (3:22–23), "Pharisees and Herod" (8:10–13), and "those outside" (4:11–12) for whom all things are in "riddles." Called (1:16–20; 3:13–19), commissioned (6:7–13), and specially taught (4:10–13, 33–34; 7:18b–23), the disciples share an integral part of Jesus' ministry as "insiders" and companions. But their response to Jesus shows them to have a bad case of myopia. They continually failed to recognize and grasp his significance (4:10, 13, 41; 6:37, 52; 7:17; 8:4, 14–21). In fact, they were almost as blind as the "Pharisees," "Herod," and "the outsiders" (8:15, 17–21). Their obtuseness only becomes more pronounced in the following sections of 8:27–10:52 and 11:1–16:8. They are in need of a "second touch" which ultimately comes after Easter.

Mark, therefore, uses this story to inform the readers about where the disciples stand in his narrative. The story comes as: (a) a clarification that despite the dangerous similarities the "disciple" is different from the opponents and outsiders, (b) a challenge to recognize their limited sight and (c) an affirmation of the hope that total sight is available through the Great Physician. At the same time, the readers themselves, who may identify with the disciples, are to hear Jesus' rhetorical questions in 8:17–21 and note their own lack of perception and precarious position that gives urgent rise to the warning against the "leaven of the Pharisees and Herod."

"Saw clearly" (διέβλεψεν), one of five different verbs for "seeing" here, signals the complete healing (aorist tense). The fuzzy images of myopia have gone. Everything is clear. But then the story underscores this point by informing the audience that the man "was restored" (ἀπεκατέστη; cf. 3:5; 9:12) and that he "continued seeing all things distinctly" (ἐνέβλεπεν τηλαυγῶς ἅπαντα). This statement provides the confirmation of the healing. The verb for seeing (ἐμβλέπειν) often connotes intense looking as "examine," "see into something," or "observe." In other words, the healing had brought thorough, complete sight to his eyes.

26 *"Jesus* sent him to his home" (ἀπέστειλεν αὐτὸν εἰς οἶκον αὐτοῦ). We find a similar dismissal in 5:19 (see *Comment*). To what extent, however, does this dismissal take on a more symbolic character of a secrecy motif? Doubtless a formal part of the pre-Markan tradition, did it connote concealment or even privacy? Mark certainly uses "house" or "home" as a place of privacy elsewhere (cf. 7:24; 9:28, 33; 10:10; see *Comment* on 7:17). But 2:1, 11; 3:20, 31–35; and 5:19–20 demonstrate that "house" or "home" per se does not necessarily imply privacy or secrecy.

"Do not enter the village!" (μηδὲ εἰς τὴν κώμην εἰσέλθῃς) only makes sense if the man did not actually live in the village. This injunction has generally been assigned to Mark's redaction as a variation of his secrecy commands (explicit in *v.l.*, see *Note* d). Read in conjunction with Jesus' having taken the man outside the village before healing him (8:23) and now sending him home without the chance to enter the village, it supposedly supports Mark's "secrecy motif" (e.g., Wrede, *Secret,* 35; Klostermann, 78; Lohmeyer, 159; Kertelge, *Wunder,* 161; Koch, *Wundererzählungen,* 69–70; Nineham, 220;

Schenke, *Wundererzählungen*, 309; Pesch, 1:419; Gnilka, 1:314; Ernst, 230; Theissen, *Miracle Stories*, 69, 147–48).

Not everyone, however, subscribes to the view that Mark added this injunction and thus the secrecy motif. For example, Luz and Roloff, for different reasons, take the injunction to have been pre-Markan. Luz argues on the basis of style, noting that Mark's secrecy commands are much more explicit (*ZNW* 56 [1965] 14–15; similarly, Johnson, *NTS* 25 [1978–79] 373). The silence commands of 1:43; 5:43; and 7:36 are quite similar to each other and straightforward. Why then this oblique approach, if all four such commands are redactional?

Roloff (*Kerygma*, 128–29) takes the command as having been related to the judgment motif associated with the woe formula in the Q saying about Bethsaida (Matt 11:21–22 // Luke 10:13–14). Accordingly, both the leaving of the village (8:23) and the command not to enter the village (8:26a) in keeping with Jesus' own actions in Nazareth (6:1–6a, 6b), and the instructions of Matt 11:21–22 // Luke 10:13–14 // Mark 6:11 regarding how to respond to places that reject the mission, signify the village's prior rejection of Jesus' "mighty works." The weakness of this suggestion lies in the absence of any hint of the village's rejection in the present story.

Even if one were to take 8:23 as a traditional thaumaturgical trait characteristic of healings and grant that 8:26b represents Mark's shifting of that special secrecy motif to a "silence command" about Jesus as in 1:44–45; 5:43; and 7:36, the injunction here would play the same role as the other silence commands. Instead of contributing to a "messianic secret," these injunctions serve as a literary device by which Mark prepares for the next scene. When the next scene requires crowds, the disregard for the silence command leads to great crowds (e.g., 1:45; cf. 2:1–2; 7:36; cf. 8:1–9). When the injunctions are apparently followed, a change of venue without crowds follows (e.g., 5:43; cf. 6:1–6a; 8:26; cf. 8:27–30). Perhaps this was Mark's way in his narrative of letting Jesus get away despite the wonder of the respective miracles (e.g., 5:35–43; 8:22–26) that inevitably would have drawn a crowd (cf. 1:22–28 and 1:32–34; 1:40–45a and 1:45b–2:2; 3:6 and 3:7–12; 5:1–20 and 8:31; 6:7–13, 30 and 6:32–44; 6:34–44 and 6:53–56; 7:31–37 and 8:1–9).

Explanation

This story, loaded with thaumaturgical traits familiar to the hellenistic world, most likely circulated in the tradition as one of a pair of healing stories with 7:32–37. The two may have concluded with the acclamation of Isa 35:5 which points to Jesus' healing ministry in terms of the prophet's promise of healing for the blind and the deaf. Though neither Matthew nor Luke uses these stories, Mark appropriately places them in a setting outside Galilee (cf. 7:31—the Decapolis; 8:22—Bethsaida).

If the story was transmitted in combination with the similar healing of the deaf-mute (7:31–37), the final acclamation drawn from Isa 35:5–6 would have served both stories since Isa 35:5–6 appropriately pertains to both "seeing" as well as "hearing" and "speaking." By combining the two stories through one acclamation, the tradition ameliorated the lack of acclamation or response after this story. Together the stories of Jesus' healing, despite their similarity to "hellenistic miracle stories," bore witness to Jesus, against the backdrop of the Scriptures, as the one in whom God was at work doing "all things well" as the one inaugurating Isaiah's promised day of salvation rather than a popular hellenistic thaumaturge.

Mark's own contribution appears limited to the literary and geographical setting. What may have been an unnamed village is now identified as Bethsaida, "the other side" from where Jesus left the Pharisees in Dalmanutha (8:10, 13). Of even more significance is the location the story has in Mark's narrative, a place that almost certainly points to its symbolical value for the evangelist.

Immediately following the highly redactional story about the Pharisees' request for a sign (8:10–13) and the leaven of the Pharisees and Herod (8:14–21), the two-stage healing helps the reader understand the previous, unflattering depiction of the disciples especially in this section (6:7–8:26) and prepares the reader for the continued focus on their myopia that follows, especially in 8:27–10:52.

Mark clearly uses the first stage of the healing to distinguish the disciples' myopia from the blindness of the "outsiders," the "Pharisees and Herod," and his own hometown and family. Their calling and response (1:16–20; 3:13–19), their special privilege as constant companions and recipients of Jesus' instruction (4:10–20, 33–34; 7:18–23), and their sharing in Jesus' ministry (6:7–13, 30; 6:34–44; 8:1–9) demonstrated their having experienced the first touch. But only a fine line separated their myopia from blindness as seen by the warning about the leaven of the Pharisees and Herod which had just preceded.

The primary focus of this story, however, is on the man's total healing. The disciples show themselves to be in need of the second touch, and the story bespeaks their experiencing it. A time must come when they see all things distinctly. That time does not, however, come at Caesarea Philippi or by the time of Jesus' suffering and death in Jerusalem. In fact, it really does not come by the end of Mark's Gospel (16:8). But Mark's readers know it came for the disciples at some point after Easter. And it came through God's gracious healing of their sight.

Mark does not appear to depict the disciples in this manner to discount them or a false Christology that they might have represented. The fact that they have been "touched" the first time sets them off from Jesus' opponents. They simply do not see clearly, as their response to Jesus indicates (e.g., 4:10–20; 4:41; 6:37; 6:52; 7:17–18; 8:4; 8:14–21). Yet the disciples do play a special role as ones with whom the reader can identify—people struggling to comprehend, to see distinctly, just what it was that God had done in and through Jesus. Informed at the outset that he is Jesus, Messiah, Son of God, the readers find supporting evidence in every pericope but only if they have eyes to see and ears to hear. Unfortunately, the "realities" of life distort the sight and the sound for them as it did for the disciples. This story offers them hope too based on the healing touch of Jesus who makes the deaf ears hear and blind eyes see—even if it comes in stages.

Index of Modern Authors

Abrahams, I. 117, 124, 130, 135
Achtemeier, P. 259, 261, 265, 267, 283, 292, 293, 304, 305, 310, 334, 342, 345, 347, 348, 354, 355, 356
Aichenger, H. 117, 123
Albertz, M. 80, 82, 130, 132
Allison, D. C. 371, 379
Ambrozic, A. M. xxxvii, xxxviii, xxxix, 40, 41, 42, 43, 44, 45, 198, 200, 201, 203, 204, 205, 208, 211, 226, 227, 231, 233, 237, 240, 241, 246, 248, 250, 253
Anderson, H. xvii, xxxi, 4, 6, 7, 9
Annen, F. 260, 265, 271
Argyle, A. W. 53, 56
Arnold, G. 5, 6, 7
Aune, D. xix, xxi, xxii, xxvii, 148, 178

Baarda, T. 271, 272, 276
Bächli, O. 53, 56, 57, 271
Bacon, B. W. 3, 4, 106, 138
Baird, T. 389
Baltensweiler, H. 237, 238, 240
Bammel, E. 15
Banks, R. 118, 123, 130, 137, 359, 367, 371–72, 375, 376
Bartsch, H. W. 96, 98, 246, 248
Bauernfeind, O. 53, 57, 271
Baumgarten, A. I. 96, 102, 279
Beare, F. W. 118, 120, 122, 123, 125
Beasley-Murray, G. 29, 40, 41, 44
Beck, N. A. 417, 418, 421
Becker, J. 15, 18, 19, 22, 23, 27, 166
Beernaert, P. M. 53
Behm, J. 226
Bennet, W. J. 130, 138
Berger, K. 118, 121, 166, 177, 359, 316, 367, 372, 373, 376, 378, 379
Berkey, R. F. 40, 44
Best, E. xvii, xxi, xxii, xxiii, xxxi, xxxvii, xl, 15, 27, 36, 38, 39, 48, 53, 57, 60, 62, 96, 99, 100, 102, 141, 142, 145, 153, 158, 166, 169, 170, 171, 173, 181, 182, 183, 184, 198, 202, 204, 215, 220, 221, 260, 313, 315, 318, 320, 322, 328, 334, 337, 338, 372, 377, 428, 430
Betz, O. 15, 17, 33, 97, 100, 148, 153, 260, 305, 309, 312, 345
Beyer, H. W. 179
Bilezikian, W. xix
Bishop, E. E. 75
Black, M. xvii, 40, 44, 166, 180, 186, 193, 198, 210, 211, 237, 238, 246, 249, 296, 324, 325, 364, 372, 378, 389, 394, 433
Blinzler, J. 166, 305
Böcher, O. 15, 21, 77, 85
Bonnard, P. 345
Bonner, C. 71, 72, 74, 271, 280, 388, 395
Boobyer, G. H. 80, 83, 91, 186, 189, 198, 205, 334, 342, 399, 417, 421, 422, 423, 425
Booth, R. P. 359, 361, 363, 364, 365, 372, 373, 375

Boring, M. E. 166, 168, 170, 171, 177–70, 170
Bornkamm, G. xxii, 206, 231
Boucher, M. 186, 188, 189, 191, 192, 198, 207, 209, 215, 217
Bousset, W. 29, 33
Bowker, J. W. 198
Bowman, J. W. 5
Branscomb, H. 80
Braun, H. 25
Braumann, G. 106, 111, 112
Bretscher, P. 29, 33
Brown, R. E. 153, 173, 198, 206, 215, 217, 218, 221, 231, 347
Brown, S. 198, 207
Brownlee, W. H. 15, 17
Bruce, F. F. 15, 18
Buchanan, G. W. 410
Bultmann, R. xvii, xxii, xxxviii, 18, 30, 32, 34, 36, 37, 43, 49, 68, 75, 81, 86, 89, 92, 104, 108, 115, 119, 120, 123, 125, 132, 169, 173, 178, 183, 188, 200, 227, 261, 264, 272, 273, 279, 282, 306, 310, 326, 327, 336, 355, 361, 373, 396, 411, 429, 432
Burkill, T. A. 53, 57, 58, 71, 74, 108, 111, 112, 113, 141, 142, 147, 198, 206, 209, 271, 279, 280, 381, 382, 383, 386, 387, 388
Buse, I. 29, 32
Bussmann, W. 118, 123
Buth, R. 153, 162

Caird, G. B. 318
Cameron, R. xix
Campbell, J. Y. 40, 44
Carlston, C. E. 97, 104, 107, 108, 110, 111, 114, 186, 189, 215, 226, 232, 246, 249, 359, 368, 372, 373, 374, 375, 376, 378
Cave, H. C. 71, 73, 74, 271, 273, 277, 278
Ceroke, C. P. 80, 91
Chilton, B. 29, 33, 34, 198, 210, 226, 232
Clark, K. W. 40, 44
Clavier, H. 334, 342, 399
Cohon, S. S. 118, 121
Cohon-Sherbok, D. M. 118, 121
Colpe, C. 89, 90, 166, 177, 178, 179, 180
Conzelmann, H. xxii, 30
Countryman, W. 417
Coutts, J. 198
Craghan, J. F. 271, 273, 277, 278, 283, 285
Cranfield, C. E. B. xvii, xxvii, xxxi, xxxiv, xxxvi, 3, 4, 6, 7, 9, 16, 17, 22, 29, 30, 41, 42, 82, 91, 98, 100, 110, 122, 136, 141, 142, 144, 147, 148, 157, 158, 159, 170, 179, 180, 192, 207, 208, 211, 215, 218, 232, 233, 262, 264, 268, 275, 276, 277, 302, 323, 328, 337, 342, 348, 350, 355, 360, 365, 378, 383, 390, 391, 392, 413, 415, 422, 423, 429

Cremer, F. G. 107
Crossan, J. D. xxxii, xxxiv, 166, 169, 170, 174, 178, 183, 184, 186, 189, 193, 194, 198, 206, 215, 217, 237, 239, 242, 243, 244, 246, 247, 249, 250, 251, 305, 309, 310, 311
Cullmann, O. 15, 17, 24, 29, 30, 33, 48, 50, 153, 160, 163

Dahl, N. 15, 17, 186–87, 198, 206, 215, 237, 240, 241, 246
Dalman, G. 29, 33, 187, 193, 195, 271, 275, 354, 356, 381, 384, 389, 392
Daniel, C. 130, 138
Danker, F. W. 399, 404
Daube, D. 53, 56, 107, 118, 120, 121, 122, 123, 141, 148, 198, 202, 215
Dautzenburg, G. 3, 4, 5, 9, 40
Deissmann, A. 396
Delling, G. 8
Dermience, A. 381
Derrett, J. D. M. 271, 273, 278, 334, 336, 345, 350, 359, 381, 385, 428
Devisch, M. xxxii, xxxiv
Dewey, J. 83, 98, 107–8, 110, 118, 120, 130, 133
Dibelius, M. xvii, xxii, xxxiii, xxxviii, 15, 27, 30, 34, 37, 92, 169, 183, 261, 267, 269, 273, 283, 346, 390, 395, 401
Dideberg, D. 53
Dietzfelbinger, C. 130, 132, 135, 136, 187, 195
Dodd, C. H. xvii, 40, 44, 107, 110, 187, 192, 215, 217, 226, 229, 237, 246, 247, 249–50, 251
Doeve, J. W. 118, 121
Donahue, J. R. 80, 83, 88, 97, 100, 101, 166, 169, 246, 289, 292
Donfried, K. P. 153, 334, 399, 401
Dormeyer, D. 324, 326
Drury, J. 215, 217
Dschulnigg, P. xxix, xxx, xxxii, xxxv
Dunn, J. D. G. 15, 22, 23, 25, 28, 80, 93, 97, 98, 118, 130
Duplacy, J. 80, 89, 91
Dupont, J. 36, 37, 237, 239

Ebeling, H. J. 107, 111
Edwards, R. A. 410, 411
Egger, W. xvii, 40, 41, 42, 43, 44, 53, 55, 63, 64, 65, 66, 67, 68, 69, 70, 141, 142, 143, 144, 146, 147, 148, 149, 189, 198, 253, 254, 313, 334, 336, 340, 354, 355, 356
Eisler, R. 15, 27
Elliott, J. K. 15, 16, 71
Ellis, P. F. xxxv
Emerton, J. 389, 395
Ernst, J. xvii, xxvii, xxxi, xxxvi, 9, 92, 98, 112, 119, 121, 125, 136, 146, 147, 149, 155, 156, 157, 159, 176, 181, 189, 190, 191, 200, 208, 227, 232, 240, 241, 242, 261, 262, 267, 273, 276, 285, 292, 293, 301, 303, 311, 312, 319, 327, 328, 330, 337,

Index of Biblical and Other Ancient Sources

A. Old Testament

B. New Testament

C. Extracanonical Jewish Literature

D. Early Christian Literature